WHO'S WHO IN SOUL MUSIC

WHO'S WHO IN SOUL MUSIC

RALPH TEE

WEIDENFELD AND NICOLSON

LONDON

First published in Great Britain in 1991 by
George Weidenfeld and Nicolson Limited
91 Clapham High Street, London SW4 7TA

British Library Cataloguing in Publication Data applied for
Printed in Great Britain by Butler and Tanner Ltd
Frome and London

Special thanks to all the following for their help:

Ian Levine, Richard Searling, Mike Allin, Bob Kilbourne, Steve Chandler, Peter Lewis, Rick Gianatos, Mark Walker, Den Christie, Damon Rochefort, Jon Williams, Caelian, Tom Graves, Martin Corteel, Allegra Huston, Natalina Bertoli, Richard Hussey, Martin Richards.

FOREWORD

The music business has always been very fond of pigeonholing its product: Black, Dance, Pop, Rap, Rock, Alternative, Country, Soul. Such tags make marketing the product more straightforward, but from the artists' point of view are simply restrictions they would rather live without. What do you call the end result when a black songwriter composes a soul song for a C & W crooner, as Lionel Richie did with 'Lady' for Kenny Rogers? What happens when a white, former teeny artist tops the black chart, as George Michael and Lisa Stansfield have both done with some panache in the States?

Artists of any pedigree do not write or perform with record company board meetings in mind, and black music (a term which, especially in soul-loving England, seems increasingly outdated) is probably more blurred around the edges than any other music form. This book gives a comprehensive guide to the artists, producers and songwriters who have contributed to the genre over the last thirty years, listing the greats and – perhaps more importantly – those whose talents are immense but largely unrecognized outside specialist circles: Bill Withers, Sam Dees and Teena Marie, to name but three personal favourites.

The unenviable task of compiling this labour of love goes to a writer whose standing in soul circles is formidable. When I first met Ralph Tee, I was an excitable seventeen-year-old who had just arrived in London from Cardiff. He was assistant editor on *Blues and Soul*, who – in conjunction with head honcho Bob Kilbourne – was responsible for serving hungry soul fans around the country their biweekly rations of info and interviews. Both men were unswerving devotees of black music, and patient enough to allow a brash, mouthy young Welshman to learn about the music and the business first-hand. Ralph is obsessed with soul music. He has dragged me around the desolate urban wastelands of Detroit, fearing for my life, just to find a little-known Keni Burke 12". If the authorities really wanted to find Lord Lucan, they should just tell Ralph that he has a rare Leroy Burgess-produced track hidden in his moustache. Lucan would be found within hours. Ralph himself would be the first to admit that this volume may be incomplete – I don't think it's possible to include everyone who's ever had anything to do with soul music. But if anyone's qualified to give it a good try, Ralph's your man.

DAMON ROCHEFORT (Nomad), July 1991

NOTE

Entries are arranged in alphabetical order, by surnames or group names where possible. Where this is not possible, e.g. Teena Marie or L L Cool J, entries are arranged according to first name or initial. Names beginning with a number have been treated as if the number was spelled out (e.g. 8th Day will be found between Effectron and Eighties Ladies).

Most entries include names shown in bold type. This indicates people/groups with separate entries of their own.

Titles of singles and songs are shown in quotation marks; album titles appear in italics.

GLOSSARY

'Motown Sound': The most innovative form of black music to come out of America. Although the Motown record company was founded in 1958, the sound was created by the label's producers in 1963 and survived until 1969. It was a combination of joyous uplifting chords on a fast 4s beat with gospel piano, prominent tambourines, driving bass lines (on and between the beat), high brass with tin-mute trumpet, and romantic strings.

'Stax Sound': The opposite of the Motown Sound, this was earthy, down-home music. It had a 4s beat with organ, punchy upfront low brass led by raw sax and trombone. The chords were simple, unsophisticated and tinged with blues.

'Northern Soul': A style of music based on the '60s Motown Sound, but produced on other labels and in other cities form the late '60s onwards. While the music existed from 1968, the phrase was coined by journalist Dave Godin in the north of England (where the sound became particularly popular) in 1970.

'Disco': A form of music which evolved from New York's gay clubs. It was a progression from the late '60s Motown Sound and matured over ten years. Initially, two copies of Motown style and 'Philly Sound' 7″ singles were played together to extend the record's playing time in discos. Disc jockeys soon became instrumental in preparing their own extended versions of records with added percussion breaks and long introductions, prior to the introduction of the 12″ disco single. The music form was officially recognised in 1973 and eventually was typified by a thumping 4s beat, rich orchestrations, slurping high-hat cymbal and often a wailing soulful vocal. It survived through to the late '70s.

'Philly Sound': Initially a part of the 'disco' sound, this was the most direct extension of the Motown Sound and was born in the early '70s with improved recording techniques. It offered more separated stereo vocals, dancing strings, melodic bass lines and strong vocals. It progressed to incorporate richer productions with jazz elements and more melancholy strings, horns and synthesisers.

'Jazz Funk': Initially referred to as 'soul jazz', this was essentially regular soul, disco, etc., with the vocal replaced by instrumental melodies and improvisation. It became an expression of the late '70s and early '80s for the fusion of jazz with funky bass lines, strings/synthesisers, and a dance beat occasionally seasoned with vocals. Later it became known simply as 'fusion'.

'High Energy': The third coming of the 4s beat after the Motown Sound and disco, but in a less soulful form. Created in the early '80s, it grew out of a desire to perpetuate the sound of late '70s disco with electric rather than acoustic instrumentations. It eventually lost all its soul elements to become a rather cheap and throwaway form of dance music.

'Brit funk': While American r & b reigned supreme in the late '70s–early '80s, this expression was coined for UK-based bands who tried to emulate the sound of American funk bands, but with a less slick, less sophisticated blend of funky bass, guitars, synthesisers, real brass, percussion and vocals. Eventually the term was dropped as British-produced soul and r & b became as good, if not better than, that imported from America!

A

A.B.s
(Group)
From Japan, The A.B.s were a funk group consisting of Fujimal Yoshino, Makoto Matsushita, Yoshihiko Ando, Naoki Watanabe and Atsuo Okamoto. The song 'Déjà Vu' from their 1983 album *A.B.'s* created some interest on the UK soul scene resulting in a single release for the song on the Streetwave label the same year.

A.C. BLACK
(Group)
A California funk/rock group consisting of Alvin Black (bass/vocals), Calvin Black (guitar/vocals), Kelvin Jones (lead vocals/keyboards), Tracy Orr (guitar/vocals), Kerry Lloyd (vocals/sampling), Larry Morgan (vocals/percussion) and Brian Haught (keyboards/programming). Their debut album *A.C.Black* was released on the Taj label via Motown in 1989.

A.R.B.
(Vocal Group)
Formed by producer **Gene Griffin** in 1990, A.R.B. stands for The Atlanta Rap Band and consists of Deirdre 'Koko' Thomas (from Atlanta), Timmy 'Artie' Arthur (from Virginia Beach, Delaware), and Idris 'X' Muhammad Jr (from New York), Idris being the son of **Idris Muhammad** Sr. Signing to Motown records, Gene produced their debut album *The Hard & Soft*, including 'All Or Nothing' (1991).

A PERFECT FIT
(Group)
British soul group released one single, 'If You Only Knew' (written by Michael Wyzgowski) on the Move label in 1986. Very little is known about the group, but the track was well received by the UK soul fraternity.

A TASTE OF HONEY
(Group)
A Taste Of Honey were **Janice Marie Johnson** (bass/vocals) and Hazel Payne (guitar/vocals), who teamed together in 1978 and recorded Janice's song 'Boogie Oogie Oogie', released by Capitol. The song became a dancefloor anthem and an international hit, reaching No. 3 in the UK charts. The track, together with parent album *A Taste Of Honey*, was produced by **Fonce** and **Larry Mizell**, better known in the field of jazz funk. *Another Taste* (1979) had little success, but 1980's *Twice As Sweet* caused ripples with 'Sukiyaki'. Their final Capitol album was *Ladies Of The Eighties* (1982) which included another popular dance item, 'We've Got The Groove' (produced by **Al McKay**) but without UK chart success.

In 1983 they contributed vocals on the **Wilton Felder** album *Gentle Fire*, following which Janice took on a solo career. In 1985 a remix of 'Boogie Oogie Oogie' (also recorded by **G.Q.**) made the UK Top 60.

ABBOTT, GREGORY
(Singer)
Gregory has made his home in various cities over the years. He went to university in Los Angeles (where he married **Freda Payne**) and Boston, worked as a researcher on Wall Street and briefly taught school in London. In 1986 he signed to CBS where 'Shake You Down' from his debut album *Gregory Abbott* was an American No. 1 and UK Top 10. He also recorded a follow-up CBS album.

ABRAMS, COLONEL
(Singer/Songwriter)
Born in Detroit, Colonel (his real name) was ten when he moved with his family to New York. Here, during the late '60s he performed with the group Conservative Manor which featured his brother Morris. In 1976 he sang lead vocals for **94 East** (a group which featured **Prince** on guitar) before joining New Jersey group **Surprise Package**.

In 1984 he recorded a ballad 'Leave The Message Behind The Door', released on New York's Streetwise label. The follow-up was 'Music Is The Answer', which established Colonel on dancefloors both sides of the Atlantic. In 1985 he signed to MCA Records for a debut album *Colonel Abrams*, including 'Trapped' (UK Top 5) and 'The Truth' (UK Top 75). A second album, *You And Me Equal Us* – including 'I'm Not Gonna Let You' (UK

Top 30) and 'How Soon We Forget' (UK Top 75) – was released in 1987.

Leaving MCA for the independent Horus label, Colonel released a single, 'Bad Timing', in 1990, produced by **Larry Blackmon**.

ACE, BUDDY

(Singer)

Buddy recorded for Duke Records 1956–69 and is best remembered for 'Nothing In The World Can Hurt Me (Except You)' which hit the American *Billboard* charts in 1966. He also recorded a ballad, 'The Inside Story', which has become a collector's item.

ACKLIN, BARBARA

(Singer/Songwriter)

Born in Chicago in 1943, Barbara was singing in the New Zion Baptist Church by the age of 11. Her cousin, highly respected musician/producer Monk Higgins, secured her a job at the local St Lawrence label, initially as a secretary. In 1964 the company's subsidiary label Special Agent released an unsuccessful debut single under the name Barbara Allen. She then concentrated on background singing with artists including **Fontella Bass** and **Etta James**. While working (in 1966) as a receptionist for Brunswick she co-wrote 'Whispers', which label boss **Carl Davis** gave to **Jackie Wilson**. The song was a hit, and Barbara began recording for the company.

After an unsuccessful start she recorded the self-written duet 'Show Me The Way To Go' with **Gene Chandler**. She and Gene scored in the US *Billboard* charts with a second duet, 'From The Teacher To The Preacher'. Her greatest solo success came with 'Love Makes A Woman' (1968), co-written with **Eugene Record**, which stayed in the American r&b charts for fifteen weeks, reaching No. 3. It was followed by her second biggest seller, 'Just Ain't Enough Love', both of which came from the album *Love Makes A Woman*.

In 1969 her second Brunswick album *Seven Days of Night* led to the single 'Am I The Same Girl', controversial in that it was the instrumental B side, 'Soulful Strut' (by **Young–Holt Unlimited**), which charted following the company's promotion of the track. In 1971 she scored her greatest songwriting success (with **Eugene Record**) with 'Have You Seen Her' for **The Chi-Lites**. Barbara continued recording with Brunswick (albums including *Someone Else's Arms*) until 1973 when she signed to Capitol. Here she recorded one album, *A Place In The Sun* (1974), which included her last American hit 'Raindrops', produced by Willie Henderson.

More recently she has worked as a background singer on projects for **Eugene Record**.

ACT 1

(Group)

Early '70s funk group produced by Raeford Gerald (who also wrote most of their songs), their main claim to fame was 1974's 'Tom The Peeper'. They cut the soul gem 'It Takes Both Of Us' in 1973.

ACTIVE FORCE

(Group)

From California, Active Force were Victor Adams, **Gerald Mallory**, Adrian Steele, Adrina Steele and Gerald Steele. They recorded one album for A&M in 1983, *Active Force* (including 'Give Me Your Love'), which was produced by **Michael Stokes**. The album featured additional keyboards by **Patrice Rushen**.

A year previously, **Gerald Mallory** of the group released 'Lay It Down On Me', a Michael Stokes production for Prelude Records.

ADAMS, ARTHUR

(Singer/Guitarist)

Born on Christmas day in America's deep South, Arthur built a reputation for his soulful guitar-playing, though he initially worked in a rock and roll band. He was a session guitarist on the movie soundtrack *Bonnie And Clyde*, during which he met **Wayne Henderson**. In 1975 Wayne took Arthur to Fantasy Records and produced his debut album *Home Brew*, an experimental set of jazz fusion cuts featuring **Ronnie Laws**, **Jerry Peters**, **Joe Sample**, **Dennis Coffey** and Motown bass player James Jamerson. Through 1976 he worked closely with Wayne's group **The Crusaders**, playing guitar on both the group's albums released that year. Wayne later returned to produce Arthur's 1977 album for Fantasy, *Midnight Serenade*.

In 1979 Arthur joined A&M for the Stewart Levine-produced album *I Love, Love, Love, Love, Love, Love, Love My Lady*. Featuring **Neil Larson** and the Seawind horns among a host of top musicians, 'I Like It Funky' did well on the jazz funk scene, while 'You Give Me Such A Good Feelin'' (on which he sang) became popular on the modern soul scene a few years later. His greatest commercial success came with the vocal dance anthem 'You Got The Floor', a UK Top 40 for RCA in 1981, originally an American import on the Inculcation label. Inculcation released a follow-up, 'Fire', which made no impact.

Arthur also recorded sessions with **David Oliver**, **Side Effect** and **Martha Reeves**.

ADAMS, GAYLE

(Singer)

Gayle Adams worked with Washington-based writers/producers from the early to mid-'80s. Signing to the Prelude label (via CBS in the UK), her album *Gayle Adams* (1980) included the UK Top 75 hit 'Stretchin' Out'. In 1981 she stirred dancefloors with 'Love Fever' and a rendition of the **Four Tops** hit 'Baby I Need Your Loving' before switching to Lester/Brown's Mainline label for a single 'I'm Warning You' (1984).

ADAMS, JOHNNY
(Singer)
From New Orleans, Johnny began recording in the late '50s for the Ric & Ron label. From 1968 to 1970 he switched to the SSS International label for acclaimed singles including 'I Won't Cry', and 1969 American r&b hits 'Release Me, Reconsider Me' and 'I Can't Be All Bad'. Over the years he has recorded for Atlantic, Ariola, Chelsea, Hep'Me and more recently Rounder. In 1978 his album *After All The Good Is Gone* won support among soul fans.

ADAMS, OLETA
(Singer/Songwriter)
From Kansas City, Oleta Adams was plucked from obscurity by British rock group **Tears For Fears**. After a concert in her hometown the group walked into a bar and heard her sing. Impressed, they exchanged albums (Oleta had recorded one locally). After touring and recording with the group on their *Seeds Of Love* album (1988), she signed to Phonogram and recorded a solo album *Circle Of One* (1990). It included 'The Rhythm Of Life' and 'Get Here'.

ADAMS, PATRICK
(Songwriter/Producer)
Born in Harlem, New York, Patrick has played an integral part in the dance music scene from the '70s to the present day. He was particularly prolific through the 'disco' era of the mid-'70s to early '80s, instigating studio-based groups whose records he wrote and produced (or co-wrote/produced with people like **Greg Carmichael** or **Lamar Thomas**). Groups he created, wrote for and/or produced include **Universal Robot Band** ('Dance And Shake Your Tambourine', 1976), **Sine** (*Happy Is The Only Way*, including 'Just Let Me Do My Thing', UK Top 40) **Musique** (including 'In The Bush', 1978), **Inner Life**, **The Main Ingredient** (*Evening Of Love/Save Me*, 1981), **Salsoul Orchestra** ('Seconds', 1982), Cloud One ('Happy Music'), Daybreak ('Everything Man'), Rare Essence ('Flipside'), Prince Charles & The City Beat Band ('We Can Make It Happen'), **Shannon** ('You Put A Spark In My Life', 1986), Venus Dodson, and **Skipworth & Turner** ('Thinking About Your Love').

Patrick also operated his own label, Pap Records, and worked as an A&R director for the Perception label.

ADEVA
(Singer)
Born 'Patricia' in Patterson, New Jersey, Adeva was a schoolteacher prior to launching a singing career on the local club scene in the mid-'80s. Her debut release was 'In And Out Of My Life' for New York's Easy Street label before she signed to Cooltempo (via Chrysalis) in 1989. Her career took off first in the UK, then back in America, with a debut album *Adeva!*, scoring hits with 'Respect', 'Warning', 'Musical Freedom', 'Beautiful Love' and 'Treat Me Right'.

AD-LIBERS
(Group)
This four-guy, one-girl American group recorded the original version of Leiber/Stoller's 'Boy From New York City' which charted for them in America (1965). After further recordings for the Phillips and Karen labels they joined writer/producer **Van McCoy** in 1968 at his Share label. At Share they released three dance singles, 'Nothing Worse Than Being Alone', 'Appreciation' and 'Giving Up'. After a brief spell at Capitol Records they split up in 1970, later to record again in 1977.

ADORABLES
(Group)
From Detroit, The Adorables were two sets of sisters, Jackie and Betty Winston, and Diane and **Pat Lewis**. Signed to Golden World in the 1960s, they were considered to be the label's equivalent to **Martha Reeves & the Vandellas**. Releases included 'School's All Over' and 'Deep Freeze'.

THE AFFAIR
(Group)
The Affair were a New York-based group featuring **Alyson Williams** (vocals), **Gwen Guthrie** (vocals), **Yogi Horton** (drums) and John Adams (keyboards), former pianist with **Change** and a one-time musical director for **Melba Moore**. The group's one single release was 'Please Don't Break My Heart' (1985) on 10/Virgin records, mixed by Van Gibbs of the group **The Limit**.

AFTER 7
(Group)
From Indianapolis, After 7 are brothers Melvin and Kevin Edmonds (brothers of **Babyface**) together with Keith Mitchell (cousin of L.A. Reid of **L.A./Babyface**). In 1989 they signed to Virgin Records and released an album *After 7*, including 'Can't Stop' and 'Heat Of The Moment'. In the UK the One World single remix of 'Can't Stop' generated a great deal of interest on the soul/dance scene in 1990. The group also recorded with **Johnny Gill** through their producers **L.A/Babyface**.

AFTERGLOW
(Group)
From Los Angeles Afterglow are Gary Herbig (sax), Sam Riney (sax/flute), Walt Johnson (trumpet), Bob Findley (trumpet/flugelhorn), John Beasley (keyboards), Domenic Genova (bass), Mike Jochum (drums/percussion), Laurence Juber (guitars), Steve Reid (percussion), Dan Foliart (keyboards/acoustic guitar) and Howard Pearl (keyboards). They met through their session work on jingles and Paramount film scores. In 1985 they recorded an album *Music Party*, (on US Riza

Records) introducing the vocals of Julie Christensen on two soul cuts, 'Running To You' and 'Afterglow'.

AGEE, TAWATHA
(Singer/Songwriter)
New York-based singer Tawatha has worked consistently as a backing singer from the mid-'70s through to the present day, predominantly with **James Mtume** who produced her one solo album *Tawatha* for Epic Records (1985). She was also a featured vocalist on **Mtume** hits including 'Juicy Fruit' (UK Top 40, 1983).

She has recorded with artists including **Bruce Fisher** (*Red Hot*, 1977), **Cabo Frio**, **Heath Brothers**, **David Sanborn**, **B.B.&Q.**, **Levert**, **Kashif**, **Keni Burke**, **Luther Vandross**, **Aretha Franklin**, **Al Jarreau**, Roxy Music, **Rena Scott** and **The O'Jays**. She co-wrote the duet 'Two Hearts' with **Mtume/Lucas** for **Stephanie Mills** and **Teddy Pendergrass**.

AIRTO
(Percussion/Producer)
Born 1941, Brazilian percussionist/producer Airto Moreiro made an impact on the UK jazz funk scene from the mid- to late '70s. As an artist he recorded albums including *Identity* (produced by **Herbie Hancock** for Arista Records, 1976) and *Touching You, Touching Me* (Warner Brothers, 1979), including 'Toque De Cuica'. As a producer he has worked with artists including **Raul De Souza** (*Colors*, 1975) and OPA (*Golden Wings*, including 'African Bird', 1976). He also recorded percussion with **Esther Phillips** (including *Home Is Where The Hatred Is*), and **Dee Dee Bridgewater** (*Sweet Rain*), among numerous other people including his wife, **Flora Purim**.

ALBRIGHT, GERALD
(Sax)
Based in Los Angeles, Gerald Albright has established himself as one of the most in-demand sax players in the business. He has recorded with artists including **Quincy Jones**, **Rockie Robbins**, **Atlantic Starr**, **Fire Fox**, **Four Tops**, **Bert Robinson**, **Bobby Womack**, **Barbara Weathers**, **Leon Ware** and numerous others. Signed to Atlantic Records as an artist, his albums include *Just Between Us* (1987) and *Dream Come True* (1990), featuring vocals by **Be Be Winans** on 'Growing With Each Other'.

ALEEM
(Group)
Aleem are identical twins Taharqa Aleem and Tunde-Ra Aleem, with **Leroy Burgess**. The brothers began their recording career with Jimi Hendrix's *Cry Of Love* and *Rainbow Bridge*, as The Ghetto Fighters.

With Leroy as lead vocalist they formed Aleem in New York during the early '80s and originally released hardcore dance songs on their own label, Nia Records. These included 'Hooked On Your Love', 'Get Down Friday Night', 'Release Yourself' and 1985's 'Confusion', which resulted in a deal with Atlantic Records. In 1986 they recorded *Casually Formal*, and worked together as producers on acts including **Fonda Rae**, Caprice, Captain Rock and **Process & The Doo-Rags**.

ALEXANDER, J.W.
(Singer/Manager)
Formerly a member of the gospel group The Pilgrim Travellers, J.W. set up the Sar Records label with **Sam Cooke** and was responsible for signing Sam to RCA, directing his music to a crossover audience. He also guided **Lou Rawls** to solo success by first trimming his Christian name from Louis and then signing him to Capitol.

ALLEN, DONNA
(Singer)
Born in Key West and raised in nearby Tampa, Florida, Donna did not know she could sing at all until she was forced to do a friend a favour and audition for a local band. The group's lead singer was planning to elope and asked Donna to be her replacement. Her musical career was launched in the early '80s.

She later joined the band Hi-Octane, touring North America for a year before joining another group, **Trama**. After leaving Trama she formed Donna Allen & Company and worked at Tampa club The Forge. Here she was approached by producer Lou Pace who went on to produce her debut album *Perfect Timing* (1986). It featured 'Serious', a UK Top 10 release in 1987 (via CBS/Portrait). The title track was a duet with **Howard Johnson**. The following year *Heaven On Earth* was released in America on the Oceana label. It featured her rendition of the **Maze** song 'Joy & Pain', released in the UK by BCM where it was a Top 40 hit.

ALLEN, RANCE
(Singer)
Born in Detroit, Rance sang with his brothers Tom, Steve and Esau as The Rance Allen Group. Their early recordings included 'Just My Salvation' (a gospel rendition of 'Just My Imagination') for the Stax label's subsidiary Gospel Truth. They also released *Smile* (1979), including 'Where Have All Our Friends Gone', prior to signing with Capitol. Here they recorded a number of songs with producer **Ronnie McNeir**.

ALPERT, HERB
(Trumpet/Industry/Singer)
Based in Los Angeles, Herb Alpert began his career as a trumpeter before becoming a co-founder of A&M Records (he's the 'A') in the early '60s. With his horn section **The Tijuana Brass** he scored instrumental hits with 'The Lonely Bull' (Top 30, 1963), 'Spanish Flea' (Top 5, 1965) and 'Tijuana Taxi' (Top 40, 1966) on the Pye label before his A&M label was launched in the UK

during 1967. While both recording and working for the label, his solo UK chart success continued with the hits 'Casino Royale' (Top 30, 1967), 'This Guy's In Love With You', marking Herb's debut as a vocalist (Top 5, 1968), 'Without Her' (Top 40, 1969), 'Jerusalem' (Top 50, 1970), 'Rise' (Top 20, 1979), 'Rotation' (Top 50, 1980), 'Keep Your Eye On Me' (Top 20, 1987) and 'Diamonds', featuring **Janet Jackson** (Top 30, 1987).

As a songwriter he worked with Lou Adler on songs for **Sam Cooke** (including 'Wonderful World'), and has produced numerous A&M acts including **Gato Barbieri**. His more recent albums include *Blow Your Own Horn*, including 'Red Hot' (1983), *Wild Romance* (1985), *Keep Your Eye On Me* (1987) produced by **Jam/Lewis**, *Under A Spanish Moon* (1988) and *North On South Street*, including 'Jump Street' (1991).

ALLEN, TIMMY
(Bass/Songwriter/Producer)
Based in New York, Timmy was the bass player with **Change**, while also recording with artists including **Hi-Gloss**, **Freddie Jackson**, and **Howard Johnson**. As writer and/or producer he has worked with **Glenn Jones** (*At Last*), **Lillo Thomas** ('Sexy Girl'), **Millie Jackson** ('Hot! Wild! Unrestricted! Crazy Love!'), **Vanessa Bell Armstrong** ('Pressing On'), **Stephanie Mills** ('A Rush On Me') and numerous others.

ALLEN, YVONNE
(Singer)
Detroit vocalist Yvonne Allen recorded with **Wilson Pickett**, **Terry Lindsay** and **The Donays** before joining **The Elgins** as a replacement for **Sandra Edwards**.

ALLSPICE
(Vocal Group)
One of the few groups to record for **Wayne Henderson**'s At Home label through Fantasy, Allspice were Doug Thomas, Deborah Shotlow, Esau Joyner, Saundra Alexander and Ned Perkins. They recorded one album in 1977, *Allspice*, very much in the Wayne Henderson '70s tradition and featuring his regular musicians including **Bobby Lyle** and **Marlon McLain**.

ALSTON, GERALD
(Singer)
Born in North Carolina, Gerald is the son of a preacher and comes from a musical family. His uncle is Johnny Fields of The Blind Boys, his aunt is Shirley Alston of **The Shirelles**. After developing his vocals in the church choir, Gerald formed the New Imperials, a teen group that also sang in churches as Gospel Jubilee. When **The Manhattans** came to perform in his town they needed some extra equipment, and hired his. When they came to collect it Gerald was rehearsing with his group. Impressed, they asked him to join The Manhattans, aged seventeen. He remained with them for seventeen years.

During this time he sang lead vocals on hits including 'Kiss And Say Goodbye' and 'Hurt' (both 1976) while winning a Grammy for his vocals on 'You Are My Shining Star' (1980). Also with the group he sang the duet 'Where Did We Go Wrong' (1986) with **Regina Belle**, her recording debut (produced by **Bobby Womack**).

In 1988 he signed with Motown as a solo artist (via the Taj label), and producers Stan Shepherd/Jimmy Varner took care of his debut album *Gerald Alston*, which included his debut single 'Take Me Where You Want To'. *Open Invitation* followed in 1990, and included 'Slow Motion' and 'Getting Back Into Love'.

ALWAYS, BILLY
(Singer/Songwriter)
Born in Chicago in 1955, Billy was the godson of gospel great Mahalia Jackson. **Aretha Franklin** treated him like a younger brother. At the age of nine he was the lead voice in his church choir, and by 11 he was touring and recording with Reverend Isaac Whittman. In 1969 he was taken on as Aretha's protégé and was given studio time by her production company Do It To It Productions. He recorded a single 'Do It Again' with the help of Aretha, **Carolyn Franklin** and **Cissy Houston**, but it was not released. Aretha's backing singer Evelyn Green introduced him to **Barrett Strong**, and from 1975 Barrett and Billy wrote a number of songs together including 'Man Up In The Sky', recorded by both Barrett (1976) and **Johnny Bristol** (1989).

In 1979 his attorney financed his debut solo album *Billy Always*, totally self-written, performed and produced. While not released officially, 'I Mean To Love You' and 'Some Kind Of Love' were bootlegged and scored success as an illegally released single. The following year he met **Willie Mitchell** who produced Billy's song 'Didn't We Do It' as the first release on Waylo. A debut Waylo album (*Billy Always*) was later released in 1982 (and **Ann Peebles** recorded 'Didn't We Do It'). Billy continues to work with Willie Mitchell and Waylo to this day, although 1988's *Trust Me* was released by Epic. His most recent album was *Let's Get Personal*, including 'One Of Them Thangs', 'Ain't Nothing But A Heartache' and 'I Need You'.

In 1981 he wrote 'Come To Me' (with Bernie Miller) for **Walter Jackson**'s album *Tell Me Where It Hurts*.

AMBASSADORS OF FUNK
(Group)
A British studio group instigated by Simon Harris, Ambassadors of Funk released 'My Mind's Made Up' for the Living Beat label in 1989. It featured a rap by **Greg Edwards**.

ANDANTES
(Vocal Group)
The Andantes are **Louvain Demps**, Jackie Hicks, Marlene Barrow and later **Pat Lewis**, all from Detroit, Michigan.

Between 1960 and 1972 they sang background vocals at Motown on everybody's releases from **Marvin Gaye** to **The Supremes** and **The Four Tops**. It is estimated that they sang on about 20,000 songs, more than any other group, as well as enjoying some success in soul circles with their solo release 'Like A Nightmare' on Motown's V.I.P. subsidiary.

In 1989 they reformed to sing backgrounds for the former Motown artists recorded by **Ian Levine**'s labels Motor City and Nightmare (named after the group's V.I.P. recording). The Andantes have since made solo recordings including 'Lightning Never Strikes Twice' (1989) for the Nightmare label.

ANDERSON, CARL

(Singer)

Born in Lynchburg, Virginia, Carl was initially inspired by **Sam Cooke**, whose records he first heard on a Nashville radio station in the early '60s. In 1969 he moved to Washington where he sang with the rock group Second Eagle prior to settling in Los Angeles in the early '70s. In 1971 he signed to Motown Records as a solo artist and worked with producer **Stevie Wonder** on a number of songs, although none were ever released. In the meantime he commenced an acting career and played Judas in both the stage and film version of *Jesus Christ Superstar* through to the mid-'70s. From here he took to singing in the bars and clubs of Los Angeles.

In 1980 Carl was spotted by CBS talent scout Larkin Arnold in a Hollywood nightclub. He was signed to Epic and recorded a debut album *A.W.O.L. (Absence Without Love)* (1982), produced by **Richard Rudolph**. The album included 'Buttercup', largely ignored at first, but a UK Top 50 hit when issued by Streetwave Records in 1985. A second Epic album, *On & On* was released in 1984, from which 'Magic' and the duet with **Vaneese Thomas** 'It's The Love' met with approval from UK soul fans. His final two Epic albums were *Protocol* (1985) with producers including Patrick Henderson, **Gary Taylor**, **Al McKay**; and *Carl Anderson* (1986), more of a greatest-hits compilation but with a new duet 'Friends And Lovers' with Gloria Loring.

In 1987 he recorded with both **Nancy Wilson** ('Forbidden Lover') and **Weather Report** before switching to the Polydor label in 1988. Here he recorded *An Act of Love* with productions by **La La** and **Al McKay**. In 1990 he returned for *Piece Of A Heart* (including 'How Deep Does it Go') for the GRP label.

His other acting work includes roles in *Hotel*, *Hill Street Blues* and *The Colour Purple*.

ANDERSON, CAROL

(Singer)

Born in Detroit, Carol began recording in the '60s with songs including 'Holding On'. She later recorded for Fee Records where her single 'Sad Girl' became a UK release for the Grapevine label in 1979. 'A Promise Is A Promise' is another of her notable releases.

ANDERSON, MAXI

(Singer)

Based in Los Angeles, Maxi has worked consistently as a session singer on the soul scene from the '70s through to the present day. She recorded a solo album *Maxi*, including 'Lover To Lover', for Blue Note Records in 1977, produced by Billy and **Gene Page**.

She has recorded with numerous artists including **Quincy Jones**, **Deniece Williams**, **Starship Orchestra**, **Beau Williams**, **The Crusaders**, **Scherrie Payne**, **John Klemmer**, **Klique**, **Rodney Franklin**, **Cherrelle** (co-writing 'I Will Wait For You' and 'Stay With Me'), **Donald Byrd**, **Lenny Williams**, **Rockie Robbins** and André Crouch.

Together with **Marlena Jeter** and Gwen Machu, Maxi also recorded as the group Silk (not to be confused with the more famous **Silk**).

ANDREWS, RUBY

(Singer)

Detroit singer Ruby Andrews recorded the original version of 'Casanova', later a popular success for both **Loleatta Holloway** and **Coffee**. In 1977 she was with ABC Records where *Genuine Ruby* included 'Merry Go Round', popular on the UK soul scene in the early '90s.

ANGLO SAXON BROWN

(Group)

This Philly group included **Debra Henry** (lead vocals), Dwight Smith (keyboards/vocals), Clemente Burnette (vocals/guitar), Tyrone Durham (drums), Alvin Brown (trumpet/flugelhorn/trombone) and Charles Manns (sax) who later became the nucleus of the group **Silk**. Also in Anglo Saxon Brown were Carlton Robinson (bass), Joe Jefferson (keyboards/producer) and Larry Washington (percussion). In the Philly tradition of the mid-'70s, the group recorded one album in 1976, *Songs For Evolution*, produced by Joe Jefferson and Charles Simmons with string and horn arrangements by Jack Smith.

ANN, SUE

(Singer)

New West Coast American singer, Sue Ann signed to MCA in 1988 for an album *Blue Velvet* including 'Love Dies Hard', written and produced by **James Mtume**. Other producers on this debut album were David and Wayne Lewis from **Atlantic Starr** and **Jesse Johnson**.

ANTHONY, C.J.

(Singer)

New West Coast American soul singer, C.J.'s only recording to date has been 1988's *Luv's Invitation* (US KMA Records), which was an early production project for

Chuckii Booker. It featured a cover version of 'You Are My Starship' alongside a strong title track.

ANY DAY NOW
(Duo)
London-based Any Day Now were Derek Green, former vocalist with **Central Line**, **Direct Drive** and **First Light**, together with Dave Hubbard, who formerly played synthesizer with the group Z6. In 1986 they signed with A&M Records and released 'Show Me The Way', produced by Mark Berry who had just scored success as a remixer with **The Bar-Kays**, **Stephanie Mills** and **Cameo**.

APOLLONIA 6
(Vocal Group)
Apollonia 6 were Apollonia Kotero with Susan and Brenda, formerly of the group **Vanity**. Apollonia began her career as an actress, mainly in films directed at the Latin American market. In 1984 the group starred in the film *Purple Rain* alongside **Prince**, who produced their album *Apollonia 6*, released by Warner Brothers.

AQUARIAN DREAM
(Group)
From the USA's East Coast, Aquarian Dream were Claude Bartee Jr (sax/vocals), Claude Bartee III (guitar/vocals/percussion), James Morrison (drums), Patricia Shannon (vocals), Dave Worthy (percussion/vocals), Winston Daley (keyboards), Ernie Adams (bass) and **Sylvia Striplin** (vocals). Signed to the Elektra label, the group worked with producer **Norman Connors** on *Fantasy*, released in 1978. The album included 'You're A Star', extremely well received on the UK funk and soul scene, but only a Top 70 hit in 1979.

ARMENTA
(Singer/Songwriter)
New York-based singer/songwriter Armenta Richardson released one dance record, 'I Wanna Be With You' (which she co-wrote with **Amir Bayaan**), on the American Savoir Faire label in 1983.

ARMSTEAD, JO
(Singer/Songwriter/Producer)
Born Josephine Armstead in Yazoo City, Mississippi, in 1944, Jo (nicknamed Joshie) sang in church prior to joining **Ike & Tina Turner** as an Ikette in 1961. As well as touring with Ike and Tina, she also recorded as an Ikette between 1961 and 1963 for the Atco subsidiary of Atlantic Records. Later the Infinity Records release 'Sitting Here Thinking' (1963) became a collector's item among Northern soul fans in the UK.

In 1964 Jo moved to New York where she survived by writing songs, many recorded by **Big Maybelle** on the Rojac label. A year later she met **Valerie Simpson**, and together with **Ashford & Simpson** she wrote two major songs for Ray Charles, 'I Don't Need No Doctor' and 'Let's Get Stoned' (1966). In 1967 Jo moved to Chicago where she married Mel Collins. Together they started two record labels, Gamma and Giant, for which Jo began to record as a solo artist. (**Garland Green** and **Jimmy Scott** also recorded for the label.) At Giant her late '60s and early '70s releases included 'I Feel An Urge Coming On', 'A Stone Good Lover', 'I've Got A Memory', 'Ain't That Good Enough', and 'There's Not Too Many More (Left Like Him)'. She was also instrumental in launching the recording career of **John Edwards** during this period.

After divorcing Mel Collins Jo returned briefly to New York and took to session work before signing to Stax's subsidiary gospel label Gospel Truth in Memphis (1973). Here she recorded 'I've Got The Vibes' and 'Give A Little Loving' (1974) before taking a break from recording. It was only in 1990 that Jo recorded again, 'Right Place' being released on her own label Praire Rose Records.

ARMSTRONG, JIMMY
(Singer/Songwriter)
New York vocalist Jimmy Armstrong recorded for Shrine Records in the early '60s. His 1960 release 'Mystery' was arranged by **Raynoma Singleton** and co-written and produced by her husband **Eddie Singleton**.

ARMSTRONG, VANESSA BELL
(Singer)
American gospel singer Vanessa Bell Armstrong originally recorded gospel albums for the Onyx label, including *Peace Be Still* (1983) and *Chosen* (1984), before switching to Jive Records and taking a more secular approach with *Vanessa Bell Armstrong* (1987); including 'You Bring Out The Best In Me' and 'Pressing On'; *Wonderful One* (1989) and *The Truth About Christmas* (1990). She also recorded a duet with **Jonathan Butler**, 'True Love Never Fails' (1988).

ARNIE'S LOVE
(Group)
Arnie's Love was essentially Arnie Joseph, half-brother of singer **Toney Lee**. Other members in the group were Debbie Allen and Arnelia Villanuea, while its name was derived from the fact that they only sing love songs. Arnie started his career as a drummer and played with **The Commodores** for one night in 1972.

When the group released their debut single, 'I'm Out Of Your Life' (US Radar Records), it was Arnie's first recording after fifteen years as a singer on the New York club scene. Produced by **Eric Matthew**, the single was released on the Streetwave label in the UK, making the UK Top 75 in 1983. It has subsequently become a collector's item. In 1985, Arnie's Love returned briefly with Profile Records, their release being a version of 'Date With The Rain' (a song earlier established by **Eddie Kendricks**, and more recently covered by **Jamie Principle**).

ARNOLD, P.P.

(Singer)

Born in Los Angeles, into a family of gospel singers, Pat Arnold took her singing seriously from the age of four. Her first professional engagement was as a backing singer with Bobby Day of Rockin' Robin. In the mid-'60s she was invited by **Ike & Tina Turner** to be one of the Ikettes, and toured with them across the States (including a tour with The Rolling Stones in 1966). While on tour in London Mick Jagger persuaded Pat to stay in London and record for the Immediate label (run by Stones manager Andrew Loog-Oldham). Andrew, Mick and Mike Hurst produced Pat's debut album *The First Lady of Immediate* (1967), which featured her debut UK single 'The First Cut Is The Deepest' (Top 20), written by Cat Stevens and later a hit again for Rod Stewart. Other UK hits on Immediate were 'The Time Has Come' (Top 50, 1967), '(If You Think) You're Groovy' (Top 50, 1968), and 'Angel In The Morning' (Top 30, 1968), following which Pat formed The Nice and toured Europe.

In 1969 she joined the cast of the play *Catch My Soul*, later acting in *Fame*, *Knot's Landing*, and as Belle in Andrew Lloyd Webber's *Starlight Express*.

Signing to 10 Records (via Virgin) in 1984 she was first asked by Boy George to sing lead on a song he had written for the movie *Electric Dreams*. In 1985 she teamed up with **Dexter Wansel** and worked with Carl and Steve from **Loose Ends** on her debut 10 Records solo single 'A Little Pain', as Pat Arnold. Leaving 10 Records she returned to the charts as lead vocalist on 'Burn It Up', a UK Top 20 on the Rhythm King label for **The Beatmasters**. Following this The Beatmasters produced her next solo release 'Dynamite', Pat's last commercial release to date.

ARRINGTON, STEVE

(Singer/Songwriter/Producer)

From Ohio, Steve Arrington originally played drums with The Young Mystics. When the group broke up, Steve moved to San Francisco while remaining members of the group combined with members of another Ohio group Black Satin Soul to form **Slave**. With the success of Slave, Steve returned to the group in 1978, initially as a backing singer but later as lead vocalist on hits 'Just A Touch Of Love', 'Watching You' and 'Wait For Me'.

Politics within the group led to Steve's departure in 1983, following which he formed a new group, Steve Arrington's Hall Of Fame. Their Atlantic Records debut was *Positive Power* (1984). In 1985 Steve scored his greatest solo success with 'Feels So Real', a UK Top 5 hit taken from his album *Dancin' In The Key Of Life*, whose title track was a UK Top 25 single in 1985. On the back of this success Steve toured the UK, and in a severe credibility blow turned his shows into lengthy spoken sermons preaching his newfound Christian faith.

Following a brief spell with EMI/Manhattan Records, Steve disappeared from the music scene.

ARTISTICS

(Vocal Group)

From Chicago, The Artistics formed in the late 1950s and were Aaron Floyd, Laurence Johnson, Jesse Bolian and lead singer Marvin Smith. Discovered by **Major Lance**, their recordings included 'Get My Hands On Some Lovin'' (1964) and their US r&b hit 'This Heart Of Mine' (1965) for the Okeh label, followed by a Brunswick album *I'm Gonna Miss You* including 'The Chase Is On'.

ASHFORD & SIMPSON

(Songwriters/Producers/Singers)

Nickolas Ashford met **Valerie Simpson** in 1963. He was 21, she 17. Val was singing in the White Rock Baptist Church choir in Harlem, and Nick joined the choir in the hope of being able to take her to dinner! They began writing songs together for fun in 1964 and were amazed when a publisher gave them $75 for a batch. They recorded three singles for the Glover label as Valerie & Nickolas before joining Scepter Records in 1965 as full-time writers. The same year the couple met **Jo Armstead**, and in 1966 the three of them took **Ray Charles** to No. 31 in the American pop charts with 'Let's Get Stoned'. Jo left to live in Chicago while Ashford & Simpson were offered a songwriting contract with Motown Records. In 1967 they wrote and arranged 'Ain't No Mountain High Enough' for **Marvin Gaye** & **Tammi Terrell**, a US Top 5 single that year and a UK Top 10 (No. 1 in the USA) for **Diana Ross** in 1970. Further Motown hits included 'You're All I Need To Get By', 'Ain't Nothing Like The Real Thing', 'The Onion Song', 'Reach Out & Touch (Somebody's Hand)' and 'Remember Me'. They worked particularly closely with both Marvin Gaye and Diana Ross during their Motown days.

In 1973 they signed as artists to Warner Brothers. In the UK they had just one single hit, 'It Seems To Hang On' (Top 50, 1978), but on both sides of the Atlantic their music was adored by both soul and disco fans. Their albums were *Gimme Something Real* (1973), *I Wanna Be Selfish* (1974), *Come As You Are* (1976), *So Satisfied* (1977), *Send It* (gold, 1977), *It Is Still Good To Ya* (gold, 1978), *Stay Free* (including 'Found A Cure') (gold, 1979), *A Musical Affair* (including 'Get Out Your Handkerchief', (1980), and *Performance* (1981). In 1982 they left Warner Brothers for Capitol where their debut album for the label was *Street Opera*, a concept album and a departure from their usual style. In 1983 the album *High Rise* was released, but it was the following year which produced their biggest UK hit (No. 3), 'Solid', from an album of the same name which also included two tracks used in the motion picture *Body Rock*. In 1985 a single 'Babies' hit the UK Top 60, followed in 1986 by an album *Real Love* and a separate single 'Time Talking' (from the stage musical *Time*) produced by Dave Clark.

From their heyday with Warner Brothers to the present day, Ashford & Simpson have maintained their work as writers and/or producers for an array of artists. These include **Chaka Khan** ('I'm Every Woman'), **Sylvester** ('Over And Over', 1977), **Randy Crawford** ('Where There Was Darkness', 1979), **Phyllis Hyman** ('I Ain't Asking', 1981), **Gladys Knight & The Pips** (two albums for CBS including *About Love*, 1980), **Diana Ross** (*The Boss*, 1979), **Brothers Johnson** ('Ride-O'Rocket'), **Stephanie Mills** ('I Can't Give Back The Love I Feel For You'/'Keep Away Girls', 1982), Dynamic Superiors ('Shoe Shoe Shine'), **Patti Labelle** ('There's A Winner In You', 1986, from the play *Pipes*), **Teddy Pendergrass** ('Is It Still Good To Ya', 'Girl You Know' and 'Only To You'), **Jennifer Holliday** ('The Game Of Love', 1983, and 'New At It'), Miami Vice star **Philip Michael Thomas** ('Baby Grew Up', 1988) and Val's brother **Ray Simpson** ('Tiger Love').

While Ashford & Simpson maintain the image of the perfect married couple, they have a reputation within the industry for endless fierce arguments with each other!

ASHFORD, NICK

(Writer/Producer/Singer)

One half of **Ashford & Simpson**, Nickolas was born in Michigan in 1942 and moved to New York in 1963 to become a singer and jazz dancer. As a solo artist he recorded one single for Verve ('When I Feel The Need'/'Young Emotions') in 1967 and one single for ABC ('Dead End Kids'/'Let's Get Stoned') in 1970.

ATLANTIC STARR

(Group)

Atlantic Starr were originally David Lewis (vocals/keyboards/guitar), Jonathan Lewis (keyboards/trombone), Wayne Lewis (vocals/keyboards), Joseph Phillips (percussion), Koran Daniels (sax), Clifford Archer (bass), William Suddeeth III (trumpet), Porter Carroll Jr (drums/vocals) and **Sharon Bryant** (vocals). Brothers David, Jonathan and Wayne first had their own bands Newban, Exact Change and Unchained Youth before moving from the East Coast to Los Angeles where they formed Atlantic Starr in the mid-'70s. In 1978 they signed to A&M and released two **Bobby Eli** produced albums, *Atlantic Starr* (1978), including 'Gimme Your Lovin'' (UK Top 75), and *Straight To The Point* (1979), including 'Losing You'. For the next three albums they worked with producer **James Anthony Carmichael**, finding a slick, soulful sound popular with UK soul fans. These were *Radiant* (1980), including 'When Love Calls'; *Brilliance* (1982), including 'Circles'/'Love Me Down', and *Yours Forever* (1983), including 'Touch A Four Leaf Clover'.

At this point Sharon left to be replaced by **Barbara Weathers**, and the line-up was reduced to just Wayne, David, Jonathan and Joseph. They began producing themselves from their most successful album in 1985, *As The Band Turns*, including 'Silver Shadow' (UK Top 50), 'One Love' (UK Top 75), 'Secret Lovers' (UK Top 10, 1986) and 'If Your Heart Isn't In It' (UK Top 50, 1986). Also in 1986 they worked briefly with producer **Maurice White** on one single 'Armed And Dangerous', released by Manhattan/EMI (mixed for 12" release by **Arthur Baker**).

In 1987 the group signed to Warner Brothers. *All In The Name of Love* included 'Always' (UK Top 5), 'One Lover At A Time' (UK Top 75) and soul gems 'Let The Sun In' and 'Don't Take Me For Granted'. 1989's *We're Movin' Up* introduced lead singer Porscha Martin, following the departure of Barbara Weathers who signed as a solo artist to the Reprise label (with Wayne Lewis a producer on her debut album). David and Wayne Lewis have also produced **George Benson**, **Billy Griffin** and **The Mac Band** (for whom they wrote 'Stalemate').

ATMOSFEAR

(Group)

Instigated by London songwriter/producer/record man Andy Sojka, Atmosfear was one of the first acts to break through on the UK black music/dance scene. As an earthy, instrumental Brit funk group, their debut was 'Dancing In Outer Space' (UK Top 50, 1979) on Andy's Elite label via MCA Records. Later singles included 'Motivation' (1980), 'Xtra Special' (1981), 'What Do We Do' (1982), and 'First/Fourmost' (1983).

AUGUSTIN, NAT

(Singer/Trombone/Keyboards)

From North London, Nat worked as an actor on TV's *Streets Ahead* and *No Problem* before joining **Light Of The World** in 1979. Here he sang lead on 'I'm So Happy' and played trombone with the band. He left in 1984 and signed to the Debut label as a solo artist. Following 'Too Busy Thinking About My Baby' and 'Summer Is Here Again' (1985) he switched to A&M for 'Ego' (1986) and 'That Girl' (1987), the latter produced by **Dexter Wansel**.

AURRA

(Group)

Aurra were born out of the group **Slave** and were originally **Steve Washington** (vocals/trumpet), Tom Lockett Jr (sax), Curt Jones and Starleana Young (vocals). They had worked together in Slave from the early '70s, but the idea for Aurra was conceived in 1980, just prior to a deal with the Dream label (via Salsoul) for a debut album *Aurra* (including 'In The Mood To Groove'). Further albums for Salsoul, *A Little Love* (1981), including 'Make Up Your Mind', and *Live And Let Live* (1983), including 'Baby Love', followed before Steve Washington took on a solo career, leaving Curt and Starleana (both from New Jersey) to take the Aurra concept to Next Plateau Records.

Here they scored their greatest commercial success with 'Like I Like It', released in the UK by Virgin/10 Records and a Top 60 hit in 1985. Further dancefloor success came in 1986 with 'You And Me Tonight' before they changed their name to **Déjà**.

AUSTIN, PATTI

(Singer/Songwriter)

From Los Angeles, Patti's father was a jazz musician and friend of producer **Quincy Jones**. Patti is Quincy's goddaughter, and began a professional relationship with him. In New York Patti sang backgrounds and jingles before eventually landing a deal with CTI Records. Here she recorded *End Of A Rainbow*, *Say You Love Me*, *Havana Candy* and *Body Language* (1980) before singing lead with Quincy Jones on his album *The Dude* (1981), including 'Betcha Wouldn't Hurt Me', 'Somethin' Special', 'Razzamatazz' and 'Turn On The Action'. Quincy then launched his Qwest label, Patti being his first signing. Here her debut album was *Every Home Should Have One* (1981), but it was in 1983 that she made her one UK chart entry with 'Baby Come To Me', a duet with **James Ingram**. Her remaining Qwest albums were *Patti Austin* (1984), including 'Hot! In The Flames Of Love' and 'Starstruck', and *Gettin' Away With Murder* (1985), including 'The Heat Of Heat' produced by **Jam/Lewis**.

In 1990 she switched to GRP for *Love Is Gonna Getcha*, including 'Through The Test Of Time' and 'Good In Love'. Elsewhere Patti sang lead with Japanese koto player Yutaka Yokokura on 'Love Light' (1978), shared lead with **Michael Jackson** on 'It's The Falling In Love' from *Off The Wall* (1979), lead on 'The Closer I Get To You' for **Tom Browne** (1979), a duet with **George Benson**, 'Moody's Mood For Love' (1980), and backgrounds with **Houston Person**, **Noel Pointer**, **Ralph MacDonald**, **Angela Bofill** and **Roberta Flack**.

AVENUE BOOGIE BAND

(Group)

Signed to Salsoul Records in New York in the late '70s, the Avenue Boogie Band were a more funky, less 'disco' conglomerate of musicians. Their releases included 'Bumper To Bumper', co-written and mixed by Billy Mersey in 1980.

AVERAGE WHITE BAND

(Group)

Formed in Scotland in 1982, The Average White Band were **Hamish Stuart** (lead vocals/guitar/bass), Alan Gorrie (lead vocals/guitar/clavinet/bass), Roger Ball (keyboards/synths/alto sax), Robbie MacIntosh (drums), Malcolm Duncan (sax/flute) and Onnie McIntyre (guitar/backing vocals). Moving to New York, they first signed to MCA for *Show Your Hand* before switching to Atlantic in 1974. Here their initial album *Average White Band* featured the million-selling instrumental 'Pick Up The Pieces' (UK Top 10, 1975), following which Robbie died of heroin poisoning. His replacement was **Steve Ferrone**, and the group continued with *Cut The Cake*, the title track from which was a UK Top 40 hit in 1975. 1976's *Soul Searching* included 'Queen of My Soul' (UK Top 30), before they recorded an album with **Ben E.King**, *Benny And Us* (1977), including 'A Star In The Ghetto'. They later switched to RCA for albums including *Feel No Fret* (1979), including 'Walk On By' (UK Top 50), 'When Will You Be Mine' (UK Top 50) and 'Atlantic Avenue'; *Shine* (1980), including 'Let's Go Round Again' (UK Top 20) and 'For You To Love' (UK Top 50); and *Cupid's In Fashion* (1982 – produced by **Dan Hartman** and released by Arista in America), including 'You're My Number One'.

During their Atlantic days, the group were also responsible for putting Dick Morrissey together with Jim Mullen for the formation of **Morrissey/Mullen**, the two groups recording together on the album *Up*. Hamish Stuart and Steve Ferrone later formed **Easy Pieces** and worked with **Diana Ross** on her *Red Hot Rhythm & Blues* (1987), Hamish co-writing 'Cross My Heart'.

A more recent album *Aftershock* (1989) featured guest appearances by **Chaka Khan**, **The Ohio Players** and **Ronnie Laws**. Hamish also co-wrote 'A Love Of Your Own' for **Millie Scott**.

AYERS, ROY

(Vibes/Singer/Songwriter/Producer)

Born in Los Angeles in 1940, Roy's mother was a schoolteacher while his father was a parking attendant and scrap-metal worker. He discovered his love for the vibes while attending a Lionel Hampton concert at the age of five. Initially, however, he studied piano during his high school years. Having mastered both piano and vibes he began to play professionally, and was soon sought after by **Chico Hamilton**, **Wayne Henderson**, **Curtis May** and **Herbie Mann**. It was with Herbie that Roy initially began recording, ultimately leading to a solo recording deal with Atlantic Records in 1967. Here he released three albums, *Virgo Vibes* (1967), *Stoned Soul Picnic* (1968) and *Daddy Bug* (1969) before he formed Roy Ayers Ubiquity in 1970. With a line-up including **Alphonse Mouzon** (drums) and **Edwin Birdsong** (keyboards/vocals), the group signed with Polydor and released *Ubiquity* the same year. By now Roy had settled in New York.

Roy began to broaden his music from straight jazz to incorporate r&b rhythms with both his own vocals and guest vocals by female singers such as **Dee Dee Bridgewater**. His Ubiquity concept continued in 1972 with *He's Coming*, offering 'He's A Superstar', 'Fire Weaver', 'We Live In Brooklyn Baby' (the break beat in 1990 for Galliano's 'Power And Glory'), and a line-up of musicians including Sonny Fortune (sax), Billy Cobham (drums), Ron Carter (bass) and Gloria Jones (backing vocals). In 1973 his releases included two Ubiquity albums, *Virgo Red* (including 'Brother Louie', 'Virgo Red' and 'Des Nude Soul'), and '*Red Black & Green* (including 'Ain't No Sunshine') together with a soundtrack album to the movie *Coffey*, before a further Ubiquity album *Change Up The Groove* (including 'Sensitize' and 'Fikisha') in 1974.

In 1975 he released *A Tear To A Smile* (including '2000 Black', 'Ebony Blaze' and 'Time And Space') and *Mystic Voyage*, from which 'Evolution' was about the first track

UK jazz funk fans seriously took notice of (although earlier recordings became sought after many years later). Musicians in Ubiquity this year included **Ricky Lawson** and **Byron Miller**. Through 1976 Roy moved further into r&b with *Everybody Loves The Sunshine* (including 'The Golden Rod' and 'It Ain't Your Sign It's Your Mind') and *Vibrations* (including 'Searching'), then in 1977 delivered his classic dance anthem 'Running Away' from the album *Lifeline*.

At this point Roy Ayers signed Ubiquity to the Elektra label (for one 1978 album, *Starbooty*), while continuing to record as Roy Ayers at Polydor. He entered what he calls his mellow period with two soul-orientated albums, *Let's Do It* (including 'Sweet Tears', 'Melody Maker', and 'Freaky Deaky') and *You Send Me* (including 'Can't You See Me', 'I Wanna Touch You Baby' and his first UK Top 50 hit 'Get On Up, Get On Down'). Also in 1978 he recorded two albums with **Wayne Henderson**, *Step In To Our Life* (including 'For Real' and a 1979 Top 50 hit 'Heat Of The Beat') and *Prime Time*. On *You Send Me* Roy had featured vocalist Carla Vaughn, who co-produced and sang on 1979's *Fever* (which included 'Love Will Bring Us Back Together', recently utilised by **The Chimes** as a break beat on 'Heaven'). His next albums were *No Stranger to Love* (1979), – including 'Don't Stop The Feeling', and *Love Fantasy* (1980).

After a tour of Africa in 1981 he changed directions again, releasing the album *Africa, Center Of The World*, influenced by African percussionist Fela Anikulapo Kuti who performed with Roy on his African tour.

His final album for Polydor was 1982's *Feeling Good* (including 'Turn Me Loose'), following which he left the label to concentrate on his own company Uno Melodic Records. In addition to his own *Lots Of Love* for the label (released in the UK as two mini-albums, *Silver Vibrations* and *Drivin' On Up* in 1983), Roy worked with **Bobby Humhrey**, **Eighties Ladies** (co-writing/producing, with **Edwin Birdsong**, 'Turned On To You', a song also recorded by Yorkshire fire-eater Nova Casper in 1986!) and **Sylvia Striplin** (producing 'Give Me Your Love') before signing to CBS in 1984. Here his music combined traditional Roy Ayers with contemporary electronic rhythms, his three albums for the label being *In The Dark* (1984), including 'Poo Poo La La'; *You Might Be Surprised* (1985, including 'Hot' and 'Virgo'); and *I'm The One (For Your Love Tonight)* (1987). His most recent studio album was *Wake Up* (1989) for the Ichiban label. Outside of his own albums he has recorded vibes with **Buster Williams**, while a live album (1991) recorded at London's 'Ronnie Scotts' for the Ronnie Scotts label offered some new songs. **David 'Fathead' Newman** (who recorded two Ayers songs, 'Foxy Brown' and 'Sweet Tears' on the 1974 Atlantic album *Newmanism*), **Whitney Houston** (1987's 'Love Will Save The Day'), **Bruce Fisher**, **Miles Jaye** ('Let's Start Love Over'), **Rick James** ('Dance Wit' me'), **Jean Carne** (*Trust Me*), **Terri Wells** ('Who's That Stranger'), **Ronnie Foster** and **Loose Ends**, among many more.

AZ ONE

(Group)

This New Jersey trio recorded one single, 'All Of My Heart', for the Profile label in 1989, released in 1990.

AZYMUTH

(Group)

From Brazil, Azymuth were formed in 1971 and comprise Jose Roberto Bertrami (keyboards/vocals/percussion), Alex Malheiros (bass/vocals), Ivan Conte (drums/synths), and Aleuda (percussion). Signed to the Milestone label, they released *Light As A Feather* in 1979. It featured 'Jazz Carnival', an instrumental which stirred UK dancefloors, became a jazz funk classic and reached the UK Top 30. Also popular on UK dancefloors was 'Dear Limmertz' from their album *Outubro* (1980), before they settled back into a mellower, more ambient style for albums including *Telecommunication* (1982), *Flame* (1984) and *Spectrum* (1985).

Individually Bertrami has recorded with **Sarah Vaughan** and released solo albums on Milestone including *Dreams Are Real* (1986) and *Blue Wave* (1983), while Alex released *Atlantic Forest* (1985), also for the Milestone label.

B

B.B.&Q.

(Studio Group)

B.B.&Q. stood for the Brooklyn, Bronx and Queens Band from New York, and was the concept of **Jacques Fred Petrus** (who also instigated **Change** and **High Fashion** comprised of session musicians). In 1981 he signed the B.B.&Q. concept to Capitol, 'On The Beat' being the debut release and a UK Top 50 dance hit. Their second album featured a further dance hit 'Imagination', written by **Kae Williams** with guest vocals by **Rick Brenna**. In 1985 B.B.&Q. was signed to Elektra Records and Kae Williams wrote, arranged and produced *Genie* which featured UK Top 40 hits in the title track and 'I'm A Dreamer'. The songs featured the vocals of **Curtis Hairston** (although there were no vocal credits on the sleeves). A further single 'Ricochet' was released by Cooltempo/Chrysalis in 1987 (UK Top 75), before Jacques was shot dead.

B&G RHYTHM

(Studio Group)

A conglomeration of West Coast jazz fusion musicians recorded an album *B&G Rhythm* produced by **Wayne Henderson** on Polydor in 1978. The musicians included Roland Bautista, **Bobby Lyle**, Dean Gant, Vance Tenort, Victor Feldman, Augie Johnson and vocalist **Sylvia St James**.

B.T. EXPRESS

(Group)

Formed by **Jeff Lane** in Brooklyn during the late '70s, B.T.Express originally recorded in the Hole In The Ground studios belonging to **Solomon Roberts**. They were Bill Risbrook (sax/vocals), Jamal Rasool (bass/lead vocals), Dennis Rowe (percussion/vocals), Rick Thompson (guitar/lead vocals), Carlos Ward (sax/flute), Wesley 'Piuke' Hall (lead guitar/vocals) and **Kashif** (keyboards). In the UK they initially appeared on the Pye International label, their debut album being *Do It Till You're Satisfied*, with 'Express' as their UK Top 40 debut in 1975. Their follow-up album was *Non-Stop*, including 'Give It What You Got' and 'Peace Pipe', although 'Does It Feel Good' was their next UK Top 75 single chart entry in 1980.

They then switched to CBS for albums including *1980* (via Calibre Records in the UK), *Energy To Burn*, *Function At The Junction*, *Old Gold, Future Gold* and *Shout It Out*. Their singles later appeared on Record Shack, Earthtone ('Your Love Is All I Need', 1984), and King Davis ('Cover Girl', 1985), although by this time Kashif had left for a solo career.

BABA, OLLIE

(Singer)

Ollie Brown released one album as Ollie Baba in 1978, before which he played drums with **Raydio** and teamed up with Jerry Knight as the recording duo **Ollie and Jerry**.

BABYFACE

(Singer/Songwriter/Producer/Guitar/Keyboards)

Born Kenneth Edmonds, in Cincinnati, Ohio, Babyface began his career as singer/guitarist/pianist with local group **The Deele**. In the mid-'80s they moved to Los Angeles where they signed to Solar Records. Also in the group was L.A.Reid, with whom Babyface began an extremely successful writing/production collaboration (see **L.A./Babyface**). As a vocalist he later recorded the duet 'Love Saw It' with **Karyn White** on *Karyn White* (1988), while as a solo artist he released *Tender Love*, featuring **Troop** and **After 7**, for Solar in 1989.

BACHARACH, BURT

(Songwriter/Arranger/Producer)

Born in New York, Burt Bacharach began a successful songwriting career with Hal David (see **Bacharach/David**) in the early '60s. Discovering **Dionne Warwick** at a recording session with **The Drifters**, he signed her to the Scepter label where he was an in-house songwriter, arranger and producer. After an extremely successful run of hits co-written/produced for Dionne Warwick and other artists, he began collaborating with Carole Bayer Sager (see **Bacharach/Bayer Sager**) which continues to this day.

BACHARACH/BAYER SAGER

(Songwriters/Producers)

Through the '60s and early '70s, **Burt Bacharach** collaborated with Hal David (see **Bacharach/David**); in the '80s Burt switched to work with Carole Bayer Sager, a New York singer who in 1977 scored a UK Top 10 hit with her solo release 'You're Moving Out Today'. They have written and/or produced songs including 'The Love Too Good To Last' (**Phyllis Hyman**), 'Makin' Love' (**Roberta Flack**), 'On My Own' (**Patti Labelle/Michael McDonald**), 'Over You'/'Perfect Lovers' (**Ray Parker Jr**), 'In My Reality' (**Natalie Cole**), 'Stronger Than Before' (**Chaka Khan**), 'Finder Of Lost Loves' (**Dionne Warwick/Glenn Jones**), 'Love Power' (**Dionne Warwick/Jeffrey Osborne**) and 'Love Is Fire, Love Is Ice' (**Gladys Knight** & The Pips).

BACHARACH/DAVID

(Songwriters/Arrangers/Producers)

Burt Bacharach and Hal David first worked together in 1956 after they met in New York. Initially their songs had no connection with soul/r&b, their early success being with white artists including Perry Como ('Magic Moments') and Tony Bennett. When Jerry Leiber and Mike Stoller at Atlantic Records brought in Burt Bacharach to arrange music for a number of their black acts, Burt met **Dionne Warwick** who was singing background vocals for **The Drifters**. In 1962 Bacharach/David wrote 'Don't Make Me Over', an American hit for Dionne followed by 'This Empty Place', 'Wishin' and Hopin'', 'Make The Music Play', 'I Say A Little Prayer' (later a hit for **Aretha Franklin**), 'Anyone Who Had A Heart' (UK Top 50, 1964) and 'Walk On By' (UK Top 10, 1964).

BAILEY, J.R.

(Singer/Songwriter)

As a solo recording artist, J.R.Bailey's releases include 'I'm Still In Love With You' (1982), while as a songwriter his credits include 'Sweet Music, Soft Lights And You' (**Issac Hayes/Millie Jackson**), and 'Just Me And You' (**Erasmus Hall**).

BAILEY, PHILIP

(Singer/Songwriter/Drummer)

Born in Los Angeles, Philip got his career break when **Earth Wind & Fire** relocated from Chicago to LA in 1971. While still signed to Warner Brothers, **Maurice White** employed Philip as the group's co-lead/falsetto vocalist and he has remained an integral part of the group to this day (his co-writing credits including 'Shining Star', 1975).

From 1983, Philip also recorded as a solo artist, both secular music for CBS and gospel music for the Myrrh/Words labels. At CBS his albums were *Continuation* (1983) produced by **George Duke**; *Chinese Wall* (1985), including the duet with Phil Collins 'Easy Lover' (UK No. 1), 'Walking On The Chinese Wall' (UK Top 40) and 'Children Of The Ghetto'; and *Inside Out* (1986).

His gospel albums include *The Wonder Of His Love* (1984) and *Family Affair* (1990). As a producer his credits include *Splendor* for **Splendor** (1979), and he also sang backgrounds with **Lonnie Hill**, **Alphonso Johnson** and numerous others.

BAKER, ANITA

(Singer/Songwriter/Producer)

Born in Detroit, Anita was acclaimed as one of the most exciting voices of the '80s, although she began her recording career by being told she couldn't sing! At that time (1979), she was a vocalist with Detroit group **Chapter 8**. Their initial record deal with Ariola was short-lived due to Ariola's alleged lack of faith. The group's guitarist **Michael Powell** kept in touch with Anita, and in 1983 secured her a solo deal with Beverly Glen records in Los Angeles. Here she released a debut album *The Songstress*, including 'Angel'/'Will You Be Mine' and Michael Powell's 'No More Tears', which became the most commercially successful song on the album.

In 1986 Anita switched to Elektra, and established Michael Powell as a producer on *Rapture*, including 'Sweet Love' (UK Top 20), 'Caught Up In The Rapture' (UK Top 75) and 'Been So Long'. The album established Anita as a major new soul singer (and songwriter) internationally. Her follow-up albums to date have been *Giving You The Best That I Got* (1988), including the **Gary Taylor**-penned 'Good Love', and *Compositions*, (1990), including 'Talk To Me,' 'Fairy Tales' and 'More Than You Know'. Elsewhere she recorded with **The Winans** ('Ain't No Need To Worry', 1987) and a duet with **Howard Hewett** ('When Will It Be', 1990).

BAKER, ARTHUR

(Artist/Producer/Industry)

Born in Boston, Arthur worked in his local record shop before moving to New York where he decided to become a producer. After taking an engineering course he found production work, and scored his first success in 1981 with 'Planet Rock' for **Afrika Bambaataa**. On the back of this success he launched his own Streetwise label with partner Paul McCravin. In 1982–84 he produced acts including **Rockers Revenge** ('Walking On Sunshine'), Michelle Wallace ('Jazzy Rhythm'), **Freeze** ('I.O.U.'), New Edition, **Loleatta Holloway** ('Crash Goes Love'), **Cuba Gooding** ('Happiness Is Just Around The Bend') and New Order for the label. He also co-wrote and produced 'No Frills Love' for **Jennifer Holliday** (1985).

1985–87 was a quiet period until he kicked a cocaine habit and launched a new label, Criminal Records. He formed two groups for the label, Wally Jump Jnr and The Criminal Element Orchestra for whom he wrote and produced. The former featured the lead vocals of **Will Downing**, whose first solo album for Island Records Arthur produced.

Through Wally Jump Jnr's association with A&M records in the UK, Arthur Baker and his group The Backbeat Disciples signed to the label in 1989 for an album which included 'The Message Is Love', and featured **Al Green**, 'Talk It Over' and **Shirley Lewis** 'It's Your Time'.

BAKER, MICHAEL
(Singer/Drummer)
Born in 1956, Michael initially took an interest in drums at the age of six while living with his parents in Japan. At seven he acquired a set of his own and moved to Minnesota where he joined a group, The M.A. Free Press, and recorded a single 'Once In A Million'. In 1977 he left to study music composition at North Texas State University, and became fully qualified by 1981. He toured with trumpeter Clark Terry and organist Jimmy Smith before moving to Los Angeles where he worked with his uncle 'Dino' Chamber who was a producer with his own label, Mo-Press Records.

Michael later recorded with **Phil Upchurch** on Phil's *Name Of The Game* album, and was a ballet student for seven years. His one solo release in the UK was 'Don't You Want My Loving' for the Passion label in 1982.

BAKER/HARRIS/YOUNG
(Musicians/Songwriters/Producers/Group)
From Philadelphia, Ronnie Baker, **Norman Harris** (guitar) and **Earl Young** (drums) first worked together as backing musicians for local group The Larks during the early '60s. From then until the late '70s they became an integral unit of musicians, songwriters and producers on the Philadelphia soul/disco music scene. Early songs on which they recorded include 'Yes I'm Ready' (**Barbara Mason**, 1964), 'It's Against The Laws Of Love' (The Volcanos, later to become **The Trammps**) and 'La La Means I Love You' (**The Delfonics**). During the early '70s they also became the nucleus of the **M.F.S.B.** rhythm section.

In 1972 they were instrumental in launching **The Trammps**, and at Salsoul Records produced for **Double Exposure** ('Ten Percent', 1976), **First Choice** ('Let No Man Put Asunder', 1977) and their own album *B.H.Y.* (1979).

BALDWIN, BOB
(Keyboards)
New York pianist Bob Baldwin recorded with **James Robinson** on his album *Guilty* (1987), while in 1988 James sang lead on 'Just A Memory' for Bob's solo debut album *A Long Way To Go* released by Malaco. In 1990 he switched to the Atlantic Jazz label for *Rejoice*, including 'The Marvin (Gaye) Medley'.

BALLARD, HANK
(Singer)
Born John Kendricks in Detroit, Michigan, in 1936, Hank and his family moved to Atlanta during his early years. Here he joined '50s group The Royals, who upon signing to the King label became known as The Midnighters. As Hank Ballard and The Midnighters the group scored with American million-sellers 'Work With Me', 'Sexy Ways' and 'Annie Had A Baby' in 1954.

In 1960 he and the group scored with 'The Twist', introducing a new dance craze, and leading the way for Chubby Checker to have an even bigger hit with the song. Follow-up hits included 'Finger Poppin' Time', and the group lived off the back of these hits until 1968 when they broke up. Much later Hank worked with **James Brown**, recording the monologue to James's 'Get On The Good Foot' (1973).

BALLOU, PHILIP
(Singer)
Philip is one of the top session singers on the American r&b music scene, and has recorded backgrounds with numerous artists including **Melba Moore**, **Glenn Jones**, **Howard Johnson**, **Luther Vandross**, **Aretha Franklin**, **General Johnson** and **Carl Anderson**. He was also the featured lead vocalist with **Hi-Gloss** and **Charles Earland** ('It's The Woman In You', 1990). He signed as an artist to RSO Records.

BAMBAATAA, AFRIKA
(Disc Jockey/Producer)
Born in the Bronx, New York, Afrika Bambaataa ('Bambaataa' means 'affectionate leader'), was one of the first disc jockeys to implement the idea of rapping words over breaks and instrumentals over records that were being played. His guest rappers became known as 'MCs' (Masters of Ceremonies), this early '80s concept leading to artists like **MC Hammer** in the early '90s!

Bambaataa also pioneered 'scratching', running the stylus of a record player back and forth across intros/breaks of records to percussive effect across another record that is being played. By 1982 he had formed a group Soulsonic Force (with Mr Biggs, Pow Wow and M.C. G.L.O.B.E), **Arthur Baker** and **John Robie** producing their releases including 'Planet Rock' (UK Top 75, 1982), 'Looking For The Perfect Beat' (1983) and 'Renegades Of Funk' (UK Top 30, 1984) for Tommy Boy Records (via Polydor in the UK). Also in 1984 Afrika scored a UK Top 50 hit duet with **James Brown**, 'Unity'.

BANBARRA
(Group)
From Washington DC, Banbarra made one significant contribution to the dance music scene, 'Shack Up', originally released by United Artists in 1975. Over the years it has become somewhat of an underground classic and has been reissued on numerous occasions.

BAND A.K.A.
(Group)
Instigated by producer Joeson James Jarrett in 1979, The Band A.K.A. consisted of Kenny Allen, Michael Fitzhugh

(lead vocals), Booker Hedlock (who also wrote the score for the TV-movie *Cindy*), Phillip Scott, Robin Holt, Stanley Hood, Jack Holmes and D'Arco Smith. Signed to Epic in 1982, their debut album *The Band A.K.A* (1982) produced a UK Top 50 single 'Grace', while the follow-up *Men Of Music* produced the UK Top 30 hit 'Joy'.

BANKS, BESSIE
(Singer)
'60s singer Bessie Banks recorded for numerous labels including Red Bird ('Go Now', 1963), and is best remembered for singles including 'Baby You Sure Know How To Get To Me' and 'Try To Leave Me If You Can (Betcha Can't Do It)'.

BANKS, DARRELL
(Singer)
'60s singer Darrell Banks recorded for the Stax label in Memphis where his albums include *Forgive Me* (1969). He is best remembered for the single 'Open The Door To Your Heart' which he recorded prior to being shot dead!

BANKS, HOMER
(Songwriter/Producer)
Born in Memphis, Tennessee, in 1941, Homer grew up in an environment of gospel music, becoming a member of the Soul Consolaters during his high-school days in the early '60s. In 1964 he recorded a solo single 'Lady of Stone' for the Genie label before becoming a staff songwriter for Stax. Here he wrote for artists including **Johnnie Taylor**. Elsewhere, he wrote and/or produced for artists including **J.Blackfoot** ('Taxi'), **Shirley Brown** (*Intimate Storm*), and **Randy Brown** (*Intimately* and *Midnight Desire*).

BANKS, RON
(Singer/Songwriter/Producer)
Born in Detroit, Ron has worked closely with **The Dramatics** over the years in addition to writing and/or producing for artists including **Five Special** ('Why Leave Us Alone'). His own solo recordings include *Truly Bad* for CBS (1983) and a single 'Heaven' on the Future label (1989), while he was also the featured vocalist on 'Dancin' Love Affair' for **Wayne Henderson** (1979).

BANKS, ROSE
(Singer)
West Coast singer signed to Motown for an album *Rose* in 1976. More recently she recorded with **Quincy Jones** on *Back On The Block* (1989).

BANKSTON, T.W.
(Singer)
Detroit singer recorded the **Sam Cooke** song 'A Change Is Gonna Come' with producer **Ronnie McNeir** for the local Straight Up label in 1989.

BARBIERI, GATO
(Sax/Songwriter)
With an individual style of playing saxophone, Gato Barbieri appealed to the UK jazz funk scene with his recordings for A&M Records during the mid-'70s. His albums include the **Herb Alpert**-produced *Caliente* (1976). His compositions include 'Last Tango In Paris', recorded by **Norman Connors**.

BARKAYS
(Group)
From Memphis, Tennessee, The Barkays were formed in the mid-'60s, and were originally James Alexander (bass), Jimmy King (guitar), Ronnie Caldwell (organ), Phalon James (Sax), Carl Cunningham (drums) and Ben Cauley (trumpet). Under the direction of Al Jackson, drummer with Booker T. & the MGs (see **Booker T. Jones**), they scored an American hit with the instrumental 'Soul Finger', shortly to become the title of their debut album (which also included 'Knucklehead', 'You Can't Sit Down' and 'Hole In The Wall') for the Volt label (via Stax) in 1965. Over the next two years they became an integral part of the Stax/Memphis sound while playing as house band for numerous artists. These included **Otis Redding** with whom they toured prior to the plane crash which killed Otis and The Barkays themselves (with the exception of James and Ben) in 1967.

At this point James formed a new line-up of the group: Lloyd Smith (guitar), Michael Beard (drums), John Colbert (vocals), Charles Allen (trumpet), Harvey Henderson (sax), Winston Stewart (keyboards), Frank Thompson (trombone), Mary Bynam (keyboards) and Sherman Gray (percussion). John (or **J. Blackfoot**), later joined **The Soul Children** and was replaced by Larry Dobson.

During the early '70s The Barkays once again became the house band at the Stax label, recording frequently with **Isaac Hayes** and establishing themselves in their own right with albums including *Gotta Groove*, *Black Rock*, *Cold Blooded* and *Money Talks*.

In 1980 the group switched to Mercury for *Injoy* (1980); *As One* (1981), including 'Open Your Heart'; *Night Cruisin'* (1982), including 'Hit And Run'; *Flying High On Your Love*; *Light Of Life*; and *Dangerous* (1984), including 'Sexomatic'.

BARNES, J.J.
(Singer)
Born in Detroit in 1943, Jimmy James Barnes sang with various gospel groups before forming Halo Gospel (which featured his sister **Ortheia Barnes**) and performing with an r&b high-school group the Five Seniors. J.J.'s postman was Fred Brown who owned a record label with **Ivy Jo Hunter**. Fred later signed him and put him to work with producer **Don Davis**.

In the meantime J.J. had also gained popularity as a nightclub singer around Detroit. His debut single was 'My Love Came Tumbling Down' (1960) featuring background vocals by The Del-Phis, later to become known as **Martha Reeves & The Vandellas**. His next five singles were released on the Mickays label (from 'Teenage Queen' in 1962), including 'Just One More Time' which established him locally. In 1964 he released 'Poor Unfortunate Me' on the Ring Records label before signing to Ric Tic. Here he released 'Please Let Me In' (1965), followed by 'Real Humdinger' in 1966 which gave him a Billboard chart debut (a UK release in 1973). His follow-up 'Day Tripper' (the Beatles song) was produced by **George Clinton** in 1966, and then came 'Say It' before Ric Tic was bought out by Motown.

At Motown **Berry Gordy** felt J.J. sang a little too much like **Marvin Gaye**, and utilised him more for his songwriting ability. He worked on songs with Dean and Weatherspoon for **The Contours**, **Martha Reeves**, **The Fantastic Four** and others, while as an artist he recorded various singles for other labels including Groovesville ('Baby Please Come Back Home'), Revilot, Buddah ('Evidence'), Volt ('Got To Get Rid Of You', also a duet album with **Steve Mancha**), Magic, Touch, Perception, Contempo, Organic and Inferno, all the time building a following on the UK Northern soul scene.

He also wrote 'Love At First Sight' for Sweet James Epps (of **The Fantastic Four**), a cult ballad on the UK soul scene (released 1983, though recorded in the '70s), while more recently he has recorded for the UK Motorcity label ('Build A Foundation', 1990) with writer/producer **Ian Levine**.

BARNES, JOHN

(Producer/Keyboards)

Based in Los Angeles, John Barnes is best known for his production work with **Michael Jackson** (co-writing 'We Are Here To Change The World', also recorded by **Deniece Williams**), **Billy Griffin** ('Hold Me Tighter In The Rain' and co-writing 'Serious'), **Herb Alpert** (*Bullish*), **Good Girls** ('Your Sweetness'), **Five Star** and **Cheryl Lynn** (co-writing 'Love Rush'). As a session keyboard player he has also recorded with **Marvin Gaye** (*I Want You*), **Benny Golson**, **G.C.Cameron**, **Chuck Cissel** ('Cisselin' Hot'), **Chocolate Jam Co.**, **Narada Michael Walden**, **Eloise Laws**, **Margie Joseph**, **Dee Dee Bridgewater** (writing 'Sweet Rain'), **The Pointer Sisters**, **The Four Tops**, **Tavares**, **Jermaine Jackson**, **Carl Anderson**, **Jennifer Holliday**, **Lamont Dozier**, **Patti Brooks**, **Lionel Richie** (co-writing 'Don't Stop'), and **Sherrick** ('Just Call').

BARNES, ORTHEIA

(Singer)

Born in Detroit, Ortheia went to school with **Diana Ross** and was singing in church from the age of nine. She was inspired to be a recording artist by her brother **J.J. Barnes** who had a hit when she was fourteen. Her first break was with Motown, who didn't record her, but hired her as an opening act on tour with **Stevie Wonder**, **Marvin Gaye** and **Gladys Knight**.

In the late '60s she signed with Coral (a subsidiary of Decca) and released the American hit single 'Waiting For Joy'. From 1970–75 she toured America with **Edwin Starr** before returning to Detroit and forming the duo **Cut Glass** with **Millie Scott**.

In 1985 she recorded a debut album *Person To Person*, produced and co-written by **Sylvia Moy** for the US MSR label, while more recently she has hosted her own radio talk show Ortheia's Special Touch (WCHB in Detroit) and has opened her own nightclub, Ortheia's Place.

In 1989 she caused a stir around Detroit and on the UK soul scene with a single 'Till You Lose It', released on the Noteworthy label. She also recorded a number of songs for the Motorcity label in the UK.

BARNUM, H.B.

(Singer/Songwriter/Arranger/Keyboards/Producer)

During the '60s H.B. Barnum recorded two albums for RCA, *The Big Voice Of Barnum – H.B. That Is*, and *Everybody Loves H.B. – Barnum That Is*, highlighting his keyboard-playing, songwriting skills and vocals. He also recorded for Capitol (*The Record*, 1965), but most of his work during the '60s/'70s was as an arranger.

He has arranged for Count Basie, Frank Sinatra, **Etta James**, **Nancy Wilson**, **Lou Rawls**, **Martha Reeves**, **The Supremes**, **The Temptations**, **The Jackson 5**, **The Marvelettes**, **O.C. Smith**, **Greg Perry**, **Lamont Dozier** ('Fish Ain't Bitin''), **Michael Wycoff** ('Looking Up To You'), **Aretha Franklin** ('When I Think About You'), **Jesse James** ('If You Want A Love Affair', which he also co-wrote), **Johnny Bristol** ('Hang On In There Baby') and **Gladys Knight & The Pips** ('Help Me Make It Through The Night').

He also wrote and produced for Jimmy Norman ('I Wanna Make Love To You', Buddah, 1975), and more recently Gloria Bare ('From The Heart').

BARRABAS

(Group)

Barrabas were a '70s funk group consisting of Ricky Morales (guitars), Juan Vidal (keyboards), Miguel Morales (bass), Daniel Louis (drums), Ernesto Duarte (percussion/sax) and J.C. Tejada (vocals). Their albums for the Atco label included *Barrabas*, *Heart Of The City* and *Watch Out* (1976).

BARRETT, RICHARD

(Singer/Songwriter/Producer)

Born in Philadelphia, Richard sang in local groups The Angels and The Valentines during the '50s. He later moved on to producing Frankie Lymon and The Teenagers – including 'Why Do Fools Fall in Love' – and also recorded himself as a solo artist.

In his capacity as an A&R man for Rama Records he was the first to sign **The Isley Brothers** and **Little**

Anthony & The Imperials, as well as discovering **The Three Degrees** (whose early recordings he produced).

BARROW, KEITH
(Singer)
Los Angeles-based singer Keith Barrow signed with CBS Records in 1978 where he worked with producer **Michael Stokes** on *Physical Attraction*. It included 'Turn Me Up', popular on the disco scene at the time, while the ballad 'You Know You Want To Be Loved' became in demand on the UK 'rare groove' scene in the early '90s when it was re-released on a number of compilation albums.

BARRY, CLAUDIA
(Singer)
Born in Canada, Claudia began her career as an actress and TV presenter before moving to England and working as a session singer with artists including Elton John and Rick Springfield. In the early '80s she signed to Chrysalis and scored American hits with 'Boogie Woogie Dancing Shoes' and 'Down And Counting'. She also made an impact on the disco scene with songs including 'Whisper To A Scream', 'Dancing Fever', 'Why Must A Girl Like Me', 'Tripping On The Moon', 'Can't You Feel My Heartbeat', 'I Don't Know If You're Dead Or Alive', 'Feel The Fire' and 'If I Do It To You', released in the UK via Ensign Records. Also recording for the Phonogram, Salsoul, Epic and TSR labels, she has scored five gold and platinum albums, while more recently she has been in the American dance charts with 'Good Time' for the Radikal label.

BARTLEY, CHRIS
(Singer)
Born in Harlem, New York, in 1949, four blocks from the Apollo Theatre, Chris joined his first group The Soulful Inspirations by the time he was ten. Changing their name to The Mindbenders, the group auditioned for **Van McCoy** who described them as 'the most horrible sound I have ever heard'! However, he was impressed by Chris's vocals and signed him as a solo artist to his Vando label. When Vando folded in 1968, Chris switched to the Buddah label and recorded 'Baby I'm Yours' and 'I Know We Can Work It Out'. He quit performing in 1971 to take care of his bedridden mother, then returned to the music scene as singer with the Ad Libs.

BARTZ, GARY
(Saxophone)
Born in Baltimore in 1941, Gary took up the alto sax at the age of eleven. As a teenager he played sax in his father's nightclub, sitting in with Art Blakey and **George Benson**. In 1964 he made his professional debut with drummer Max Roach, joined Art Blakey in 1965 and by 1967 had his own group Ntu Troop with whom he recorded for Milestone Records. In 1970 he worked with **Miles Davis**, then in 1972 switched to the Prelude label and moved towards fusing soul r&b with jazz in his music. His albums included *Home*, *Juju Street Songs*, *I've Known Rivers & Other Bodies*, and *Slingerella, A Ghetto Fairy Tale*. In 1974 he began recording with **Norman Connors** (from the album *Slewfoot*). Further albums include *The Shadow Do* (1975), produced by **Larry** and **Fonce Mizell**, and for the Catalyst label *Ju Ju Man* (1976), featuring **Syreeta**, before a switch to Capitol for *Music Is My Sanctuary* (1977) and *Love Affair* (1978). His next move was to Arista where he worked with writers/producers **Mtume/Lucas** on *Music* and *Bartz* (1980). He also recorded with **The Blackbyrds** and **Rena Scott**.

BASIC BLACK
(Vocal Group)
New to Motown in 1990, Basic Black are Kelvin 'K.B.' Bradshaw, Lloyd 'Spec' Turn, Darryl 'Dezo' Adams and Walter 'Dis Mucho' Scott. Their debut album was the **Gene Griffin**-produced *Basic Black*, including 'Nothing But A Party'.

BASS, FONTELLA
(Singer)
Born in St Louis, Missouri, in 1940, Fontella began her musical career at the age of five playing keyboards in a church ensemble of which she later became music director. Her mother sang with the Clara Ward singers. Duly impressed, **Oliver Sain** took Fontella to sing in his band in 1960, and to the Chess label for 'Don't Mess Up A Good Thing', her American hit duet with **Bobby McClure** (1964). Her vocal talents had also been recognised by **Ike Turner**, who recorded her on a number of his own labels, although it was at Chess that she scored her biggest hit with 'Rescue Me' (UK Top 20) in 1965. The follow-up was 'Recovery' (UK Top 40) in 1966, while in 1969 she recorded an album in Paris with her husband, trumpet player Lester Bowie, before signing to Jewel Records for further productions by Oliver Sain.

Her younger brother, incidentally, is **David Peaston**.

BATAAN, JOE
(Singer/Producer)
Based in New York during the '70s, Joe first made an impact on the disco scene in 1975 with his version of the **Gil Scott-Heron** song 'The Bottle', released by RCA. From here through to 1980 he recorded for the Salsoul label with releases including 'Ordinary Guy' (1975), 'Rap-O-Clap-O' (1979) and the **Leon Bryant**-penned 'You Are My Latin Lover' (1980). As a producer he worked with artists including **Laso** ('Another Star').

BATTLE, HINTON
(Singer)
Los Angeles-based singer Hinton Battle worked in Hollywood as a dancer and actor in addition to signing a recording deal with Qwest Records in 1986. Here he worked with producer Laythan Amor on a debut album *Untapped*.

BAYAAN, AMIR
(Songwriter/Producer/Keyboards)
Amir Bayaan is the brother of Robert 'Kool' Bell of **Kool & The Gang**, a group Amir played with prior to becoming a freelance musician and producer. His production projects include work with **Third World**, **Tomorrow's Edition**, **LaToya Jackson** (co-writing 'Hot Potato'), **Armenta** ('I Wanna Be With You') and **Freddie Jackson**.

BAYLOR, HELEN
(Singer/Songwriter)
Born in Tulsa, Oklahoma, Helen moved to Los Angeles during her childhood and aged thirteen recorded her debut single 'The Richest Girl'. In New York she performed as an opening act for **Aretha Franklin**, **Stevie Wonder** and **B.B.King** as Little Helen while also landing a role in the Broadway musical *Hair* prior to a stint with the group **Side Effect**. Here (as Helen Lowe) she sang lead on the group's album *What You Need* (1976), her voice being particularly prominent on the group's version of 'Always There'. She also co-wrote 'S.O.S.' for the album. Her roots were in the church, and in 1982 she rededicated her life to religion after suffering under the pressures of the music business and becoming a cocaine addict.

Fully recovered, she signed to Word Records in Nashville and released an album, *Highly Recommended*, including 'There's No Greater Love' (released back to back on a single in the UK by Expansion Records, 1990).

BE BE & CE CE WINANS
(Group)
From Detroit, Be Be and Ce Ce Winans are brother and sister and members of the gospel family **The Winans**. Be Be's wife is also a gospel singer, Debra Winans. Be Be and Ce Ce first appeared as a duo in 1984 singing a rendition of 'Up Where We Belong', later featured on their debut album *Lord Lift Us Up*, including 'Worth The While', for the PTL label. In 1987, after numerous concerts and American TV appearances they signed with Capitol where their albums have been *Be Be & Ce Ce Winans*, including 'I.O.U. Me' and 'Love Said Not So'; *Heaven* (1988), including 'Lost Without You', 'Hold Up The Light' (featuring **Whitney Houston**) and 'Meantime'; and *Different Lifestyles* (1991). In 1990 Be Be guested with **Gerald Albright** as lead vocalist on 'Growing With Each Other' from *Dream Come True*. Although gospel singers, their music has wide appeal on the secular r&b scene.

BEASLEY, WALTER
(Sax)
New York-based saxophonist made his recording debut for Elektra in 1986 with 'Back In Love Again'. The song was later featured on his debut album *I'm So Happy* for Polydor. From here he switched to Mercury for *Just Kickin' It* (1989), all his material being produced by **Lionel Job**.

BECK, KENNY
(Singer/Songwriter/Producer)
Born in South Bronx, New York, Kenny has written and/or produced for artists including **Octavia** ('2 The Limit'), **The Main Ingredient** ('Do Me Right') and **Cashflow** ('Mine All Mine') through the '80s. For GTI Records in the UK, he also released a solo single 'Shut Your Crack'.

BECK, ROBIN
(Singer)
When Robin Beck scored a UK No.1 hit with 'First Time' in 1988, the pop scene thought they had discovered a brand new white singer from America. In fact she had made a major impact on the '70s disco scene with her **Chic**-like single 'Sweet Talk' (from *Robin Beck*). Robin also sang backgrounds on recordings for **Patti Austin**.

BEE GEES
(Group)
Not strictly a soul group, but Australian brothers Barry, Robin and Maurice Gibb made a major impact on the mid-'70s disco scene with a string of hits from the movie soundtrack *Saturday Night Fever* for RSO Records (via Polydor). The movie burst the burgeoning New York/San Francisco/London-based disco music scene wide open, while the Bee Gees scored hits including 'Jive Talkin'' (UK Top 5, 1975), 'You Should Be Dancing' (UK Top 5, 1976), 'How Deep Is Your Love' (UK Top 5, 1977), 'Stayin' Alive' (UK Top 5, 1977) and 'Night Fever' (UK No.1, 1978).

Having established themselves on the soul/disco scene, the group continued to score with 'Too Much Heaven' (UK Top 5, 1978), 'Tragedy' (UK No.1, 1979), 'Love You Inside Out' (UK Top 20, 1979), 'Spirits Having Flown' (UK Top 20, 1980), 'Someone Belonging To Someone' (UK Top 50, 1983) and 'You Win Again' (UK No.1, 1987). In 1990 Bruce Forest gave 'You Should Be Dancing' a 'house' remix, served as a 12" B-side to a reissue of 'How Deep Is Your Love'.

BEGGAR & CO
(Group)
Formerly the horn section of London-based group **Light Of The World**, Kennie, Baps and Breeze formed an offshoot group in 1981. Initially they worked with Spandau Ballet on their UK Top 5 hit 'Chant No.1', making their own chart debut with '(Somebody) Help Me Out' (UK Top 20) the same year. Later in 1981 they returned with a follow-up single 'Mule (Chant No. 2)' (UK Top 40) and an album *Monument* before switching to RCA for *We All Work Out* (1982), and then to Polydor for 'Anybody See My Trial' (1983).

BEGINNING OF THE END
(Group)
From Nassau, Beginning Of The End recorded 'Funky Nassau' in 1971, which became a local hit before Atlantic made it an American Top 20 record later in the year. An

evergreen on the UK funk scene, the song came from the group's one album *Funky Nassau* (1971).

BELL, AL

(Producer/Industry)

Born in 1941, Al began his career as a disc jockey, and then became station manager for WUST in Washington DC. In 1961 he joined the Stax label as national sales director. He later became owner of Stax, having transformed it from a local independent to an internationally successful and respected soul/r&b label, selling 55 million albums in 14 years.

Stax artists included **Otis Redding**, **Isaac Hayes**, **The Staples Singers**, Booker T. and the MGs (see **Booker T. Jones**), **Sam & Dave** and **Johnnie Taylor**, many of whom Al worked with as either producer or consultant. During the early '70s, Stax signed a distribution agreement with CBS, but after the departure of Clive Davis in 1973, Al wanted independence back for Stax. CBS didn't agree, and the combination of this together with bad investments, and financial difficulties at the Memphis bank which held the Stax account, led to the demise of the label. In 1975 Al was accused of embezzling over $18 million from the Memphis bank, and although he was cleared of all charges, the Stax label was finished, and Al retired from the record business for eleven years.

In 1986 he moved to Los Angeles and launched the Edge label, his artists at this time including **J. Blackfoot**, **The Main Ingredient** and **Bobby McClure**. He also spent a period of time at Motown, while more recently he has worked as a producer with **Mavis Staples**.

BELL, ARCHIE

(Singer)

Born in Houston, Texas, Archie formed his own vocal group while at Phillis Wheatley Senior High School (better known for producing outstanding basketball players). Archie Bell & The Drells were formed in 1965, The Drells being Lee Bell, James Wise, and Willie Pernell. In 1967 they won a talent contest organised by Skipper Lee Frazier, who decided to manage them. The same year he secured them a recording contract with Atlantic Records. Among the first songs they recorded was 'Tighten Up', initially issued as a B side at a time when Archie had temporarily left the group to serve in the army. The record took off across America, and by the time he returned it had sold four million copies! *Tighten Up* became the title of the group's first album (1968). In the early '70s the group were put together with writers/producers **Gamble/Huff**, and while still at Atlantic first collaborated on a million-seller 'I Can't Stop Dancing'. In the UK their early taste of Gamble/Huff success came with 'Here I Go Again' (Top 20, 1972) and 'There's Gonna Be A Showdown' (Top 40, 1973), both from their *Here I Go Again* album.

After leaving Atlantic they recorded briefly for the Florida label Glades (including 1973's 'Girls Grow Up Faster Than Boys', released by President in the UK), before signing with Philadelphia International (PIR) in 1975. Later that year they released *Dance Your Troubles Away*, which firmly established them as a household name with the **McFadden & Whitehead** soul anthems 'Let's Groove' and 'The Soul City Walk' (UK Top 20). A follow-up album, *Where Will You Go When The Party Is Over*, was released in 1976 and featured 'Don't Let Love Get You Down', a song which only took off in the UK during the mid-80s after a huge revival on the soul scene, reaching the UK Top 50 in 1986. In the meantime the group had released two further albums, *Hard Not To Like It* (1977) and *Strategy* (1979). A single 'Everybody Have A Good Time' also made the UK Top 50 in 1977, but the group left PIR in 1979.

Archie signed as a solo artist with Becket Records in New York and released the one album *I Never Had It So Good* from which 'Any Time Is Right' was popular in 1981. More titles were recorded but were not released by the label. In 1982 he recorded a solo single with the WMOT label, 'Touching You', before rejoining the Drells for 'Look Back Over Your Shoulder', released on the Nightmare label in 1986 (and by Achievement in the USA in 1988). Today he lives in Houston where he has a production company. He has been working on songs for his daughter, and still performs dates as a solo artist or with The Drells.

BELL, JERRY

(Singer)

Los Angeles-based singer Jerry Bell recorded for MCA in the early '80s. His albums included *Winter Love Affair* (1981), on which 'Tell Me You'll Stay' was written, arranged and produced by **Michael Wycoff**. The song became popular on the UK soul scene in the late '80s.

BELL, SAM

(Singer/Songwriter)

Born in Philadelphia, Sam sang with **The Gainors**, and later **Garnet Mimms & The Enchanters**, taking over as lead singer of The Enchanters when Garnet left to pursue a solo career. Following the demise of the group he managed **Lorraine Ellison** and wrote 'I Dig You Baby' for her before becoming a preacher.

BELL, THOM

(Songwriter/Producer/Musician)

Born in Philadelphia to West Indian parents, Thom had mastered piano, drums and flugelhorn by the time he was nine. His twin sister Barbara went to the same school as **Kenny Gamble**; they later formed a vocal duo Kenny And Tommy. In 1959 they recorded a single 'Someday' for the Heritage label before forming **The Romeos**, although Thom left soon after to get married.

At the age of 23 Thom was employed by Cameo Records, and came to the UK with Chubby Checker as his music director. His first move into production was when **The Delfonics** approached him with their song 'He Don't Really Love You'. He continued to work with the group on hits including 'Didn't I (Blow Your Mind This Time)' and 'La La Means I Love You' (both 1971).

With co-writer **Linda Creed** (see also **Bell/Creed**), Thom established himself alongside **Gamble & Huff** as one of the pioneers of the 'Philly sound' through the '70s, with songs and/or productions for artists including **New York City** ('I'm Doin' Fine Now', 1972), **The Stylistics** (most of their major hits), **Detroit Spinners** ('I'll Be Around', 1973), Elton John, **Deniece Williams** (*My Melody* and *Niecey*, including 'It's Your Conscience'), **Dee Dee Bridgewater** ('Lonely Disco Dancer'), **Lou Rawls**, **Teddy Pendergrass**, **Brandi Wells**, **Phyllis Hyman** ('We Should Be Lovers') and **The Temptations** ('Aiming At Your Heart', 1981).

In 1974 he formed his own Tommy label (via PIR/CBS), artists on the label including **Force Of Nature**, while as an artist he recorded duets with **Bobby Taylor** as BT & TB for the Philadelphia International label (PIR). More recently he has produced for **James Ingram** and **Phyllis Hyman** ('First Time Together' and 'Old Friend').

BELL/CREED

(Songwriters)

From Philadelphia, **Thom Bell** and **Linda Creed** collaborated on numerous songs and productions through the '70s. These included songs and/or productions for **Diana Ross/Marvin Gaye** ('You Are Everything', 1973), **Phyllis Hyman** ('Loving You, Losing You'), **Eloise Laws** ('Love Comes Easy') and **The Detroit Spinners** ('Ghetto Child'), among many more.

BELL, WILLIAM

(Singer/Songwriter)

Born William Yarbrough in Memphis in 1939, William's win in a talent contest led to his debut solo release 'Alone On A Rainy Night' for the local Meteor label. He briefly formed a vocal group The Del Rios before resuming his solo career with Stax Records. Here he became one of the label's most prominent artists during the '60s. After creating an initial impression in 1962 with 'You Don't Miss Your Water (Till The Well Runs Dry)', he scored American r&b chart success with songs including 'I Forgot To Be Your Lover', 'Everybody Loves A Winner', 'Happy', 'Every Day Will Be Like A Holiday' and 'Private Number' (a duet with **Judy Clay**). His Stax albums included *Relating* and *Bound To Happen*.

In 1969 he formed his own Peachtree label, but as an artist switched to Mercury for two albums including *Coming Back For More* and an American r&b hit single 'Trying To Love Two' (recently re-recorded by **Barbara Lynn**) and 'If Sex Was All We Had' (1977).

He later recorded *Survivor* for the Kat Family label before forming his new label Wilbe Recording Corporation (via Ichiban) in 1985 and recording *Passion* and *On A Roll*. Other artists he signed to Wilbe included **Eddie Floyd** and **Janice Bullock**. As a songwriter he wrote a number of titles with **Booker T. Jones**, and had a million-seller with 'Born Under a Bad Sign' which was recorded by Eric Clapton.

BELLE, REGINA

(Singer)

Born in New Jersey, Regina grew up in a gospel music environment before discovering secular r&b at the age of five. From here she took up trombone, tuba and steel drums at school before taking her vocals seriously. Aged twelve she sang a version of The Emotions hit 'Don't Ask My Neighbours' at a school contest and won $25. She joined a local vocal group before studying opera and jazz at college. Personality disc jockey Vaughn Harper at WBLS radio in New York put Regina in touch with **The Manhattans**, and they began working together opening live shows for **Patti Labelle**, **Dionne Warwick**, **Gladys Knight** and other leading acts who came to town. She also recorded with the group on 'Where Did We Go Wrong', a song produced by **Bobby Womack** from 1986's *Back To Basics*.

Through the Manhattans connection she signed a solo contract with CBS in 1987, soon releasing a debut single 'Show Me The Way' and album *All By Myself*, including 'Please Be Mine' and 'After The Love Has Lost Its Shine'. Producers on the album were **Nick Martinelli** and **Michael J. Powell**. In 1988 she guested with **Surface** on 'You Are My Everything' and 'Hold On To Love' for their *2nd Wave* album and sang a duet with **Peabo Bryson**, 'Without You', on his album *Positive*. Regina's second album was *Stay With Me* (1989), including 'Good Lovin'', 'Baby Come To Me' and 'What Goes Around'.

BENDETH, DAVID

(Singer/Guitarist)

Based in Canada, David made an impact on the early '80s dance scene with his song 'Feel The Real', released in the UK by Ensign Records. The follow-up was 'Love Collect'/'Goldmine'.

BENELUX AND NANCY DEE

(Group)

This small group out of Belgium made one record 'Switch' in 1979 which was released in the UK on the Scope label. The instrumental version became a dancefloor anthem that year.

BENOIT, DAVID

(Keyboards/Songwriter)

American pianist David Benoit worked with producers **Rinder/Lewis** on 'Life Is Like A Samba' (1979), a fusion of Latin jazz and dance music, popular in the UK through the early '80s on AVI Records. He remained at the label for jazz funk albums including *Stages* (1982), before switching to GRP where his albums include *Inner Motion* (1990).

He has written and produced for artists including Mark Winkler (*Ebony Rain*, 1987).

BENSON, GEORGE

(Guitarist/Singer)

Born in Pittsburgh in 1944, George took up the guitar at the age of eight, but was also singing with his cousin in an r&b group by the time he was a teenager. In 1963 he moved to New York where he landed his first professional gig playing with a jazz ensemble led by **Jack McDuff**. At this time he made his little-known recording debut for CBS, on which he sang and played guitar. Signing to CTI in the early '70s he became strictly an instrumentalist, initially as house guitarist for the New Jersey label. He recorded on albums for **Hubert Laws**, **Esther Phillips**, **Herbie Hancock** and **Freddie Hubbard**, before recording his own debut album *White Rabbit* for the label in 1971.

Establishing himself in the field of fusion jazz, his other CTI albums included *Body Talk*, *Benson & Farrell* with flautist **Joe Farrell** and *Good King Bad* (1976), from which CTI released one of their few 12" singles, 'Summertime'/'2001', showcasing George once again as a vocalist. George Butler at Blue Note Records suggested Benson produce organist **Ronnie Foster**, resulting in *On The Avenue* (1974). Ronnie became part of George's recording and touring band (as pianist/synth player), George also producing a second Ronnie Foster album *Cheshire Cat* for Blue Note in 1975.

In 1976 George signed to Warner Brothers and under the direction of producer Tommy LiPuma recorded *Breezin'*, including 'This Masquerade' and *In Flight* (1977), including 'Nature Boy' (UK Top 30) and 'The World Is A Ghetto'. Also in 1977 he sang the original version of 'Greatest Love Of All' (UK Top 30), a song released on Arista Records from the movie soundtrack *The Greatest* and later a hit for **Whitney Houston**. Having now established himself as a major vocal artist (while continuing to play guitar), he made *Weekend In L.A.* (1978), including 'On Broadway' and 'Lady Blue'; *Livin' Inside Your Love* (1979), including 'Love Ballad' (UK Top 30); *Give Me The Night* (1980), including the title track (UK Top 10), 'Love X Love' (UK Top 10), and 'Moody's Mood For Love', a duet with **Patti Austin**; *What's On Your Mind* (1981) (UK Top 50–1981), 'Turn Your Love Around' (UK Top 30–1981), 'Never Give Up On A Good Thing' (UK Top 20–1982); *In Your Eyes* (1983), including 'Inside Love (So Personal)' (UK Top 75); *20/20* (1984), including the title track (UK Top 30, 1985), 'I Just Wanna Hang Around You', 'Beyond The Sea' (UK Top 75, 1985) and 'Kisses In The Moonlight' (UK Top 75, 1985); *While The City Sleeps* (1986), including 'Shiver' (UK Top 20, 1986), 'Teaser' (UK Top 50, 1987); and *Twice The Love* (1988), including 'Let's Do It Again' (UK Top 75) and 'Tender Love'.

In 1989 he returned to strictly jazz with *Tenderly* and *Big Boss Band* (1990) featuring the Count Basie Orchestra, including 'Baby Workout' and 'Basie's Bag'. Elsewhere he has recorded either vocals or guitar with **Harvey Mason** ('What's Going On'), Tony Williams ('Hip Skip'), **Chaka Khan** ('We Got The Love', 1978), **Aretha Franklin** (duet 'Love All The Hurt Away', 1981), **Jimmy Smith** (*Off The Top*, 1982), and **Earl Klugh** (duet album *Collaboration*, 1987), among others.

BENSON, RENALDO

(Singer/Songwriter/Producer)

Born in Detroit, Renaldo is best known in his role as one of the **Four Tops** from the '60s through to the present day. He is also a skilled songwriter and co-wrote the classic 'What's Going On' for **Marvin Gaye** in addition to forming a songwriting partnership with **Ronnie McNeir** on songs including 'For Your Love' (1975) through to 'Searching' (1990). Benson/McNeir songs have also been recorded by artists including **Klique** ('Ain't Nothing Better').

BENTON, BROOK

(Singer/Songwriter)

Born Benjamin Franklin Peay in Camden, South Carolina, in 1931, Brook Benton grew up singing gospel and joined the Camden Jubilee Singers as a young child. At the age of 17 he moved to New York where he joined the Bill Landford Spiritual Singers before forming his own r&b group The Sandmen. By day he maintained a job as a truck driver. He also secured part-time work recording demos for other artists, before signing to Epic as a solo artist where his early recordings included 'The Wall' and 'A Million Miles From Nowhere'. In 1959 he switched to Mercury Records, and scored an instant American hit with 'It's Just A Matter Of Time'. In the UK his success during this era included 'Endlessly', later recorded by **Randy Crawford** (Top 30, 1959), 'Kiddio' (Top 50, 1960), 'Fools Rush In' (Top 50, 1961) and 'Boll Weevil Song' (Top 30, 1961), scoring twenty gold records in total back in America.

From Mercury he switched to Reprise (via Warner Brothers) for one album *Laura What's He Got (That I Ain't Got)* before moving to Cotillion in 1970. Here he recorded the original version of 'Rainy Night In Georgia' – again, later covered by Randy Crawford. His albums for the label were *Brook Benton Today*, *The Gospel Truth* and *Do Your Own Thing*. He also recorded *Mister Bartender* for the All Platinum label in 1976.

BERRY, CHUCK

(Singer/Songwriter/Guitarist)

Born Charles Edward Berry in San Jose, California, in 1926, Chuck and his family settled in St Louis, Missouri, during the early '30s. Here he took to singing, both in school and in church, eventually forming his own group.

Originally he trained as a hairdresser, but in 1955 he was offered a recording deal with Chess Records in Chicago. Here he scored immediately with an American No. 1 r&b hit 'Maybellene'. This was followed by songs including 'Brown-Eyed Handsome Man' and 'Roll Over

Beethoven' while in the UK (via Columbia) he scored in the late '50s with 'School Day' (Top 25, 1957) and 'Sweet Little Sixteen' (Top 20, 1958). He also appeared in the movies *Go Johnny Go* and *Fun Fun Fun* during this period.

In 1959 he landed himself in jail for an alleged offence involving a child, emerging four years later to find new success with songs including 'Go Go Go' (Top 40, 1963), 'Let It Rock' (Top 10, 1963), 'Run Rudolph Run' (Top 40, 1963), 'Nadine (It Is You)' (Top 30, 1964), 'No Particular Place To Go' (Top 5, 1964), 'You Never Can Tell' (Top 30, 1964) and 'Promised Land' (Top 30, 1965).

In 1966 he signed with Mercury for one album *Club Nitty Gritty* before returning to Chess in 1969 for *Back Home* and further success with 'My Ding-A-Ling' (No. 1, 1972), and 'Reelin' And Rockin'' (Top 20, 1973). He also recorded one album *Rock It* for Atlantic in 1979.

BEVERLY, FRANKIE
(Singer/Songwriter/Producer)
Born in Philadelphia, Frankie formed his first group Frankie Beverly & The Butlers in 1966. On the local Rouser label they released a single 'Because Of My Heart', before Frankie released a solo single 'If That's What You Wanted' for the Gamble label in 1968 (as Frank Beverly). In 1971 he formed the group Raw Soul, recorded two singles with the group, performed locally and then took the group away from Philadelphia as he didn't want them to be associated with the Philly sound that was emerging through the **Gamble/Huff** empire. Re-locating to San Francisco Frankie developed a new musical style with the nucleus of Raw Soul, later changing the name to **Maze** and signing to Capitol in 1976.

BIDDU
(Songwriter/Arranger/Producer)
Born into an Indian family, Biddu moved to the UK and worked in a doughnut factory before becoming a songwriter and producer at Beacon Records. During the mid-'70s he signed to Epic as The Biddu Orchestra where he scored on the more commercial end of the disco scene with the instrumentals 'Summer Of '42' (UK Top 20, 1975), 'Rain Forest' (UK Top 40, 1976), 'Soul Coaxing' (1977) and 'Journey To The Moon' (UK Top 50, 1978).

Also on the more commercial end of the disco scene he wrote and/or produced for artists including **Tina Charles** ('Dance Little Lady Dance'), and **The Real Thing**. More recently Biddu resurrected The Biddu Orchestra for a single 'Humanity' released on the Trax label (1989), and worked with vocalist Chris Johnson (cousin of **Paul Johnson**).

BIG MAYBELLE
(Singer)
Born in Jackson, Tennessee, in 1926, Maybelle Smith established herself as a blues singer at venues like the Apollo in New York during the '50s. During the early '60s she became known as Big Maybelle and was a pioneer of soul music, earning a new nickname 'Mother Of Soul' and recording *Pure Soul* for the Epic label. She later switched to the Scepter label where she recorded *The Soul Of Big Maybelle*, including 'Don't Let The Sun Catch You Cryin''.

BILLY & BABY GAP
(Group)
Consisting of Billy Young and Anthony Walker (aka Baby Gap), Billy & Baby Gap signed to Total Experience after touring extensively with **The Gap Band**. Billy, from Buffalo, NY, made his professional debut in 1977 playing keyboards with Spyro Gyra. Anthony, from Chicago, was influenced by The Gap Band's Charlie Wilson and made his debut with this group. Their debut single was 'Rock The Nation'.

BIRDSONG, CINDY
(Singer)
Born in Detroit, Cindy was a teenager when she formed The Ordettes with three other ladies including **Patti Labelle**. She later joined **The Supremes**, where she replaced Florence Ballard and stayed with the group until being replaced by **Lynda Laurence**.

BIRDSONG, EDWIN
(Singer/Songwriter/Producer)
Born in Los Angeles, California, Edwin was the son of a minister and grew up in a strict church-going environment. Joining the Los Angeles Community Choir he became acquainted with such artists as **Merry Clayton**, **Billy Preston** and **D.J.Rogers**, with whom he eventually toured. After serving in the Vietnam War, Edwin ended up in Germany where he played in clubs and entertained servicemen. Building up his confidence, he moved to New York where he assembled the Edwin Birdsong Trio playing blues and jazz. He went to the Manhattan School Of Music, and later the Juilliard School of Music as a composition major. Following his days at Juilliard he played with the Youth Symphony Orchestra, an association which fused synthesizers with classical music. From here he signed to Polydor and released two albums, *What It Is* (1971) and *Supernatural* (1973), describing his music as 'the missing link between rock and funk'.

After one album for Bamboo Records, *Dance Of Survival* (1975), he signed with Philadelphia International where he released the one album *Edwin Birdsong* (1979) which included a single 'Phiss-Phizz'. He also worked closely with **Roy Ayers** during the '70s, co-writing 'Running Away' and 'Freaky Deaky', while co-producing Roy's three albums *Vibrations*, *Lifeline* and *Let's Do It*. Also with Roy Ayers he worked with **Eighties Ladies**, co-writing/producing 'Turned On To You' in 1981.

His other solo singles include 'Perfect Love' for the Sound Of New York label (1984) and 'Son of A Rapper Dapper Snapper' for the Singh label (1985). As a top session keyboard player he is known as 'Bird' and has worked with numerous artists including **Stevie Wonder** ('Spiritual Walkers').

BLACK IVORY

(Group)

New York-based '70s group Black Ivory originally consisted of **Leroy Burgess**, Russell Patterson and Stuart Bascombe. Signing to the Today label they scored an American r&b hit with the **Patrick Adams**-produced 'Don't Turn Around' and built a following with two albums for the label. They later recorded three albums for the Buddah label, returning on Panoramic Records in 1985 for 'I've Got My Eyes On You'.

BLACKBYRDS

(Group)

The Blackbyrds were Keith Killgo (drums), Joe Hall III (bass/vocals), Orville Saunders II (guitar), **Kevin Toney** (keyboards), Stephen Johnson (sax). Originally Barney Perry (guitar), Allan Barnes (sax) and Perk Jacobs (percussion), all musical protégés of **Donald Byrd**. Donald was the group's mentor and producer, landing them a record deal at Fantasy Records. Here they made their debut in 1974 with *The Blackbyrds*, which immediately won UK dancefloor acclaim on the soul/jazz funk scene with 'Do It, Fluid' and 'Gut Level'. In 1975 they reached the peak of their success with two albums, the first of which, *Flying Start*, included their one UK Top 25 hit 'Walking In Rhythm'. The second was *City Life* featuring 'Rock Creek Park', which today remains a classic soul/funk track in the UK.

Continuing to record with Fantasy, their other albums were *Unfinished Business* (1976); *Action* (1977), including 'Soft And Easy'; then in 1988 *Night Grooves*, which featured popular new mixes of their leading tracks up to this point. The Blackbyrds also recorded a soundtrack album to the film *Cornbread, Earl And Me*. In 1980 they returned with a final album *Better Days*, produced by **George Duke**, which made little impact. **Kevin Toney** then pursued a solo career.

BLACKFOOT, J.

(Singer)

Born John Colbert in Memphis, Tennessee, in 1947, 'J. Blackfoot' is a nickname he acquired as a child due to his habit of walking barefoot on the tarred sidewalks of Memphis during the hot summers. He spent his teen years in jail after being picked up in a stolen car, but the experience fired his ambition to be a successful singer. When he was released he spent six months as lead singer with a new line-up of **The Barkays** (after original members were killed with **Otis Redding** in a plane crash).

In 1968 **Isaac Hayes** and David Porter put together a vocal group **The Soul Children** at Stax Records, and John became lead singer. When the group split up, he began a solo career and in 1983 signed to the Sound Town label for *City Slicker*, including the single 'Taxi' (UK Top 50, 1984). *U-Turn* was later released by the Edge label (1986).

BLACKMAN, DON

(Keyboards/Singer/Songwriter)

Born in Queens, New York, in 1953, Don's cousin was a close friend of **McCoy Tyner**, and McCoy played keyboards with one of Don's main influences John Coltrane (who lived less than a mile away). Furthermore, Don's next-door neighbour was saxophonist Charles McPhearson and by the time Don was fifteen he was playing in Charles's band with Sam Jones and Louis Hayes. During the '70s he was influenced by **Herbie Hancock** and **George Duke**, and took to electric keyboards, later playing with **Parliament/Funkadelic**, and becoming a founder member of Lenny White's group **Twennynine**.

In 1981 his song 'Haboglabotribin'' was recorded by pianist **Bernard Wright** (Don singing lead vocals on the track) for the GRP label, following which GRP signed him for his one album for the label, *Don Blackman*, including 'Never Miss A Song' and 'Heart's Desire'. He later played keyboards with **Roy Ayers** on Roy's album *You Might Be Surprised* (1985), and with **La La**.

BLACKMON, LARRY

(Singer/Songwriter/Producer)

Born in New York, Larry Blackmon developed an interest in music as a child. Every Sunday after church he attended shows at The Apollo Theatre in Harlem where he was inspired by artists including **James Brown**, **Otis Redding** and **The Temptations**. He began his formal music training at junior high school, and later put together a succession of groups including The Mighty Gees, Concrete Wall, East Coast and The New York City Players. The name of the latter proved cumbersome, so he changed it to **Cameo**.

In addition to fronting Cameo as lead singer, songwriter and producer, he also formed Atlanta Artists Records in the early '80s and worked with artists including **Cashflow** and **Barbara Mitchell**. Elsewhere he worked as songwriter and/or producer with artists including **Charles Earland** ('The Only One'), **Bobby Brown** and **Colonel Abrams** ('Bad Timing').

BLACKSMITH

(Group)

London-based brothers Carl and Tim Atkins worked as session musicians before realizing that school friend Peter Trotman sang just like **Leroy Burgess**! After hearing some demos, 4th & Broadway signed them as The Beat Lads for a debut single 'It's You' (1988). From here they switched to Phonogram at which point they changed their name to Blacksmith. They have released singles including 'Get Back To Love' and 'Hold You Back' in addition to 'The Brixton Bass Mix' remixes for artists including Bananarama, **David Grant**, **D-Mob** and The Cookie Crew.

BLACKWELL, DEBBY
(Singer)
Born in Paterson, New Jersey, Debbie initially sang with the Bethel Church Of Christ Choir from the age of seven. She later appeared on stage with Shirley Caesar and The Edwin Hawkins Singers, and recorded with Darnel Williams and as lead singer with **The Jammers**. Teaming up with songwriter/producer **Leroy Burgess**, her debut solo single was 'Once You Got Me Going', released in the UK via Virgin/10 Records in 1986.

BLAIR, ARNOLD
(Singer)
Chicago singer Arnold Blair worked with **Leroy Hutson** who produced the single 'Trying To Get Next To You' in the early '70s, popular in the late '80s on the UK soul scene.

BLAKE, JOHN
(Violin/Songwriter)
After studying jazz theory, harmony and composition, John took up the violin and worked in American r&b/jazz circles playing with artists including **James Brown**, **Barry White**, **Isaac Hayes** and Alice Coltrane during the '70s. When **Grover Washington** wanted his own string section, John assembled it and became part of it (they later became **Locksmith**).

Through the '80s he recorded with artists including **McCoy Tyner** (writing 'Horizon'), **Bob Thompson** and **Norman Connors**. He also recorded a solo album for the Gramavision label, *Adventures Of The Heart* (1987), featuring **Gwen Guthrie** on the title song.

BLAND, BOBBY
(Singer)
Born Robert Calvin Bland in Rosemark, Tennessee, in 1930, Bobby Bland moved with his family to Memphis in 1944. He worked as a valet and driver for **B.B. King** before Ike Turner recognised his talent and produced some songs for him released on the Modern label during the '50s. He also joined a group the Beale Streets before going into the army. While on leave, in 1953, he was signed to Duke Records, first recording 'Army Blues' and later scoring in America with 'Further On Up The Road' (1957). Through the '60s his American hits included 'I Pity The Fool', 'That Did It', 'The Feeling Is Gone', 'Turn On Your Lovelight', 'Call On Me' (1963), 'Ain't Nothing You Can Do', 'Ain't Doing Too Bad' and 'Rocking In The Same Old Boat'.

In 1972, Duke was bought out by ABC which became MCA and released Bobby's albums including *Dreamer* (1974), including 'I Ain't Gonna Be The First To Cry', and *You've Got Me Loving You* produced by Monk Higgins and **Al Bell** (1984). In 1985 he began recording for the Malaco label, albums including *After All* (1986).

BLAST, C.L.
(Singer)
Born in Birmingham, Alabama, C.L. grew up singing gospel before turning to secular music and singing with a number of local groups. He recorded a solo single 'I'll Take The Case' and album *I Wanna Get Down* for the Atlantic label prior to working with producer **Frederick Knight** on Park Place Records. Here an album *C.L.Blast* (1984) included 'Lay Another Log On The Fire', 'Fifty Fifty Love' and 'I Just Don't Know'.

BLAZE
(Group)
From Newark, New Jersey, Blaze are Chris Herbert (vocals), Josh Milan (keyboards) and Kevin Hedge (drums). They formed in the mid-'80s: Chris had established himself as a fine church singer, Josh was playing keyboards in the same church and Kevin was a DJ who tried to emulate Larry Levan from the New York club Paradise Garage. Together they wrote 'Yearning' which they released on their own label, Ace Beat Records. New York DJ Freddy Bastone put them together with Curtis Sabina who owned the Quark label in New York. Here they released 'Whatcha Gonna Do For Lovin'', 'If You Should Need A Friend' and 'Can't Win For Losing' which established them across the East Coast and in the UK, where the tracks were issued by Republic Records.

Their blend of soul and contemporary dance attracted major record companies to hire them to mix for artists including **Diana Ross**, **Mica Paris**, **Coldcut** ('People Hold On' featuring **Lisa Stansfield**), **Womack & Womack**, ABC, **Isaac Hayes**, **Babyface**, **Phase II** and **Kool & The Gang**. In October 1989 they signed with Motown where they immediately started work on a debut album *25 Years Later*. The initial single release was 'So Special', followed by the 1990 release of the album, including 'Get Up' and 'Lover Man'.

BLEU, MIKKI
(Singer)
Born in Houston, Texas, Mikki began performing with school bands from the age of twelve. After leaving school he played in clubs, recording 'Bedrock' in 1982. Its popularity lead to tours with **The Gap Band**, **The Barkays** and **Con Funk Shun** before he joined the line-up of **Club Nouveau** in 1986 (with whom he toured but did not record). In 1985 he signed briefly to Elektra as a solo artist, but switched to EMI in 1989 for *I Promise*.

BLOOD SWEAT AND TEARS
(Group)
'60s soul group scored with one UK hit 'You've Made Me So Very Happy' (Top 40, 1969), written by **Brenda Holloway** and released by CBS.

BLOODSTONE
(Group)
Charles Love (vocals/guitar), Harry Williams (vocals/percussion) and Charles McCormick (vocals/bass) first worked together in Kansas City as The Sinceres before moving to Los Angeles and changing their name to Bloodstone. Willis Draffen and Ronald Wilson later replaced Charles McCormick and Harry. In 1972 they toured the UK supporting **Al Green** and were signed by Decca. In 1973 (joined by drummer **Steve Ferrone**) they scored their one UK Top 30 hit 'Natural High' from their debut album of the same name. Other Decca albums included *Unreal* (1973), *I Need Time* (1974) and *Ride Of The Sphinx* (1975), before Steve Ferrone left to join **The Average White Band** in 1976.

They later recorded for Motown (*Don't Stop*, 1978), before a switch to T-Neck Records (via CBS) and albums including *Go On And Cry* (1982) and *Party* (1984).

BLOW, KURTIS
(Rapper/Producer)
Born in New York in 1961, Kurtis is one of the pioneers of rap music, and first scored a rap hit in 1979 with the seasonal 'Christmas Rappin'' (UK Top 30) for Mercury Records. His other UK hits have been 'The Breaks' (Top 50, 1980), 'Party Time' (Top 75, 1985), 'If I Ruled The World' (Top 30, 1986) and 'I'm Chillin'' (Top 75, 1986). In 1985 he starred in the hip hop movie *Krush Groove*, and was the featured rapper on the **Rene & Angela** hit 'Save Your Love For No. 1'. He instigated a star line-up of singers/musicians, King Dream Chorus & Holiday Crew, for a tribute to Martin Luther King ('King Holiday', 1986), co-wrote/produced 'It's Yours' for **Oran 'Juice' Jones** (1986) and recorded with **Trouble Funk** ('Break It Up') in 1987.

BLU, PEGGI
(Singer)
New York-based singer Peggi Blu signed to MCA Records in the late '70s where she worked with producers including **Jerry Ragovoy** on her debut album *I Got Love* (1980). It was only in 1987 that she returned for a second album *Blu Blowin'* including 'Tender Moments', 'Once Had Your Love', 'Over & Over', 'Two Can Play At That Game' and a **Bert Robinson** duet 'All The Way With You' produced by **Nick Martinelli**.

Over the years she has worked as a session singer with artists including **Lou Courtney**, **Quincy Jones** ('The Places You Find Love'), **The Manhattans** and **Stephanie Mills**.

BLUE FEATHER
(Group)
Based in Holland, Blue Feather played on their local club scene before recording a few of their songs with an aim to release a single. 'Let's Funk Tonight' was licensed to the Siamese label in Canada. Imports of this record reached the UK where its popularity led to a Top 50 hit for Mercury Records in 1981. Their follow-ups included 'Let It Out' (1983).

BLUE MAGIC
(Vocal Group)
Based in Philadelphia, Blue Magic are vocal group Vernon Sawyer, Keith 'Duke' Beaton, Ted 'Wizzard' Mills, Wendell Sawyer and originally Richard Pratt (who left in 1981). Signing to the WMOT/Atlantic label they worked with producer **Norman Harris** on million-selling American hits including 'Side Show' (1974), 'What Comes Over Me' (1974), 'Chasing Rainbows' (1975) and 'I Like You' (1975). They also recorded seven albums for WMOT, and two for Atco, *The Magic Of The Blue* and *Blue Magic*.

In 1989 they signed to OBR/CBS, a division of Def Jam Records in New York for *From Out of The Blue*, including the **Moody/Bell** penned/produced 'Romeo And Juliet'. They also sang backgrounds for **Alyson Williams** and for The Rolling Stones on the song 'If You Really Want To Be My Friend' on their album *It's Only Rock And Roll*.

BLUE MODERNE
(Studio Group)
Blue Moderne was a concept instigated by **Ish**. A debut dance single 'Through The Night' was released on Roll Records (1986) before the group switched to Atlantic for a single 'Do That Again' and album *Where Is Love* (1988). Sandy Barber sang vocals while Ish played all the instruments and produced the songs.

BLUE NOTES
(Group)
Working independently of **Harold Melvin**, The Blue Notes recorded the album *The Truth Has Come To Light* for Glades (via TK) in 1977.

BLUE ZONE
(Songwriters/Producers/Group)
UK band Blue Zone were **Lisa Stansfield** (lead vocals), Ian Devaney and Andy Morris, who signed with Rocking Horse Records (via Arista) in the mid-'80s. In 1987 they worked with writer/producer Paul O'Duffey on songs including 'On Fire' and 'Thinking About His Baby', the B-side of the latter before their own song 'Big Thing' which established themselves on the London club scene.

Lisa Stansfield then began a solo career while Ian and Andy continued to co-write and produce with her.

BLUE, BARRY
(Singer/Songwriter/Producer)
Based in the UK, Barry scored a series of early '70s dance hits with 'Dancing On A Saturday Night' (Top 5, 1973), 'Do You Wanna Dance' (Top 10, 1973), 'School Love' (Top 20, 1974), 'Miss Hit And Run' (Top 30, 1974) and 'Hot Shot' (Top 25, 1975), all for Bell Records (which later became Arista). From here Barry concentrated on

production work with a number of UK singers and groups including **Heatwave**.

BMP

(Group)

Butch Neil, Marlon Holland and Pete DaCosta recorded one album, *Loc-It-Up*, released by Epic in 1985. It was produced by Gene Redd Jr, brother of **Sharon Redd**.

BOB AND EARL

(Duo)

In the late '50s, Bob and Earl were originally **Bobby Byrd** and Earl Nelson. They had met as members of **The Flames**, but worked together recording for a number of small labels before Bobby Byrd left to be replaced by Bobby Relf in 1959. Together the new duo released 'Harlem Shuffle' for the Marc label in 1963, a US Top 50 which made No. 7 in the UK charts when re-issued on the Island label in 1969.

The group's producer/road manager was **Barry White**, for whom Bobby Relf wrote 'Walking In The Rain', a debut hit for **Love Unlimited**.

BOBO, WILLIE

(Timbales/Vocals)

Born William Correa in New York's Spanish Harlem, Willie recorded as a session percussionist with numerous artists including Count Basie, Rod Stewart, Tito Puente and Cal Tjader. His roots were in Latin music, and he was a pioneer of latin/jazz fusion. In the '60s he recorded for the Verve label (including *A New Dimension* and *Boogaloo In Room 802*), and then Sussex (including *Do What You Want To Do*) before he signed to CBS in the late '70s. In 1978 his **Wayne Henderson**-produced album *Hell Of An Act To Follow* included versions of the **Ronnie Laws** classic 'Always There' and **The Crusaders/Side Effect** 'Keep That Same Old Feeling', popular on the UK jazz funk scene. His follow-up album *Bobo*, including 'Palos' and 'Latin Lady', was released in 1979. He died in the early '80s.

BODY

(Vocal Group)

From Detroit, Michigan, Letitia, Peggy and Francina Body are three sisters who took to singing as a vocal group in their teens. Becoming involved in the city's performing arts programme with **Kim Weston**, they sang at local concerts and festivals during their high-school days. They moved to California and caught the attention of **Stevie Wonder** who was planning his own label Wondirection. Stevie put them in a studio to record a song. The label didn't materialize, but the song led to a deal with MCA Records where their debut single was 'In The Middle Of The Night'.

They toured with **Earl Klugh** (1985), **Jermaine Jackson** (1986) and sang vocals on 'Sweetest Tabu' for **George Howard** (1987) before working with writer/producer **Angela Winbush** on 1990's *Easy To Love*, which included 'Touch Me Up' and 'Body'.

BOFILL, ANGELA

(Singer/Songwriter)

Born in New York, in high school Angela Bofill formed a group The Puerto Rican Supremes. She had played piano from the age of ten, and sang from the age of four. Her father was a Latin music singer who once sang with Cuban bandleader Machito. After graduating she sang with a number of groups on the Latin circuit and recorded a single 'My Friend' for which *Latin New York* magazine nominated her as best Latin female vocalist. In her early twenties she composed the jazz suite *Under The Moon And Over The Sky*, and became lead soloist with New York's Dance Theater of Harlem chorus. Moving further into jazz she performed at Madison Square Garden with Stan Getz, Benny Goodman and other jazz greats.

In 1978 **Dave Valentin** introduced her to producers **Grusin/Rosen** who signed her to their GRP (Grusin Rosen Productions) label. Her debut album *Angie* (1978) included her own songs 'Under The Moon And Over The Sky', 'Baby, I Need Your Love' and 'The Only Thing I Would Wish For'. The label at the time was distributed through Arista, to which she signed directly after a second GRP album *Angel Of The Night* (1979). Moving from jazz fusion to soul/r&b, Angela worked with producer **Narada Michael Walden** on the albums *Something About You* (1981) including 'Tropical Love'; and *Too Touch* (1983), including 'Is This A Dream' and 'I Can See It In Your Eyes' before **The System** produced *Let Me Be The One* (1984) and her final two Arista albums *Teaser* (1984) and *Tell Me Tomorrow*, including 'Still In Love' (1985).

Between labels Angela toured with the New York Jazz Explosion, and played her first dates in the UK. In 1986 she sang 'Where Do We Go' for **Stanley Clarke** on his album *Hideaway* before signing with Capitol in 1988. Here she recorded *Intuition*, with a number of producers including **Norman Connors**.

Angela also recorded twice with **Dave Valentin**, performing lead vocals on 'We'll Make Love' (1979) and 'Can't Change My Heart' (1986).

BOHANNON, HAMILTON

(Singer/Songwriter/Producer/Drummer)

Born in Newnan, Georgia, Hamilton played drums in a high-school band while still in elementary school. After taking a music degree he was fortunate to meet **Stevie Wonder** who hired him as a drummer. As a result of this he settled in Detroit where he worked with numerous artists on the Motown label during the mid-'60s.

In 1972 he signed with the Brunswick label where in 1975 he had a run of UK hits with 'South African Man' (Top 25), 'Disco Stomp' (Top 10), 'Foot Stompin' Music' (Top 25) and 'Happy Feeling' (Top 50). In 1976 he signed to Mercury where he recorded a string of albums including *On My Way*, *Cut Loose*, *Summertime Groove* and *Too Hot To Hold*. From *Summertime Groove* came 'Let's Start The Dance' featuring **Carolyn Crawford**, a massive dancefloor anthem in 1978 (UK Top 75) which remained popular through to 1982 when it was released again and reached the UK Top 50.

By now he had launched his own Phase 11 label where 1980's *One Step Ahead* included a version of 'Baby I'm For Real' featuring **Liz Lands**. He has also worked consistently with **Carolyn Crawford** on tours, writing and producing her solo release 'Coming On Strong' (1978).

In 1984 he signed to MCA where his albums include *Motions* (1984) and *Here Comes Bohannon* featuring **Altrinna Grayson** (1989).

BOILING POINT
(Group)
'70s funk group scored in the UK with 'Let's Get Funktified', a 1978 Top 50 hit released for the group on the Bang label.

BOMB THE BASS
(Studio Group)
Based in the UK, Bomb The Bass is the brainchild of writer/producer Tim Simenon. Initially for the Mister-ron label the group scored with 'Beat Dis' (Top 5, 1988), and 'Megablast'/'Don't Make Me Wait' featuring Lorraine McIntosh of **The Cool Notes** (Top 10, 1988), before switching to Rhythm King Records. Success continued with a version of 'Say A Little Prayer' featuring Maureen Walsh (Top 10, 1988) and 'Winter in July' (1991).

BOMBERS
(Group)
Based in Canada, The Bombers recorded a song called '(Everybody) Get Dancin'' in 1979 which was originally released by West End Records in New York. Via Flamingo Records in the UK, the song became a Top 40 hit later in the year, 'Let's Dance' (Top 75) being the follow-up single later in the year.

BONEY M
(Vocal Group)
While Boney M are generally regarded as a pop group, it should be recognized that it is through the appeal of their music that people have become interested in more serious dance/black music. Instigated by Frank Farian in 1975, the group made their debut on Creole Records with 'Baby Do You Wanna Bump'. From here they switched to Atlantic Records for a string of UK hits including 'Daddy Cool' (Top 10, 1976), 'Sunny' (Top 5, 1977), 'Ma Baker' (Top 5, 1977), 'Belfast' (Top 10, 1977), 'Rivers Of Babylon'/'Brown Girl In The Ring' (No. 1, 1978), 'Rasputin' (Top 5, 1978), 'Mary's Boy Child–Oh My Lord' (No. 1, 1978), 'Painter Man' (Top 10, 1979) and 'Hooray Hooray It's A Holi-Holiday' (Top 5, 1979).

Formed in Germany, Boney M were Bobby Ferrell, Liz Mitchell and Marcia Barrett.

BOOKER T. & THE M.G.s
See **Jones, Booker T.**

BOOKER, CHUCKII
(Singer/Songwriter/Producer/Keyboards)
Born in Los Angeles, Chuckii was proficient with the guitar and drums by the time he was fourteen. At school he studied graphic art, and it was his friends who persuaded him to concentrate on music and play in their group. In 1984 **Barry White** signed them to his production company, Barry being Chuckii's godfather, and Barry's wife Glodean being a close friend of Chuckii's mother! Unfortunately their album recorded at this time was not released, and Chuckii left to join the group **Tease**. Here he played keyboards for three years before moving into production and working with artists including **C. J. Anthony** (*Luv's Invitation*), **Barry White** (*The Man Is Back!*), **Geoffrey Williams** ('The World Is Full Of Other People') and **Lalah Hathaway** ('Sentimental').

He has also recorded with **Vanessa Williams**, **Troop** and **Kool & The Gang**, and as a solo artist for Atlantic Records.

BOOM, TAKA
(Singer)
Born Yvonne Stevens in Chicago in 1954, Taka (meaning 'love of my people' in Swahili) Boom (a name derived from her former husband who was a demolition expert!) is the sister of **Chaka Khan**. Together they sang locally before Chaka joined **Rufus** and Taka moved to Los Angeles where she worked with **George Clinton** (as a 'Bride Of Funkenstein'), **The Gap Band** and **Carl Carlton**. In 1975 she became lead singer with **Undisputed Truth**, following which she signed to the Ariola label which released her debut album *Taka Boom*, including 'Night Dancing', in 1979. Switching to Mirage (via Polydor in the UK), an album *Climate For Love*, including 'In The Middle Of The Night', was released in 1985.

BOONE, LEN
(Singer/Songwriter)
Little-known artist wrote and sang 'Love Won't Be Denied', released in the USA on Chrysalis (1978). The track became a sizable dance track on the UK soul and funk scene, but Len was never to be seen or heard from again.

BOOTHE, PATRICK
(Singer)
Born in Chelsea, London, Patrick began singing at the age of seven. After vocal training and club work he joined British funk band Midnite Express in the late '70s. As a solo artist he recorded 'Dance All Night' and 'Never Knew

Love Like This Before' for the Streetwave label in 1982, both featuring the **Earth Wind & Fire** horn section.

BOYS

(Vocal Group)

The four Abdul Samad brothers were born in Compton, California, and now live in Northridge, California. They are Khiry, Hakeem, Tajh and Bilal, who from their talent show days to signing with Motown were compared with The Jackson 5. Their career took off after performing together on Venice beach, where they built up a following performing karate moves to dance music during Sundays. Progressing to singing, they landed an appearance on TV's *Junior Star Search*, appearing alongside twelve-year-old **Shanice Wilson**. From this they were persuaded by Motown to record a demo.

Originally accepting a deal from MCA, they moved to Motown when Jheryl Busby at MCA moved to become president of Motown. Here their debut album *Message From The Boys* (1988), including 'Dial My Heart', was produced by **L.A./Babyface**. They also recorded with **Earth Wind & Fire**.

As actors, Tajh was in *Cagney & Lacey* and *St Elsewhere*, Hakeem was in *Diff'rent Strokes* and *Facts Of Life*, while as gymnasts the group were members of The Ebony Fliers who performed at the 1984 Olympics.

BRAINSTORM

(Group)

'70s group Brainstorm recorded for Los Angeles-based Tabu Records where they are best remembered for 'Wake Up And Be Somebody', taken from the **Jerry Peters**-produced *Stormin'* (1977). The group featured vocalists Belita Woods and Trudy Womack, Belita co-writing 'Say You Will' for **L.J.Reynolds** and also having a solo release 'I Just Love You' for Epic in 1973.

BRAMBLE, DEREK

(Singer/Producer)

Born in the East End of London in 1962, Derek soon moved with his family to Slough where he grew up playing in reggae bands. His sister was a friend of **Roy Carter** who was with the group **Heatwave**. Derek shortly joined as bass player, replacing Mario Mantese in 1978, and staying with the group until 1982. Fellow group member/writer **Rod Temperton** taught him the fundamentals of songwriting, and they collaborated on 'The Spice of Life' for **Manhattan Transfer**.

After leaving Heatwave he worked briefly with **Linx**. When lead singer **David Grant** began a solo career, Derek worked with him as songwriter and producer, a successful liaison which led to further writing and production for **Jaki Graham**. Songs written during this period include 'Stop And Go' and 'Watching You Watching Me' (David Grant); 'Set Me Free', 'Round And Round' and 'Step Right Up' (Jaki Graham), 'Still In Love' (**Angela Bofill**, and later Jaki Graham) and 'Heaven Knows' (Jaki Graham, and later **Lalah Hathaway**). He also contributed a vocal on his Jaki Graham duet 'Let's Get Blue'. After producing David Bowie (*Tonight*, 1985) and Jaki Graham (*Breaking Away*, 1986) he moved to Los Angeles. Here, to date, he has produced **Gerald Albright**, **Vanessa Williams** and Tim Owens. He also co-wrote 'I Belong To You' for **Whitney Houston** (1990).

BRANCH, CLIFF

(Singer/Songwriter/Pianist/Producer)

New Yorker Cliff Branch recorded one single 'Don't Give Up (On Love)' released on the Sutra label in 1988. He later formed a jazz group Ready For Reality and recorded for Next Plateau. From the group's album, his production 'Give In To The Fight' was a popular jazz dancer at the latter end of 1990.

BRAND NEW HEAVIES

(Group)

From London, the Brand New Heavies are Jan Kincald (drums/keyboards/percussion), Lascelles (percussion/guitar), Simon Bartholomew (guitar), Andrew Levy (bass/keyboards), Mike Smith (sax), Paul Dias (trumpet), Jim Wellman (sax/keyboards) and Jay Ella Ruth (vocals). The nucleus of the group came together during the mid-'80s when '70s funk and soul was enjoying a revival. Capitalizing on what was known as the 'rare groove' scene in London, they came together as The Brothers International to play live in clubs that were also getting into **James Brown**-style music on vinyl. In the late '80s the group became the Brand New Heavies and recorded a debut single 'Got To Give' for the Cooltempo label. By the time they switched to the Acid Jazz label (1990), the group had widened their style to incorporate jazz. Their debut album *Brand New Heavies*, featuring the vocal cuts 'Dream Come True', 'Ride In The Guy' and 'Stay This Way', was one of the most popular soul and jazz albums of 1990.

BRASHEAR, OSCAR

(Trumpet/Flugelhorn)

Top American horn player Oscar Brashear has recorded with numerous artists through the '70s and '80s. He has recorded as part of the **Earth Wind & Fire** horn section, and was the featured soloist on 'Do It, Fluid' for **The Blackbyrds** (1974).

BRASS CONSTRUCTION

(Group)

The brainchild of **Randy Muller**, New York's Brass Construction stormed their way onto the dance music scene in 1975 with a platinum album *Brass Construction*, including 'Movin'' (UK Top 30) and 'Changin'', for the United Artists label. The line-up was Randy Muller (vocals/keyboards/flute/percussion), Larry Payton (drums), Wayne Parris (trumpet/vocals), Joe Arthur Wong (lead guitar), Sandy Billups (vocals/congas), Michael Grudge (sax/vocals), Morris Price (trumpet/vocals/percussion), Jesse Ward (sax/vocals) and Wade Williamson (bass). Initially working with producer **Jeff Lane** they became one of the first black American funk bands to establish themselves as a major act on the UK scene. Their albums continued with *Brass Construction II* (1976) including 'Ha Cha Cha' (UK Top 40); *III* (1977), *IV* (1978) and *V* (1979) including 'Music Makes You Feel Like Dancin'' (UK Top 40) and 'Shakit', before they switched to the EMI America label.

Here Randy Muller took over production, at first taking the group in a more synthesizer-orientated direction on *Attitudes* (1982), including 'Can You See The Light'. Moving to Capitol, they returned to their earthier sound for *Conversations* (1983) including 'Walkin' The Line' (UK Top 50) and 'We Can Work It Out' (UK Top 75); *Renegades* (1984), including 'Partyline' (UK Top 75) and 'International' (UK Top 75); and *Conquest* (1985), including 'Give And Take' (UK Top 75).

More recently the group's classic dance hits were remixed and released on EMI's Syncopate dance label, these being 'Movin'' (UK Top 30, 1988) and 'Ha Cha Cha'.

BRASS FEVER

(Group)

Top West Coast jazz fusion musicians teamed together for two albums, *Brass Fever* (1975) and *Time Is Running Out* (1976), both released by ABC Records. The title track of the latter album featured vocals by **The Jones Girls**, drawing Brass Fever to the attention of Philly soul fans. Other personnel involved included George Bohanon, **Ernie Watts, Oscar Brashear**, **Lee Ritenour**, James Jamerson, **John Handy** and **James Gadson** on essentially instrumental recordings.

BRATHWAITE, WAYNE

(Bass/Producer/Songwriter)

Based in New York, Wayne emerged on the r&b/fusion jazz scene during the mid-'80s, initially as a bass player and then as a writer/producer. He has worked with artists including **Ruby Turner**, **Jonathan Butler** (producing *Deliverance*), **Najee**, **Billy Ocean** (co-writing 'When The Going Gets Tough' and 'Love Zone'), **Glenn Jones**, **George Benson** ('Tender Love'), **Kenny G** ('Hi How Ya Doin''), **Stephanie Mills**, **Genobia Jeter** (co-writing 'Blessing In Disguise') and **Millie Jackson** (co-writing 'Mind Over Matter').

BREAKFAST BAND

(Group)

Based in the UK, The Breakfast Band were a seven-piece instrumental group who were popular on the jazz funk scene in the early '80s. In 1981 Disc Empire Records (a subsidiary of the shop Disc Empire run by London's Kiss FM disc jockey Tony Monson) released their debut single 'L.A. 14'.

BREAKWATER

(Group)

From Philadelphia, Breakwater were **Kae Williams** (keyboards), Gene Robinson (lead vocals/trumpet), James Gee Jones (drums), Linc 'Love' Gilmore (guitar), Steve Green (bass), Vince Garnell (woodwinds), Greg Scott (woodwinds) and John 'Dutch' Braddock (percussion). They met at school. In 1978 they signed to Arista and released two albums, *Breakwater* (1978), including 'Work It Out', 'You Know I Love You', 'No Limit' and 'Feel Your Way', and *Splashdown* (1980), including 'Say You Love Me Girl', produced by Kae Williams and Rick Chertoff. The group split up after leaving Arista and all left the music business with the exception of Kae who became a freelance pianist, songwriter and producer. 'Say You Love Me Girl' was issued in the UK for the first time in 1986.

BRECKER BROTHERS

(Duo)

Brothers Michael (sax) and Randy (trumpet/flugelhorn) Brecker have worked consistently as a horn section and a group on the American r&b and jazz scene through the '70s and '80s. As The Brecker Brothers they joined **Billy Cobham** on *Crosswinds*, *Eclipse* and *Shabazz* during the mid-'70s for Atlantic, switching to Arista for their own albums *The Brecker Brothers* (1978), *Heavy Metal Be-Bop* (1979), *Detente* (1980) and *Straphangin'* (1981).

Individually, Randy Brecker recorded *Amanda* (1985) with vocalist Eliane Elias and recorded with **Breakwater**, while Michael Brecker has recorded with **Ashford & Simpson** and **Spyro Gyra** among numerous others.

BRENDA AND THE TABULATIONS

(Group)

Philadelphia-based group featuring **Terry Jeffries**, Brenda and The Tabulations scored American hits in the '60s including 'Dry Your Eyes' and 'Right On The Tip Of My Tongue'. In the mid-'70s they signed with the Chocolate City label where they worked with producers **Bobby Eli**, **Norman Harris** and **John Davis** on *I Keep Coming Back For More* (1977). It included 'Let's Go All The Way (Down)', popular on the UK 'rare groove' scene during the mid-'80s.

BRENNA, RICK

(Singer)

Leading New York session singer, Rick recorded background vocals for artists including **Lillo Thomas** and **Howard Johnson** before singing lead with **B.B.&Q.** on the single 'Imagination'. In 1982 he joined **Change** as lead singer, his recordings with the group including 'Change Of Heart' (1984).

BRICK

(Group)

From Atlanta, Georgia, Brick were Jimmy Brown (lead vocals/flute/sax/horns), Regi Hargis Hickman (vocals/guitar/bass), Ray Ransom (lead vocals/bass/keyboards/percussion) and Eddie Irons (lead vocals/drums/keyboards). In the mid-'70s they signed to the Bang label (via CBS) and established themselves on the UK funk/soul scene with 'Dazz' (disco jazz) which reached the UK Top 40 in 1976. Their albums included *Brick* (1977), *Stoneheart* (1978), *Good High* (1979), *Waiting On You* (1980) and *After 5* (1982), including 'Free Dancer'. More recently they worked with producer **Michael J. Powell** on *Too Tuff* (1988) for the Magic City label.

BRIDES OF FUNKENSTEIN

(Group)

The concept of **George Clinton**, The Brides Of Funkenstein were an ensemble of various female backing singers who accompanied George and his groups **Parliament/Funkadelic** etc. in concert and on their recordings.

BRIDGES, ALICIA

(Singer)

New York vocalist Alicia Bridges made one album, *Alicia Bridges*, released by Polydor in 1978. It included 'I Love The Nightlife (Disco Round)', popular on UK dancefloors and a Top 40 hit.

BRIDGEWATER, DEE DEE

(Singer/Keyboards)

Born in Memphis, Tennessee, Dee Dee moved with her family to Flint, Michigan, where she became a professional singer and pianist by the age of 16. In 1970 she joined Thad Jones and Mel Lewis as featured vocalist with their big band. She recorded one album *Suite For Pops* with them before being discovered by **Norman Connors**. Norman took her away from traditional jazz and introduced her to fusion/r&b music circles. From here she began to record with artists including **Stanley Clarke** (*Unexpected Days*, 1973), **Roy Ayers** (*A Tear To A Smile*, 1975), and **Pharaoh Sanders**. In 1974 she played Glinda in the Broadway production of *The Wiz*, and signed to Atlantic for *Dee Dee Bridgewater* (1976), including 'He's Gone'.

In 1978 she switched to Elektra where she worked with producer **Stanley Clarke** on *Just Family*, including 'Sweet Rain' and 'Night Moves'; producer **George Duke** on *Bad For Me* (1979) and producer **Thom Bell** on *Dee Dee Bridgewater* (1980), including 'One In A Million (Guy)' and 'Lonely Disco Dancer'. In the mid-'80s she toured with the stage show *Billie*, playing Billie Holliday.

BRISTOL, JOHNNY

(Singer/Songwriter/Producer)

Born in Morganton, North Carolina, Johnny began his recording career singing duets with Jackey Beavers in Detroit. Together they released four singles on Gwen Gordy's Tri-Phi label, including the original version of 'Someday We'll Be Together'. The song was later recorded by **Diana Ross & The Supremes** as their 'farewell' record in 1969, with Johnny as producer and male voice. Johnny married into the Motown family by becoming the husband of Iris Gordy. Writing and producing with partner **Harvey Fuqua**, his initial success came with a gold record 'How Sweet It Is' for **Junior Walker** & The All Stars in 1966 (and later the follow-up 'What Does It Take'). Both on his own and in collaboration with Harvey, he also wrote and/or produced for numerous Motown artists including **Diana Ross**, **Marvin Gaye/Tammi Terrell** ('Ain't No Mountain High Enough'), **Smokey Robinson**, **David Ruffin**, **Edwin Starr/Michael Jackson** ('25 Miles'), **Gladys Knight & The Pips** ('I Don't Want To Do Wrong' and 'Help Me Make It Through The Night'), **Martha Reeves** ('No One There'), **Jimmy Ruffin**, **The Detroit Spinners**, **The Four Tops** and **Stevie Wonder** ('Yester-Me, Yester-You, Yesterday').

In 1974 he left Motown to sign with MGM Records as a solo artist. He scored immediately with 'Hang On In There Baby' (UK Top 5) and a string of popular soul singles through the mid-'70s, 'Do It To My Mind', 'Memories Don't Leave Like People Do', 'You & I' and 'Love Me For A Reason', the latter being a Bristol-penned UK No. 1 hit for The Osmonds. Switching to Ariola Records, 'Take Me Down' became a cult single on the New York disco scene, following which 'Love No Longer Has A Hold On Me', released by Handshake Records, endeared him to UK soul/dance audiences again. He switched to Atlantic Records where his albums include *Strangers* (1978). More recently he has recorded for the UK Motorcity label, co-writing and producing with **Ian Levine**. Here he stirred the UK soul scene with a rendition of 'Man Up In The Sky' (1989), while his own songs for the label include 'Keep This Thought In Mind'. He also recorded 'Come To Me' (1991) for Whichway Records.

He has also written and/or produced for artists including **Tavares** ('Check It Out', 1973), **Buddy Miles** ('Just A Kiss Away', 1975), **Tamiko Jones** ('Touch Me Baby'), **Real Thing** ('Love Takes Tears'), **O.C.Smith** ('La La Peace Song'), **Margie Joseph** (*Feeling My Way*, 1978), and in 1985 returned to Motown to produce a version of **Holland/Dozier/Holland**'s 'I'm Ready For Love' for **The Four Tops**.

BRITT, MEL

(Singer)

When **Jerry Butler** formed his FIP label in the '60s, Mel was one of his artists. In 1968 a single release 'She'll Come Running Back' became popular on the UK 'Northern soul' scene.

BROCK, TOM
(Singer/Songwriter)
Based in Los Angeles, Tom worked with **Barry White** during the '70s, also recording as a solo artist for 20th Century Records. As a songwriter his work includes 'A Case Of Too Much Love Makin'' for **Gloria Scott**.

BROCKINGTON SINGERS
(Vocal Group)
Philadelphia-based group The Brockington Singers recorded briefly with the **Gamble/Huff** TSOP subsidiary of Philadelphia International Records in 1975. Their single 'Stretch Out' was produced by Bruce Hawes.

BROOKINS, ROBERT
(Singer/Songwriter/Producer)
As a teenager Robert performed in front of Ronald Reagan at the White House in Washington prior to becoming a prominent producer on both the West and East Coast of America during the mid-'80s. In 1986 he was the featured singer on the **George Duke** album *George Duke*, following which he signed to MCA as a solo artist where his albums have been *In The Night* (1986), including 'Come To Me' and the **Stephanie Mills** duet 'In The Night (Making Love)'; and *Let It Be Me* (1988), including another **Stephanie Mills** duet 'Where Is The Love'.

As a writer and/or producer he has worked with **The Reddings**, **Bobby Brown** ('Seventeen'), **Jackie Jackson**, **Stephanie Mills**, **Deniece Williams** ('Blind Dating'), **Jeffrey Osborne** ('All Because Of You') and **The Whispers** ('Innocent'). He has also recorded keyboards with artists including **George Howard** (*A Nice Place To Be*), **Ramsey Lewis and Nancy Wilson** (*The Two of Us*), **Stanley Clarke** ('Find Out') and **Roy Ayers**.

BROOKS, PATTI
(Singer)
New York-based singer Patti Brooks recorded for Casablanca Records in the early '80s, her albums including *Patti Brooks*, including the **Michael Lovesmith**-penned/produced 'Reach For My Love'. In 1985 she switched to Easy Street Records for 'Lifeline Dancing'.

BROOM, BOBBY
(Guitarist)
Born in New York, Bobby had mastered the guitar by the time he was thirteen. Soon he was given a professional break by **Weldon Irvine** who employed him in a stage production of *Young Gifted And Broke*. At 16 he was playing at Carnegie Hall with **Sonny Rollins** and **Donald Byrd**. In 1979 **Tom Browne** invited him to be the guitarist on his first two albums for the GRP label (via Arista). Impressed, label owners **Grusin/Rosen** signed him as an artist in 1981 for *Clean Sweep* (1981) and *Living For The Beat* (1984), both of which were popular on the UK jazz funk scene.

BROOMFIELD, AL
(Singer)
From Miami, Al is the brother of Ronald Broomfield (aka **Eugene Wilde**). Al has so far recorded one album, *Broomfield* (1987), for the Vision label in Miami, issued in the UK via CBS.

BROTHERLY LOVE
(Duo)
From Philadelphia, brothers Al and Tyrone Chestnut first recorded 'Super Lovin'' for the Paramount label as The Chestnut Tree in 1972. They later released 'Sweet Loretta' as The Chestnut Brothers on Street Level Records (1983) before becoming Brotherly Love for 'Whole Lotta You In Me'/'Hey Sweet Lady' in 1990.

BROTHERS BY CHOICE
(Group)
Los Angeles-based group Brothers By Choice featured vocalist Chris Higgins and recorded for the ALA label during the '70s where their albums included *She Puts The Ease Back Into Easy* (1978).

BROTHERS JOHNSON
(Singers/Songwriters/Instrumentalists/Producers)
The Brothers Johnson are George Johnson (guitar/vocals, born 1953) and **Louis Johnson** (bass/vocals, born 1955) from Los Angeles. While at school with elder brother Tommy and cousin Alex Weir they formed a group Johnson Three Plus One, playing at school functions and parties. As they became more professional they were hired to support touring r&b acts such as **Bobby Womack** and **The Supremes**. George and Louis began a serious music career playing in **Billy Preston**'s band. Here they wrote songs for Billy including 'Music In My Life' and 'The Kids And Me' before parting company in 1973. They were later hired by **Quincy Jones** to play on *Mellow Madness*. Quincy recorded four of their compositions on the same album. These were 'Is It Love That We're Missin'', 'Listen (What Is It)', 'Trying To Find Out About You' and 'Just A Taste of Me'. Quincy later invited them on his tour of Japan before producing their first album, *Look Out For No. 1* (1976) after they had signed to A&M, the label Quincy was with at the time, and the label they remain with today. The album included 'Get The Funk Out Ma Face' and the American hit single 'I'll Be Good To You', certified gold within three months of release, and later going platinum. Quincy himself recorded the track with vocalists **Ray Charles** and **Chaka Khan** in 1989.

The Brothers' second album, *Right On Time* (1977) went gold within three days of release in the USA, and platinum in seventy-seven. It included 'Strawberry Letter 23', one of the first tracks to be released by A&M in the UK on 12" format and a Top 40 hit. Also on the album was an instrumental tribute to Quincy Jones called 'Q'. Quincy was also on hand as producer for the Brothers' third album *Blam* (1978), which included UK hit singles 'Ain't We Funkin' Now' (Top 50) and 'Ride-O-Rocket' (Top 50) together with the jazz funk instrumental classic 'Streetwave'. Their greatest commercial success in the UK came in 1980 with a Top 10 single 'Stomp', a dancefloor anthem that year. *Light Up The Night* (also including 'Smilin' On Ya') was again produced by Quincy Jones, and the title track hit the UK Top 50.

In 1981 'The Real Thing', in the style of a Quincy production but produced by the Brothers themselves, reached the UK Top 50. The track was featured on 1982's *Blast*, a greatest-hits compilation with four new tracks. Around this time both Louis and George began to embark on their own ventures, Louis playing bass with **Michael Jackson** on *Thriller* and recording a gospel album as part of **Passage**. George Johnson recorded with **Steve Arrington** among various ventures.

In 1984 the Brothers returned with *Out Of Control*, featuring 'You Keep Me Coming Back' produced by **Leon Sylvers**. They next recorded in 1988 at the invitation of their label, A&M; *Kickin'* contained the single 'Kick It To The Curb'. In 1989 it was back to work with Quincy Jones, co-writing 'Tomorrow' with **Sideah Garrett** for his *Back On The Block*, which also included the new version of 'I'll Be Good To You'.

BROWN, BOBBY

(Singer)

Born in Boston, Bobby Brown rose to fame as lead singer with **New Edition** before **Johnny Gill** took his place and Bobby began a solo career. His debut album *King Of Stage* was jointly produced by **Larry Blackmon**, **John Luongo**, **Michael Lovesmith** and **Robert Brookins**, but his solo career only took off in a big way when writers/producers **L.A./Babyface** took over for 1988's *Don't Be Cruel*, including title track hit (UK Top 50), 'My Prerogative' (UK Top 5), 'Every Little Step,' 'Roni' and 'Rock Wit'Cha'.

BROWN, BOE

(Singer/Drummer/Songwriter)

Beginning his professional career as a drummer, Boe joined New York group **The Strikers** before becoming the lead singer of **Warp 9**. Impressed by his vocal skills, Bob Dylan and Jeff Beck later hired him as a backing vocalist. In 1985 Boe Brown & The Uptown Horns cut a version of 'Sound Your Funky Horn', originally a '70s hit for **K.C. & The Sunshine Band**.

BROWN, CHUCK

(Singer/Songwriter)

Born in Washington DC, Chuck Brown and his group The Soul Searchers were pioneers of the 'go-go' sound in the late '70s. The Soul Searchers were John 'JB' Buchanan (synths/trombone/vocals), Donald Tillery (trumpet/vocals), Leroy Flemming (sax/flute/timbales/vocals), Jerry 'Wildman' Wilder (bass/vocals), Gregory 'Bright Moments' Gerran (congas/percussion), Curtis Johnson (organ), Skip Fennell (keyboards), Ricardo 'Tricky Sugar Foot' Wellman (drums) and Le Ron Young (lead guitar). In 1979 they released the single/album *Bustin' Loose* (Source Records) which stirred UK dancefloors without making a major impact (a follow-up Source album *Funk Express* was released in 1980). In 1985 at the height of the go-go craze in the UK, *Bustin' Loose* was re-released due to popular demand (the album also including 'Berro & Sombaro' and the 'Philly'-style **Gamble/Huff/Butler**-penned 'Never Gonna Give You Up'). A year previously, Chuck and his group had teamed up with Maxx Kidd's T.T.E.D. label and started the ball rolling with 'We Need Some Money'. In 1991 he returned on Goff Records with *90s Goin Hard*.

BROWN, GLORIA D.

(Singer)

Born in Montgomery, Alabama, in 1959, Gloria moved to Washington at the age of 12 and sang in gospel groups before fronting her own band New Breed and singing backgrounds for **The Detroit Spinners**, **Major Harris**, **James Brown** and others. In 1984 her debut single 'The More They Knock The More I Love You' was released by Krystal Records (via Virgin/10 Records in the UK where it reached the Top 60). She later worked with **Roy Ayers**.

BROWN, INEZ

(Singer)

Born in New York, Inez studied music at Queens College in the city prior to establishing herself as a singer on the local club scene. Hired by West End Records, she became a staff vocalist for many of the label's artists in addition to working as lead vocalist with Lovelace, Gary Tom's **Empire** and **Sleeque**. She occasionally tours as vocalist with '60s vocal group **The Marvelettes**.

BROWN, JAMES

(Singer/Songwriter/Producer)

Born in South Carolina in 1932, James was raised by his aunt in Augusta, Georgia, following the separation of his parents. He also spent some time in a remand home, and first made an income from shining shoes. In the early '50s he formed a gospel group The 3 Swanees with **Bobby Byrd** and Johnny Terry. Settling in Macon, Georgia, where Little Richard and The Five Royals were scoring success, the group became The Famous Flames (after a brief spell as The Avons) and hooked up with Little Richard's former manager Clint Brantley. In 1956 they recorded a demo of James's 'Please Please Me' which impressed Ralph Bass, talent scout for King Records in Cincinnati. He drove to Macon and signed the group for the release of the single.

That single was the first of a string of ten influenced by popular hits of the day with an added gospel ingredient. None were as successful as 'Please Please Me', and the group was nearly dropped by the label. In 1958 their fortunes changed with the release of 'Try Me', an American Top 50 (later gold) and the first of twelve hits in a row up to 1960. By now The Flames had expanded to a twenty-piece band with four warm-up soloists, two vocal groups, a comedian and a troupe of dancers. James learned every dance routine of the day to perfection and invented a few himself, making his stage presence the most energetic anyone had seen. His live show recorded at the Apollo Theatre in New York in 1962 was one of the most important releases of his career, establishing him across America. The following year he was voted America's No. 1 r&b singer.

In 1964 James played his first concert in the UK (a legendary performance in Walthamstow), and started his own production company Fair Deal. These recordings he took to Smash Records in Chicago after differences of opinion with his old label, King. From this point James Brown & The Flames recorded as just James Brown, and 'Out Of Sight' was his first release on the label (1964). It was soon followed by 'Papa's Got A Brand New Bag' (about the civil rights battle being fought in America), his first chart entry in the UK (Top 30, 1965), released on the London label.

Briefly returning to King (after legal problems with Smash), he recorded 'I Got You (I Feel Good)' (Top 30, 1966 on Pye), followed by 'Don't Be A Drop Out' which was part of a 'Stay At School' campaign and was rewarded by a citation from vice-president Hubert Humphrey at the White House. Also in 1966 James reached the UK Top 20 with 'It's A Man's Man's Man's World', his last hit on the Pye label (UK) before he signed to Polydor. In response to the American street riots of 1968 James recorded 'Say It Loud, I'm Black And I'm Proud', and found himself on a political soapbox following the assassination of Martin Luther King. This era (which included a TV appearance later praised by white politicians) put him in a delicate position which at one point sent his record sales plummeting. He shortly announced that he was to retire as a 'black leader' and return to making music.

In 1970 James moved into his 'funk' era creating a charged syncopated rhythm formula which has inspired numerous artists and records to this day. In America he started the ball rolling with 'Funky Drummer', a record utilizing a drum pattern copied unashamedly on countless dance records during the late '80s and early '90s. In the UK his career picked up with 'Sex Machine' (Top 40, 1970), recorded in Nashville and his most popular recording of all time. His other hits, including 'Hey America' (UK Top 50, 1971), 'Soul Power', 'Get On The Good Foot', 'King Heroin', 'Funky President' (1974), 'Don't Tell Him', 'Get Up Offa That Thing' (UK Top 25, 1976), 'Body Heat' (UK Top 40, 1977) and 'It's Too Funky In Here' (1979), further established him as 'The Godfather' (of soul) worldwide.

Also during this time James had moved into writing and/or producing for his singers and musicians in what had become known as The James Brown Revue. These included individual projects with **Bobby Byrd** ('I Know You Got Soul', 1971), **Lyn Collins** ('Think About It', 1972), Sweet Charles ('Yes It's You', 1974) and **Maceo Parker** (including 'Cross The Track', 1975).

In 1980 James recorded 'Rapp Payback' on Henry Stone's TK label (UK Top 40 on RCA) following which his erratic recordings included 'Bring It On, Bring It On' for Augusta Sound (UK Top 50 on Sonet, 1983) and 'King Of Soul' for MCA the same year (from the movie *Doctor Detroit*). When the hip hop scene emerged, James returned as an artist in partnership with **Afrika Bambaataa** for 'Unity', about the fight against nuclear war (Top 50 on Tommy Boy, 1984). His vocal grunts, made him the 'most sampled' artist on the rap/hip hop scene. In 1985 he recorded 'Living In America' (UK Top 5 on Scotti Brothers/ CBS) for the movie soundtrack *Rocky IV* (and his own album *Gravity*), following which all his early recordings and productions enjoyed a revival on the mid-'80s 'rare groove' scene. During this period 'Sex Machine' was re-released twice in the UK and reached the Top 50 in both 1985 and 1986.

In 1988, amongst further re-releases, **Coldcut** enjoyed some UK success with their James Brown medley 'Coldcut Meets The Godfather', while Polydor unearthed an unreleased '70s recording 'She's The One', which reached the UK Top 50. Also in 1988 James returned to the studio for a **Full Force**-produced album *I'm Real*, including 'Static', and recorded a historic duet 'Gimme Your Love' with **Aretha Franklin** for her album *Through The Storm*. In 1989 he landed himself in jail on a reckless driving charge, but was released, after a year.

BROWN, JOCELYN

(Singer)

Born in North Carolina, Jocelyn grew up in a family of seven brothers and two sisters, of which she was the eldest. (She is also related to **Barbara Roy** and **La-Rita Gaskin**.) Acappella singing among the family became a way of life, and upon moving to New York (when she was six), Jocelyn developed her singing further in the churches of Harlem. From here Jocelyn established herself on the New York session circuit, working with a broad spectrum of artists including Bruce Springsteen, Bette Midler, Bob Dylan, **Kleeer** and numerous names on the r&b scene.

In the early '80s she joined Salsoul group **Inner Life**, her lead vocals featuring on cuts including 'Aint No Mountain High Enough' (1981), 'Moment Of My Life' (1982) and 'I Like It Like That' (1983).

In 1984 she launched her solo career with 'Somebody Else's Guy', a song she had written herself and an instant smash hit. It reached No. 13 in the UK charts on 4th & Broadway Records (licenced from the American label Vinyl Dreams).

'Somebody Else's Guy' was produced by **Fred McFarlane/Allen George**, who brought Jocelyn back to the UK

Top 60 later in 1984 with 'I Wish You Would'. About the same time, various releases by Jocelyn came out on other New York labels who had previously recorded sessions with her. These included 'Picking Up Promises' (Easy Street), 'So In Love' (Silver Cloud) and 'Hands Off' (Urban Rock). None were hits or were released in the UK. She also recorded two singles for the US Posse label, 'Too Through' (later re-released by Malaco) and 'If I Can't Have Your Love', while returning to session work with artists including Robert Owens, **Chuck Stanley**, **Curtis Hairston**, **Pieces of a Dream** and **Diana Ross**.

In 1985 Jocelyn teamed up with **Jellybean** who had just signed a production agreement with Warner Brothers. 'Love's Gonna Get You' reached the UK Top 70 that year; the American 12" pressings featured an acappella version of the song during which she sings 'I've Got The Power'. A sample of this vocal was utilized by the group Snap who scored a massive hit in 1990 with 'The Power'. Upon the success of the Snap record she moved to London where she took legal action against the group and recorded a 1990 remix of 'Somebody Else's Guy' together with a new song 'Freedom' for the W.A.M. label. She also took up session work and became the guest lead vocalist with **Incognito** on their version of 'Always There' (1991).

BROWN, KEISA

(Singer)

Frederick Knight signed Keisa Brown to his Park Place label in 1985 and wrote/produced the majority of songs on *Keisa Brown*, including 'I Betcha Didn't Know That'.

BROWN, MAXINE

(Singer/Songwriter)

Born in Kingstree, South Carolina, Maxine first established herself as a gospel singer in New York around the late '50s. In the early '60s she moved into secular music and found success with American and UK soul fans with 'All In My Mind' (1961). This self-written song was followed by 'Funny', both singles released on the independent Nomar label. After a brief spell with the ABC label she switched to Scepter/Wand Records where she recorded the albums *Saying Something* and *Hold On I'm Comin'* with **Chuck Jackson**.

Although she also made an impact with solo singles like 'Ask Me, It's Gonna Be Alright' and 'Oh No, Not My Baby' (a hit for Manfred Mann), it is felt that her chances at Scepter were restricted as the label had **Dionne Warwick** to promote at the same time. Her other memorable '60s recordings include 'One In A Million', 'Since I Found You', 'I Cry Alone' and 'I Wonder What My Baby's Doing Tonight'.

BROWN, MORRIE

(Producer/Songwriter)

New York producer Morrie Brown worked with artists including **B.T.Express** (*1980*), before teaming up with **Kashif** and **Paul Laurence Jones** as a third of Mighty M Productions during the early '80s. During this time he worked with artists including **Evelyn 'Champagne' King** ('Love Come Down' and 'I'm In Love') and **The Manhattans** ('You Send Me'). He also wrote 'This Is Heaven' for **Howard Johnson** in 1982.

BROWN, O'CHI

(Singer)

From Tottenham, North London, O'Chi made her recording debut in 1983 with a reggae version of Procul Harem's 'A Whiter Shade Of Pale'. Signing to Magnet Records (where Pete Waterman worked prior to **Stock/Aitken/Waterman**), her follow-ups were 'Why Can't We Be Friends' and the Stock/Aitken/Waterman-produced 'Whenever You Need Somebody', later a hit for Rick Astley.

BROWN, OLLIE

(Singer/Songwriter/Drummer)

Born in Detroit in 1952, Ollie was eight years old when he formed The Stingrays with a six-year-old **Ray Parker** and an eight-year-old Nathan Watts. Ollie later played as a session drummer for the Motown, Invictus and Hot Wax labels with artists including **The Originals**, **Billy Preston** and **Syreeta** ('With You I'm Born Again') before moving to Los Angeles in the early '70s.

In 1978 he reunited with Ray Parker to play drums with **Raydio**, during which time he met **Jerry Knight** with whom he later formed **Ollie And Jerry**. The following year he recorded with **Sly & The Family Stone**, before making a solo album as **Ollie Baba** and forming his own production company Brown Sugar Productions to work with artists including **Klique** and **Fire Fox**.

In 1981 he toured with **Quincy Jones** which led to production work for **Patti Austin** and **Deco**, while back at Motown he moved into sessions and/or production with artists including **Billy Preston**, High Inergy, **Syreeta** ('I Must Be In Love') and MCA.

BROWN, PETER

(Singer/Songwriter)

Born in Chicago, Peter landed himself a record deal with TK Records in Miami after sending them demos of his songs. For the company's subsidiary label Dream he recorded *Stargazer* and scored two UK disco hits in 1978 with 'Do Ya Wanna Get Funky With Me' (Top 50) and 'Dance With Me' (Top 75). After 1980's *Can't Be Love*, Peter signed with CBS for *Snap* (1983) which included 'They Only Come Out At Night', mixed for the dancefloors by **Jellybean**. Through Jellybean, Peter also wrote 'Material Girl' for Madonna.

BROWN, RANDY
(Singer)
Born in Memphis, Tennessee, Randy built something of a cult status on the UK soul scene with the release of his debut album *Welcome To My Room* for the Parachute label in 1978. His other albums included *Intimately*, written and produced by **Homer Banks** and Chuck Brooks (Parachute, 1979), and *Midnight Desire* (Chocolate City, 1980), including 'The Next Best Thing To Being There'/'Do You Love Me'. More recently he released a three-track EP, 'Are You Lonely'/'Lifetime Of Happiness'/'Trying To Hold On', in the UK on Three-Way Records (1988).

His brother, incidentally, is William Brown from **The Mad Lads**.

BROWN, RUSS
(Singer/Songwriter)
Born in New York in 1952 Russ has a gospel background and studied music theory in earlier years. He's a hairdresser by profession, although in 1986 he cut 'Gotta Find A Way' which was well received on the UK dance scene, released by 10 Records (via Virgin). 'Take My Love' came in 1987 before Russ returned to his salon.

BROWN, SHARON
(Singer)
New York club/session singer signed with the city's Profile record company in 1982 and recorded a debut single 'I Specialize In Love'. Released in the UK via Virgin, it became a major dance record that year, also reaching the UK Top 40. The follow-up, 'You Got Me Where I Want To Be', was co-written/produced by **Patrick Adams** but had less of an impact.

BROWN, SHEREE
(Singer/Songwriter/Guitar)
Los Angeles-based Sheree has to date only recorded two albums (both for Capitol) *Straight Ahead* (1981), including 'You'll Be Dancing All Night' and 'It's A Pleasure', and *The Music* (1982), including 'Happy Music'. Both albums were showcases for her songwriting, with 'It's A Pleasure' recognized as her finest moment, and later re-recorded by **Francis Nero**. She has also worked closely with **Patrice Rushen** (co-writing both 'Haven't You Heard' in 1979 and 'Watch Out' in 1986), and has been a backing singer with **Fire Fox** and **Marilyn Scott**.

BROWN, SHIRLEY
(Singer)
Born in West Memphis, Arkansas in 1947, Shirley sang gospel in church before progressing to club work by the time she was 14. By then she had moved with her family to St Louis. Her first recordings were 'I Ain't Gonna Tell' and 'Love Is Built On A Strong Foundation', released on the Abet label and produced by Oliver Sain. It was **Albert King**, however, who took her to Stax in 1974 and teamed her with producer **Al Jackson** for her debut on the label, the million-seller 'Woman To Woman'. *Woman To Woman* was released in 1975 and included 'Between You And Me', 'It Ain't No Fun', and 'Stay With Me'. Soon after its release the Stax label folded, and Shirley switched to Arista. Here, in 1977, she delivered *Shirley Brown* which included 'I Need Somebody To Love Me', 'I'll Be Right There Lovin' You', 'I Need You Tonight' and 'A Mighty Good Feeling'.

In 1979 a compilation of early Stax recordings was issued, *For The Real Feeling*, but Shirley didn't officially release a new album until 1984 when she signed to Sound Town for *Intimate Storm*, which included 'I Don't Play That', 'Looking For The Real Thing' and 'This Used To Be Your House', co-written and produced by **Homer Banks**. 1986 delivered a Black Diamond release 'If This Is Goodbye' from Shirley before she signed to Malaco in 1989 and recorded a duet 'Ain't Nothin' Like The Lovin' We Got' with **Bobby Womack**. It was released in the UK by Cooltempo/Chrysalis.

BROWN III, WILLIAM C.
(Singer)
Born in Memphis, William is the brother of **Randy Brown** and originally sang with **The Mad Lads**. In 1982 he recorded a solo single 'Shining' for the HcRc label.

BROWNE, TOM
(Trumpeter)
Born in Queens, New York, in 1959, Tom originally played piano, having take lessons from the age of 11. Switching to trumpet, inspired by his collection of jazz albums, his first gig was in a Queens club The Village Door. In 1975 he landed his first professional gig with **Weldon Irvine**. From here he played with **Sonny Fortune** (*Infinity Is*) and Lonnie Smith (*Gotcha*) and was later introduced to **Dave Grusin & Larry Rosen** at GRP Records via **Earl Klugh**. Grusin & Rosen signed him to GRP (via Arista) and Tom broke onto the music scene in 1979 with a highly acclaimed instrumental jazz fusion album *Browne Sugar*, not released in the UK. His first real breakthrough came in 1980 with the release of 'Funkin' For Jamaica', taken from his second album *Love Approach*. The single was a UK Top 10 hit, and featured the lead vocals of **Toni Smith** (later a voice allegedly utilized by S-Express on 'Theme From S-Express').

Continuing his association with producers Grusin & Rosen, his next albums were *Yours Truly* (1981), including 'Fungi Mama' and 'Bye Gones', and *Magic* (1982), before he signed directly to Arista. Here he progressed into an electro style of jazz with 'Rockin' Radio' from a 1983 album of the same name (which also included a final GRP production 'Brighter Tomorrow').

In 1984 he recorded a final Arista album *Tommy Gun*, which featured **Siedah Garrett** singing lead on the leading moment 'Secret Fantasy' produced by **Maurice Starr**. Also in 1984 he recorded with Fuse One on their

Ice album, and with **Roy Ayers** on 'Goree Island' from his album *In The Dark*. More recently Tom has recorded for Malaco Records' jazz label subsidiary and has been involved in numerous sessions.

BROWNMARK

(Singer/Bass/Songwriter/Producer)

Born in Minneapolis, Brownmark was playing electric bass by the time he left high school and aged 18 was hand-picked by **Prince** to play with his group The Revolution. After instigating the group **Mazarati**, he signed to Motown and released *Just Like That* in 1988. In the UK they changed his name to Mark Brown and released a single 'Next Time' from the album. As a songwriter and/or producer he has also worked with **Chico Debarge**, **Stacy Lattisaw** and **Lakeside**.

BRUNSON, TYRONE

(Singer/Bass/Producer)

From Washington DC, Tyrone played bass and sang with local bands during his teen years through the '70s. His solo demos later impressed the Believe In A Dream label (via CBS) which signed him in 1982. His debut single release was an instrumental, 'The Smurf' (UK Top 75), inspired by a New York dance craze and an anthem on the UK 'electro' dance scene. The track was included on his debut album *Sticky Situation*, the follow-up being *Fresh* (1984). In 1987 he switched to MCA for the **James Mtume**-produced *Love Triangle*. He also sang backgrounds with **Levert**.

BRYANT, LEON

(Singer/Songwriter/Producer)

From Queens, New York, Leon took music lessons from the age of two, began classical training by the age of five and was musical director of a choir by the age of twelve! After encouraging reactions to a composition he entered in the American Song Festival, he looked for a record deal. In 1980 his song 'You Are My Latin Lover' was an American hit for **Joe Bataan**, and the following year his debut, self-titled album (a mixture of gospel and r&b) was released by De-Lite Records. He released a second album for De-Lite, *Finders Keepers*, in 1984, the same year he wrote and produced an album for **The Intruders**, *Who Do You Love*, which included 'Warm And Tender Love'.

An opera fan, his favorite tenor is Luciano Pavarotti.

BRYANT, SHARON

(Singer)

Born in New York, Sharon joined **Atlantic Starr** in the late '70s and was their lead singer when the group signed to A&M in 1979. Here she sang songs including 'When Love Calls' and 'Circles'. After leaving Atlantic Starr in 1984 she married Rick Gallway, a one-time member of the group **Change**. After working as a session singer, Sharon returned to the spotlight in 1989, releasing an album on the Wing label (via Polygram) *Here I Am*, including 'Foolish Heart'.

BRYSON, PEABO

(Singer/Songwriter)

Born in Greenville, South Carolina, Peabo initially worked as a songwriter and in-house producer for Bang records in the early '70s. In 1975 he recorded a debut single 'Underground Music' for the company's subsidiary Bullet, produced by **Michael Zager**. *Peabo* was later released the same year. He then signed to Capitol for whom his first album *Reaching For The Sky* reached gold status in America in 1978. His follow-up albums at Capitol included *Crosswinds* (1979), *Paradise* (1980), *Turn The Hands Of Time* (1981) and *Don't Play With Fire* (1982) before a duet album *Born To Love* (1983) with **Roberta Flack** which included the UK Top 5 hit 'Tonight I Celebrate My Love'. (Back in America Peabo had already scored a hit duet album *We're The Best Of Friends* with **Natalie Cole** in 1979.)

In 1984 Peabo switched to Elektra for *Straight From The Heart* (1984), *Quiet Storm* (1986) and *Positive* (1988), including his duet with **Regina Belle** 'Without You', before returning to Capitol in 1989 for *All My Love* which included 'Show And Tell' and his duet with **D'Atra Hicks** and 'Palm Of Your Hand'. In 1991 he changed labels to Columbia (CBS changing their name to Columbia this year) for *Can You Stop The Rain*, including 'Closer Than Close'.

As a songwriter, Peabo's credits include 'Feel The Fire', recorded by **Stephanie Mills** and **Teddy Pendergrass**.

BULLARD, FREDERICK

(Singer)

From West Palm Beach, Florida, Frederick toured American soul clubs during the '70s and '80s while building up a following. In 1984 he released 'You've Got To Give It Up' for Encore Records (via Move in the UK).

BULLOCK, JANICE

(Singer)

Memphis singer Janice Bullock signed to Wilbe Records owned by writer/producer **William Bell**, who produced her 1987 album *Don't Start A Fire*.

BURGESS, LEROY

(Singer/Songwriter/Producer)

Born in New York, Leroy began his music career at the age of 14 as a member of **Black Ivory**. He worked with the group until around 1977 when he left to concentrate on his own songwriting and productions. Black Ivory's producer was **Patrick Adams** who had worked at Salsoul Records. In the early '80s, Leroy wrote and/or produced for the label with artists including **Inner Life** (*Inner Life*), and later himself when 'Heartbreaker' was his solo release in 1983.

He later wrote 'Once You Got Me Going' (Debbie

Blackwell–ex-**Jammers**), 'Fly Girl' (**Intrigue**), 'Together Forever' (**Intrigue**), and 'Over Like A Fat Rat' (**Fonda Rae**), co-writing 'No Way' (**Bobbi Humphrey**) and 'Big Time' (**Rick James**), while in the meantime getting to know the **Aleem** brothers who lived in the same apartment block. Shortly he joined Aleem as vocalist from their club hit 'Hooked On Your Love' onwards.

He also sang backgrounds with **B.B.&Q.**, and became rather a cult producer on the UK black music scene in the '80s. More recently he has recorded as a solo artist again for the Konkrete label, and released 'Running After You' in 1991.

BURKE, KENI

(Singer/Songwriter/Bass/Producer)

Born in Chicago, Keni began his career in the 1960s with brothers James, Clarence, Dennis and sister Aloha in his family group **Stairsteps**. Keni was the bass player and when they split up in 1971 he moved to Los Angeles in search of session work. In 1974 he toured with **Billy Preston** who was a friend of ex-Beatle George Harrison. George met Keni at a time The Stairsteps were discussing a reunion album, and signed the group to his Dark Horse label. The result was one Billy Preston-produced album *2nd Resurrection* including Keni's song 'Tell Me Why' (later recorded by **Pockets**). In 1977 the group split up again, but, determined to succeed as a solo artist, Keni recorded a solo album for Dark Horse. The album *Keni Burke* (1977), including 'Keep On Singing' and 'You Are All Mine', wasn't a great success so Keni returned to session work with his bass guitar. He played with **Smokey Robinson**, **Sly and The Family Stone** (*On The Right Track*, 1979), **Terry Callier**, **Linda Clifford** ('Runaway Love', 1978), Dusty Springfield, **Diana Ross**, **Ramsey Lewis** (*Routes*, 1980), **Gladys Knight**, **Four Tops**, **Curtis Mayfield**, **Eugene Record**, **The Emotions** and **Bill Withers** among many more.

He later recorded two albums for RCA, *You're The Best* (1981), including 'Let Somebody Love You', 'Gotta Find A Way Back In Your Heart', 'Paintings Of Love' and 'Never Stop Loving Me'; and *Changes* (1982), including 'Hang Tight' and 'One Minute More'. The latter also included 'Risin' To The Top' which has become a cult song on the UK soul scene, although it has never charted (though twice released as a single). The song has been used as a sample on numerous rap records, while the bass line could well have been the influence for **The Mary Jane Girls** hit 'All Night Long'. In 1987 Keni played some dates in the UK but there has been no solo record release since *Changes*. A number of new songs have been recorded, however. These include 'Overnight' and 'Friends Or Lovers', but they remain unfinished.

As a songwriter/producer he has worked with **The Jones Girls** (1984's *Keep It Comin'* including 'You Can't Have My Love' and 'Ah Ah Ah Ah'), **The O'Jays** ('Put Our Heads Together'), **The Whitehead Brothers**, Mavis Staples ('Chocolate City'), **The Whispers** (co-writing 'Let's Go All The Way), **Perri** (co-writing 'I'm The One', also playing bass on *The Flight*), and **Bill Withers**, his most recent work being with Polygram group The Drama Club in 1990. Other bass sessions include the 1984 **George Howard** album *Steppin' Out*, while he also arranged vocals on **Peabo Bryson**'s *Positive*. He is planning new solo releases for 1991.

BURKE, SOLOMON

(Singer)

Born in Philadelphia in 1936, Solomon had a gospel upbringing, singing in his own church, 'Solomon's Temple' (founded by his grandmother) by the age of nine. He also sang on local radio as 'The Wonder Boy Preacher' before his voice broke. Moving to New York, he recorded for the Apollo and Singular labels in the mid- to late '50s before signing to Atlantic where he became one of the first major soul voices of the '60s. His debut single for the label was 'Keep The Magic Working' (1960), an American Top 30 hit, followed by the successful 'Just Out of Reach (Of My Two Empty Arms)' (1961). Further American hits followed with 'Cry To Me', 'Down In The Valley', 'If You Need Me' (a 1962 cover of the **Wilson Pickett** hit), 'You're Good For Me' (1963), 'Everybody Needs Somebody To Love' (1964), and 'Got To Get You Off My Mind' (1965), one of his producers during this era being **Tamiko Jones**.

In 1969 he switched to Bell Records for *Proud Mary* before changing labels again to MGM for *Electronic Magnetism*. In 1974 he signed to ABC/Dunhill for a Martin Luther King tribute album *I Have A Dream* before working with arranger **Gene Page** on 'Midnight And You' and his Chess Records debut 'You And Your Baby Blues' (1975). In 1979 he moved labels again, this time to Infinity (via MCA) for *Sidewalks Fences And Walls*.

BURRELL

(Group)

From New York, twins Rheji and Ronald Burrell are self-taught musicians who developed singing skills through the church and joined the group Inner Spirit when they were 13. Entering the New Jersey Teen Arts Festival they won first place four years in a row. Developing playing and recording skills on their own four-track recorder, they put together demos, eventually getting a record deal in their early twenties. Their debut was 'I'll Wait For You (Take Your Time)', released via Virgin/10 Records in the UK (1988).

Individually Ronald created, wrote and produced for **Bas Noir**, and numerous projects for the New York-based label Nu Groove.

BURTON, JENNY

(Singer)

Born in New York and raised as a foster child, Jenny took a fancy to the music business while still at high school. She eventually got a break in 1970 while working as a receptionist at Bell Records. A voice was urgently needed to sing a demo, and Jenny volunteered. The demos landed her a small deal with Cotton Records which included one single 'Nobody Loves Me Like I Do', a duet with **Dooley Silverspoon**, and some backing vocal sessions. In 1983 she was put forward as the artist to record 'One More Shot', a song written by John Robie. The success of the single, released by Plateau in the USA, lead to a deal at Atlantic. Around this time she married Peter Link, a major figure in the theatre world who writes songs and has his own recording studio and publishing company. She released *In Black And White* and recorded a duet ballad with Patrick Jude called 'Strangers In A Strange World' that was featured in the film *Beat Street*.

In 1985 *Jenny Burton* was released and featured the dance hit 'Bad Habits', a **George/McFarlane** composition/production in the style of **Jocelyn Brown**'s 'Somebody Else's Guy'. Her UK chart entry from the album, however, was 'Let's Get Back To Love' which made the Top 70. *Souvenirs* was released in 1986 and was produced by John Luongo.

BUTCH AND THE NEW PORTS
(Group)
From Detroit, this group originally recorded as the **Young Sirs** before signing to Uptight Records in the early '70s and releasing 'Driftin' Away', 'I'm Gonna Get You', 'Just Like Magic' and 'Just Because Of You'. Lead vocalist with the group was **Oliver Cheatham**.

BUTLER, JERRY
(Singer/Songwriter/Producer)
Born in Sunflower, Mississippi, in 1939, Jerry moved to Chicago when he was three. Here he sang with various church choirs, becoming a member of the Northern Jubilee Gospel Singers at 15. In 1957, he met **Curtis Mayfield**, whose group **The Impressions** he joined after spending some time with a doo-wop group The Quails.

In 1958 Jerry co-wrote 'For Your Precious Love' which he recorded as lead singer with The Impressions. Its success across America launched his solo career which initially involved Curtis Mayfield as songwriter (on 'He Will Break Your Heart', for example) and guitarist. On the Vee-Jay label he scored American hits including 'Moon River' (1961), 'Make It Easy On Yourself' and 'I Stand Accused' (1964). He recorded a duet album *Delicious Together* with **Betty Everett** (1964) and wrote songs for Count Basie, **Jackie Wilson** and **Otis Redding**. During 1967, after the demise of Vee-Jay, Jerry met writers/producers **Gamble/Huff** in the Philadelphia nightclub Prep's. Jerry signed to Mercury, and worked with them on *The Ice Man Cometh* (1968), including 'Hey Western Union Man' and 'Only The Strong Survive'; and *Ice On Ice* (1969), including 'Moody Woman' and 'What's The Use Of Breaking Up'. He had been nicknamed 'The Ice Man' by legendary Philadelphia DJ Georgie Woods.

In the early '70s he recorded a couple of duet projects, *One Plus One* with **Gene Chandler** (1970) and the million-selling 'Ain't Understanding Mellow' with **Brenda Lea Eager** (1971). He also launched his own FIP label (artists including **Mel Britt**), and took on various production projects (including **The Sylvers** 1972 album). In 1975 he switched to Motown to record both as a solo artist and in partnership with **Thelma Houston** while in 1977 he began a production company, Fountain Productions (projects including **Mystique** 'If You're In Need'). Signing to the Philadelphia International label (PIR) he recorded *Nothing Says I Love You Like I Love You* (1978), including '(I'm Just Thinking About) Cooling Out' and a duet with **Debra Henry**, 'Don't Be An Island'. Also while at PIR he co-wrote and produced 'Was That All It Was' and 'When I Find You Love' for **Jean Carne** (later a 1989 release for **Kym Mazelle**), and co-produced **Dee Dee Sharp Gamble** ('Breaking And Entering') prior to his own second album for the label, *Best Love I Ever Had* (1980).

As a guest vocalist he also recorded with **Stix Hooper** on 'Let's Talk It Out' from *Touch The Feeling* (1982).

BUTLER, JONATHAN
(Singer/Songwriter/Guitarist)
Born in Athlone (Cape Town), South Africa, the youngest of 17 brothers and sisters, Jonathan became a proficient vocalist and guitarist by the time he was six. He shortly became the chief family breadwinner, and had established a career for himself by the time he was 13. Due to his disillusionment with apartheid, he emigrated to London in 1985 at the invitation of fellow South Africans Clive Calder and Ralph Simon, founders of Jive Records. Signing to the label he recorded with **Ruby Turner** on her remake of 'If You're Ready (Come Go With Me)' before the release of his own debut album *Introducing Jonathan Butler* (1986).

Teaming up with producer **Barry Eastmond**, his follow-up double album *Jonathan Butler* (1987) created a great deal of interest on the UK soul scene for songs including 'Lies' (UK Top 20), 'Love Songs, Candlelight & You' and 'Overflowing'. His next Jive albums were *More Than Friends* (1988), including 'True Love Never Fails', a duet with **Vanessa Bell Armstrong**, *Deliverance* (1990) and *Heal Our Land* (1990).

His songs have also been recorded by **Al Jarreau**, **Billy Ocean**, **George Benson** ('Tender Love') and **Millie Jackson** ('I Fell In Love').

BY ALL MEANS
(Group)
Based in Los Angeles, By All Means are James Varner (lead vocals/trumpet/trombone), Lynn Roderick (vocals) and Billy Shepherd (guitar). Lynn previously worked as an actress in TV shows including *Moonlighting* and *Cagney & Lacey*, while Billy was an integral part of the group **Skool Boyz**. James and Lynn met in 1985 while touring with **Bill Withers**. Stan Sheppard (producer) was

in the audience and suggested they form a band with his brother Billy. Signing to 4th & Broadway (via Island) their albums have been *By All Means* (1988), including 'I Surrender' and 'You Decided To Go'; and *Beyond A Dream* (1989).

As writers and producers they have also worked closely with **Gerald Alston** on his two solo albums for Motown.

BYRD, BOBBY
(Singer/Musician)
Born in South Carolina, Bobby played in a gospel group The 3 Swanees with **James Brown** and Johnny Terry before expanding the group and changing their name to The Flames in the early '50s. While James spent a spell in prison, Bobby recorded with the group's Earl Nelson as **Bob And Earl** before forming a new group The Avons.

When James Brown was freed he joined The Avons and instigated their change of name back to The Flames and ultimately James Brown And The Famous Flames during the '60s. It is claimed that Bobby wrote as many as forty of James's major hits (including 'Sex Machine'), although his credits are missing from many of the releases. Bobby also sang consistently with The James Brown Revue (as did his wife Vickie Anderson), and produced for James during the '60s and '70s too.

As a solo artist he is best remembered for the James Brown-produced 'I Know You Got Soul' (1971) and 'If You Got A Love You Better Hold On To It' (1972), popular on the UK 'rare groove' scene in the mid-'80s.

BYRD, DONALD
(Trumpet)
Born in Detroit, Michigan, in 1932, Donald formed his first band during his teen years, shortly to establish himself on the New York jazz scene while working with Max Roach, Art Blakey and **Herbie Hancock**. He also recorded as a solo artist for the Prestige label, his albums here including *House Of Byrd*. After acquiring a teaching degree he taught at Howard University (where he also became chairman), one of his students during the late '60s being **Larry Mizell**.

Until this point Donald had played traditional jazz, but inspired by Larry Mizell he experimented with fusion jazz, 'jazz funk' as the UK soul scene called it. Amidst much initial criticism he recorded *Ethiopian Knights* (1972) for Blue Note Records. Continuing in a jazz funk vein (with Mizell as writer/producer) his other albums for the label included *Blackbyrd* (1973), *Street Lady* (1974), *Caricatures* (1976) and what has become his 'cult' and much-sought-after release, *Places And Spaces* (1976), including 'Change (Makes You Wanna Hustle)', 'Wind Parade' and '(Fallin' Like) Dominoes'. Also in 1976 he recorded a live version of '(Fallin' Like) Dominoes' in Central Park, New York, which was included on *Blue Note Live At The Roxy*. It became a UK jazz funk classic anthem during the late '70s and early '80s. In the meantime he switched to Elektra, where he recorded as Donald Byrd And 125th Street NYC. Here he recorded *Thank You For Funking Up My Life* (1978), including 'Loving You', and two **Isaac Hayes**-produced albums: *Love Byrd* (1981), including 'Love Has Come Around' (UK Top 50), and *Words, Sounds, Colours And Shapes* (1982).

He also instigated groups **N.C.C.U.** and **The Blackbyrds**, writing ('Do It Fluid') and producing their albums *The Blackbyrds* and *City Life*. He also produced **Three Pieces** and recorded with his nephew **Alex Bugnon**.

BYRD, GARY
(Rapper/DJ)
During the '60s Gary Byrd met **Stevie Wonder** and wrote the lyrics to his songs 'Black Man' and 'Village Ghetto Land'. From there he established himself as a top DJ on American radio. In 1983 he worked with Stevie Wonder again, this time on 'The Crown', a debut Gary Byrd single (12″ only). It became the first and only release on Stevie's Wondirection label, co-written by Stevie who produced and sang on it. In 1984 Gary could be heard presenting the BBC's Sunday gospel radio show 'Sweet Inspiration', while in 1986 he wrote a poem about Halley's Comet for a broadcast made by the European Space Agency.

C-BRAND

(Group)

Detroit-based group C-Brand recorded for the Spring label in the early '80s where the popular 'Wired For Games' was taken from their one album *In Growth* (1982). A new line-up of C-Brand later worked with former **Contours** vocalist Billy Gordon (lead on 'Do You Love Me') on the **Ian Levine**/**Bobby Taylor**-penned/produced 'Half Hearted' for the Motorcity label.

C.C.R. CREW

(Group)

Instigated by British DJ 'Froggy' (Steve Howlett), C.C.R. Crew was a studio concept for Froggy's Circle City Records label. 1987 saw the release of 'Stretchin' The Pieces', a reworking of **The Average White Band**'s 'Pick Up The Pieces'.

C.J. & CO.

(Studio Group)

During the 'disco' era of the late '70s, Cornelius Brown Jr, Joni Tolbert, Connie Durden, Curtis Durden, **Earl Van Dyke** (occasional keyboards) and Charles Clark worked together as C.J. & Co., making 'disco symphony' albums with dance beats and heavy orchestrations. With producers including **Mike Theodore** and **Dennis Coffey**, their albums for Westbound Records included *Devil's Gun* (1977) and *Deadeye Dick* (1978). The vocalists within the group also sang on Mike Theodore's own album *Cosmic Wind*.

CABO FRIO

(Group)

From Rochester, New York, Cabo Frio formed in 1982 and are a jazz fusion group consisting of Curtis Kendrick (drums), Glen Cummings (guitar), George Sessum (bass), Kenny Blake (sax) and Joey Santora (keyboards), all top pedigree musicians who had previously played with leading jazz/r&b artists. In 1986 they signed to Zebra Records (via MCA) where their albums have been *Right On The Money* (1986) and *Cabo Frio* (1987), featuring **Eugene Wilde** on 'I'll Get Back To You' and 'Love Talk'.

CAESAR, VIC

(Songwriter/Producer/Vibes)

Based in Los Angeles, Vic was a session musician who in 1979 instigated the group **Cook County** and signed them to Motown Records.

CAIRO

(Group)

From East London, Cairo are Lennox Cameron (lead vocals/keyboards) and Thomas Ribeiro Jr, who first met at school. They signed to Citybeat Records in the late '80s where their singles included 'On The Rebound', 'Dancing On The Nile' and '(I Want You) In My Life'.

CALDERA

(Group)

West Coast jazz fusion group consisted of Steve Tavaglione (flute/sax), Jorge Strunz (guitars), Mike 'Baiano' Azevedo (congas/percussion), Carlos Vega (drums), Dean Cortez (bass), Hector Andrade (timbales/percussion) and Eduardo del Barrio (keyboards). Their 1977 album *Sky Islands* on Capitol featured a **Dianne Reeves** lead vocal on 'Ancient Source', which also featured Larry Dunn from **Earth Wind & Fire** on keyboards.

CALDWELL, BOBBY

(Singer/Songwriter/Guitar)

Bobby Caldwell emerged during 1978 with the highly acclaimed **Bobby Caldwell** including 'Down For The Third Time', 'What You Won't Do For Love' and 'Love Won't Wait', for the Miami-based Clouds label (via TK). In 1980 he returned with *Cat In The Hat* before switching to Polydor for *Carry On* (1982). He found trouble being accepted as a black music singer during the late '70s/early '80s because he was white.

CALIFORNIA EXECUTIVES

(Group)

From Santa Barbara, The California Executives featured the lead vocals of Ronald Dudley. In 1987 the group signed to the Parliament label and delivered *Dancing And Romancing*.

CALLIER, TERRY

(Singer/Songwriter)

Chicago-based singer recorded for the Chess/Cadet labels from the mid-'60s to the early '70s, his songs including 'Look At Me Now', 'I Just Can't Help Myself' and 'Gotta Get Closer To You'. During the mid-'70s he recorded 'I Don't Want To See Myself (Without You)' which became popular on the UK 'rare groove' scene during the mid-'80s. In the late '70s he signed to Elektra where his albums included *Turn You To Love* (1979) including 'Ordinary Joe' and 'Sign Of The Times'.

CALLOWAY

(Duo/Songwriters/Producers/Multi-Instrumentalists)

From Kentucky, Reggie, Vincent and Greg Calloway first played together professionally in a jazz trio Sun Child, accompanying **Sonny Stitt**. In 1979 Greg left the group while Reggie and Vincent formed **Midnight Star**.

After establishing themselves the brothers worked on outside projects as writers and/or producers with a number of artists including **Levert** ('Casanova'), **Natalie Cole** ('Jump Start', and Reggie also writing 'I Wanna Be That Woman'), **Gladys Knight & The Pips** ('Love Overboard'), **The Whispers** ('Joy'), **Klymaxx** ('The Men All Pause'), and **Teddy Pendergrass**.

After leaving **Midnight Star**, Reggie and Vincent formed Calloway and scored an American hit with 'I Wanna Be Rich', taken from their debut album *All The Way* (1990) for Los Angeles-based Solar Records.

CALVIN, BILLIE

(Singer/Songwriter)

Los Angeles singer Billie Calvin worked with writer/producer **Norman Whitfield** during the '70s, and sang in the original line-up of **Undisputed Truth**. As a songwriter, her most successful composition was 'Wishing On A Star', originally a hit for another Whitfield-produced act **Rose Royce**. More recently she has recorded as a solo singer on the UK Motorcity label with producer **Ian Levine**.

CAMEO

(Group)

Formed in 1976 by **Larry Blackmon**, the thirteen-member group was originally known as The New York City Players. Their first recording was 'Find My Way', after which they built up a live following and signed to the Casablanca label as Cameo. Here they established themselves with two early albums: *Cardiac Arrest* (1977), including 'Smile', 'Rigor Mortis' and 'We All Know Who We Are'; and *Ugly Ego* (1978), including 'Insane' and 'Give Love A Chance'. Their reputation as a premier funk band extended to the UK, while in America *Secret Omen* (1979), including 'I Just Want To Be' and 'Sparkle', was the first of five gold albums in a row. The others were *Cameosis* (1980), including 'Shake Your Pants'; *Feel Me* (1980), including 'Keep It Hot' and 'Your Love Takes Me Out'; *Knights Of The Sound Table* (1981) – their first to be released in the UK – including 'Freaky Dancin'' and 'Knights By Knights'; and *Alligator Woman* (1982), including 'Just Be Yourself' and 'Flirt'.

By this time the group had trimmed down from thirteen to a nucleus of four members, these being **Larry Blackmon** (lead vocals/drums), Tomi Jenkins (vocals), Nathan Leftenant (trumpet), and **Charlie Singleton** (guitar), although Charlie left in 1985 (while initially continuing to record with the group). They had settled in Atlanta, and in 1981 launched their own Atlanta Artists label (via Phonogram), artists including **Cashflow** and **Barbara Mitchel**. In 1984 they created a new formula which fused '70s funk with '80s technology and entered their most commercially successful period in the UK with *She's Strange*, including 'You're A Winner' and 'Hangin' Downtown', and their UK chart debut with the title track (Top 40). 1985's *Single Life* furthered their popularity with UK hits 'Attack Me With Your Love' (Top 75), 'Single Life' (Top 20), 'A Goodbye' (Top 75) and strong album tracks 'I'll Never Look For Love' (a duet with Barbara Mitchell) and 'I've Got Your Image'. Then came *Word Up* (1986), from which the title track was a UK Top 5 hit, followed by 'Candy' (Top 30), 'Back And Forth' (Top 20), and 'She's Mine' (Top 40).

Also in 1986 Cameo wrote 'Baby, I Wanna Tell You Something' recorded by **Bobby Brown**, **Larry Blackmon** producing three cuts on Bobby's debut solo album.

CAMERON, G.C.

(Singer/Songwriter)

Born in Jackson, Mississippi, G.C.'s parents and their ten children moved to Detroit in 1955. G.C. joined the marines to serve in Vietnam before being demobbed in 1967. Back in Detroit G.C. was auditioned by **Marvin Gaye** to replace Chico Edwards as lead singer of **The Detroit Spinners**. G.C. was the voice on the Motown classic 'It's A Shame', a UK Top 20 hit (1970), before commencing a solo career. He married Gwen Gordy (who had just left **Harvey Fuqua**) and moved to Los Angeles where he recorded for the Motown subsidiary Mowest. Here he released 'Act Like A Shotgun' (1971), 'I'm Gonna Get You' (1971), 'What It Is, What It Is' (1972), 'Come And Get This Thang' – a duet with **Willie Hutch** (1973), 'Don't Wanna Play Pyjama Games' (1973) and an album *7th Son* (1973), including 'Pyjama Games', before a move back to Motown for *Love Songs and Other Tragedies* (1974), *G.C.Cameron* (1974), *You're What's Missing In My Life* (1977), whose title track became popular on the UK 'rare groove' scene in the mid-80s, and a duet album with **Syreeta** (*Rich Love, Poor Love*, 1977).

Gwen then left G.C. and returned to Harvey, while Harvey (strangely) produced G.C. for Honey Records in 1980, 'Live For Love' being a single release in the UK (via Flamingo Records). Returning to Mississippi he signed to the Malaco label for *Give Me Your Love* (1983). In 1989 he hooked up with a couple of UK record labels to release 'Wait Until Tomorrow' for the Ardent label, and a remake of 'It's A Shame' for the Motorcity label, which was later featured on *Right Or Wrong* for the label (1991).

CAMERON, RAFAEL
(Singer/Songwriter)
Born in Georgetown, Guyana, in 1951, Rafael sang in high-school bands before moving to New York in 1973. Here he joined fellow Guyanese in a local band. In 1979 Rafael signed to Salsoul Records, where **Randy Muller** produced his debut album *Cameron* accompanied by music from **New York Skyy**. Randy continued to work with Rafael on his follow-up *Cameron's In Love* (1981), including 'Funtown USA', 'All That's Good To Me' and 'Boogie's Gonna Get Ya'.

CAMOUFLAGE
(Studio Group)
One of many disco concept groups to emerge from New York during the '70s, Camouflage were session musicians/singers who came together for one album *A Disco Symphony*, including 'Bee Sting' (State Records, 1977).

CAMPBELL, TEVIN
(Singer)
A voice for the '90s, Tevin was discovered by **Bobbi Humphrey** and made his recording debut aged fourteen with **Quincy Jones** on *Back On The Block* (1989), singing lead on 'Tomorrow'.

CANDELA
(Group)
From New York, Candela are Lisa Dean (keyboards), Fernando Luis (guitar), Isidro Ross (percussion) and Michelle Pratt (vocals), who was 16 when the group released their debut single 'Love You Madly' on Arista in 1982. Michelle landed the job of lead singer after 115 female vocalists auditioned!

CANDIDO
(Congas/Percussionist)
Percussionist Candido signed to New York's Salsoul label in the late '70s where he worked with vocalist Woody Cunningham from the group **Kleeer**. From the albums he made, *Dancin' And Prancin'* (1979) made the most impact, tracks including 'Thousand Finger Man' and the dance classic 'Jingo'. While 'Jingo' only reached the UK Top 75 (1981, on Excalibur Records), it dominated dance floors for ten years!

CAPTAIN SKY
(Singer/Songwriter/Producer)
From Philadelphia, Captain Sky made a series of recordings in the early '80s for a number of local labels including WMOT (*Concerned Party No.1*, 1980 and single 'Station Break', 1981) and Philly World ('Don't Touch That Dial', 1982).

CARLTON, CARL
(Singer)
Born in Detroit in 1953, Carl was twelve years old when the Golden World label signed him, hoping he would be their answer to **Little Stevie Wonder**. After one single, 'Nothin' No Sweeter Than Love', he left the label and recorded for others including Lando and eventually the Houston-based Backbeat (releases including 'Competition Ain't Nothing' and 'Look At Mary Wonder'). In 1974 he had an American pop hit with 'Everlasting Love' before he switched to 20th Century Records where he scored his one UK pop hit with 'She's A Bad Mama Jama' (Top 40, 1981).

CARLTON, LARRY
(Guitar/Producer/Songwriter)
Born Larry Eugene Carlton in Torrance, California, in 1948, Larry first worked professionally with the house band at Disneyland prior to becoming a staff music writer for NBC TV in 1969. In 1973 he joined **The Crusaders**, who accompanied Larry on his solo album *Singing/Playing* (1974) for MCA. He also spent some time as guitarist with **The 5th Dimension** in addition to a great deal of session work with artists including **Al Jarreau**, **Minnie Riperton** and **Randy Crawford**.

Towards the end of the 70s he moved into production and signed to Warner Brothers as an artist. In 1978 he produced the *Suite Lady* album for **Gap Mangione** and recorded his own album *Larry Carlton*. His other solo Warner Brothers albums were *Strikes Twice* (1980), *Sleepwalk* (1982) and *Friends* (1983) before he switched to MCA for *Alone, But Never Alone* (1986), *Last Nite* (1987) and *Discovery* (1988).

Larry also co-wrote and produced 'Oh Yeah!' for **Bill Withers** and can be found as the featured guitarist on Mike Post's theme to TV's *Hill Street Blues*.

CARMAN, PAULI
(Singer)
Pauli first sang with a group called Coalkitchen before becoming the lead singer with **Champaign**. The group were with CBS, the label Pauli signed to as a solo artist in 1986. Here he released *Dial My Number* (the title track single produced by **The System**) and *It's Time* (1987). More recently he has rejoined Champaign at Malaco Records.

CARMICHAEL, GREG
(Songwriter/Producer)
Based in New York, Greg worked closely with **Patrick Adams** during the late '70s and early '80s on projects for numerous disco artists including **Inner Life**. His own work includes songs and/or productions for artists including Wish ('Nice & Soft', 1981), **Universal Robot Band** and **Roshelle Fleming**.

CARMICHAEL, JAMES ANTHONY
(Producer/Arranger)
Based in Los Angeles, James has been closely involved in the careers of **The Commodores** and their former lead singer **Lionel Richie** as an arranger and producer from the '70s through to the present day. He has also arranged and/or produced for artists including **The Miracles**, **Atlantic Starr** and **The Pointer Sisters**.

CARNE, JEAN
(Singer)
Jean's father came from New Orleans and was deeply into the music of Satchmo. Jean's own musical roots were in jazz, and it was in this field that she began a recording career with her husband. She had met pianist Doug Carn in college, and they moved to California and secured a deal with Ovation Records in 1971. Their albums *Infant Eyes* (1971), *Spirit Of The Newland* (1972) and *Revelation* (1973) featured versions of instrumental classics including Horace Silver's 'Peace' and McCoy Tyner's 'Contemplation', to which Jean added her own lyrics.

In 1974 she was a featured vocalist on *Rebirth Cycle*, a jazz album recorded by **James Mtume**. A fourth Doug & Jean album, *Higher Ground*, featuring the best tracks from the first three albums, was released in 1976. Doug and Jean's marriage came to an end and they left the Ovation label.

As a solo artist she performed with Duke Ellington just prior to his death, and then at numerous nightclubs before being spotted by producer **Norman Connors**. Norman invited her to become a featured vocalist on *Slewfoot* (1974) and then *Saturday Night Special* (1975) (including 'Valentine Love', 'Dindi' and 'Skin Diver'). This took her to Philadelphia where she met **Gamble/Huff**. Signing to their Philadelphia International label (as Jean Carn) she recorded a total of four albums (the last for the TSOP subsidiary): *Jean Carn* (1976), including 'Free Love', 'I'm In Love Once Again' and 'If You Wanna Go Back'; *Happy To Be With You* (1978), including 'Don't Let It Go To Your Head' (the song for which she is best remembered in the UK), 'I Bet She Won't Love You Like I Do' and 'No No You Can't Come Back Now'; *When I Find You Love* (1979), including 'My Love Don't Come Easy' and 'Was That All It Was' (her one dance anthem, greatly extended on 12" release); and *Sweet And Wonderful* (1981), including 'Love Don't Love Nobody' and 'We Got Some Catching Up To Do'. Also at the label she recorded with **Dexter Wansel** (lead vocals on 'Dreams of Tomorrow'), and worked on various background arrangements for the label's artists. Later, when Philadelphia International wound down their recording activities, **Kenny Gamble** helped Jean to secure a deal with Motown. In 1982 she worked with **Norman Connors** on her one Motown album *Trust Me*, and was the featured vocalist on a version of 'Let's Stay Together', a single by **Bobby M** released by the company. 'Trust Me', incidentally, was written by **Al Johnson** with whom she recorded the duet 'I'm Back For More' in 1980; it remains one of her most popular recordings.

From 1982 she returned to her jazz audiences playing the club circuit, and also added an 'e' to her name for numerological reasons. She visited the UK for the first time with the New York Jazz Explosion in 1985, shortly to return with her own band. As Jean Carne, a new recording deal came her way with Omni/Atlantic Records in 1986. Here she recorded *Closer Than Close* (1986) and *You're A Part Of Me* (1988). 'Closer Than Close' became a US No. 1 r&b record, but she still failed to make an impact on the charts this side of the Atlantic.

She sang lead vocals on 'You Might Be Surprised' and 'Can I See You' for **Roy Ayers** on his album *You Might Be Surprised* (1985); 'The Look of Love' and 'Keep In Touch' for **Grover Washington** on *Strawberry Moon* (1987); 'Night Breeze' for **Stanley Turrentine** on *L.A. Place* (1989). She also sang backgrounds with artists such as **Rick James**.

CARSTAIRS
(Group)
Popular on the UK 'Northern soul' scene in the early '70s, The Carstairs recorded for the Red Coach label where 'It Really Hurts Me Girl' (1973) has become somewhat of a classic.

CARTER, CLARENCE
(Singer)
Born in Alabama, Clarence lost his sight at an early age. His first recordings were with Calvin Scott as Calvin and Clarence with the C & C Boys between 1963 and 1966, but Clarence went solo after Calvin was injured in a car accident. In 1967 Clarence signed with the Fame label and scored an American Top 10 hit that year with 'Tell Daddy'. He also discovered **Candi Staton**, whom he married and brought to Fame as a recording artist.

Clarence switched to the Atlantic label for a string of American hits including 'Looking For A Fox', 'Slip Away', 'Too Weak To Fight', 'I Can't Leave Your Love Alone', and a 1970 pop hit 'Patches', a **General Johnson** song which reached No. 2 in the UK that year. A further American hit followed in 1971 with 'Slipped, Tripped, & Fell in Love', a song originally written for Ann Peebles. Clarence's next chart success in the USA was 'I Got Caught Making Love To Another Man's Wife'. By now he had signed with ABC where his albums included *Loneliness And Temptation* (1975). In 1981 he resurfaced on Venture Records for two albums before joining the Certain label and releasing 'Messin' With My Mind' in 1985. Later in 1987 he recorded *Doctor C.C.* for the Ichiban label.

CARTER, ROY
(Singer/Songwriter/Producer)
Based in London, Roy worked with **The Foundations** before joining **Heatwave** in the late '70s. From here he

became a major influence on the UK 'Brit funk' scene as producer for a number of groups including **Central Line**. He also worked as producer with American groups including **Mission**.

CASEY, HARRY W.
(Singer/Songwriter/Producer)
Born in Florida, Harry Wayne Casey gained his first musical experience in the early '70s while working in a small recording studio belonging to TK Records. During the day he worked at the label's warehouse where he met **Rick Finch** and together they formed **K.C. & The Sunshine Band**. Also at TK, Harry wrote and/or produced for artists including **George McCrae** ('Rock Your Baby'), **Jimmy 'Bo' Horne** ('Dance Across The Floor') and **Gwen McCrae**.

CASH, ALVIN
(Singer)
Born in St Louis, Missouri, in 1939, Alvin formed Alvin Cash & The Crawlers with his four brothers during the mid-'50s. For the Mar-V-Lus label they scored American r&b success with 'Twine Time'. In 1960 he met Muhammad Ali, later to inspire his single release 'Ali Shuffle'. Alvin recorded solo discs 'Alvin's Got A Boogaloo', 'The Philly Freeze' and 'Funky Washing Machine' during the '60s.

CASHFLOW
(Group)
From Atlanta, Georgia, Cashflow were Gaylord Parsons (drums/vocals/raps), Kary Hubbert (lead vocals), James Duffie (keyboards/backing vocals) and Regis Ferguson (keyboards). Signing to the Atlanta Artists label belonging to **Larry Blackmon** of **Cameo**, the group recorded one album *Cashflow* (1986), including 'Mine All Mine' (UK Top 20).

CASHMERE
(Group)
Cashmere were two top session musicians Daryl Burgee (from Philadelphia) and Dwight Ronnell Dukes (from Chicago). Dwight had previously recorded as lead singer with **Heaven & Earth**. In 1982 Daryl and Dwight worked with producer **Bryan Loren** on a debut album *Let The Music Turn You On*, including 'Do It Anyway You Wanna' for the Philly World label, released by 4th & Broadway in the UK in 1983. They added pianist/songwriter Mick Horton, **Eugene Wilde**'s co-writer (on 'Gotta Get You Home With Me Tonight'), making the group a trio. Their second album *Cashmere* (1985) featured 'Can I' (UK Top 30) and 'We Need Love' (UK Top 75).

CASIOPEA
(Group)
From Japan, this instrumental group made an impact on the UK jazz funk scene in the early '80s. Their albums for Alfa Records (via CBS in the UK) included *Mint Jams* (1982).

CASTON, LEONARD
(Singer/Songwriter/Producer)
Based in Los Angeles, Leonard worked with **Frank Wilson** producing **Eddie Kendricks** at Motown, the label where he and his wife recorded as Caston & Majors (including 'I'll Keep A Light In The Window', 1974). As songwriter and/or producer, Leonard worked with artists including **Alice Clark** ('Don't Wonder Why') and **Philip Bailey** ('God Is Love' and 'Safe In God's Love'), while Caston & Majors also sang backing vocals for artists including **Minnie Riperton** ('Can You Feel What I'm Saying').

CASTOR, JIMMY
(Singer/Songwriter/Sax)
Born in New York in 1943, Jimmy began his career in local doo-wop groups before turning professionally to the saxophone in 1960. From here he played numerous sessions, and scored a solo hit on the mid-60s Latin jazz scene with 'Hey Leroy, Your Mama's Callin'' for Smash Records (1966). The following year he produced the jazzy samba 'Hey Leroy, Your Mama's Callin' You' for Smash Records.

In 1972 he formed the Jimmy Castor Bunch and signed to RCA where the group's debut *It's Just Begun* featured the dance hit 'Troglodyte', (the 'Bunch' featuring Gerry Thomas who later joined **Fatback**). In 1974 the group were with Atlantic for *Butt Of Course* (including 'The Everything Man'). His subsequent American dance hits were 'Bertha Butt Boogie', 'E-Man Boogie' and 'King Kong'. In 1982 *E Man Boogie 82* was released by Salsoul, following which Jimmy launched his own label Long Distance Records and released a single 'Can't Help Falling In Love'. In 1984 Jimmy returned to Salsoul (via the Dream label subsidiary) for *Don't Waste The Time*, from which 'Amazon' did well in the States as a single.

CAYENNE
(Group)
Featuring Roy Davies (keyboards), Ron Carthy (trumpet), Jeff 'Bud' Beadle (flute/saxes), Paul Nieman (trombone), Chris Fletcher (timbales/percussion), Gary Griffiths (congas/percussion), Jeffrey Jai Seopardie (drums), Geoff Dunn (drums), John McKenzie (bass), Jesus Alfredo Merchan (bass) and Danny Schogger (clavinet), London group Cayenne was the brainchild of Roberto Campoverde (guitars). An album *Roberto Who ...?* (inspired by Roberto's unusual surname) was produced by **Chris Palmer** on his Groove Productions label in 1981. The title track/single featured vocals by **Linda Taylor**, while the album featured a version of Freddie Hubbard's 'Little Sunflower'.

CELI BEE & HER BUZZY BUNCH

(Vocal Group)

Celi Bee and her Buzzy Bunch recorded one album *Celi Bee & Her Buzzy Bunch* for the Miami-based TK label in 1977. It included 'One Love', popular on the UK disco scene of the late '70s.

CENTERFOLD

(Duo)

Minneapolis-based duo Keni Towns and Phil Jones recorded as Centerfold on a CBS album *Centerfold* (1988), written and produced by Keni and Phil with **Monte Moir** and Ricky Peterson.

CENTRAL LINE

(Group)

The nucleus of London-based group Central Line were Linton Breckles (vocals/percussion), **Camelle Hinds** (bass/vocals), Lipson Francis (keyboards) and Henry Defoe (guitars). One of the first British soul groups (or 'Brit funk' as it was termed back then), they scored mild success for the Mercury label with the **Roy Carter**-produced songs '(You Know) You Can Do It' (Top 75, 1981), 'Walking Into Sunshine' (Top 50, 1981), 'Don't Tell Me' (Top 75, 1982), 'You've Said Enough' (Top 75, 1982), 'Nature Boy' (Top 25, 1983) and 'Surprise Surprise' (Top 50, 1983).

CERRONE

(Songwriter/Producer/Instrumentalist)

From France, Cerrone moved to Los Angeles where he amassed no less than 32 gold and platinum records. His initial success came after signing to Atlantic for the UK Top 40 hit 'Love In C Minor' from the 1976 album of the same name. However, he is probably best remembered for 'Supernature', a Top 10 UK hit in 1978 (re-recorded and re-released by Streetwave Records in 1986). In 1979 he switched to CBS and returned to the UK Top 40 with 'Je Suis Music'. His next move was back to France in 1983 where he wrote bestselling novels including *Nevrose*, which later became a movie. In 1985 he returned to LA to work as a session musician, initially with **Colonel Abrams**.

CHAIN REACTION

(Group)

New York funk band caused a stir on UK dancefloors with 'Dance Freak' (1977), sold as an import on the Sound Of New York label.

CHAIRMAN OF THE BOARD

(Group)

Formed by **General Johnson** in the late '60s, Chairman of The Board were the aforementioned General with Danny Woods, Eddie Custis and Harrison Kennedy (later also Ken Knox and Jackie Myers). Through the General's association with **Lamont Dozier**, **Holland/Dozier/Holland** signed the group to their Invictus label and gave them a string of hits with 'Give Me Just A Little More Time' (UK Top 5, 1970), 'You've Got Me Dangling On A String' (UK Top 5, 1970), 'Everything's Tuesday' (UK Top 20, 1971), 'Pay To The Piper' (UK Top 40, 1971), 'Chairman Of The Board' (UK Top 50, 1971), 'Working On A Building Of Love' (UK Top 20, 1972), 'Elmo James' (UK Top 25, 1972), 'I'm On My Way To A Better Place' (UK Top 30, 1973) and 'Finders Keepers' (UK Top 25, 1973).

From here the group split up and pursued solo projects, General signing to Arista Records. In 1984 he reformed the group and 'Loverboy' was released to wide acclaim on the American 'beach music' scene. Three years later the track was released in the UK (through Syncopate/EMI), remixed by **Ian Levine** and featuring a keyboard solo by Mick Talbot of The Style Council. It reached the Top 75. In 1987 they recorded *The Music*, including remakes of 'Don't Walk Away' and 'Loverboy', on the Surfside label.

CHAMPAIGN

(Group)

From Champaign, Illinois, Champaign were originally **Michael Day**, **Pauli Carmen** (lead vocals), Rena Jones (formerly with Andre Crouch), Howard Reeder (guitar), Dana Walden (keyboards) and Michael Reed (bass). They were later joined by **Marshall Titus**. Signing to CBS, their debut single was 'How 'Bout Us', a 1981 UK Top 5 hit from their debut album of the same name (which also included 'Can You Find The Time') produced by **Leo Graham**. Their follow-ups were *Modern Heart* (1982) and the self-produced *Woman In Flames* (1984), including 'Off And On Love', before Pauli began recording as a solo artist. He returned to the group in 1991 to record *Champaign Four*, released by Malaco Records.

CHANDLER, GENE

(Singer)

Born Eugene Dixon in Chicago in 1937, Gene sang gospel and then doo-wop with groups The Gaytones and The Dukays before a spell with the American air force. Upon his return in 1960 he rejoined The Dukays and recorded 'Night Owl' with the group.

Under the direction of **Carl Davis**, Gene signed to Vee-Jay Records and took the surname Chandler as Jeff Chandler was Carl's favorite actor at the time. In 1962 he recorded his solo debut 'Duke Of Earl' which sold millions across America. From here he worked with **Curtis Mayfield** on a song 'Rainbow' (which he has now recorded three times!) before switching to the Constellation label for 'Just Be True' (1964) and 'Nothing Can Stop Me' (1965).

He then switched to Mercury and recorded duets with **Barbara Acklin** ('Show Me The Way To Go' and 'From Teacher To Preacher') and an album with **Jerry Butler** before changing labels again to MCA in 1969 for 'Bet You Never Thought It' and an album *Here's To Love*.

Also in 1969 he signed **Mel And Tim** to his own Bamboo label and sold a million copies of 'Blackfield In Motion'.

In 1972 he teamed up with **Curtis Mayfield** again and signed to the Curtom label, but after little success switched to Chi-Sound in 1978 to work once again with **Carl Davis**. Here his fortune changed with the Carl Davis-produced/Rick Gianatos-mixed 'Get Down' (UK Top 20, 1978), from an album of the same name. His follow-up hit was 'When You're Number One' (UK Top 50, 1979). His final Chi-Sound album was *Gene Chandler '80*, including 'Does She Have A Friend' (UK Top 30, 1980).

In 1984 he returned with a single 'I'll Make The Living If You Make The Loving Worthwhile' and in 1985 an album *Your Love Looks Good On Me* for the Fast Fire label.

CHANDLER, GEORGE
(Singer)
George made an impression on the 'Brit funk' scene in the early '80s. At Polydor he sang with both **The Olympic Runners** and as a solo artist on singles including 'This Could Be The Night' (1982). He also sang backing vocals with **Central Line**.

CHANDLER, LORRAINE
(Singer)
From Detroit, Lorraine worked with the song-writing/production team of Ashford/Terry/Lewis, known as Pied Piper Productions. Her recordings include 'She Don't Want You' (for RCA Victor) and in 1966 'What Can I Do' (on Giant).

CHANDLER, OMAR
(Singer)
Born in Harlem, New York, Omar began a professional singing career during his teens, but subsidized his earnings by driving a taxi. One evening in 1983 his passengers included Teddy Riley who was duly impressed by Omar's vocals and suggested they work together.

Later that year they performed as a duo at the Apollo Theater in Harlem and won first prize. Through further work at the Apollo he secured a recording deal with MCA Records in 1988. His debut album *Omar Chandler*, including 'Do You Really Want It' and 'This Must Be Heaven', a duet with **Audrey Wheeler**, was released in 1990, while in between times he sang lead on 'Joy & Pain' for hip hop act Rob Base and D.J.E.Z. Rock on Profile Records. He is now married to Teddy Riley's sister!

CHANELLE
(Singer)
New Jersey singer Chanelle signed to New York's Profile label in 1989 where she scored a dance hit with 'One Man'.

CHANGE
(Group)
The brainchild of **Jacques Fred Petrus** (recently shot dead) and Mauro Malavasi, Change was originally a French studio concept put together with hand-picked New York session musicians in 1980. For the RFC label (via Atlantic) their debut album was *The Glow Of Love* (1980), featuring lead vocals by **Luther Vandross** on the double-header single 'A Lover's Holiday' 'Glow Of Love' (UK Top 20) and 'Searching' (UK Top 20). The success of this album prompted a live tour, for which an official group was put together. For lead vocals, Luther was replaced by **James Robinson** who remained with the group for *Miracles* (1981) and *Sharing Your Love* (1982), including 'The Very Best In You'. Debra Cooper and **Rick Brenna** took over as lead vocalists while the lineup settled as **Timmy Allen** (bass/songwriter), **Vince Henry** (sax) and Michael Campbell (guitar).

In 1984 they hired the services of writers/producers **Jam/Lewis** for *Change Of Heart* including the title track single (UK Top 20) and 'You Are My Melody' (UK Top 50). Group founder **Jacques Fred Petrus**-produced (with Timmy Allen) the follow-up *Turn On Your Radio* (1985, via Cooltempo in the UK), including 'Let's Go Together' (UK Top 40), 'Oh What A Feeling' (UK Top 75) and 'Mutual Attraction' (UK Top 75).

CHANSON
(Group)
Under the guidance of David Williams and J.Jamerson Jr, French group Chanson shocked with their pink vinyl release 'Don't Hold Back', somewhat of a disco anthem during its year of release (1978). In the UK it was a Top 40 hit for Ariola Records.

CHAPTER 8
(Group)
From Detroit, the nucleus of Chapter 8 is **Michael Powell** and **David Washington**, who formed the group in 1972. Originally they worked as a backing band for **The Detroit Emeralds** before adding vocalist Rick Means and later **Carolyn Crawford**. Carolyn left to be replaced by Barbara Love, and later **Anita Baker**, whom David had discovered singing backgrounds with another local Detroit band Osmoses. Rick was replaced by Gerald Lyles. When the group signed to Ariola in 1979 the line-up was Derek Dickson, Michael Powell, Allen E.Nance, Courtlen Hale, Scott Guthrie, David Washington, Van Cephus and lead vocals by Anita Baker and Gerald Lyles. Their debut album *Chapter 8*, including 'Ready For Your Love' and 'I Just Wanna Be Your Girl', was released in 1979, but the group were dropped by Ariola shortly afterwards as the company told them Anita couldn't sing!

In 1985 the group became Valerie Pinkston (co-lead vocals), Gerald Lyles (co-lead vocals), Vernon Fails (keyboards), Courtlen Hale (sax), **David Washington** (bass) and **Michael Powell** (guitars/producer). The group recorded their second album, *This Love's For Real*, including 'Don't Stop Loving Me', 'How Is It Possible', 'How Can I Get Next To You' and 'It's My Turn' for the Beverly Glen label, firmly establishing the group with UK soul fans. The line-up remained the same for *Forever* (1988), including 'Give Me A Chance' and 'So In Love', this time for Capitol Records. Produced by **Michael Powell**, who by now had established himself as a hit-making producer for **Anita Baker** and **Regina Belle**, the lavish production was well received by soul fans but Capitol dropped the group.

More recently Michael Powell and musicians from the group have recorded with **Anita Baker**, **Peabo Bryson** (*Positive*), **David Peaston** and **James Ingram** ('You Make Me Feel Like A Natural Man').

CHARLES, LEE
(Singer)
Lee was one of the many soul vocalists **Holland/Dozier/Holland** worked with on their Invictus label in the early '70s. His recordings include 'Get Your House In Order' (1974).

CHARLES, RAY
(Singer/Songwriter/Producer)
Born Ray Charles Robinson in Albany, Georgia, in 1933, Ray was left totally blind after an attack of glaucoma in 1939. At this point he was living in Greenville, Florida, where he attended a blind school and studied music. After the death of both his parents in 1948 he became a full-time musician and moved to Seattle. In 1949 he went to Los Angeles and began a series of recordings for the Swingtime label (including 'St Pete Florida Blues') before signing to Atlantic in 1952. His early recordings included 'Mess Around', 'It Should Have Been Me' and 'Don't You Know' before he found his soul/gospel sound in 1954 with 'I Got A Woman', 'Should've Been Me' and 'Tell All The World About It'.

In 1959 Ray recorded what was to become a pop standard, 'What I'd Say', before his first UK success in 1960 with 'Georgia On My Mind' (Top 50). Here his recordings were released by HMV, and single hits flowed with 'Hit The Road Jack' (Top 10, 1961), 'I Can't Stop Loving You' (No. 1, 1962), 'You Don't Know Me' (Top 10, 1962), 'Your Cheating Heart' (Top 20, 1962), 'Don't Set Me Free' (Top 40, 1963), 'Take These Chains From My Heart' (Top 10, 1963), 'No one' (Top 40, 1963), 'Busted' (Top 25, 1963), 'No One To Cry To' (Top 40, 1964), 'Makin' Whoopee' (Top 50, 1965), 'Cryin' Time' (Top 50, 1966), 'Together Again' (Top 50, 1966), and 'Here We Go Again' (Top 50, 1967).

Back in America Ray had left Atlantic (in 1960) and signed to ABC where critically his music was less acclaimed by the soul fraternity, especially his cover versions of Beatles songs 'Yesterday' and 'Eleanor Rigby', released in the UK on the Stateside label in 1967–8. Also during this period he had ventured into country and western music, especially with the aforementioned 'I Can't Stop Loving You'. In 1968 he formed his own label Tangerine Records (via ABC) where artists included **Tyrone Davis** before the label changed its name to Crossover (now via Atlantic) in 1973. Through the '70s and '80s Ray continued to tour extensively with his band and backing singers The Raelettes.

More recently (1989) Ray was one of the featured vocalists on 'I'll Be Good To You' (with **Chaka Khan**) on the **Quincy Jones** single taken from Quincy's *Back On The Block* album. He also signed to Warner Brothers for a new album due for release in 1991.

CHARLES, SONNY
(Singer/Songwriter)
American singer Sonny Charles recorded one album *The Sun Still Shines* for the Highrise label in 1982. It included 'Put It In A Magazine', popular on the UK soul scene.

CHARLES, SWEET
(Singer)
Sweet Charles recorded one album *For Sweet People, From Sweet Charles* produced by **James Brown** and released by Polydor in 1974. The album included 'Yes It's You', re-released in the UK (1987) after becoming popular on the mid-'80s 'rare groove' scene.

CHARME
(Studio Group)
Formed in New York, Charme were session musicians and singers who recorded one album *Let It In* for RCA Records in 1979. It included a version of the song 'Georgy Porgy' featuring the lead vocals of **Luther Vandross** (UK Top 75, 1982) and 'Never (Gonna Let You Go)' featuring the lead vocals of **Gwen Guthrie**.

CHARO
(Singer)
Charo was already a famous TV personality in Spain before she met producer **Vince Montana** in the mid-'70s. Vince took her to New York to record with **The Salsoul Orchestra**, and produced an album *Charo And The Salsoul Orchestra* (1977). In the spirit of mid-'70s Philly/disco, the album included 'Dance A Little Bit Closer' which reached the UK Top 50 in 1978.

CHEATHAM, OLIVER
(Singer)
Born in Detroit, in 1948, Oliver was first encouraged to sing by his gospel-trained mother. His first experiences were with groups **The Young Sirs** (later known as **Butch And The New Ports**), Mad Dog And The Pups (for whom he also worked as choreographer) and Gaslight. His first solo release was 'Hard Times' recorded for the local Tier label, following which he met **Al Perkins** and became lead singer with Sins Of Satan, a group who later recorded for MCA as **Round Trip**, and then **Oliver**. After two Oliver albums for MCA he signed to the label as a

solo artist, releasing his debut *Saturday Night* in 1983. It included 'Get Down Saturday Night' (UK Top 40) and 'Bless The Ladies' (German Top 10).

After MCA, Oliver moved briefly to Move Records ('Mama Said', 1985) and then Champion for *Go For It* (1987) including 'S.O.S.' He also sang backing vocals with **One Way**, Leo Sayer and **Melissa Manchester**.

CHERRELLE
(Singer)
Born Cheryl Norton in Los Angeles, Cherrelle (pronounced 'sheh-rell') moved with her family to Detroit during her teens. Her next-door neighbour was **Michael Henderson** who invited her to join him in the studio while he recorded *In The Night Time* (1978). Cherrelle spent four years touring with Michael.

Moving back to Los Angeles she signed with Tabu Records and worked with **Jam/Lewis** on three albums commencing with *Fragile* in 1984. It included 'I Didn't Mean To Turn You On', later a hit for Robert Palmer, and 'When I Look In Your Eyes', popular among UK soul fans. 1985's *High Priority* album included 'Saturday Love', a duet with **Alexander O'Neal** (UK Top 10) and 'Will You Satisfy' (UK Top 60, 1986). Also in 1985 Cherrelle guested with Alexander O'Neal on 'Innocent' from his debut album *Alexander O'Neal*. A third album *Affair* was released in 1988 and included 'Everything I Miss At Home' which initially created interest. Later the title track was remixed to good reactions, but it was a 1990 remix of 'Saturday Love' which briefly put Cherrelle back in the charts.

CHESS, PHIL AND MARSHALL
(Industry)
Phil and brother Marshall Chess were the founders of Chess Records in Chicago. The Chess recording studios were recently made an official landmark in the city.

CHEYANNE
(Singer)
Born in New York, Cheyanne (pronounced Shy-Ann) graduated from high school with a degree in folk music and vocal theory. She had been singing gospel in church since the age of five. After performing with a number of groups in the New York area she launched a solo career. Upon meeting producer Kyle West she signed to Capitol (via Syncopate in the UK) where her debut single was the self-penned 'I've Waited Too Long' (1988).

CHI-LITES
(Vocal Group)
From Chicago, **Eugene Record**, Marshall Thompson, Robert 'Squirrel' Lester and Creadel 'Red' Jones first sang together as The Hi Lights before discovering another group with the same name. In 1961 they added an extra 'C' and signed to the Daran label, owned by Marshall's uncle. After making little impression on a number of other local labels, they were signed by Brunswick (via MCA in the UK) in 1969 where they began working with producer **Carl Davis**. From here they made an immediate impression across America with 'Give It Away' before the release of their first million-seller 'Give More Power To The People' (UK Top 40, 1971). They followed this success with 'Have You Seen Her' (UK Top 5, 1972), 'Oh Girl' (UK Top 20, 1972), 'Homely Girl' (UK Top 5, 1974), 'I Found Sunshine' (UK Top 40, 1974), 'Too Good To Be Forgotten' (UK Top 10, 1974), 'It's Time For Love' (UK Top 5, 1975) and 'You Don't Have To Go' (UK Top 5, 1976).

At this point **Eugene Record** left the group to sign as a solo artist with Warner Brothers and was temporarily replaced by Vandy 'Smokey' Hampton. Eugene returned in the late '70s when the group signed to **Carl Davis**'s new label Chi-Sound. Here their albums were *Heavenly Body* (1980) and *Me And You* (1981), including 'Try My Side Of Love'. In 1983 Creadel left the group, reducing them to a trio for *Bottoms Up*, including 'Changing For You' (UK Top 75), for the Larc label (via PRT in the UK).

Larc Records in Los Angeles shortly became Private I Records (via CBS) on which the group recorded one album *Steppin' Out* (1984), including 'Stop What You're Doing', before the group switched to Nuance in 1986 for 'Hard Act To Follow' (via Certain in the UK). Eugene left again and was replaced by **Anthony Watson** and the group signed to Ichiban for *Just Say You Love Me* (1990), including 'There's A Change'.

CHIC
(Group)
Formed in New York in 1977 by **Bernard Edwards** (bass) and **Nile Rodgers** (guitar) (see also **Rodgers/Edwards**), a debut single 'Dance Dance Dance Dance' was signed to Atlantic before an official group lineup was put together. The record became a UK Top 10 hit and the Rodgers/Edwards sound proved a successful formula on the disco scene, so the group was extended to include drummer Tony Thompson and lead singers Alfa Anderson and Luci Martin.

Further hits came with 'Everybody Dance' (Top 10, 1978), 'Le Freak' (UK Top 10, 1978), 'I Want Your Love' (UK Top 5, 1979), 'Good Times' (UK Top 5, 1979), 'My Forbidden Lover' (UK Top 20, 1979) and 'My Feet Keep Dancing' (UK Top 30, 1979), their albums including *Chic* (1978), *Risqué* (1979), *Les Plus Grandes Success*, *Real People* (1980), *Take It Off* (1982) and *Believer* (1983), including 'You Are Beautiful'.

CHILL FAC-TOR
(Group)
Based in Philadelphia, Chill Fac-tor were Lark Lowery (vocals/percussion), Lennie Sampson (vocals/keyboards), Nate Clory (bass), Tyrone Lewison (vocals/keyboards), **Tony Fountain** (vocals/guitar) and Gus Wallace (vocals/drums). Recording for the Philly World

label, their album *Chill Fac-tor* included a dance version of Hank Ballard's 'Twist' (1983).

CHIMES
(Group)
The Chimes came together in the late '80s when musicians Mike Peden and James Locke from Edinburgh met vocalist Pauline Henry from North London. Signing to CBS they immediately made an impression on the UK dance scene with **Jazzie B**-produced songs including 'Heaven' and '1-2-3', taken from their debut album *The Chimes* (1989/90), also including 'True Love', 'Love Comes To Mind', 'I Still Haven't Found What I'm Looking For' and 'Love So Tender'.

CHOCOLATE MILK
(Group)
From Memphis, Tennessee, Chocolate Milk were Dwight J.Richards (drums/vocal), Joseph Foxx III (trumpet/vocals), Frank J.Richard (lead vocals), Amadee Castanell (sax/vocals), Robert Dabon (keyboards) and Mario G.Tio (guitar). With producer **Allen Toussaint** the group recorded for RCA Records from the mid-'70s to the early '80s, and are best remembered for the title track of their album *Action Speaks Louder Than Words* (1975). Their later RCA albums include *Blue Jeans* (1981).

CHRISTOPHER, GAVIN
(Singer/Songwriter)
Based in Chicago, Gavin worked with **Rufus** and **Chaka Khan** during the mid-'70s, also writing 'Life Is A Dance' for Chaka who wrote the sleeve notes to his debut album *Gavin Christopher* for Island Records in 1976. A second album, also called *Gavin Christopher*, was released by the RSO label (via Polydor) in 1979 where its most popular song 'We're In Love' was produced by Philadelphia man **Bobby Eli**. Gavin also wrote and/or produced for **Charles Jackson** ('Gonna Getcha Love') and **Cuba Gooding** ('Got The Hots'), and has been the featured vocalist on recordings for **Herbie Hancock** (*Magic Windows* and *Monster*, including 'Stars In Your Eyes'), **Jeff Lorber** ('Best Part Of The Night') and **Tyzik** ('Love Won't Wait').

CIRCLE CITY BAND
(Group)
This New York funk group stirred UK dancefloors in 1983 with 'Magic', a single on the Circle City label. The follow-up was 'My Place', released by Becket Records in 1984.

CISSEL, CHUCK
(Singer/Songwriter)
From Tulsa, Oklahoma, Chuck was the first black member of the Tulsa Little Theatre, and danced in the company's production of *South Pacific*. He was seen by an Oklahoma oil baron who offered to finance Chuck's entire college education! After studying dance and drama at the University of Oklahoma, he won a Best Actor award in 1970 for his role in *Your Own Thing*. He landed big parts on and off Broadway in the casts of *A Chorus Line*, *Purlie* and *Hello Dolly*, as well as working in the lucrative advertisement market. While shooting a TV commercial for Coke in Atlanta, Chuck met Larkin Arnold, who signed him to Arista after hearing a demo of three of his songs. His first album *Cisselin' Hot* (1979), included the American hit 'Just For You' and 'Do You Believe' which was popular with UK soul fans. A second Arista album, *If I Had The Chance* (including 'Love Is Missing From Our Lives') was released in 1982.

CITY LIMITS
(Group)
From Philadelphia, City Limits featured Bruce Hawes and **Terri Wells**, whose impression on the soul scene was later to come individually. After playing together since high school, **Gamble/Huff** signed City Limits to the TSOP subsidiary of Philadelphia International in 1975 and released *Circles*. It included the single 'Love Is Everywhere' which performed well in the American disco charts. The following year the group split up, Terri turning to session singing and Bruce becoming an integral part of the Philly musician scene, also co-writing such songs as 'Where There Is Love' (**The Whispers**), 'Tonight You And Me' (**Phyllis Hyman**), 'Let No Man Put Asunder' (**First Choice**) and numerous tracks for **Melba Moore** (including 'Closer' and 'Something On Your Mind' which he also co-produced). Bruce also co-produced with **Eugene Record** 'Mellow Mellow Right On' for **Lowrell** (1979).

CLARK, ALICE
(Singer)
American East Coast singer Alice Clark scored success on the UK 'Northern soul' scene in 1967 with 'You Hit Me Where It Hurts', written by **Sylvia Moy/Mike Valvano** and released by Warner Brothers. During the early '70s she recorded for the Mainstream label where *Alice Clark* (1972) included 'Never Did I Stop Loving You', popular on the UK soul scene.

CLARK, CHRIS
(Singer/Songwriter)
Chris began her career singing r&b around the clubs of San Francisco, before signing to Motown as one of the label's first white artists in the '60s. Five singles were released, 'Do Right Baby', 'Love's Gone Bad', 'I Want To Go Back There Again' (for which she is best remembered), 'From Head To Toe' and 'Whisper You Love Me Baby'. There were also two albums, *Soul Sounds* and *C.C. Rides Again* (1969).

CLARK, DEE
(Singer/Songwriter)
Born Delecta Clark in Blythville, Arkansas, in 1938, Dee grew up in an environment of gospel music in Chicago. Here he joined the Hambone Kids who recorded for the Okeh label in 1952 before Dee changed his musical direction towards r&b and joined The Goldentones. They became the Kool Gents, who recorded for Vee-Jay prior to Dee signing to the label as a solo artist. He later worked closely with guitarist **Phil Upchurch** for whom he co-wrote 'You Can't Sit Down'. As a solo artist, Dee later recorded for the Constellation, CBS, Wand and EMI labels.

CLARKE, RICK
(Singer)
London singer Rick Clarke initially recorded as a solo artist for RCA where his singles included 'Looking Out For You' and 'Perfect Lady' (1987). Rick and Emma Haywoode also released a duet single 'I Really Want To Be With You' for RCA. In 1988 he switched to the Wa label where 'I'll See You Along The Way' reached the UK Top 75.

CLARKE, SHARON DEE
(Singer)
From North London, Sharon was introduced to the music business by her manager Damon Rochefort (who she had met through a mutual friend **Juliet Roberts**. Damon hooked her up with producer **Ian Levine** who took her into the studio for 'Dance Your Way Out Of The Door', released by Arista in 1986. Since then she has recorded for a number of labels including Debut ('He's Coming Back'), Nightmare ('Past Present And Future', and 'Awesome'/'I Can't Stay Mad At You', 1987), Urban ('Something Special', 1989) and Rumour ('Keeping My Faith In Love', 1989). She also sang as featured lead vocalist with FPI Project ('Going Back To My Roots', 1989) before joining **Nomad** who in 1991 scored with the hit singles 'I Wanna Give You Devotion' (UK Top 5) and 'Just A Groove' (UK Top 20). Sharon has also maintained a full-time career as an actress on stage and screen. On stage she has played a jazz singer in *A Taste Of Honey* and a singing plant in *Little Shop Of Horrors*. On TV she has been in *Eastenders* and *The Singing Detective*.

CLARKE, STANLEY
(Bass/Songwriter/Producer)
Born in Philadelphia in 1951, Stanley's mother was a top opera and church singer who encouraged him to study the violin. He later switched to double bass. He felt a violin looked ridiculous on him due to his height! With an appetite for improvisational jazz he went to study at the Philadelphia Music Academy before relocating to New York in 1970. Here he found work as a session player with artists including Stan Getz, Art Blakey, Dexter Gordon, **Gato Barbieri, Deodato, Aretha Franklin** and **Quincy Jones**.

In 1971 Stanley joined forces with Chick Corea and Joe Henderson to form Return To Forever. He and Chick remained the nucleus of the band until mid-1976 when Stanley undertook his first tour as headlining artist. From 1973 Stanley was being voted top electric bass player in every major music poll. He joined Polydor Records for *Children Of Forever* (1973) featuring Chick Corea, **Dee Dee Bridgewater** (vocals on 'Unexpected Days') and **Lenny White**. The same year he also wrote and arranged 'Dr Jive' for **Flora Purim** on *Butterfly Dreams*, also teaming up with **George Duke**.

The next year he switched to Nemperor Records (via Atlantic) for *Stanley Clarke*, followed in 1975 by *Journey To Love*, which included 'Silly Putty'. In 1978 he moved into outside productions, an early project being Dee Dee Bridgewater's *Just Family* (for which he also co-wrote the title track). The same year he signed with Epic Records with whom he remains today, combining his funky bass playing with guest vocalists and musicians. These albums include *Schooldays* (1977); *Modern Man* (1978); *I Wanna Play For You* (1979), including 'Together Again'; *Rocks, Pebbles And Sand* (1980), including 'We Supply'; *Let Me Know You* (1982), including 'Straight To The Top', 'Time Exposure', (1984), including **Howard Hewett**'s lead vocal on 'Heaven Sent'; *Find Out* (1985), featuring **Robert Brookins**; and *Hideaway* (1986), featuring **George Howard**, **Angela Bofill** and **Herbie Hancock**.

Stanley met Howard Hewett after they shared a recording studio in Los Angeles. They first worked together when Howard sang with **Shalamar**. Stanley worked on the group's album *The Look*, and later co-wrote/produced 'I'm For Real' for Howard's first solo album. As producer he has also worked with Kent Jordan, **Roy Ayers** ('In The Dark'), Rodney Salsbury, **Rodney Franklin** (*Learning To Love* and *Marathon*) and **Ramsey Lewis/Nancy Wilson** (*The Two of Us*), and has also recorded and toured with **George Duke** as The Clarke/Duke Project (three albums to date, the last being *3* in 1990). It was while on tour with The Clarke/Duke Project that **Jeffrey Osborne** first graced the UK stage as a solo artist.

Stanley has also recorded with **McCoy Tyner**, Jeff Lorber, **Aretha Franklin, Donna Summer** ('Dinner With Gershwin'), and was musical director of **Fuse One**.

CLASS ACTION
(Studio Group)
Instigated by Sleeping Bag records in New York, Class Action was centred around the vocals of Chris Wiltshire who sang their one release 'Weekend', a UK Top 50 hit (via Jive Records) in 1983. Chris's vocal was later utilized by **Todd Terry** on his remake in 1988. Chris sang sessions with **Major Harris** and **Luther Vandross** before becoming lead singer with **Musique**.

CLAUSELL

(Singer)

New York vocalist recorded an anti-drug dance record 'Don't Let It Be Crack', mixed by **Paul Simpson** for the Easy Street label in 1986.

CLAY, OTIS

(Singer)

Born in Waxhaw, Mississippi, Otis began his career as a gospel singer and after moving to Chicago in 1957 made his debut vinyl appearance as lead singer of The Gospel Songbirds. In 1965 he signed with the local One-der-ful label (after one single for CBS which was not issued). Working with writers/producers Jimmy Jones and Eddie Silvers, his early recordings included 'A Flame In Your Heart', 'I'm Satisfied', 'That's How It Is' and 'Got To Find A Way'. In 1968 he switched to Cotillion Records (via Atlantic) for singles including 'She's About A Mover' before producer **Willie Mitchell** signed him to Hi Records. Here he scored American r&b success with 'Precious Precious', 'If I Could Reach Out' and 'Trying To Live My Life Without You' during the early '70s (albums including *I Can't Take It*).

From here he launched his own Echo label where he recorded 'Victim Of Circumstance' in 1975 before changing labels again to Glades (via TK) for 'All I Need Is You' in 1976, and then Kayvette in 1977 for releases including 'All Because Of Your Love', 'Today My Whole World Fell', 'Let Me In' and 'Sweet Woman's Love'.

In 1980 he worked with Memphis songwriter George Jackson, and recorded a number of songs including 'Cheatin' In The Next Room', 'Messin' With My Mind' and 'The Only Way Is Up', later a UK No.1 hit for **Yazz**. The latter was issued on *Check It Out* on the Blues r&b label in 1985. More recently Otis has returned to work with **Willie Mitchell** on *Watch Me Now* for Waylo Records (1989).

CLAYTON, MERRY

(Singer)

Born in Gert Town, New Orleans, Merry 'Baby Sister' Clayton is the daughter of a Baptist reverend and naturally grew up in a strict gospel environment. Her professional career, however, has been divided equally between rock & roll and r&b. She has recorded with artists from Elvis Presley and The Rolling Stones to **The Supremes** and **Ray Charles** (becoming one of the Raelettes). In 1962 she recorded 'You're The Reason I'm Living', a duet with Bobby Darin which gave her a taste of American chart success. She moved to Los Angeles where she founded **Sisters Love** and scored success with the group at A&M Records. When they switched to Motown, Merry stayed at A&M, signing as a solo artist to the Ode label subsidiary.

At Ode, her albums included *Gimme Shelter* (1975) and *Merry Clayton* (1976), while as a featured vocalist she recorded with artists including **Gene Page** (*Lovelock*), **Harvey Mason** (*Earth Mover*), **Michael Wycoff** (*Come To My World*), **Leslie Smith** ('Before The Night Is Over'), **Roy Ayers** ('Can't You See Me'), **Webster Lewis** ('Give Me Some Emotion'), and sang backgrounds with **Gene Harris**, **The Blackbyrds** and **Bobby Womack**.

She also signed to MCA where **The Crusaders** wrote and produced 'When The World Turns Blue', popular on the UK soul scene.

CLAYTON, WILLIE

(Singer)

Born in Indianola, Mississippi, in 1956, Willie was one of eleven brothers and sisters. Raised on black music, he eventually fronted a college band which went on to play at local club venues during the late '60s. From here he made his debut recording as a solo artist, 'That's The Way Daddy Did' for the local Duplex label.

In the early '70s he moved to Chicago with his band and established a local reputation. He auditioned to appear with **Al Green**, an opportunity which introduced him to Al's producer **Willie Mitchell**. Willie signed him to the Pawn label, a division of Hi, and produced a series of singles including 'Baby You Are Ready', 'Say Yes To Love' and 'Abracadabra', following which he toured with **Al Green**, **Barry White** and **James Brown**.

In 1980 Willie launched his own label, Sky Hero Records, and released 'Living With You, But My Heart Is Somewhere Else'. In 1983 he formed another label Kirstee Records and released 'Where Has Love Gone'. In 1984 **General Crook** produced his next singles 'Tell Me' and 'What A Way To Put It' for the Compleat label. Another single 'Happy' was released on the Big City label.

Back on Kirstee, Willie's singles continued with songs including 'Running In And Out Of My Life' (1985), 'Show And Tell' (1986), 'Weak For You' (1986) and the most popular of all, 'Your Sweetness' (1987), the latter released in the UK by Timeless Records. The label also issued *Forever*, including a selection of brand new songs, of which 'Rocking Chair' was later released in America on the Warlock label. He then switched to Polydor to record one album as *Will Clayton* before returning to Kirstee.

CLIFFORD, LINDA

(Singer)

Born in Brooklyn, New York, Linda is a former Miss New York State. She is also an actress, having appeared in *Rosemary's Baby*, *Sweet Charity* and *The Boston Strangler*. Her first recording deal was with Paramount which released a debut single 'March Across The Land' in 1973. A few years later she moved to Chicago and landed her first major recording contract in 1977 with Curtom Records, a label owned and run by **Curtis Mayfield**. Her first album was *Linda Clifford* (1977). In 1978 came the follow-up *If My Friends Could See Me Now*, from which the title track was a UK Top 50 single. It was the B-side 'Runaway Love', however (also on the album), which became regarded as a soul/dance classic and is constantly revived to this day. In 1979 she recorded a disco version of Simon & Garfunkel's 'Bridge Over Troubled Water', released on the RSO label and a Top 30 UK hit. She also recorded a duet album with Curtis Mayfield, *The Right Combination*, but when Curtis moved his recording operation to Atlanta, Linda stayed in Chicago to raise a family. Her next recording was 1982's *I'll Keep On Loving You*, released by Capitol.

In 1984 Linda recorded *Sneakin' Out* for the Chicago-based Red Label, gaining some interest for 'We've Got Our Chance', though it was not released as a single. Her second album for Red Label was *My Heart's On Fire* (1985). Linda is still recording and in 1991 hopes to find a label to release brand new tracks produced by Rick Gianatos.

CLINTON, GEORGE

(Singer/Songwriter/Producer)

Born in New York, George sang doo-wop on street corners from the early '50s, and formed his first group **Parliament** in 1955. Turning professional by the '60s, he produced 'Day Tripper' for **J.J.Barnes** (1966), and first recorded with Parliament on the 1967 single release 'Poor Willie' for ABC Records. Later that year he scored an American r&b hit with '(I Wanna) Testify' (which he later produced for **The Dells** in 1978). George shortly became one of the pioneers of 'funk' music, later naming his own 'P'funk' style to distinguish it from classic funk! By the mid '70s he had firmly established his P'funk sound, creating a number of groups: **Funkadelic**, **Bootsy's Rubber Band**, **The Brides Of Funkenstein** and maintaining Parliament in this style. A number of these groups employed the same musicians, some benefiting from being signed to different labels at the same time.

Towards the end of the '70s George decided to form his own label and signed a multi-million-pound deal with CBS to distribute it. The deal led to legal problems with Warner Brothers with whom he was having his greatest success. This situation put a stop to his recordings until 1982 when he signed to Capitol as a solo artist. Here he released a debut album *Computer Games* (1982) including 'Loopzilla' (UK Top 75) and 'Atomic Dog'. Follow-up albums included *You Shouldn't Nuf Bit, Fish!* (1983), *Some Of My Best Jokes Are Friends* (1985), *R&B Skeletons (In The Closet)* (1986), including 'Do Fries Go With That Shake' (UK Top 75). In 1989 he signed with **Prince**'s Paisley Park label and released *The Cinderella Theory* (1990).

CLIVILLES/COLE

(Songwriters/Producers)

Robert Clivilles and David Cole have worked as writers and producers on the New York dance music scene since the late '80s. They established themselves with artists including Seduction, Richard Valentine ('Come Back Lover'), **Evelyn 'Champagne' King** and Trilogy ('I ove Me Or Love Me Not'). In 1990 they formed C & C Music Factory and scored UK chart success with the title track of their debut album *Gonna Make You Sweat* (featuring **Martha Wash**), which also included 'Here We Go' and 'Let's Rock & Roll'.

CLUB NOUVEAU

(Group)

Formed in Sacramento, California, in 1987, Club Nouveau consisted of Jay King, Denzil Foster, Thomas McElroy, Samuelle Pratter and Valerie Watson. Jay had earlier been the brains behind the pop hit 'Rumours' (UK Top 20, 1986) by the Timex Social Club, and upon switching his interests to Club Nouveau formed King Jay Records to which the group signed (via Tommy Boy). Their one UK hit was a version of the **Bill Withers** song 'Lean On Me' (Top 5, 1987), while other singles include 'Jealousy' (1987).

Subsequently, Thomas McElroy and Denzil Foster set themselves up as writers/producers, and have to date scored success with **En Vogue** and former Club Nouveau vocalist Samuelle ('So You Like What You See').

COBHAM, BILLY

(Drummer/Producer)

Born in Panama in 1944, Billy moved to New York where he played on various sessions before joining the **Miles Davis** band in 1968. After recording three albums with Miles he played with a group Dreams before joining The Mahavishnu Orchestra where he became resident drummer until 1972 when he was replaced by **Narada Michael Walden**.

He then recorded sessions with artists including **James Brown, Herbie Mann, Charles Earland** and **Roy Ayers** (*He's Coming*, including 'He's A Superstar' and 'Fire Weaver'), before signing with Atlantic in 1974 and recording *Crosswinds*, *Total Eclipse* and *Shabazz* with **The Brecker Brothers**. His next recording liaison was with **George Duke**: The Cobham Duke Band recorded *Funky Thide* and *Life And Times*.

Billy switched to CBS Records where his solo albums included *Magic* (1977), *Simplicity Of Expression, Depth Of Thought* (1978), including 'Bolinas', and the **Wayne Henderson**-produced *Billy Cobham* (1979) including 'What Is Your Fantasy'. During this time he produced two albums for Pete and Sheila Escovedo (see **Sheila E**), *Solo Two* (1977) and *Happy Together* (1978).

He later recorded for labels including Elektra Musician (*Billy Cobham's Glass Menagerie*), Phonogram ('Same Ole Love') and GRP (*Warning*, 1985).

COFFEE

(Vocal Group)

New York-based vocal trio Coffee were Lenora Dee Bryant, Glenda Hester and Elaine Sims. Signing to the De-lite label (via Phonogram), they recorded a **Leo Graham**-produced album *Slippin' And Dippin'* (1980) which included the most popular version of 'Casanova', earlier recorded by **Ruby Andrews** and **Loleatta Holloway**. Their follow up single 'Slip And Dip'/'I Wanna Be With You' made the UK Top 75 (1980). They returned with *Second Cup* in 1982.

COFFEY, DENNIS
(Guitar/Producer)
During the early '70s Dennis recorded fusion jazz albums for the Sussex label (including *Evolution*) before working as a session guitarist with a number of Detroit artists including **Marvin Gaye** (*I Want You*), **R.J.'s Latest Arrival** and **David Ruffin**. Through the late '70s/early '80s disco era he continued his sessions at Westbound Records (via Atlantic), also recording *Instant Coffee*, *A Sweet Taste Of Sin* and *Back Home*, including 'Free Spirit' and 'Wings Of Fire', the latter particularly popular on the UK jazz funk scene in 1977. He also coproduced *Devils Gun* for **C.J. & Co** that year.

In 1982 he worked with **Mike Theodore** and **Kashif** producing an album for **High Fashion**, then in 1990 returned with *Under The Moonlight* for the Orpheus label (via Capitol).

COGNAC
(Studio Group)
Cognac were one of the many studio groups put together by Salsoul Records in New York during the disco era. They are best remembered for their single 'How High' (1978).

COLD FIRE
(Group)
Los Angeles-based group Cold Fire were Ray Towns Sr, Ray Towns Jr, William Reese, Warren Petty, Roland Jennings, Ronald Rillera, Jimmie Weaver, Michael Loatman and Douglas Stevens. Signing to Capitol they released *Too Cold* (1981), from which 'Daydreamin'' was popular on the UK soul scene.

COLE, NATALIE
(Singer)
Born in Los Angeles in 1950, Natalie is the daughter of the legendary Nat King Cole. She was 11 when she made her stage debut, later joining a university band as lead vocalist. By the '70s she was working as a club singer and in 1973 met writers/producers **Jackson/Yancy**. In 1974 they worked together on an album at **Curtis Mayfield**'s Curtom studios in Chicago. From these sessions Natalie landed a deal at Capitol Records. With Jackson/Yancy, Natalie's albums were *Inseparable* (1975), including 'This Will Be' (UK Top 40); *Natalie* (1976) – the year she married Marvin Yancy, including 'Mr Melody'; *Thankful* (1977) including 'Lovers' and 'Annie Mae'; *Unpredictable* (1977), including 'Be Mine Tonight'; *I Love You So* (1979), including 'Stand By', 'Happy Love' and 'Don't Look Back' (1980) before she switched to Epic for her final Jackson/Yancy-produced album *Movin' On* (1983).

After an album for the independent Modern label, and a duet 'Over You' with **Ray Parker** for his album *After Dark*, she rejoined the Capitol family (Manhattan Records via EMI) in 1987. Here her albums have been *Everlasting* (1987), including 'Jump Start' (UK Top 50, 1987/Top 40, 1988), 'Pink Cadillac' (UK Top 5, 1988) and 'I Live For Your Love' (UK Top 40, 1988); and *Good To Be Back* (1989) including 'Miss You Like Crazy' and 'Gonna Make You Mine'. In 1989 she also scored with 'Wild Women Do' from the movie soundtrack *Pretty Woman*. The 1988 remix of 'Pink Cadillac' featured the B side 'I Wanna Be That Woman', not featured on any album but popular with UK soul fans. In 1991 she switched to Elektra where she recorded *Unforgettable*, which featured her own versions of her father's hits.

COLEMAN, DESIREE
(Singer)
Based in Los Angeles, Desiree signed to Motown in 1988 where her debut album *Desiree Coleman* featured a line-up of producers including **Craig T.Cooper** and **Ollie Brown**.

COLEMAN, DURELL
(Singer/Songwriter)
Born in Roanoke, Virginia, in 1958, Durell moved to Los Angeles during the '70s. In 1982 he recorded 'Lovely Girl' as lead singer of All Directions, then 'I'm Serious' as lead singer of Third Party before auditioning for the TV show *Star Search*. Here he won fifteen weeks in a row and was signed by Island Records. A debut album *Durell Coleman* (1985) featured the popular soul single 'Do You Love Me'.

COLLAGE
(Group)
Los Angeles-based group Collage were Richard Aguon (drums/vocals), Dean Boysen (trumpet), Emilio Conesa (guitar/vocals), Kirk Crumpler (bass/keyboards), Albert DeGracia (keyboards), Ruben Laxamana (sax/vocals), Melecio Magdaluyo (sax), Lee Peters (lead vocals), Larry White (guitar/synths) and Ross Wilson (trombone/trumpet). The name of the group was derived from the different ethnic backgrounds of the members. In the early to mid-'80s they recorded for Solar where they worked with producer Nicholas Caldwell of **The Whispers** on *Get In Touch* (1983) and *Shine The Light* (1985) including 'Romeo Where's Juliet?' (UK Top 50).

COLLINS AND COLLINS
(Duo)
Tonee and Bill Collins recorded for A&M Records in 1980 where the **John Davis**-produced *Collins And Collins* included a version of the **Gamble/Huff** song 'You Know

How To Make Me Feel So Good', popular on the UK soul scene.

COLLINS, BOOTSY

(Singer/Guitar/Bass/Keyboards/Drums)

Born in Detroit, Bootsy formed his own group The Pacesetters during the '60s. It included **Philippe Wynne** as a full-time member, while one of the group's sidemen was **George Clinton** with whom Bootsy began collaborating on the 'P'funk' music scene.

Later, while recording with George for his groups **Funkadelic** and **Parliament**, he formed Bootsy's Rubber Band with Bernie Worrell and **Fred Wesley** and a host of 'P'funk' musicians. In 1976 they signed to Warner Brothers where his albums include *Stretching Out In Bootsy's Rubber Band* (1976), *Ahh ... The Name Is Bootsy* (1979) including 'The Pinocchio Theory', *Player Of The Year* (1978), *This Boot Is Made For Fonk-N* (1979) and *The One Giveth* (1980).

Another ten years later (1990), Bootsy's Rubber Band signed to 4th & Broadway (via Island) for 'Jungle Bass'. In the meantime Bootsy has recorded with **Trouble Funk** (*Trouble Over There*), **L.J.Reynolds** and a number of Detroit artists.

COLLINS, LYN

(Singer)

From the early to mid-'70s, Lyn worked closely with **James Brown**, projected by him as 'The Female Preacher' in his legendary revues. She also sang backgrounds for James who secured her a solo deal at the People label (via Polydor), and wrote/produced her 1972 release 'Think (About It)'. This song was much revived on the mid-'80s 'rare groove' scene in the UK where it was sampled and eventually re-released. Her **James Brown**-produced albums on Polydor include *Check Me Out* and *If You Don't Know Me By Now* (1975), including 'Rock Me Again & Again & Again'.

COLLINS, WILLIE

(Singer)

Born in New York, Willie worked as a postman before his singing talents were recognized by Capitol who signed him in 1986 for *Where You Gonna Be Tonight.*

COLON, WILLIE

(Trumpet/Trombone/Vocals)

Born in the Bronx, New York, in 1950, Willie was seventeen when he founded the Willie Colon Orchestra, soon to become one of the most popular Latin music bands in the city. In 1986 he signed with A&M Records and released 'Set Fire To Me' which was an American r&b hit and a floor-filler in the UK that year. He has amassed four Grammy awards.

COLORBLIND

(Group)

Formed in 1981, Colorblind were Donny Horner (guitars), Dwight Carter (guitar), Tre Burton (drummer/songwriter), Ronnie Balfour (percussion), Jerry Bowie (keyboards/vocals), Marvin McDonald (lead vocals) and Bob Fisher (keyboards). After touring with Chocolate Milk, **The S.O.S. Band**, **The Gap Band**, **Con Funk Shun** and **Slave**, the group recorded a mini-album *Crazy*, released by Capitol in 1984 and produced by **Rhani Harris**.

COMMODORES

(Group)

The Commodores formed in Tuskegee, Alabama, in 1969. They were **Lionel Richie** (lead vocals), William King (guitar/keyboards/trumpet), Walter 'Clyde' Orange (drums/keyboards/vocals), Milan Williams (guitar/keyboards/vocals), Ronald LaPread (bass) and **Thomas McClary** (guitar/vocals). Most of the members met at college. After establishing themselves locally they performed at New York's Town Hall where they were spotted by talent scout Benjamin Ashburn. Ben took the group under his wing as manager and got them auditioned by Motown. The label signed them, though originally to tour as a support act for **The Jackson 5**.

Their own success came in 1974 when their debut *Machine Gun*, including 'The Zoo (The Human Zoo)', written and produced by **Pam Sawyer** and **Gloria Jones**, went gold in five countries. In the UK the single 'Machine Gun' was their debut hit, and a UK Top 20 entry. Following this success they continued to make earthy funk records, but further UK chart success eluded them until 1977 when a ballad 'Easy' hit the Top 10. The record established Lionel Richie as a songwriter and balladeer, eventually leading to his own solo career. Then The Commodores scored UK Top 40 hits with 'Brick House', 'Zoom' (another ballad and Motown's first ever 12" single release in the UK), and 'Flying High' through 1977–8 before in August 1978 the group reached No. 1 with another ballad, 'Three Times A Lady'. The song reached the Top 5 in twenty-five countries. By now their first four albums had gone gold, followed by two platinum albums, one double platinum album and two triple platinum albums. They were also working with arranger and producer **James Anthony Carmichael** who brought further ballad hits for the group with songs like 'Sail On' and 'Still' (both 1979). When Lionel Richie left to become a solo artist, James moved with him.

In 1984, Following Lionel's eventual departure, the role of lead singer was handed to **J.D.Nicholas** whose vocals are featured on 'Nightshift', a Grammy Award-winning song in 1985 (and a UK Top 5 hit) from the album of the same name. The group were still at Motown, but following the departure of Thomas McClary in 1985, the group switched to Polydor. The line-up was now William King, J.D.Nicholas, Walter Orange and Milan Williams. 'Goin' To The Bank' reached the UK Top 50 in 1986, but they didn't reach the charts again until 'Easy' was reissued by Motown in 1988. The same year a new Polydor album *Rock Solid* had little success.

CON FUNK SHUN
(Group)
The origins of Con Funk Shun date back to 1968 when **Michael Cooper** (lead vocals/guitar) and Louis McCall (drums/percussion/vocals) formed a high-school band Project Soul in California. The group became Con Funk Shun when Michael and Louis moved to Memphis in 1972. By now the line-up had grown to include Cedric Martin (bass/keyboards/vocals), Danny Thomas (keyboards/vocals), Karl Fuller (horns/percussion/vocals), Melvin Carter (keyboards/lead vocals) and Zebulon Paulle Harrel (sax/percussion/vocals). Initially they worked as an in-house studio band at Stax Records, a situation which also allowed them to record their own material (released by the local Fretone label). In 1976 they signed to Mercury Records. Here their albums were *Secrets* (1977), including 'Fun'; *Loveshine* (1978), including 'Shake And Dance With Me'; *Candy* (1979); *Spirit Of Love* (1980); *7* (1981); *Touch* (1982); *Fever* (1983), produced by **Deodato**; *Electric Lady* (1985); *Burnin' Love* (1987) including 'You Make Me Wanna Love Again' produced by **Leon Ware** and the title track, a UK Top 75 single; and *Secrets*.

CONLEY, ARTHUR
(Singer/Songwriter)
Arthur owes his career break to Stax artist **Otis Redding** who signed him to his Jotis label (via Atlantic) in the mid-'60s. Here Arthur recorded songs including 'I'm A Lonely Stranger', the Redding/Conley-penned 'Sweet Soul Music' (UK Top 10, 1967) and 'Funky Street' (UK Top 50, 1968). He later released *More Sweet Soul* for the Atco label (1969).

CONLEY, DAVID 'PIC'
(Producer/Flute)
David is best known for his role as member of New York-based group **Surface**, although as a producer he has worked with artists including **Gwen Guthrie** ('Close To You'), **Visions**, **Jermaine Jackson** ('Don't Take It Personal'), **Barbara Weathers**, **Rebbie Jackson**, **The Mac Band** ('The Best Of Love') and **Melba Moore** ('Do You Really Want My Love').

CONNORS, NORMAN
(Drummer/Producer/Songwriter)
Born in Philadelphia in 1948, Norman took up drums and began composing music at the age of five. After leaving school he worked with **Billy Paul**, **Jack McDuff**, John Coltrane and **Charles Earland** before leaving home for New York. Here he was hired by **Pharaoh Sanders** in 1971; he toured the world and recorded five albums with Sanders. In 1972 he signed with the Cobblestone label, a division of Buddah Records and recorded his first album *Dance of Magic*. After his follow-up *Dark Of Light*, the label folded and Norman signed directly to Buddah. With *Live From The Sun* (1973) and *Slewfoot* (1974), including 'Mother Of The Future', he began to make an impression on the UK 'jazz funk' scene before commercial success in America came his way with the help of songwriter/vocalist **Michael Henderson**.

They first collaborated in 1975 on Norman's *Saturday Night Special*, including 'Valentine Love' (a duet with **Jean Carne**) and 'Dindi' (featuring **Jean Carne**), before major American chart success came in 1976 with 'You Are My Starship' featuring Michael as solo lead vocalist. The album *You Are My Starship*, also including 'Betcha By Golly Wow' (featuring **Phyllis Hyman**), went platinum in America. (The boat on the cover, incidentally, belonged to the late actor John Wayne.)

By now Norman had built a reputation for finding talented new vocalists and bringing them to the attention of the soul scene, something he continues to do to this day. His next albums were *Romantic Journey* (1977), including 'You Are Everything' (featuring **Eleanor Mills**) and 'Once I've Been There' (featuring **Prince Phillip Mitchell**), the jet on the cover belonging to Henry Fonda!; and *This Is Your Life* (1977), including 'Captain Connors', 'Stella' and 'You Make Me Feel Brand New'; before two albums for Arista, *Take It To The Limit* (1980), including 'Melancholy Fire' (featuring **Glenn Jones**) and 'Justify' (featuring **The Jones Girls**); and *Mr C* (1981) including 'She's Gone' (featuring **Beau Williams**).

During this time Norman also formed **The Starship Orchestra** (1978) and also worked as a producer with artists including **Aquarian Dream** (*Fantasy*, including 'You're A Star') **Pharaoh Sanders** (including *Love Will Find A Way*, 1978), **Al Johnson** (*Back For More*), **Phyllis Hyman** (*Can't We Fall In Love Again*) and **Jean Carne** (*Trust Me*).

In 1988 he signed to Capitol and released *Passion*, including 'I Am Your Melody' (featuring Spencer Harrison), as well as producing an album by **Angela Bofill** (*Intuition*) for the label.

CONQUEST, JUNE
(Singer)
Chicago singer June Conquest recorded a series of duets with **Donny Hathaway** (as June And Donny) for Curtom Records during the early '70s.

CONTOURS
(Vocal Group)
This Detroit group formed in the late '50s, and were originally known as The Blenders. They were Billy Hoggs, Sylvester Potts, Hubert Johnson, Billy Gordon and Joe Billingslea, Billy and Joe having previously been members of **The Majestics**. The group became The Contours after a record company turned them down as The Blenders. On their way out of the office, they noticed the word

Contour on the door. Hubert's cousin was **Jackie Wilson**, and via this connection the group were auditioned by **Berry Gordy** at Motown. In 1962 Berry wrote 'Do You Love Me' for them, a debut single which went straight to No. 2 in the American charts. In the UK, Brian Poole & The Tremoloes took the song to No. 1 in 1963. Further American hits included 'Don't Let Her Be Your Baby', 'Can You Jerk Like Me', and their one UK hit 'Just A Little Misunderstanding' (Top 40, 1970). In 1987 'Do You Love Me' was featured on the *Dirty Dancing* movie soundtrack, and The Contours reformed for a live 'Dirty Dancing' tour (without Billy Gordon).

In 1989 they began recording with the UK Motorcity label, working with writer/producer **Ian Levine** on *Flashback* (1990), including 'Face Up To The Fact'.

CONTROLLERS
(Vocal Group)
The Controllers are Reginald McArthur, Leonard Brown, Ricky Lewis and Larry McArthur, who met in the late '60s at their high school in Fairfield, a suburb of Birmingham, Alabama. Originally a gospel group The Soul Controllers, they recorded two singles while still at school, 'Right On, Brother, Right On' and 'Hate Is The Thing, Peace Is The Rap'. Signing to Juana (via TK) Records in the late '70s, they established themselves on the soul scene in 1977 with the ballad 'Somebody's Gotta Win, Somebody's Gotta Lose', also the title of their debut album for the label, produced by **Frederick Knight**.

1979's *Next In Line* featured 'I Can't Turn The Boogie Loose', which in its extended form on American 12″ release (at two speeds, back to back) enjoyed a revival on the UK 'rare groove' scene in the mid-80s. After three Juana albums they recorded 'Distant Lovers' (the **Marvin Gaye** song) on their own label CMP (1982) prior to signing with MCA. Here, a debut single 'Crushed' (featuring **Stevie Wonder** on harmonica) came from 1984's *The Controllers*, which also included 'Undercover Lover' and 'Givin' Up On Love'. Their other MCA albums were *Stay* (1986) including 'My Secret Fantasy'; and *For The Love Of My Woman* (1987) including 'Sleeping Alone', 'Keep In Touch', and 'My Secret Fantasy' again. In 1988 they signed with Capitol, releasing *Just In Time* the following year.

CONWAY BROTHERS
(Group)
From Chicago, The Conway Brothers were Huston (lead vocals/bass), James L. (guitar/vocals), Hiawatha (drums) and Frederick Conway (keyboards/vocals). In 1971 they began performing professionally and built a local reputation. Their debut single was 'Set It Out', successful locally in 1983. They signed to Paula Records in 1985 and released 'Turn It Up', a UK Top 20 hit via Virgin/10 Records. Their follow-up single was 'Raise The Roof', released later the same year.

CONWAY AND TEMPLE
(Singers/Songwriters)
New York-based artists Margaret Conway and Robert Temple recorded together as Conway And Temple during the early '80s. For Jive Records, their releases include the single 'You Can Lay Your Head On My Shoulder (Love Lights)' in 1982.

COOK COUNTY
(Studio Group)
Vic Caesar instigated Cook County, a group of musicians including Everett D. Bryson (percussion), Steve Turner (drums), Bill Von Ravensberg (bass), George Gaffney (keyboards), Bruce Wyndham (guitar), Ralf Rickert/Bob Ojeda/Gene Goe (trumpets), Peter Christlie/Jim Coile/Pat Rizzo (saxes) and Victor himself on vibes. In 1979 they released one album on Motown, *Cook County*, which included 'Pinball Playboy' and 'State Street Samba', popular on the UK 'jazz funk' scene.

COOKE, SAM
(Singer/Songwriter)
Born in Chicago in 1931, Sam grew up in an environment of gospel music and as a young teenager joined a gospel group The Highway Q.C.s. In the meantime a group The Soul Stirrers had an American hit with 'By And By' with lead vocals by Ray Harris. When Ray left the group in 1950, Sam took over and built himself a following with his fresh vocal interpretations of gospel standards. After six years of building to the peak of popularity on the gospel scene he turned to secular r&b/soul, and the group took on **Johnnie Taylor** as their new lead singer. For Specialty records in Los Angeles (for whom he had recorded with The Soul Stirrers), Sam recorded a debut solo single 'Lovable' as Dale Cooke (his father's name), prior to using his real name.

In 1957 he officially launched his solo career with 'You Send Me', a No. 1 single in America (on the Keen label) and a UK Top 30 for London Records. After two further UK Top 30 hits (on HMV), 'Only Sixteen' (1959) and 'Wonderful World' (1960), Sam signed with RCA. Here his classic soul hits continued with 'Chain Gang' (Top 10, 1960), 'Cupid' (Top 10, 1961), 'Twistin' The Night Away' (Top 10, 1962), 'Another Saturday Night' (Top 30, 1963), and 'Frankie And Johnny' (Top 30, 1963), although he was nearly killed in an air crash in 1960. Across America he also scored hits with 'Bring It On Home To Me' and 'A Change Is Gonna Come' (1964).

In 1963 he had formed his own label SAR Records (with his manager **J.W. Alexander**), his artists including **Johnnie Taylor**, The Sims Twins and **The Valentinos**. In December 1964 he was shot dead by Bertha Franklin, the owner of a motel in Los Angeles, in order to protect Linda Boyer from an alleged sexual offence, a case both the media and the music business appeared to cover up at the time.

In 1984 RCA were excited to find a master tape of a

concert recorded ten months before Sam's death. *Live At The Copa* was released for the first time in 1985.

Sam Cooke's vocal style was considered to be unique at the time and a great influence on **Otis Redding**, **Wilson Pickett**, **Solomon Burke** and other artists of the day and beyond. He also had a brother, L.C.Cooke, who at one time was a protégé of **Aretha Franklin**, and his daughter Linda is now the wife of **Cecil Womack** and one half of **Womack & Womack**.

COOL NOTES
(Group)
From South London, The Cool Notes were originally Steve McIntosh (keyboards/vocals), Lorraine McIntosh (lead vocals), Heather Austin (lead vocals), Joseph 'J.C.' Charles (guitar), Ian Dunstan (bass), Peter 'Lee' Gordon (guitar) and Peter 'Rattie' Rolands (drums), who first worked together as a reggae band during the mid-'70s. Initially they recorded for the Jama label, run from a record shop in Brixton. Here 'My Tune' topped the reggae charts before they became a soul group in 1983. Recording for the Abstract Dance label, run by their manager, the group first made an impression on the UK soul scene with 'You're Never Too Young' (Top 50, 1984), then 'I Forgot' (Top 75, 1984), 'Spend The Night' (Top 20, 1985), 'In Your Car' (Top 20, 1985), 'Have A Good Forever' – the title track of their one album (Top 75, 1985), 'Into The Motion' (Top 75, 1986) and 'Momentary Vision' (1986).

As a trio of Steve, Lorraine and J.C., they later recorded for Risin' Records ('Magic Lover'/'House Of Love', 1988) and Jet Star ('Tell Me', 1989). Lorraine also sang lead with **The Beatmasters** ('Don't Make Me Wait') while Steve now manages The 49'ers.

COOPER, BERNADETTE
(Drummer/Singer/Producer)
Born in Los Angeles, Bernadette was the founder member of all-girl group **Klymaxx** prior to signing to MCA as a solo artist. Her debut album *Drama According To Bernadette Cooper* was released in 1990. She also sang backgrounds with **Deele**.

COOPER, CRAIG T.
(Songwriter/Guitar/Singer/Producer)
Based in Los Angeles, Craig emerged on the American soul and jazz scene during the late '80s as a session musician and producer with artists including **The Main** ('All Of Me'), **Ronnie Laws** ('Identity'), **Lever Krystol**, **Bert Robinson** and **Lalah Hathaway**. As an artist he signed to Valley Vue Records where his recordings include *The Craig T. Cooper Project* (1989) and 'Quality Time' (1990).

COOPER, MICHAEL
(Singer/Songwriter/Guitar)
Born in California, Michael Vernon Cooper began a music career at high school, forming a group Project Soul with Louis McCall. In 1972 he and Louis moved to Memphis where they formed **Con Funk Shun**. Michael became lead singer and wrote songs for the group before signing to Warner Brothers as a solo artist in 1987. His albums have been *Love Is Such A Funny Game* (1987) including 'To Prove My Love'; and *Just What I Like* (1989). He co-wrote 'Do Me Right' for **Pebbles**.

COPELAND, JOHNNY
(Singer)
Texas-based singer Johnny Copeland began a career as a boxer before making a name for himself on the '60s soul scene. His singles include 'The Invitation', 'Down On Bended Knees', 'Suffering City' and 'No Puppy Love', recorded for a number of labels and made more generally available across America by Wand and Atlantic. In the mid-'70s he sang blues for Rounder Records.

CORYELL, LARRY
(Guitar/Keyboards)
Born in Texas in 1943, Larry initially took up piano from the age of four. By the time he was twelve he switched to guitar, and in 1961 moved to Seattle where he worked as both a journalist and a musician. In 1965 he moved to New York and made his recording debut with **Chico Hamilton** before joining The Free Spirits.

One of the pioneers of fusion jazz, Steve recorded with artists including **Spaces**, Chick Corea and **Miroslav Vitous**. His solo albums for Arista appealed to the UK's jazz funk scene.

COSTA, PAULINHO DA
(Percussion)
Based in Los Angeles, Paulinho Da Costa was without a doubt the most prolific percussionist on the American soul and jazz scene in the '70s and '80s. He has recorded with countless artists on the black music scene from **Michael Jackson** through to virtually every name you could think of! As a recording artist he is signed to Pablo Records where his albums have included *Agora* (1977), *Happy People* (1979), including 'Deja Vu' and 'Love Till The End Of Time', and *Sunrise* (1984).

COURTNEY, DEAN
(Singer)
Dean was popular on the UK 'Northern soul' scene during the late '60s and '70s. He recorded for labels including MGM ('Love You Just Can't Walk Away'), RCA ('I'll Always Need You') and Paramount.

COURTNEY, LOU
(Singer/Songwriter/Producer)
Lou Courtney worked in Detroit during the '60s, particularly in partnership with **Robert Bateman** on songs/productions for **Barbara Lewis** (including 'Thankful For What I Got'). In the mid-'60s he recorded for the Riverside label where his singles include 'If The Shoe Fits', 'Skate Now' and 'You Ain't Ready'. During the early

'70s he recorded for **Jerry Ragovoy**'s Rags label (via Epic) where the title track of *I'm In Need Of Love* (1973) was a disco hit. The album also included 'What Do You Want Me To Do', popular on the UK soul scene during the late '80s. He also recorded for a series of other labels, including RCA where *Buffalo Smoke* was released in 1976.

His song 'I Don't Need Nobody Else' was later re-recorded by **Norman Connors** on *Take It To The Limit*.

COVAY, DON

(Singer/Songwriter)

Born in Orangeburg, South Carolina, in 1938, Don was the son of a Baptist preacher. His family had a gospel group, the Cherry-Keys, with whom Don sang as soon as he was old enough. He grew up in Washington where in the '50s he joined vocal group **The Rainbows** with **Marvin Gaye**, John Berry, and **Billy Stewart**. He also performed live as a solo artist with Little Richard, who recorded Don as 'Pretty Boy' on the Atlantic release 'Bip Bop Bip'. In 1960 he had some solo success with 'Pony Time' (written by Don and John Berry) on the Arnold label, though it was Chubby Checker who had an American No. 1 hit with the song about the dance craze in 1961.

In 1964 he was back with Atlantic, this time as Don Covay and the Goodtimers, scoring further American hits with 'Mercy Mercy', 'Sookie Sookie' and 'See Saw'. His songs were also recorded by **Aretha Franklin** and Gene Chandler. During the early '70s he recorded (predominantly blues) for the Janus and Mercury labels. These included *Super Dude I* (1973), including 'Leave Him', 'It's Better To Have (And Not Need)' (UK Top 30, 1974) and 'Hot Blood' (1975). In 1976 he recorded one album for the Philadelphia International label, *Travellin' In Heavy Traffic*, which included strange song titles, 'Chocolate Honey' and 'Six Million Dollar Fish'.

CRAWFORD, CAROLYN

(Singer)

Born in Detroit, Carolyn signed with the Motown label after winning a talent contest. She was 14 years old, and had qualified for the contest by collecting bread wrappers! Here in 1965 she recorded 'Forget About Me', 'When Someone's Good To You' and 'My Smile Is Just A Frown Turned Upside Down'. In 1971 she spent a brief period with **Hodges, James & Smith** before joining **Chapter 8** where she met fellow group vocalist **Rick Means** (whom she married). After leaving the group she sang backing vocals with **Charo** until 1975. In 1976 she recorded three singles for the Philadelphia International label, 'Just Got To Be More Careful', 'It Takes Two To Make One' and 'Good And Plenty' (with 'When You Move, You Lose' on the B-side of the record). While at the label she also co-wrote 'Just Because You're Mine' with **McFadden & Whitehead**, recorded by **Teddy Pendergrass**.

By now she was also performing and recording with **Bohannon** as his vocalist, Carolyn's voice contributing the much sampled 'Everybody, get on up and dance' on the classic dance anthem 'Let's Start The Dance' (a UK hit in both 1978 and 1982). Bohannon also wrote and produced her 1978 solo Mercury album *My Name Is Caroline* which included 'Coming On Strong'. More recently she has recorded for the UK Motorcity label: *Heartaches* (1990), including 'Which Way Do I Turn' and 'Timeless'.

CRAWFORD, HANK

(Sax)

Born in Memphis, Tennessee, in 1934, Hank formed his first band in 1963, and played with **Ike Turner** before joining the **Ray Charles** band in the late '50s. Here he became music director as well as lead sax player. He began a solo career at Atlantic Records with albums including *Mr Blues* and *After Hours*, before switching to the Kudu subsidiary of CTI. Here he became one of the pioneering fusion jazz sax players of the mid- to late '70s with albums including *Help Me Make It Through The Night*, *We Got A Good Thing Going*, *Don't You Worry 'Bout A Thing*, *Cajun Sunrise Wildflower* (1974) and *Tico Rico* (1977), including the soulful 'Teach Me Tonight'.

Also at Atlantic he played with artists including **Esther Phillips** prior to leaving for the Milestone label for which he records today. His most recent album is *Night Beat* (1989).

CRAWFORD, RANDY

(Singer)

Born in Macon, Georgia, in 1952, Randy grew up in Cincinnati, Ohio, where her first singing experience was in church and at school. Accompanied by her father, she was performing in clubs by the time she was 15, and shortly afterwards sang in a group which featured **Bootsy Collins**. In 1972 she toured America as an opening act for **George Benson**, during which time she came to the attention of Cannonball Adderly, who invited her to sing on his album *Big Man*. At this point she signed briefly to CBS and recorded a debut single 'Don't Get Caught In Love's Triangle' (produced by **Johnny Bristol**) before switching to Warner Brothers in 1976. Here her albums have included *Everything Must Change* (1976); *Miss Randy Crawford* (1977); *Raw Silk* (1979), including 'Endlessly'; *Now We May Begin'* (1980), produced by **The Crusaders** and including 'Last Night At Danceland' (UK Top 75) and 'One Day I'll Fly Away' (UK Top 5); *Secret Combination* (1981), produced by **Tommy LiPuma** and including 'You Might Need Somebody' (UK Top 20), 'Rainy Night In Georgia' (UK Top 20), the title track (UK Top 50) and 'Rio De Janeiro Blue'; *Windsong* (1982), including 'Imagine' (UK Top 75) and 'One Hello' (UK Top 50); *Abstract Emotions* (1986), including 'Almaz' (UK Top 5); and *Rich & Poor* (1989), including 'Knocking On Heaven's Door' featuring Eric Clapton.

In addition to her solo hits, she also gave **The Crusaders** their most commercially successful release with 'Street Life' (UK Top 5, 1979) on which she was the featured vocalist. She was also a featured artist on the album *Casino Lights* recorded live by Warner Brothers at Montreux, Switzerland, in 1982.

CREATIVE SOURCE
(Group)
Based in Los Angeles, early '70s funk/soul group Creative Source consisted of Barbara Berryman, Barbara Lewis, Don Wyatt, Steve Flanagan and Celeste Rose. Initially they recorded for the Sussex label where their albums included the **Michael Stokes**-produced *Creative Source* (1973) and *Migration* (1974), including 'I Just Can't See Myself Without You' and 'Who Is He And What Is He To You', before they switched to Polydor for *Consider The Source* (1976).

CREED, LINDA
(Songwriter/Producer/Percussion)
Born to French parents in Philadelphia in 1949, Linda landed herself a recording contract at Philly Groove Records but nothing was released. Instead she met **Thom Bell** who, impressed by her poems, suggested she write lyrics to his music. Together they wrote a string of Philly classics during the '70s including 'Betcha By Golly Wow' (**Stylistics/Phyllis Hyman**), 'Stone In Love With You' and 'You Make Me Feel Brand New' (**Stylistics**) and 'One Of A Kind Love Affair' (**Detroit Spinners**). She also wrote 'The Greatest Love Of All' (**George Benson/Whitney Houston**) with **Michael Masser**. As a solo producer she worked with **Eloise Laws** (*Eloise Laws*, 1980), having co-produced 1977's *Eloise* with **Jerry Goldstein** and **Johnny Gill** (writing 'Half Crazy'). She died of cancer in 1986.

CROOK, GENERAL
(Singer/Songwriter/Producer)
Born in Chicago, General Crook recorded for the Wand label in the mid-'70s where he is best remembered for 'Best Years Of My Life'. His albums include *General Crook* (1974), including 'Thanks, But No Thanks', while more recently his single 'I Can't Stand It'/'Main Squeeze' was released in the UK by Expansion Records (1986). He has also been working closely with **Willie Clayton** as producer in recent years.

CROWN HEIGHTS AFFAIR
(Group)
From New York, Philip Thomas (lead vocals), Bert Reid (sax), Raymond Reid (guitar), William Anderson (guitar/vocals), James 'Ajax' Baynard (trumpet), Raymond Rock (vocals/drums/percussion), Howie Young (keyboards) and Muki Wilson (bass/vocals) first formed Crown Heights Affair in the early '70s. They first recorded for RCA and had a regional hit with 'Super Rod' (1973) before switching to De-Lite Records (via Phonogram), recording eight albums to 1983. In 1975 they established themselves on the international scene with 'Dreaming A Dream', released by Polydor in the UK. This was followed by *Do It Your Way* (1976), including 'Far Out'; *Dancin'* (1977), released in the UK via Contempo; and their most successful album, *Dream World* (1978), including 'Galaxy Of Love' (UK Top 30), 'I'm Gonna Love You Forever' (UK Top 50) and 'Say A Prayer For Two' – one of the first tracks ever to be remixed for commercial release.

In 1979 the group scored a UK Top 50 hit with 'Dance Lady Dance', while *Sure Shot* marked a change in musical direction with the double-headed single 'You Gave Me Love'/'Use Your Body And Soul' (UK Top 10) in 1980. Further singles continued with 'You've Been Gone' (UK Top 50, 1980), 'Somebody Tell Me What To Do' (1982), 'Rock The World'/'Heavy Lovin'' (1983), 'Make Me The One' (1986) – following the departure of the Reid brothers, and the Marshall Jefferson-mixed 'I'll Do Anything' (1989).

In the meantime William Anderson and Ray Reid had embarked on productions together for artists including **Unlimited Touch** ('Searching To Find The One', 1981), **France Joli** ('Gonna Get Over You', 1981) and **Trilark**.

CRUSADERS
(Group)
From Houston, Texas, The Crusaders were originally known as The Swingsters and then The Jazz Crusaders with an original line-up of **Joe Sample** (keyboards), **Wilton Felder** (sax), **Stix Hooper** (drums), Robert 'Pops' Popwell (bass) and **Wayne Henderson** (trombone). The group first played together in high school before relocating to Los Angeles in the '60s in search of a record deal. Here they recorded jazz for the Pacific label before becoming simply The Crusaders in 1970.

They switched to the Blue Thumb/ABC label and became pioneers of fusion jazz ('jazz funk'), their albums including *Second Crusade*, *Unsung Heroes* and *Scratch* before they were joined by guitarist **Larry Carlton** in 1973 (and also recorded on his solo album *Singing/Playing* that year). Further albums, *Southern Comfort* (1974), *Chain Reaction* (1975), including 'I Felt The Love', and *Those Southern Knights* (1976) were released before Wayne Henderson left the group to pursue solo recordings and production activities.

The Crusaders recorded two more ABC albums, *Free As The Wind* (1976) and *Images* (1978) before the label merged with MCA. At this point Pops Powell left, and the group began to introduce vocals to their recordings. The first of these was 'Street Life', a UK Top 5 single from their 1979 album of the same name. The song featured the vocals of **Randy Crawford**, whose album *Now We May Begin* the group produced and played on in 1980. Later that year they employed the services of **Bill Withers** on 'Soul Shadows' for their new album *Rhapsody & Blues*. In 1981, 'I'm So Glad I'm Standing Here Today' featuring the vocals of Joe Cocker reached the UK Top 75.

Stix Hooper left the group at this point, reducing The Crusaders to Will and Joe who in 1982 produced 'Don't Take Your Love To Hollywood' for **Kelly Marie**. Later they replaced Stix with drummer **Ndugu**, and returned with the albums *Ghetto Blaster*, including 'Night Ladies' (UK Top 75) and *Access All Areas* (live) in 1984. In the meantime Will and Joe recorded solo albums, and after the departure of Ndugu a final Crusaders album for MCA, *The Good And Bad Times*, was released in 1986, including 'The Way It Goes' featuring **Nancy Wilson**.

CRYSTAL WINDS

(Group)

From Chicago, Crystal Winds are Martin Dumas Jr (guitar), Jimmy Allen (bass), Henry Johnson (guitar), Bruce Gaitsche (guitar), Tony Brown (bass), Wayne Stewart (drums), Frank Donaldson (drums), Paul Colman (keyboards/vocals), Cortez Brown (sax/vocals) and Theresa Davis (vocals). In 1982 they released *First Flight*, including 'So Sad' and 'Lovers Holiday', for the Cash Ear label, popular with UK soul fans.

CUNNINGHAM, WOODY

(Drummer)

Woody originally played drums with the rock group Pipeline before they moved into r&b/funk in the mid-'70s and toured as **The Universal Robot Band**. The musicians later formed the nucleus of **Kleeer**, Woody remaining the drummer with the group while also maintaining session dates with **Sylvester**, **Faith Hope & Charity** and **Luther Vandross** among others. In the '70s he also toured the UK as drummer with Disco Tex And The Sexolettes, and played an integral role with **Candido**.

CURIO

(Group)

Formed in the late '80s, Curio are Rodney Shelton, Michael H. Williams and Jake Hunter. In 1990 they signed with Motown and released *Special Feeling*, including 'I Can't Stay'.

CURRY, MINI

(Singer)

Born in Detroit, Mini worked with producer **Michael Powell** on 'I Think I'm Over You', released by Total Experience Records in 1987. In the UK it was released on her one album *100%* for the Timeless label. In 1991 Mini recorded the duet 'With You' with **Teddy Pendergrass** from his *Truly Blessed* that year. Mini has also recorded duets with her brother Tyrone Curry, whose own solo recordings include 'I'm So In Love' for the Digital Soul Records label.

CURTIS, CHANTEL

(Singer)

In 1979 Chantel worked with French arrangers and producers on 'Get Another Love', initially released on the Key label in New York where it became a hit on the disco scene. It was similarly popular on the UK disco scene and reached the Top 75 after being released on Pye Records.

CURTIS, KING

(Saxophone)

Born Curtis Ousdey in Texas, King Curtis first established himself after moving to New York where he made a series of jazz albums for the Status and Prestige labels. To supplement his income he also recorded sessions with artists including The Coasters, **Aretha Franklin** and **Sam Cooke**.

He was the forerunner of artists like **Grover Washington** and **David Sanborn** with his recordings in the '60s for Atlantic including 'Memphis Soul Stew', 'Night Train', 'Soul Serenade' and 'Soul Twist', and an album *Changes*. *King Curtis Live At Fillmore West* was released the year he was stabbed to death in New York (1971). Another live performance, this time with **Sam Cooke**, was later discovered by RCA Records and released in 1985 on a Sam Cooke album *Live At The Copa*.

CURTIS, T.C.

(Singer/Songwriter/Producer)

Born William Alexander Smith in London, 'T.C.' is derived from his old stage name Terry Curtis, used during his days with local dance bands. Turning to dance music in the mid-'80s, he recorded a debut single 'Body Shake' and licensed it to the Groove Productions label. The reaction to the record prompted him to start his own label, Hot Melt, on which he released his next singles 'Bump And Slide' and 'Dance To The Beat' in 1984. Strong reactions to these led to a call from Virgin Records who licensed the Hot Melt label which released a further single 'You Should Have Known Better' (1985). At this point T.C. decided he would rather run his label independently and took it away from Virgin. His next singles included 'Step By Step' (1986), 'Let's Make Love' (1986) and 'Slave Of Love' (1986), while he also signed Dotty Green to his label for two singles, 'I Want You' and 'I Caught You Out', also in 1986.

T.C. is also an experienced window-maker and mechanical engineer. He can make made-to-order window frames, double-glazing and parts for engines and dishwashing machines.

CUT GLASS

(Duo)

From Detroit, Cut Glass were **Ortheia Barnes** and **Millie Scott**. They formed the partnership in 1979 and performed locally before recording the dance hit 'Without Your Love' in 1979.

CYMONE, ANDRE

(Singer/Songwriter/Producer)

Andre originally played bass with **Prince** in a band **94 East** during the mid-'70s. He signed to CBS as a solo artist where his albums included *Survivin' In The 80s*, including 'Make Me Wanna Dance' (1983) and the **Prince**-produced 'The Dance Electric' (1985). Andre then moved into songwriting and production himself for other artists including **Jody Watley** ('Looking For A New Love' and 'Real Love').

D

D-MOB
(Songwriter/Mixer/Producer)
D-Mob is the brainchild of London DJ producer/mixer Danny D, a former record promoter who first recorded under the banner of DSM. *Warrior Groove* was a UK Top 75 release for Elite Records in 1985. Danny then worked at Chrysalis as an A&R man before signing to FFRR (via Phonogram) as D-Mob in 1988. Here his debut was *We Call It Acieed* (UK Top 5), followed by singles including 'C'Mon And Get My Love', 'The Way Of The World', 'It's Time To Get Funky' and 'Put Our Hands Together'.

D-TRAIN
(Singer/Songwriter)
D-Train was the name **James Williams** used to record under prior to signing to CBS under his real name. As D-Train, he signed to Prelude Records (via CBS) in 1982 where 'You're The One For Me' was perhaps the most original dance record that year and a UK Top 30 hit. His debut album of the same name included 'Walk On By' (UK Top 50, 1982) and 'Keep On'. He later scored with 'Music' (UK Top 30, 1983), 'Keep Giving Me Love' (UK Top 75, 1983) and 'The Shadow Of Your Smile' (1983). In 1984 he released 'Thank You' for the Prelude label (now via RCA), before returning to CBS under his real name.

DAMARIS
(Singer)
Born in Puerto Rico, Damaris Cortese Carbauth met **Luther Vandross** when they both sang on Kentucky Fried Chicken commercials. In 1981 she sang backgrounds with Luther on 'You Stopped Loving Me' (a song for his first Epic album), and for Luther's **Dionne Warwick** song/production 'So Amazing'. In 1982 she won the American Song Festival prize of a $200,000 budget to make an album for CBS. *Damaris* (1984) featured a cover of 'What About My Love' (a song established by **Johnnie Taylor**) and featured Luther on background vocals!

DANIELS, EDDIE
(Sax)
Eddie has worked as a top session saxophonist, as well as recording fusion jazz albums as a solo artist (including *Morning Thunder* for CBS in 1980). He has recorded with numerous artists including **Ashford & Simpson**, **Kleeer**, **Charles Earland** and **Michael Franks**.

DANTE
(Group)
Not to be confused with singer **Steven Dante** or American singer **Dante**, the British group Dante was a funk band instigated by Jean Paul Maunick ('Bluey'), a former guitarist and founder member of **Light Of The World**.

DANTE
(Singer)
Not to be confused with singer **Steven Dante** or the British group **Dante**, the American singer Dante was born Dennis Sanders in Phoenix, Arizona, where he sang in church with his brothers. Aged seventeen he moved to California to sing with the Love Center Choir, and became a session singer with artists including **Sylvester**, Edwin Hawkins, **Narada Michael Walden**, **Stacey Lattisaw** and **Johnny Gil**. Moving to Philadelphia he hooked up with songwriter Tony Collins for 'Freak In Me', released in the UK on Virgin/10 Records. The track featured backing vocals by **Patti Labelle**'s backing singers, The Sweeties.

DANTE, STEVEN
(Singer)
Born in Hackney, London, Steven began to take his singing seriously from the age of fifteen. A demo of his voice was heard by Jean 'Bluey' Paul of the group **Light Of The World** who wrote him some songs and arranged some vocal tuition. With some new demos Bluey and Steven went to New York in search of a record deal, eventually working with **Marcus Miller** and **Ray Bardini** (two thirds of **Luther Vandross**'s production team) on 'So Long', released by Chrysalis in 1986. Steven's voice also impressed John '**Jellybean**' Benitez who hired him to sing lead vocals on 'The Real Thing' (UK Top 20, 1987), taken from Jellybean's *Just Visiting This Planet*.

From here Steven went to Minneapolis where, still for Chrysalis, he worked on *Find Out* (1988), including 'I'm

Too Scared' (UK Top 40), with producers including **Jam/ Lewis**.

D'ARBY, TERENCE TRENT

(Singer)

Born in Florida in 1963, Terence emigrated to London in his early twenties where he was groomed by CBS Records. Here he appealed to soul but mainly pop audiences with songs from his debut album *Introducing The Hardline According To Terence Trent D'Arby* (1987) which included 'If You Let Me Stay' (Top 10), 'Wishing Well' (Top 5), 'Dance Little Sister' (Top 20) and 'Sign Your Name' (Top 5). His second album, *Neither Fish nor Flesh*, was released in 1989.

DASH, SARAH

(Singer)

Born in Philadelphia, Sarah Dash joined the group **Labelle** before signing to the Kirschner label as a solo artist in 1978. Here her debut album featured 'Sinner Man'. *Ooh La La* was released in 1979. In the mid-'80s she teamed up with **Dr York** for the duet 'It's Too Late', then in 1988 signed to Manhattan (via EMI) for *You're All I Need*, including a title track duet with **Patti Labelle**, a duet 'Don't Make Me Wait' with **Ray, Goodman & Brown**, and 'To Tell You The Truth'.

DAVIS, CARL

(Producer)

Carl has played an integral role on the Chicago black music scene from the '60s through to the present day. As a producer his early work included 'I Get The Sweetest Feeling' and '(Your Love Keeps Lifting Me) Higher And Higher' for **Jackie Wilson**, while through the '70s he was particularly prolific with his work at the Brunswick and Chi-Sound labels. His productions include 'All About The Paper' (**The Dells**), 'Get Down' (**Gene Chandler**) and 'Touching In The Dark' (**Walter Jackson**), and countless others.

DAVIS, DARLENE

(Singer)

Born in New York, Darlene is the daughter of Rosetta Davis who sang frequently with Duke Ellington. Her stepmother was a founder member of '50s girl group The Crystals. She sang with the Crystals for seven years before Chuck Berry suggested she considered a solo career. Signing to Jamaica Funk Productions (belonging to **Tom Browne**) she recorded 'Frantic Lover' before working with New York disc jockey Elai Tubo on a single 'I Found Love' which became a UK Top 75 hit (via Serious Records) in 1987.

DAVIS, DON

(Songwriter/Producer/Industry)

Born in Detroit, Don has owned and run numerous soul/r&b labels since the '60s, and has also been actively involved as a songwriter and/or producer with artists including **Johnnie Taylor** (*Who's Making Love To Your Old Lady* and *Rated Extraordinaire*), **L.J.Reynolds** (*Travelin'*), **Marilyn McCoo & Billy Davis Jr** ('You Don't Have To Be A Star'), **Bobby Womack**, **David Ruffin** (*So Soon We Change*/'Sexy Dancer'), **Steve Mancha**, **The Dramatics**, **Ronnie McNeir** and **The Holidays** ('No Greater Love'/'Your Song'). Not all were recorded for his own label; some were made for Stax (where he worked as a writer/producer) and other companies including Motown, Capitol, CBS and MCA.

The labels he has owned include Groovesville and Grove City, while he also has his own recording studio, United Sound Systems in Detroit, where numerous soul/r&b classics have been recorded over the years. Today Don is more actively involved in his banking business in Detroit.

DAVIS, JOHN

(Songwriter/Arranger/Producer)

In the late '70s, John Davis & The Monster Orchestra scored on the disco scene with 'Up Jumped The Devil' (Sam Records, 1977) and 'Ain't That Enough For You' (Miracle Records, 1978). He also worked as an arranger and/or producer for artists including **Diana Ross** ('The Boss'), **Collins And Collins** ('You Know How To Make Me Feel So Good'), **Ray Simpson**, **Touch Of Class** ('I Love You Pretty Baby'), **Phyllis Hyman** ('One Thing On My Mind' and 'I Don't Want To Lose You') and more recently **Richard Rogers**.

DAVIS, MARY

(Singer)

Born in Savannah, Georgia, Mary taught herself to sing by listening to **Aretha Franklin** and **Gladys Knight** records. Aged nineteen she moved to New York and worked with **King Curtis** before signing to a production company owned by Bill Curtis (from the group **Fatback**). She moved to Atlanta and joined a group Santa Monica. Shortly they changed their name to **The S.O.S. Band** with whom Mary recorded six albums (four gold) prior to taking on a solo career in 1986. An album, *Mary Davis*, was released in 1989 by Tabu Records (via CBS).

DAVIS, MILES

(Trumpet)

One of the greatest trumpet players there has ever been, Miles has broadened the boundaries of jazz considerably over an incredible career that stretches back to the '50s. While his music itself remains the property of his loyal and solid following, its influence has been phenomenal on countless soul, funk and r&b groups and artists including **George Clinton**, **Earth Wind & Fire**, **Return To Forever** and **Weather Report**.

Many members of The Miles Davis Band have had successful recording careers after working with Miles, including **James Mtume/Reggie Lucas** (see **Mtume/**

Lucas), **Michael Henderson**, Keith Jarrett, **Gary Bartz** and **Ndugu**. A classic Miles quote is, 'Don't play what you know, play what you don't know.'

DAVIS, TYRONE

(Singer)

Born in Greenville, Mississippi, in 1938, Tyrone first recorded for the Tangerine label owned by **Ray Charles**, but without success. His next move was to the Dakar label (via Atlantic), where his fortune changed with the American hit 'Can I Change My Mind' (1968), also the title of his debut album. Follow-up success came his way with the release of 'All The Waiting Is Not In Vain' (1969), 'Turn Back The Hands Of Time' (also the title of his second album, 1970), 'You Keep Me Holding On' (1971), 'I Had It All The Time' (1972) and 'It's All In The Game' (1973), before he switched to CBS. Here his first single was 'Give It Up' (1976), following which he released albums including *Let's Be Closer* (1977), *In The Mood* (1979), *I Just Can't Keep On Goin'* (1980) and *Love Ain't Over There* (1981), working closely with producer Leo Graham. Leo also worked with Tyrone on later albums for the Future label including *Sexy Thing* (1985) and *Man of Stone* (1987).

DAWSON, CLIFF

(Singer/Songwriter)

Based in New York, Cliff recorded a single 'Somehow' for the Rondelet Music & Recordings label in 1981 before signing to Broadwalk Records the following year. Here he worked with producer **Lionel Job** on *Cliff Dawson* (1982), including 'It's Not Me You Love' and 'Don't Hide Away From Love'. As a songwriter he has worked for artists including **Pieces Of A Dream** ('We Belong To Each Other') and **Willie Collins** ('Where You Gonna Be Tonight').

DAWSON, JOHNNY

(Singer/Songwriter/Producer)

Detroit vocalist Johnny Dawson has sung with The Sensations, The Five Emeralds, The Downbeats and more notably **The Elgins**, with whom he continues to perform to this day. In between the break-up and reforming of The Elgins Johnny worked as a session singer with **Norman Whitfield**.

DAY, MICHAEL

(Singer)

From Champaign, Illinois, Michael was thirteen when he played truant from school to earn $200 a week singing in nightclubs. Moving to Chicago he came to the attention of Clive Davis who signed him for one album at CBS, but due to its lack of success he moved back to Champaign where he formed the group **Champaign**.

DAY, MORRIS

(Singer/Drummer)

Born in Minneapolis, Morris formed a band Enterprise which became a rival to another local group **Flytetime**. Shortly after **Jesse Johnson** had joined Enterprise, the two groups amalgamated as **The Time**. Morris would have been the group's drummer had **Alexander O'Neal** (lead singer with Flytetime) not left the group, leaving Morris to step in as lead vocalist. As a solo artist he signed to Warner Brothers for albums *Color Of Success* (1985), including 'The Oak Tree', and *Daydreaming* (1987). Recently he has rejoined The Time.

DAY, PATTI

(Singer)

From Washington, DC, Patti sang locally on the jazz scene before signing to the Starway label in 1987. Here she recorded *Love Crazy*, including 'Right Before My Eyes' produced by **Michael Zager**. The song was bootlegged in the UK where it had become in demand on the dance scene. It was released by Debut Records in 1989, then again in 1991.

DAYE, EDDIE

(Singer)

From Washington, Eddie's group Eddie Daye And The 4 Bars recorded such 'Northern soul' singles as 'Guess Who Loves You' in 1966 on Shrine Records.

DAYTON

(Group)

Formed in Ohio, Dayton was formed by **Shawn Sandridge** (lead vocals/guitar) and Chris Jones (lead vocals/keyboards/trumpet), formerly of the group **Sun**. Other members were Dean Hummons (keyboards), Derrick Armstrong (vocals), and Jenny Douglas (vocals), who originally recorded as **Magnum**. Kevin Hurt (drums/percussion), Rachel Beavers (background vocals) and Karen Harris Chappel (lead and background vocals) completed the line-up. Signing to United Artists, Shawn and Chris wrote all the songs on the first two Dayton albums, *Dayton* (1980), including 'Eyes On You', and *Cutie Pie* (1982). The group also toured as musicians for **Quincy Jones**, **Stephanie Mills** and **Ashford & Simpson**. Their third album *Hot Fun In The Summertime* (1983) introduced the services of **Rahni Harris** as producer, writer, vocalist and keyboard player. Rahni also wrote and produced the group's most highly acclaimed album *Feel The Music*, including 'The Sound Of Music' (UK Top 75), 'It Must Be Love' and 'Promise Me', for Capitol in 1983.

DAZZ BAND

(Group)

Formed in Ohio, The Dazz Band were instigated by Bobby Harris and began their career in 1971 as jazz band Bell Telephunk. Moving into danceable *jazz* and incorporating vocals into their music, the group changed their name to **Kinsman Dazz** and signed to 20th Century Records. When they switched to Motown in 1981, the line-up was Bobby Harris (sax/vocals), Pierre Demudd (trumpet/lead vocals), Keith Harrison (keyboards/vocals), Sennie 'Skip' Martin II (trumpet/vocals), Eric Fearman and **Marlon McClain** (both guitar), Kevin Kendrick (keyboards), Kenny Pettus (percussion/vocals), Issac Wiley Jr (drums), Michael Wiley (bass) and Juan Lively (lead vocals). They had now become The Dazz Band and released the albums *Invitation To Love* (1981), including 'Everyday Love'; *Keep It Live* (1982), including 'Let It Whip'; *Joystick* (1983); *Jukebox* (1984), including 'Let It All Blow' (UK Top 20); *Hot Spot* (1985); and *On The One* (1986). Their later albums were released by Geffen (*Wild And Free*, 1986) and RCA (*Rock The Room*, 1988).

DE LA SOUL

(Group)

Based in New York, De La Soul are 'Posdinous', 'Mace' and 'Truhgoy The Dove' who combined an unusual blend of funk, rap and fashion across two highly successful albums, *3 Feet High And Rising* (1989), including 'Me Myself & I', and *De La Soul Is Dead* (1991), including 'Ring Ring Ring', for Tommy Boy Records.

DEAN, JOHNNY

(Singer/Songwriter)

Born in Coldwater, Mississippi, Johnny sang gospel with his two brothers during the late '50s and early '60s. Through the mid-'60s and early '70s he worked as a freelance songwriter for the Stax label, then retired from the music business to be a printer. In 1983 he returned to the studio and recorded 'Sitting Around My Table', released by the Memphis-based Magic 7 label in 1984.

DEBARGE

(Group)

Los Angeles family group Debarge originally consisted of **El Debarge** (keyboards/vocals), James (keyboards/vocals), Randy (bass/vocals), Mark (trumpet/sax/vocals), and Bunny Debarge (vocals). Their elder brothers Bobby and Tommy played with the group **Switch** and it was through them that Debarge signed to Gordy Records (via Motown) in 1982. Here their albums included *All This Love* (1982) and *In A Special Way* (1983), while their greatest commercial success came in 1985 with the singles 'Rhythm Of The Night' (UK Top 5) and 'You Wear It Well' (UK Top 75) from the album *Rhythm Of The Night*. At this point, El and Bunny Debarge signed as solo artists with Motown (Bunny recording one album *In Love*, 1987) while the remaining group signed to the Stripped Horse label. James Debarge also attracted publicity for eloping with **Janet Jackson**.

DEBARGE, CHICO

(Singer)

From the **Debarge** family group, Chico recorded one solo album for Motown, *Chico Debarge* (1986), including 'Talk To Me'. Also on the album was 'I Like My Body', written and produced by **Gary Taylor**.

DEBARGE, EL

Singer/Songwriter/Producer)

El Debarge was lead singer of the family group **Debarge**, before Gordy (via Motown) signed him as a solo artist in 1986. Here his albums included *El Debarge*, including 'Who's Johnny' (UK Top 75, 1986) and *Gemini* (1989) including 'Broken Dreams', 'Real Love' and 'Turn The Page', before **Quincy Jones** utilized him as co-lead vocalist on 'The Secret Garden' (which El also co-wrote) with **James Ingram**, **Al B.Sure** and **Barry White** (1989). From here El signed to Warner Brothers.

DEBONAIRES

(Vocal Group)

From Detroit, The Debonaires members featured Joyce Vincent (lead singer) and Telma Hopkins, both of whom later became members of the pop group Dawn. As The Debonaires they recorded for the Golden World label from the early to mid-'60s, and then switched to the Solid Hit label where their releases included their best-remembered single 'Loving You Takes All Of My Time' (1966). Telma Hopkins later appeared in the science fiction movie *Trancers*.

DECO

(Group)

Recording for **Quincy Jones**'s label Qwest Records in Los Angeles, Deco were a mid-'80s funk band featuring the vocals of **Philip Ingram**, brother of **James Ingram**.

DEELE

(Group)

From Cincinnati, Ohio, The Deele were Antonio 'L.A.' Reid (drums/percussion), Kenny 'Babyface' Edmonds (vocals/guitar/keyboards), Kevin 'Kayo' Roberson (bass), Darnell 'Dee' Bristol (vocals) and Carlos Greene (vocals). In 1984 the group signed with Solar Records in Los Angeles and worked with producer Reggie (**Calloway**) on a debut album *Street Beat*. The follow-up *Material Thangz* (1985) was produced by the group themselves, as was 1987's *Eyes Of A Stranger*. In 1988 the group scored a single hit with 'Two Occasions' with Babyface on lead vocals.

By this time **L.A./Babyface** had established themselves as leading songwriters and producers both with the group and with other artists including **The Whispers**, **The Mac Band**, **Pebbles** and **Karyn White**.

DEES, JOEY

(Singer)

Born in Morgan City, Mississippi in 1940, Joey sang in church choirs before joining spiritual group The Southern Bells. In 1957 he moved to Los Angeles to join The Zion Travellers, and by the late '60s had established himself as a top backing singer with leading names on the r&b music scene. In 1975 he toured America as a solo artist before winning a top blues award back in Los Angeles. In 1977 he was involved in an accident and it wasn't until 1980 that he was well enough to perform again.

DEES, SAM

(Singer/Songwriter/Producer)

Born in Birmingham, Alabama, in 1945, Sam was nine when he won a song contest. He formed The Bossanovians in 1959, and later moved briefly to New York before returning in 1965 to record his debut solo single 'I Need You Girl'/'Lonely For You Baby' for the SSS label. He then recorded for Lolo ('It's All Wrong, It's All Right'/'Easier To Say Than Do', 1969), then Chess ('Can You Be A One-Man Woman'/'Maryana', 1971), mainly in Memphis, Tennessee. Meanwhile his songs were being recorded by artists including **Z.Z.Hill**, **Clarence Carter**, **Tyrone Davis**, **Ben E.King**, **Frederick Knight** and **The Persuaders**. In 1972 Sam switched to the Clinton label for 'I'm So Very Good'/'Claim Jumping', the popularity of which led to a deal with Atlantic, and *The Show Must Go On* (1975). In the UK 'Fragile, Handle With Care' was Sam's first single release, followed by a duet with **Bettye Swann**. Sam switched to Polydor in 1977 (including 'My World'). Two years later he moved to Los Angeles, which remains his home today.

His next solo release was the instrumental 'Survive' (with 'Fly Angel Fly' on the B-side of the record) for the UK Move label (1986), before in 1988 he launched his own label Pen Pad and signed himself as an artist. From his album *Secret Admirer* 'Just Wait Until I Get You Home' and 'After All' were released as American singles, the latter issued in the UK by RCA (1989). Primarily as a songwriter he has a cult status on the UK soul scene, his songs having been recorded by **Anita Ward** ('Sweet Splendor'), **Charles Jackson** ('For The Sake Of The Memories'), **Dorothy Moore/Millie Jackson** ('Special Occasion'), **Loleatta Holloway** ('Cry To Me' and 'Worn Out Broken Heart'), **Colonel Abrams** ('Never Change', co-written with Abrams), **Salsoul Orchestra/Johnnie Taylor** ('Seconds'), **Larry Graham** ('One In A Million You'), **Rockie Robbins** ('Hang Tough', 'After Loving You' and 'For The Sake Of A Memory'), **Tavares** ('Let Me Heal The Bruises'), **Margie Joseph** ('Just As Soon As The Feeling's Over'), **Aretha Franklin/George Benson** ('Love All The Hurt Away'), **Gladys Knight** ('Save The Overtime For Me', co-written with Gladys, and 'All Our Love'), **Atlantic Starr** ('All In the Name Of Love'), **Whitney Houston/Manhattans** ('Just The Lonely Talking') and **Regina Belle** ('After The Love Has Lost Its Shine'). More recently his song 'Lover For Life' was recorded by Whitney Houston on her 1990 album *I'm Your Baby Tonight*. His co-written songs include '(You're My) Aphrodisiac' (**Dennis Edwards**), 'Drop My Heart Off At The Door' (**Barbara Hall**) and 'I Betcha Didn't Know That' (**Keisa Brown/K.C. & The Sunshine Band**).

DEJA

(Group)

Vocalists Curt Jones and Starleana Young recorded as **Aurra** prior to becoming Déjà in 1987 and were originally part of the group **Slave**. Their singles for Virgin/10 Records were 'Serious' (1987), 'That's Where You'll Find Me' (1988) and the **Teddy Riley/Gene Griffin**-produced 'Made To Be Together' (1989).

DELEGATION

(Group)

Formed in Birmingham, England, in 1976, Delegation were originally Ricky Bailey, Ray Patterson and Len Coley. Signing to State Records, they scored with UK hits 'Where Is The Love We Used To Know' (Top 30) and 'You've Been Doing Me Wrong' (Top 50) in 1977 before scoring in America with 'Oh Honey' (1978). In 1979 Len was replaced by Bruce Dunbar, and the group switched to Ariola for the *Eau De Vie*, including 'One More Step To Take' which became popular on the UK soul scene during the mid-'80s.

Upon signing to Epic they added Texas-born vocalist Kathy Bryant whom they had met while working in Germany. Here they delivered 'It's Your Turn', around which time Ricky and Ray wrote 'Stand Up, Reach For The Sky' for **Revelation**.

DELFONICS

(Vocal Group)

From Philadelphia, William Hart, Wilbert Hart, Randy Cain and Ritchie Daniels originally sang together in the '60s as The Four Gents. In 1971 they acquired a fifth member, **Major Harris**, and became The Delfonics. Their debut release 'He Don't Really Love You' was the first ever **Thom Bell** production and was released on Moonshot Records. It had been leased to them by **Cameo** who released the follow-up 'You've Been Untrue' themselves. When the label closed down, their manager Stan Watson formed his own label Philly Groove, on which the Delfonics had UK hits with 'Didn't I (Blow Your Mind This Time)' (Top 50), 'La La Means I Love You' (Top 20) and 'Ready Or Not, Here I Come' (Top 50) again produced by Thom Bell (in 1971).

DELLS

(Group)

From the outskirts of Chicago, Illinois, The Dells are Chuck Barksdale, Laverne Allison, John Carter, Michael McGill and Marvin Junior who first worked together as

The El Rays in 1953. In 1956 they became local heroes after a successful visit to New York where they performed 'Oh What A Night' at Harlem's Apollo Theatre.

Changing their name to The Dells in 1962, they recorded a debut single '(Bossa Nova) Bird' for the Argo label before switching to Chess Records. They toured with Dinah Washington and took session work in Chicago, providing backgrounds to recordings including 'Hello Stranger' for **Barbara Lewis** in 1963. They also toured with **Ray Charles** before returning to Chicago to record their classic soul song 'Stay In My Corner' (1968). Their one UK Top 20 hit was 'I Can Sing A Rainbow – Love Is Blue' (1969). In 1974 they recorded a joint album with **The Dramatics**, *The Dells V. The Dramatics*, continuing the liaison on 'Love Is Missing From Our Lives' from The Dells' 1975 album *We Got To Get Our Thing Together* for the Cadet label. After a brief stop with Mercury Records (*No Way Back*), they switched to ABC where *New Beginnings* featured **Al Hudson** & Soul Partners and productions by **George Clinton** (1978).

One further ABC album, *Face To Face* (1979), followed before the group worked with producers **Carl Davis**/**Eugene Record** at 20th Century for *I Touched A Dream* (1980), including 'All About The Paper', and *Whatever Turns You On* (1981), including 'Happy Song'. They later worked with writers/producers **Jackson/Yancy** on *One Step Closer* (1984). Their next album, *The Second Time*, (1988) was for the Veteran label.

DEMPSEY, JANICE

(Singer)

New York-based vocalist sang backgrounds with artists including **Najee**, **Freddie Jackson**, **John Whitehead**, **Lillo Thomas** and **Smokey Robinson**. Her own solo career got off to a false start at Geffen Records, where her debut album was not officially released. In 1990 she switched to Epic which released her **Paul Laurence**-co-produced *Thirsty* in 1990.

DEODATO, EUMIR

(Songwriter/Producer/Arranger/Keyboards)

Born in Rio de Janeiro, Deodato taught himself music as a child and in his teens was playing in pop bands. At the age of seventeen he was asked to arrange the music for an orchestral recording session, which led to a career in arranging and producing. In 1970 he arranged *Chapter Two* for **Roberta Flack** before emerging as a recording artist on the New Jersey-based label CTI Records in 1972. His debut release was '2001', a jazz fusion version of Strauss's 'Also Sprach Zarathustra' adapted for the Stanley Kubrick film. By this time he had emigrated to America, where he worked on the East Coast writing jingles for radio and TV.

At CTI he released *Prelude* (1973) and *Deodato 2* (1974), before switching to MCA where his albums included *First Cuckoo* and *Very Together* (1976), including 'Peter Gunn'. On UK dancefloors, he made his most significant impact after signing to Warner Brothers, where his first album *Love Island* (1978) included the anthemic instrumental 'Whistle Bump'. The follow-up *Night Cruiser* offered a similar anthem in the title track. His other Warner Brothers albums included *Happy Hour* (1982) and *Motion* (1984), while more recently he has recorded for Atlantic (including *Somewhere Out There*, 1989).

As a producer he was instrumental in changing the musical direction of **Kool & The Gang**, producing the group from their hit 'Ladies' Night' in 1979 onwards. He has also worked as a producer with artists including **Juicy** (*It Takes Two*), **Kleeer** ('Take Your Heart Away'), **Con Funk Shun** (*Fever*, 1983), **One Way** (*You Better Quit*, 1986) and **The Dazz Band** (*Anticipation*). As an arranger he has worked with **Aretha Franklin** (*Let Me In Your Life*), Wes Montgomery (*Down Here On The Ground*), Bette Midler and Frank Sinatra.

DESIGN

(Group)

A UK based soul/funk group, Design were Tidu Mankoo (guitar/synths/vocals), Raj Nagi (lead vocals), Raj Jagdev (bass), Biddy Mankoo (drums/percussion/vocals) and Sam Birdi (percussion/vocals). Their debut single was 'I Want You, I Need You', released by Dental Records in 1989.

DETROIT EMERALDS

(Vocal Group)

From Detroit, The Detroit Emeralds were originally James Mitchell (lead singer) and Marvin Willis, with brothers Abe Tilmon and Ivy Tilmon. In the late '60s the group recorded for the Ric Tic label, 'Show Time' being an r&b hit during this period. In the early '70s they recorded for the Janus label, 'Feel The Need' becoming an international hit in 1973 (UK Top 5). From here they signed with Westbound (via Atlantic) where UK hits followed with 'You Want It You Got It' (Top 20) and 'I Think Of You' (Top 30) the same year. 'Feel The Need' was later extended for 12″ release during the disco era, and was a UK Top 20 hit in 1977. Also in 1977 James and Marvin formed an off-shoot group **The Floaters**, while their backing band became **Chapter 8**.

Carl Johnson then replaced Abe in the original Detroit Emeralds, while Abe formed his own group of the same name. Both worked in cabaret during the late '70s and '80s. Other vocalists who have sung with the line-ups include **Jimmy Scott** and a thirteen-year-old **Michael Henderson**.

DETROIT SPINNERS

(Vocal Group)

From Detroit, Henry Famborough, Billy Henderson, Pervis Jackson, **C.P.Spencer** and Bobby Smith were friends at high school and first sang together as The Domingos in 1955. Their first professional gig was on the same bill as

The Four Ames (who later became **The Four Tops**). They changed their name in 1957 after being confused with The Flamingos and The Dominoes. In America they became The Spinners, while in the UK 'Detroit' was added to avoid confusion with the British folk group The Spinners. ('Spinners' were huge hubcaps on Cadillacs, trendy in the '50s.) In 1961 they were signed to the Tri-Phi label (owned by Gwen Gordy and **Harvey Fuqua**) before the company became part of Motown in 1964. By now the group consisted of Bobby, Pervis, Henry, Billy and Chico Edwards. Switching to the VIP subsidiary of Motown, American hits began with 'Sweet Thing' (1966), 'I'll Always Love You' (1967) and 'Truly Yours' (1967), before **G.C.Cameron** replaced Chico in 1970 and the group scored their first gold single with 'It's A Shame' (UK Top 20). At this point G.C. left to be replaced by **Phillippe Wynne** and the group left Motown.

In 1972 they signed with Atlantic on the recommendation of **Aretha Franklin**. Here they teamed up with writer/producer **Thom Bell** where the hits began rolling with 'Mighty Love', 'Could It Be I'm Falling In Love' (UK Top 20, 1973), 'Ghetto Child' (UK Top 10, 1973), 'I'll Be Around' (1973), 'Then Came You' featuring **Dionne Warwick** (UK Top 30, 1974), 'Rubberband Man' (UK Top 20, 1976), 'Wake Up Susan' (UK Top 30, 1977), 'Working My Way Back To You' (UK No. 1, 1980), and 'Body Language' (UK Top 40, 1980). Their albums during this era included *Spinners*, *New And Improved* (1975), *Happiness Is Being With The Spinners* (1976), *Mighty Love*, *Pick of The Litter*, *Can't Shake This Feeling* and *Labour of Love*.

By now **John Edwards** had joined the group, replacing Phillippe who left due to poor health. With John as lead singer they scored a further hit with the **Michael Zager**-produced medley 'Cupid – I've Loved You For A Long Time' (UK Top 5, 1980). Remaining with Atlantic the group returned in 1984 with *Cross Fire*, including 'Two Of A Kind', 'Right Or Wrong' and 'Love Is In Season' (produced by **Leon Sylvers**), and sang on the soundtrack album to the movie *Twins*. *Lovin' Feelings* followed in 1985.

In 1989 the group signed with the Fantasy-distributed Volt label for *Down To Business*, following which Atlantic remixed 'Ghetto Child' for UK release in 1990.

DEVAUGHN, WILLIAM

(Singer/Songwriter/Guitarist)

From Washington, William worked for the government as a draftsman and was a Jehovah's Witness. In 1974 he went to Philadelphia with a song he had written called 'Be Thankful For What You Got'. He recorded it with the nucleus of **M.F.S.B.** and producer **Alan Felder**; it became a Philly classic when released on the Roxbury label. Follow-ups including 'Blood Is Much Thicker Than Water', 'Give The Little Man A Great Big Hand' and 'Figures Can't Calculate' (for the Tec label) were not so popular.

DIAMOND, GREGG

(Songwriter/Producer/Keyboards)

Based in New York, Gregg emerged in the mid-'70s as a producer, initially on the jazz fusion scene with artists including Impact Of Brass on albums including *IOB* (1977) for Polydor. During the disco era of the late '70s he produced albums for his groups Star Cruiser and Bionic Boogie. 'Gregg Diamond's Star Cruiser' delivered *Star Cruiser*, including 'Starcruisin'' and 'Holding Back' for the Miami-based Marlin label (via TK) in 1978, while the same year 'Gregg Diamond's Bionic Boogie' delivered *Hot Butterfly*, featuring **Luther Vandross** as lead vocalist on the title song and 'Cream (Always Rises To the Top)'. 'Hot Butterfly' was written by Gregg and later recorded by **Chaka Khan** on *Naughty*.

Gregg stayed at Polydor for two further albums, *Tiger Tiger* (1979) and *Hardware* (1979).

DIAMOND, KEITH

(Songwriter/Producer)

Keith originally wrote and produced for UK artists including **Richard Jon Smith** ('In The Night') and **Billy Ocean** ('Caribbean Queen'), the success of which brought him work in America. Here he continued his services for artists including **Melba Moore** ('When You Love Me Like This'), **Freddie Jackson** ('Calling') and **James Ingram** (*Never Felt So Good*).

DIBANGO, MANU

(Sax)

Born in Douala, Cameroon, in 1934, Manu Dibango settled in Europe as a teenager and was a given his first saxophone as a gift from a group of Africans he worked with. He has recorded a mixture of jazz and African music since the early '50s, but is best remembered for 'Soul Makosa', originally released in 1973 and popular on the UK jazz funk scene when revamped and reissued in 1978. In 1986 he re-recorded 'Big Blow' with Bill Laswell and the group Material, also working with them on new songs including 'Abele Dance' and 'Pata Pia' for Celluloid Records (via Streetwave in the UK). He also worked with **Herbie Hancock** on 'Electric Africa' (1986).

DICKEY, GWEN

(Singer)

Gwen sang in clubs around Miami, Florida, before being discovered by members of **Undisputed Truth**. The group introduced her to their producer **Norman Whitfield** who made her lead singer of **Rose Royce**. Gwen sang all the early Rose Royce hits including 'Car Wash' (1976) and 'Wishing On A Star' (1978), later recording these hits as a solo artist in the late '80s.

DIGGS, DAVID

(Keyboards)

West Coast pianist David Diggs recorded for the Palo Alto Jazz label in the early '80s. *Realworld* (1983) featured

Paul Jackson and Larry Williams and was popular on the UK jazz funk scene. His follow-up was *Streetshadows* (1985), featuring **Dianne Reeves** and **George Howard**.

DIRECT DRIVE

(Group)

Direct Drive were Mick Ward, Robert Williams, Helen Rogers and Pete Quinton. Earlier members included **Paul Hardcastle** and **Derek Green** who left to form **First Light**. The group worked as a rhythm section called Ritual before becoming one of the pioneering 'Brit funk' bands of the early '80s. Through a music paper advert they signed to Oval Records, their debut release being a 3-track 12": 'Time Machine', 'Don't Depend On Me' and 'Take A Stand'. It was followed by a double A side 'Time's Running Out' and 'I'm The One', originally recorded as a session for Capital Radio.

Through working with **Shakatak** (after the departure of Paul and Derek), Direct Drive signed to the Passion label where they released one single 'In The Middle Of Spring'. From here they formed their own label D.D.R. to release 'Pass The Paper' and 'Anything'. The latter was licensed by Polydor, taking the group to the UK Top 75 in 1985. Later that year they reached the Top 75 again with 'A.B.C. (Falling In Love's Not Easy)'.

DOHENY, NED

(Singer/Songwriter)

From a Japanese family, Ned grew up in America where in 1978 he recorded *Prone*. The single release 'To Prove My Love' was popular on the UK dance scene, while elsewhere Ned's songs were recorded by artists including **Average White Band** ('Love's A Heartache'), **Tata Vega** ('Get It Up For Love') and **Millie Scott** ('A Love Of Your Own').

DORSEY, LEE

(Singer)

Born in New Orleans in 1927, Lee originally took a career in boxing before working in a car-repair garage. Here, while singing under a car, he was invited to record for the local Rex label, his single debut being 'Rock Pretty Baby' in 1957. His follow-up 'Little Moe' (1958) was recorded for the Valiant label, and later reissued by ABC where Lee signed to them directly. In the meantime he met producer **Allen Toussaint** and co-writer/producer Marshall Sehorn, and scored an American million-seller with 'Ya Ya' for the independent Fire label in 1961. The follow-up was 'Do-Re-Mi' (1962), but it wasn't until 1965 that he scored again with 'Ride Your Pony' followed by 'Get Out Of My Life Woman', 'Confusion', 'Working In The Coalmine' and 'Holy Cow' (1966). He also recorded duets with Betty Harris.

He recorded one album for Polydor, *Yes We Can*, including 'Everything I Do Gonnah Be Funky', before signing to ABC for one last album, *Night People* (1978). During the '80s he toured as support act for punk rock group The Clash and died from emphysema in 1986.

DOUBLE EXPOSURE

(Vocal Group)

A mid-'70s vocal group from Philadelphia, Double Exposure worked with producers **Baker/Harris/Young** (BHY) on their classic disco record 'Ten Percent' for Salsoul Records in 1976.

DOUGLAS, CAROL

(Singer)

New York-based singer capitalized on the disco scene of the mid-'70s by recording 'Doctor's Orders', a popular dancefloor record during 1976. Recording for Midsong (via RCA), she also scored with 'Midnight Love Affair' (1976) and an album *Full Bloom* (1977).

DOUGLASS, JIMMY

(Songwriter/Producer)

Based in New York, Jimmy was closely involved in the success of **Slave**, producing their finest moments including 'Just A Touch of Love' (1980). He also produced for artists including **Odyssey** ('Inside Out', 1982) and **Evelyn 'Champagne' King** ('Out Of Control', 1984).

DOWNING, AL

(Singer/Pianist)

From Texas, Al Downing recorded with the Fats Domino Band in addition to numerous small labels during the '60s and '70s. In Philadelphia he was briefly signed by V-Tone Records, while he is perhaps best remembered for his 1974 single 'I'll Be Holding On' for Chess Records. His brother is **Don Downing**.

DOWNING, DON

(Singer/Songwriter)

From Texas, Don is the brother of **Al Downing** and initially scored on the soul scene in 1973 with 'Lonely Days And Lonely Nights' (UK Top 40) for the People label. In 1978 he released *Doctor Boogie* for the RS International label which included 'Doctor Boogie', in demand in the mid-'80s on the UK 'rare groove' scene.

DOWNING, WILL

(Singer)

From New York, Will worked as a session singer before meeting producer **Arthur Baker** and singing in his group Wally Jump Jnr. When Arthur recorded 'Love Is The Message', Will was all set to be the lead singer before **Al Green** stepped in at the last minute. Signing to Island as a solo artist, Will employed Arthur to produce his debut album *Will Downing*, including 'A Love Supreme' (UK Top 20), 'In My Dreams' (UK Top 40) and 'Free' (UK Top 75) in 1988. In 1989 he recorded/produced a duet 'Where Is The Love' with **Mica Paris** and returned with a second album *Come Together As One*, including 'Test Of Time'.

His third album was the more jazz-orientated *A Dream Fulfilled* (1991) including 'The World Is A Ghetto' and 'I Try', his popularity in all cases being greater in the UK than back home in America to date.

As a session singer he has recorded with **Daryl Payne** (lead on 'I Can't Believe It's Over', 1983), **Marc Sadane**, **Warp 9** and **Jennifer Holliday** ('No Frills Love'), among others.

DOZIER, LAMONT

(Singer/Songwriter/Producer)

Born in Detroit, Michigan, in 1941, Lamont made his recording debut in 1956 with The Romeos. His school friend Ty Hunter had scored a record deal with the Anna label (via Motown), and it was Ty who introduced Lamont to **Berry Gordy**. Initially he recorded as a solo artist for the Anna and Melody Labels (as Lamont Anthony Dozier) before ultimately becoming part of **Holland/Dozier/Holland**, with whom he wrote and produced numerous classic Motown hits during the '60s.

In 1970 Holland/Dozier/Holland moved to Los Angeles to launch the Hot Wax/Invictus labels. When they recorded as an act in 1972, Lamont sang lead on 'Why Can't We Be Lovers' (UK Top 30) before the partnership came to an end and Lamont began a solo career. Signing to ABC (and later Warner Brothers), his albums include *Black Bach*, *Out Here On My Own* (1973), including 'Fish Ain't Bitin'', *Bittersweet*, *Right There* (1976), *Peddlin' Music On The Side*, *Bigger Than Life* and *Love & Beauty*. In 1977 he stirred UK dancefloors with 'Going Back To My Roots' (later a hit for **Odyssey**/F.P.I. Project), before a final Warner Brothers album *Boogie Business* in 1979. He later recorded for CBS (*Working On You*, including 'Starting Over', 1981) and A&M (*Lamont*, including 'Shout About It' and 'I Ain't Playing', 1981).

As a solo writer and/or producer, he has worked with artists including **Z.Z. Hill** (*That Ain't The Way You Make Love*, 1975), **Margie Joseph** (*Hear The Words, Feel The Feeling*, 1976), **Aretha Franklin** (*Sunshine Will Never Be The Same* and the majority of *Sweet Passion*, 1977), **Ziogara** (*I Surrender* and *Love's Calling*, 1981) and Alison Moyet ('Invisible').

His son is **Lamont Dozier Jr**, by his former wife Ann Dozier who at one time worked for Motown.

DOZIER JR, LAMONT

(Singer/Songwriter)

Born in Detroit, Lamont is the son of **Lamont Dozier** (of **Holland/Dozier/Holland**). He is currently recording solo material which he has written with his mother Ann Dozier, although to date nothing has been released. He has competed in syndicated TV shows and most recently played The Wizard in a Detroit staging of *The Wiz*.

DR STRUT

(Group)

West Coast session musicians David Woodford (sax/flute), Kevin Bassinson (keyboards), Tim Weston (guitar), Peter Freiberger (bass), Claude Pepper (drums) and Everett Bryson (percussion) teamed together for one album, *Dr Strut*, released by Motown in 1980. The instrumental album was produced by Lee Young Sr, who produced a similar set for Motown instrumentalists **Flight**.

DR YORK

(Singer/Songwriter/Producer/Musician)

From Brooklyn, Dr York began his career as a session musician around New York and Philadelphia. After recording with **Harold Melvin & The Blue Notes**, The **Delfonics** and **Evelyn 'Champagne' King** he formed his own groups Jackie and The Starlights, The Students and **Passion** as lead singer. He later launched his own Passion label, recording himself as a solo artist. His debut release was the single 'It's Only A Dream' which came from the album *New* (1985). He also teamed up with **Sarah Dash** for the duet 'It's Too Late', and recorded with **T.C.Curtis** on the Hot Melt label in the UK.

DRAMATICS

(Vocal Group)

From Detroit, The Dramatics were formed in 1962, and were originally Ron Banks, Larry Reed, Robert Ellington and Arthur Phillips. All were students at Pershing High School where they first performed together. After turning professional in 1964, Larry, Robert and Arthur were replaced by Larry 'Squirrel' Demps, Elbert Wilkins and Roderick Davis, their dance routines inspired by watching **The Contours**. Their debut single was 'Inky Dinky Wang Dang Doo', although their first American r&b success was with 'All Because Of You' released on the local Sport label in 1967. The following year **Don Davis** signed them to the Volt label (via Stax) in Memphis, Roderick being replaced by Willie Ford, while a fifth member William 'Weegee' Howard was added. (William had previously recorded one solo album for the Cotillion label.) Their initial release for Volt was 'Your Love Was Strange' which did so badly the group were dropped. Two years later they were re-signed when Don Davis put them together with producer Tony Hester.

In 1971 the group established themselves on the American charts and on the UK soul scene with 'Whatcha See Is Whatcha Get', a gold record from an album of the same name (also including 'Get Up And Get Down' and 'In The Rain'). The group toured America with **James Brown** before William and Elbert left to form a splinter group (1972), and for four years there were two groups working as The Dramatics! With Dupree Sims and Isaac Reed, Howard and Wilkins signed to Mainstream Records and had a minor American hit with 'No Rebate On Love', while the remaining members became Ron Banks & The Dramatics, adding **L.J. Reynolds** as lead singer and

Lenny Mayes. Ron's group continued to record successfully for labels including Volt (*A Dramatic Experience*, 1973, including 'Hey You! Get Off My Mountain'), Cadet, ABC (*Drama V*, 1975, including 'You're Fooling You' and 'Spaced Out Over You', 1977), and MCA (*Any Time, Any Place*, 1979, including 'Stranger In My Life').

When L.J. and Larry left in 1980, Craig Jones became a new member of Ron's group and *New Dimensions* was released by Capitol in 1982. The group temporarily disbanded in 1983, but Ron, L.J., Howard, Lenny and Willie reunited for *Positive State Of Mind*, including 'Please Say You'll Be Mine', for Volt in 1989. The follow-up was *Stone Cold* (1990).

DREAMBOY
(Group)
From Detroit, Dreamboy are Jimi Hunt (keyboards), Dewey Twymon (drums), Paul Stewart (bass), Jeff Stanton (lead vocals/keyboards/guitar) and Jeff Bass (guitar), who first worked together in 1981 as Foreplay (changing their name to Dreamboy a year later). In 1984 they released a mini-album of their own songs on a local Detroit label. This made its way to **Quincy Jones** who signed the group to his Qwest label (via Warner Brothers). An album *Contact* was released in 1985.

DRIFTERS
(Vocal Group)
The Drifters were originally formed by lead singer **Clyde McPhatter** and the group's manager George Treadwell (married to **Sarah Vaughan** at the time). Alongside Gerhard Thrasher, Andrew Thrasher and Willie Ferbee this original line-up signed to Atlantic in 1953 and released six singles (including 'Money Honey' and 'White Christmas') until Clyde left the group in 1955.

David Baughn stepped in as lead vocalist from 1956, shortly followed by Johnny Moore. The line-up included about thirty people over the next twenty years. These included **Bill Fredericks** and **Ben E.King** (with former members of his group The Crowns). In the UK hits began to roll from 1960 with 'Dance With Me' (Top 20) and 'Save The Last Dance For Me' (Top 5). These were followed by 'I Count The Tears' (Top 30, 1961), 'When My Little Girl Is Smiling' (Top 40, 1962), 'I'll Take You Home' (Top 40, 1963), 'Under The Boardwalk' (Top 50, 1964), 'At The Club' (Top 40, 1965), 'Come On Over To My Place' (Top 40, 1965), 'Baby What I Mean' (Top 50, 1967), 'Saturday Night At The Movies' (Top 5, 1972), 'Like Sister And Brother' (Top 10, 1973), 'Kissin' In The Back Row Of The Movies' (Top 5, 1974), 'Down On The Beach Tonight' (Top 10, 1975), 'There Goes My First Love' (Top 5, 1975), 'Can I Take You Home Little Girl' (Top 10, 1975) and 'You're More Than A Number In My Little Red Book' (Top 5, 1976).

As so many members had come and gone over the years, there were various legitimate and not so legitimate line-ups many calling themselves The Drifters at the same time.

DRIZA BONE
(Group)
The nucleus of London band Driza Bone are Vince Garcia and Billy Angel, who recorded an original version of their debut song 'Real Love' in 1990. It featured an anonymous female vocalist who was later replaced when the song was officially released in 1991. Billy also remixed the Alison Limerick hit 'Where Love Lives' (1991).

DUKE, DORIS
(Singer)
Born Doris Curry in Sandersville, Georgia, Doris sang with numerous gospel groups in the '50s before moving to New York in the early '60s. Here she found work as a backing singer, moving her direction into secular r&b and enjoying recording sessions with **Aretha Franklin** and **Jackie Wilson**. In 1967 she recorded briefly as Doris Willingham before hooking up with producer Swamp Dogg as Doris Duke for an album *I'm A Loser*, including 'To The Other Woman (I'm The Other Woman)' which was an American r&b hit in 1970 (released by Canyon). Her next album was *A Legend In Her Own Time*, released by Mankind Records. She then came to England and recorded for the Contempo label.

DUKE, GEORGE
(Singer/Keyboards/Songwriter/Producer)
Born in San Raphael, California, in 1946, George was aged four when musically inspired by a Duke Ellington concert. Taking up the piano shortly afterwards, he had turned professional before he left high school. He played in a rock group before joining a Latin band called Jaxx Co-Op. Moving to San Francisco, he led a resident jazz trio at a local nightclub while studying at the San Francisco Conservatory where he majored in trombone and composition. He spent three years touring as pianist with **Al Jarreau** before discovering the electric piano and working with Jean-Luc Ponty. Overheard by Frank Zappa in 1969, George was invited to join The Mothers Of Invention. In 1970 he replaced Joe Zawinul in Cannonball Adderly's band, rejoining Mothers Of Invention in 1972, when Frank Zappa encouraged George to develop his vocals and work with synthesizers. This he did, primarily as a session player while forming the Cobham/Duke Band with **Billy Cobham** and signing to Atlantic for *Funky Side Of Things* and *Life And Times*.

By the mid-'70s he had signed with the MPS label where his albums were *The Aura Will Prevail* (1975) and *Liberated Fantasies* (1976) before he switched to Epic and began to make an impact on what was to become the UK jazz-funk scene. His Epic albums included *From Me To You* (1977), including 'Scuse Me Miss'; *Reach For It* (1977); *Don't Let Go* (1978); *Follow The Rainbow* (1979), including 'Party Down' and 'Say That You Will'; *Master*

Of The Game (1979), including 'I Want You For Myself'; *A Brazilian Love Affair* (1980), the title track being a UK Top 40 hit; *Dream On* (1982); *Guardian Of Light* (1983); and *Rendezvous* (1984). Also at Epic he recorded with **Stanley Clarke** as the Clarke/Duke Project on three albums. In 1985 he switched to Elektra for *Thief In The Night* (1985) and *George Duke* (1986).

As a producer he has worked consistently through the '70s and '80s with artists including **Flora Purim** (*Carry On*, 1979), **Dee Dee Bridgewater** (*Bad For Me*, 1979), **The Blackbyrds** (*Better Days*, 1980), **Jeffrey Osborne** (*Jeffrey Osborne*, 1982, *Stay With Me Tonight*, 1983 and *Don't Stop*, 1984), **Rufus** ('Take It To The Top), **Raul De Souza** (*Sweet Lucy* and *Don't Ask My Neighbours*), **Deniece Williams** (*I'm So Proud*, 1983, and 'Let's Hear It For The Boy', 1984), **Angela Bofill** (*Tell Me Tomorrow*, 1985), **Seawind**, **Howard Hewett**, **Larry Graham**, **Smokey Robinson**, **Sister Sledge** ('Smile'), **Stephanie Mills** and **101 North**.

As a session player he has recorded with numerous artists including **Sarah Vaughan**, **Aretha Franklin**, **Quincy Jones**, **T-Connection**, **Airto** and **The Whispers**. He has also written a movie soundtrack, *The Heavenly Kid*, and a three-part opera which he hopes a record company will release one day along with music for a ballet that he wants to compose.

DUKES
(Duo)
Male vocal duo The Dukes signed to WEA in the early '80s and made an impression on the UK soul scene with their classy single 'Mystery Girl' (Top 50, 1981), one of the best British soul productions there had been up to this point. Their follow-up was 'Thank You For The Party' (Top 75, 1982).

DUNBAR, ERNESTA
(Singer)
Philadelphia-based singer recorded one album *Ernesta Dunbar* for the local World Records label (1986). The album included 'Checking Out', popular on the UK soul scene and released here by Streetwave Records.

DUNCAN, CELENA
(Singer)
Born in London, Celena made her recording debut at thirteen before presenting her own TV show *Celena & Friends* and appearing in the series *Angels*. At the age of sixteen she played Dorothy in *The Wiz* (Crucible Theatre, Sheffield) and later Mary Magdalene in a stage version of *Jesus Christ Superstar*. She also recorded 'Shine On' with Bucks Fizz producer Andy Hill, which became a popular dance record in the mid-'70s.

From here she went to New York and worked with **Odyssey**'s producer Sandy Linzer together with Steve Levine on a song called 'I Want Your Love Back'. She also recorded for the RCA and Nightmare labels.

DUNCAN, DARRYL
(Singer/Songwriter/Producer)
Born in Chicago in 1963, Darryl was bought an organ by his parents when he was nine, but fell in love with the piano by the time he was a teenager. At high school he joined a band called Cashmere (not to be confused with the Philly group) and after performing around Chicago for four years left to develop his own songwriting skills. After building up a catalogue of songs he landed a job as staff writer at A&M Records. This moved him to Los Angeles where he also found work for artists including **Maurice White**, **Chaka Khan** and **Michael Jeffries** (co-writing 'We Loved') before Motown signed him as an artist in 1988 and released his self-written/arranged/produced debut *Heaven*.

As a producer, Darryl has also worked with **Billy Always**, **E.U.** (writing 'I Confess') and **Sarah Dash** (writing 'Feel Good').

DUNLAP, GENE
(Drummer)
Born in Detroit, Gene began to play the drums from the age of four although his first job was in a music store. While still at school he met **Earl Klugh** with whom he formed a group. By the mid-'70s Gene was playing drums for Earl professionally, Earl also helping to secure Gene a solo recording deal with Capitol in the early '80s. His three albums were *It's Just The Way I Feel* (1981), including 'Before You Break My Heart'; *Party In Me* (1982) and *Tired Of Being A Nice Guy* (1983). He also played drums with **Roy Ayers** on *Don't Stop The Feeling*.

DUNN, LARRY
(Producer/Keyboards)
Larry has played an integral part in the group **Earth Wind & Fire** over the years, in addition to his work as a producer and musician with artists including **Ronnie Laws**, **Caldera** and **Stanley Turrentine**.

DYKE, EARL VAN
(Keyboards)
Born in Detroit, Earl Van Dyke was employed by Motown during the late '60s and early '70s as pianist and music director on tours with most of the label's top acts. From 1962 to 1972 he was instrumental in shaping the 'Motown sound', and released the albums *That Motown Sound* and *The Earl Of Funk* on the label's Soul subsidiary. Six solo singles were also released on the label, 'Too Many Fish In The Sea' and 'Six By Six' being particularly popular. He also recorded with **C.J.& Co**, **R.J.'s Latest Arrival**, **Lenny Williams**, **Terry Callier**, **Ruby Andrews** and numerous other artists away from Motown. In 1989 he began recording with UK writer/producer **Ian Levine** for the Nightmare/Motorcity labels, 'Detroit City' being his first release.

DYNASTY
(Group)
Instigated by Solar Records label boss Dick Griffey and producer **Leon Sylvers** in Los Angeles, Dynasty were Kevin Spencer (bass), Nidra Beard and Linda Carriere. Their debut album *Your Piece Of The Rock* included the dance classic 'I Don't Want To Be A Freak (But I Can't Help Myself)', a UK Top 20 hit in 1979. The follow-ups were *Adventures In The Land Of Music* (1980) and *The Second Adventure* (1981), including 'Love In The Fast Lane'.

DYSON, RONNIE
(Singer)
Born in Washington in 1950, Ronnie grew up in Brooklyn and took to gospel music in his early years. In 1968 he landed a part in the Broadway musical *Hair*, which eventually led to a recording deal with CBS Records. His debut single 'If You Let Me Make Love To You' (1970) was an American hit. In 1971 he made his one UK chart entry with a Top 40 single 'When You Get Right Down To It'. His other American hits included 'Why Can't I Touch You', 'The More You Do It', 'Don't Be Afraid', 'I Think I'll Tell Her', 'One Man Band (Plays All Alone)' and 'I Just Don't Want To Be Lonely' (later a hit for **The Main Ingredient**). In 1974 he toured the UK as support for **The Supremes**, and teamed up with **The Trammps** in 1975, who produced 'Lady In Red' for him. All his recordings up to this point were made in Philadelphia.

In 1976 he switched producers to **Chuck Jackson/Marvin Yancy** and scored a hit 'The More You Do It' (also the name of his album that year, which featured 'A Song For You'). Further CBS albums, *Love In All Flavours* (1977) and *If The Shoe Fits* (1979) followed before a return to Philadelphia. Here, in 1981, he worked with **Bobbi Eli** on a Cotillion album *Phase 2* (including 'Heart To Heart'), and in 1983 **Butch Ingram** brought him success on the dancefloors with 'All Over Your Face', also for the Cotillion label.

Before his next recording, Ronnie appeared in the film version of *Hair* and starred in a further film, *Putney Swope*. In 1989 he teamed up with **Thomas & Taylor** for 'See The Clown', released in the UK by Ardent Records in 1990. He died of a heart attack later that year.

E., SHEILA
(Vocals/Percussion)
The daughter of percussionist **Pete Escovedo**, Sheila was discouraged from taking up percussion by her father who had spent years struggling in the business. Instead she was made to take up the violin and play football (which she did for eight years!). At the age of fifteen she joined her father's group Azteca while they rehearsed at home. When the group's percussionist went sick one night, Sheila persuaded her father to let her take over at a date in San Francisco in front of an audience of 8,000 people. The experience hooked her on percussion and a music career for life.

In 1977 she recorded the first of two albums with her father, *Solo Two*, then *Happy Together* in 1978. Both were released as by Pete and Sheila Escovedo and featured **Mark Soskin**, **Bill Summers** and **Willie Colon**, and were produced by **Billy Cobham**. Proceeding to session work, Sheila toured and/or recorded with **Jeffrey Osborne**, **The Crusaders**, **Herbie Hancock**, **Diana Ross**, **Marvin Gaye**, **Bill Summers**, **Johnny Hammond**, **The Blackbyrds**, **Flora Purim**, **Dee Dee Bridgewater** and **George Duke**. She took up singing after deciding it would be difficult to be successful playing only percussion.

When **Prince** invited her to work on the *Purple Rain* soundtrack, they discussed a Sheila E. solo project. Prince shortly found her a manager through the Starr Company (which also managed **The Time** and **Vanity 6**), and helped her sign to Warner Brothers. He has also been closely involved in her albums *The Glamorous Life* (1984), *Romance 1600* (1985), including 'A Love Bizarre', and *Sheila E.* (1987). In the UK, 'The Belle Of St Mark' reached the UK Top 20 in 1985.

E.U.
(Group)
Experience Unlimited, as they were originally known, were formed in Washington during 1970. They met as teenagers at Ballou High School and first played together at Valley Green Community Center. In 1973 they worked with Maxx Kidd and released a debut single 'Hey You', following which they signed to Maxx's T.T.E.D. label. In 1975 the group opened their own record shop, The E.U. House Of Peace, and by 1978 they were firmly established on the Washington go-go music scene. The same year they recorded their debut, self-titled album. Under the leadership of Gregory 'Sugar Bear' Elliot the group underwent a slight change of line-up before releasing singles 'Rock Yer Butt', 'E.U. Freeze', and 'Knock Him Out Sugar Ray' (all in 1979). Two albums followed, *E.U. Just The Way You Like It* (1979) and *Future Funk* 1980.

In 1981 **Kurtis Blow** heard an E.U. record in a nightclub, and decided to collaborate with them on 'Party Time', very popular on the British go-go music scene (and a UK Top 60 hit) in 1985. In 1987 E.U. shot to prominence on the UK dance scene with 'Da Butt', a **Marcus Miller**-produced song featured in Spike Lee's film *School Daze*. In 1988 the group hit the UK Top 25 as guests of Salt 'N' Pepa on 'Shake Your Thang (It's Your Thing)'. The following year a debut Virgin album, *Livin' Large*, featured a 1989 remix of 'Da Butt' alongside a ballad 'Taste Of Your Love' which won acclaim with UK soul fans. Their most recent album *Cold Kickin' It* (including 'I Confess') was released in 1990.

EAGER, BRENDA LEE
(Singer/Songwriter)
Based in Los Angeles, Brenda originally sang in a group of backing singers, Peaches, formed by **Jerry Butler**. In addition to touring with Jerry, Brenda co-sang his million-selling American hit duet 'Ain't Understanding Mellow' (1971), while elsewhere she has recorded backgrounds with **Grey & Hanks**, **Smokey Robinson**, **C.J. Anthony** and **Bobby Womack**. In 1984 she recorded a single 'Watch My Body Talk' for the Private I label (via Epic), and later co-wrote 'Why You Wanna Love Me Like That' for **The Manhattans** and songs for group 3 For 3 (guesting as vocalist on the group's 'My Beloved' in 1990).

EARLAND, CHARLES
(Keyboards/Sax)
Born in Philadelphia, Charles preferred to study the saxophone even though his mother was a pianist. At the age of sixteen he played his first professional gig with Pancho Villa, a bandleader who had a jazz background playing with **George Duke** and **Herbie Hancock**. His next major

engagement was with organist **Jimmy McGriff** for whom he played sax until Jimmy convinced him he was a talented organist and should change his instrument. Having done this Charles soon landed a recording contract, his debut album being *Black Talk* for the Prestige label in the early '70s. By now he was experimenting with jazz fusion, and put together an ensemble of similar-minded musicians who played together as Charles Earland And Odyssey. In 1976 the group recorded *Odyssey* for Mercury, and immediately won acclaim on the UK jazz funk scene with the album's strongest track 'Intergalactic Love Song'. Next came *The Great Pyramid* (1976) and *Revelation* (1977), further exploring his fusion direction, both highly acclaimed and collectable.

Charles's greatest solo success came in 1978 when he teamed up with **Brass Construction**'s **Randy Muller** who produced his next Mercury album *Perceptions*. Featuring the vocals of **New York Skyy**, the album's single release 'Let The Music Play' became a huge jazz funk anthem on UK dancefloors, also making the UK Top 50. From here Charles changed labels to CBS for *Coming To You Live* (1980). The title track proved popular with UK dance audiences but not on the same scale as the previous hit. In 1982 he teamed up with **Cameo**'s **Larry Blackmon** for 'The Only One' (from *Earland's Jam*), by which time virtually all jazz elements had disappeared from his music.

In early 1983 he returned with a final CBS album *Street Themes*. Later that year he made a surprising record, 'Doggie Boogie Baby' (US Strut 12"), which made a big impact on the emerging electro dance scene. It was released in the UK by MCA but didn't chart.

EARTH WIND & FIRE

(Group)

Founded by **Maurice White** in 1970, this supergroup were originally known as The Salty Peppers and had two single hits, 'La La Time' and 'Love Is Life', in their Chicago hometown before becoming Earth Wind & Fire. Signing to Warner Brothers in 1971, the original line-up was Maurice White (drums/percussion/kalimba/vocals), brother Verdine White (bass), Wade Flemons (vocals), Don Whitehead (keyboards/vocals), Sherry Scott (vocals), Michael Beal (guitar/harmonica), Yackov Ben Israel (percussion), Chet Washington (sax) and Alex Thomas (trombone). On 1971's *The Need Of Love*, guest musicians were **Oscar Brashear**, **Doug** and **Jean Carne** before their switch to CBS in 1972 and a change in line-up to Maurice, Verdine (bass), **Philip Bailey** (vocals), **Larry Dunn** (keyboards), Ralph Johnson (drums), **Ronnie Laws** (sax) and Roland Bautista (guitar). By now the group had settled in Los Angeles.

Their debut CBS album was *Last Days And Time* (1972), following which **Al McKay** (guitar) replaced Roland Bautista, Andrew Woolfolk (sax) replaced Ronnie Laws and Johnny Graham was added on guitar. Their next albums were *Head To The Sky* (1973), *Open Our Eyes* (1974) and *That's The Way Of The World* (1975), by which time Maurice's brother Fred White had taken over as drummer. After forming Kalimba Productions in 1976 (still via CBS), Maurice produced a string of hit singles for the group: 'Saturday Night' (Top 20, 1977), 'Fantasy' (Top 20, 1978), 'Jupiter' (Top 50, 1978), 'Magic Mind' (Top 75, 1978), 'Got To Get You Into My Life' (Top 40, 1978), 'September' (Top 5, 1978), 'Boogie Wonderland' with **The Emotions**, the first non-limited edition 12" single issued by CBS in the UK (Top 5, 1979), 'After The Love Has Gone' (Top 5, 1979), 'Star' (Top 20, 1979), 'Can't Let Go' (Top 50, 1979), 'In The Stone' (Top 75, 1980), 'Let Me Talk' (Top 30, 1980), 'Back On The Road' (Top 75, 1980), 'Let's Groove' (Top 5, 1981) and 'I've Had Enough' (Top 30, 1982). Albums during this period included *Spirit* (1976), *All 'N' All* (1977), *I Am* (1979), *Faces* (1980) and *Raise* (1981). In the meantime their stage shows had grown to incorporate magic, visual illusions and an array of impressive special effects.

1983's *Powerlight*, including 'Fall In Love With Me' (UK Top 50), failed to meet with the usual euphoria, and the group took a few years off to concentrate on other ventures. Both **Maurice White** and **Philip Bailey** recorded solo albums while **Al McKay** and Ralph Johnson worked as producers before the group returned to the studio for *Touch The World* (1987), including 'System Of Survival' (UK Top 75) and 'Thinking Of You'. Their most recent album was *Heritage* (1990), featuring **M.C. Hammer**.

EARTHLINE CONNECTION

(Group)

From New Cross, South London, Earthline Connection were a soul/funk group consisting of Rudy François (guitars), Teddy Trevor Ashaye (vocals/percussion), Elson Charles (bass/rhythm guitars), Albert Loren (sax) Peter Regis (sax), Michael Parkinson (drums/percussion), Dean Mark Edwards (songwriter) and Michael Matovu (keyboards/vocals).

EASTBOUND EXPRESSWAY

(Studio Group)

The concept of writer/producer **Ian Levine**, Eastbound Expressway made an impact on the disco scene with singles 'Danger Zone' (1976), 'Cloudburst' (1977) and 'Never Let Go' (1977), and an album *Eastbound Expressway*, including 'Better Look Before You Leap'. In 1983 Ian reformed the group with partner Fiachra Trench for 'Primitive Desire', a 'high energy' dance hit in the UK and a Top 10 hit in Holland. The group's next single 'Frantic Love' was used as the theme tune to UK Channel 4's pop programme *Earsay*, and in 1986 the group released 'You're A Beat', a 'Eurobeat' anthem.

The group's line-up changed frequently, but for a tour consisted of vocalists Bonnie Anderson (formerly with Skin On Skin), Karen Freeman and Jocelyn Phillips.

EASTMOND, BARRY J.
(Songwriter/Arranger/Producer)
Barry initially worked as an arranger on the Philly music scene during the early '80s. After rhythm arrangements for artists including **The O'Jays** he settled in New York where he has worked as producer with numerous artists including **Jonathan Butler** (*Jonathan Butler*, 1977), **Najee**, **The Controllers** ('Stay'), **Billy Ocean** (co-writing 'When The Going Gets Tough' and 'Love Zone'), **Glenn Jones**, **George Benson**, **Howard Hewett/Anita Baker** (*When Will It Be*, 1990) and **Regina Belle** (co-writing *All Our Love*).

EASTSIDE CONNECTION
(Group)
Seven-guy one-girl group scored with one disco hit 'You're So Right For Me' in 1977. Released in the States on the Rampart label (on multi-colour vinyl), in the UK it was available on the Creole label where it was a Top 50 hit in 1978.

EASY PIECES
(Group)
Easy Pieces, derived from the **Average White Band** in the mid-80s, consisted of **Hamish Stuart** (vocals/guitar), **Steve Ferrone** (drums), Anthony Jackson (bass) and Renee Geyer (vocals). In 1988 they released an album *Easy Pieces* for A&M, co-produced by **Hawk Wolinski** of **Rufus**. **Neil Larsen** and Randy Brecker (see **Brecker Brothers**) also played on the album.

EATON, CLEVELAND
(Bass/Songwriter/Producer)
Born in Chicago, Cleveland replaced Eldee Young as bass player with **Ramsey Lewis** in 1965 before forming his own record label Cle-An-Thair. Here he released 'It's Mookie Time' and 'I Feel Trouble On Its Way Again' as Cleveland Eaton & The Kats. His album *Half & Half* for Cle-An-Thair was later reissued on the Philly-based Gamble label owned by **Kenny Gamble**. With the popularity of jazz fusion increasing he switched to this style for *The Eaton Menu, Plenty Good Eaton* (1975), including 'Chi-Town Theme', on the Black Jazz label before switching to Ovation records in 1976 for *Instant Hip*, including his dance classic 'Bama Boogie Woogie'. *Keep Love Alive*, including the UK single 'Birmingham Train', was released in 1978. More recently Cleveland has recorded with **George Benson** (1990).

EAVES, HUBERT
(Songwriter/Arranger/Producer)
Based in New York, Hubert Eaves played keyboards with **Gary Bartz** in his group Ntu Troop (recording with them for Prestige Records) prior to becoming prominent as a writer and/or arranger for artists including **Stephanie Mills** ('Sweet Sensations'), **Roberta Flack/Donny Hathaway** ('Back Together Again'), **Phyllis Hyman**, **Norman Connors**, **Pharaoh Sanders** and productions for **Mtume/Lucas** from the mid-'70s.

His son is drummer/bass player Hubert Eaves Jr, who went to the same school as **James 'D-Train' Williams**. Hubert Jr persuaded Hubert Sr to help James launch his career, and after 'D-Train' signed with Prelude Records, Hubert Sr co-wrote/produced his debut release 'You're The One For Me' (1982). From here he wrote and/or produced for artists including **The Strangers** ('Step Out Of My Dream'), **Miles Jaye** ('Let's Start Love Over'), **Luther Vandross** ('She Won't Talk To Me'), **Whitney Houston** ('Who Do You Love'), **Cheryl Lynn** ('Let Me Love You'), **Genobia Jeter**, **Stacy Lattisaw** and **Phyllis Hyman** ('Children Of The World').

EBONY BROTHERS
(Group)
London dancers/singers Tony and Pinky teamed up for the Phil Harding-produced 'Brighten Up Your Night' for RCA Records in 1983. Tony and Pinky were also in-house dancers for the UK TV show *Top Of The Pops* during the early '80s.

EBONY RHYTHM FUNK CAMPAIGN
(Group)
From Chicago, Ebony Rhythm Funk Campaign were Pamela 'Doyle' Tanner and Tony 'Fast Black' Roberts (vocals), Lester 'Lammy' Johnson (bass), Dwayne 'Buzzard' Garvin (drums), Lloyd 'T.J.' Jones (guitar), Michael 'Corleone' Woods and George 'Butch' Dennie (keyboards), and Henry 'Du Du' Miles (sax). In 1975 they recorded 'How's Your Wife (And My Child)', for the Innovation II label (via EMI in the UK), releasing a **Carl Davis**-produced album *Watching You, Watching Me* for Chi-Sound (also via EMI) in 1976. The group's music direction was in the care of **Sonny Sanders**. Don Myrock (sax) from **Earth Wind & Fire** recorded with the group on their album.

EBONYS
(Vocal Group)
From Camden, New Jersey, The Ebonys were Clarence Vaughn, James Tuten, David Beasley and Jenny Holmes who formed in the late '60s. While singing together in a local nightclub they were spotted by **Gamble/Huff** who signed them to their Philadelphia International label in 1971. Here a debut single release 'You're The Reason Why' became the label's first American hit, although their follow-ups did not do as well. In 1973 they recorded their one album *The Ebonys*, a Gamble/Huff production which included the Philly ballad classic 'It's Forever'.

ECKSTINE, BILLY
(Singer)
Billy Eckstine was a forerunner of the black music singers from the 60s onwards, and was scoring million-sellers in the mid-'40s with songs including 'Prisoner Of Love' (later

recorded by **James Brown**). He later recorded for labels including Motown, Stax and A&M, the latter liaison being 'The Best Thing', produced by **Quincy Jones** and **Herb Alpert** in 1976. He also recorded a series of duets with **Sarah Vaughan**.

More recently (1990) he has worked with songwriter/producer **Ian Levine** on the UK-based Motorcity label (including duets with **Susaye Green**).

ECSTASY, PASSION & PAIN
(Group)
Formed in Philadelphia in 1973, Ecstasy, Passion & Pain consisted of **Barbara Roy** (lead vocals/guitar), Althea Smith (drums/vocals), Carl Jordan (percussion), Joseph Williams (bass), Jimmy Clark (guitar/vocals) and **Ronnie Foster** (keyboards). Recording with top Philly musicians including **Norman Harris**, **Bobby Eli**, **Earl Young** and **Vince Montana**, their albums for Roulette Records (via PRT in the UK) included *Ecstasy Passion & Pain* (1974).

EDWARDS, ALTON
(Singer/Songwriter)
From Zimbabwe, Alton moved to Zurich in 1978 and then to London in 1981 where he had the one solo hit single 'I Just Wanna Spend Some Time With You' (UK Top 20) on the Streetwave label (via Epic). Prior to that he performed with South African groups Sabu and Unity, and spent some time developing his own style in Los Angeles with former Motown producer **Clay McMurray**.

EDWARDS, CANDYE
(Singer)
Born in Detroit, Candye is the daughter of Lee 'Toni Wallace' Clark who sang as an Ikette with **Ike & Tina Turner**. In 1981 she became a member of the group **One Way** and married group member **Kevin McCord**. With One Way Candye sang lead on the song 'Lady You Are'.

Kevin later wrote and produced solo songs for Candye on both MCA Records (*Lady*, 1985), and Presents Records (*Candye Right Now*, including 'Right Now', 1986).

EDWARDS, DEE
(Singer)
This Detroit-based singer recorded for labels including Deto ('I Can Deal With That') and Cotillion (*Heavy Love*) during the '70s without making a major impression on the UK soul scene.

EDWARDS, DENNIS
(Singer/Keyboards)
Born in Birmingham, Alabama, in 1943, Dennis was seven when he moved with his family to Detroit. During his high-school days he sang with gospel group The Crowns Of Joy before forming a jazz ensemble Dennis Edwards & The Firebirds inspired by the music of Richard 'Groove' Holmes. Out performing one night he met James Jamerson, session bass player with Motown who suggested Dennis audition as a solo artist for the label. Motown, however, needed a lead singer for **The Contours**, and Dennis became their lead singer on songs including 'It's So Hard Being Alone'.

He also recorded a solo single 'I Didn't Have To (But I Did)' for the International Soulsville label, but put his solo career on hold after replacing **David Ruffin** as lead singer of **The Temptations** in 1968. Here he maintained the group's chart success with songs including 'Cloud Nine' and a total of over thirty albums with the classic Motown group. In 1977 he temporarily left the group, but returned in 1979 only to leave again in 1983.

Gordy records (via Motown) eventually signed Dennis as a solo artist in 1984 where he worked with producer Dennis Lambert (who had produced Dennis on 'Love On My Mind' with **The Temptations**). There were two albums for Gordy, *Don't Look Any Further* (1984), including the title track hit featuring **Siedah Garrett** (UK Top 50), and *Coolin' Out* (1985), before he rejoined **The Temptations** again for a brief period in 1987.

More recently he has worked with **David Ruffin** and **Eddie Kendricks** as a third of Ruffin/Kendricks/Edwards, although as yet they haven't recorded together.

EDWARDS, GREG
(Disc Jockey)
One of the pioneers of the soul scene in the UK, Greg (alongside Robbie Vincent and Chris Hill) was primarily responsible for the UK's jazz funk & soul scene from the mid-'70s with a highly influential London-based radio programme. Greg also recorded a rap on 'My Minds Made Up' for **Ambassadors Of Funk**.

EDWARDS, JOHN
(Singer)
Born in St Louis, Missouri, in 1944, John first pursued his interest in singing while in the army during the early '60s. From 1963 he sang in army men's clubs in Germany before proceeding to a series of talent contests. Back in the States he settled in Columbus, Georgia (performing once with **Wilson Pickett**), before a series of dates in Chicago introduced him to **Curtis Mayfield** in 1968. It was through Curtis that John recorded for Weis Records, his debut release being 'If I Don't Lose My Head', produced by **Jo Armstead** in 1969. Jo continued to co-write and produce John's releases, these including 'There'll Never Be Another Woman' (Weis, 1970), and 'One More Time' (Twin Stacks Records, 1971), before a switch to Bell Records in 1972. Here he recorded 'The Look On Your Face' (written/co-produced by **Floyd Smith**) before another change of label to Aware in 1973. Again with producer Floyd Smith he released an album *John Edwards*, from which the single 'Messing Up A Good Thing' remains popular with UK soul fans.

Following the demise of the Aware label, John worked briefly with **The Detroit Spinners** in 1973, eventually joining the group full-time in 1977. In 1976 he had recorded one further solo album, *Life Love and Living*, released on the Cotillion subsidiary of Atlantic.

EDWARDS, REO

(Producer)

One of the founders of go-go music in Washington DC, Reo managed and produced for the group **Trouble Funk**, nurturing the sound with late '70s releases including 'Arcade Funk Tilt' and 'Drop The Bomb'. Also as a producer he worked with **Chuck Brown** & The Soul Searchers on 'We Need Some Money'.

8TH DAY

(Group)

Originally from Detroit, 8th Day were formed by Tyrone 'Ty' Douglas and Virginia 'Vee' McDonald. Ty had previously played trumpet on recording sessions for Motown while Vee had a classical piano background. The couple moved to Los Angeles in the early '70s and extended the group to incorporate Barrington 'Bo' Henderson, Denzel Broomfield, **Steve Mancha** and Adrienne Robinson. At Motown, Ty had worked with **Holland/Dozier/Holland** who by now had their own Invictus label in Los Angeles. It was here 8th Day signed in the mid-'70s where they scored an American hit with 'She's Not Just Another Woman'. Their albums included *8th Day.*

EIGHTIES LADIES

(Vocal Group)

Instigated by **Roy Ayers**, The Eighties Ladies featured the lead vocals of **Sylvia Striplin** on their one album for Roy's Uno Melodic label, *Ladies Of The Eighties* (1981), including 'Turned On To You'.

EL CHICANO

(Group)

Featuring songwriter/producer Aaron Ballesteros, El Chicano made an impression on the American r&b scene during the '70s. In 1984 they signed to CBS and stirred UK dancefloors with singles 'Do You Want Me' and 'Let Me Dance With You' (via Streetwave).

EL COCO

(Instrumentalist)

Multi-instrumentalist El Coco worked with producers **Rinder & Lewis** during the late '70s for AVI Records in Los Angeles. During this time two instrumentals, 'Cocomotion' (1977) and 'Let's Get It Together' (1980), became anthems on the UK dance scene.

ELBERT, DONNIE

(Singer)

Based in Chicago, Donnie originally recorded for the De Luxe label and scored American r&b success with 'What Can I Do?' (1957) before he switched to Vee-Jay Records for further success with 'Will You Ever Be Mine'. From here he joined the army, but returned in 1961 to record for a number of independent labels before launching his own Gateway label in 1964. He cut a string of American r&b hits including 'Run Little Girl', 'You Can Push It Or Pull It' and 'A Little Piece Of Leather' (the latter establishing Donnie on the UK soul scene). From here he moved to the UK where he settled until 1970, marrying an English lady and recording an album of **Otis Redding** cover versions for Polydor. Back in America he scored further hits with 'Can't Get Over Losing You', and remakes of 'Where Did Our Love Go' and 'I Can't Help Myself', his most recent success (1972).

ELECTRIK FUNK

(Studio Group)

Electric Funk were a studio project instigated by writers/producers **Eric Matthew** and **Darryl Payne** for Prelude Records (via Epic in UK) in New York. Making an impact on the early '80s 'electro' scene, their singles included 'On A Journey (I Sing The Funk Electric)' in 1982.

ELGINS

(Group)

Detroit group The Elgins were originally **Johnny Dawson**, Norman McLean, Jimmy Charles and Saundra Edwards, Saundra was later replaced by **Yvonne Allen**. The guys were originally known as The Sensations, the name with which they recorded American r&b hits 'Uncle Sam's Man', 'Music, Music, Music' and 'Let Me In' on the Flip label. They also briefly recorded with The Five Emeralds for the State label. They became The Elgins after joining Motown, the name having once been used by **The Temptations**. It was Berry Gordy's idea that they have a female vocalist. Their biggest hit was 'Heaven Must Have Sent You', originally released in 1966 (UK No. 3, 1971, following a live tour). The song was a hit for the second time in 1979 recorded by **Bonnie Pointer**, and the group recorded it again themselves in the style of the Pointer version in 1989.

Their only other American hit was 'Darling Baby'; in the UK 'Put Yourself In My Place' was a follow-up hit (Top 30, 1971), although the group had already been dropped from Motown by June 1967. In 1988 the group re-formed to record for the Motorcity label, *Take The Train* being released in 1990.

ELI, BOBBY

(Songwriter/Producer/Guitar)

Born in Philadelphia, Bobby has been an integral part of the Philly black music scene since the '60s, but particularly during the '70s and early '80s as a session guitarist, songwriter and producer. Most people assume him to be black, although he is in fact white! As writer and/or producer he has worked with artists including **Major Harris** ('Love Won't Let Me Wait', 1974), **Blue Magic** ('Sideshow'), **Brenda And The Tabulations** ('Let's

Go All The Way Down'), **Booker Newberry III** ('Love Town'), **Ronnie Dyson** ('Heart To Heart'), **Atlantic Starr** (*Straight To The Point*), **Gavin Christopher** ('We're In Love'), **Joanna Gardner** ('I Could Never Love Another Like You'), **Jean Carne** ('Givin' Up On Love') and **Jackie Moore** ('This Time Baby'). His guitar sessions are far too numerous to mention.

ELLIMAN, YVONNE
(Singer)
'70s singer Yvonne Elliman first hit the UK charts in 1972 on MCA Records with 'I Don't Know How To Love Him', released back to back with 'Superstar' by Murray Head. In 1976 she switched to RSO (via Polydor) where she worked with the Gibb Brothers (of the **Bee Gees**) during the *Saturday Night Fever*/disco era. During this time the group wrote and/or produced her hits including 'Love Me' (UK Top 10, 1976), 'Hello Stranger' (UK Top 30, 1977), 'I Can't Get You Out Of My Mind' (UK Top 20) and 'If I Can't Have You' (UK Top 5, 1978). 'Love Me' was re-released in 1991 due to popular demand.

ELLINGTON, LANCE
(Singer)
Lance is the son of English bandleader Ray Ellington who was prolific on radio during the '50s and '60s (on programmes including *The Goon Show*). Lance initially worked with the National Youth Jazz Orchestra before becoming one half of the cabaret act Koffee 'n' Creme. In the meantime he established himself as a top session singer and recorded with artists including **Tina Turner**, **Al Green**, **Deniece Williams**, **Terence Trent D'Arby** and **Johnny Gill**, before A&M Records signed him as a solo artist. His debut album was *Pleasure and Pain* (1990).

ELLISON, LORRAINE
(Singer/Songwriter)
From Philadelphia, Lorraine sang gospel before fronting **The Golden Chords** and The Ellington Sisters. Under the management of **Sam Bell** she signed with Mercury in 1965, and released 'I Dig You Baby' (written by Sam) followed by 'Call Me Anytime You Need Some Lovin''. In 1967 she signed with Loma (via Warner Brothers), and got a break when Frank Sinatra cancelled a studio appointment leaving a whole orchestra standing. Lorraine was called in at the last minute and used the session to lay down 'Stay With Me', regarded today as a soul classic though not a big hit at the time. She released an album *Heart And Soul* that year. She remained at the Loma label for 'Heart Be Still', 'I Want To Be Loved', 'Try Just A Little Bit Harder' and the album *Stay With Me* (1969) before *Lorraine Ellison* was released by Warner Brothers in 1974. With Sam Bell she also wrote songs for **Garnet Mims** and **Howard Tate**.

ELLISON, WILLIE JOHN
(Singer/Songwriter/Guitarist/Producer)
Born in Montgomery, West Virginia, Willie was the lead singer of '60s group **The Soul Brothers Six** which he reformed in the '70s after moving to Ontario, Canada. After the group eventually disbanded in 1977 Willie moved to the UK where he recorded a version of 'Wild World' (the Cat Stevens song) for Red Bus Records.

He was later approached by **Choker Campbell** who was launching his own Campo label. Here Willie recorded a single 'I Don't Just Want Your Body' in 1989.

EMOTIONS
(Vocal Group)
From Chicago, The Emotions are primarily a sister group comprising Wanda, Sheila, Pamela and Jeanette Hutchinson, although Wanda and Sheila have been the only two consistent members of the group and there are never more than three members in the line-up at any one time. There are five Hutchinson sisters in all, four of whom can sing, and in the mid-'80s the group 'adopted' a new sister Adrianne Harris. Jeanette, Wanda and Sheila Hutchinson first sang together as a gospel trio The Heavenly Sunbeams with their father during the early 1960s.

Turning to secular music, they began to build a local following and in 1968 met a male vocal group The Emotions. The guys were not too serious about their music career and offered the sisters their name in a friendly gesture. Becoming The Emotions they met Pervis Staples of the **Staples Singers**, who initially recorded the sisters for Twin Stacks, prior to landing a deal with the Volt subsidiary of Stax in 1969. Here they teamed up with songwriter/producer **Isaac Hayes**, and in 1969 they scored Stateside with 'So I Can Love You' (produced by Isaac, written by Sheila) from a debut album of the same name. The following year Jeanette took time off to be replaced by Theresa Davis, and following *Untouched* (1971) the group continued to score Stateside with r&b hits 'Show Me How' (1971), 'My Honey And Me' (1972) and 'From Toys To Boys' (1973).

Prior to leaving the Stax family the group wrote 'I Don't Wanna Lose Your Love', which Isaac Hayes intended to produce as a ballad. They were soon to play the song to **Maurice White** who suggested it would work better as an earthy dance track. In 1976 they went with this idea, signing with CBS through Maurice White's Kalimba Productions. The group's debut CBS album was *Flowers*, which firmly established the sisters on the UK soul scene. Remaining with Maurice White's Earth Wind & Fire production style, the sisters had their greatest solo commercial success the following year with 'Best Of My Love', a UK Top 5 hit taken from their second CBS album *Rejoice* (which also included 'Don't Ask My Neighbors'). Then 'I Don't Wanna Lose Your Love' from the first album was issued as a UK single (Top 40). Maurice White and The Emotions continued to work together, and in 1979 collaborated on 'Boogie Wonderland' as **Earth Wind &**

Fire featuring The Emotions. Another UK Top 5 hit, the track was the first 12" single issued in the UK by CBS that was not a 'limited edition'. The Emotions stayed with Maurice and his ARC label (still via CBS) for a further three albums, *Sunbeam* (1979), *Come Into My World* (1979) and *New Affair* (1981), but were unable to repeat their earlier chart status.

In 1984 they switched to the American Red Label for *Sincerely*, which though critically acclaimed for the extremely classy 'All Things Come In Time' was not released in the UK. Through the same Chicago-based production company they landed a deal with Motown in 1985, though *If I Only Knew* has been their only Motown album to date.

More recently, the title track of the group's first CBS album *Flowers* was remixed in the UK by Gaz Anderson and Tony Thorpe for CBS (1990). Various members of the group have also written for **Patti Labelle** ('Deliver The Funk'), **Charles Jackson** ('At The Party') and others. Pam and Jeanette sang backing vocals with **Helen Baylor** on her 1990 gospel anthem 'There's No Greater Love', while Wanda and Jeanette appeared on **Earth Wind & Fire**'s 'Heritage' (1990). Sheila can also be found as a featured vocalist on **Garry Glenn's** 1987 'Feels Good To Feel Good'.

EN VOGUE
(Vocal Group)

En Vogue are Dawn Robinson (from Connecticut), Terry Ellis (from Texas), Cindy Herron (from San Francisco) and Maxine Jones (from New Jersey), who all auditioned at the same time for **Club Nouveau**'s producers Denzil Foster and Thomas McElroy in 1988. They wanted a female vocal group to feature on the album *FM2*, and these four ladies got the job! Impressed, **Foster/McElroy** put them together officially, and wrote/produced their debut album *Born To Sing*, including 'Hold On', 'Lies' and 'You Don't Have To Worry', for the Atlantic label in 1990.

ENCHANTERS
(Group)

From Philadelphia, The Enchanters was the combination of Zola Pearnell with local groups **The Gainors** and The Ambassadors. The complete line-up was Zola, **Garnet Mimms**, Charles Boyer and **Sam Bell**. In 1963 'Cry Baby' was an American r&b hit for the United Artists label, following which they scored with 'Baby Don't You Weep', 'For Your Precious Love' and an album *Cry Baby And Eleven Other Hits*. In 1964 Garnet left the group. Sam took over lead vocals and signed the group to Warner Brothers.

ENCHANTMENT
(Vocal Group)

Los Angeles-based group Enchantment featured Emanuel (EJ) Johnson, David Banks, Joe (Jobie) Thomas, Ed (Mickey) Clanton and Bobby Green. They recorded albums for a series of labels including United Artists (*Enchantment*, 1978), RCA (*Journey To The Land Of Enchantment*, produced by **Michael Stokes**, 1979; and *Soft Lights, Sweet Music*, produced by **Don Davis**, 1980) and CBS (*Utopia*, again produced by **Michael Stokes**, 1983). They also released a single 'Feel Like Dancing' on Prelude Records (1984).

EQUALS
(Group)

This 70s group featured **Eddy Grant** prior to his solo career in the reggae world. Here Eddie wrote/produced 'Funky Like A Train' (1976), much resurrected in the mid-'80s in the UK.

ERRISON, KING
(Congas)

Born in Barbados, King Errison settled in Los Angeles during the mid-'70s where he established himself as a top conga player on the disco and r&b music scene. He recorded with artists including **Bobbi Humphrey**, **Lenny Williams**, **Quincy Jones**, The Carpenters, **Z.Z.Hill**, **The Four Tops**, **Merry Clayton**, **Martha Reeves**, Cannonball Adderley and numerous others. He also recorded a solo album *L.A.Bound* for Westbound Records (1977), and later a solo single 'Living Up On Jupiter' for the Shatter label (1983). As an actor, he appeared in the James Bond movie *Thunderball*.

ERUPTION
(Vocal Group)

Eruption was instigated by producer **Frank Farian** (who also put together **Boney M**, and featured the lead vocals of **Precious Wilson**. Recording for Hansa Records (via Atlantic), their two biggest hits were 'I Can't Stand The Rain' (Top 5, 1978) and 'One Way Ticket' (Top 10, 1979).

ESCOVEDO, PETE
(Percussion/Vocals)

Percussionist Pete Escovedo is the father of **Sheila E.** and used to run a group Azteca in which Sheila played as a fifteen-year-old. In 1977 he and Sheila signed to the San Francisco-based Fantasy label where they recorded *Solo Two* (1977) and *Happy Together* (1978). Pete also played on albums for **Bill Summers** (lending his vocals) and more recently **Sheila E**.

ETORIA, TONY
(Singer/Songwriter)

While the Americans scored the most success on the late '70s soul/dance scene, UK singer Tony Etoria made a major impression on the charts with his song 'I Can Prove It' (Top 30) for GTO Records in 1977. Sadly he was unable to follow up this great start!

EVANS, RICHARD

(Producer/Arranger)

Based in Los Angeles, Richard established himself as an arranger and producer during the '70s where he worked with soul and jazz artists including **Ahmad Jamal** (1973–80), **The Valentine Brothers** (*The Valentine Brothers*, 1979), **Rockie Robbins** (A&M/MCA albums), **Leroy Hutson**, **Samuel Jonathan Johnson**, **Natalie Cole** ('Mr Melody') and **Linda Williams** ('City Living'). Linda was also the vocalist on Richard's one album *Richard Evans*, including 'Burning Spear' and 'Capricorn Rising', for Horizon Records (via A&M) in 1979.

EVERETT, BETTY

(Singer)

Born in Greenwood, Mississippi, in 1939, Betty gained her initial experience singing gospel before relocating to Chicago. Here she moved into the secular r&b field, initially with a solo release 'Your Love Is Important To Me', and an American hit 'You're No Good' during the early '60s. In 1964 she scored a million-seller in America with 'The Shoop Shoop Song (It's In His Kiss)'. During the year she also recorded duets with **Jerry Butler** on an album *Delicious Together* (including 'Let It Be Me'). In the UK her hits were 'Getting Mighty Crowded' (Top 30, 1965) and the former American hit 'It's In His Kiss' (Top 40, 1968). After further recordings for the ABC and MCA labels she worked with Fantasy Records during the late '70s on songs including 'Sweet Dan'.

EXCITERS

(Group)

American duo Herb Rooney and Brenda Reid originally formed The Exciters in the '60s, when they scored some success with 'Tell Him' (UK Top 50, 1963) and 'Do Wah Diddy Diddy' (later a UK hit for Manfred Mann). In 1967 they recorded 'Blowing Up My Mind', which became a popular record in the UK on the 'Northern soul' scene of the early 70s. In 1975 they re-recorded the song, signed to 20th Century Records and scored a UK Top 40 hit with 'Reaching For The Best' (co-written by **Ian Levine**).

In 1989 **Ian Levine** re-recorded 'Reaching For The Best' with Brenda Reid (as The Brand New Exciters) for the UK Nightmare label.

EXECUTIVE SUITE

(Group)

Philadelphia-based group Executive Suite recorded a number of singles during the early '70s, 'When The Fuel Runs Out' is regarded as somewhat of a classic.

F

FAIR, YVONNE
(Singer)
Born in Virginia, Yvonne grew up in New York where she sang with both The Chantells and **James Brown**. After five years with James she met **Norman Whitfield** who produced her Motown album *The Bitch Is Black*. Her one Motown hit was 'It Should Have Been Me' (UK Top 5, 1976). More recently she has worked as personal manager to **Dionne Warwick**.

FALCONS
(Vocal Group)
Consisting of **Wilson Pickett**, Sir Mack Rice, **Eddie Floyd** and **Joe Stubbs**, The Falcons were a late '50s/early '60s group who scored American hits with songs including 'She's So Fine' (1960) and 'I Found A Love' (1962).

FAMILY
(Group)
From Minneapolis, The Family were a five-man group featuring **St Paul** and **Jellybean** who recorded one album *The Family*, released on **Prince**'s Paisley Park label via Warner Brothers in 1985. 'High Fashion' and 'Susannah's Pajamas' were the tracks to generate interest at the time, though the album also contained the original version of the Prince song 'Nothing Compares 2 U', later a smash hit for Sinead O'Connor.

FANTASTIC FOUR
(Vocal Group)
From Detroit, The Fantastic Four are James Epps, Joseph Pruitt, Paul Scott and Cleveland Horne. Originally recording for the Ric Tic label, their singles included 'Girl Have Pity' (1966), 'Can't Stop Looking For My Baby' (1967), 'Ain't Love Wonderful' (1967), 'You Gave Me Something' (1967), 'As Long As I Love' (1967), 'As Long As The Feeling Is There' (1967), 'Goddess Of Love' (1968), 'Man In Love' (1968), 'I've Got To Have You' (1968) and 'I Love You Madly' (1968). What **The Temptations** were to Motown, The Fantastic Four were to Ric Tic until Motown bought out the label and re-issued 'I Love You Madly' in 1968. Following this, Motown's 'Soul' label, issued *Best Of The Fantastic Four* (1969), featuring the early Ric Tic singles.

During the mid-'70s, the group enjoyed popularity on the dance and disco scenes with their albums for the Westbound label (via Atlantic), *Night People* (1976) and *Got To Have Your Love* (1978), and the **Dennis Coffey**-produced single 'B.Y.O.F. (Bring Your Own Funk)' (1978). More recently the group have worked with producer **Ian Levine** on the UK Motorcity label, releases including 'Working On A Building Of Love' (1990).

FANTASTICS
(Vocal Group)
This '60s vocal quartet from America scored one UK Top 10 in 1971 with 'Something Old, Something New' for the Bell label. During one UK tour their promoter billed them as **The Temptations**, which Motown were not too pleased about. The group, meanwhile, thought they were supporting the Temps!

FANTASY
(Studio Group)
Instigated by Tony Valor, Fantasy were a collection of session musicians and singers from New York who worked together for one release 'You're Too Late', a popular dance record released by Epic in 1980.

FARIAN, FRANK
(Producer)
Based in Europe, Frank is best remembered for instigating the group **Boney M** for whom he also produced. He also instigated and produced **Eruption** in addition to being closely involved in numerous disco acts through the '70s and '80s.

FARRELL, JOE
(Sax/Flute)
Born in Chicago in 1937, Joe initially studied the flute before moving to New York where he took up the sax as a second instrument. In 1959 he joined the Maynard Ferguson Big Band playing both instruments, then in 1972 he became a co-founder member of **Return To Forever**. In the mid–late '70s he recorded as a member

of **Players Association**, while he also made solo albums for labels including Xanadu (*Flute Talk*), CTI (*Moon Germs*, *Outback*) and Warner Brothers (*Night Dancing*, the title track being a UK Top 75 single in 1978).

His session activities included work with artists including **James Brown**, **Aretha Franklin** (solo on 'Angel' and 'Until You Come Back To Me, That's What I'm Gonna Do'), Santana and **Billy Cobham**.

FAT LARRY'S BAND

(Group)

From Philadelphia, Fat Larry's Band or F.L.B. was founded by **Larry James** (drums/vocals/producer), and further consisted of Theodore Cohen (guitar), Larry La Bes (bass/percussion), Terry Price (keyboards/vocals), Frederick Campbell (vocals), Alfonzo Smith (percussion/vocals) and Douglas Jones (sax/vocals). The group was founded in the mid-'70s and recorded for the WMOT/Fantasy labels until the early '80s. During this time they released a string of melodic dance/disco records, their debut single 'Center City' making the UK Top 40 in 1977. Further UK dancefloor success came with 'Boogie Town' (Top 50, 1979) and 'Lookin' For Love Tonight' (Top 50, 1979). Their albums during this time were *Feel It*, *Lookin' For Love*, *Stand Up* and *Off The Wall*. In 1979 the group also played with Larry under two pseudonyms, **Slick** and **Philly Cream**, also for Fantasy Records.

Fat Larry's Band managed to survive the end of the disco boom, and returned in 1982 with a popular dance single 'Act Like You Know'. The track was taken from *Breakin' Out* which featured the ballad 'Zoom', soon to be the group's biggest hit (reaching No. 2 in the UK charts that year). In 1983 the group released a cover of the Motown classic 'Stubborn Kind Of Fellow', but Larry James died of a heart attack shortly after its release.

In 1986 Omni Records in Philadelphia reissued 'Zoom' in the States, the flipside offering the previously unreleased 'Which One Should I Choose'.

FATBACK

(Group)

The Fatback Band, as they were originally known, was the concept of Bill Curtis, the name being inspired by the '60s 'fatback' jazz beat from New Orleans. Bill's initial intention was to start a production company and sign artists to record with his selection of session musicians. His first signing was **Mary Davis**, but he soon decided to write/produce for himself and his musicians, forming The Fatback Band in the early '70s. Signing to the Perception label, they released three classic albums, *Let's Do It Again* (1980), *People Music* and *Feel My Soul* (1974), all of which established their earthy instrumentation style blended with dance rhythms and vocal refrains. The group at this time was Bill Curtis (drums/percussion), Johnny King (guitar), Johnny Flippin (bass/percussion), George Adams (trumpet), Earl Shelton (sax), Wayne Woolford (congas), Artie Simmons (trombone), Gerry Thomas (keyboards) and Jayne & Gerry (backing vocals). To this day, Gerry remains the second longest surviving member, having previously worked with the **Jimmy Castor** Bunch.

Switching to the Spring/Event label (via Polydor) they recorded a further sixteen albums featuring many UK dance classics of the '70s and '80s, including 'Yum Yum Gimme Some' (Top 40, 1975), '(Are You Ready) Do The Bus Stop' (Top 20, 1975), '(Do The) Spanish Hustle' (Top 10, 1976), 'Partytime' (Top 50, 1976), 'Night Fever' (Top 40, 1976), 'Double Dutch' (Top 40, 1977) and 'Backstrokin'' (Top 50, 1980). The group always invited a live audience to recording sessions to give their tracks a spontaneous feel. Albums during this period included *Raising Hell* (1975), *Night Fever* (1976), *Man With The Band* (1977), *Nycnyusa* and *Hot Box* (1980). Not a UK hit but a dance classic, 'King Tim III' has been regarded as the first rap record. It featured fast spoken dialogue long before the **Sugarhill Gang** began the craze with 'Rappers' Delight'.

In 1982 the group became known as simply Fatback, changed musical direction and added vocalist Michael Walker who co-wrote and sang 'She's My Shining Star', a **Maze**-style soul record. The following year they stirred dancefloors with 'The Girl Is Fine (So Fine)' and the spoken 'Is This The Future'. Later in 1983 came the release of *With Love*, including what was to become one of the '80s' dance anthems, 'I Found Lovin''. In the UK, the song reached the Top 50 in 1984, the Top 75 in 1986 and the Top 10 in 1987. It was remixed by the late London disc jockey Steve Walsh who also scored a UK Top 10 hit with it in 1987.

By now the group were Bill Curtis and Gerry Thomas with Ed Jackson (sax/flute), Robert Damper (synths), Westley Watson (keyboards), Linda Blakely (vocals), Michael Walker (vocals) and Johnny Flippin (bass). Following the initial recording of 'I Found Lovin'' they had switched American labels in 1984 to Cotillion (via Atlantic). Here they released *Phoenix* (1984) and *So Delicious* (1985), including 'Lover Undercover'.

FEARON, PHIL

(Singer/Songwriter/Producer)

Born in Northwest London, Phil performed with **Kandidate** before forming his own group **Galaxy**. He switched to Chrysalis as a solo artist in 1986, where his hits were 'I Can Prove It' (UK Top 10) and 'Ain't Nothing But A House Party' (UK Top 75). He also built his own recording studio and formed a record label, 20/20.

FEEL

(Studio Group)

Feel was derived from **The Players Association** and was the work of two of its members, Chris Hills and Danny Weiss. In 1982 Chris wrote 'I'd Like To', released in New York on the Sutra label (Buddah in the UK).

FELDER, ALAN

(Songwriter)

Born in Philadelphia, Alan's sister Nadine Felder was lead singer with **Honey And The Bees**. In 1971 Alan began to write songs with **Norman Harris**, scoring success with **First Choice** ('Smarty Pants' and 'Armed And Extremely Dangerous') and **Double Exposure** ('Ten Percent'). He also worked with **The Manhattans**. Alan produced 'Be Thankful For What You Got' (**William DeVaugn**) and 'Boogie Fund' (Solar Flare), and wrote 'Keep Smilin'' (**Bunny Sigler**) with Bunny Sigler, and 'You Can't Have My Love' (**Jones Girls**), 'Rising To The Top' and 'Hang Tight' with **Keni Burke**.

FELDER, WILTON

(Sax/Bass)

From Texas, Wilton is an integral part of **The Crusaders** where he is predominantly known for his sax-playing. He is also a seasoned bass player and has played bass at countless sessions over the years, with **Chuck Jackson** (*Through The Times*, 1973); **Gene Redding** (*Blood Brother*, 1974); **Arthur Adams** (*Home Brew*, 1975); **Gene Page** (*Lovelock*, 1976); **Al Jarreau** (*Glow*, 1976); **Marvin Gaye** (*I Want You*, 1976); **Minnie Riperton** (*Can You Feel What I'm Saying*, 1977); **Brenton Wood** (*Come Softly*, 1977); Dizzy Gillespie (*Free Ride*, 1977); **Paul Kelly**; **Eloise Laws**; and **Z.Z.Hill**.

As with his fellow members of **The Crusaders**, Wilton recorded simultaneously as a solo artist, (although accompanied and produced by the group) his debut album being *We All Have A Star*, including 'Let's Dance Together' for ABC Records (1978). It included a popular dance track 'Let's Dance Together', and featured members of The Crusaders. In 1980 an MCA album *Inherit The Wind* featured the vocals of **Bobby Womack** on the title track, which reached the UK Top 40 that year. His next album *Gentle Fire* (1983) featured vocals by **A Taste Of Honey** and a popular jazz instrumental 'Summer Nights In Rio'. 1984's *Secrets* included '(No Matter How High I Get) I'll Still Be Looking Up To You', a vocal duet featuring **Bobby Womack** and **Alltrinna Grayson**. The song reached the UK Top 75 in 1985. His next album was *Love Is A Rush*, released by MCA in 1987.

As a sax session player, Wilton can be found on recordings by **O'Bryan** (*Doin' Alright*), **Bobby Womack** (*Through The Eyes Of A Child*), **Howard Hewett** ('I'm For Real'), **Rosie Gaines** ('Skool-Ology') and many others.

FERGUSON, SHEILA

(Singer)

Born in Philadelphia, Sheila recorded as a solo artist for the Jamie label before her producer **Richard Barrett** instigated her move to become lead singer of **The Three Degrees**. She recorded with the group on all their '70s hits for the Philadelphia International label before going solo in the late '80s. She is also the author of a cookery book, *Soul Food*.

FERRONE, STEVE

(Drummer)

Born in Brighton, England, Steve played drums with groups including Brian Auger Oblivion Express and **Bloodstone** before joining **The Average White Band** as replacement for Ronnie MacIntosh in 1976. From here he established himself as a top session drummer across America recording with artists including **George Duke**, **The Four Tops**, **Jeffrey Osborne**, **Keni Burke** ('Risin' To The Top'), **Peabo Bryson**, **Angela Bofill**, **Rahmlee** (*Think*), **Chaka Khan** ('I'm Every Woman' and 'Be-Bop Medley'), **Diana Ross**, **Patti Austin**, **Jennifer Holliday** and **Roberta Flack**.

FEST, MANFREDO

(Songwriter/Arranger/Keyboards)

Born blind in Porto Alegre, Brazil, Manfredo was originally taught classical music by his father, a distinguished German concert pianist. Throughout his career, Manfredo composed music using Braille, and recorded for a number of labels through the '60s and '70s after moving to São Paulo. He recorded five albums for the Brazilian RGE label, and then moved to Minneapolis where his albums for the Daybreak label included *After Hours* (1972). On the UK 'jazz funk' scene, he made his greatest impression in 1979 with a **Jerry Peters**-produced album for the Tabu label, *Manifestations* including 'Jungle Kitten'.

FEVA, SANDRA

(Singer/Songwriter/Producer)

Based in Detroit, Sandra has built a solid reputation as a local club singer, while as a recording artist she established herself with UK soul fans through her albums *The Need To Be* (1979), including 'Choking Kind', and *Savoir Faire* (1981), including 'Leaving This Time', for Venture Records. During the late '80s/early '90s she has worked closely with **Aretha Franklin**, touring as a backing singer, while also recording singles for labels including Krisma ('You Can't Come Up In Here No More', 1986), Jerni ('Love Came Right On Time', 1988) and Grandstand ('Sexyonic', 1989). Her real name is Sandra Dance.

FEVER

(Group)

West Coast funk group Fever consisted of Dale Reed (sax/songwriter/producer), Joseph Bomback (keyboards), Dennis Wadlington (bass), Steven Bailey (lead vocals) and Tip Wirrick (guitar/clavinet). Signing to the Fantasy label, their albums included *Dreams and Desire* (1980).

FIELDS, ALVIN

(Singer/Songwriter)

Los Angeles-based artist Alvin Fields was featured vocalist with **Michael Zager** on *Zager* (1980), before Michael arranged and produced his debut album for A&M Records, *Special Delivery* (1981).

FIELDS, RICHARD 'DIMPLES'
(Singer/Songwriter/Producer)
Born in San Francisco, Richard's early ambitions lay in athletics where his preoccupation was baseball. While at high school he formed a band with some friends which built up a following in the Bay Area. In 1980 he signed as a solo artist with Broadwalk Records (via Epic in the UK) for three self-penned/produced albums. From *Dimples* (1981), 'Like Your Loving' and 'She's Got Papers On Me' (the latter featuring **Betty Wright**) established Richard on the soul scene, the album reaching gold status in the USA. 1982's 'I've Got To Learn To Say No' was Richard's one UK Top 60 chart single, and a second album *Mr, Look So Good* also reached gold status in the USA that year. He co-wrote and produced a whole album *Ouch* for **The Ohio Players**. Later in 1982 his album *Give Everybody Some* was released by Broadwalk before the label went out of business.

In 1984 he returned with an RCA album *Mmm* (including 'I Need You Baby'). He wrote and produced an album for RCA group **9.9** (1985), who more recently joined him for 'I Can't Stop Lovin' You' on Richard's 1990 album *Dimples* for the independent Life label.

FIFTH DIMENSION
(Vocal Group)
Formed in Los Angeles during the mid-'60s, The Fifth Dimension were **Marilyn McCoo & Billy Davis Jr**, Lamonte McLemore, Florence LaRue and **Ron Townson**, originally known as The Versatiles. While on tour with **Ray Charles** they came to the attention of Marc Gordon who became their manager and signed them to the Soul City label in 1967. Here they scored American hits with 'Go Where You Wanna Go', 'Up Up & Away' and 'One Less Bell To Answer' from their seven gold albums for the label through to 1972. In the UK their recordings were released on the Liberty label, their hits here being 'Aquarius – Let The Sunshine In' (Top 20, 1969) and 'Wedding Bell Blues' (Top 20, 1970). **Ron Townson** later formed a group Wild Honey with **Vesta Williams** while **Marilyn McCoo & Billy Davis Jr** scored hit duets on their own.

FIFTH OF HEAVEN
(Group)
Formed in Manchester, Fifth Of Heaven were Denise Johnson (vocals), Steve Williams (bass/keyboards) and Andy Hickey (keyboards). In 1987 they recorded 'Just A Little More' which they released on their own DFM ('Done For Money') label to good reactions from the UK soul scene. In 1989 they returned with 'Without You (Baby I'm Lost)' on Mix Out Records.

52ND STREET
(Group)
From Manchester, England, 52nd Street were eventually Tony Henry (guitar/vocals), John Dennison (keyboards/bass), Diane Charlemagne (vocals) and Tony Bowry (bass/synths/vocals). In 1982 the group signed with Factory Records and had local success with their debut 'Look Into My Eyes'. (The previous year 'Checkin' You Out' was promo'd but not released by WEA). Their follow-up 'Cool As Ice' was remixed by **Jellybean** and did well in the US dance charts in 1983. A further single 'Can't Afford' followed on Factory but at the end of the year the group temporarily split up (disillusioned by the lack of success) but re-formed the following year with the amended line-up above. Again they did well in the US dance charts with 'Can't Afford'.

Greater recognition in the UK came with *Children Of The Night*, produced in Philadelphia by **Nick Martinelli** following the group's signing to Virgin/10 Records in 1985. The album featured 'Tell Me (How It Feels)', a popular UK dance record and Top 60 entry. Early in 1986 the group charted again with 'You're My Last Chance' (UK Top 50) and 'I Can't Let You Go' (UK Top 60), both from the first album.

In 1987 the group changed producers to work with **Lenny White** on 'Are You Receiving Me', which wasn't particularly well received. The group have not charted since.

FINCH, RICK
(Songwriter/Producer)
Born in Miami, Florida, Rick was only fifteen when he engineered (in the studio) **Betty Wright**'s hit recording 'Clean Up Woman' and was still in his teens when he co-wrote 'Rock Your Baby' for **George McCrae** with **H.W.Casey** (of **K.C. & The Sunshine Band**). As a lead member of K.C. & The Sunshine Band he co-wrote 'Sound Your Funky Horn', later arranging and producing a new version of the song for **Boe Brown** & The Uptown Horns.

FINE QUALITY
(Studio Group)
Instigated by **Sylvia Robinson**, Fine Quality were an early '80s group who stirred dancefloors in 1981 with their single 'Aah Dance' for the Sugar Hill label.

FINISHED TOUCH
(Group)
Based in Los Angeles, Finished Touch were a group of singers who worked together on one Motown album *Need To Know You Better* in 1979. The group consisted of Harold Johnson (keyboards/vocals), Kenny Stover (vocals/producer), **Mike & Brenda Sutton** (vocals/songwriters/producers), Michael McGloiry (guitar), Larry Brown and the services of **Jermaine Jackson**.

FINISHING TOUCH

(Vocal Group)

Based in Philadelphia, Finishing Touch worked locally in the late '60s/early '70s, their recordings including 'Your Love Has Put A Spell On Me', written by **Bunny Sigler** and **Al Felder** for the Philly Groove label.

FIRE FOX

(Vocal Group)

Fire Fox were vocalists **Paulette McWilliams** and Toi Overton. Signing to Atlantic in 1985, they delivered one album *Fire Fox* produced by **Ollie E. Brown**. The album featured guest appearances by **Paul Jackson**, **Gerald Albright** and guest vocals by **Larry Graham**, **Ray Parker** and **Howard Hewett**.

FIRST CHOICE

(Group)

From Philadelphia, First Choice were **Rochelle Flemming**, Annette Guest and Joyce Jones, who first sang together at high school as The Debronettes in the late '60s. In 1972 they met writers/producers **Norman Harris** and **Alan Felder** and released a debut single 'This Is The House Where Love Died' on the Wand label. Remaining under the direction of Harris/Felder they switched to the Philly Groove label (via Bell) and scored UK success with 'Armed And Extremely Dangerous' (Top 20) and 'Smarty Pants' (Top 10), both in 1973. Also on Philly Groove came 'The Player' (1974) before they switched to the Salsoul label. In 1977 they hit the dancefloors with 'Doctor Love' and their classic 'Let No Man Put Asunder', of which the **Shep Pettibone** mix is revived regularly to this day (although it has never been a UK hit).

FIRST CIRCLE

(Group)

From New York, Larry Marsden (guitar/vocals), Glenn 'Chango' Everett (drums/vocals), Albert Lee (lead vocals), Anthony McEwan (bass) and Richard Sinclair (percussion) first recorded as Full Circle, but had to change their name due to a rock band which used the same name. Initial pressings of their **Randy Muller**-produced debut *Boys Night Out* 1987 including 'Working Up A Sweat' (UK Top 50), 'Miracle Worker' and 'Can't Find A Love', were under the name Full Circle before it was re-pressed as First Circle.

FIRST LIGHT

(Duo)

London-based duo First Light are Derek Green and **Paul Hardcastle** who first worked together as members of **Direct Drive**. As First Light their debut release was 'AM' for Charlie Gillett's Oval label before they switched to London Records to score UK chart success with 'Explain The Reasons' (UK Top 75, 1983) and 'Wish You Were Here' (UK Top 75, 1984). In 1990, after Paul had a run of success as a solo artist, First Light was re-formed for the release 'So Easy' on the Sgt. Pepper label.

FIRST LOVE

(Vocal Group)

From Chicago, First Love were Denise Austin, Demetrice Henrae (former lead singer with Chicago funk bands Phoenix and Power) and Martha Jackson (formerly with Chicago group Power Line). They formed in 1977, the year of their debut single release 'Don't Say Goodnight' for the Brunswick label. In 1982 they switched to the Chicago International Music label (via Epic) and released *Love At First Sight*, on the strength of which they toured with **Marvin Gaye** on a forty-two-date tour. In 1984 they were with the Mirage label (via Virgin in the UK) for the release of 'Things Are Not The Same (Without You)'.

FISCHER, ANDRE

(Drums/Producer)

Originally based in Chicago, Andre played drums with **Rufus** before establishing himself as a producer on the Los Angeles scene with artists including **Martha Reeves**, **Gloria Gaynor**, **Brenda Russell** ('In The Thick Of It'), **Sheree Brown** (*The Music*), **Lalah Hathaway** ('Smile' and 'Somethin''), **Natalie Cole** and many more.

FISHER, BRUCE

(Singer/Songwriter/Guitar)

Based in Los Angeles, Bruce initially recorded for United Artists where his single 'At The End Of A Love Affair' is fondly remembered on the 'Northern soul' scene of the early '70s. In 1973 he co-wrote 'Body Heat', the title track of what was to become the first gold-selling album for **Quincy Jones** on Mercury Records. He later signed to Mercury himself where *Red Hot* featured an all-star line-up of musicians including **Roy Ayers**, **Keni Burke** (with whom he wrote the title song), **Charles Earland**, **Mtume** and the **Brecker Brothers** (1977).

He later played guitar with **Sunfire**, sang backgrounds with **Roy Ayers** (co-writing 'Get On Up, Get On Down'), and more recently co-wrote/produced songs for the group 3 For 3 (1990).

FIVE SPECIAL

(Vocal Group)

Late '70s funk vocal group Five Special consisted of Steve Boyd, Bryan Banks, Mike Pettilo, Steve Harris and Greg Finley. In 1981 they stirred UK dancefloors with their Elektra release 'Why Leave Us Alone' from *Track'n*.

FLACK, ROBERTA

(Singer)

Born in Black Mountain, North Carolina, in 1940, Roberta grew up in Arlington, Virginia, where she took piano lessons from the age of nine. Aged fifteen she studied music at Howard University where she began experimenting with her voice and joined a vocal quartet.

Moving to Washington, she accompanied opera singers on the piano at the city's Tivoli Club while also moving into the blues and r&b field by playing in local nightclubs. In 1968 she was overheard by an Atlantic executive who brought her to the label that year. In 1969 she released a debut album *First Take* which included 'The First Time Ever I Saw Your Face'. The album was followed by *Chapter Two* (1970).

In the UK Roberta first made an impression on the charts in 1972 when 'The First Time Ever I Saw Your Face' was released and reached the Top 20. The same year she teamed up with **Donny Hathaway** for a duet album *Roberta Flack And Donny Hathaway* which featured 'Where Is The Love', a UK Top 30 hit and a soul classic (written by **Ralph MacDonald**, Roberta's percussion player for five years between 1970–5). The album also included 'You've Got A Friend' and 'You've Lost That Lovin' Feeling'. She continued to deliver classic hits with 'Killing Me Softly With His Song' (UK Top 10, 1973) and 'Feel Like Making Love' (UK Top 40, 1974), prior to 1975's *Feel Like Making Love*.

1977's *Blue Lights In The Basement* featured a new Donny Hathaway duet, 'The Closer I Get To You', which reached the UK Top 50 in 1978. The same year an album *Roberta Flack* included 'If Ever I See You Again'. Roberta was soon working with Donny Hathaway again, though after a few new songs were completed Donny took it upon himself to end his life. The songs, including the **Mtume/Lucas**-penned UK No. 3 hit 'Back Together Again', were included on 1979's *Roberta Flack Featuring Donny Hathaway*. The album also included the **Stevie Wonder**-penned 'Don't Make Me Wait Too Long' (UK Top 50, 1980).

For the movie soundtrack *Bustin' Loose*, Roberta recorded a **Luther Vandross** song 'You Stopped Lovin' Me', following which Luther toured with Roberta as backing singer after his departure from **Change**. In 1982 she was back in the studio for *I'm The One*, which included 'Making Love' and 'Til The Morning Comes'. It was co-written and produced by **Ralph MacDonald**, following which she moonlighted to Capitol to record a duet album *Peabo Bryson And Roberta Flack*. 1983's *Born To Love* included the UK No. 2 duet ballad 'Tonight I Celebrate My Love', with **Peabo Bryson**.

The next year she joined forces with **Sadao Watanabe** for a single 'If I'm Still Around', again produced by Ralph MacDonald. 1988's *Oasis* included the **Ashford & Simpson** song 'Uh-Uh Ooh-Ooh', remixed by **Arthur Baker** to popular dancefloor reactions that year.

FLEMING, ROSHELLE

(Singer)

Roshelle sang lead vocals with Philadelphia-based group **First Choice** prior to recording a solo debut, 'Love Itch', released in the UK by Crossover Records in 1986.

FLEMMING, GARFIELD

(Singer)

New York-based singer Garfield Flemming made one record for the Becket label in 1981. The song was 'Don't Send Me Away', a UK soul anthem which remains popular to this day. He later recorded for a number of small labels including Gimme Five ('Let's Turn In Early').

FLIGHT

(Group)

Flight were West Coast jazz/fusion musicians Pat Vidas (trumpet/vocals), Jim Vaeger (keyboards), Ted Karczewski (bass), John DeNicola (Fender bass) and Steve Shebar (drums/vibes). 1980's *Excursions Beyond* for Motown featured a version of **The Jacksons**' 'Shake Your Body (Down To The Ground)', but was popular with UK 'jazz funk' fans for the instrumental title track.

FLOATERS

(Vocal Group)

From Detroit, The Floaters were a vocal quintet formed by James Mitchell and Marvin Willis, formerly members of the **Detroit Emeralds**. In 1977 they signed to ABC Records and made a major impact with the title track of their debut album *Float On* which was a UK No. 1 hit. The song, one of the first to be released on a 12" single, ran for just under twelve minutes! Their follow-up albums included *Magic* (1978) and on Fee Records *Get Ready For The Floaters & Shu-Ga* (1981).

FLOYD, EDDIE

(Singer)

Memphis singer Eddie Floyd signed with Stax Records in the '60s, 'Knock On Wood' being a major hit in 1967 (UK Top 20). His follow-ups included 'Raise Your Hand' (UK Top 50) and 'Things Get Better' (UK Top 40) the same year. His Stax albums included *Soul Street* before he switched to Malaco in the '70s. More recently he recorded *Flashback* for **William Bell**'s Wilbe label (via Ichiban).

FLYTETIME

(Group)

Originally formed by **Terry Lewis** and **Jellybean Johnson** during their school days, this group employed the services of **Jimmy 'Jam' Harris** and performed locally without any name for several years during the mid-'70s. Expanding to eleven members, the group became Flytetime when **Alexander O'Neal** (lead vocals), Monte Moir (keyboards) and a four-piece horn section (including Cynthia Johnson of **Lipps Inc.**) joined the line-up. Building up a following in Minneapolis, they were soon working as concert support for visiting artists to the city including **Dynasty**, **Cameo**, **Switch**, **The Barkays**, **One Way** and **Maze**.

In the meantime **Morris Day** had formed a group called Enterprise and was working on the road with **Prince**. When guitarist **Jesse Johnson** left Enterprise to join Flytetime, and Prince signed to Warner Bros, Terry Lewis, Jimmy Jam, Jesse Johnson and Morris Day hooked up together to form **The Time**.

More recently the name Flytetime has been used for the production company of Jimmy Jam and Terry Lewis.

FORCE

(Group)

The Force were probably the Philadelphia International label's least successful group. They released one album *The Force* (1979), a disco dance confection which featured a cover version of 'Rock Your Baby'.

FORCE MDs

(Vocal Group)

From Staten Island, New York, The Force MDs are TCD, Stevie D, Jessie D, Trisco and Mercury. They began by singing doo-wop together locally and made pocket money by entertaining passengers on the Staten Island ferry. When rap music took off in the early '80s, the group incorporated rapping into their repertoire, and soon landed a deal at Tommy Boy Records. Here a debut release 'Let Me Love You' (1983) began to build them a following prior to the release of *Love Letters* (1984). In 1985 the group worked with **Jam/Lewis** on 'Tender Love', which reached the UK Top 30 when released in the UK in 1986. The following year they returned with *Touch And Go* which included 'Love Is A House'.

FORCE OF NATURE

(Group)

From Philadelphia, Force Of Nature were a funk band who came to the attention of **Thom Bell** in 1974. Signing them to his Tommy label (via CBS), they released an album *Force Of Nature* prior to switching to the Philadelphia International label in 1976. Here they released *Unemployment Blues*, from which 'Do It (Like You Ain't Got No Backbone)' and 'Discomite' served pre-disco dancefloors in the USA.

FORD, PENNYE

(Singer)

Born in Cincinnati, Ohio, Pennye's father Gene Redd was an executive producer for King Records (the label James Brown was signed to early in his career). Her sister is **Sharon Redd**. After studying various musical instruments Pennye joined a group called Reach and toured Japan. Upon returning to the USA she decided to relocate to Los Angeles where she found a job with Motown's publishing company Jobete Music singing demos of their songs. From here she signed with Total Experience and released a debut solo single 'Change Your Wicked Ways' and an album *Pennye* in 1984. Her next single 'Dangerous' (1985) reached the UK Top 50.

More recently Pennye has sung as the uncredited lead vocalist with Snap on their 1990 hits 'Ooops Up' and 'Mary Had A Little Boy'. She has also become close friends with **Chaka Khan** and sang backgrounds on Chaka's duet with **Edwin Starr**, 'Our Day Will Come' (1991).

FORTUNE, SONNY

(Sax/Flute)

Born in Philadelphia in 1939, Sonny moved to New York in the '60s where he played with Buddy Rich and **McCoy Tyner**, among others. In the early '70s he joined **Miles Davis**, and later recorded fusion albums for Atlantic. These include *Infinity Is* (1977) and *Serengeti Minstrel* (1978).

FOSTER/McELROY

(Songwriters/Producers)

From Oakland, California, Denzil Foster and Thomas McElroy played an integral role in **Club Nouveau** before branching out into writing and production in the late '80s. Initially they put together a group of singers to front their album *FM²*, later giving them the name **En Vogue** and signing them to Atlantic. They have also written and produced for artists including **Con Funk Shun**, **Robert Brookins**, **Samuelle** ('So You Like What You See') and **Alexander O'Neal** ('Midnight Run').

FOSTER, IAN

(Singer/Songwriter/Producer)

Born to Jamaican parents in South London, Ian initially worked with reggae group One Love, during which time he developed his songwriting skills. By the time he reached his mid-twenties, his songs had been recorded by artists including **Loose Ends**, **Five Star**, **Jean Carne** and **Quincy Jones**. As a solo artist he signed to MCA Records in 1986 where he worked with producer **Nick Martinelli** on *Ian Foster*. He now lives in Los Angeles where he has branched into production with artists including **Perri**.

FOSTER, RONNIE

(Keyboards/Singer)

Born in Buffalo, New York, in 1950, Ronnie was a competent pianist by the age of ten. His first professional instrument was the organ and he was initially hired by artists including **Stanley Turrentine** and Grant Green prior to his solo recording deal with Blue Note Records in the early '70s. Here his albums included *Two-Headed Freak* (1972), *Sweet Revival* (1973), and then the **George Benson**-produced *On The Avenue* (1974) and *Cheshire Cat* (1975), featuring **Mtume**, William Allen (**Roy Ayers**'s bass player) and Ronnie himself on vocals. Moving from organ to synths and Rhodes electric piano, Ronnie was hired by **George Benson** as his pianist, although he also moonlighted as keyboard player and vocalist with **Ecstasy, Passion & Pain** during the mid-'70s. In 1978 he signed to CBS as a solo artist where his albums were *Love Satellite* (1978), including 'Happy Song' (featuring

Stevie Wonder on drums) and 'Midnight Plane' (featuring **Roy Ayers** on vibes), and *Delight* (1979).

As a songwriter and/or producer he has worked with **David Sanborn** (*A Change Of Heart*, 1987) and **Dee Dee Bridgewater** ('Open Up Your Eyes'), while he has also recorded with **Flora Purim**, **The Temptations**, **Stevie Wonder** ('Summer Soft'), and **Chaka Khan** ('Night In Tunisia'). More recently he has been co-writing with **Susaye Greene** for a forthcoming solo album.

FOUNDATIONS
(Group)
Featuring the lead vocals of **Clem Curtis**, London-based group The Foundations scored UK hits from the mid-'60s on Pye Records with songs 'Baby, Now That I've Found You' (No. 1, 1967), 'Back On My Feet Again' (Top 20, 1968), 'Any Old Time' (Top 50, 1968), 'Build Me A Buttercup' (Top 5, 1968), 'In The Bad Bad Old Days' (Top 10, 1969) and 'Born To Live And Born To Die' (Top 50, 1969). The group included **Roy Carter** who later joined **Heatwave**.

FOUR TOPS
(Vocal Group)
From Detroit, The Four Tops are Levi Stubbs, Renaldo 'Obie' Benson, Lawrence Payton and Abdul 'Duke' Fakir who started out as The Aims in the mid-'50s. They went to the same school as **Aretha Franklin**, and sang in talent shows as teenagers before becoming a local nightclub act. They also began recording, originally for the Chess label, then Red Top Records and CBS before meeting **Berry Gordy** via **Jackie Wilson** (Levi's cousin). Berry saw potential and signed them to Motown as The Four Tops in 1963, their debut album being *Breaking Through*. They also helped out as backing singers before teaming up with writers/producers **Holland/Dozier/Holland** later in the year for their first American hit 'Baby I Need Your Loving'. The Four Tops polished up their live act which took them all over America, opening in some cases for artists including **Billy Eckstine**, **Brook Benton** and Count Basie.

In the UK the group established themselves in 1965, their hits being 'I Can't Help Myself' (Top 30, 1965), 'It's The Same Old Song' (Top 40, 1965), 'Loving You Is Sweeter Than Ever' (Top 25, 1966), 'Reach Out I'll Be There' (No. 1, 1966), 'Standing In The Shadows Of Love' (Top 10, 1967), 'Bernadette' (Top 10, 1967), 'Seven Rooms Of Gloom' (Top 20, 1967), 'You Keep Running Away' (Top 30, 1967), 'Walk Away Renee' (Top 5, 1967), 'If I Were A Carpenter' (Top 10, 1968), 'Yesterday's Dreams' (Top 25, 1968), 'I'm In A Different World' (Top 30, 1968), 'What Is A Man' (Top 20, 1969), and 'Do What You Gotta Do' (Top 20, 1969). They were one of the few American black acts to compete in the UK with The Beatles during the '60s, Brian Epstein being the organizer of their first tour. Back in America they remained at Motown until 1972, their early '70s UK hits being 'It's All In The Game' (Top 5, 1970), 'Still Water Love' (Top 10, 1970), 'Just Seven Numbers' (Top 40, 1971), 'Simple Game' (Top 5, 1971) and 'Walk With Me, Talk With Me Darling' (Top 40, 1972).

In 1972 they switched to the ABC/Dunhill label (Probe in the UK), where 'Keeper Of The Castle' (UK Top 20) became the title of their first album for the label in 1973. Their second UK hit single during this period was 'Sweet Understanding Love' (Top 30, 1973), while albums for the label included *Main Street People* (1973), and *Meeting Of The Minds* (1974), including 'Midnight Flower' and 'Tell Me You Love Me'. Also at ABC Lawrence recorded a solo album.

After an absence from the UK charts during the later '70s, their fortunes changed in 1981 after switching labels to Casablanca. Here, *Tonight* featured 'When She Was My Girl' (Top 5), 'Don't Walk Away' (Top 20) and 'Tonight I'm Gonna Love You All Over' (Top 50), following which they returned to Motown and a reunion with **Holland/Dozier/Holland** on *Back Where I Belong*. They remained at Motown for two further albums, *Magic* (1985) including 'Sexy Ways' and 'Maybe Tomorrow' featuring **Phyllis Hyman**, and *Hot Nights* (1986), before leaving the label again. In 1988 a radical remix of 'Reach Out I'll Be There' made the UK Top 20, following which the group returned on Arista with *Indestructible* including 'Loco In Acapulco' (UK Top 10), from the movie soundtrack *Buster*.

FOWLER, BARBARA
(Singer)
This New York-based session singer was the voice on early '80s club hits for studio groups including **Sinnamon** ('Thanks To You'), in addition to which she recorded the single 'Come And Get My Lovin'' as a solo artist for the Radar label.

FOXX, INEZ & CHARLIE
(Duo)
From Greensboro, North Carolina, brother and sister Inez and Charlie Foxx had independent careers away from the music business before hooking up in 1962 to sign with Symbol Records, owned by **Juggy Murray Jones**. Here they scored American hits with 'Mockingbird', 'Ask Me' and 'Hurt By Love' before a label switch to Musicor for 'I Stand Accused' and 'Count The Days'. Later in 1969 Inez released a solo album on Volt, *At Memphis*.

FOXY
(Group)
'70s dance band Foxy were formed by **Ish** (vocals/guitar) in Miami and further consisted of Carl Driggs (lead vocals), Arnold Paseiro (bass), Richie Puente Jr (percussion/clavinet), Charlie Murciano (keyboards/woodwinds/vibes) and Joe Galdo (drums/percussion/vocals). After signing to the Dash label (via TK), they scored on the disco scene with 'Get Off' (1976), their most popular record in the UK, while across America they also reached

No. 1 in the dance charts with 'Hot Number' and 'Rock'. 'Get Off' was remixed and issued by Sunnyview Records in 1986.

FRANKLIN, ARETHA

(Singer/Songwriter/Keyboards/Producer)

Born in Memphis, Tennessee, in 1942, one of four children and the second daughter of Baptist minister Revd C.L.Franklin (one of the early leaders of the civil rights movement), Aretha grew up with her family on the East Side of Detroit where her father was appointed pastor of the New Bethel church. By the age of five she was playing piano and singing gospel, while by fourteen she was touring and performing alongside her father at his sermons. By the late 1950s she developed a taste for **Sam Cooke**, Fats Domino and the popular artists of the day. At this point her father, while not keen on her interest in secular music, took Aretha to the small JVP label in Detroit where her first recordings were made.

In 1960 she moved to New York after securing a record deal with CBS, and worked with producer John Hammond (who had produced Billie Holliday). Her first single was 'Today I Sing The Blues', an American Top 10 r&b hit alongside the follow-up 'Won't Be Long'. Her debut album *Aretha* was released in 1961. The next album was *The Electrifying Aretha Franklin*, featuring jazzy big band numbers in contrast to the jazz quartet accompaniments of her first recordings (when she also played her own piano). Growing unhappy with this music, with the support of manager Ted White she changed musical direction. She worked with producers including Bob Mersey and Clyde Otis, emulating popular female singers of the day (including **Dionne Warwick** with a version of 'Walk On By'). Albums were *The Tender, Moving, Swinging Aretha Franklin*, *Laughing*, *Unforgettable – Tribute To Dinah Washington* and the jazzier *Yeah*. In 1962 she was crowned 'The Queen Of Soul' and married Ted White.

Her last CBS album was *Soul Sister* (1965), and in 1967 she signed to Atlantic. Under the direction of **Jerry Wexler** she released her first million-seller, 'I Never Loved A Man (The Way I Loved You)', the title of her debut Atlantic album. By 1968 she had five gold records and made her first impression on the UK charts with 'Respect' (written by **Otis Redding**), a UK Top 10 single in 1967 from her third Atlantic album *Lady Soul*. Her UK single hits included 'Baby I Love You' (Top 40, 1967), 'Chain of Fools' (Top 50, 1967), 'Since You've Been Gone' (Top 50, 1968), 'Think' (Top 30, 1968) and 'I Say A Little Prayer' (Top 5, 1968), the latter two from *Aretha Now* (which also included 'You Send Me'). Following *Soul 69* she divorced Ted White and temporarily returned to the church and her family. She also worked on a few production projects with her protégés L.C.Cooke (brother of Sam) and **Billy Always**, although these recordings were not released.

Her next album was *This Girl's In Love With You* (1970), including 'Call Me'. 'Don't Play That Song' was a UK Top 20 hit from her next American album *Spirit In The Dark*, which was called *Don't Play That Song* in the UK after the success of the single. Following a live album recorded at the San Francisco rock venue Fillmore West, Aretha returned to the studio for *Young Gifted And Black* and *Amazing Grace*. Her only UK chart success during this era was 'Spanish Harlem' (Top 20, 1971).

In 1973 Aretha hooked up with producer **Quincy Jones** for *Hey Now Hey* which included the UK Top 40 hit 'Angel' (written by sister **Carolyn Franklin** and **Sonny Sanders**). Quincy also produced a USA-only released track 'Master Of Eyes (The Deepness Of Your Eyes)', Aretha's only single not to appear on any of her albums. The following year she scored further success (UK Top 30) with 'Until You Come Back To Me (That's What I'm Gonna Do)' co-written by **Stevie Wonder**, Clarence Paul and Morris Broadnax. The song (recently recorded again by **Miki Howard**) came from Aretha's first album of 1974, *Let Me In Your Life*, including 'I'm In Love'. Her second was *With Everything I Feel In Me*, which included the Barry Mann song 'When You Get Right Down To It' (later recorded by **Brandi Wells**) and 'You'll Never Get To Heaven'.

Her next album was *You* (1975), including 'It Only Happens (When I Look At You)', although this and her subsequent albums through to 1979 failed to sell well. There are still some golden moments to be found during this era on albums *Sparkle*, a movie soundtrack produced by **Curtis Mayfield** (1976); *Sweet Passion* (1977), including the **Lamont Dozier**-produced 'Sunshine Will Never Be The Same' and Aretha-penned 'When I Think About You'; *Almighty Fire* (1978), produced by Curtis Mayfield and including 'I Needed You Baby'; and *La Diva* (1979), produced by **Van McCoy** and including 'I Was Made For You'.

The year Aretha departed from Atlantic (1979), her father was shot, leaving him in a coma for five years. Instead of allowing this tragedy to get her down, Aretha signed to Arista. She released *Aretha* (1980) from which 'What A Fool Believes' re-established her in the UK Top 50. Next, *Love All The Hurt Away* (1981) featured the hit duet of the same name with **George Benson** (UK Top 50). Arista releases continued with two **Luther Vandross**-produced albums, *Jump To It* (1982), including '(It's Just) Your Love' and 'This Is For Real', and *Get It Right* (1983), including 'Better Friends Than Lovers'. Hooking up with producer **Narada Michael Walden**, hits continued in 1985 from the album *Who's Zoomin' Who*, including 'Freeway of Love' (Top 75), the title track (Top 20) and 'Another Night' (Top 60). Also in 1985 her duet with The Eurythmics 'Sisters Are Doin' It For Themselves' reached the UK Top 10 (on RCA).

In 1986, after 24 gold records and 14 Grammy awards, Aretha scored her first UK No. 1 with George Michael on the duet 'I Knew You Were Waiting (For Me)' from her album *Aretha* that year. The album also included 'Rock-A-Lott' (the 'Lott' being a discreet tribute to Arista company man Roy Lott), the a cappella from the song forming the basis for the recent 49ers hit 'Touch Me'. It also included 'Jimmy Lee' (UK Top 50), a Keith Richards production of 'Jumpin' Jack Flash' and a **Larry Graham** duet 'If You Need My Love Tonight'.

Aretha later sang duets with Elton John, **Whitney Houston** ('It Isn't, It Wasn't, It Ain't Never Gonna Be') and **James Brown** ('Gimme Your Love', remixed on 12" by **Prince**) on her 1989 album *Through The Storm* (which included a remake of 'Think'). Her most recent album is *What You See Is What You Sweat* (1991), including the **Sly Stone** song 'Everyday People'.

FRANKLIN, CAROLYN

(Singer/Songwriter)

Born in Memphis, Tennessee, in 1944, Carolyn was the youngest sister of **Aretha Franklin** for whom she wrote songs including 'Without Love', 'Sing It Again – Say It Again', 'Baby Baby Baby' and 'I Was Made For You'. She sang backgrounds for Aretha, while as a solo artist she signed to RCA Records for *This Is Carolyn*. She also wrote 'Don't Wait Too Long' for **Erma Franklin**.

FRANKLIN, ERMA

(Singer)

Younger than sister **Aretha Franklin**, but older than her other sister **Carolyn Franklin**, Erma grew up in a musical environment and sang in church before making various recordings for labels including Shout, Epic and MCA.

FRANKLIN, RODNEY

(Keyboards)

Born in Berkeley, California, in 1958, Rodney was taking jazz piano lessons by the age of six at Washington Elementary School. His Administrator at the school was Dr Herb Wong, a noted jazz journalist, DJ and teacher. Prior to signing with CBS in 1978, Rodney worked extensively with **John Handy** in San Francisco, and toured with **Bill Summers**, **Freddie Hubbard** and **Marlena Shaw**.

His debut CBS album was *In The Center* (1978), an underground jazz fusion album (not released in the UK) featuring 'On The Path' and 'I Like The Music Make It Hot' (with Freddie Hubbard). 1980's *You'll Never Know* saw some major chart success with 'The Groove' (UK Top 10), even creating a brief UK dance craze 'The Freeze' (instigated by disc jockey Chris Hill). His other CBS albums were *Rodney Franklin* (1980), *Endless Flight* (1981), *Learning To Love* (1982), *Marathon* (1984), produced by **Stanley Clarke**, *Skydance* (1985) and *It Takes Two* (1986). In 1988 he switched to BMG for *Diamond Inside Of You* which featured lead vocals by **Jennifer Holliday** on the single 'Gotta Give It Up'.

FRANTIQUE

(Group)

Frantique were an all-girl dance/disco group put together by the Philadelphia International label in 1979. They recorded one album *Frantique* which included the disco hit 'Strut Your Funky Stuff', a UK Top 10 that year.

FRAZIER, BILLY

(Singer/Songwriter/Producer)

Born in New York, Billy worked with local groups King Davis, **B.T.Express**, The 11th Commandment (on Chess Records) and The Night Hawks (on Atlantic) before recording briefly for Capitol. In 1980, as Billy Frazier And Friends he recorded 'Billy Who?' for the local Bijuma label. The song was released in the UK by DJM records where it enjoyed dancefloor success. Billy also owns a nightclub in Queens, New York.

FRAZIER, CAESAR

(Singer/Songwriter/Producer/Keyboards)

Based in Los Angeles, Caesar recorded *Caesar Frazier '75* for the 20th Century label (1975) before working with producers including Mike Theodore on *Another Life*, released by Westbound (via Atlantic) in 1978. The title track came in vocal and instrumental versions, the latter being particularly popular in the UK.

FREDERICK

(Singer/Songwriter)

From Ohio, Frederick Davis recorded one album *Frederick* for the Heat label in 1985. It featured his co-penned composition 'Games', popular on the UK soul scene.

FREEEZ

(Group)

London-based group Freeez were instigated by **John Rocca** who produced their debut recordings 'Keep In Touch' (UK Top 50) and 'Stay' for the Pink Rhythm label in 1980. Making an impression on the early '80s 'Brit funk' scene they were signed by Beggars Banquet where they continued to be successful with home-made productions 'Southern Freeez' (UK Top 10, 1981), 'Flying High' (UK Top 40, 1981) and 'One To One' (1982).

In 1983 John spent some time in New York where he worked with producer **Arthur Baker** on a new single 'I.O.U.', an 'electro' anthem and UK Top 5 hit later in the year (also released in America on Arthur's Streetwise label). The follow-up was 'Pop Goes My Love' (UK Top 30, 1983). Here, Billy Crichton (vocals/guitar) and Louis Smith (keyboards) joined the group, replacing **John Rocca** who embarked on a solo career. The new line-up released 'That Beats My Patience' followed by 'Train Of Thoughts', and an album *Idle Vice*. Ian Johns then joined the group as new vocalist, leaving Billy as the group's guitarist.

FRIENDS OF DISTINCTION

(Group)

Based in Los Angeles, Friends Of Distinction were popular on the late '60s/early '70s American soul scene with songs including 'Grazing In The Grass' and 'I Really

Really Hope You Do'. Their musical director was **Billy Osborne**, brother of **Jeffrey Osborne**.

FULL FORCE
(Group)
From New York, Full Force are B-Fine, Shy-Shy, Paul Anthony, Gerry, Bow-Legged Lou, and Curt. At the more commercial end of rap and hip hop, the group first made an impression in 1985 as guests of Lisa Lisa and Cult Jam on the 1985 UK Top 20 hit 'I Wonder If I Take You Home'. Later in the year they released their own CBS debut album *Full Force*, including 'Alice, I Want You Just For Me' (UK Top 10), before turning to writing/production for artists including **La La** ('If You Love Me Just A Little' and 'My Love Is On The Money', 1987) **Cheryl Pepsii Riley** (*Me, Myself & I*, 1988), **James Brown** (*I'm Real*, 1988) and British singer/Page 3 girl Samantha Fox ('Naughty Girls', 1988).

FUNK DELUXE
(Group)
From New York, Funk Deluxe were Rick (guitar), Jesse (guitar), Chris (bass), Zack (drums), Stevie (keyboards), Jeff (vocals) and Lois (vocals) who signed to the Salsoul label under the direction of **Randy Muller** in 1984. They delivered one album *Funk Deluxe*, including 'This Time' and 'Tender Lovin''.

FUNK FUSION BAND
(Studio Group)
Instigated by producer **Nick Martinelli**, the Funk Fusion Band were a handful of musicians from Philadelphia who came together for one single release 'Can You Feel It' for the WMOT label in 1981.

FUNK MASTERS
(Group)
London-based group utilized the lead vocals of **Juliet Roberts** on their one UK chart success 'It's Over' (Top 10) for Master Funk Records in 1984.

FUNKADELIC
(Group)
Formed by **George Clinton**, Funkadelic were essentially the members of **Parliament**, a group name George temporarily lost the rights to during a deal with Atlantic Records. He officially formed Funkadelic in 1975 and signed them to the Westbound label, although he also won back the rights to the Parliament name at the same time. He decided to sign Parliament to 20th Century Records which meant at one point there was one set of musicians recording with two different names for two different labels.

Funkadelic's albums at Westbound included *Let's Take It To The Stage* (1975), although the group's finest moment came in 1978 when they delivered the dancefloor anthem 'One Nation Under A Groove' (UK Top 10) for Warner Brothers.

FUQUA, HARVEY
(Singer/Songwriter/Producer)
Born in Chicago, Harvey formed a vocal group The Moonglows in 1959 with three members of The Marquees, one of whom was **Marvin Gaye**. After two single releases, their record company Chess acquired a share in Gwen Gordy's Anna label in Detroit. Harvey went to the Motor City to meet Gwen, fell in love and married her! Anna became the Tri-Phi label with artists including **The Detroit Spinners** before the company was taken over by Motown, and Harvey instigated **Marvin Gaye**'s move to Detroit and subsequent work for Motown as a drummer.

During Harvey's stay at Motown he co-wrote songs including 'Twenty-Five Miles' (with **Johnny Bristol** and **Edwin Starr**), and also produced 'Yester-Me, Yester-You, Yesterday' with **Johnny Bristol** for **Stevie Wonder**. After leaving Motown in 1970 he instigated **New Birth**, for whom he wrote and arranged at RCA through to 1975.

From here he formed his own Milk and Honey label (via Fantasy) and discovered **Jeanie Tracey** who initially wrote songs for Harvey's gospel group Voices Of Harmony. Also during this period and through to the late '70s he wrote and/or produced for artists on his label including Water and Power and **Two Tons Of Fun**, co-writing their 'Taking Away Your Space' with **Sylvester**, for whom he also co-produced 'You Make Me Feel (Mighty Real)'.

FUTURES
(Vocal Group)
From Philadelphia, this quintet formed in 1968 while together in high school. They were **James King**, Kenny Crew, Richard Wright, Jon King, Frank Washington and Harry McGilberry. In 1970 they teamed up with **Kenny Gamble** to record 'Breaking Up', a small hit on the US Amjo label. In 1972 Richard Wright died from a brain tumour and was replaced by Frank Washington. Next they recorded 'Love Is Here' and 'Stay With Me' on Kenny's Gamble label prior to recording for Buddah (*Castles In The Sky*), United Artists and finally the Philadelphia International label in 1978. Here their albums were *Past, Present And The Futures* (1978), which included the group's most memorable recording 'Ain't Got Time Fa Nuthin'' together with 'You Got It'; and *The Futures* (1980).

On the Philly scene they sang backgrounds for **Lou Rawls**, **Melba Moore** ('Pick Me Up I'll Dance' and 'Standing Right Here'), **McFadden & Whitehead**, **Billy Paul** and many others. More recently James King has pursued a solo career, his single 'Memory' proving popular with UK soul fans.

G., KENNY

(Saxophone/Producer)

From Seattle, Washington, Kenny Gorelick was playing saxophone by the time he reached high school. Here he met **Philip Woo**, with whom he formed a couple of groups Energy and Cold, alongside Bold & Together. At the age of seventeen he played with **The Love Unlimited Orchestra** when it came to Seattle. A later professional engagement was in Liberace's orchestra which took him to Portland, Oregon. Here he decided to audition for **Jeff Lorber** who was looking for a new sax player. He was immediately invited to join the Jeff Lorber Fusion which was signed to the Arista label. Here Jeff co-produced with **Meco** Kenny's solo debut album *Kenny G* in 1982.

While still working with the Jeff Lorber Fusion, Kenny met **Kashif** backstage after a concert. He was invited to play on 'Say Something Love' for Kashif's own debut album in 1983, also for Arista. Also under the direction of Kashif, Kenny recorded a 1983 album *G Force*. It included 'Hi How Ya Doin'', a UK Top 70 hit in 1984 on which Kenny did not sing vocals. Vocalist on 'Love On The Rise' in 1985 was Kashif himself, but this together with the album *Gravity* was the last time they worked together. 1986's *Duotones* included a version of 'What Does It Take' featuring the vocals of **Ellis Hall** from **Tower of Power**. The song was a UK Top 75 hit, following which the instrumental 'Songbird' (from the same album) was a UK Top 25 hit in 1987.

In 1988 the self-produced *Silhouette* (featuring **Smokey Robinson**) was released by Arista. Kenny can also be found on recordings by **Collage, Jennifer Holliday, Whitney Houston, The Four Tops** and **Johnny Gil** ('My My My').

In the USA, incidentally, his music is considered 'New Age' (meaning atmospheric, esoteric and relaxing). While in the mid-'80s he moved to Los Angeles, he returns to Seattle frequently where as a producer he has worked with the jazz fusion group 206 (206 also being the telephone area code for Seattle).

G.Q.

(Group)

From New York, G.Q. were Keith 'Sabu' Crier – later known as **Keith Sweat** (bass/vocals), Emmanuel Rahiem LeBlanc (guitar/lead vocals), Paul Service (drums/vocals) and Herb Lane (keyboards/vocals). Keith and Emmanuel initially worked together as Sabu And The Survivors, Sons of Darkness, Third Chance and **Rhythm Makers**, at which point they were joined by Paul and Herb. Changing their name to G.Q. (standing for Good Quality) the group signed with Arista and released their dance classic 'Disco Nights – Rock Freak' (UK Top 50, 1979). It came from a debut album *Disco Nights* which was followed by two further albums, *GQ Two* (1980), including 'Standing Ovation' and 'GQ Down', and *Face To Face* (1981).

In 1984 they released one last single 'You Are The One For Me' on the independent Stadium label before Keith launched his solo career.

GADSON, JAMES

(Drummer/Vocals)

Based in Los Angeles, James Gadson has been about the most prolific drummer on the '70s/'80s r&b scene. In 1970 he played with **Charles Wright** in The Watts 103rd Street Rhythm Band on their cult track 'Express Yourself', from which point he has played on numerous classic tracks for artists including **Marvin Gaye** (*I Want You*), **Aretha Franklin** ('Sunshine Will Never Be The Same'), **The Supremes**, **Minnie Riperton** ('Can You Feel What I'm Saying'), **Martha Reeves, Bill Withers, Margie Joseph** ('I Feel His Love Getting Stronger'), **Ramsey Lewis, Teena Marie, Patrice Rushen, Eloise Laws, Cheryl Lynn** ('Got To Be Real'), **Tavares, Randy Crawford** ('Endlessly'), **Womack & Womack** (*Love Wars*), **David Oliver, Phyllis Hyman** ('Don't Tell Me, Tell Her'), **Michael Wycoff, David Ruffin, Jerry Knight, Johnnie Taylor** ('What About My Love' and 'Just Ain't Good Enough'), **Johnny Bristol, Johnny 'Guitar' Watson, G.C.Cameron** ('You're What's Missing In My Life'), **Lenny Williams, Leon Ware** ('Why I Came To California'), **Prince Phillip Mitchell** ('One On One'), **Randy Brown, Linda Evans** ('Elevate Our Minds'), **Rockie Robbins** ('You

And Me'), **Sherrick, Gwen McCrae** ('Keep The Fire Burning'), **Smokey Robinson, Anita Baker** (*Songstress*), **Wilton Felder** ('Let's Dance Together'), **John Handy** ('Hard Work'), **John And Arthur Sims** ('Love Will Getcha'), **Magic Lady, Patti Brooks, Terry Callier** ('Ordinary Joe'), **Beau Williams, Booker T.Jones, Natalie Cole, Benny Golson** (lending his vocals to 'High On Sunshine') and **Bobby Womack** (both *Poet* albums, co-producing *The Poet II*, and *So Many Rivers*, including 'I Wish He Didn't Trust Me So Much'). He also worked with **Bobby McClure**, arranging and producing 'You Never Miss Your Water' and 'It Feels So Good (To Be Back Home)' for Edge Records.

GAINES, ROSIE

(Singer/Songwriter/Keyboards)

Rosie sang lead vocals with the San Francisco-based group Flash before signing to Epic as a solo artist in 1985. Here she released *Caring*, including 'Good Times', followed in 1987 by the **Patrick Moten**-penned/produced single 'Crazy'. This single was later withdrawn while her second album was shelved.

As a songwriter she co-wrote 'You' on the **Curtis Ohlson** album *So Fast*, on which she also sang the title cut (1987), while in 1990 she toured as part of **Prince**'s band. She also sang backgrounds with **Narada Michael Walden** and **Michael Jeffries**, while in 1991 'Crazy' was issued in the UK for the first time on CBS compilation album *Soul Souvenirs*.

GAINORS

(Vocal Group)

Based in Philadelphia, late '50s/early '60s vocal group The Gainors consisted of **Garnet Mimms** (lead singer), **Howard Tate**, Sam Bell, Willie Combo and John Jefferson. After recording for local labels including Red Top ('Follow Me', 1958), Cameo and Talley-Ho Records, Garnet and Sam joined **The Enchanters**.

GALAXY

(Group)

Galaxy was the concept of North Londoner **Phil Fearon** who was the featured singer on all their UK hits: 'Dancing Tight' (Top 5, 1983), 'Wait Until Tonight My Love' (Top 20, 1983), 'Fantasy Real' (Top 5, 1983), 'What Do I Do' (Top 5, 1984), 'Everybody's Laughing' (Top 10, 1984), 'You Don't Need A Reason' (Top 50, 1985), and 'This Kind Of Love' (Top 75, 1985), all for Ensign Records.

GALE, ERIC

(Guitar)

Born in Brooklyn, Eric first took up the guitar in his teen years. After leaving high school he played professionally and over the years has become one of the most in-demand musicians on the r&b scene. As a solo artist, he signed to the Kudu subsidiary of CTI Records in 1973 where his debut album was *Forecast*. Switching to CBS in 1976 his albums included *Ginseng Woman* (1977), *Multiplication* (1978), *Part Of You* (1979), *Touch of Silk* (1980) and *Live To Love* (1980). More recently he has recorded for labels including Elektra Musician (*Blue Horizon*, 1982), and Artful Balance Records (1989).

As a session player he has worked with numerous artists including **Jackie Wilson, The Drifters, Maxine Brown**, The Flamingos, **Aretha Franklin, Marvin Gaye, The O'Jays**, Frank Sinatra, **Diana Ross**, Steely Dan, Mongo Santamaria, **Ashford & Simpson, Stuff, Charles Earland, Teddy Pendergrass, Angela Bofill, Grover Washington** and **Jimmy Smith**. He also worked as music director for **Roberta Flack**, during which time he met **Richard Tee**. Through the '70s and '80s Eric and Richard have worked together on numerous projects for Roberta and other artists.

GAMBLE/HUFF

(Songwriters/Producers)

Kenny Gamble and **Leon Huff** first met in 1984 during a recording session for 'The 81', a song for Candy & The Kisses which Kenny had written and on which Leon played keyboards. By 1965 they were writing together, 'Gee I'm Sorry Baby' for **The Sapphires** being an early collaboration. Deciding to move further into joint writing/production projects they formed Excel Records and signed **The Intruders**. After one release they changed the name of the label to Gamble Records for further hits by The Intruders and other local acts **Frank Beverly** (of **Maze**), The Cruisers, Baby Doll and Madman. Away from their own label they also worked with numerous artists including **Jerry Butler**, co-writing and producing his two classic albums *The Ice Man Cometh* (1989) and *Ice On Ice* (1969).

It was The Intruders who gave them their first million-seller with 'Cowboys To Girls' in 1971. By now they had not only started the Philadelphia International (PIR) label but ran the smaller North Bay label which was set up to develop new acts. One of these acts was Talk Of The Town, a group instigated by **McFadden & Whitehead** who soon became key figures within the Gamble/Huff empire. At PIR Gamble/Huff songs/productions included the '70s Philly classics 'For The Love Of Money', 'Now That We Found Love', 'Love Train', 'I Love Music', 'Darlin' Darlin' Baby', 'Used To Be My Girl', 'Extraordinary Girl', 'My Favourite Person' and 'Lovin' You' (**The O'Jays**); 'When Will I See You Again', 'Dirty Ol' Man', 'Year Of Decision' and 'Take Good Care Of Yourself' (**The Three Degrees**); 'Satisfaction Guaranteed', 'The Love I Lost', 'If You Don't Know Me By Now' and 'Don't Leave Me This Way' (**Harold Melvin & The Blue Notes**); 'Come Go With Me', 'Turn Off The Lights', 'Close The Door' and 'Only You' (**Teddy Pendergrass**); 'Sexy' and 'T.S.O.P' (**M.F.S.B.**); 'Show You The Way To Go' (**The Jacksons**); 'Don't Let It Go To Your Head', 'If You Wanna Go Back' and 'Free Love' (**Jean Carne**); 'You'll Never Find Another

Love Like Mine', 'Let Me Be Good To You', 'See You When I Get There' and 'What's The Matter With The World' (**Lou Rawls**); 'You Gonna Make Me Love Somebody Else' (**The Jones Girls**); 'Me & Mrs Jones' and 'Let's Make A Baby' (**Billy Paul**).

They ran the PIR label until the mid-'80s, originally via CBS and later EMI, but in 1987 shelved the label to launch the Gamble & Huff Records label. Here they recorded **Lou Rawls** before Lou left to sign with Blue Note. While Gamble/Huff are far from retired, the r&b world awaits their next move!

GAMBLE, KENNY
(Singer/Songwriter/Producer)
Born in Philadelphia, Kenny went to school with Barbara Bell, twin sister of **Thom Bell**. Through their friendship, Kenny met Thom and formed a vocal duo, recording a duet 'Someday' for the local Heritage label in 1959. Expanding to a group and calling themselves The Romeos, they attracted local attention and recorded for Cameo Records. While at Cameo, Kenny met in-house producer Jerry Ross who taught him about the music business and helped develop his songwriting. Together they wrote 'The 81' which the label decided to record for their group Candy And The Kisses. Keyboard player for the session was **Leon Huff** whom Kenny first met at the recording of the song in 1964.

From the mid-'60s to the mid-'80s, Kenny wrote and/or produced numerous classic soul hits with Leon (see **Gamble/Huff**) on labels including his own Gamble and the mighty Philadelphia International Records he formed with Leon. He was also briefly married to **Dee Dee Sharp**.

GAMBLE, LENNY
(Singer)
Lenny Gamble was allegedly a pseudonym for UK Radio DJ/personality Tony Blackburn who recorded the **Gamble/Huff** song 'I'll Do Anything' for DJM in 1978.

GAP BAND
(Group)
From Tulsa, Oklahoma, The Gap Band are the Wilson brothers Ronnie, Charlie and Robert. Their father was a minister, and the brothers spent their early years in their father's church choir. The name GAP comes from the first three letters of Tulsa's three major black business communities, Greenwood, Archer and Pine Streets. The band was formed by eldest brother Ronnie. Their first break came via rock star Leon Russell (also from Tulsa) who took them on the road as his opening act in 1973. In 1978 they came to the attention of Lonnie Simmons who signed them to his Total Experience production company. They remained with Lonnie for ten years, recording initially for the Mercury label, and then for Lonnie's own Total Experience label.

Numbering their albums rather than inventing titles, the group released *Gap Band I* (1979), including 'Open Up Your Mind (Wide)' and 'Shake', before scoring commercial success with 'Oops Up Side Your Head' (UK Top 10) and 'Party Lights' (UK Top 30) from *Gap Band II* (1980). Further UK hit singles were 'Burn Rubber On Me' (Top 25, 1980), 'Humpin'' (Top 40, 1981), 'Yearning For Your Love' (Top 50, 1981), 'Early In The Morning' (Top 75, and the only American platinum r&b single in 1982), 'Outstanding' (Top 75, 1983), 'Someday' featuring **Stevie Wonder** (Top 20, 1984), 'Jammin' In America' (Top 75, 1984) and 'Big Fun' (Top 5, 1985). The group's last Total Experience album was *Straight From The Heart* (1987), following which they stopped briefly at Arista for 'I'm Gonna Git You Sucka' from the film soundtrack of the same name (1988). In 1989 they signed to Capitol for *Round Trio*, including 'Addicted To Your Love'.

More recently the group's music has been regarded as the inspiration for the 'swing beat' sound instigated by **Teddy Riley** and his group **Guy** in the late '80s.

GARCIA'S SUPER FUNK
(Group)
Formed by Guille Garcia in Miami, Florida, Garcia's Super Funk recorded the one Guille and **Ish**-penned dance record 'I Didn't Know That You Could Dance' for the TK label in 1978.

GARDIER, DONNA
(Singer)
Born in North London, Donna is the daughter of French Caribbean parents. Having sung in her local Pentecostal choir from the age of five she became lead vocalist by the time she reached her teens. She also sang with a gospel group Destiny, while building a steady interest in soul music and ultimately breaking into London session work in the late '80s. Her debut solo release was 'I'll Be There', swiftly issued commercially by Virgin Records to whom she signed in 1990. The follow-up was 'Reach Out' (1991).

GARDNER, BURGESS
(Trumpet/Flugelhorn)
From Chicago, session musician Burgess Gardner lead the Chicago Regal Theater house band from 1967, and performed with Count Basie, Horace Silver, Ramsey Lewis and many leading jazz musicians. In 1983 he released one solo album *Music Year 2000*, a collaboration with **Al Perkins**, recorded in Detroit. It contained a track 'Gemstone' which sounded exactly like the original backing tape to the **Al Hudson**/Soul Partners classic 'Spread Love'. A trumpet lead replaced the vocals, and the result lead to brief success on the UK fusion scene.

More recently Burgess has taught jazz at the California State University.

GARDNER, JOANNA
(Singer)
Born in Philadelphia in 1962, Joanna is the daughter of a police force mechanic and a social/community director for a nursing concern. At the age of sixteen she decided to sing full-time, eventually forming her own group Joanna's Band which performed at her mother's nightclub. She also worked as a barmaid at the club during weekends! Taking a part-time job in a jeweler's shop she met British group **Loose Ends** who walked in the store. Fascinated by their clothes and accent she talked to them and became friends. Loose Ends were recording in Philadelphia with **Nick Martinelli**.

Excited by her voice, Nick took her to Philly World Records who signed her up within five days. She debuted by singing 'Today's Your Lucky Day' with **Harold Melvin**, and then joined Loose Ends as a backing singer on 'Hangin' On A String' (also appearing on their *So Where Are You* album). This was soon followed by a debut album, *Joanna Gardner* (1985), released in the UK via Polydor. Here the tracks 'I Could Never Love Another Like You', 'Pick Up The Pieces', 'We Can Make It' and 'Special Feelings' established her with UK soul fans, many of whom went to see her London stage debut while on a playback tour with Loose Ends later that year.

Joanna also made a film appearance with **Eugene Wilde**, singing a duet 'First Love Never Dies' (featured on the soundtrack *Rappin'*), but this was the last we heard of her.

GARDNER, TAANA
(Singer)
Based in New York, Taana has worked as a session singer on numerous r&b/dance records through the '80s in addition to recording as a solo artist for labels including West End ('We Can Work It Out'). More recently she has recorded for the Yes Records label, 'Over You' being a single release in 1991.

GARRETT, LEE
(Singer/Songwriter)
Born blind in Mississippi, Lee developed a friendship with **Stevie Wonder** which led to a collaboration on Stevie's album *Where I'm Coming From*. Their joint songwriting projects extended to artists including **Jermaine Jackson** ('Let's Get Serious'), **The Detroit Spinners** ('It's A Shame') and back to Stevie again for 'Signed, Sealed, Delivered'.

As a solo artist, Lee signed to Chrysalis in the mid-'70s where his one album *Heat For The Feats* (1976) included 'You're My Everything' (UK Top 20), 'Better Than Walkin' Out' and 'Heart Be Still.'

GARRETT, SIEDAH
(Singer/Songwriter)
Based in Los Angeles, Siedah Garrett is a top name on the West Coast session singer scene, and a protégé of **Quincy Jones**. While she has been signed to Quincy's Qwest label, her finest moments have included guest lead/co-lead vocals for artists including **Tom Browne** ('Secret Fantasy'), **Dennis Edwards** ('Don't Look Any Further'), **Michael Jackson** ('I Just Can't Stop Loving You'), **Sergio Mendes** ('Brasil '86') and **Quincy Jones** himself ('One Man Woman').

As a songwriter her work has been recorded by artists including **Michael Jackson** ('Man In The Mirror'), **Aretha Franklin** ('Mercy'), **Natalie Cole** ('As A Matter Of Fact') and once again **Quincy Jones** (co-writing 'One Man Woman', 'Wee B. Dooinit', 'The Secret Garden' and 'Tomorrow'). She has recorded background vocals with **George Howard, The Commodores**, **Sarah Vaughan**, **El Debarge**, **Glenn Jones**, **Hinton Battle** and numerous others.

GARY TOMS EMPIRE
(Group)
New York-based '70s group Gary Toms Empire featured Gary Toms (songwriter/arranger/singer/keyboards) with Norbert Sloley (bass), Rick Aikens (drums), John Sussewell (drums), Butch Campbell (guitar) and **Patrick Adams** (keyboards). On tour they utilized the services of **Inez Brown** as lead singer. Their albums for Mercury Records included *Let's Do It Again* (1978).

GARY'S GANG
(Group)
The brainchild of Gary Turnier in New York, Gary's Gang were a small group of musicians who recorded live in a friend's garage. It was here they made their debut single 'Keep On Dancin'' which sold half a million copies around the world and was a UK Top 10 hit (1978). It was co-written by **Eric Matthew** and released in the UK by CBS (licenced from Sam Records). Their CBS follow-up was 'Let's Love Dance Tonight' (UK Top 50, 1979).

In 1982 they returned with 'Knock Me Out' (UK Top 50) for Arista before Eric Matthew wrote and produced 'Makin' Music' for the Radar Records label in 1983. In 1990 'Keep On Dancin'' was remixed by Hollywood Impact, and released by BCM Records in the UK.

GASKIN, LA-RITA
(Singer)
The niece of **Barbara Roy** and a cousin of **Jocelyn Brown**, La-Rita began a serious music career after moving from Washington to New York. Through Jocelyn she found session work with artists including **Stevie Wonder, Roberta Flack, Millie Jackson, Melba Moore, Candi Staton, The Fatback Band, Inner Life** and **Ben E.King**. As a solo artist she recorded 'Nice & Slow' which was released in the UK on the Excalibur label in 1981.

GATLING, TIMMY
(Singer/Songwriter/Producer)
Timmy began his career with a New York group called Fame before joining Kids At Work where his fellow

members included **Teddy Riley**. Via Teddy he wrote and produced tracks for **Guy**, while through his manager Cassandra Mills he wrote and/or produced **Stephanie Mills** ('Ain't No Cookin''), **Ralph Tresvant** ('Last Night') and **Bell Biv Devoe** ('When Will I See You Smile Again', with **Alton 'Wokie' Stewart**, before signing with Tommy Boy Records. His debut album *Help* was released in 1989.

GAYE, FRANKIE

(Singer/Songwriter)

Born in Washington DC in 1941, Frankie is the younger brother of **Marvin Gaye** He also has another brother and two sisters, all of whom grew up in a strict church environment (their father being a preacher). When Marvin and **Harvey Fuqua** left Washington for Detroit, Frankie stayed behind and established himself as a singer on the Washington club circuit.

In 1964 Frankie was drafted to serve in Vietnam, where he fought until 1967. Upon his return he began working with Marvin, generally in the organization of his live shows and business interests. When Marvin moved to Los Angeles with Motown, Frankie moved too. He sang backing vocals on many of Marvin's recordings including 'What's Going On', a song inspired by Frankie's own account of his experience in Vietnam.

As a writer he composed the complete soundtrack to the film *Penitentiary 1* in 1972, while as a performer he has worked extensively in California, his voice sometimes being compared with Marvin's. He also began a series of visits to the UK, meeting his Scottish wife while on tour in 1980. In 1989 he signed to the Motorcity label and recorded 'It Takes Two' with Kim Weston. (Marvin had originally recorded the song with Kim in 1966.) As a solo artist on the label his singles to date include 'Extraordinary Girl' (1989) and 'My Brother' (1990).

GAYE, MARVIN

(Singer/Songwriter/Producer/Keyboards/Drums)

Born in Washington in 1938, Marvin Pentz Gaye was the son of a minister and first took to singing in his father's church choir. While at high school he learned piano and drums and decided on a musical career, influenced by a recurring dream about being a performer. He broadened his musical interests beyond gospel to r&b and formed a group The DC Tones with some friends. After a brief spell in the Air Force he joined leading Washington vocal group **The Rainbows** with **Don Covay** and **Billy Stewart**. In 1957 he and two former Rainbows became The Marquees, and met Bo Diddley who instigated their one album for Okeh Records. They also accompanied Bo on his Chess release 'I'm Sorry'.

In 1959 the group auditioned for **Harvey Fuqua** who invited The Marquees to team up with him to become The Moonglows. After two singles for Chess, Harvey moved to Detroit where he married Gwen Gordy (sister of **Berry Gordy**) and became a director of her Anna label before it was taken over by Motown. Once at Motown, Harvey brought Marvin to Detroit as a session drummer. Marvin's first recordings with Motown were playing drums for artists including **Smokey Robinson** & The Miracles.

The idea that Marvin should record as a singer was originally greeted with some resistance by Berry Gordy, but 'Let Your Conscience Be Your Guide' became Marvin's debut solo release in 1961. It was followed by an album *The Soulful Moods Of Marvin*, featuring two further singles, 'Mister Sandman' and 'Soldier's Plea'. In 1962 Marvin wrote 'Stubborn Kind Of Fella' which he recorded with background vocals from **Martha Reeves & The Vandellas**. The single was an American hit and his first release in the UK (on the Oriole label). At this point he married Anna Gordy (another sister of Berry Gordy) for whom he wrote his next release 'Pride And Joy', another American hit. In the UK Marvin first made an impression on the charts with 'How Sweet It Is', (Top 50, 1964), also a hit in America where its success was followed up by 'Can I Get A Witness'.

In 1964 Marvin began to explore the duet concept, initially with **Mary Wells** and an album *Together*, including 'Once Upon A Time' (UK Top 50). When Mary left Motown later in the year, Oma Heard recorded a number of sides with Marvin (never released) before **Kim Weston** stepped in for *Take Two*, including 'It Takes Two' (UK Top 10, 1966). Then Marvin was joined by **Tammi Terrell** for 'Ain't No Mountain High Enough' (later a hit for **Diana Ross**), which established this partnership in America. In the UK their hits were 'If I Could Build My Whole World Around You' (Top 50, 1968), 'Ain't Nothin' Like The Real Thing' (Top 40, 1968), 'You're All I Need To Get By' (Top 20, 1968), 'You Ain't Livin' Till You're Livin' (Top 25, 1969), 'Good Lovin' Ain't Easy To Come By' (Top 50, 1969), and 'The Onion Song' (Top 10, 1969). In the meantime Marvin had also teamed up with producer **Norman Whitfield** for solo hits including the classic 'I Heard It Through The Grapevine', one of Motown's all-time biggest selling singles (UK No. 1, 1969) and 'Too Busy Thinking 'Bout My Baby' (Top 5, 1969). In 1970 Tammi Terrell died (from a brain tumour) during one of their shows in Cleveland, Ohio.

Deeply shocked, Marvin became almost a recluse for two years, some thinking he would never record or perform again. In the meantime his brother **Frankie Gaye** returned from Vietnam and it was Frankie's account of this experience, together with the social climate in America, which motivated him to record *What's Going On*, including 'Save The Children' (UK Top 50), 'Inner City Blues' and 'Mercy Mercy Me', in 1971. Originally rejected by Motown, the album became a classic.

In 1972 he worked on the soundtrack album to the movie *Trouble Man*, before returning for more of an official album to 'What's Going On' with the album *Let's Get It On* in 1973 (including the UK Top 40 title track single). Later that year he teamed up with **Diana Ross** for *Diana & Marvin*, including 'You Are Everything' (UK Top 5, 1974) and 'Stop, Look, Listen (To Your Heart)'

(UK Top 25, 1974). Back in concert, Marvin made his first live concert appearance in six years at the Oakland Coliseum in 1974 (an event captured and released as a live album).

His next album *I Want You* (1976) including 'All The Way Around' and 'Come Live With Me Angel', was mainly written and produced by **Leon Ware**. A later rumour was that the songs were originally intended for Leon himself, but handed over at Marvin's request! In the UK, however, singles from the album were not hits, and it was 'Got To Give It Up' which next saw Marvin in the UK Top 10 (1977). The album on which it appeared was *Love Man*, including 'Ego Tripping Out'. Marvin then had a painful divorce from his wife Anna which inspired album *Here My Dear* (1979). Royalties were supposed to go to Anna in part settlement of the divorce but he attracted publicity by trying to withhold them.

His final album for Motown was *In Our Lifetime* (a re-recording of *Love Man*) which met with unfavourable reviews. He left the label, vowing never to record for them again. By now Marvin was living in Belgium, and it was here that Larkin Arnold from CBS Records went to tempt him with a new recording deal. In 1982 Marvin signed to CBS where his first release was the Grammy award-winning 'Sexual Healing' (UK Top 5) from *Midnight Love*, also including 'My Love Is Waiting' (UK Top 40, 1983) and 'Joy'.

Following an argument, Marvin was shot dead on 1st April 1984 by his father who was arrested, but later walked free proving he was acting in self-defense. Following this tragic death of a soul legend, CBS released two further albums, *Dream Of A Lifetime* (1985) including 'Sanctified Lady' and 'Symphony', and *Romantically Yours* (1985) including previously unreleased tracks leased from Motown, assembled and mixed by **Harvey Fuqua**. Motown themselves released *Motown Remembers Marvin Gaye* (1986), including 'The World Is Rated X', while various other previously unreleased tracks have surfaced between then and now (including a single 'My Last Chance', recorded in 1973 and released in 1990). After much campaigning, Marvin was finally honoured with a star on Hollywood's 'Walk of Fame' in 1990.

GAYNOR, GLORIA
(Singer)
Born in Newark, New Jersey, Gloria was one of six sisters and a brother. During her teens she worked in local clubs both as a solo singer and with local band the Soul Satisfiers. While performing in New York she met Jay Ellis who became her manager and secured her a recording deal with CBS in the early '70s.

In 1974 she switched to the MGM label (via Polydor) and scored a string of hit singles which in the UK were 'Never Can Say Goodbye', a cover of the **Jackson 5** hit (Top 5, 1974); 'Reach Out I'll Be There', a cover of the Four Tops hit (Top 20, 1975); 'All I Need Is Your Sweet Lovin'' (Top 50, 1975); 'How High The Moon' (Top 40, 1976); 'I Will Survive' (No. 1, 1979); and 'Let Me Know I Have The Right' (Top 40, 1979). During this era she appealed to both disco and Philly soul fans. 'This Love Affair' (1978) and 'Let's Mend What's Been Broken', written/produced by **McFadden & Whitehead** (1981), weren't major hits but remain soul gems.

Her albums included *Never Can Say Goodbye* (1974); *Experience Gloria Gaynor* (1975), including 'How High The Moon'; *I've Got You* (1976); *Glorious* (1978); *Stories* (1980) and *I Kinda Like Me* (1981). In 1983 she switched to Chrysalis for 'I Am What I Am' (UK Top 20), a song from *La Cage Aux Folles* which holds Gloria in high esteem on the gay scene to this day.

GAZ
(Studio Group)
On the late '70s disco scene, studio group Gaz emerged out of New York on the Salsoul label with 'Sing Sing', a huge dancefloor record in 1978 which reached the UK Top 75 in early 1979.

GENERAL KANE
(Group)
Based in Los Angeles, General Kane are an eight-piece group led by Mitch McDowell. They released two albums for Tabu Records before joining Motown for singles 'Crack Killed Applejack' and 'Hairdooz' in the late '80s.

GEORGIO
(Singer)
Born in San Francisco, Georgio Allentini started his career as a disc jockey hiring venues and staging parties. Teaching himself how to play a handful of instruments he moved to Los Angeles, raised some money and spent it recording his first single 'Sex Appeal'. He released it on his own label, Picture Perfect in 1986 but when sales took off, Georgio and his record were signed exclusively by Motown. The song was the title of his debut album *Sex Appeal* (1987) also including 'Lover's Lane' and 'Tina Cherry'.

GEYER, RENEE
(Singer)
Based in Los Angeles, Renee signed to Polydor in 1977 and worked with former Motown writer/producer **Frank Wilson** on *Renee Geyer*, including a version of a song Frank co-wrote for **The Supremes** called 'Touch'.

GIBSON BROTHERS
(Group)
Chris (vocals/percussion/guitar), Patrick (drums/vocals) and Alex Gibson (piano/vocals) were born in Martinique in the French West Indies and lived most of their lives in Paris, France. In 1976 they signed to the Zagora label, and their debut release was 'Come To America' which entered the French and Italian charts. It was followed up by 'Non Stop Dance', a No. 1 hit in the Benelux countries.

In 1979 they scored on the 'disco' scene with 'Cuba' (Top 50), 'Ooh What A Life' (Top 10) and 'Que Sera Mi Vida' (Top 5), released in the UK by Island Records. Further success on the label followed with 'Mariana' (Top 20, 1980). In 1981 they released 'Quartier Latin', a single/ album for Epic Records, while in 1983 they were with Stiff Records for 'My Heart's Beating Wild' (Top 75).

GIL, GILBERTO
(Singer/Musician/Songwriter)
Born Gilberto Passos Gil Moreira in Salvador in 1942, Gilberto discovered the drums by the age of three. Aged seven he was playing samba rhythms and took up the trumpet. In 1950 he took up the accordion and joined a group The Desafinados. He also took up the guitar and developed his vocal skills. In 1960 he composed his first song 'Felicidade Vem Depois' (a bossa nova), and found work composing jingles and working on TV programmes. Moving to São Paulo in 1965, Gilberto sang regularly in the João Sebastiao Bar nightclub.

In 1966 he moved to Rio de Janeiro and recorded his debut album for the Phillips label. He was also involved in the 'Tropicalista' music/culture movement with Gal Costa, Tom Ze, Caetano Veloso, Mutantes, Rogerio Duprat, and poets Torquato Neto and Luis Carlos Capinam. In 1969 he scored with 'Aquele Abraco' ('That Hug'), and moved to London after a second album. There he recorded a new album for Phillips (with English lyrics) and worked in European theatre/TV before returning to Brazil in 1972. From *Gilberto 2222* he scored with 'Back In Bahia' and 'Oriente'. Two more albums on Phillips followed in 1974 before he teamed up with Jorge Ben for *Gil And Jorge*.

Further success came with *Refazenda* in 1975 and *Refavela* in 1977, before he signed with WEA the same year. His albums here included *Nightingale* and *Realce* (1979), including 'Toda Menina Balana'. His 1982 release 'Palco', also with WEA, was popular on the dance scene with its Earth Wind & Fire-style vocal effects.

GILES, ATTALA ZANE
(Songwriter/Producer/Guitar)
Based in Los Angeles, Attala established himself in the mid-'80s as a songwriter/producer and has since worked for artists including **Con Funk Shun**, **The Emotions**, **The Jacksons** (the majority of *2300 Jackson Street*), **Barry White** (tracks on *The Man Is Back!*), **Howard Hewett** ('Shadow'), **Meli'sa Morgan** (*The Lady In Me*), **Will Downing** ('The Love We Share'), **Patti Labelle** ('Fine Fine Fella'), **Shirley Jones** ('Caught Me With My Guard Down') and **Gladys Knight** ('Men').

He also recorded with **Billy Osborne** (brother of **Jeffrey Osborne**) as Osborne & Giles for a company called Red Label, Billy co-writing a number of songs for other artists with Attala.

GILL, JOHNNY
(Singer)
Born in Washington, Johnny took up singing at the age of eight and formed a gospel quartet with his three brothers, Gill Special. His childhood friend was **Stacey Lattisaw** whose success as a child star inspired him to record a demo tape. Stacey took it to her company, Cotillion, who signed Johnny in 1983.

Here his albums were *Perfect Combination* (1984), a duet album with Stacey Lattisaw, and *Chemistry* (1985), including 'Can't Wait 'Till Tomorrow'. In 1987 he was lined up to replace **Bobby Brown** in **New Edition** and recorded as lead singer with the group on songs including 'Can You Stand The Rain' and 'Boys To Men' (1988). In 1989 he reunited with Stacey Lattisaw for 'Where Do We Go From Here' on her album *What You Need*, and signed to Motown as a solo artist where 1990's *Johnny Gill* included 'Rub U The Right Way', 'My My My' and 'Wrap My Body Tight' – remixed by **Jazzie B**. The album was jointly produced by **Jam/Lewis** and **L.A./Babyface**.

Johnny has also sung backgrounds with **Jeffrey Osborne** and contributed fingersnaps on 'Escapade' for **Janet Jackson**!

GIOVANNI, NIKKI
(Poet)
Highly respected poet Nikki Giovanni wrote four books, *Recreation* (1970), *Black Feeling, Black Talk, Black Judgement* (1970), *My House* (1972) and *The Women And The Men* (1975), excerpts from which she read to music on a self-titled album for Niktom Records (via Atlantic) in 1975. She was accompanied by session musicians including Cornell Dupree, **Richard Tee**, **Steve Gadd** and **David Newman**. **Cissy Houston** was among the background singers, and the album was produced by **Arif Mardin**. **Roberta Flack** wrote the sleeve notes!

GLASS HOUSE
(Vocal Group)
Los Angeles-based '70s group Glass House comprised **Scherrie Payne**, Ty Hunter, Pearl Jones and Larry Mitchell. With songwriters/producers **Holland/Dozier/ Holland** they recorded for the Invictus label, their albums including *Inside The Glass House*.

GLASS, PRESTON
(Songwriter/Producer)
Preston worked consistently on the '80s r&b scene in both New York and Los Angeles, writing and/or producing for artists including **Anita Pointer** (*Love For What It Is*), **Audrey Wheeler** (*Let It Be Me*), **Tyka Nelson**, **Natalie Cole** ('Miss You Like Crazy'), **Aretha Franklin** ('Who's Zoomin' Who'), **Bert Robinson**, **Pieces Of A Dream** ('We Belong To Each Other'), **George Benson** ('Twice The Love'), **Kenny G** ('Songbird'), **Diana Ross** ('Bottom Line') and **Margie Joseph**.

GLAZE

(Group)

From Detroit, Glaze are Rick Kitchen (vocals), Pam Dixson (vocals), Tyrone Hornaday (keyboards), Freddie Guy Hudson (bass), William Wooten (keyboards), Harold Thomas (sax) and Charles Williams (guitar). Their debut single release was 'Promises' (1988) for the local Rivertown label, later issued in the UK as a B-side to 'Love Hurts' on the Expansion label.

GLENN, GARRY

(Singer/Songwriter/Producer)

Born in Detroit, Garry was one of seven children. His sister Beverly was a professional gospel singer who encouraged him to sing as a young child, and by the time he reached high school he was the director of an eighty-voice choir.

During the mid-'70s he realized he had songwriting skills, and in 1977 **The Dramatics** recorded his song 'Sing And Dance Your Troubles Away'. His songs have since been recorded by **Al Hudson** & The Soul Partners ('Spread Love', 1978), **Eddie Kendricks** ('Intimate Friends'), **Philip Bailey** ('It's Our Time', 1983), **Chuck Cissel** ('I've Been Needing Love So Long'), **Phyllis Hyman** ('Be Careful How You Treat My Love'), **Anita Baker** ('Caught Up In The Rapture', 1986 and 'Priceless', 1988), **R.J.'s Latest Arrival** ('Heaven In Your Arms', 1986), **Jean Carne** ('Flame Of Love', 1986), **Pieces of a Dream** ('Winning Streak' and 'Love Of My Life' – Garry also sang lead vocals – 1986), **Natalie Cole** ('Gonna Make You Mine'), **Geoff McBride** and Byron Woods ('You Don't Even Know').

As a recording artist he made a debut album *Garry Glenn*, including 'Got You On My Mind', for PPL Records (1980), and switched to Motown for *Feels Good To Feel Good* (1987), including 'Running Away' and 'Torch For You'. More recently he has signed with the Zing label in the UK.

GLOVER, BOBBY

(Singer)

Born in Ohio, Bobby worked with **Roger Troutman** and **Zapp** before making one Roger Troutman-produced solo album *Bad Bobby Glover* (1984), including 'Happy' and 'Bright Skies, Sunny Days', for CBS Records. Bobby also sang backgrounds with groups including **Dayton**.

GOLDSMITH, GLEN

(Singer/Songwriter)

Based in Notting Hill, London, Glen's singing career took off after he answered an advert in the magazine *Melody Maker* placed by the songwriting/production team **Jolley/Harris/Jolley**. Together they scored three UK Top 40 hits with 'I Won't Cry' (1987), 'Dreaming' (1988) and 'What You See Is What You Get' (1988) for the Reproduction label. A further single 'Save A Little Bit' reached the UK Top 75 (1988) before **Jolley/Harris/Jolley** became the driving force behind **Innocence**. Glen also wrote songs with Leee John and Errol Kennedy of **Imagination**.

GOLDSTEIN, JERRY

(Producer/Songwriter)

Based in Los Angeles, Jerry has been closely involved with the group **War** both as manager and producer. His own company, Far Out Productions, has also worked for other artists including **Eloise Laws**, whose album *Eloise* (1977) he co-produced with **Linda Creed** (co-writing 'Baby You Lied').

GOLSON, BENNY

(Sax/Producer)

Born in Philadelphia, Benny played tenor sax with jazz artists including Lionel Hampton (1953), Dizzy Gillespie (1956–8) and Art Blakey (1959) before forming a group Jazztet with **McCoy Tyner** and Art Farmer (trumpet) in 1959.

On the UK jazz funk scene, Benny is best remembered for his 1977 CBS recording 'The New Killer Joe', adapted from an instrumental he had already written, 'Killer Joe', but now featuring a spoken rap written by **Quincy Jones**. The track came from an album of the same name, the follow-up being *I'm Always Dancing To The Music* in 1978.

GOODING, CUBA

(Singer)

After a brief career as a debt collector and door-to-door salesman (of encyclopedias, no less), Cuba Gooding joined **The Main Ingredient** as their lead singer in 1969. Taking time off from the group he recorded two solo albums for Motown, *The First Cuba Gooding Album* and *Love Dancer*. In 1983 he took 'Happiness Is Just Around The Bend', a song The Main Ingredient had recorded on *Euphrates River* in 1974, and re-recorded it as a solo artist on **Arthur Baker**'s Streetwise label. The track became Cuba's one UK Top 75 single release. The follow-up was 'Got The Hots', written and produced by **Gavin Christopher**.

More recently Cuba has returned to the line-up of The Main Ingredient on a full-time basis.

GOODY GOODY

(Group)

Instigated by **Vince Montana** in Philadelphia, Goody Goody made a major impression on the disco scene of the late '70s with Vince's song/production 'No. 1 Dee Jay' for Atlantic Records in 1978.

GORDY, BERRY

(Industry/Songwriter/Producer)

Born in Detroit, Berry worked on a car factory assembly line and enjoyed a little success as a boxer before dedicating himself to songwriting and producing. In 1956 he met **Jackie Wilson** and offered to write him songs. A string of hits followed including 'Reet Petite' (UK Top 10, 1957/UK No. 1, 1986), 'To Be Loved' (UK Top 25, 1958), 'Lonely Teardrops' and 'That's Why I Love You So'. In these early days of rock & roll, many black singers and groups were having their songs taken to greater heights by white acts. Berry had the foresight to cross over colour lines and realized that rhythm was the most important thing in making records, and that people only listened to the words once the beat had caught their attention.

In 1959, with borrowed money, Berry formed Motown Records and over the years made it the most successful black music company there has ever been. Initially he continued his songwriting (including 'Do You Love Me' for **The Contours**), but soon spent all his time developing his roster which was to include **Stevie Wonder**, **Diana Ross**, **The Jackson 5**, **Smokey Robinson**, **Marvin Gaye**, **The Temptations**, **The Four Tops**, **Gladys Knight**, **Martha Reeves & The Vandellas** and many more.

In 1971 Berry moved Motown from Detroit to Los Angeles where he expanded his company into films with movies including *Lady Sings The Blues* and *The Last Dragon*. He sold Motown to MCA Records in the late 80s for around 60 million dollars. In 1991 he returned to the record business by forming West Grand Music Productions, signing his first artist **Louis Price** back to Motown.

GORMAN, FREDDIE
(Singer/Songwriter)
Born in Detroit, Freddie had left high school and was working in a post office before he met songwriters/producers **Holland/Dozier/Holland** through a mutual friend. At this point he joined a group The Fidelatones, although he continued his work as a postman and eventually met **Berry Gordy** by delivering mail to his mother's house.

In 1961 he recorded for Motown's Miracle label for a single 'The Day Will Come' and remained at Motown to write songs for artists including **The Marvelettes** (co-writing 'Please Mr Postman', later a hit for The Beatles and The Carpenters), **The Supremes**, **Martha Reeves** & **The Vandellas**, **Marvin Gaye** and **The Four Tops**.

As a solo artist he switched to Ric Tic ('In A Bad Way', 1964, and 'Can't Get It Out Of My Mind', 1965), the label for which he also co-wrote songs including 'School's All Over' (**The Adorables**), 'Don't You Tell A Lie' (Patti Gilson) and 'Like Columbus Did' (The Reflections).

Later in 1965 he joined **The Originals** and returned to Motown, moving with both the group and the label to Los Angeles in the early '70s. More recently he has recorded as Freddie G for the Airwave label, and again with The Originals for the UK-based Motorcity label with writer/producer **Ian Levine**. Motorcity also released a solo Freddie Gorman single 'I Just Keep Falling In Love' in 1990.

GRACE, FREDI
(Singer)
In the early '80s, Fredi recorded with her own group Fredi Grace & Rhinestone for RCA in Los Angeles. Their albums included *Get On Your Mark* (1982). More recently she replaced **Mary Davis** as lead singer of **The S.O.S. Band**.

GRAHAM, JAKI
(Singer)
Born in Birmingham, Jaki sang with The Medium Wave Band prior to teaming up with **Derek Bramble** and signing to EMI as a solo artist. Here she recorded a debut single 'What's The Name Of Your Game' (1984) with 'Hold On' on the B-side, but she first made a chart impression with 'Could It Be I'm Falling In Love', a duet recorded with **David Grant** (UK Top 5). The year was 1985, a good year for Jaki as her Derek Bramble-penned/produced solo UK hits flowed with 'Round And Round' (Top 10) and 'Heaven Knows' (Top 60), prior to a second duet hit with David Grant 'Mated' (Top 20). Her debut album *Heaven Knows* was also released that year.

A second album *Breaking Away* came in 1986, again penned/produced by Derek Bramble and featuring further UK single hits 'Set Me Free' (Top 10), 'Breaking Away' (Top 20), 'Step Right Up' (Top 20), and a highly acclaimed ballad 'Let's Get Blue'.

GRAHAM, LARRY
(Singer/Bass/Songwriter/Producer)
Born in Beaumont, Texas, Larry grew up in Oakland, California, where he played guitar in a family trio. Taking up the bass guitar he was recruited by **Sly & The Family Stone** in the mid-'60s, with whom he stayed for six years. Moving into production, he worked initially with a band called Hot Chocolate (not the British group of the same name), shortly becoming part of the group himself and renaming them Graham Central Station. The group were David Vega (guitar), Robert Sam (keyboards), Hershall Kennedy (keyboards), Willie Sparks (drums) and Patrice Banks (percussion). During the mid-'70s the group scored American success with 'Can You Handle It' (1974), 'Feel The Need' (1974) and 'Your Love' (1975) from albums including *Ain't No Bout-A-Doubt It*, *Graham Central Station*, *Mirror* (1976), *Now Do U Wanna Dance*, *Release Yourself* and *My Radio Sure Sounds Good To Me*.

In 1980 he began a solo career with 'One In A Million You', penned by **Sam Dees**. The song became the title of his first solo album, followed by *Just Be My Lady* (1981) and *Sooner Or Later* (1982). The instrumental of the title track of *Sooner or Later* was Larry's one UK Top 75 entry.

As a songwriter he has written with **Sam Dees** and **Lenny Williams**, and has sung with **Fire Fox** ('Stand Up For What You Believe In', 1985) and **Aretha Franklin** (duet 'If You Need My Love Tonight' from *Aretha*, 1986).

GRANT, DAVID

(Singer/Songwriter)

Born in Hackney, East London, David shot to prominence on the 'Brit funk' scene of the early '80s as one half of the group **Linx**. From here he pursued a solo career, working with writer/producer **Derek Bramble** on a series of UK hits 'Stop And Go' (Top 20), 'Watching You Watching Me' (Top 10), 'Love Will Find A Way' (Top 25) and 'Rock The Midnight' (Top 50) from his debut album *David Grant* (1983) for Chrysalis.

His next run of success came in 1985 with two hit duets 'Could It Be I'm Falling In Love' (Top 5) and 'Mated' (Top 20) with **Jaki Graham**. In 1987 he switched to Polydor and scored a UK Top 75 single with 'Change', while more recently David has recorded songs including 'Life' and 'Anxious Edge' for the 4th & Broadway label.

A David Grant collector's item is an unreleased 7" single of 'Have Yourself A Merry Little Christmas', issued as a promotional item only in 1984.

GRAY, DOBIE

(Singer/Songwriter)

Born in Brookshire, Texas, in 1943, Dobie first started making records after moving to Los Angeles. Here he scored with 'Look At Me' for the Cordak label (1963) and later his classic 'The In Crowd' recorded for the Charger label and a UK Top 25 hit for London Records in 1965. Moving to Nashville, he found success with 'Drift Away' for MCA and went on to record three albums for the label, *Drift Away*, *Loving Arms* and *Hey Dixie*, before switching to Capricorn for *New Ray of Sunshine*. He hit the UK Top 50 in 1975 with 'Out On The Floor', released on the Black Magic label. In 1979 he scored on the disco scene with 'You Can Do It' from *Dobie Gray* (released by Infinity) which included a remake of 'The In Crowd'. As a songwriter, his 'City Stars' was recorded by **David Ruffin**.

GRAYDON, JAY

(Guitar/Producer/Songwriter)

Based in Los Angeles, Jay initially established himself during the '70s as a guitarist and recorded with numerous artists including **Marvin Gaye**, **David 'Fathead' Newman**, **Booker T. Jones**, **Norman Connors** and **Eloise Laws**. From the early '80s he developed his own sophisticated production style which adapted particularly well to the music of **Al Jarreau**. Jay produced Al's albums *This Time* (1980), *Breakin' Away* (1981), *Jarreau* (1983) and *High Crime* (1984), also playing guitar on many of the sessions, and co-writing many of his finest moments including 'Easy', 'Roof Garden' and 'Mornin''.

Jay also wrote and/or produced for artists including **Herbie Hancock**, **George Benson**, **Aretha Franklin**, **Debarge**, **El Debarge** ('Someone' and 'After You'), **Earth Wind & Fire** ('After The Love Has Gone'), **Dionne Warwick** ('Friends In Love' and 'For You') and **Lou Rawls** ('Stop Me From Starting This Feeling').

GRAYSON, ALLTRINNA

(Singer)

Born in Cleveland, Ohio, Alltrinna's vocal skills were first recognized by **Bobby Womack** who discovered her singing in the burger bar where she worked! Later, when **Patti Labelle** was unable to tour with Bobby to promote *The Poet II*, Alltrinna was invited on a world tour and got standing ovations wherever she went! In 1985 she made her recording debut on '(No Matter How High I Get) I'll Still Be Looking Up To You', a duet with **Bobby Womack** for a **Wilton Felder** album. She also sang backgrounds with **Bobby Womack**, Run DMC, and **Tramaine** ('The Joy That Floods My Soul'). In 1989 she sang two lead vocals for **Hamilton Bohannon** ('House Over The Hill' and 'Over The Rainbow'), but her best work is still to come!

GREAVES, R.B.

(Singer)

A nephew of **Sam Cooke**, R. B. Greaves's moment of glory was in 1969 when his single 'Take A Letter Maria' was a multi-million-seller for Atlantic Records across America. His follow-up, a rendition of 'Always Something There To Remind Me' was also successful.

R.B. also recorded *To Be Continued* for Polydor as Sonny Childe.

GREEN, AL

(Singer)

Born in Forest City, Arkansas, in 1946, Al Green's father was bass player Robert Green who put Al to work with brothers Robert, William and Walter as The Green Brothers. The group toured the gospel circuit in the South and later the Midwest after the family moved to Grand Rapids, Michigan. After singing in the church through these early years, Al formed a rock/r&b group The Creations in 1964. Changing their name to Al Green and The Soul Mates, 'Back Up Train' was a small regional hit on their own Hotline label. While performing in local venues, Al came to the attention of **Willie Mitchell** in Midland, Texas (1969). Willie signed him to a solo recording contract to the Hi label, and the two set about writing songs together. Their first album was *Green Is Blues* (1970), and the following year '(I'm So) Tired Of Being Alone' was Al's first million-seller, released in the UK by London Records and a Top 5 hit here in 1971.

Over the next five years he recorded nine albums which collectively sold over thirty million copies, establishing Al as a major soul star of the '70s. Between 1971 and 1974 he had seven Top 10 hits including 'Let's Stay Together' (UK Top 10, 1972, later a hit for **Tina Turner**), 'Look What You Done For Me' (UK Top 50, 1972), 'I'm Still In Love With You' (UK Top 40, 1972) and 'Sha-La-La' (UK Top 20, 1974). He had seven gold albums by 1975 including *Gets Next To You* (1971), *I'm Still In Love With You* (1972), *Call Me* (1973) and *Explores Your Mind* (1974).

In 1976 Al moved into gospel music, recording two

soul-blended-with-gospel albums *Belle* (1977) and *Truth 'N' Time* (1978). During this time he still performed his soul hits, but turned exclusively to gospel in 1979 after an accident on stage in Cincinnati, when he fell twelve feet off stage onto a steel instrument case and spent fifteen days in hospital. He felt he was disobeying his calling from God. In 1980 he recorded his first all-gospel album *The Lord Will Make A Way* on Myrrh Records, which won him a Grammy for Best Soul Gospel Performer. In the UK 'Tired Of Being Alone' was re-released by Cream Records (via PRT). Three albums followed, *Higher Plane* (1982), *Precious Lord* (1983) and *Trust In God* (1984). By now Al had also been ordained a Baptist minister and become the Reverend Al Green.

In 1985 Al signed to A&M and joined forces again with producer **Willie Mitchell** for *Going Away*, which was essentially gospel but with a slight move back to secular music. The mix of soul and gospel continued with *Soul Survivor* (1986) and then *I Get Joy* (1989), his third A&M album (which featured the contemporary 'As Long As We're Together' with **Al B. Sure**). The same year Al found himself back in the UK charts as guest vocalist on 'The Message Is Love', an inspirational single by **Arthur Baker**, also on the A&M label.

GREEN, GARLAND
(Singer)
Born in Dunleath, Mississippi, in 1942, Garland went to the same school as **Tyrone Davis** and moved to Chicago when he was sixteen years old. Here he met Argia Collins, the owner of a chain of food stores who recognized his talent and put him on the road to success.

Garland initially recorded for the Giant label where his debut single was 'Girl I Love You' (1968), later issued by the Uni label (via MCA). Further singles 'Mr Misery' and 'Ain't That Good Enough' preceded his first album *Jealous Kind Of Fella* (1969), the title track from which was a million-seller across America. In 1971 he switched to the Cotillion label (via WEA) where he scored further American chart success with 'Plain And Simple Girl' arranged by **Donny Hathaway** (1971), one of five singles for the label. Other singles, 'Girl I Love You', 'Forty Days And Nights', 'Ain't That Good Enough' and 'Just Loving You' later became in demand on the UK soul scene.

From 1973 he recorded for Spring (via Polydor) including the singles 'Let The Good Times Roll', 'He Didn't Know (He Kept On Talking)' and 'Send Him My Best Wishes') before he departed the label in 1976. Later in the year he released one single 'I.O.U' with 'It's A Backdoor World' on the B-side for Casino Records prior to signing with RCA. Here he recorded 'Don't Let Love Walk Out On Us' and a **Leon Haywood**-produced album *Love Is What We Came Here For* (1977), including 'I Quit Running The Streets'.

In 1979 he moved to Los Angeles where in 1983 he returned with a **Lamont Dozier** co-produced album *Garland Green* for the Ocean Front label. The album was also co-produced by Arleen Schesel who became Garland's wife. In 1985 his five-track gospel album was released on his own Love L.A. Music label. His cousin is **Jimmy Scott**.

GREEN, JESSE
(Singer/Musician)
Born in St James, Jamaica, Jesse moved to Britain in 1965 after performing with local groups in Kingston, Jamaica. As a session player he worked in the UK with Judge Dredd, The Pioneers, Greyhound and Desmond Dekker before joining Jimmy Cliff for a worldwide tour.

Deciding to go solo, he scored immediately in 1976 with 'Nice And Slow' (Top 20, remixed and re-released in 1982), following which he had hits with 'Flip' (Top 30, 1976), 'Come With Me' (Top 30, 1977), 'I Believe In You' and 'Disco Crazy', all for EMI Records.

GREENE, SUSAYE
(Singer/Songwriter)
While growing up in Los Angeles, Susaye Green began her professional career as a twelve-year-old. Through her mother's involvement in the record business, Susaye sang with Harry Belafonte before she reached her teens, also singing background for Harry on *Streets I Have Walked*. She later graduated from the School Of Performing Arts, made famous by the TV show *Fame*, before her debut single 'Please Send Him Back' was released on the New York label Tru-Glo-Town. From here she sang with **Ray Charles** as one of The Raelettes before **Harvey Fuqua** made her the original lead singer with his group **New Birth** (singing lead on 'Until It's Time For You To Go').

Susaye was briefly married to **Leon Ware** (with whom she made an unreleased album) before she joined **Stevie Wonder** as a member of Wonderlove in 1974. Here she met **Deniece Williams** for whom she co-wrote 'Free'. She also wrote a number of songs with Stevie himself, one of which 'I Can't Help It' was recorded by **Michael Jackson** on *Off The Wall*. (On Stevie's 'Joy Inside My Tears', incidentally, Susaye was the exclusive backing singer.)

In 1976 Susaye joined **The Supremes**, replacing **Cindy Birdsong** and recording with the group on their two albums that year, *High Energy*, including 'I'm Gonna Let My Heart Do The Walking', and *Mary, Scherrie & Susaye*. After **Mary Wilson** left the group in 1977, Susaye recorded one Motown album *Partners* (1979), including 'Luvbug' (featuring **Ray Charles**) and 'You've Been Good To Me', with **Scherrie Payne** as Scherrie & Susaye while also hosting her own TV show *Hollywood Hot*.

In 1984 Susaye came to London where she met her present husband and decided to stay. She resumed her recording career with saxophonist Courtney Pine, singing lead on his recording of 'Children Of The Ghetto' before Motorcity Records worked with her on new solo singles 'Stop I Need You Now' (1990) and her own version of 'Free' (1991). Also at Motorcity she recorded a number of duets with **Billy Eckstine**.

GREY AND HANKS

(Singers/Songwriters)

Zane Grey and Len Ron Hanks established themselves as a songwriting force on the r&b scene during the '70s. Their songs include 'Back In Love' (**L.T.D.**), 'Rising Cost Of Love' (**Millie Jackson**), 'If You're In Need' (**Lenny Williams/Mystique**), 'Party Town' (**Norman Connors**), 'How Long' (**Debra Laws**) and 'Never Had A Love Like This Before' (**Tavares**).

They also made an impression as artists after signing with RCA and delivering *You Fooled Me* (1978), including 'Dancin'', and *Prime Time* (1980), including 'Now I'm Fine'.

BILLY GRIFFIN

(Singer/Songwriter)

Born in 1951, Billy auditioned for Motown in Los Angeles in the early '70s and was thrown into the world spotlight as lead singer with **The Miracles** in 1971. Replacing **Smokey Robinson**, Billy had never been a professional singer, and many thought he wouldn't last. In 1975 The Miracles released *City Of Angels* featuring the multi-million selling 'Love Machine' (UK Top 5, 1976). The song was co-written by Billy along with other songs on what became one of Motown's most successful albums. *Power To The Music* (1976) was the last Miracles album on Motown before the group switched to CBS and later split up.

In 1983 Billy signed to CBS as a solo artist and worked with writer/producer **John Barnes** on *Be With Me*. It included the UK Top 20 hit 'Hold Me Tighter In The Rain', following which he returned to the studio for *Respect* (1983), which included the UK Top 75 hit 'Serious'. His final CBS album *Systematic* was co-produced by **Leon Ware** and Wayne Lewis (1985). In 1986, he switched labels to Atlantic and released the single 'Believe It Or Not'. An album was recorded, but did not materialize due to differences of opinion with the label. Instead Billy sang backgrounds with artists including **Rodney Franklin** ('Women Of The World'), **Gerald Albright** and **Teena Marie** before recording for the UK Motorcity label from 1989. Here his debut single was 'First In Line', co-written and produced by **Ian Levine**.

Billy has also had an acting career in a few American soap operas.

GRIFFIN, DONALD

(Guitar)

Brother of **Billy Griffin**, guitarist Donald Griffin has recorded and/or toured with **Anita Baker**, **The Four Tops**, **Bobby Lyle**, **Donna Summer** ('Dinner With Gershwin') and **Lalah Hathaway**.

GRIFFIN, GENE

(Songwriter/Producer)

New York-based producer Gene Griffin first established his name as a major new force in dance music in the late '80s. One of the pioneers of 'New Jack Swing' with partner **Teddy Riley**, Gene has written and/or produced for artists including **Guy** ('Groove Me'), **Today**, **Pieces Of A Dream**, **Basic Black**, **James Ingram** ('It's Real') and **Stephanie Mills**.

GRIFFIN, HERMAN

(Singer)

From Detroit, Herman began his recording career in the late '50s, 'I Need You' being the first song recorded for Berry Gordy's Motown production company. It was also the first song published by Jobete Music. The year was 1957, but the track was released on the H.O.B. label as the Motown label wasn't operational at this time.

Berry Gordy produced several follow-ups released on the Kudo label prior to Herman signing with the Motown subsidiary Anna Records. Here 'Hurry Up And Marry Me' was released in 1960. The same year he switched to the Tamla label for 'True Love'. Also in 1960 Herman married **Mary Wells**, bringing her to the label and also switching to the main Motown label himself in 1962 for 'Sleep Little One'. Herman was also responsible for taking Mary away from Motown, though they divorced shortly after this.

Through the remainder of the '60s Herman recorded for Epic, Mercury and Double L ('Mr Heartbreak'), as well as becoming promotion manager. He also worked as a producer, and in 1971 formed a group The Boys In The Band, penning the million-seller 'How About A Little Hand For The Boys In The Band' released on Polydor. On Spring Records, the group also scored in the mid-'70s with 'Money Music'. In 1989 he recorded 'Not One Chance In A Million', his one single for the Motorcity label before he died later in the year.

GRUSIN/ROSEN

(Songwriters/Producers/Instrumentalists)

Dave Grusin (keyboards) and Larry Rosen (drums) first met in Los Angeles during the mid-'60s. In 1976 they decided to form their own company Grusin/Rosen Productions (GRP) and worked with artists including **Earl Klugh**, **Noel Pointer**, **Patti Austin** and **Lee Ritenour** on a series of r&b-flavoured jazz recordings. In 1978 the company extended to a record label, which originally (via Arista) delivered a series of recordings by artists including **Tom Browne** ('Funkin' For Jamaica'), **Dave Valentin**, **Bernard Wright**, **Bobby Broom**, **Jay Hoggard** and **Angela Bofill**, all of which made a major impression on the UK's jazz, funk & soul scene.

More recently the label (now via MCA) has concentrated on adult contemporary jazz recordings for artists including **The Crusaders**, **Spyro Gyra**, **George Howard** and **Carl Anderson**.

GRUSIN, DAVE

(Keyboards/Arranger/Songwriter/Producer)

Dave was introduced to jazz by his father, and was playing piano by the time he was four. Enrolling at the University of Colorado's music school, he played with various jazz groups, while as a writer his music was inspired by film composers such as André Previn. In 1959 he moved to New York and became director of *The Andy Williams Show*, a position which eventually moved him to Los Angeles. In 1964 he left Andy Williams to move into the world of music for TV and films. His first film soundtrack was *Divorce American Style*. In 1979 he had an Academy Award nomination for *Heaven Can Wait* and *The Champ*.

In the mid-'60s **Sergio Mendes** introduced Dave to the record industry by hiring him to arrange hits including 'Fool On The Hill' and 'The Look Of Love'. This lead to further offers from **Quincy Jones**, who put him to work with **The Brothers Johnson**. In 1976 Dave and long-time friend Larry Rosen decided to form their own production company **Grusin/Rosen** Productions (GRP) and worked with numerous artists on a series of r&b-flavoured jazz recordings. This led to the GRP record label in 1978.

As a solo recording artist, Dave made his own impression on the UK jazz funk scene with albums for GRP including *Mountain Dance* (1980), *Out Of The Shadows* (1982), *Night Lines* (1984), *One Of A Kind* (1984) and *Harlequin* with **Lee Ritenour** (1985).

GUINN

(Group)

From Philadelphia, the Guinn family are Randy (bass), Michael (lead vocals), Skip (vocals), Bonnie, Earl (guitars) and Marjorie, together with Lori Fulton (from Harrisburg) who joined the group in 1985. The sister members of the group originally worked together as **The Passionettes**. Prior to recording one self-titled Motown album as Guinn (which included 'Dreamin'', 'Open Your Door' and 'People Will Be People'), they recorded some songs as **New Experience** for the Philly World label.

GUTHRIE, GWEN

(Singer/Songwriter/Producer)

Born in New Jersey, Gwen began her career as a backing singer during the mid-'70s. She also enjoyed some success as a songwriter prior to launching her solo career in the early '80s. She first made an impact on UK dancefloors with 'It Should Have Been You' (1982), having signed to Island Records where she continued to score with producers **Sly/Robbie** on 'Padlock', 'Seventh Heaven' and 'Hopscotch' and an album *Portrait* (1983).

Just For You (1985) followed before she switched to Polydor for her most commercially successful album in the UK *Good To Go Lover* (1986), including the self-penned/produced 'Ain't Nothing Going On But The Rent' (UK Top 5) and a cover version of '(They Long To Be) Close To You' (UK Top 25). In 1988 she changed labels again to Warner Brothers for 'Can't Love You Tonight', prior to *Hot Times* (1990) including 'Sweet Bitter Love', 'Hot Time In Harlem' and the duet with **George Benson** 'I'll Give My Best To You'.

Gwen has also sung with **The Affair**, **George Howard**, **Houston Person**, **Noel Pointer**, **Angela Bofill**, **John Blake** (lead vocal on 'Adventures Of The Heart'), **Billy Griffin**, **Aretha Franklin**, **Margie Joseph**, **Roberta Flack** and **Thelma Jones** among others. Her co-written song credits include 'This Time I'll Be Sweeter' (a hit for **Linda Lewis**), and seven songs for the debut **Sister Sledge** album *Circle Of Love*. She wrote 'God Don't Like Ugly' for **Roberta Flack**, and 'Second Chance' and 'Love Strong Enough To Move Mountains' for **Martha Reeves**.

Her brother is music attorney and producer Karl Guthrie.

GUY

(Group)

New York-based group Guy are **Teddy Riley** with brothers Aaron Hall and Damion Hall. Their debut album *Guy* (1988), including 'Groove Me', was one of the instigators of the 'New Jack Swing' style of music which remains prominent on the dance scene in the early '90s. It was produced jointly by Teddy Riley and **Gene Griffin**.

In 1990 the group returned with a second album *The Future*, including 'Her'.

GUY, JASMINE

(Singer)

Jasmine initially worked as an actress both on stage and in Hollywood. She starred in the Spike Lee movie *School Daze* and had a part in the American TV sit-com *It's A Different World*. As a recording artist she sang with **Peabo Bryson** before she signed to Warner Brothers in 1990. Here she worked with producers including **Full Force** and **Timmy Gatling** on her debut album *Jasmine Guy*, including 'Try Me'.

H

HAIRSTON, CURTIS
(Singer)
Born in Winston-Salem, North Carolina, Curtis was singing by the age of three. Locally he was known for a dramatic rendition of 'We Are All God's Children' which he sang in his grandfather's church. He decided to make music his career at the age of thirteen. In the meantime, basketball great Earl Monroe had decided to start a record label, and on a visit to his old town Curtis called him at his hotel. Having mentioned that they had been to the same school and that he had a demo tape, he was invited over and later signed to Earl's Pretty Pearl label.

His debut was 'I Want You (All Tonight)', released by RCA in the UK where it became a Top 50 hit in 1983. The follow-up 'I Want Your Lovin' (Just A Little Bit)' was released in the UK by London in 1985, charting even higher as a Top 15 entry that year. Back in America he also scored r&b success with his version of 'We All Are One', despite Jimmy Cliff's hit with the song at the very same time.

Signing to Atlantic, he began developing his songwriting skills, writing with Nona Hendryx for his debut albums. His initial Atlantic single was 'Chillin' Out', which to date has been his last UK chart entry (Top 60 in 1986). About the same time Curtis fronted an album of songs for **B.B.&Q.** (although uncredited), before the group's **Kae Williams** worked with him on 1987's *Curtis Hairston* which featured the popular UK soul dance track 'The Morning After'.

More recently Curtis recorded with the jazz group Ready For Reality on their 1990 Next Plateau release *Ready For Reality.*

HAKIM, OMAR
(Songwriter/Drummer)
Since the early 1980s Omar Hakim has been establishing himself on the East Coast's r&b and jazz scenes, primarily as a drummer but also as a songwriter. Early credits go back to 1982 when he sessioned with **Roy Ayers** on *Turn Me Loose*, later to record with Roy again on his albums *Love Fantasy* and *Africa, Center Of The World.* In 1983 he played drums on the **Glenn Jones** dance anthem 'I Am Somebody', and also wrote 'Being With You' recorded by **Smokey Robinson** that year.

Through the eighties he can be found on recordings by **Melba Moore**, **La La**, **Weather Report** and numerous others. His solo album *Rhythm Deep* (featuring saxophonist **Najee**) was released by GRP in 1989. In 1990 he teamed up with **Joe Sample** for the former Crusader's album *Ashes To Ashes.*

HALE, WILLIE 'BEAVER'
(Singer/Guitar/Songwriter)
Born in Forrest City, Arkansas, in 1945, Willie first established himself as a guitarist during his teens, playing with a group The Savoys. The group's sax player, Arthur Pryor, dubbed him 'Little Beaver' because of his two protruding front teeth. His first releases were during the mid-'60s when he recorded for the Phil-L.A. Of Soul label as Frank Williams & The Rocketeers Featuring Little Beaver. From here he switched to the Cat label (a subsidiary of the Florida based TK company) to record as a solo artist. After a studio date with **Betty Wright**, playing guitar on her hit 'Clean Up Woman', he recorded his debut album *Joey* (1972) under the name Little Beaver, before establishing himself on the UK soul scene with 'Party Down' in 1974. The track was also the title of his 1975 album, released in the UK on President Records. In the States he continued to record for Cat/TK, further albums including *Black Rhapsody* (1976) and *When Was The Last Time* (1977), before in 1980 he began to record as Willie 'Beaver' Hale. At this time he released *Beaver Fever*, from which an American-issued single 'Groove On' became an anthem on the UK soul scene (though never released here). Willie has also recorded numerous guitar sessions with artists including **Aretha Franklin**, **Timmy Thomas**, **Latimore**, **Gwen McCrae**, and more recently with **Betty Wright** again on her *Mother Wit* (1987).

HALL, BARBARA
(Singer)
Chicago singer Barbara Hall recorded the double-header 'Can I Count On You'/'V.I.P' for the city's Innovation II label in 1974. The following year she returned with the **Sam Dees/Frederick Knight** song 'Drop My

Heart Off At The Door' for the label, released via EMI in the UK.

HALL, CARL

(Singer)

New York singer Carl Hall first began recording in the mid-'60s, his single 'My Baby's So Good' for Mercury being one of his few solo releases. In 1971 he recorded briefly for CBS, 'What About You' being a highly in-demand and collectable single on the UK modern soul scene. As a background singer Carl can be found on the Lou Courtney soul classic 'What Do You Want Me To Do', and various tracks by **Stephanie Mills**.

HALL, ELLIS

(Singer)

Ellis replaced **Lenny Williams** in the Oakland, California-based group **Tower Of Power** in the mid-'70s. More recently he has been the featured vocalist on a number of r&b-orientated jazz albums for artists including **101 North**, **Kenny G**, **Tower Of Power** and **Byron Miller** ('Gotta Get It Right').

HALL, ERASMUS

(Singer)

The California-based singer emerged in the early 1980s with *Your Love Is My Desire* for the Westbound label. It featured 'Just Me And You', which today remains a popular and highly collectable track among UK soul fans. Later in 1984 Erasmus returned on Capitol with the **George Clinton**-produced *Go Ahead*.

HALL, RANDY

(Singer/Songwriter/Producer)

Born in Chicago in 1960, Randy took up classical piano at the age of eight. Inspired by Elvis Presley movies he later switched to guitar. Aged thirteen he formed the Windy City Four before **The Staples Singers** took him on as their guitarist for two years.

Drummer in the Windy City Four was Vincent Wilburn, the nephew of **Miles Davis**. Through Vincent, Miles heard a few of Randy's compositions and asked him to write some lyrics to the one he liked the most, 'Man With The Horn'. The track became the title of one of the most successful Miles Davis albums ever, and it was Randy who sang the vocals on this song together with 'Shout', also on the album.

Moving into session work Randy worked with **Ramsey Lewis**, **Roberta Flack** and then Wayne Shorter (of **Weather Report**) who introduced Randy to **Ray Parker Jr**. Ray invited him to play on a number of sessions and was also impressed by his songwriting. In 1983 Randy's song 'Up Front' was recorded by **Diana Ross**, and produced by Ray Parker Jr on the album *Ross*.

In 1984 Randy signed with MCA and delivered a debut album *I Belong To You*, produced by **Ray Parker Jr**. It included 'I Want To Touch You' with sexual overtones from Anita Sherman. The follow-up *Love You Like A Stranger* was released in 1988.

HAMMER, M.C.

(Rapper/Songwriter/Producer)

Born in Oaktown, California, M.C. Hammer first took rapping seriously at the age of eight while still at school. He established a local reputation and released a debut album *Feel The Power* on his own Bustin Records label. He established himself on the international rap scene upon signing to Capitol Records and releasing his album *Let's Get Started* (1988). In 1990 his second album *Please Hammer Don't Hurt 'Em*, including 'U Can't Touch This' and 'Pray', sold five million copies to become the best selling black music release since *Thriller* by **Michael Jackson**.

His latest move is to launch a label Bust It Records (via Capitol), where he will be releasing/producing records for a number of his own productions on artists including Special Generation, Soft Touch and New Look Posse.

HAMMOND, JOHNNY

(Organ/Songwriter)

Born John Robert Smith, Johnny established himself on the popular 'jazz organ' scene of the '60s, before the UK jazz funk fraternity adopted him in the late '70s/early '80s, as a result of his albums for Milestone Records: *Gears* (1975), including 'Los Conquistadores Chocolates' and 'Fantasy', produced by **Larry** and **Fonce Mizell**, and *Forever Taurus* (1976), produced by **Wade Marcus**. He also recorded for the Prestige and Salvation labels during the '70s.

HANCOCK, HERBIE

(Keyboards/Songwriter/Producer)

Born Herbert Jeffrey Hancock in Chicago in 1940, Herbie took up classical piano at the age of seven before moving into jazz during his high-school days. Here he formed his first band before joining **Donald Byrd** as pianist at the age of 20 in 1960. Donald was so impressed he convinced his record company, Blue Note, to sign him and in 1963 his debut album *Takin' Off*, including 'Watermelon Man', was released. Follow-up albums on Blue Note included *Maiden Voyage*, *Inventions And Dimensions*, *Empyrean Isles*, *Speak Like A Child* and *The Prisoner*, while between 1963 and 1968 he also played with **Miles Davis** and recorded with him (including his own compositions).

In 1968 he signed to Warner Brothers with his own sextet, and by the early '70s was experimenting with electronic keyboards, first reflected on his album *Mwandishi* in 1971. The following year he moved to Los Angeles and signed to CBS, releasing *Sextant* (1972), *Headhunters* (1973), featuring his regular group of musicians the **Headhunters** and including 'Chameleon' and a new version of 'Watermelon Man', *Thrust* (1974), *Death Wish* (1974), *Man-Child* (1975) and *Secrets* (1976), including the Grammy-winning 'Doin' It', co-written with **Wah Wah Watson** and **Ray Parker**.

From 1976 he took on two parallel recording careers, one aiming towards the 'jazz funk' scene and ultimately crossover pop music, the other aiming at the traditional jazz scene with his group V.S.O.P. 1978's *Sunlight* introduced his use of the vocoder on the single 'I Thought It Was You' (UK Top 20), his following funk/pop albums being *Feets Don't Fail Me Now*, including 'You Bet Your Love' (UK Top 20, 1979); *Monster* (1980), including 'Making Love' and 'Stars In Your Eyes', featuring **Gavin Christopher**; *Mr Hands* (1980); *Magic Windows* (1981); *Lite Me Up* (1982); *Future Shock* (1983), including 'Rockit' (UK Top 10) and 'Auto Drive' (UK Top 40); and *Sound-System* (1984).

Herbie has also produced or co-produced albums for artists including **Airto** (*Identity*, 1976) and **Webster Lewis** (*Give Me Some Emotion*, 1979), and has recorded with **Alphonse Mouzon**, **Chaka Khan** ('Night In Tunisia') and numerous artists over the years. He also appeared in and was music director of the film *Round Midnight* (1986).

HANDY, JOHN

(Sax/Vocals)

Born in Dallas, Texas, in 1933, John began career as an alto sax player in the early '60s with Charlie Mingus. Shortly after he formed a quintet with **Michael White** recording *Jazz At Monterey* (released by CBS). He has spent the majority of his life as a saxophone teacher, but is fondly remembered on the UK 'jazz funk' scene for his classic 'Hard Work' (1976) on the Impulse label. *Hard Work* was also the title of the album which featured the single of the same name. He also recorded albums for labels including MPS (*Karuna Supreme*) and Warner Brothers (*Carnival*).

HARDCASTLE, PAUL

(Keyboards/Songwriter/Producer)

From Pimlico, London, Paul grew up with London DJ Steve Walsh. They lived in the same street and went to the same school, but while Steve took an interest in music, Paul got into motorcycles and raced them until the day he crashed into the side of a car and spent four months in hospital. His musical skills, meanwhile, were encouraged by his father who was a professional musician. In earlier years Paul had taken up guitar and drums while also spending four years on the road with his father in Europe. Becoming an assistant at a hi-fi store in Chelsea he saved up some money to buy a synthesizer. After learning how to play it he answered an ad in a music paper for a keyboard player. The group was **Direct Drive** where he met vocalist Derek Green with whom he later left to form **First Light**.

In the meantime he reacquainted himself with Steve Walsh, and together they formed a record label Total Control. Their first release was a medley of 'You're The One For Me/Daybreak/Am' which reached the UK Top 50 (1984) as a solo Paul Hardcastle record (with vocals by Kevin Henry). A follow-up 'Guilty' was a Top 60 entry on Total Control. From here Paul released one single 'Rain Forest' for the Bluebird label (1984) which did even better (Top 50), resulting in a recording deal with Cool Tempo/Chrysalis. His first single for the label was 'Eat Your Heart Out' (recorded in his house at Leyton, mixed in New York) again featuring Kevin Henry and a Top 60 single in 1984. In 1985 Paul reached the pinnacle of his commercial success with '19', an instrumental with dialogue about the Vietnam War which went to No. 1 in thirteen countries. Also that year he wrote 'The Wizard', the theme for TV's *Top Of The Pops* through the late '80s – early '90s.

Paul's other Chrysalis hits in the UK included 'Just For The Money' (Top 20, 1985), 'Don't Waste My Time' (Top 10, 1986), and 'Foolin' Yourself (Top 60, 1986). More recently he has re-formed **First Light**.

HAREWOOD, DORIAN

(Singer/Actor)

From Dayton, Ohio, Dorian developed his musical expertise at high school and music school before graduating and landing the role of Judas in *Jesus Christ Superstar*. After many prestigious stage roles he moved to Los Angeles where in 1975 he starred in his first film *Foster and Laurie*. He later starred on Broadway with **Stephanie Mills** in *To Sir With Love* and played a lead role in the Stanley Kubrick film *Full Metal Jacket*.

In 1988 he began his solo recording career with *Love Will Stop Calling* for the Emerick label, although these days he is acting more or less full time.

HARRELL, GRADY

(Singer)

Born in Los Angeles, Grady's mother sang with **The Friends Of Distinction**. While at high school he formed a group Poppa's Results with sister Raquel (who later sang backgrounds with **Diana Ross**), and later met **Jeffrey Daniel** and **Jody Watley** at the American TV show *Soul Train*. At this point he almost became lead singer of **Shalamar**, though **Howard Hewett** just beat him to it.

Signing to the Constellation label (via Solar), he worked with producer **Fred Wesley** on an album *Mwana* (1984) before his friend Andre Cleveland (son of Revd James Cleveland) secured him a deal at RCA. Here his albums have been *Come Play With Me* (1987), featuring two songs produced by **Stevie Wonder**, and *Romance Me* (1990).

HARRIET

(Singer/Songwriter)

Born in London, Harriet moved to Cambridge and then Canada for a year before settling in Sheffield. Aged fifteen she joined a local group before meeting drummer Russ Courtney, who used to play with **Jimmy James** &

The Vagabonds. Together they began writing songs, and eventually landed a publishing deal.

Harriet's own songwriting success took off with 'One Man Woman', written with **Ian Prince** and recorded by **Quincy Jones** on *Back On The Block* (1989). Shortly afterwards, 'Discover Me' found its way to **Alisha Warren** who recorded it for RCA. From here Harriet signed to East West Records where she worked with producers including **George Clinton** on her debut album *Woman To Man* (1990), including 'Temple Of Love'.

HARRIS, BARBARA

(Singer)

Based in New York, Barbara was lead singer with **The Toys** on their '60s recording 'Lover's Concerto', while more recently she has worked on the '80s dance scene as a session singer with groups including **Kreamcicle** ('Dancing In The Street').

HARRIS, BETTY

(Singer)

Betty was an early '60s deep soul singer who initially recorded songs including 'Cry To Me' for the Jubilee label (1963). Switching to the Sansu label in New Orleans she recorded duets with **Lee Dorsey** before moving on to the SSS International label for releases including 'There's A Break In The Road'.

HARRIS, CORTEZ

(Singer/Guitarist)

Based in Detroit, Cortez played guitar with **One Way** prior to recording as a solo artist. For Chance Records he worked with producer **Kevin McCord** on 'Say That You Will' before releasing *All About Love* on the Tez-Ru label in 1990.

HARRIS, DAMON

(Singer)

Damon spent a brief period as lead singer of legendary Motown group **The Temptations** before Fantasy Records signed him as a solo artist for the disco song 'It's Music' in the late '70s. Damon also sang backgrounds with **Rose Royce**.

HARRIS, EDDIE

(Sax/Singer)

From Chicago, Eddie recorded for the Liberty label prior to signing to Atlantic in 1967 and originating a new style of electric sax playing with the album *Tender Storm*. He continued to record over forty more albums in this style, two with pianist Les McCann and others utilizing his own vocals.

HARRIS, GENE

(Keyboards)

Based in Los Angeles, Gene's albums for Blue Note Records during the '70s were highly acclaimed on the UK jazz funk scene. They included *Gene Harris And The Three Sounds* (1971), *Gene Harris Of The Three Sounds* (1972), including 'Killer Joe', *Astralsignal* (1974) and *In A Special Way* (1976) featuring Verdine White of **Earth Wind & Fire**, **Harvey Mason**, **James Gadson**, **Philip Bailey**, **Deniece Williams** and **Merry Clayton**.

HARRIS, JIMMY 'JAM'

(Songwriter/Producer/Drummer/Keyboards)

Born in Minneapolis, Jimmy played drums in his father's jazz band before meeting Terry Lewis at school. Here he developed keyboard and vocal skills, and played his father's organ in a school group. A while after the end of the school year he left to join a vocal group Mind And Matter and then became a club/local radio disc jockey while also working in a record store.

One night after being dumped by his girlfriend he happened to overhear local group **Flytetime** rehearse, and feeling dejected he accepted an invitation to join their group as second keyboard player (the other was **Monte Moir**). He later became one half of **Jam/Lewis**, writing and producing a string of hits from the mid-'80s onwards.

HARRIS, MAJOR

(Singer)

Born in Richmond, Virginia, in 1947, Major is Mr Harris's real Christian name. His father was christened Major, as was his grandfather. He also christened his son Major Harris so not to break with family tradition! (His brother is Philly songwriter Joe Jefferson and his cousin was **Norman Harris**.) While in Virginia Major recorded his debut single 'Just A Bad Thing' with The Charmers (1959) and briefly spent some time in California where a single 'Just Love Me' was released by Epic.

Still in high school he moved to Philadelphia where he furthered his singing experience with The Jarmels (recording 'A Little Bit of Soap'), The Impacts and Nat Turner's Rebellion. He also recorded 'Call Me Tomorrow' which was released on the Okeh label. His first major break was with **The Delfonics**, a group he joined in 1971 and scored hits with including 'La La Means I Love You'.

His debut solo album *My Way* was released by Atlantic in 1974 and featured the classic ballad 'Love Won't Let Me Wait' (featuring a groaning **Barbara Ingram**!), co-written by **Bobby Eli**. The single (UK Top 40, 1975) sold over 2 million copies worldwide and was later covered by **Luther Vandross**. Major recorded five further albums for Atlantic, including *Jealousy* and *Major Harris And The Boogie Blues Band*, and one for RCA, *How Do You Take Your Love* produced by **Jerry Ragovoy** in 1978.

In 1983 Major returned to the recording scene with a single 'All My Life', originally released on the Pop Art label in the USA. In the UK it was released by London and reached the Top 75. The following year *I Believe In Love* was released by Streetwave in the UK.

HARRIS, NORMAN
(Guitar/Songwriter/Producer)
Norman is the cousin of **Major Harris**, and first made his impression on the Philadelphia music scene in the early '60s. As a guitarist he first worked as part of **Baker/Harris/Young** as backing musicians for local group The Larks (1964), this trio of musicians later becoming the nucleus of **M.F.S.B.** and 'the Philly sound'.

Independently of BHY he co-wrote/produced a series of releases for **First Choice**, commencing with 'This Is The House Where Love Died' (1972) followed by 'Armed And Extremely Dangerous' (1973). His writing and/or production credits can also be found on records by **The Trammps** ('Disco Inferno'), **Blue Magic** ('Side Show'), **Curtis Mayfield** ('Body Guard'), **Loleatta Holloway** ('Hit And Run'), **The Whispers** (*One For The Money*) and **The Manhattans** ('That's How Much I Love You'). As an arranger, his credits include **Bunny Sigler** ('Keep Smilin''), **Barbara Mason** ('Half Sister, Half Brother') and more recently **Eugene Wilde** ('Chey Chey Kule').

His 'Philly guitar' became synonymous with the sound of Philadelphia, as he played on hundreds of soul classics during the '70s and early '80s. He also recorded a solo album *The Harris Machine* for the Philadelphia International label (1980), but passed away in 1986. His niece, incidentally, is **Liz Hogue**.

HARRIS, RAHNI P.
(Singer/Musician/Producer)
In 1978, Rahni Harris with F.L.O. made a major impact on UK dancefloors with the instrumental 'Six Million Steps (West Runs South)', originally released on the Inspirational Sounds label, and issued in the UK by Mercury (via Phonogram) where it was a UK Top 50 hit. Through the '80s Rahni worked consistently on the r&b scene as musician, songwriter and producer with artists including **Melba Moore**, **Colourblind** (*Crazy*), **Dayton** (*The Sound Of Music*) and **Xavier** ('Work That Sucker To Death' and 'Love Is On The One').

HARRIS, SIMON
(Disc Jockey/Songwriter/Producer)
London-based disc jockey moved into production in the mid-'80s and became a co-founder of the Music Of Life label. On FFRR Records (via Phonogram) he scored solo success with 'Bass (How Low Can You Go)' (UK Top 20, 1988) and 'Here Comes That Sound' (UK Top 40, 1988). He is also a champion yo-yo player!

HARTMAN, DAN
(Singer/Songwriter/Producer)
Based in New York, Dan rose to prominence on the late '70s disco scene with his anthem 'Instant Replay' (UK Top 10) for the Blue Sky label (via CBS). Only a 7″ single was made available at the time in the UK, the 12″ being available as an American import. His follow-up was 'This Is It' (UK Top 20, 1979), although in America the title song of his album *Relight My Fire*, featuring **Loleatta Holloway**, was another anthem, enjoying greater popularity in the UK on the late '80s 'house' music scene.

In 1985 he signed to MCA where he scored again with 'Second Nature' (UK Top 75) and 'I Can Dream About You' (UK Top 20). In between times he has written and/or produced for artists including **Diana Ross** ('It's Never Too Late'), **Average White Band** (*Cupid's In Fashion*, including 'You're My Number One'), **Loleatta Holloway** ('Love Sensation'), **James Brown** ('Living In America') and **Chaka Khan** ('Can't Stop The Street').

HARVEY, STEVE
(Singer/Songwriter/Producer)
Born in Aberdeen, Scotland, Steve trained as a drummer initially, encouraged by his father who was also a musician and a big black music fan. After mastering the instrument he formed a rhythm section with some friends, but found it difficult to find work. In 1979 they moved to London, but were still unable to find work. After splitting up, Steve joined the group Private Lives and was able to subsidise his income with session work. After saving up some money he hired a demo studio to experiment with a few of his own compositions. He also taught himself the rudiments of guitar and keyboards.

During this time he wrote 'Something Special' at the request of New York singer **Sharon Redd**. It was declined and Sharon released 'Love How You Feel' instead, but Steve's manager persuaded him to sing the song himself, and the result was released on his manager's Pressure label. It was followed up by 'Tonight'.

As writer and/or producer, Steve later worked with **Total Contrast**, **Steven Dante**, **Nia Peeples** and Karyn White ('Slow Down'). More recently he has signed as an artist to A&M, 'I'm The One' being his debut single for the label in 1990.

HARVEY, VICKI
(Singer)
From Detroit, Vicki first took to singing in church where she met local producer **Kevin McCord**. Recording for Kevin's Chance label she recorded a single 'Play Your Cards Right' in 1989.

HATHAWAY, DONNY
(Singer/Songwriter/Producer)
Born in Chicago in 1945, Donny grew up in St Louis with his grandmother Martha Cromwell, a well known gospel singer. He studied music at Howard University in Washington where he shared a room with **Leroy Hutson**. Together they wrote 'The Ghetto'.

After leaving university he performed on the Washington club circuit, including work with the Ric Powell Trio and soon branching out into studio sessions. Through his club work he met **Curtis Mayfield** who employed him at Curtom Records as a staff producer. It was through Donny that Curtis met Leroy Hutson, who was to become the new lead singer of **The Impressions**. While at Curtom, Donny recorded duets with **June Conquest** and later worked at the Chess and Stax labels with **The Staples Singers**, **Carla Thomas** and **Jerry Butler**.

While at a music fair he met **King Curtis** who took him to Atco/Atlantic Records, who signed him as a solo artist. An album *Donny Hathaway* was released in 1970, fast establishing him with 'The Ghetto'. Now highly respected as a singer and songwriter, he recorded consistently through the '70s but had no solo UK hits. His albums included *Everything Is Everything*, *Come Back Charleston Blue* (soundtrack) and *Extensions Of A Man*, including 'Love Love Love', 'Someday We'll All Be Free' and 'Valdez In The Country'. His greatest commercial success was with **Roberta Flack** with whom he recorded *Roberta Flack and Donny Hathaway*, and scored with the UK Top 30 hit 'Where Is The Love' in 1972. Their other duets included 'The Closer I Get To You' (UK Top 50, 1978) from Roberta's album *Blue Lights In The Basement* and 'Back Together Again' (UK Top 5, 1980) released just after Donny took his life by throwing himself out of a window. Towards the end of his life he suffered from personal/identity problems. He left a number of children including daughter **Lalah Hathaway**.

He also worked as an arranger ('Plain And Simple' for **Garland Green**) and played keyboards with **Aretha Franklin** ('Until You Come Back To Me (That's What I'm Gonna Do)'.

HATHAWAY, LALAH
(Singer)
Born in Chicago, Lalah Hathaway is the daughter of the late **Donny Hathaway**. She was ten when her father died, and twenty-one when she signed to Virgin Records. Her debut album *Lalah Hathaway* (1990) included 'Heaven Knows', 'Something', 'Smile' and 'I'm Comin' Back'.

HAVENS, RICHIE
(Singer)
Born in New York in 1941, Richie joined the McCrae gospel singers at the age of fourteen. His early recordings were for the Verve label, his music being a mixture of soul, folk and rock. Here his albums included *Somethin' Else Again* (1969). He performed at Woodstock, and also recorded for labels including Polydor and A&M, making an impression in 1976 with *The End Of The Beginning*, including 'I'm Not In Love'.

HAYES, ISAAC
(Singer/Songwriter/Producer/Musician)
Born in Covington, Tennessee, in 1938, Isaac Hayes grew up with his grandparents, moving to Memphis during his teens. Here he took up sax in a high-school band, and after mastering the keyboards he was accepted at the Stax label as a studio musician, initially playing on early **Otis Redding** recordings. Moving into songwriting, he collaborated with **David Porter** on 'You Don't Know Like I Know' and 'Soul Man' (**Sam & Dave**), 'B-A-B-Y' and 'Let Me Be Good To You' (**Carla Thomas**), 'I'm A Big Girl Now' (**Mable John**) and various songs for **Wilson Pickett**, Don Covay, **Johnnie Taylor**, The Soul Children and **The Emotions**.

In the meantime (during 1967) Isaac had recorded *Presenting Isaac Hayes* (later re-issued as 'Blue Hayes'), but it was in 1969 that he first made an impact with *Hot Buttered Soul*, including 'By The Time I Get To Phoenix'. The album, along with follow-ups *The Isaac Hayes Movement*, *To Be Continued* and *Shaft* (1971) reached platinum status in America, the classic 'Shaft' soundtrack reaching the UK Top 5 and establishing him internationally. Further Stax albums followed with *Black Moses* – his 'nickname' (1971), *Tough Guys* (soundtrack, 1974), *Truck Turner* (soundtrack, 1974), and *Movement* before he switched to ABC in 1975. Here he scored with a single 'Disco Connection' (UK Top 10, 1976) and formed his own label, Hot Buttered Soul Records, where he produced **The Masqueraders**.

Switching to Polydor he continued with *New Horizon* (1977), including 'Moonlight Lovin' (Ménage A Trois)', and *For The Sake Of Love* (1978), including 'Zeke The Freak', before he teamed up with **Millie Jackson** on the Spring label for a duet album *Royal Rappin's* (1985), including 'Sweet Music, Soft Lights And You'.

He also arranged/produced/co-wrote two albums for **Donald Byrd** (*Love Byrd* and *Words, Sounds, Colours & Shapes*), while as an actor he appeared in TV's *Starsky & Hutch*, *The Rockford Files* and most notably John Carpenter's movie *Escape From New York*.

More recently he has recorded for CBS and in 1990 sang lead on 'Just Be My Lady' on the album *All Because Of You* for saxophonist Kim Waters.

HAYWOOD, LEON
(Singer/Songwriter/Producer)
Born in Houston, Texas, Leon began his career as a pianist and moved to Los Angeles where he became a session player. In 1963 he began to record as a solo artist, his American chart successes over the years including 'She's With Her Other Love', 'Mellow Moonlight', 'I Want To Do Something Freaky To You', 'It's Got To Be Mellow' and the instrumental 'Soul Cargo'.

In 1978 he was recording for MCA – *Double Pleasure*, including 'You Bring Out The Freak In Me' – before he switched to 20th Century for *Leon Haywood Naturally*, *Come And Get Yourself Some* and *Naturally*, including his most noted dance classic 'Don't Push It, Don't Force It' (UK Top 20, 1980).

He later recorded for CBS (*Intimate*), Casablanca ('I'm Out To Catch', 1983), and Modern ('Tenderoni', 1984). In 1983 he also produced half an album for **Jerry Knight**, *Love's On Our Side*, including 'She's Got To Be A Dancer' which he co-wrote.

HAYWOODE, EMMA

(Singer)

Emma grew up in Leeds, the daughter of Russian parents. She originally signed with RCA and recorded the duet 'I Really Wanna Be With You' with **Rick Clarke**. Switching to Boss Records she released 'Need Your Lovin'', 'Rescue Me', and sessions with Hot House. She later worked with Liverpool producer Jon Williams on 'People (Round & Round)'.

HEADHUNTERS

(Group)

Bennie Maupin, Mike Clark, Paul J. Jackson, **Bill Summers**, DeWayne McKnight, Paul Potyen (keyboards) and Derric Youman (vocals) were among the line-up of musicians who accompanied **Herbie Hancock** both on tour and in the studio during the mid-'70s. They signed as Headhunters to Arista where their albums were *Survival Of The Fittest* and *Straight From The Gate*.

HEARD, LARRY

(Songwriter/Producer/Drummer/Keyboards)

Born in Chicago, Larry took up the drums as a child and played in a number of local jazz rock groups during his teens. One of his brothers overheard a song he had written called 'Mysteries Of Love' and persuaded him to release it as a single. Released under the pseudonym of Mr Fingers, the song became a classic on the Chicago 'house music' scene of the mid-'80s, and was later re-recorded with vocalist **Robert Owens**.

Robert then sang a number of Larry's songs including 'The Path', 'Break Down The Walls' and 'Can You Feel It', all under the group name of Fingers Inc, (which also included a second vocalist Ron Wilson). By now Larry had established his own production style (incorporating his own keyboard-playing), developing something of a cult following on the UK house scene. A Fingers Inc. album *Another Side* on the UK Jack Trax label is now a collectors item (never released in America).

Broadening his horizons beyond Fingers Inc., Larry's services as a writer and/or producer were utilized by Chicago artists including **The Nightwriters**, The It, **Lil Louis** ('Touch Me' and '6 a.m.'), **Kym Mazelle** ('Treat Me Right'), Blakk Society ('Just Another Lonely Day'), Trio Zero ('Twilight') and **Mondee Oliver** ('Stay Close'). He revived Mr Fingers for 'What About This Love' (1989).

HEATH BROTHERS

(Group)

The Heath Brothers are Percy (bass, founding member) and Jimmy (saxes/flute). Percy was born in North Carolina in 1923, Jimmy in Philadelphia in 1926. They first went on the road together in 1948 playing with trumpeter Howard McGhee. Adopting Stanley Cowell (keyboards), Tony Purrone (guitar) and Akira Tana (drums), The Heath Brothers veered into jazz fusion in 1974, and after building an American following signed to CBS in 1978. Their albums here were *Passing Thru*, *In Motion* (1979), *Live At The Public Theater* (1980), including 'For The Public' (produced by the Heaths' son/nephew **James Mtume**) and 'Watergate Blues', and *Expressions Of Life* (1981), including a further Mtume production 'Dreamin'', which has become a collector's item among fusion jazz fans in the UK.

In 1982 the group switched to the Antilles label for *Brotherly Love*.

HEATWAVE

(Group)

Formed in Germany during the mid-'70s by **Johnnie Wilder** and Tommy Harris, the success of Heatwave began after **Rod Temperton** joined them as keyboard player and chief songwriter. Tommy then left to be replaced by drummer Ernest 'Bilbo' Berger (from Czechoslovakia), Keith Wilder (Johnnie's brother), guitarist Eric Johns (later to be replaced by Johnnie's cousin Billy Jones), bass player Mario Mantese (later replaced by **Derek Bramble**) and **Roy Carter**. (Rod was later replaced by Calvin Duke, and lead singers have included J.D.Nicholas.)

In 1976 they signed to GTO (via Epic) in the UK, and made an immediate impression with 'Boogie Nights' (Top 5) from their debut album *Too Hot To Handle* (1977), also including 'Ain't No Half Steppin'' and a Top 20 hit in the title track. Success continued with *Central Heating* (1978), including 'The Groove Line' (Top 20), 'Mind Blowing Decisions' (Top 20) and 'Always And Forever' (Top 10), which sold in excess of ten million copies around the world.

Further albums were *Hot Property* (1979) including 'Razzle Dazzle' (Top 50), *Candles* (1981), including 'Gangsters Of The Groove' (Top 20), and *Current* (1982), including 'Mind What You Find', although their heyday passed following an accident which left **Johnnie Wilder** paralysed from the waist down.

In 1990 the group returned on the Brothers Organisation label for a remake of 'Mind Blowing Decisions' and a number of new songs.

HEAVEN & EARTH

(Group)

Heaven & Earth featured the lead vocals of Chicago-born singer Dwight Ronnell Dukes. During the late '70s they recorded for Mercury (including *Fantasy*, 1979), although they are best remembered for their single 'I Really Love You', released by WMOT Records in 1981. Dwight later joined the group **Cashmere**.

HEBB, BOBBY

(Singer/Songwriter)

Bobby originally played spoons and sang with the Smokey Mountain Boys. He also studied guitar with Chet Atkins and Hank Garland before writing and recording the original version of 'Sunny', a mid-'60s r&b/country & western/pop hit which later became a hit for **Boney M**.

HELMS, JIMMY
(Singer)
This UK singer made one major contribution to the world of soul music, 'Gonna Make You An Offer You Can't Refuse' for Cube Records, a UK Top 10 hit in 1973. It was remixed and re-released in 1983.

HENDERSON, EDDIE
(Trumpet/Flugelhorn/Songwriter)
Born in New York in 1940, Eddie has maintained a career as both a top-grade doctor and a musician from the '60s through to the present day. His early music experience came by performing with artists including **Herbie Hancock** before he signed with the Capricorn label for *Realization* and *Inside Out* before switching to Blue Note in the early '70s.

During the jazz funk era of the mid–late '70s Eddie recorded for Capitol and made a major impression on UK dancefloors with 'Say That You Will' from *Comin' Through* (1977), and 'Prance On' (UK Top 50) from his follow-up album *Mahal* (1978). He has also recorded with artists including **Pharaoh Sanders**, **Charles Earland**, **Will Downing** ('The World Is A Ghetto'), and wrote *Dreams* recorded by **Norman Connors**.

HENDERSON, FINIS
(Singer/Songwriter)
Born in Chicago, Finis grew up in a show-business environment where his father was a dancer and later vice-president of **Sammy Davis** Enterprises. He also managed artists including **Jerry Butler** and **Brook Benton**. As a teenager Finis worked with a group Dynamic 4 before joining Weapons Of Peace in 1970 (recording for the Playboy label). When the group split up in 1978 Finis moved to Los Angeles where initially he worked as a comedian. Here he was discovered by Richard Pryor who employed him as his opening act in San Francisco.

He also shared an apartment with **Al McKay** of **Earth Wind & Fire**, and together they formed a group Prophecy with **Bill Wolfer** (for whom Finis wrote 'Call Me' on the 1982 album *Wolf*). However Motown offered him a solo contract, and Al McKay worked as producer on his one album *Finis*, including 'Skip To My Lou'.

HENDERSON, MICHAEL
(Singer/Bass/Songwriter)
Born in Mississippi in 1951, Michael moved to Detroit as a child and was only thirteen when he was employed as bass player with **The Fantastic Four**, **The Detroit Emeralds**, **Billy Preston** and numerous Motown artists between 1964 and 1965. From here he toured with both **Aretha Franklin** and **Stevie Wonder** before being recruited by **Miles Davis** with whom he played and toured for seven years.

Upon meeting **Norman Connors**, Michael insisted Norman record some of his songs. Accepting, Norman recorded 'Valentine Love', a duet Michael sang with **Jean Carne** (from *Saturday Night Special*, 1975). The song was Michael's first vocal recording and an American hit single. He also sang the classic follow-up 'You Are My Starship' from the platinum Norman Connors album of the same name, Michael writing both this and 'We Both Need Each Other' for the album. As a result of his vocal success with Norman, Michael signed to Buddah Records as a solo artist and released *Solid* (1976), *Goin' Places* (1977), *In The Night Time* (1978), *Do It All* (1979), *To Be Loved*, *Wide Receiver*, *Slingshot* (1981) – featuring Michael virtually nude on the cover! – and *Fickle* (1983). He later recorded one album for EMI, *Bedtime Stories* (1986).

Michael has recorded with **Phyllis Hyman** (duet 'Can't We Fall In Love Again', 1981), **Bobby Womack** and **Johnnie Taylor**, and produced **The Dramatics**. His next-door neighbour, incidentally, was **Cherrelle** who he gave a break to in 1978 by employing her as a backing singer and taking her on tour for four years.

HENDERSON, WAYNE
(Trombone/Producer/Songwriter)
Born in Houston, Texas, Wayne was one of the original members of **The Crusaders** and played trombone with the group until 1976. From here he signed to ABC as a solo artist and recorded *Big Daddy's Place* (1977), including 'I'm Staying Forever' and 'Keep That Same Old Feeling', which later became highly sought after on the UK 'jazz funk' scene. In 1978 he switched to Polydor where his albums were *Living On A Dream* (1978), including 'Hot Stuff', and *Emphasized* (1979), including 'Dancing Love Affair', as well as two duet albums with **Roy Ayers**. By this time he had moved to Los Angeles and launched his At Home Productions company with a selection of top West Coast session musicians including **Bobby Lyle**, **Ronnie Laws**, **Augie Johnson**, **Marlon McClain** and **Roland Bautista** (plus a regular string section).

His unique At Home production style made a significant contribution to the r&b scene of the late '70s/early '80s, Wayne working on numerous projects for artists including **Ronnie Laws** (*Pressure Sensitive*, including 'Always There'), **Bobby Lyle** (*The Genie*), **Pleasure** (most albums), **Side Effect** (most albums), **Arthur Adams** (*Home Brew*), **Gabor Szabo** (*Nightflight*), **Michael White** (*White Night*), **Hilary** (*Just Before After Hours*), **Smoke** (*Smoke*), **Chico Hamilton** (*Nomad*), **Ramsey Lewis** (two tracks on *Ramsey*), **Narada Michael Walden** and **David Oliver** (all three albums). He also launched his own At Home label (via Fantasy), with artists including **Allspice**.

In the '80s, following the demise of the 'At Home'

company, he was less prolific, although he continued to produce artists including **The McCrarys** (*All Night Music*, co-writing 'Love On A Summer Night'), **Mary Wells** ('My Guy' re-make), **Rebbie Jackson**, **Hiroshima** (*Odori*) and **Lawrence Hilton Jacobs**. He continued to produce **Ronnie Laws** from 1986's *All Day Rhythm* through to *True Spirit* in 1990.

HENDERSON, WILLIE
(Singer/Songwriter)
From Chicago, Willie was an established arranger/producer in the early '70s, also working closely with **Carl Davis**. As a solo artist his recordings include *The Dance Master* for the New Sounds label (1973).

HENDRYX, NONA
(Singer)
Born in Trenton, New Jersey, Nona began by singing in church. Here she met **Sarah Dash** with whom she formed a duo the Del Capris. Their friends **Patti Labelle** and **Cindy Birdsong** had a group The Ordettes, and the four decided to team up as The Bluebelles. They later joined Patti Labelle in both **Patti Labelle & The Bluebelles** and **Labelle**.

Nona later recorded as a solo artist for both Epic (during the '70s) and RCA (during the '80s).

HENRY, DEBRA
(Singer)
From Philadelphia, Debra originally sang with **Anglo Saxon Brown**, a group which later became **Silk** and signed to the Philadelphia International (PIR) label in the late '70s. Here she caught the attention of **Kenny Gamble** who had intended to help her with a solo career before the winding down of the label. While at PIR she recorded with **Jerry Butler** on the duet 'Don't Be An Island'.

HEWETT, HOWARD
(Singer/Songwriter)
Born in Ohio, Howard settled in Los Angeles where from 1979 he became one-third/lead vocalist of the group **Shalamar**. After a string of hits through to 1985 he signed to Elektra as a solo artist. Here he has recorded *I Commit To Love* (1986), including 'I'm For Real' and 'Stay', *Forever And Ever* (1988), and *Howard Hewett* (1990), including 'Show Me', and 'When Will It Be', a duet with **Anita Baker**.

Elsewhere he has worked with **LaToya Jackson** (co-writing/producing 'Frustration' from *Heart Don't Lie* (1984), **Stanley Clarke** (lead vocal on 'Heaven Sent You' from *Time Exposure*, 1984), **George Duke** (lead vocal on 'King For A Day', 1986), **Fire Fox**, **Stacy Lattisaw** (duet 'Ain't No Mountain High Enough', 1988) and **Donna Summer** (backgrounds) among many others.

HI-GLOSS
(Studio Group)
Hi-Gloss was the concept of Giuliana Salerni who arranged and produced 1981's *Hi-Gloss* released by Prelude Records. The group featured a line-up of top session musicians including **Timmy Allen** (bass) and **Kae Williams** (keyboards), with lead vocal by **Phillip Ballou** and backgrounds from **Luther Vandross** and **Ullanda McCullough**. Lyrics for the album were co-written by **Phil Hurtt**, with 'You'll Never Know' later recorded by **Shakatak**.

HI-TENSION
(Group)
From North London, **David Joseph** (chief song-writer/keyboards/lead vocals), Ken Joseph (bass/vocals), Paul Phillips (guitar/vocals), Leroy Williams (percussion), Jeff Guishard (percussion/lead vocals), Paul McLean (sax), David Reid (drums), Paapa Mensah (drums), Guy Barker (trumpet), Peter Thomas (trombone), Bob Sydor (sax) and Ray Alan Eko (sax) were school friends who originally performed as Hott Waxx. In 1977 they changed their name to Hi-Tension and became one of the innovators on the 'Brit Funk' scene of the mid-'70s. Signing to Island Records, their debut single 'Hi-Tension' became a dancefloor anthem in 1978 (UK Top 20) and became the title track of a highly acclaimed album which featured 'British Hustle' (UK Top 10), 'Peace On Earth', 'Autumn Love' and the instrumental 'Power And Lightning'.

David Joseph later left the group. In 1984 Ken, Leroy and Jeff returned as Hi-Tension on Streetwave Records and released 'Rat Race' (1984) and 'You Make Me Happy' (1985).

HICKS, D'ATRA
(Singer)
Born in Harlem, New York, in 1968, D'Atra sang in her grandfather's church choir from the age of four. As a teenager she joined her sister Miriam in a vocal duo The Hicks Sisters and saved up enough money to make a recording. This was heard by the producer of *Mama I Want To Sing*, the most successful non-Broadway black musical in theatre history, in which D'Atra went on to play the lead role of Doris Winter.

In 1989 she signed with Capitol as a solo artist and worked with producers including **Narada Michael Walden** and **Nick Martinelli** on a debut album *D'Atra Hicks*.

HICKS, MARVA
(Singer/Songwriter)
Born in Petersburg, Virginia, Marva grew up in a gospel enviroment prior to a trip to New York. Here she saw a Broadway show and became hooked on being a performer, following which she took acting classes in Washington DC. After developing her vocals she recorded a series of demos, one of which landed her a deal at Infinity

Records where her debut single was 'Looking Over My Shoulder' (1981). Unfortunately the label went out of business, but Marva found work on Broadway with Lena Horne for two and a half years. Lena took the show to London where Marva met **Stevie Wonder**.

In 1984 Marva began to tour with Stevie, also contributing backing vocals to his album *Characters*. While singing with Stevie she was approached by Polydor in 1988, following which her debut album *Marva Hicks*, including 'One Good Reason' and 'I Got You Where I Want', was released in 1991.

HIGH FASHION
(Vocal Group)
Instigated by producer **Jacques Fred Petrus**, High Fashion were Erick McClinton, **Alyson Williams** and **Meli'sa Morgan** from New York. Meli'sa co-wrote many of the songs, while their 1982 Capitol debut album *Feelin' Lucky* was co-produced by **Mike Theodore**, **Dennis Coffey** and **Kashif**. It included 'Feelin' Lucky Lately' and three songs by Kashif. *Make Up Your Mind* was released in 1983.

HIGH, MARTHA
(Singer)
Vocalist with **James Brown**, Martha released one single on Salsoul Records, 'Showdown', produced by James himself in 1979.

HILARY
(Flute)
Born in Glens Falls, New York, in 1951, Hilary Schmidt was the third of nine children. When she was ten the family moved to Long Island, where Hilary took up the trombone (her brother took up French horn). After leaving school Hilary taught herself sax and flute before enrolling in Boston's Berklee School of Music in 1970. By 1972 she was studying classical music in New York. In the mid-'70s she played with local groups including Calliope, Blues Busters, Simbora and Mulatto. In 1978 Dr George Butler signed her for one album at CBS, sending her to Los Angeles to work with **Wayne Henderson** on her debut album *Just Before After Hours* which included 'Do It' and fusion jazz favourite 'Amazona'.

HILL, LONNIE
(Singer)
From Austin, Texas, Lonnie was a member of his family's spiritual group The Gospel Keynotes by the age of 17. Their successful recordings included 'Keep On Walking', 'Don't Look Back' and 'We Need Prayer'. His interest in secular r&b lead him to Denver where he recorded *You Got Me Running* for the Urban Sound label. It was released in the UK in 1986 by Virgin/10 Records, and included the much acclaimed single 'Galveston Bay' (UK Top 75). The album also featured **Philip Bailey** on backing vocals.

HILL, Z.Z.
(Singer)
Born Arzel Hill in Naples, Texas, in 1940, Z.Z. began his recording career in Los Angeles under the guidance of his brother Matt. Through the '60s he recorded numerous songs for the Kent label including 'You Were Wrong', 'You Don't Know Me' and 'If I Could Do It All Over' before forming his own Hill label during the '70s. Here he scored an American hit with 'Don't Make Me Pay For His Mistakes' (1972) which led to a recording deal with United Artists. Following albums including *The Best Thing That's Happened To Me* (1973) and *Keep On Lovin' You* (1975), including the **Lamont Dozier**-produced 'That Ain't The Way You Make Love', he switched to CBS for *Love Is So Good When You're Stealing It* (1977), *Let's Make A Deal* (1978), including 'This Time They Told The Truth', and *The Mark Of Z.Z.* (1979).

Prior to his death he recorded albums for Malaco including *I'm A Blues Man* and *Bluesmaster* (both 1984).

HINDS, CAMELLE
(Songwriter/Producer)
Based in London, Camelle played bass and sang with **Central Line** before establishing himself as a producer. In 1986 he formed his own group Hindsight, and for Circa released a series of singles including 'Small Change' (1986), 'Lowdown' (Top 75, 1987) and 'Heaven's Just A Breath Away' (1987).

HINES, GREGORY
(Singer/Actor)
Primarily a dancer and actor, Gregory teamed up with **Luther Vandross** for the hit American duet 'There's Nothing Better Than Love', taken from Luther's 1986 album *Give Me The Reason*. The track was later included on Gregory's debut album for Epic Records *Gregory Hines* (1988) including 'Love Don't Love You Anymore', produced by Luther Vandross.

As an actor he was in *The Cotton Club*, *Running Scared* and *White Nights*, among other films.

HIROSHIMA
(Group)
Formed in Los Angeles during the late 70s, Hiroshima consists of Dan Kuramoto (vocals/sax/flute), June Okida Kuramoto (bass/koto), Teri Kusumoto (vocals/percussion), Johnny Mori (taiko/percussion), Danny Yamamoto (drums), Jess Acuna (vocals/congas/percussion), Dane Matsumara (bass), Peter Hata (guitar) and Richard Mathews (keyboards/synths), all of whom are Japanese-American. Signing to Arista in 1980, their debut album was *Odori*, produced in Los Angeles by **Wayne Henderson**.

HODGES, JAMES & SMITH

(Vocal Group)

Formed in Detroit, Hodges, James & Smith were Pat Hodges, Denita James and Jessica Smith, although for a time they featured the additional vocals of **Carolyn Crawford**. They recorded backgrounds for artists including **Bobby Womack** (*Roots In Me*) and **Ronnie McNeir** (*Ronnie McNeir*). Their albums for London Records include *What's On Your Mind* (1977).

HOGGARD, JAY

(Vibes)

Born in Washington DC in 1954, and raised in New York, Jay studied piano and saxophone before taking up the vibes in 1970. He was given his first professional engagement by Clifford Thorton in 1973 during his days as a freshman at Wesleyan University in Middletown, Connecticut. In 1977, after travelling to Tanzania to study East African xylophone music, he returned to New York as a session musician and found work with artists including **Roberta Flack** and **Candi Staton**. In 1979 he released *Solo Vibraphone* and *Days Like These*, the latter for GRP Records making an impact on the UK 'jazz funk' scene (followed by a London appearance at The Horseshoe Hotel).

Moving back into more traditional/Latin jazz, his albums included *Under The Double Moon* (with pianist Anthony Davis) for GRP Records (1980), *Rain Forest* including 'Reverend Libra', for Contemporary Records, (1981), and *Mystic Winds, Tropical Breezes* for India Navigation Records (1981).

More recently, he contributed a vibes solo for **Will Downing** on 'Love Call'.

HOGUE, LIZ

(Singer)

From Philadelphia, Liz Hogue is the niece of **Norman Harris**. During the '80s she worked as a session singer with **Jean Carne**, **Grover Washington** and **Norman Connors** prior to meeting **Chris Jasper**. After leaving both **The Isley Brothers** and **Isley/Jasper/Isley**, Chris launched his Gold City label (via CBS) and produced Liz's debut album *Vicious & Fresh* (1989), including 'Dream Lover'.

HOLIDAYS

(Vocal Group)

Formed by Jimmy and Jack Holland in Detroit, this Chicago-based vocal group began their career as the Forsandos in 1958. In 1963 (after a few years off for army service) the group was re-formed and released 'Step By Step' on the Markie label. In 1965 they moved to Detroit where they released 'Deep Down In My Heart' on Master Records before switching to Golden World Records. **Edwin Starr** believes his voice was taken from a demo and used as the lead vocal on the group's release 'I'll Love You Forever' for the Golden World Records label in 1966. Their final release on Golden World was 'Watch Out Girl' (1966) before later recordings for labels including Solid Hit, Revilot, Soul Hawk (apparently a different line-up), Marathon and Rob-Ron.

HOLLAND/DOZIER/HOLLAND

(Songwriters/Producers)

From Detroit, Michigan, Holland/Dozier/Holland were **Eddie Holland**, **Lamont Dozier** and Brian Holland. Eddie Holland (born 1939) recorded 'Jamie' as a solo artist for United Artists. The single (and subsequent album of the same name) was instigated by **Berry Gordy** at Motown who paired Eddie's brother Brian Holland (born 1941) with Lamont Dozier as producers in the early '60s. When Eddie's own recording career seemed unlikely to survive on a long-term basis, he joined Brian and Lamont in a three-way partnership to engineer what became the 'Motown sound' through the '60s.

Their hits as songwriters/producers at Motown include 'Where Did Our Love Go', 'Baby Love', 'Stop! In The Name Of Love', 'You Can't Hurry Love', 'You Keep Me Hangin' On', 'Love Is Here And Now You're Gone,' 'My World Is Empty Without You' and 'Reflections' (**The Supremes**); 'Reach Out I'll Be There', 'Standing In The Shadows Of Love', 'I Can't Help Myself' and 'Seven Rooms Of Gloom' (**Four Tops**); 'Nowhere To Run' and 'Jimmy Mack' (**Martha Reeves & The Vandellas**); 'How Sweet It Is' and 'Road Runner' (**Junior Walker & The All Stars**); 'This Old Heart Of Mine' and 'Put Yourself In My Place' (**Isley Brothers**); and 'Heaven Must Have Sent You' (**The Elgins**).

In 1970 they left Motown to concentrate on their own projects. Moving to Los Angeles they launched their own Hot Wax/Invictus labels and scored immediate hits with **Freda Payne**'s 'Band Of Gold' (UK No. 1), **Chairman of the Board**'s 'Give Me Just a Little More Time' and 'You've Got Me Danglin' On A String' (both UK Top 5) and **100 Proof Aged In Soul**'s 'Somebody's Been Sleeping In My Bed'. Both for their own labels and outside productions (including 'Just Being Myself' for **Dionne Warwick** in 1972), the unit of Holland/Dozier/Holland remained together until 1973. After the release of their own r&b classic 'Why Can't We Be Lovers', lead singer Lamont Dozier left to start a solo career.

Invictus, however, continued to 1977 with Brian Holland producing one of the label's last releases, 'I Got It' by **New York Port Authority**.

HOLLAND, EDDIE

(Songwriter/Producer)

Born in Detroit, Eddie recorded as a solo artist for Motown (singles including 'Candy To Me', 1964) before he became a third of the legendary **Holland/Dozier/Holland**.

HOLLIDAY, JENNIFER

(Singer)

Born in Houston, Texas, Jennifer developed her vocal skills in church during her days with the Pleasant Grove Choir. On one occasion the choir was invited to perform on TV, at which point Jennifer was spotted by a local theatre production company. The company were staging a version of *Don't Bother Me, I Can't Cope*, and Jennifer was approached for a major role. Still in her teens she left for New York where she landed a Broadway role in *Your Arm's Too Short To Box With God*. In 1981 Jennifer joined the cast of *Dreamgirls*, in addition to which she signed as a solo artist to Geffen Records. Her solo debut became the Grammy Award-winning 'And I'm Telling You I'm Not Going' (UK Top 40, 1982), taken from the show (as was the follow-up 'I am Changing').

In 1982 she took leave from *Dreamgirls* to work with producer **Maurice White** on her debut album *Feel My Soul* (1983), her temporary replacement being Julia McGirt (see **Julia & Co**). She later returned to the show while her liaison with Geffen continued with *Say You Love Me* (1985), including 'No Frills Love' and 'Hard Time For Lovers', and *Get Close To My Love* (1987), including 'Heart On The Line'.

She later sang lead vocals on 'Gotta Give It Up' for **Rodney Franklin** from his album *Diamond Inside Of You* (1988), before switching as a solo artist to Arista (1991).

HOLLOWAY, BRENDA

(Singer)

Born in California in 1948, Brenda recorded her debut single 'Hey Fool' (1962) for the Donna label when she was fourteen. Two years later she signed with Motown and scored American hits with 'Every Little Bit Hurts' and 'What Are You Going To Do When I'm Gone', both regarded as classics by Motown fans alongside 'Operator', 'Together Till The End Of Time', 'Hurt A Little Every Day', 'How Many Times Did You Mean It', 'I'll Always Love You' and 'You Make Me So Very Happy' (later a hit for Blood Sweat & Tears).

Her 1968 recording 'Just Look What You've Done' is also acclaimed as one in the first of a handful of records to shape the face of disco music in the early '70s. After Motown she teamed up with **Holland/Dozier/Holland** to record two singles for the Music Merchant label, 'Let Me Grow' and 'Some Quiet Place', before returning to her gospel roots with an album released by the Birth Right label in 1980.

In 1988 she recorded 'Give Me A Little Inspiration' and a duet 'On The Rebound' with **Jimmy Ruffin** for the UK Nightmare label. She has also sung backgrounds with **Barry White** ('Sho' You Right'), Joe Cocker and **Leon Ware**. Her most recent album is *All It Takes* (1991), including 'You Gave Me Love' for the Motorcity label.

Her sister is Patrice Holloway, who recorded 'Stolen Hours' for Capitol and was a top West Coast session singer in the '70s.

HOLLOWAY, LOLEATTA

(Singer)

Loleatta was born in 1946 in Chicago where, apart from a few years in Atlanta, she has lived all her life. During her teens she sang with The Holloway Community Singers, a gospel group co-founded by her mother. From here she sang with famed gospel group The Caravans during the mid-'60s, and recorded for the Gospel and Hob labels. In 1971 Loleatta met producer **Floyd Smith** who not only introduced her to secular recording, but also became her husband. Floyd produced her debut secular single 'Rainbow 71', a version of an earlier **Gene Chandler** song. Loleatta also joined the Chicago cast of the stage musical *Don't Bother Me, I Can't Cope*.

From here Loleatta signed with GRC Productions and recorded a string of songs commencing with 'Mother Of Shame' and an album *Loleatta Holloway* (1973), released by Atlanta-based label Aware Records. Her next album was *Cry To Me* (1975), from which the title track ballad was written by **Sam Dees** and is regarded as a soul classic. After the Aware label folded, Loleatta switched to the Gold Mine subsidiary of Salsoul Records. Here, during the late '70s she recorded a string of albums, scoring success on the disco scene with single hits including 'Hit And Run' (1977) produced by **Norman Harris**, 'Seconds' (1982) with **The Salsoul Orchestra** and 'Love Sensation' (1983) produced by **Dan Hartman**. Her vocal on this last track was in 1989 utilised by Black Box who featured it in their UK smash hit 'Ride On Time', which stayed at No. 1 in the charts for six weeks. To get her voice in shape for each recording session, incidentally, Loleatta drinks Vicks Vapour Rub. She's been drinking it since the age of seven!

Until 1984 Loleatta continued to work with husband **Floyd Smith**, his version of 'Sweet Thing' (the **Rufus/Chaka Khan** classic) landing her a deal with Streetwise Records just prior to his death. The song was released as a B side to an **Arthur Baker** production 'Crash Goes Love', but an album was never released. Since then Loleatta has recorded for independent dance labels DJ International and Saturday Records, her last recording to date being 'Heart Stealer' (1989) which became 'Do That To Me (Set Me Free)' in 1991. The sampling of her voice from '70s recordings has been trendy on late '80s-early '90s dance records made predominantly in Italy.

HOLMAN, EDDIE

(Singer/Songwriter)

Born in Norfolk, Virginia, in 1946, Eddie came from a strict church-going family which moved to New York in the '50s. Here he established himself as child performer Little Eddie Holman in Off-Broadway theatres and on NBC-TV's *The Children's Hour*. He also recorded for the Leopard and Ascot labels before moving to Philadelphia in the '60s. In 1965 he recorded 'This Can't Be True' for Cameo Parkway Records. Follow-ups included 'Am I A

Loser (From The Start)' which later became collector's items on the Northern soul scene in the UK.

After 'I'll Cry 1000 Tears' for Bell Records (1968), Eddie signed with ABC Records, scoring with 'I Love You' and his classic 'Hey There Lonely Girl' (UK Top 5, 1974). Other American hits on ABC included 'Don't Stop Now', 'Since I Don't Have You' and 'Cathy Called'. He then recorded for GSF and Silver Blue Records before signing to Salsoul in 1977. That year he recorded 'This Will Be A Night To Remember' which became a disco classic.

In the 80s Eddie became a born-again Christian and studied for a degree in theology. In 1985 he recorded the gospel album *United*, including 'Give It All To The Lord' and 'Holy Ghost', for his own Agape label in Philadelphia. His secular music activities continued, especially in the UK where he has recorded 'I Surrender' for the Action label and 'Whatever Happened To Our Melody' for Nightmare Records (1989).

HONEY AND THE BEES
(Vocal Group)
From Philadelphia, Honey And The Bees were Nadine Felder (sister of **Alan Felder**), Gwen Oliver, Ann Wooten and Jean Davis. They formed officially in 1965 after having previously sung together as both The Superiorettes and The Yum Yums. With arrangements by **Bobby Martin** and productions by local DJ Jimmy Bishop, the group recorded singles including 'I'm Confessin' That I Love You' and 'Sunday Kind Of Love' on the Arctic label from 1966 to 1968. Switching to the Jubilee label in 1970, releases continued with '(I Want You) To Make Love', 'Love Can Turn To Hate' and 'It's Gonna Take A Miracle' before they signed to Bell Records. Here in 1972 they released 'That's What Girls Are Made For' and 'Song For Jim'.

HONEY CONE
(Vocal Group)
Based in Los Angeles, Honey Cone were Carolyn Willis, Shellie Clark and Edna Wright who in 1969 signed with the **Holland/Dozier/Holland** label Hot Wax and scored American r&b success with 'While You're Out Looking For Sugar'. Their follow-ups included 'One Money Don't Stop No Show' and 'Want Ads' together with albums *Honey Cone*, *Sweet Replies* and *Soulful Tapestry* through the early '70s.

HOOKER, FRANK
(Singer/Songwriter)
Based in Washington DC, Frank made one major impression on the dance scene with 'This Feelin'', a single for the Panorama label in 1980. The label was run by Cory Robbins who discovered the group. The song, meanwhile, was mixed by Rick Gianatos who later co-produced the 1991 hit for **Frances Nero** 'Footsteps Following Me'. Cory Robbins went on to launch his own label Profile in New York.

HOOPER, STIX
(Drums/Songwriter/Producer/Singer)
Born in Houston, Texas, Stix was one of the founder members of **The Crusaders** during the early '60s. He played consistently with the group through to the mid-'80s, also recording two solo albums for MCA, *The World Within Stix Hooper* (1979), including the **Joe Sample**-penned 'Cordon Bleu', and *Touch The Feeling* (1982), featuring vocalist **Jerry Butler** on 'Feeling Happy', during this time.

After leaving **The Crusaders** he signed to the Artful Balance label in Los Angeles and released *Lay It On The Line* (1989). It included a version of 'I Felt The Love', a song he had originally co-written and recorded with **The Crusaders**. In 1990 he produced an album for eighteen-year-old jazz keyboard player Vernell Brown Jr.

HORNE, JIMMY 'BO'
(Singer)
Based in Miami, Jimmy is best remembered for his 1978 release 'Dance Across The Floor', a major disco single for TK Records.

HORTON, McKINLEY
(Keyboards/Songwriter)
Born in Philadelphia, McKinley wrote and/or produced songs for **Eugene Wilde**, **Terri Wells**, **Norwood** and **Harold Melvin & The Blue Notes** before joining the group **Cashmere** as keyboard player/songwriter.

HORTON, YOGI
(Drummer)
New York-based top session drummer Yogi Horton played with artists including **Grover Washington**, **Ashford & Simpson**, **B.B.&Q.**, **High Fashion**, **Charles Earland** and **Luther Vandross** before tragically taking his own life in the mid-'80s.

HOT BUTTERED SOUL
(Vocal Group)
This vocal group was instigated by **Isaac Hayes** and consisted of **Pat Lewis**, Diane Lewis, Rose Williams and Diane Davis. In addition to their work with Isaac they recorded two albums with **Donald Byrd**, *Love Byrd* (1981), including 'Love Has Come Around', and *Words, Sounds, Colours And Shapes* (1982).

HOT STREAK
(Group)
Originally known as A Different Flavor, Hot Streak are Derrick Dupree (lead vocals), Ricci Burgess (drums), Jacob Dixon (bass) and Al Tanner Jr (lead guitar). The group performed throughout New York, New Jersey and Connecticut before hooking up with producers Curtis Hudson and Lisa Stevens for 'Body Work', released by Easy Street in the USA and a Top 20 UK release for Polydor (1983).

HOUSTON, CISSY

(Singer)

Based in New York, Cissy recorded for RCA in the late '50s as one of The Drinkyard Singers before teaming up with nieces Dee Dee and **Dionne Warwick** and Judy Clay to form a group of background singers. Together they worked with artists including **Aretha Franklin**, Dusty Springfield and Neil Diamond before Cissy formed The Sweet Inspirations.

After scoring late '60s American success on Atlantic Records with songs including 'Sweet Inspiration' and 'Why Am I Treated So Bad', the group split up and in 1970 Cissy commenced a solo career. She recorded for numerous labels including Commonwealth International, Janus, Private Stock (*Cissy Houston*, 1977), CBS (*Warning – Danger*, 1979) and EMI (*Step Aside For A Lady*, 1980). In the meantime she became a minister at the New Hope Baptist Church, which her daughter **Whitney Houston** joined at the age of eleven. She later recorded a duet with Whitney 'I Know Him So Well' on *Whitney* (1987).

Cissy is a favourite singer of **Luther Vandross** who invited her to record with him on his first two albums. Her most recent solo release was 'With You I Could Have It All' for the Glitter label (via Creole in the UK) in 1985.

HOUSTON, THELMA

(Singer)

Born in Leland, Mississippi, Thelma was taught to sing by her babysitter at the age of three. She grew up in Long Beach, California, from the age of ten, and after her high-school days toured there with gospel group The Art Reynolds Singers. She later became resident singer at The Factory Club. Here she met Marc Gordon (**Fifth Dimension**'s manager) who secured her a recording deal with ABC in 1969. Her debut album was *Sunshower*, although her first American hit single was 'Save The Country' which was not on the album. In the UK her first single was a rendition of the Rolling Stones classic 'Jumpin' Jack Flash' (released on the Stateside label).

In 1972 she signed to Motown's sister label Mowest for one album, *Thelma Houston*, before signing to Tamla (also via Motown) in 1974 and winning a Grammy nomination for 'You've Been Doing Wrong For So Long'. Following this she recorded two albums of duets with **Jerry Butler**, *Thelma And Jerry* and *Two Tone* (1975) before scoring her biggest success to date with 'Don't Leave Me This Way', a UK Top 20 hit despite another version by **Harold Melvin** & The Blue Notes climbing the charts at the same time. It was taken from her album *Any Way You Like It* (1976). Her other Tamla albums were *Ride To The Rainbow*, *The Devil In Me* (1977) and *Ready To Roll* (1979), including 'Saturday Night, Sunday Morning', a popular soul/disco track in the UK, before she switched to RCA. Here she recorded three albums but only two were released. 'If You Feel It' reached the UK Top 50.

Thelma's next move was to MCA where she worked with **Jam/Lewis** on 'You Used To Hold Me So Tight' (UK Top 50) and *Qualifying Heat* (1984). She appears not to have recorded again as a solo artist until 1990 when 'Hold On' was released as a single (on the Century 2000 label), taken from the film soundtrack *Olympus Force*. In the meantime Thelma had recorded three songs on the Richard Pryor movie soundtrack *The Bingo Long-Travelling All-Stars And Motor Kings*, a duet with **Dennis Edwards** 'Why Do People Fall In Love' (1985), and a duet with **The Winans** 'Lean On Me' from the *Lean On Me* movie soundtrack (1989).

She is now signed to the Reprise label (via Warner Brothers) where *Throw You Down*, including 'Out Of My Hands', was produced by **Richard Perry** and released in 1990.

HOUSTON, WHITNEY

(Singer)

Born in New Jersey in 1964, Whitney is the daughter of **Cissy Houston** and a niece of **Dionne Warwick**. Aged eleven she began developing her vocal skills at the New Hope Baptist Church where her mother is Minister of Music. Four years later she was singing backgrounds with her mother in nightclubs, and in the studio with **Lou Rawls** and **Chaka Khan**. She also became a fashion model, appearing in *Cosmopolitan* and on the front cover of *Seventeen* by the time she was eighteen.

Through working with her mother she came to the attention of Clive Davis who signed her to the Arista label in 1983. Her debut album *Whitney Houston* (1985) featured UK hit singles 'Saving All My Love For You' (No. 1), 'How Will I Know' (Top 5), 'The Greatest Love Of All' (Top 10, 1986), 'Hold Me', a duet with **Teddy Pendergrass** (Top 50, 1986), and 'You Give Good Love'. It sold over 13 million copies worldwide and established her as an international star. Her second album *Whitney* (1987) included UK hit singles 'I Wanna Dance With Somebody' (No. 1), 'Didn't We Almost Have It All' (Top 20), 'So Emotional' (Top 5), 'Where Do Broken Hearts Go' (Top 20, 1988), 'Love Will Save The Day' (Top 10, 1988) and 'One Moment In Time' (No. 1, 1988), and soul gems 'Just The Lonely Talking Again' and 'For The Love Of You'.

Also in 1988 she recorded 'Hold Up The Light' with **Be Be & Ce Ce Winans** on their album *Heaven*, while in 1989 she recorded 'It Isn't, It Wasn't, It Ain't Never Gonna Be' with **Aretha Franklin** on her album *Through The Storm*. In 1990 she returned with a third album *I'm Your Baby Tonight*, including 'We Didn't Know', a duet with **Stevie Wonder** and 'Lover For Life', although soul fans went for B sides (including 'Feels So Good') of the first singles which were not on the album.

HOWARD, AUSTIN

(Singer)

Born in England after his parents emigrated from Jamaica, Austin began his musical career in 1983 as founder member of British soul/funk group The Biz (one club hit 'Falling'). He later became part of B-Biz-R (one club hit 'Sucker For Love'). His first solo release was 'I'm The One Who Really Loves You', produced by **Stock/Aitken/Waterman** and released by 10 Records in 1986. The song was also featured in the film *Knights And Emeralds*.

HOWARD, GEORGE

(Sax)

From Philadelphia, George first established himself in the '70s as a session sax player on the Philly r&b scene. He worked with groups including **Harold Melvin & The Blue Notes**, **First Choice** and **Blue Magic** and later toured with **Grover Washington Jr** before moving to Atlanta and commencing a solo career. In 1982 he signed with the Palo Alto Jazz label and delivered a debut album *Asphalt Gardens* before inviting Dean Gant, **Keni Burke**, **Ndugu** and **Gwen Guthrie** to record with him on *Steppin' Out* for the TBA label (1984). After moving to Los Angeles, his next albums were *Dancing In The Sun* (1985) and *Love Will Follow* (1986), featuring **Siedah Garrett** and former members of **Maze**, before he signed to MCA.

Here his albums included *A Nice Place To Be* (1987), including 'Sweetest Taboo' featuring **Body**, and *Personal* (1989), including 'Fakin' The Feelin'' featuring **Syreeta**. In 1991 he switched to GRP where his most recent album is *Love And Understanding*.

HOWARD, MIKI

(Singer)

From Chicago, Miki's mother sang with The Gospel Caravan, while her father was a member of The Pilgrim Jubilees. During Miki's gospel singing days as a child she performed with the Reverend James Cleveland. At the age of sixteen she joined **Side Effect** with whom she performed and sang between 1977 and the early '80s. The group's producer had been **Wayne Henderson** who gave Miki session work on various At Home Productions with **Michael White** (vocal scats on 'Time Has No Ending'), **David Oliver** and **Chico Hamilton**, in addition to sessions with **Roy Ayers** (female lead on 'Poo Poo La La'), **Billy Cobham**, **Stanley Turrentine** and **L.A.Boppers** (backgrounds and co-lead on 'Are We Wrong', 1980).

In 1986 she signed as a solo artist to Atlantic Records and released her debut album *Come Share My Love*, including 'Imagination'. After the release of her second, *Love Confessions* (1987), including 'Crazy', she took a year off to get married before the release of her third album *Miki Howard* (1989), including 'Love Under New Management' and 'Until You Come Back To Me'.

HUBBARD, FREDDIE

(Trumpet/Songwriter)

Born in Indianapolis in 1938, Frederick Dewayne Hubbard initially played the French horn for which he won a music scholarship. At the age of twenty he moved to New York where he worked with **Sonny Rollins** and **Quincy Jones** before becoming a member of Art Blakey's Jazz Messengers.

His initial solo recordings were for the Blue Note label in the '60s, and 1967's *Backlash* included his original version of 'Little Sunflower'. He then recorded for Atlantic (*High Blues Pressure*) and in the early '70s CTI (*First Light*, *Red Clay* and *Keep Your Soul Together*) before switching to CBS where he made his greatest impression on the UK jazz funk scene with albums including *High Energy* (1974), *The Love Connection* (1970), including 'Little Sunflower' (featuring **Al Jarreau**) and 'Brigitte', and *Skagly* (1980). From here he recorded for labels including Liberty (*Mistral*, 1981), Fantasy (*Splash*, 1981), Pablo Today (*Born To Be Blue*, 1982, including 'Gibraltar') and Elektra Musician (*Ride Like The Wind*, 1983).

Also on the jazz funk scene he has recorded with artists including **Charles Earland**, **Jeff Lorber**, **Norman Connors** and **Rodney Franklin**.

HUDSON PEOPLE

(Group)

The Hudson People made one of the very first British dance records to make an impact on the burgeoning 'jazz funk & soul' scene of the late '70s. 'Trip To Your Mind' was released on their own Hithouse label (later via Phonogram) in 1979.

HUDSON, AL

(Singer)

Based in Detroit, Al formed a group Al Hudson & The Soul Partners during the mid-'70s and signed to ABC Records. They made an impression on the soul/dance scene with songs from their albums *Especially For You* (1977), including 'Trying To Prove My Love', and *Cherish* (1977). In 1978 they recorded with **The Dells** on 'My Life Is So Wonderful (When You're Around)', and also scored their most significant dancefloor victories with songs 'How Do You Do' and 'Spread Love'. Directly after this the group changed their name to **One Way**.

While the group were signed to Capitol, Al co-produced songs for **Bert Robinson**. More recently he has recorded a solo album (as yet unreleased).

HUDSON, DAVID

(Singer)

David recorded *Honey Honey* (1980) for the Miami-based TK label before working with producer **Willie Mitchell** in Memphis on *Nite & Day* (1987) for Waylo Records.

HUDSON, LAVINE

(Singer)

From Brixton, London, Lavine sang in her pastor father's gospel choir before moving to the USA and studying at the Berklee School Of Music. Here she stayed for two and a half years and built up a gospel following through her performances in church. Her popularity led to an invitation to sing on the gospel TV show presented by The Clark Sisters. She moved back to the UK and worked with the London Community Gospel Choir before landing a role on the gospel TV show *People Get Ready*. In the meantime tapes of her compositions landed her a recording deal with Virgin and a debut single 'Intervention' was released in 1988 (UK Top 60). A debut album *Intervention* was released later in the year and included 'Flesh Of My Flesh' remixed for the dancefloors by **Loose Ends**.

HUDSONS
(Group)
From West London, The Hudsons were brothers Vince and Jude who played with several bands before getting a recording break with Morgan Khan's Streetwave label in 1982. Here they released the 'Brit funk' dance record 'Show Me You Care'.

HUES CORPORATION
(Group)
From Los Angeles, The Hues Corporation were St Clair Lee, Fleming Williams and Ann Kelley. In 1974 they signed to RCA and scored with 'Rock The Boat' (UK Top 10).

HUFF, LEON
(Songwriter/Producer/Keyboards)
From Camden, New Jersey, Leon taught himself piano by studying hit records on the radio. In the late '50s he travelled to New York and found work as a session keyboard player. Hooking up with Leiber and Stoller he played on a number of recordings with Phil Spector, The Ronettes and Carole King. Soon he was working in Philadelphia leading a group of musicians called The Locomotions for the city's Cameo and Swan labels. Here he recorded on 'The 81', a song for Candy And The Kisses co-written by **Kenny Gamble**. The two met in 1964.

Leon's manager was record producer Leroy Lovett who taught him the basics of production. Leon had already taught himself the rudiments of songwriting and had penned an American hit 'Mixed Up Shook Up Girl' for Patty And The Emblems prior to working with either Kenny Gamble or Leroy Lovett (who also managed **The Intruders**). Leroy and Leon collaborated on 'All The Time', a hit for The Intruders alongside Leon's work as half of **Gamble/Huff**. In 1971, Gamble/Huff launched their own record label Philadelphia International (PIR) and scored classic upon classic through the '70s. In addition to these Leon also released one solo album *Here To Create Music* (1980), including 'I Ain't Jivin'', 'I'm Jammin'' and 'Tight Money'.

Independently Leon wrote 'It's Forever' (**The Ebonys**), 'Do It Any Way You Wanna'(**People's Choice**), 'If You Move, You Lose' (**Carolyn Crawford**) and, prior to launching PIR, 'Girl Don't Make Me Wait' and 'Follow Your Heart' for **Bunny Sigler**.

HUGHES, FRED
(Singer)
Born in Arkansas, Fred Hughes moved to the West Coast where he worked with his own band The Creators in the early '60s. In 1965 he signed with Vee-Jay Records for 'Oo Wee Baby, I Love You', an American Top 25 hit and regarded by some in the UK as a soul classic.

HUGHES, RHETTA
(Singer/Actress)
New York-based Rhetta Hughes worked with writer/producer **Jo Armstead** during the '60s where she is perhaps most fondly remembered for 'I Can't Stand Under This Pressure', released on the Tetragrammaton label in 1968. She also had an American hit with 'Hip Old Lady On A Honda' (1969). Through the '70s she worked as a session singer with artists including **Roberta Flack**, while releasing occasional solo recordings for CBS and later Aria Records where 'Angel Man' was a single release in 1983. She has also worked as an actress.

HUGO & LUIGI
(Songwriters/Producers)
Of Italian descent, Hugo Peretti and Luigi Creatore invested in the music business by acquiring the Roulette company in 1957. Two years later they sold it and began to produce a string of hits with **Sam Cooke** through to his death. From here they worked with **The Isley Brothers** before setting up their own label with Atco/Phonogram, and enjoying a run of hits with **The Stylistics** and **Van McCoy**.

HUMPHREY, BOBBI
(Flute/Singer)
From Dallas, Texas, Bobbi moved to New York after leaving high school and landed a job with Duke Ellington on her first weekend in the city. In 1971 she signed to the Blue Note label and recorded albums including *Satin Doll* (1971) and *Black And Blues* (1973), including 'Harlem River Drive', by which time she was singing as well as playing the flute. Her producers at this time were **Larry** and **Fonce Mizell** who gave her music a fusion jazz taste popular among UK jazz funk audiences.

In 1977 she signed to Epic for *Freestyle*, *Home Made Jam* (1978) and *The Good Life* (1979), including 'Love When I'm In Your Arms', all produced by **Ralph MacDonald**. From here she signed with the Uno Melodic label and worked with **Roy Ayers** on a single 'Baby Don't You Know' in 1982.

In 1986 Bobbi made an impact with a new single 'No Way' featuring **Stevie Wonder**, co-written by **Leroy Burgess** and produced by Ralph MacDonald for Mercury Records. She later had an album *City Beat* released on the Malaco label (1988) before signing to Warner Brothers for 'Let's Get Started' in 1990. Bobbi also discovered **Tevin Campbell**.

HUNT, GERALDINE
(Singer/Songwriter)
New York singer Geraldine Hunt first recorded in the '60s for labels including Bombay ('Two Can Live Cheaper Than One', 1964) and Roulette ('Never Never Leave Me', 1968) before making an impact during the end of the disco era with 'Can't Fake The Feeling' (UK Top 50) from a 1980 Prism album *No Way* (via Champagne in the UK), which included 'Gotta Give A Little Love', recorded in Philadelphia.

HUNTER, IVY JO
(Singer/Songwriter/Producer)
From Detroit, Ivy Jo Hunter was employed by Motown during the early '60s as staff songwriter and producer (in addition to having a couple of single releases on the company's VIP subsidiary label). His co-written songs include 'Dancing In The Street' (**Martha Reeves & The Vandellas**), 'Behind A Painted Smile' (**The Isley Brothers**) and 'Loving You Is Sweeter Than Ever' (**The Four Tops**). He also wrote 'Without Love' for **Aretha Franklin** with her sister Carolyn.

In 1989 he began work for the UK Motorcity label. Here he has to date released a solo single 'Eyewitness News' and with **Ian Levine** wrote 'Footsteps Following Me' for **Frances Nero**.

HURTT, PHIL
(Singer/Songwriter/Producer)
From Philadelphia, Phil established himself in the early '70s as one of the Young Professionals, a group of talented songwriters and producers on the Philly r&b scene. As a songwriter his biggest success was 'I'll Be Around' which he co-wrote with **Thom Bell** in 1973, a classic soul recording for the **Detroit Spinners** and later a UK hit for **Terri Wells**. At the same time he began working closely with **Bunny Sigler**, an early co-production being a 1973 Atlantic album *Sweet Charlie Babe* for **Jackie Moore**. He also co-produced 'The Weathermen' and 'Mama Never Told Me', the first two singles for **Sister Sledge** that year.

As a recording artist he signed briefly with Fantasy in 1978, his single release 'Giving It Back' being a popular soul/dance record that year and a UK Top 40 hit. He was also involved in the **Hi-Gloss** album for Prelude, for which he co-wrote all of the songs.

HUTCH, WILLIE
(Singer/Songwriter/Producer/Guitarist)
Born in Los Angeles in 1946, Willie McKinley Hutchinson grew up in Dallas where he sang with The Ambassadors. A keen and ambitious singer/songwriter as a teenager, Willie first came to the attention of the music business in 1964 when his debut single 'Love Has Put Me Down' was released by the Soul City Records label. His songs attracted the attention of **The Fifth Dimension** who recorded a number of them. Willie himself recorded with Venture prior to two albums in the early '70s with RCA (including *Let's Try It Over*).

In 1970, he received a phone call from producer Hal Davies who urgently needed a song written to a backing track he had entitled 'I'll Be There'. By 8 am the next morning **The Jackson 5** were in the studio recording it. Willie later co-arranged vocals on 'Got To Be There' and 'Never Can Say Goodbye' for the group, impressing **Berry Gordy** who employed him at Motown on a more permanent basis.

Willie produced the first **Smokey Robinson** album without The Miracles, and when **Sisters Love** had a cameo role in *The Mack*, the group's manager suggested Willie record the soundtrack. The result was *The Mack*, including 'Brother's Gonna Work It Out' and 'Slick', Willie's first album for Motown in 1973. (Willie also worked with Sisters Love on 'Mr Fix-It Man'.) His other albums at the label included *The Mark Of The Beast* (1975); *Concert In Blues* (1976), including 'Party Down'; *Color Her Sunshine* (1976), including 'I Like Everything About You'; *Havin' A House Party* and *Fully Exposed* before he joined the Whitfield label for two albums, *In Tune* (1978), including 'Easy Does It, and *Midnight Dancer*.

In 1982 he wrote 'Keep The Fire Burning' for **Gwen McCrae** and returned to Motown for three collaborations with **Berry Gordy**. The first was a duet for **The Four Tops** and **Aretha Franklin** 'What Have We Got To Lose' (1983), the second a song/production for **Sammy Davis Jr** 'Hello Detroit' (1984), and the third a soundtrack album for Berry's film *The Last Dragon* (1985). This soundtrack included a Willie Hutch single 'The Glow'. During this period at Motown he wrote/produced *Sexy Ways* for The Four Tops and released two albums, *In And Out* (1985) and *Making A Game Of Love* (1985), including 'Keep On Jammin''.

Willie has also written and/or produced for **The Miracles**, **The Main Ingredient** ('California My Way'), **Junior Walker**, **Diana Ross** and **Marvin Gaye**, among others.

HUTSON, LEROY
(Singer/Songwriter/Producer)
Through sharing a room with **Donny Hathaway** at Howard University in Washington DC, Leroy met **Curtis Mayfield**. Leroy and Donny wrote 'The Ghetto' together before Leroy replaced Curtis as lead singer with **The Impressions** in 1970.

After recording/touring with the group for three years, Leroy signed directly to the Curtom label in 1973. His debut album was *Love Oh Love* from which he scored an American r&b hit with 'So In Love With You'. His other albums were *The Man* (1973), including 'The Ghetto'; *Leroy Hutson* (1975), including 'All Because Of You' and 'Lucky Fellow'; *Hutson II* (1976), including 'Love To Hold You Close'; *Feel The Spirit* (1976); *Closer To The Source* (1978), including 'In The Mood' and 'Get To This (You'll Get To Me)'; and *Unforgettable* (1979), including 'So

Nice'. Following this he took a three-year break before returning with *Paradise* (Elektra, 1982) which included 'Classy Lady' and 'Nice And Easy', co-produced by Nicholas Caldwell of **The Whispers**.

As a writer and/or producer Leroy has worked with **Deon Jackson** ('I'll Always Love You'), **Roberta Flack** ('Tryin' Times' and 'Gone Away'), **The Natural Four** ('You Bring Out The Best In Me'), **Linda Clifford**, **Voices Of East Harlem** ('Cashing In'), **Arnold Blair** ('Trying To Get Next To You') and **The Next Movement** ('Let's Work It Out').

In the UK Leroy has had a cult following rather than commercial hits (or indeed releases), although 'All Because Of You' was issued in 1989.

HYMAN, PHYLLIS

(Singer)

Born in Pittsburgh though raised in Philadelphia, Phyllis was the eldest of seven children. She took up singing naturally, won a scholarship to music school and began her professional career in 1971 with a group The New Direction. (She had also trained as a legal secretary in case her singing career didn't take off.) The group toured America before disbanding leaving Phyllis to join a Miami group All The People. While in Miami she also worked with another local group The Hondo Beat and made an appearance in the film *Lenny*. In 1974 she formed Phyllis Hyman & the P/H Factor, and toured with them for two years before settling in New York. Here she built up a local reputation on the club scene where artists including **Roberta Flack**, **George Benson**, **Stevie Wonder** and **Ashford & Simpson** would go out of their way to hear her perform. She was also invited by **Jon Lucien** to sing on his album *Premonition*.

Norman Connors was looking for a female singer and soon got to hear about Phyllis. Shortly she became a Norman Connors featured vocalist, commencing with 'Betcha By Golly Wow' on *You Are My Starship* (1976). The same year she recorded two solo singles 'Baby I'm Gonna Love You' and 'Leaving The Good Life Behind' while also recording with The **Fatback** Band on 'Night Fever'. In 1977 her debut album *Phyllis Hyman* was released by Buddah Records, and featured 'Loving You – Losing You', 'No One Can Love You More' and 'Beautiful Man of Mine'. She was guest vocalist with **Pharaoh Sanders** on his 1978 album *Love Will Find A Way*.

In 1978 Phyllis signed directly to Arista for *Somewhere In My Lifetime*, which included 'Kiss You All Over', 'Living Inside Your Love', 'The Answer Is You' and 'Be Careful How You Treat My Love'. The album was followed in 1979 by a **Mtume/Lucas** written/produced album *You Know How To Love Me*, the title track which firmly established Phyllis with UK soul fans and was a dance anthem that reached the Top 50 in 1980. Also on the album was another huge dance record, 'Under Your Spell'. Her other Arista albums were *Can't We Fall In Love Again* (1981), including 'Don't Tell Me Tell Her' and 'The Love Too Good To Last', and the **Narada Michael Walden/Thom Bell**-produced *Goddess Of Love* (1983), including 'Riding The Tiger', 'Why Did You Turn Me On' and 'We Should Be Lovers'.

In 1986 she signed to the Philadelphia International label (via EMI) for *Living All Alone*, including 'First Time Together' and the **Loose Ends**-penned 'Ain't You Had Enough Love'. More recently she has recorded *Phyllis Hyman In The Prime Of Her Life*, due for 1991 release.

Phyllis played a fashion model in the movie *Too Scared To Scream* (recording the title song with Charles Aznavour), and has recorded with **McCoy Tyner** (*Looking Out*, 1982), **Joe Sample** ('The Survivor', 1985), **The Four Tops** ('Maybe Tomorrow', 1985), **Ronnie Foster**, Barry Manilow (*Swing Street*, 1987) and **Grover Washington** ('Sacred Kind Of Love', 1989).

I

I.C.Q.

(Group)

British fusion jazz group, the Ivan Chandler Quintet are Ivan Chandler (keyboards), Andy Hamilton (sax), Brad Lang (bass), Theodore Thunder (drums), Miguel Acciaioly (percussion), and Spike (trombone). They first established themselves on the UK jazz funk scene in 1981 when they began a regular Sunday residency at The Belvedere Arms in Ascot. During this time they released a single 'Final Approach' on a limited edition single which broadened their popularity across the country.

In 1983 they officially launched their own label Unsquare Records and continued to entertain fusion jazz fans with titles including 'Soak It Up', 'Flight Of The Vendohair' and 'Dutch Ovens'.

I-LEVEL

(Group)

UK funk band I-Level were Duncan Bridgeman and Jo Dworniak from Essex, together with Sam Jones from Freetown, Sierra Leone. Duncan and Jo met through an advert in *Melody Maker* and played in groups Scrambled Egos and Shake Shake prior to I-Level. Sam had earlier toured Europe with reggae band Brimstone. Recording for Virgin Records, they first made an impact on UK dancefloors with 'Give Me' (1982), the track later being a Top 5 r&b single in the USA where it was released on the Epic label. In 1983 they scored two UK Top 50 hits with 'Minefield' and 'Teacher', their albums being *Cat Amongst The Pigeons* (1984) and *Shake* (1985).

IMAGINATION

(Group)

London group Imagination were originally **Leee John** (lead vocals/keyboards), Ashley Ingram (bass/vocals) and Errol Kennedy (drums/percussion). Working with producers/songwriters Steve Jolley and Tony Swain they created a unique blend of British soul/dance which won them a following in the early '80s. For the R&B label (via PRT), their UK albums were *Body Talk* (1981), including the title track debut single (Top 5), 'In And Out Of Love' (Top 20) and 'Flashback' (Top 20); and *In The Heat Of The Night* (1982), including 'Just An Illusion' (Top 5), 'Music And Lights' (Top 5), the title track single (Top 20) and 'Changes' (Top 40).

Further success came with 'Looking At Midnight' (Top 30, 1983), 'New Dimensions' (Top 75, 1983), 'Burnin' Up' (1983), 'State Of Love' (Top 75, 1984), and 'Thank You My Love' (Top 30, 1984) before the group switched to RCA. Here their recordings include 'Instinctual' (Top 75, 1988) and 'The Last Time' (1988), featuring **Kenny G**.

IMPRESSIONS

(Vocal Group)

From Chattanooga, Tennessee, The Impressions were originally known as The Roosters and consisted of **Curtis Mayfield**, Sam Gooden, Fred Cash, and brothers Richard and Arthur Brooks, with the slightly later addition of **Jerry Butler**. In 1958 Richard, Arthur and Jerry wrote 'For Your Precious Love', recorded by the group and initially released on the Falcon label. It was shortly re-released by Vee-Jay Records where it became an American hit single and launched a solo career for Jerry who was the lead singer. In the meantime the group were reduced to a trio of Curtis (lead singer), Sam and Fred, although Curtis spent some time as Jerry's co-songwriter and guitarist.

In 1961 The Impressions picked up their recording career and signed with Paramount Records. Here they scored American success with songs including 'Gypsy Woman' (1961), followed two years later with another big hit 'It's All Right' (1963). From here the group further established themselves with 'You Must Believe Me' (1963), 'I'm So Proud' (1963), 'Amen' and 'People Get Ready' (1963), switching to ABC Records for further success with 'I've Been Trying' (1964).

When Curtis formed Curtom Records in 1968, the group switched to the label for albums including *This Is My Country* (1968), *Check Out Your Mind* (1969) and *The Best Impressions* (1970), at which point Curtis left the group. He was replaced by **Leroy Hutson** who was a friend of the group's regular keyboard player **Donny Hathaway**. From here the group scored success with 'Love Me' (1972), on the back of which they toured the UK.

When Leroy left the group later in 1972, Reggie Torrian

and lead singer Ralph Johnson (later to front **Mystique**) took the group back to a quartet and recorded the soundtrack album *Three The Hard Way* (1973). Further success followed with American hits including 'Finally Got Myself Together' (1974), 'Sooner Or Later' (1974), 'Sunshine' (1974) and 'Same Thing It Took' (1974), before their one UK hit with 'First Impressions' (Top 20, 1975).

They later recorded for labels including Chi-Sound (*Fan The Fire*, 1981) and Ric-Ett (*Something Said Love*, 1990).

INCOGNITO

(Group)

Based in London, Incognito were originally Paul 'Tubbs' Williams (bass), Peter Hinds (keyboards), Jean Paul Maunick (guitar) and Jeff Dunn (drums). The group's nucleus evolved from another group **Light Of The World**, this offshoot veering more towards jazz funk. Their debut release was 'Parisienne Girl' (1981) for the Ensign label where they also recorded *Jazz Funk* (1981), including 'Shine On'. Nine years later, in 1990, they reformed and signed to Talkin' Loud Records (via Phonogram), where with the addition of vocalist Linda Muriel their singles have included 'Can You Feel Me' (1990), 'Inside Life' (1991) and 'Always There' featuring **Jocelyn Brown** (UK Top 10, 1991).

INCREDIBLES

(Group)

This '60s group featured the lead vocals of Mike Kirkland who later created interest with his solo album *Doin' It Right* (1975), including 'You Put It On My Mind'.

INDEEP

(Studio Group)

From New York, Indeep made a major impression on the dance scene with their 1982 release 'Last Night A D.J. Saved My Life' (UK Top 20) for the S.O.N.Y. label. Their follow-up was 'When Boys Talk' (UK Top 75, 1983).

INDEPENDENT MOVEMENT

(Vocal Group)

This West Coast American group was instigated by writers/producers **Jackson/Yancy** and consisted of Jayne Hall, Jerry Whittington, John Brown and Steve Wilson, on original line-up of **The Independents**.

Signed to Polydor they released *Slippin' Away* in 1978, produced by Tom Washington.

INDEPENDENTS

(Vocal Group)

The Independents were Chuck Jackson, Maurice Jackson, Helen Curry and later Eric Thomas. Recording for the Scepter label (Pye in the UK), the group scored American success from 1973 with singles including 'Leaving Me', 'It's All Over', 'The First Time We Met', 'Just As Long As You Need Me' and 'I Just Want To Be There'. Their principal songwriters were Chuck Jackson and Marvin Yancy (see **Jackson/Yancy**), who later established themselves as writers and producers with **Natalie Cole** and **Ronnie Dyson**.

INDEX

(Group)

From West London, this Brit-funk group consisted of Curtis Paul (bass), Dennis Palmer (guitar), Jeff St Paul (percussion), Attlee Baptiste (lead vocals), Cosmo Bowen (drums) and Alexander 'Boo' (keyboards). Cosmo and Dennis were formerly with the group Breeze, and Jeff was with Prime Cut. Their debut single 'Starlight' was released on the Record Shack label via Arista in 1981.

INGRAM

(Group)

A family group from Camden, New Jersey, Ingram were officially launched after lead member **Norman 'Butch' Ingram** was forced to give up a professional basketball career after an accident. Other members were James (vocals/keyboards/sax/flute/principal songwriter – not to be confused with **James Ingram**), **Barbara** (also a top session singer), Billy (guitar/bass/trombone), John (drums/lead vocals/tuba), Timmy (drums/percussion/trumpet), Francis, Edith and Virginia Ingram (vocals), who prior to Butch's accident had been a group called The Ecstasies. All the family were encouraged to study music by their minister father who also was a DJ on WIMR in Philadelphia. Butch taught himself the bass, acquired some recording equipment and put the family to work on their first album *Ingram's Kingdom*. When it sold 25,000 copies they signed to H&L the following year for their second album *That's All* (1977). The album featured an instrumental 'Mi Sabrina Tequana' which became a cult dance record on the UK's underground soul scene.

H&L went out of business, but the name Ingram was tied up contractually for two years, preventing the group from using it. Around the same time **Butch Ingram** began work producing an album for **Philly Cream**, but the group split up before the album was finished. Ingram stepped in to finish it off, and adopted the name for the album later released by WMOT Records. Ingram continued to record as Philly Cream after the first album, and in 1979 had an American hit with 'Ain't No More Motown Review'. They also worked as a studio group with **The Stylistics**, **Blue Magic**, **Barbara Mason**, **David Simmons**, **Brandi Wells** and **Ronnie Dyson**.

In 1983 they recorded as Ingram once again, releasing *Would You Like To Fly*, including 'Smoothin' Groovin'' (UK Top 75) and 'DJ's Delight' on the Mirage label (via Streetwave in the UK). Their follow-up was *Night Stalkers* (1984).

In 1985 James Ingram produced **The Sweethearts**, while John released a solo single debut 'Can I Take You Home Tonight'.

INGRAM, BARBARA
(Singer)
From Camden, New Jersey, Barbara is one of the **Ingram** family, but as a singer in her own right was one of the most in-demand session voices in '70s r&b, especially in Philadelphia. With Carla Benson and Yvette Benton, the trio toured as Flower And The Sweethearts, and recorded together too with numerous artists. Barbara is the seductive voice on the **Major Harris** classic 'Love Won't Let Me Wait'.

INGRAM, BUTCH
(Singer/Songwriter/Producer)
Born in Camden, New Jersey, Butch is the spearhead of the **Ingram** family group, and began his music career after giving up basketball due to injury. In addition to instigating Ingram, he also worked as a writer and/or producer with numerous artists including **Booker Newberry III**, **Brandi Wells** ('I Love You'), **The Emotions**, **Odyssey**, **Major Harris**, **Ronnie Dyson** ('All Over Your Face'), Michelle Gold ('Lost In Love'), **Roz Ryan** ('Boy Where Have You Been'), **David Simmons** and **Barbara Mason** ('She's Got The Papers' and 'Another Man').

INGRAM, JAMES
(Singer)
From Ohio, James moved to Los Angeles in 1973 in search of a music career. His first date was as a keyboard player with **Leon Haywood**, after which he formed his own group Revelation Funk. He was pulled from virtual obscurity by **Quincy Jones** who had heard a demo tape and was impressed by James's vocals. Quincy hired him to record on *The Dude* (1981) where he was featured lead vocalist on 'Just Once', 'One Hundred Ways' and the title track.

Quincy signed him to his Qwest label (via Warner Brothers), and they initially worked together writing 'P.Y.T. (Pretty Young Thing)' which was recorded by **Michael Jackson** on 1982's *Thriller*. James's debut album *It's Your Night* was released in 1983 and included 'Yah Mo B There' (featuring **Michael McDonald**) which charted twice in 1984 and once (Top 20) in 1985 in the UK. Also in 1983 James had reached the UK Top 20 with 'Baby, Come To Me', a duet with **Patti Austin**. In 1986 James returned with *Never Felt So Good* produced by **Keith Diamond**, following which he signed directly to Warner Brothers for 1989's *It's Real*, featuring productions by **Gene Griffin** and **Michael Powell**. Also in 1989 James was a featured singer on the Quincy Jones album *Back On The Block*, in particular 'The Secret Garden'.

James has also sung backgrounds with **The Brothers Johnson**, **Howard Hewett** and **Luther Vandross**.

INGRAM, LUTHER
(Singer)
Born in Jackson, Tennessee, Luther sang in church before moving to New York. Here he was signed by the Koko label (via Stax) and released *I've Been Here All The Time*, including 'My Honey And Me', and *If Loving You Is Wrong (I Don't Want To be Right)* (1972) which sold 50,000 copies on import in the UK without being released.

Later albums included the Koko release *Do You Love Somebody* (1977) and *Luther Ingram* for Profile (1986).

INGRAM, PHILIP
(Singer)
Philip is the brother of **James Ingram**, and sang with the Motown group **Switch** between 1978 and 1980, before joining Deco and recording for the Qwest label. As a backing singer he has worked with **George Howard**, **The Commodores**, **Fire Fox**, **The Four Tops**, **El Debarge** and **Linda Clifford**, while he has been a featured vocalist with **The Kazu Matsui Project** ('Standing On The Outside', 1983), **Jeff Lorber** ('Don't Say Yes', 1984), and **Bobby Lyle** ('Reach Out For Love', 1990).

INNER CIRCLE
(Group)
Inner Circle were initially brothers Roger Lewis (lead guitar) and Ian Lewis (bass) who formed the group in Jamaica in 1968. The brothers were accompanied by musicians who later became the nucleus of **Third World**. After a fire destroyed a club in Kingston where the group were residents, the brothers formed a new group with Calvin McKensie (drums), Bernard Harvey (keyboards) and Charles Farquharson (keyboards) and recorded for the Top Ranking label. In 1974 the group was joined by lead singer Jacob Miller, and in 1977 they switched to Capitol for *Reggae Thing* (1977) and *Ready For The World* (1978). Their next move was to Island Records where the title track of *Everything Is Great* (1979) made an impact with UK soul/dance fans and became a UK Top 40 hit. 'Stop Breaking My Heart' made the UK Top 50 later in the year.

In 1980 Jacob was killed in a car crash, and the group returned to the Top Ranking label with new vocalist Trevor Brown. They also moved to Miami where they opened a recording studio and worked with **Joe Tex** and more recently 2 Live Crew. In 1990, with new vocalist Carlton Coffey, they signed to Warner Brothers and recorded 'Bad Boys', the theme to the TV programme *Cops*.

INNER CITY
(Group)
Based in Detroit, Inner City are Kevin Saunderson and Paris Grey who made an impact on the commercial end of the techno dance scene during the late '80s/early '90s. Signed to Virgin Records, their biggest hits were 'Big Fun' (UK Top 10, 1988) and 'Good Life' (UK Top 5, 1988),

while they also stirred dancefloors with songs including 'Ain't Nobody Better' (1989), 'Do You Love What You Feel' (1989), 'Whatcha Gonna Do With My Love' (1989, a cover of the **Stephanie Mills** soul classic) and 'Till We Meet Again' (1991).

INNER LIFE
(Studio Group)
From New York, Inner Life were first put together by producers **Patrick Adams** and **Greg Carmichael** in the late '70s and featured the lead vocals of **Jocelyn Brown**. After *I'm Caught Up* (1979) for Prelude Records they switched to Salsoul where they first made an impression on the disco scene with a version of 'Ain't No Mountain High Enough' in 1981. In 1982 producer **Leroy Burgess** took over for *Inner Life*, featuring disco hits 'I Like It Like That' and 'Moment Of My Life'. Leroy also co-wrote 'Let's Change It Up', released by the Personal label in 1984.

INSTANT FUNK
(Group)
Based in Philadelphia, Instant Funk were singers and musicians assembled by **Bunny Sigler** in the mid-'70s. They provided the instrumentation on Bunny's albums (including *Keep Smilin'*) and also signed as a group to the T.S.O.P. label (via CBS) where Bunny worked as writer/producer on their debut *Get Down With The Philly Jump* (1976) including 'It Ain't Reggae (But It's Funky)'. In 1978 they made their most significant impact on the dance scene with 'I Got My Mind Made Up' (UK Top 50), again produced by Bunny Sigler, although by now the group had switched to Salsoul Records. Their following Salsoul releases included *The Funk Is On* (1980), singles 'No Stoppin' That Rockin'' (1982) and 'Why Don't You Think About Me' (1982), and a final album *Kinky* (1983) including 'Just Because You'll Be Mine'. In 1985 they briefly returned with a single for the Pop Art label, 'Tailspin', featuring Yves Sterling.

The group can also be found providing the instrumentation to an album *Callin'* (1978) for **The Pips** without **Gladys Knight**!

INTRIGUE
(Group)
Featuring the lead vocals of **Dino Terrell**, New York-based group Intrigue were instigated by **Leroy Burgess**, although **McFarlane/George** produced their one dance success 'Fly Girl' for the World Trade label (1984).

In 1987, McFarlane/George produced 'Together Forever' on the American Cooltempo label for Intrigue (presumably the same group).

INTRUDERS
(Vocal Group)
From Philadelphia, The Intruders were originally Sam 'Little Sonny' Brown, Eugene 'Bird' Daugherty, Phil Terry and Robert Edwards, who grew up together in the '50s. They were recording for the local Gowen label by 1961. Their manager was Leroy Lovett who also took care of affairs for **Leon Huff**. In 1964 Leon first produced an Intruders record for the Musicor label before the group took off with 'All The Time' (1965) on Excel, a new label Leon had formed with **Kenny Gamble**. The label shortly became Gamble Records.

The group continued to record for the Gamble label (they were the major act), with successful singles 'United', 'Devil With An Angel's Smile', 'Baby I'm Lonely', 'A Love That's Real' and a million-seller in 1968 with 'Cowboys To Girls'. This was all before the launch of Gamble & Huff's Philadelphia International (PIR) label in 1971, or UK chart success. In 1973 The Intruders released *Save The Children* for PIR, and scored the biggest hit of their career with 'I'll Always Love My Mamma', a UK Top 40 hit and a Philadelphia classic. The same year they joined **The O'Jays** and **Billy Paul** for some concert dates to launch the PIR label in the UK.

In 1974 the group were back in the UK charts with '(Win Place Or Show) She's A Winner' before they split up in 1975. Two members became Jehovah's Witnesses, one a politician, and the other a truck driver. However, in 1984 Eugene Daugherty (the truck driver) formed a new line-up with Lee Williams, cousin Al Miller and brother Fred Daugherty. This new Intruders line-up had earlier worked as Lee Williams And The Cymbals, recording a single 'I Love You More Than Anything' for the De-Lite label. As The Intruders they recorded *Who Do You Love* (1985) including 'Warm And Tender Love', produced by **Leon Bryant** and released in the UK by Streetwave, where the title track reached the UK Top 75.

INVISIBLE MAN'S BAND
(Group)
The Invisible Man's Band was instigated by Clarence Burke, brother of **Keni Burke** and originally a member of the Chicago family group The Stairsteps. Together with Alex Masucci, Clarence took the group to Island Records in the late '70s and enjoyed success on the UK soul scene with 'All Night Thing' in 1979. A follow-up single 'Love Can't Come/Love Has Come' was released by Island in 1980, but in 1981 they switched to the Broadwalk Entertainment label. Here they released 'Rated X' (1981), before a further change to the Move N Groove label for 'Sunday Afternoon' (1983). More recently there has been talk of Clarence joining the Stairsteps for a reunion.

IRVINE, WELDON
(Songwriter/Producer/Keyboards)
Based in New York, Weldon grew up in a jazz environment, his mid-'70s albums for RCA making an impact on the UK jazz funk scene. These include *Cosmic Vortex* (1974), including 'Walk That Walk, Talk That Talk', and *Spirit Man* (1975), including 'We Gettin' Down'. He also recorded with artists including **The Friends Of Distinc-**

tion, **Charles Earland**, **Bernard Wright** and **Sonny Fortune**.

IRWIN, BIG DEE

(Singer/Songwriter/Producer)

Born Defosca Erwin in New York in 1939, Big Dee Irwin first came to prominence in 1957 as lead singer with The Pastels on their recording 'Been So Long'. In 1963 he scored success with the duet 'Swinging On A Star' (UK Top 10) for the Colpix label, and is also fondly remembered for 'You Satisfy My Needs' on Rotate Records (1965). As Dee Irwin he also recorded 'One Part Two Part' for the Signpost label in addition to writing and producing for the group **Ripple** during the '70s.

ISH

(Singer/Songwriter/Producer/Guitarist)

Born in Cuba, Ish was influenced by the Afro-Latin rhythms of the Caribbean before moving with his family to Chicago in the early '60s. Here he studied guitar and developed his vocals before moving to Miami where he worked as a club singer during the '70s. He also found work with the local TK label as a session guitarist and worked with many of the groups on the label before forming **Foxy**.

Following the demise of TK Records, Foxy split up and Ish formed a new group Oxo. Signing to Geffen Records the group scored an American Top 20 hit with 'Whirly Girl' before Ish signed to the label as a solo artist and released *On This Corner* (1984). He also spent a great deal of time in New York working with Henry Stone (the founder of TK) on projects for his new labels including Sunnyview Records.

In 1986 he created a studio group **Blue Moderne**, and wrote/performed/produced their album *Where Is Love* for Atlantic in 1988. He also worked as a producer with **The Dazz Band**.

ISLEY BROTHERS

(Group)

From Cincinnati, Ohio, the original three Isley Brothers (Ronald, Rudolph and O'Kelly) sang gospel with their mother prior to moving to New York in 1957. Here they recorded doo-wop for small labels, their first ever release being 'An Angel Cried' for the Teenage label before signing to the Gone label in 1958. After four singles, which were essentially rock and roll, they signed to RCA in 1959. That year a debut American hit came their way with 'Shout'. The group's guitarist, incidentally, was Jimi Hendrix, who later left to enjoy international success as a solo artist.

Their next hit was not until 1962 when after a brief spell with Atlantic they moved to Wand Records for 'Twist & Shout', a song which became a standard for British beat groups and a UK Top 50 hit on the Stateside label when released in 1963. On the move again, they signed briefly to United Artists for one album (including their original version of 'Who's That Lady') before forming their own T-Neck record label in 1964.

After a few unsuccessful recordings they were offered a deal at Motown, where **Berry Gordy** put them together with **Holland/Dozier/Holland** in 1965. A year later they scored with the classic 'This Old Heart Of Mine', a UK Top 50 hit in 1966. The Isleys remained with Motown for two albums, *This Old Heart Of Mine* (1966) and *Soul On The Rocks* (1968). In the UK, follow-up Motown single hits were 'I Guess I'll Always Love You' (Top 50, 1966/Top 20, 1969), a re-release of 'This Old Heart Of Mine' (Top 5, 1968), 'Behind A Painted Smile' (Top 5, 1969) and 'Put Yourself In My Place' (Top 20, 1969). Also in 1969 they revived their T-Neck label (via Buddah) for *It's Your Thing*, from which the title track was a UK Top 30 when issued on the Major Minor label. The song was also the title track of a movie which the group financed. By now they had added younger brothers Marvin Isley (bass) and Ernie Isley (drums/guitar), together with cousin **Chris Jasper** (keyboards). In the USA, other successful T-Neck releases included 'I Turned You On (Now I Can't Turn You Off)', 'Black Berries', 'Was It Good To You', 'Work To Do', 'Layaway', 'Get Into Something', 'Love The One You're With', and a 1972 album *Brother Brother Brother*.

In 1973 they signed to Epic, their first album *3+3* containing the UK hits 'That Lady' (Top 25), 'Highway Of My Life' (Top 25) and 'Summer Breeze' (Top 20) alongside 'Don't Let Me Be Lonely Tonight'. Further Epic albums were *Live It Up* (1974), *The Heat Is On* (1975), *Harvest For The World* (1976), *Forever Gold* (1977), *Showdown* (1978), *Winner Takes It All* (1979), *Go All The Way* (1980), *Grand Slam* (1981), *Inside You* (1981) and *Between The Sheets* (1983). From these, 'Harvest For The World' reached the UK Top 10 (1976), and 'It's A Disco Night (Rock Don't Stop)' the Top 20 (1979).

In 1984 The Isley Brothers divided into two groups. The original trio of Ronald, Rudolph and O'Kelly carried on The Isley Brothers name at Warner Brothers, while the younger trio became **Isley/Jasper/Isley**. Over at Warner Brothers *Masterpiece* was released in 1985 before O'Kelly died of a heart attack in March 1986. A 1987 album *Smooth Sailing* featured only Ronald and Rudolph Isley and featured songs, backgrounds and productions by **Angela Winbush** whom Ronald now manages as an artist.

ISLEY/JASPER/ISLEY

(Group)

Marvin Isley (bass), Ernie Isley (drums/guitar) and cousin **Chris Jasper** (keyboards) originally worked together as members of **The Isley Brothers** from 1969. In 1984 they decided to make a break from the group and form their own trio. Signing to a division of CBS they debuted with a single 'Look The Other Way' and an album *Broadway's Closer To Sunset Boulevard*. The following year the title track of their *Caravan Of Love* album made a UK Top

60 single. It was the Housemartins, however, who took the song to the UK No. 1 position in 1986.

More recently **Chris Jasper** has become a solo artist/producer, while Ernie Isley (co-writer of 'Harvest For The World' and 'Between The Sheets') released a solo album *High Wire* on the Elektra label in 1990.

IVY

(Group)

Ivy are Christopher McCants (drums/vocals), Samual McCants (keyboards/vocals), Greg Smith (keyboards/vocals), David Miller (bass/vocals), Carl McCaskey (guitar/vocals), Rex Lee (percussion/vocals), Sharon Jones (keyboards/vocals) and Laddie Fair (sax). The original nucleus of the group recorded as **Rumple-Stilt-Skin** in 1983 before signing to the Ohio-based Heat label in 1985. Here they released *Hold Me*, *Ivy II* (1986), including 'Tell Me', and *Ivy III* (1987).

J

JBs

(Group)

The JBs were the backbone to the music of **James Brown**. Over the years members included **Lyn Collins**, Pee Wee Ellis, **Fred Wesley**, **St Clair Pinckney**, **Marva Whitney** and Vicki Anderson.

JACKSON SISTERS

(Vocal Group)

Based in Detroit, The Jackson Sisters made little impression on the UK soul scene at the time of their mid-'70s recordings. In the late '80s, however, the **Johnny Bristol**-penned/produced 'Shake Her Loose' (1975), and in particular, the **Bobby Taylor**-produced/co-written 'rare groove' anthem 'I Believe In Miracles' (1976), both for Polydor Records, became popular.

JACKSON/YANCY

(Songwriters/Producers)

Chuck Jackson (not to be confused with **Chuck Jackson**), born in Greenville, South Carolina, in 1945, originally sang with **The Independents** where he wrote songs with Marvin Yancy (born in Chicago, 1950). In addition to their own songwriting success with the group, they further established their reputation by writing with **Jerry Butler**, their collaboration 'You' being the title song on an **Aretha Franklin** album in 1975.

In 1976 Marvin married **Natalie Cole** who launched the Jackson/Yancy partnership in a major way with a string of successful albums and singles across America. Elsewhere they wrote and/or produced for artists including **Ronnie Dyson** ('The More You Do It'), **Natural Four** ('Night Chaser') and **The Dells** (*One Step Closer* and 'Passionate Breezes').

JACKSON, BRIAN

(Producer/Songwriter/Musician)

New York-based Brian Jackson first came to prominence in the early '70s through his collaboration with **Gil Scott-Heron** (whom he met at Lincoln University). While still in his teens, Brian worked on songs for Gil including 'The Bottle' (1974), 'H20 Gate Blues', and 'Johannesburg'. Through the late '70s and '80s he worked live on keyboards with artists including **Earth Wind & Fire** and **Stevie Wonder** before returning to studio work to write and/or produce for artists including **Will Downing**, **Gwen Guthrie**, High C, Sefus and Aja.

JACKSON, CHARLES

(Singer)

Often confused with **Chuck Jackson**, Charles Jackson was also known as Chuck Jackson, especially in reference to his songwriting work with **Marvin Yancy**. His solo albums include *Gonna Getcha' Love* for Capitol (1979), produced by **Gavin Christopher**.

JACKSON, CHUCK

(Singer)

Born in North Carolina in 1937, Chuck Jackson's singing potential was recognized very early on, and he was singing in church as a young child. Aged only seven, he was taken on by a local radio station to sing gospel on air. Later as a student he performed at weekends with a touring group The Raspberry Gospel Singers. His first recordings were with the Del-Vikings, a famous doo-wop group of the '50s who scored success with 'Come Go With Me'. He was first given a break by **Jackie Wilson**, who gave him a solo spot in a revue he was putting together for a tour. After going solo he moved from label to label, appearing on Beltone, Clock and Atco, but it wasn't until Detroit producer Luther Dixon signed him to New York's Scepter company that his true potential was realized in the early '60s.

Scepter created a new label, Wand, for whom Chuck began recording. His first single 'I Don't Want To Cry' reached No. 5 in the American r&b charts and was a Top 60 pop hit. It also became a standard song for many soul acts to follow. Most of his Wand singles were hits of varying degrees; his biggest ever was the **Burt Bacharach**/Bob Hilliard classic 'Any Day Now' which won him many British fans with its Pye International release in 1962. The following year Lennon/McCartney cited Chuck as their favourite singer (alongside **Ben E.King**). Around this time he recorded an album of Elvis Presley songs, *Dedicated To The King*, his first dance record 'Hand It

Over' (1964), and several successful duets with **Maxine Brown** (including 'Oh No Not My Baby').

In 1967 Chuck switched to the Tamla subsidiary of Motown. He stayed there until the early '70s, during which time songs like 'What Am I Gonna Do Without Your Love', 'Girls Girls Girls', 'These Chains Of Love', 'I've Got To Be Strong' and 'Good Things Come To Those Who Wait' kept UK soul fans happy. The songs came from the three albums he recorded for the label (two on the V.I.P. subsidiary).

In 1973 he could be found on the ABC label for *Through All Times*, but it wasn't until the late '80s that he made a serious impact on the soul scene again, having signed to the Nightmare label in London. Following a live performance at President Bush's inauguration (he is George's favourite singer), he recorded 'All Over The World' (1989) which remains one of his most popular recordings, being re-released in 1991 by Debut Records.

Incidentally, Chuck should not be confused with the Chuck Jackson of the group **The Independents** and the **Jackson/Yancy** songwriting/production partnership.

JACKSON, DEON

(Singer)

Mid-'60s soul singer Deon Jackson recorded songs including 'Love Makes The World Go Round' (1965) and 'Oh Baby' for Atlantic Records before working with writer/producer **Leroy Hutson** on 'I'll Always Love You', released on the Shout label in 1972.

JACKSON, FREDDIE

(Singer)

From Harlem, New York, Freddie sang at the White Rock Baptist Church as a child, and entered the music business as a session singer in the mid-'70s. His mother was a singer who actually went into labour with Freddie while performing on stage! During his church years he became good friends with **Paul Laurence Jones** whom he had met as a child. They later wrote songs together (including 'Trust Me' for Lillo Thomas), and performed in the same group LJE, with Freddie as lead singer.

After singing on one anonymous disco record with Edna Holt during the disco boom, he was offered the role of lead singer with the group **Mystic Merlin**. He recorded one album with the group in Los Angeles, *Mr Magician*, before leaving to take up solo singing back on the New York club circuit.

At the New York club Freddie's he was spotted by **Melba Moore**. Impressed, she invited him to meet her manager, and he was immediately signed up and taken on tour with **Angela Bofill**, **Lillo Thomas**, Harry Belafonte and others before landing a record deal at Capitol. Before recording as a solo artist, however, he embarked on a period of songwriting, particularly with Paul Laurence with whom he wrote 'Jam Song' for **Howard Johnson** (1982), and 'Keepin' My Lover Satisfied' for Melba Moore (1983). In 1985 his debut album *Rock Me Tonight* was released, from which the title track was an immediate hit in the USA, while 'You Are My Lady' was Freddie's UK Top 50 debut that year. 'Rock Me Tonight' was the follow-up in the UK, reaching the Top 20 in 1986.

Also in 1986 he arranged background vocals for **Glenn Jones**'s 'Stay', sang a duet with **Melba Moore**, 'A Little Bit More', on her album *A Lot Of Love*, and returned with a new album *Just Like The First Time*, which included 'I Don't Want To Lose Your Love', 'Tasty Love' and a UK Top 40 hit 'Have You Ever Loved Somebody'. His next album *Don't Let Love Slip Away* (1988) featured two UK Top 60 hits, 'Nice 'N' Slow' and 'Crazy (For Me)'. In 1989 he recorded a duet 'I Do' with **Natalie Cole** on her album *Good To Be Back*. In 1990 he released a fourth album, *Do Me Again* (including 'Don't It Feel Good').

JACKSON, JACKIE

(Singer/Songwriter)

Born Sigmond Esco Jackson in Gary, Indiana, in 1951, Jackie is a member of the famous Jackson family, although his initial career plans were in baseball. Jackie signed to Motown as the eldest member of **The Jackson 5** in 1967. He later recorded a solo album at Motown, *Jackie*, in 1973, then *Be The One* for Polydor in 1989.

JACKSON, JANET

(Singer/Songwriter/Producer)

Born in Gary, Indiana in 1966, Janet is the sister of **Michael Jackson** and the youngest member of the Jackson family. Her stage debut was at the age of seven when she joined **The Jackson 5** at the MGM Grand in Las Vegas doing impressions of Mae West! When she was nine she featured on the *Jackson Family* TV specials, later playing Penny Gordon in *Good Times* before switching to another American TV show, *Diff'rent Strokes*. Janet's father Joe Jackson set up a recording deal with A&M Records in 1982, and a debut album *Janet Jackson* was jointly produced by teams **Foster Sylvers**/Jerry Weaver, and **Rene & Angela**. The follow-up was *Dream Street* (1984), including a duet with Cliff Richard 'Two To The Power', this time with writers and producers including **Jesse Johnson**, **Giorgio Moroder**, and her brothers Michael and **Marlon Jackson**. She also married James Debarge of the group **Debarge**, but this was short-lived.

Success in a major way came when she worked with writers/producers **Jam/Lewis** on *Control* (1986), which included 'What Have You Done For Me Lately' (UK Top 5), 'Nasty' (UK Top 20), 'When I Think Of You' (UK Top 10), 'Control' (UK Top 50), 'Let's Wait A While' (UK Top 5), 'Pleasure Principle' (UK Top 30) and 'Funny How Time Flies' (UK Top 75).

In 1987 she was the vocalist on the **Herb Alpert** hit 'Diamonds' (UK Top 30), before returning with a fourth album *Rhythm Nation*, including 'Miss You Much' and 'Escapade', in 1989.

In 1991 she switched to Virgin Records in a deal worth several million pounds.

JACKSON, JERMAINE
(Singer/Producer)
Born in Gary, Indiana, in 1954, Jermaine Lajuane Jackson was an original member of family group **The Jackson 5** from 1969. He remained with the group until 1975 when they switched labels from Motown to Epic, leaving Jermaine as a solo artist at Motown. One reason for this was that he married Hazel Gordy, daughter of Motown founder **Berry Gordy**. His solo albums at Motown included *My Name Is Jermaine* (1976), *Feel The Fire* (1977) and *Frontiers* (1978) before **Stevie Wonder** wrote him a hit single 'Let's Get Serious' (UK Top 10) in 1980. Albums continued with *Jermaine* (1981), *I Like Your Style* (1981) and *Let Me Tickle Your Fancy* (1982), including 'Very Special Part' featuring Devo!, before taking the time to rejoin his brothers for the TV special *Motown 25*, an album *Victory* (for Epic) and a worldwide tour.

In 1984 he switched to Arista and released *Dynamite*, including 'Sweetest Sweetest' (UK Top 75), 'Do What You Do' (UK Top 10), 'Take Good Care Of My Heart' (duet with **Whitney Houston**) and 'Tell Me I'm Not Dreaming' (duet with **Michael Jackson**). His work with Whitney Houston at this time extended to producing songs (including 'Someone For Me') for her debut album. Further Arista albums followed with *Precious Moments* (1986) and *Don't Take It Personal* (1989). Also in 1989 Jermaine rejoined **The Jacksons** on *2300 Jackson Street* as vocalist, songwriter and producer.

He has written and/or produced for artists including **Howard Johnson** ('All We Have Is Love') and **Finished Touch** (*Need To Know You Better*).

JACKSON, JERRY
(Singer)
Based in Philadelphia, this '60s soul singer is best remembered for his single 'It's Rough Out There' for Cameo Parkway Records in 1966.

JACKSON, LATOYA
(Singer)
Born in Gary, Indiana, LaToya is one of the **Jacksons** family; in fact she's the fifth of nine children. She took up music later in life than **The Jackson 5**, originally wanting to become either a nurse or a nun.

Encouraged by her father to perform with the group as part of their revue, LaToya began her stage career in 1976 by perfecting a tap-dancing routine which became an opening act. By 1979 she had developed her vocal skills and signed to Polydor where she recorded *LaToya Jackson* (1979) and *My Special Love* (1980). She also recorded with **The Jacksons** on their *Triumph* album and sang on 'P.Y.T.' for brother **Michael Jackson**.

In 1984 she switched to the Private I label (via CBS) in Los Angeles to release *Heart Don't Lie*, including 'Hot Potato' (an American dance hit). From here she signed briefly to the UK Streetwave label where she released one single 'Oops Oh No' in 1985. Next she appeared nude in a men's magazine, starred in the film *Cry Of The City*, and appeared in the video for the Paul McCartney/**Michael Jackson** duet 'Say Say Say'. In 1986 a four-track EP appeared on a limited edition 12" single featuring 'Stay The Night', 'Special Love', 'Camp Kuchi Kaiai' and 'Fill You Up', although there was no label credit. In 1991 she spent some time in London working on new songs with producer Damon Rochefort from the group **Nomad**.

LaToya has her own line of cosmetics, Mahogany Image, and in 1989 she was voted the worst dressed woman in the world!

JACKSON, MARLON
(Singer/Songwriter/Producer)
Born in Gary, Indiana, in 1957, Marlon David Jackson is a member of the **Jacksons** family and is an original member of **The Jackson 5**. As a solo artist he has recorded for the Capitol label, while his credits as a producer include **Betty Wright**'s *Wright Back At 'Cha*.

JACKSON, McKINLEY T.
(Songwriter/Producer/Keyboards/Arranger)
McKinley worked consistently on the American soul scene through the '70s and '80s, arranging music for artists including **Aretha Franklin**, **The Jones Girls**, **Greg Perry**, **Marvin Gaye** (horns on 'Sexual Healing'), **Norman Connors**, **Starship Orchestra** and **Aquarian Dream**, among many more.

As a writer and/or producer, his work extends to artists including **Lamont Dozier** ('Fish Ain't Bitin'' and 'Out Here On My Own'), **Z.Z.Hill** and Reggie Garner ('That Ain't The Way You Make Love'), **Jean Carne** ('We Got Some Catchin' Up To Do'), **Sweet Talks** (*Sweet Talks*), **Bloodstone** (*Party*), **Shirley Jones** ('Love Is Comin' At Cha') and **Margie Joseph** ('Hear The Words, Feel The Feeling').

JACKSON, MICHAEL
(Singer/Songwriter/Producer)
Born in 1959 in Gary, Indiana, Michael was an original member of **The Jackson 5**, and sang lead vocals on the group's debut hit 'I Want You Back' (UK Top 5) in 1970. While working with his family group, Michael launched his solo career at Motown in 1972 with 'Got To Be There' (UK Top 5), continuing his solo success that year with 'Rockin' Robin' (UK Top 5), 'Ain't No Sunshine' (UK Top 10) and 'Ben' (UK Top 10).

When The Jacksons switched to Epic records, Michael signed as a solo artist to Epic where his albums have rated among the top-selling of all time. These have been the **Quincy Jones**-produced *Off The Wall* (1979), including 'Don't Stop 'Till You Get Enough' (UK Top 5), the title track single (UK Top 10), 'Rock With You' (UK Top 10) and 'She's Out Of My Life' (UK Top 5); The 40-million-selling *Thriller* (1983), including 'The Girl Is Mine' duet with Paul McCartney (UK Top 10), 'Billie Jean' (UK No. 1), 'Beat It' (UK Top 5), 'Wanna Be Startin' Somethin'' (UK Top 10), title track single (UK Top 10), 'P.Y.T.' (UK Top 20) and 'Human Nature' (1983); and *Bad* (1987), including 'I Just Can't Stop Loving You' featuring **Sideah Garrett** (UK No. 1), title track single (UK Top 5), 'The Way You Make Me Feel' (UK Top 5), 'Man In The Mirror' (UK Top 30), 'Dirty Diana' (UK Top 5), 'Another Part Of Me' (UK Top 20) and 'Smooth Criminal' (UK Top 10).

All through this period Motown released previously unissued recordings of Michael's solo work and scored in the UK with 'One Day In Your Life' (No. 1, 1981), 'We're Almost There' (Top 50, 1981), 'Happy' (UK Top 75, 1983), 'Farewell My Summer Love' (UK Top 10, 1984) and 'Girl You're So Together' (UK Top 40). He also recorded a second duet with Paul McCartney on Parlophone Records, 'Say Say Say' (UK Top 5, 1983), and later teamed up with **Stevie Wonder** for a duet 'Get It' on Stevie's *Characters* (1987).

In 1991 he re-signed with CBS (now known as Sony), on a deal worth £500 million which includes funds for his new label Nation Records.

Michael has also written and/or produced for artists including **Diana Ross** ('Muscles'), **Greg Phillinganes**/ Eric Clapton ('Behind The Mask'), **Jennifer Holliday** ('You're The One'), USA For Africa ('We Are The World', co-written with **Lionel Richie**) and sister **Rebbie Jackson** ('Centipede'). As an actor, he has played the role of Scarecrow in a film version of *The Wiz*, and starred in the 3-D film *Captain Eo* made for Disneyland.

JACKSON, MILLIE

(Singer/Songwriter)

Born in Thompson, Georgia, in 1944, Millie grew up with her grandparents but ran away from home aged fourteen to join her father in New Jersey. She later worked as a model in New York before an impromptu singing debut with a live band for a bet. That evening in 1964 was the start of her singing career!

Her first single was 'A Little Bit Of Something' for the MGM label before she signed with Spring Records (via Polydor). Her debut album *Millie Jackson* included 'My Man Is A Sweet Man' (UK Top 50), 'A Child Of God' and 'Ask Me What You Want' (1972). She soon became established for her outspoken lyrics, many of which had to be censored for radio but won her a strong live following. At Spring her albums included *It Hurts So Good* (1973), *Caught Up* (1974), *Still Caught Up* (1975), *Feeling Bitchy* (1977), including 'If You're Not Back In Love Again By Monday', *For Men Only* (1980), *Lovingly Yours* and *Free And In Love*. She also recorded a duet album *Royal Rappin's* with **Isaac Hayes**, and a duet with Elton John, 'An Act Of War'.

In 1984 she scored some UK success with 'I Feel Like Walkin' In The Rain' (UK Top 75) before switching to Jive Records for *An Imitation Of Love* (retitled from the American release 'Back To The S--t'), including 'Love Is A Dangerous Game' and 'Hot! Wild! Unrestricted! Crazy Love', and *The Tide Is Turning* (1988).

Millie's daughter is Keisha Jackson, who recently signed a recording deal with CBS.

JACKSON JR, PAUL

(Guitar)

Los Angeles-based guitarist Paul Jackson Jr established himself as one of the most in-demand session players on the r&b music scene in the '70s and '80s. A mere few of his credits include recordings with **The Temptations**, **Barry White**, **Bobby Womack**, **Booker T. Jones**, **Gerald Alston**, **Glenn Jones**, **Luther Vandross**, **Gene Page**, **Patrice Rushen**, **Howard Hewett**, **Jeffrey Osborne**, **Jermaine Jackson**, **Peabo Bryson**, **Beau Williams**, **Natalie Cole**, **Ramsey Lewis**, **Nancy Wilson** and **The Pointer Sisters**.

In 1984 he arranged, co-produced and played guitar on 'Don't Look Any Further' for **Dennis Edwards**, while his solo albums for the Atlantic label have been *I Came To Play* (1988), featuring **George Duke/Gerald Albright/ O'Bryan**, and *Out Of The Shadows* (1990), including 'Days Gone By' and 'The New Jazz Swing'.

JACKSON, TONY

(Singer)

Tony Jackson sang backgrounds with artists including **Stevie Wonder**, **Luther Vandross** and Paul Young during the '80s. As lead singer with the group Ritz, their version of 'Locomotion' went to No. 1 in France, Belgium, Australia and New Zealand. In 1990 he signed as a solo artist to Tivoli Records and released a debut single 'Don't Push'.

JACKSON, RANDY

(Singer/Songwriter/Musician)

Born Steven Randall Jackson in Gary, Indiana, in 1962, Randy is one of the **Jacksons** family, but was too young to be one of **The Jackson 5**. Initially as a songwriter he worked with the group, co-writing 'Shake Your Body (Down To The Ground)' for The Jacksons' album *Destiny* (1978). Also in 1978 he recorded a debut solo single 'How Could I Be Sure', a much sought-after soul single he co-wrote which was released by Epic. While recording his first solo album in 1980 he was involved in a near-fatal car accident in which he temporarily lost the use of his legs. That recording project was later abandoned.

His official function with The Jacksons involves selecting musicians and overseeing their sound system, though in 1988 he formed a group Randy & The Gypsies and signed to A&M. 1989's *Randy & The Gypsies* included the popular soul cut 'Love You Honey'.

JACKSON, REBBIE
(Singer)
Born in Gary, Indiana, Rebbie (pronounced 'ree-bee') is one of the **Jacksons** family and is the eldest of the three sisters. As far as a recording career is concerned, she kept very much out of the limelight until 1984 when she signed to CBS. In the meantime she had worked as a cabaret and session singer (with, among others, **Betty Wright** and **The Emotions**), and embarked on some TV work (alongside *Wonder Woman*'s Lynda Carter at one point).

Her CBS debut album was *Centipede*, the title track of which was written and produced by brother **Michael Jackson**. Also on the album, essentially produced by **Wayne Henderson**, was a version of **Prince**'s 'I Feel For You'. She recorded two further CBS albums, *Reaction* (1986) and *R U Tuff Enuff* (1988). In 1991 she signed to Motown.

JACKSON, TITO
(Singer/Songwriter/Guitar/Keyboards)
Born Toriano Adarryll Jackson in Gary, Indiana, in 1953, Tito is one of the **Jacksons** family, and an original member of **The Jackson 5**. He has also worked as a producer with **Howard Hewett** and his own sisters **LaToya** and **Rebbie Jackson**.

JACKSON, WALTER
(Singer)
Born in Pensacola, Florida, in 1939, Walter began his career singing in nightclubs before producer **Carl Davis** took him to the Okeh label in the late '60s. Here he stayed for six years recording a series of songs including 'It's An Uphill Climb To The Bottom' and 'Where Have All The Flowers Gone'. From 1973 he worked with Carl at a number of labels including Brunswick ('Let Me Come Back'), Epic, Cotillion, Wand, Chi-Sound (*Feeling Good*, 1976, *I Want To Come Back As A Song*, 1977, and *Good To See You*, 1978), and CBS (*Tell Me Where It Hurts*, 1981).

In 1983 Chi-Sound issued *A Portrait Of Walter Jackson* which included 'It's Cool' and 'Touching In The Dark', both popular on the UK soul scene in the mid-'80s at the time of his death.

JACKSONS/JACKSON 5
(Group)
From Gary, Indiana, the Jacksons story started with brothers **Jackie**, **Tito** and mother Katherine Jackson when one night the family's TV broke down! Having nothing to do, the trio sang harmonies together and discovered a mutual love of singing. Later they were joined by **Marlon**, **Jermaine** and **Michael**, while their mother dropped out when father Joe officially formed The Little Jackson Brothers.

It was under this name that they first worked professionally before coming to the attention of **Bobby Taylor** who took them to Motown in the late '60s. After a series of showcases at the Apollo in New York, the Regal Theater in Chicago and Uptown in Philadelphia, Motown signed the group as The Jackson 5. Here they initially worked with Bobby Taylor who wrote and produced their debut hits 'I Want You Back' (UK Top 5), 'ABC' (UK Top 10), and 'The Love You Save' (UK Top 10) in 1970. Their other hits in the UK as The Jackson 5 were 'I'll Be There' (Top 5, 1970), 'Mama's Pearl' (Top 30, 1971), 'Never Can Say Goodbye' (Top 40, 1971), 'Lookin' Through The Windows' (Top 10, 1972), 'Santa Claus Is Coming To Town' (Top 50, 1972), 'Doctor My Eyes' (Top 10, 1973), 'Hallelujah Day' (Top 20, 1973) and 'Skywriter' (Top 25, 1973).

At Motown they recorded with **Stevie Wonder** on his *Fulfillingness First Finale* album (1974), and **Michael Jackson** scored some solo hits prior to their departure from the label in 1975 (although **Jermaine Jackson** stayed on as a solo artist).

Upon signing to Epic in 1976 they became The Jacksons, as 'The Jackson 5' was a name that belonged to Motown (much like 'The Supremes'). Initially at Epic they were sent to work with **Gamble/Huff**, and *The Jacksons* (1976) included a UK No. 1 hit 'Show You The Way To Go'. Gamble/Huff also produced the follow-up *Goin' Places* (1977), UK single hits that year being 'Enjoy Yourself' (Top 50), 'Dreamer' (Top 30) and 'Goin' Places' (Top 30). 1978's *Destiny* featured UK Top 10 hit singles 'Blame It On The Boogie' and 'Shake Your Body (Down To The Ground)', while 1980's *Triumph* kept the group in the UK charts with 'Heartbreak Hotel' (Top 50), 'Can You Feel It' (Top 10) and 'Walk Right Now' (Top 10).

By now The Jacksons had become the most successful music business family, and various members took on solo projects. They reunited in 1984 for *Victory* (including UK Top 30 hits 'State of Shock' and 'Torture') and again in 1989 for *2300 Jackson Street* which included the **L.A./Babyface** song/production 'Nothin' Compares To U'.

JACOBS, LAWRENCE HILTON
(Singer/Keyboards/Actor)
From Los Angeles, Lawrence Hilton Jacobs recorded three albums for three different labels. These were *Lawrence Hilton Jacobs* (1978), including 'When We Can', produced by **Lamont Dozier** on ABC; *All The Way Love* (1979), produced by **Freddie Perren** on MCA; and an unreleased third album in 1984 produced by **Wayne Henderson**. Only a single, 'I Never Been Here Before', was released from this third set (on the Street City label).

As a session pianist/backing singer Lawrence has recorded with **The Sylvers**, **The Impressions**, **Rick James** and **The Gap Band**, although he is better known in Hollywood circles for his acting. He played a high-school student in TV's *Welcome Back Kotter* and Calvin James in *Hill Street Blues*. He also had a leading role in the movie *Young Blood* for which **War** recorded the soundtrack album, featuring a drawing of Lawrence prominently on the cover!

JAM/LEWIS
(Songwriters/Producers)
From Minneapolis, **Jimmy 'Jam' Harris** and **Terry Lewis** met one summer at school. Terry persuaded Jimmy to play keyboards with his group (which included **Jellybean** Johnson on drums), although at the end of the school year Jimmy left leaving Terry and Jellybean as the nucleus of the group which they later called **Flytetime**.

Jimmy rejoined the group a few years later by which time they had a rival in Morris Day's local outfit Enterprise. The groups shortly amalgamated to become **The Time**. During a five-month break between tours, Jam and Lewis decided to investigate the Los Angeles music scene, taking with them a Casio keyboard on which they wrote a few tunes. One of these was 'Wild Girls' which they played to Dick Griffey, president of Solar Records. Dick felt the song could be right for his all-girl group **Klymaxx**, and the track became their first song/production.

Playing in a celebrity basketball game (representing **The Time**), Jam and Lewis met **Leon Sylvers III** who was looking for songs to record with **Real To Reel**. Through Leon came songwriting work with **Gladys Knight** ('When You're Far Away') and **The SOS Band** ('High Hopes'). Until 1983, Jam and Lewis both toured with The Time and maintained recording commitments in Los Angeles during time off. But then a freak storm prevented them from making it to a Time concert in Texas, and they were axed from the group.

Concentrating full-time on writing and producing, their first major commitment became an album for **The SOS Band**, from which 'Just Be Good To Me' became their first American No. 1 hit single, and a Top 20 hit in the UK. The Tabu record company were so pleased that label president Clarence Avant gave them further work with **Alexander O'Neal** (*Alexander O'Neal*, including 'What's Missing', 'Innocent' and 'A Broken Heart Can Mend') and **Cherrelle** (*Fragile*, including 'I Didn't Mean To Turn You On' and 'When I Look In Your Eyes').

From that point in the mid-'80s through to the present day they have remained prolific as songwriters and producers for numerous artists including **Change** ('Change Of Heart' and 'You Are My Melody'), **Cheryl Lynn** ('Encore' and 'Fidelity'), **Thelma Houston** ('You Used To Hold Me So Tight'), **Howard Johnson** ('Knees'), **Patti Austin** ('The Heat Of Heat'), **Force MDs**, **Janet Jackson** ('What Have You Done For Me Lately', 'Control', 'When I Think Of You', 'Let's Wait A While', 'Pleasure Principle' and 'Escapade'), The Human League, **New Edition**, **Michael Jeffries** ('Not Thru Being With You'), **Johnny Gill** ('Rub You The Right Way' and 'Wrap My Body Tight'), **Ralph Tresvant** ('Sensitivity') and further work with **Alexander O'Neal** ('Fake', 'Criticize', 'Never Knew Love Like This' and 'The Lovers') and **Cherrelle** ('Saturday Love', 'Will You Satisfy', 'Everything I Miss At Home' and 'Affair').

In 1990 both Jimmy 'Jam' Harris and Terry Lewis reunited with **The Time** for an album and tour. In 1991 they launched their own record label Perspective Records (via A&M), their first release being an album by The Sounds of Blackness, *The Evolution of Gospel*, including 'Optimistic'.

JAMAL, AHMAD
(Keyboards)
Based in Los Angeles, keyboard player Ahmad Jamal made an impression on the UK 'jazz funk' scene with albums for 20th Century Records including *Ahmad Jamal* (1975), including 'The World Is A Ghetto' and 'Superstition' (co-produced by **Richard Evans**), *One* (1978) and *Genetic Walk* (1980) before his switch to Motown *Night Song* (1980), including 'Deja Vu'.

JAMES BARNES AND THE AGENTS
(Group)
Sometimes confused with **J.J.Barnes**, James Barnes is in fact a percussionist from Detroit, for whom J.J.Barnes did write a song 'Free At Last' in 1968 (released on the Golden Hit label).

JAMES TAYLOR QUARTET
(Group)
The nucleus of UK-based jazz/soul quartet The James Taylor Quartet are James Taylor (keyboards), David Taylor (guitar) and John Willmott (sax). Their music encompasses jazz, rap and soul, their album for Polydor being *Do Your Own Thing* (1990), including 'Love The Life'.

JAMES, BOB
(Keyboards/Songwriter/Producer)
Born in New York in 1939, Bob studied the keyboards and became an established pianist and music director by the '60s. During the mid-'60s he was working with artists including **Sarah Vaughan**, **Quincy Jones**, **Roberta Flack** and **Dionne Warwick**. In 1973 he signed as an artist to the CTI label, and worked with producer Creed Taylor on a numerical set of fusion jazz albums, *One* (1974), *Two* (1975), *Three* (1976), including 'One Mint Julep' and 'Westchester Lady', and *Four* (1977). Also at the label he worked with fellow artists including **Grover Washington**, **Stanley Turrentine** and **Eric Gale**.

In 1978 he launched his own label Tappan Zee (via CBS), both for his own recordings and various artists for whom he decided to write and produce. His own albums include *Touchdown* (1978), *Lucky Seven* (1979) and *H* (1980), before he attempted a pop/crossover album *Sign Of The Times* (1981) utilising a number of **Rod Temperton** songs (including 'The Steamin' Feelin''). Artists he signed and worked with at Tappan Zee were **Wilbert Longmire** (including 'Black Is The Colour,' 1978), Mongo Santamaria (including 'Watermelon Man', 1979), **Richard**

Tee (including 'Strokin'', 1979), and Joanne Brackeen ('Keyed In', 1979).

In 1982 Bob teamed up with **Earl Klugh** for two duet albums, *Two Of A Kind* released by Capitol, and *One On One* released by CBS. A solo album *Foxie* (1983) was the last release on Tappan Zee before Bob gave up the label as a business while maintaining the logo on his recordings to this day.

Also in 1983 *The Genie* was released, featuring Bob's theme for the TV series *Taxi*. The following year he released two CBS albums, *12* (jazz fusion) and *Rameau* (his interpretation of music by the baroque composer). In 1986 he switched to Warner Brothers, initially teaming up with **David Sanborn** on *Double Vision* (which also featured **Al Jarreau**). His first solo album for the label was *Obsession*, released later in the year.

Bob has recorded with **Aretha Franklin**, **Roberta Flack** and David Chesky, and more recently produced two albums for saxophonist Kirk Whalum, *And You Know That* (1988) and *The Promise* (1989). Away from music Bob is a keen golfer, regularly teaming up for matches with **Harvey Mason**.

JAMES, ETTA

(Singer)

Born in Los Angeles in 1938, Etta sang gospel music in church before diverting her attention to rock and roll. In 1955 she was discovered by **Johnny Otis** who signed her to Modern Records and launched her on the r&b scene with 'Dance With Me Henry'. In 1959 she was signed to Argo Records (via Chess) for 'All I Could Do Was Cry', followed closely by a duet with **Harvey Fuqua** 'If I Can't Have You' and albums including *Top Ten*, *Queen Of Soul* and *At Last*, by the late '60s.

Seven Year Itch and *Stickin' With My Guns* were released by Island Records during the late '80s, then in 1989 she recorded with West Coast rapper Def Jef on 'Droppin' Rhymes On Drums'.

JAMES, FREDDIE

(Singer/Songwriter)

American child star Freddie James scored a UK Top 75 hit with his debut single 'Get Up And Boogie' for Warner Brothers in 1979. He later switched to Arista where he enjoyed dancefloor success with 'Don't Turn Your Back On Love' (1982).

JAMES, JESSE

(Singer)

Born James McClelland in 1943 in Eldorado, Arkansas, Jesse moved to the Bay Area of California as a young child. His 'James' surname was handed to him by a compere at a concert who couldn't pronounce his real name during one of his early shows. In the '60s he recorded for the Shirley label where 'I Will Go' (featuring **Sly Stone** on guitar), was the first of six singles before he switched to Hit Records for 'I Call On You' in 1966.

He later recorded for labels including 20th Century (including 'Believe In Me Baby' and *Jesse James*), Uni ('Ain't Much Of A Home'), Zea ('Don't Nobody Want To Get Married' and 'I Need You Baby'), Zay ('I Know I'll Never Find Another'), and back to 20th Century in 1974 ('No Matter Where You Go', 'You Ought To Be Here With Me' and 'If You Want A Love Affair'). Through the '80s he recorded for labels including Moonlite Hope, Midtown ('I Can Feel Your Love Vibes', 1984), TTED (*It Takes One To Know One*, 1988), and two albums for Gunsmoke, *I Can Do Bad By Myself* (1989) and *Looking Back* (1990).

JAMES, JIMMY

(Singer)

From the West Indies, Jimmy James and his group The Vagabonds settled in the UK during the '60s and established themselves on the club scene playing a mixture of reggae and soul/r&b. In 1966 they recorded *The New Religion* for the Piccadilly label before Pye Records gave them a UK chart hit with 'Red Red Wine' (1968).

In 1975 Jimmy and the group had a dance hit 'You Don't Stand A Chance If You Can't Dance', following which they scored further UK chart success with 'I'll Go Where Your Music Takes Me' (Top 25) and 'Now Is The Time' (Top 5), both in 1976 for Pye Records. The group continue to work on the UK cabaret circuit.

JAMES, JOSIE

(Singer/Songwriter)

From Los Angeles, Josie has established herself as one of the finest session singers on the West Coast r&b scene. Over the years she has worked with artists including **Stevie Wonder** (*Songs In The Key Of Life* and *Hotter Than July*), **George Duke** (lead vocal on 'I Want You For Myself'), **Joe Sample** (lead vocal on 'Burnin' Up The Carnival'), **Raul De Souza**, **Flora Purim**, **Billy Ocean**, **Howard Hewett** and **Randy Brown**.

On a visit to the UK she recorded as a solo artist for the TPL label, singles including 'Call Me (When You Need My Love)' (1985) and 'Dance You Up'.

JAMES, LARRY

(Singer/Songwriter/Producer/Drummer)

From Philadelphia, Larry James earned a nickname 'Fat Larry' due to a weight problem which ultimately led to his death a few years ago. He began his career as a drummer, initially playing with groups including **The Delfonics** and **Blue Magic**. During the '70s he instigated a group **F.L.B.** (Fat Larry's Band), and upon signing the group to the Fantasy label used the musicians to record as **Philly Cream** and **Slick** for the label too.

Also at Fantasy records he produced 'Everybody's Singin' Love Songs', a dance anthem for another Philly group **Sweet Thunder**.

JAMES, RICK
(Singer/Songwriter/Producer)
Born James Johnson in Buffalo, New York, in 1955, Rick James joined the US Navy as a teenager but fled to Canada without leave where he shared an apartment with Neil Young (who was unknown at the time). Rick and Neil formed a group The Mynah Birds, and it was a Canadian witch who told the then James Johnson to change his name to Rick. The duo left Canada for Detroit and scored a deal with Motown, though their recordings weren't released.

Rick then came to the UK where he formed Main Line, a blues band in which he sang and played guitar and harmonica. Returning to the States he recorded some solo material in a new funkier vein. In 1974 A&M released 'My Mama' prior to Rick presenting his new sound to Motown who signed him in 1978. Later that year a debut album *Come Get It* featured 'You And I' (UK Top 50) and established his original blend of funk and soul. His follow-up albums at Motown included *Bustin' Out of L Seven* (1979), including 'High On Your Love Suite'; *Fire It Up* (1979); *Garden Of Love* (1980); *Street Songs* (1981), including 'Give It To Me Baby' (UK Top 50, 1981), 'Super Freak' and 'Ghetto Life'; *Throwin' Down* (1982), including 'Dance Wit' Me' (UK Top 75, 1982) and 'Standing On The Top'; *Cold Blooded* (1983), including 'Ebony Eyes', a duet with **Smokey Robinson**; *Glow* (1985); and *The Flag* (1986).

Also while at Motown he wrote and produced a debut album for **Teena Marie**, *Wild And Peaceful* (1979), including 'I'm A Sucker For Your Love'; produced an album for his backing band **The Stone City Band**, *In 'N' Out* (1980); instigated a **Temptations** album *Reunion* (1982), featuring early members **David Ruffin** and **Eddie Kendricks**, on which he performed and produced 'Standing On The Top'; while also writing and producing his protégés **The Mary Jane Girls** (two albums) and **Val Young** (*Seduction*).

Away from Motown he sang a duet with **Chaka Khan**, 'Slow Dancin'' from *Chaka Khan* (1982); instigated the group **Process And The Doo-Rags** after creating a concept around one of his backing singers James Hawkins, producing their CBS debut album *Too Sharp* (1984); and reunited with **Teena Marie** for two duets, 'Call Me' and 'Once And Future Dream', on her *Naked To The World* (1988).

As a solo artist he later signed to the Reprise label (via WEA), while in 1990 a breakbeat of Rick's took **MC Hammer** to the top of the international charts with 'U Can't Touch This'.

JAMES, VICTORIA WILSON
(Singer/Songwriter)
Born in Gary, Indiana, Victoria worked as a session singer on the local music scene before moving to London in 1985. Here she performed on the club scene before joining The Ghastly Girls, a female equivalent to The Beastie Boys. After plenty of media attention (but no record deal), the group split up, and in 1988 Victoria released a debut solo single 'I Want You In My Movie' for the Risin' label.

From here she met Nellee Hooper and **Jazzie B** who were looking for new singers for their group **Soul II Soul**. Victoria became the voice on 'A Dream's A Dream' and toured extensively with the group through 1989 and 1990. Jazzie also took her to Epic Records in New York who signed her as a solo artist. Here Victoria co-wrote the songs for *Perseverance* (1991), including 'Through' and 'Woman of Colours'.

JAMM
(Group)
Freddy Boy (lead vocals) and Keecho (keyboards) recorded as Jamm for the Epic label, which released a debut album *Jamm* in 1988.

JAMMERS
(Group)
New York-based group The Jammers established themselves on the dance scene during the early '80s with their recordings for Salsoul. Featuring the lead vocals of **Debby Blackwell**, they worked with writer/producer **Richie Weeks** on *The Jammers* (1982), including 'Be Mine Tonight', 'What Have You Got To Lose' and 'And You Know That'.

JARREAU, AL
(Singer/Songwriter)
Born in Milwaukee, Wisconsin, Al Jarreau studied psychology at university, and originally worked as a rehabilitation counsellor. His singing was originally confined to private parties before the opening of the Half-Note Club in San Francisco. Here he was persuaded to be the resident singer, and remained at the club for three years during the mid-'60s. His pianist was **George Duke**.

Moving on to further club work in Los Angeles he came to the attention of Reprise Records (via Warner Brothers), who signed him in 1975. From here he established himself with both jazz and soul audiences with his unique voice that sang both melodies and 'scat' jazz solos like a musical instrument. His Reprise albums included *We Got By* (1975) and *Glow* (1976) before he signed directly to Warner Brothers for albums including *All Fly Home* (1978); *This Time* (1980), including 'Alonzo', 'Spain' and 'Distracted'; *Breakin' Away* (1981), including 'Easy', 'Roof Garden', 'We're In This Love Together' (UK Top 75) and 'Our Love'; and *Jarreau* (1983), including 'Mornin'' (UK Top 30), 'Trouble In Paradise' (UK Top 40), 'Boogie Down' (UK Top 75) and 'Love Is Waiting'

Al's producer through the late '70s/early '80s was **Jay Graydon**, although he used a mixture of different people following his commercial peak in 1983 (when there was much less 'scat' in his recordings). The last recording in the style of his *Breakin' Away* album (the most highly acclaimed by UK soul fans) was 'I Keep Callin'', a popular B side to 'Let's Pretend', a single taken from 1984's *High Crime*, which also included 'Raging Waters'. He later worked with producer **Nile Rodgers** on *L Is For Love* (1986), including 'Tell Me What I Gotta Do', while in 1987 he scored a UK Top 10 hit with the theme to TV's *Moonlighting*.

Outside of his own solo recordings he has recorded with **Flora Purim** ('Carry On', 1979), **Freddie Hubbard** ('Little Sunflower' – on which he wrote lyrics – from *The Love Connection*), **Bob James/David Sanborn** ('Since I Fell For You' from *Double Vision*); **Sister Sledge** ('Betcha Say That To All The Girls', 1983), **Kashif** ('Edgartown Groove', 1984), **Shakatak** ('Day By Day', 1984), **Melissa Manchester** (duet 'The Music Of Goodbye', UK Top 75, 1986), **Joe Sample** (*Spellbound*, 1989), **Larry Carlton**, and **Quincy Jones** (*Back On The Block*, 1989).

JASPER, CHRIS
(Singer/Songwriter/Producer)

Chris Jasper played an integral role in **The Isley Brothers** before becoming one third of **Isley/Jasper/Isley**. As a solo artist he formed a label Gold City (via CBS) and released *Superbad* in 1987.

Also at the label he co-wrote and produced *Vicious & Fresh* for **Liz Hogue**.

JAY & THE TECHNIQUES
(Group)

Based in Philadelphia, Jay & The Techniques enjoyed popularity on the American r&b scene from the mid-'60s (with songs including 'Apples, Peaches & Pumpkin Pie', 1967) through to the mid-'70s (including 'Number Onederful' for Polydor, 1976). In the UK, they also scored on the 'Northern soul' scene with 'Baby Make Your Own Sweet Music'.

JAYE, MILES
(Singer/Songwriter/Producer/Violin)

From New York, Miles initially studied violin and had ambitions to play in an orchestra. During five years with the air force he took up keyboards and bass, and developed vocal skills too. Returning to New York he played club dates and hooked up with guitarist **Eric Gale**. From here he worked with **Phyllis Hyman** as instrumentalist while moonlighting for two years as a member of the **Village People** (the Policeman).

After sending a tape of his songs to **Teddy Pendergrass** he was signed to Teddy's Top Priority Productions and recorded an album *Miles*, including 'Let's Start Love Over', released by Island Records in 1987. Miles also wrote and produced 'Good To You' and 'I'm Ready' for the Teddy Pendergrass album *Joy* before signing directly to Island. In 1989 Miles released a follow-up album *Irresistible*, including 'Objective', 'Heaven' and 'Message', highly acclaimed within the UK soul fraternity. His third album for the label was *Strong*, including 'Sensuous' (1991).

JEFFERSON, MARSHALL
(Songwriter/Producer)

Born in Chicago, Marshall pursued rock music until he developed a taste for dance and soul in the early '80s. By 1983 he had acquired a keyboard and drum machine with which he tried to emulate the disco of the late '70s. Soon he found himself at the centre of Chicago's new 'house' music scene, and in 1986 emerged as an artist/producer on twelve local dance hits. Four of these were released by the Trax label under his own name (including 'Move Your Body'), others under various pseudonyms such as On The House (including 'Ride The Rhythm').

From here he moved into major-league productions for artists including **Ten City** ('Whatever Makes You Happy'), **Kym Mazelle**, **Ce Ce Rogers**, Vicky Martin, The Truth ('Open Your Eyes'), Big Fun and **Evelyn 'Champagne' King** ('Day To Day'). One of his trademarks is the use of real string sections in many of his productions.

JEFFRIES, MICHAEL
(Singer)

Los Angeles-based vocalist made his debut recording alongside **Karyn White** as vocal guests of **Jeff Lorber** on *Private Passion* in 1985. The following year he signed directly to Warner Brothers where his debut solo release 'Razzle Dazzle' was featured on the soundtrack album to the film *Wildcats*. He later worked with writers/producers **Jam/Lewis** on *Michael Jeffries* (1989), including the duet with **Karyn White** 'Not Thru Being With You'.

JEFFRIES, TERRY
(Singer)

Terry originally sang with **Brenda & The Tabulations**, wrote 'On The Shelf' for **B.B.&Q.**, and more recently featured as lead singer with **Paul Simpson**.

JELLYBEAN
(Remixer/Producer/Artist)

Born John Benitez in South Bronx, New York, in 1959, John was given the nickname Jellybean by his sister who jazzed up his initials. He moved into DJ'ing at the invitation of friends who wanted him to spin records at local parties. In 1976 he turned professional and began working around New York and New Jersey. Establishing a fine reputation for mixing records he became very much in demand, also appearing as a DJ in the Sylvester Stallone movie *Nighthawks*. He also started The Funhouse, a one-time top nightspot in New York City where he worked every weekend spinning for often 14 hours to a 3,500 capacity crowd!

In the early '80s he moved into production, his first being 'Nuke' for Warp 9. He also worked alongside Soulsonic Force, **Michael Jonzun**, **Arthur Baker**, **John Robie** and **Afrika Bambaataa** on a number of pioneering electro/hip hop records. Once established as a mixer, remixer and producer his services became in demand by artists including Madonna ('Physical Attraction', 'Holiday' and 'Lucky Star'), Elvis Costello, **Michael Jackson**, Rockers Revenge and **Whitney Houston**.

In 1984 he signed as an artist to Liberty Records (via EMI) and delivered an EP *Wotupski!?!* which included 'Was Dog A Doughnut', 'The Mexican' and a Madonna-written song 'Sidewalk Talk' which hit the UK Top 50 in 1986. About this time he launched his own production company with Warner Brothers, his first artist being **Jocelyn Brown** whose Jellybean-produced single 'Love's Gonna Get You' featured the vocal sampled by Snap on 'The Power'.

In 1987 Jellybean switched labels to Chrysalis and hit the UK charts again with 'The Real Thing' (with **Stephen Dante**, Top 15), 'Who Found Who' (Top 10) and 'Jingo' (Top 15). He charted again in 1988 with 'Just A Mirage' (Top 15) and 'Coming Back For More' (Top 50). He also produced **Stacy Lattisaw** ('Nail To The Wall') and **Michael Jeffries** (the 1989 album *Michael Jeffries*), before switching as an artist to the East West label in 1990. Here his debut album was *Spillin' The Beans* (1991), including 'What's It Gonna Be'.

JENKINS, KECHIA

(Singer)

Born in New Jersey, Kechia sang on the local club scene before being invited to sing backgrounds at a local recording session. The producers Guy Vaughan and Cedric Guy put together a demo of 'I Need Somebody', later released by Profile Records in 1987 (via City Beat in the UK).

JENKINS, TOMI

(Singer)

Tomi Jenkins has spent the majority of his career with **Cameo**, although the group's front man **Larry Blackmon** produced Tomi's solo debut *Tomi* for Elektra Records in 1989.

JEROME, STEVE

(Singer/Songwriter)

British singer/songwriter Steve recorded as an artist for the DJM label, 'You're Supposed To Be My Friend' and 'It's Mine And You Don't Own It' (1981), while also writing 'Dressing Up' for the **Street Angels** and 'Fool For You' for **Juliet Roberts**.

JESSUP, MICK

(Singer/Songwriter/Producer)

Born in Washington, Mick's career took off in the early '80s writing, arranging and performing with top vocal groups. During 1983 he was a member of **Special Delivery**, for whom he wrote songs featured on *Living On The Run*. In 1986 he teamed up with producer Reo Edwards to create a commercialized form of go-go music. To showcase their results they put together a group called Effectron who released the cut 'Don't Stop That Go-Go Beat'.

JETER, GENOBIA

(Singer/Songwriter)

Born in Washington, Genobia is the niece of legendary gospel performer Reverend Julius Cheeks and cousin of disco diva Julie Cheeks. She signed to the Savoy label in 1980 and released gospel albums *Heaven* (1980), *Things 'Have' Got To Get Better* (1981) and *Genobia Jeter* (1981), including a duet with **Glenn Jones**, 'Not Just For Today'. On the gospel scene, incidentally, she has the nickname 'Doosie'.

In 1983 she teamed up with Glenn Jones again for 'Keep On Doin'', a cult modern soul duet from Glenn's album *I Am Somebody* for RCA. Signing to RCA herself in 1986, she turned further towards secular music for *Genobia*, including 'All Of My Love' (written/produced by **Meli'sa Morgan/Lesette Wilson**), 'Blessing In Disguise' and 'Take A Look'. Other producers on the album included **Hubert Eaves**, **Robert Wright** and Wayne Brathwaite.

She has sung background vocals with **James 'D-Train' Williams**.

JETER, MARLENA

(Singer)

Based in Los Angeles, Marlena is a top session singer who has recorded with numerous artists including **David Oliver**, **Donald Byrd**, **Lenny Williams**, **Rockie Robbins**, **Norman Connors**, **Starship Orchestra**, **Beau Williams** and **Debra Laws**. She also sang in a group Silk (not to be confused with **Silk**) alongside **Maxi Anderson** and Gwen Machu.

JIANI, CAROL

(Singer)

Born in Nigeria, Carol settled in Canada where she first took to singing in high-school musical productions. At university she joined a group Montreal and appeared in a Canadian stage production of *Cabaret*. Here she was spotted by producer Joe Le Greca, and under his guidance she made an impression on the '70s disco scene with 'Hit And Run Lover' and 'Mercy'. She is known to her fans as 'The Bitch Of Disco'. More recently she has recorded for MCA and (in 1990) Lanmere Records (including a version of the **Yvonne Fair** hit 'It Should Have Been Me').

JIVE FIVE

(Vocal Group)

From New York, The Jive Five were originally Eugene Pitt, Beatrice Best, Casey Spencer, Norman Johnson and Jerome Hammer. They were formed in 1959 by Eugene who had previously sang with The Genies. In 1961 they signed to the Beltone label and released 'My True Story', a debut single which remained an American No. 1 for seven weeks. Tragedy struck when Norman and Jerome were killed in a car crash, following which Eugene's brothers Herbert and Frank joined the group.

In 1965 they released an album for the United Artists label *I'm A Happy Man*, whose title track was an American Top 5 hit. They later sang backgrounds with **Gloria Gaynor** ('Never Can Say Goodbye') while continuing to record until 1985 with albums including *Here We Are* and *Way Out*.

JOB, LIONEL

(Producer)

New York-based producer Lionel Job played an integral role in the group **Starpoint** and has worked with numerous artists through the '70s, '80s and '90s including **Walter Beasley**, **Bert Robinson**, **Audrey Wheeler**, **Cliff Dawson** and **Omar Chandler**.

JOCKO

(Disc Jockey)

Philadelphia DJ wrote his own rap to the instrumental of 'Ain't No Stoppin' Us Now', the **McFadden & Whitehead** classic, and released it as 'Rhythm Talk' on the Philadelphia International label in 1979. His follow-up was 'The Rocketship', produced by Douglas Henderson and released later in the year.

JOHN, ADAM

(Singer)

From Greenville, Alabama, Adam is one of five brothers and five sisters. He has worked with **Clarence Carter**, **Marvin Gaye**, **King Floyd** and **Chuck Jackson** as a backing singer. He also produced and managed the '70s group The Village Soul Choir who had an American hit with 'Cat Walk'. He has toured consistently with his own band since the '70s, being particularly popular in the Southern states of America.

JOHN, LEEE

(Singer)

British singer Leee John is best known for his role as lead singer with the group **Imagination**. He also released a solo single 'Rock Me Slowly' for the R&B label.

JOHN, MABLE

(Singer)

From Detroit, Mable is the sister of Little Willie John, a popular singer on the r&b scene between 1955 and 1960. In 1956 she met **Berry Gordy** when her brother worked with **Jackie Wilson** (for whom Berry was writing songs). Berry gave her vocal lessons before she signed to the Motown label.

She is best remembered, however, for her recordings on the Stax label between 1966 and 1968. These include 'Your Good Thing (Is About To End)' (1966), 'You're Taking Up Another Man's Place', 'I'm A Big Girl Now', 'Don't Hit Me No More', 'Able Mable', 'Same Time, Same Place' and 'Shouldn't I Love Him'. She was then invited by **Ray Charles** to be leader and music director of The Raelettes, a position she held for nine years. In the late '70s she turned to Christianity and graduated from the Crenshaw Christian Center School of Ministries. More recently she recorded a gospel album *Where Can I Find Jesus* for the US Meda label, and two songs in 1990 for the Motorcity label.

JOHNSON & BRANSON

(Duo)

In 1989 **Howard Johnson** and Regis Branson teamed together as Johnson & Branson. Produced by Bryan Loren, their album *Johnson & Branson* was released that year by A&M Records, for which Howard had previously recorded as a solo artist.

JOHNSON, AL

(Singer/Songwriter/Keyboards/Arranger)

From Washington, Al began his career as lead singer with The Unifics in the mid-'60s. In 1968 the group recorded *Sittin' In The Court Of Love* for the Kapp label. Singles 'It's A Groovy World' (1969) and 'Got To Get To You' (1970) were released before they switched to the Fountain label for 'Dawn Of A New Day' in 1971.

In 1978 Al recorded his debut solo album *Peaceful* for the Marina label (including his original version of 'I've Got My Second Wind'), following which he played keyboards on **Bobby Thurston**'s *You Got What It Takes* and *The Main Attraction*, and with Gayle Adams on *Stretchin Out*. The following year he teamed up with **Norman Connors** to be lead vocalist on the song 'Your Love' for Norman's album *Invitation*. In 1980 Norman produced Al's CBS album *Back For More* which included the duet with **Jean Carne** 'I'm Back For More' and a new version of 'I've Got My Second Wind'. The same year Al sang lead on 'I Don't Need Nobody Else' from a further Norman Connors album *Take It To The Limit*.

Al co-produced tracks with **The Whispers** on their album *Love For Love* (1983), sang lead with C.J's Uptown Crew ('Forever On My Mind' released by Washington Hit Makers in 1990), worked as arranger for **Tata Vega**, Bloodstone, **Evelyn King**, **Peabo Bryson** and **Roberta Flack**, while also writing 'We Have Love For You' for **Deniece Williams** and 'Trust Me' for **Jean Carne**.

JOHNSON, ALPHONSO

(Bass)

Alphonso established himself as a top American session bass player during the '70s and worked with artists including **The Crusaders**, **Airto** and **Dee Dee Bridgewater** ('Sweet Rain'). He also recorded *Yesterday's Dreams*, featuring **Grover Washington, Patrice Rushen** and the vocals of **Dianne Reeves/Philip Bailey**, for Epic Records in 1976.

JOHNSON, AUGIE
(Singer/Arranger/Producer)
Based in Los Angeles, Augie was the driving force behind **Side Effect** and also worked as a backing singer with the group's producer **Wayne Henderson** on other projects for artists including **David Oliver** and **Pleasure**.

Elsewhere he has recorded with **Gene Page** (*Lovelock*), **The Brothers Johnson** and **Morris Day**. He also instigated the group **L. A. Boppers** and produced their albums in addition to one album *Round Trip* for **Light Of The World**.

JOHNSON, GENERAL
(Singer/Songwriter)
Born in Norfolk, Virginia, in 1944, Norman 'General' Johnson performed on the Southern State gospel circuit under the name Boy Wonder as a six-year-old child. At high school he formed Norman Johnson and The Showmen, and built a reputation which led to a recording session in New Orleans with **Allen Toussaint**.

In 1965 Norman and his group signed to Swan Records in Philadelphia and recorded there until 1968 when the group split up. Returning to Virginia he pursued his songwriting and wrote 'Patches', a major hit for **Clarence Carter** (UK Top 5, 1970). Developing a friendship with **Lamont Dozier**, he spent a period of time in Detroit where he eventually put together a new group, **Chairman Of The Board**.

In 1977, after the success of Chairman Of The Board (primarily in the UK), General Johnson (as he was now known) signed as a solo artist to Arista Records and released *General Johnson*, including 'Don't Walk Away'. Also at Arista he wrote and produced two tracks for **Martha Reeves**, including the title track of her one Arista album *The Rest Of My Life*.

From here he established himself on the 'beach music' scene (the style of beach music being a nostalgic throwback to the '60s, popular in clubs and lounges along America's Atlantic coastline). Signing to the Surfside label he rejuvenated **Chairman Of The Board** for re-recordings of songs including 'Don't Walk Away' and 'Loverboy'.

JOHNSON, HOWARD
(Singer/Songwriter/Percussion)
From Miami, Howard began his career singing in local bars and clubs. In one small Miami bar he was spotted by **Sandy Torano** who was looking to form a group. In 1977 they formed **Niteflyte** and signed to Ariola for two albums. He remained with the group until the early '80s when he signed with A&M Records as a solo artist. His debut solo album, *Keepin' Love New* (produced by **Kashif**, **Paul Laurence Jones** and **Morrie Brown**) was released in 1982 and featured the Top 50 UK hit 'So Fine'. In the following year came his **System**-produced album *Doin' It My Way*, before a final solo A&M album *The Vision* (1985) which featured 'Stand Up' and 'Knees' produced by **Jimmy Jam & Terry Lewis**.

In 1986 he recorded a duet 'Perfect Timing' with **Donna Allen** for her album, before returning to A&M in 1989 as one half of **Johnson & Branson**.

JOHNSON, J.J.
(Singer)
Born in St Petersburg, Florida, J.J. first took his singing seriously as a teenager. His early releases were 'Ooh Ooh Baby' and 'I Want To Know What Love Is' on the Big Apple label from New York, before a move to TCC with 'Don't You Go Away'.

In 1988 J.J. won a talent contest sponsored by Capitol Records and Budweiser. His prize was a recording contract with Capitol which has so far led to the single release 'I Am Serious'.

JOHNSON, JESSE
(Singer/Guitarist/Songwriter)
Born in Rock Island, Illinois, Jesse's father was a professional guitarist who encouraged his son to take up the instrument as a child. Mastering the guitar during his teens, Jesse joined local groups Treacherous Funk, Dealer and Pilot (the latter two rock groups). Moving to Minneapolis he met **Morris Day** and joined his group Enterprise before they and rival group **Flytetime** joined forces to become **The Time** and went on tour with **Prince**. Jesse appeared with The Time in Prince's film *Purple Rain*, and through Prince went on to write and/or produce for **Vanity 6**, **Janet Jackson** (two tracks for *Dream Street*) and **Ta Mara & The Seen**.

Away from The Time, Jesse formed The Jesse Johnson Revue consisting of Mark Cardenas (keyboards), Bobby Vandell (drums), Michael Baker (guitar), Gerry Hubbard (bass) and Brad Marshall (keyboards). His debut solo album *Jesse Johnson's Revue* was released by A&M in 1985, the follow-up being *Shockadelica* (1986), including 'She (I Can't Resist)' and featuring **Sly Stone** on 'Crazay'. A third album, *Every Shade Of Love*, including 'Love Struck', was released in 1988 before Jesse returned to The Time for a reunion album.

Jesse has also written and/or produced for **Sue Ann**, Kool Skool and **Debarge**.

JOHNSON, L.V.
(Singer/Guitarist)
Born in Chicago in 1946, L.V.Johnson grew up among blues musicians. His uncle was Elmore James, and **B.B.King** was a family friend who taught L.V. how to play blues guitar. In 1965 he was hired by **Tyrone Davis** to be the guitarist in his group, recording on songs including 'Turn Back The Hands Of Time'. He also worked at Stax Records as a guitarist, playing on sessions for **The Barkays**, **Johnnie Taylor** and **The Soul Children**, while as an artist he has recorded for labels including Phono (*We Belong Together*, 1981), ICA ('I Don't Really Care'

and 'It's Not My Time'), and Ichiban (*Cold And Mean*, 1989). He also part-owns a steakhouse and nightclub in Chicago.

JOHNSON, LAMONT

(Singer/Bass)

Born in Detroit, Lamont worked as a session bass player with local groups including **Chapter 8**, and also recorded *Music Of The Sun* for Tabu Records (1978), produced by **Jerry Peters**.

JOHNSON, LORRAINE

(Singer)

Based in Memphis, Tennessee, Lorraine Johnson's major contribution to the disco scene was her song 'Feed The Flame', released on the Prelude label in 1978.

JOHNSON, LOUIS

(Bass/Vocals/Songwriter)

Born in Los Angeles in 1955, Louis and brother George Johnson established themselves professionally in the early '70s as musicians and songwriters for **Billy Preston**. Becoming **The Brothers Johnson** they have worked closely with **Quincy Jones** since the mid-'70s. Through Quincy, Louis played bass on the **Michael Jackson** albums *Off The Wall* and *Thriller*, while also playing on numerous other Quincy productions over the years.

In 1981 he formed a group **Passage** with his wife Valerie and recorded one album which he produced. Later in 1985 he recorded one solo album *Evolution* for Capitol. His bass-playing can also be found on recordings with **Jeffrey Osborne**, **Side Effect**, **Sister Sledge**, **Donna Summer** ('State of Independence') and many more.

JOHNSON, MARV

(Singer/Songwriter/Producer)

Born in Detroit in 1938, Marv's vocal talents were first recognized by **Berry Gordy** who produced his first recording 'Come To Me' in 1958. It took off so fast in America that Berry licenced it to the United Artists label, where Marv's follow-up was the million-seller 'You Got What It Takes' (UK Top 5, 1960). Released via London Records in the UK, further success came in 1960 with 'I Love The Way You Love' (Top 40) and 'Ain't Gonna Be That Way' (1960). In America, meanwhile, Marv remained popular with songs including 'Happy Days', 'Move Two Mountains' and 'Merry Go Round', before he signed to the Gordy label (via Motown) in 1965.

Here he scored further American hits with 'Why Do You Want To Let Me Go' and 'I Miss You Baby (How I Miss You)', while in the UK his two Motown hits were 'I'll Pick A Rose For My Rose' (Top 10, 1969) and 'I Miss You Baby' (Top 25, 1969). His final release for Motown was 'So Glad You Chose Me' in 1970.

After eighteen years, Marv signed to the Nightmare label in the UK where he worked with writer/producer **Ian Levine** on 'By Hook Or By Crook' (1988). He later switched to the Motorcity label where he continued to work with Ian on *Come To Me* (1990). Elsewhere he wrote/produced for artists including **Sue Perrin** ('Candy Store Man').

JOHNSON, ORLANDO

(Singer/Songwriter)

From New York, Orlando's group Trance signed with the Easy Street label in 1983 and recorded the popular 'Turn The Music On' which he both co-wrote and sang. More recently he was the featured singer on 'Keep On Jammin'' for Secchi, recorded in Italy (1991) for the Energy label.

JOHNSON, PAUL

(Singer)

London-based singer Paul Johnson originally sang with the group **Paradise** before CBS signed him as a solo artist in 1987. Here he worked with producers including **Junior** on songs 'Half A World Away' while his first UK chart success came with 'When Love Comes Calling' (Top 75, 1987). In 1988 he recorded a duet 'Words Into Action' with **Mica Paris** on her album *So Good*, while his more recent singles have included 'Don't Make Me Wait Too Long' (1990). His cousin Chris Johnson is a top recording engineer who was once a member of the **Biddu** Orchestra and more recently fronted a UK soul band Breeze.

JOHNSON, SAMUEL JONATHAN

(Singer/Songwriter)

Based in Los Angeles, Samuel made one contribution to the soul scene with his **Richard Evans**-arranged album *My Music* for CBS (1978). It included the disco single 'You'.

JOHNSON, 'SUGAR BEAR' LOUIS

(Singer/Songwriter/Bass/Producer)

As a songwriter Louis co-wrote 'We Held On' and 'Hungry For Your Love' with **Joe Tex**. He also recorded with Joe Tex, **George Duke** and **Lou Rawls**, and had UK solo releases on Move Records.

JOHNSON, SYL

(Singer/Guitar)

Born in Mississippi, Syl began his career as a guitarist during his early teens. His first professional gig was as a member of the Eddie Boyd band. Between 1958 and 1962 he played and toured with Howlin' Wolf before **Willie Mitchell** signed him to the Hi label. Here he scored American r&b success with 'I'm Still Here', 'We Did It' and 'Back For A Taste of Your Love', utilizing his bluesy vocals to the maximum.

During the early '80s he signed briefly to the Broadwalk label and made an impression on UK dancefloors with 'Ms Fine Brown Frame' (1982), released via Epic.

JOLI, FRANCE
(Singer)
Born in Montreal, France was singing live on stage by the age of five. When she was eleven she performed on children's TV and appeared at Montreal's Queen Elizabeth Hotel in a benefit for crippled children. Her performance was in front of an audience of 3000 people, and inspired her to make singing her career. In 1978 she met producer Tony Green through whom she signed a recording contract and released her debut single 'Come To Me' the following year. From here she established herself as an artist on the disco scene. In 1981 the more soulful 'Gonna Get Over You' (for Prelude Records) was written by William Anderson of **Crown Heights Affair**.

JOLLEY/HARRIS/JOLLEY
(Writers/Producers)
Comprising Mark Jolley (former bass player/studio engineer), Brian Harris (musician/singer/songwriter) and Anna Jolley (former artist on RCA), the trio first experimented as a songwriter/production team on 'Slap You Back' for Exception (1986). It reached twenty-five in the American dance charts (via Jump Street records) and persuaded the team to carry on working together.

In 1987 they placed an advert in *Melody Maker* magazine for singers, and found **Glen Goldsmith**. For Glen they delivered hits including 'I Won't Cry' (Top 40) and 'Dreaming' (Top 20), the success of which brought them work with other artists including **Reid** ('One Way Out' and 'Real Emotion') and **Shirley Lewis**. They remixed a series of records for **Mica Paris**, **Barry White** ('For Your Love I'll Do Most Anything'), **Pieces Of A Dream** and **Chic** among others. More recently they have been the driving force behind a string of hits for **Innocence**.

JOMANDA
(Group)
Jomanda are Joanne Thomas, Renee Washington and Cheri Williams from New Jersey. As individuals they sang in local church choirs before forming the group in 1986. They released 'On Top' and 'I'll Give It To You' before scoring a UK hit with 'Make My Body Rock' in 1989.

JONES GIRLS
(Vocal Group)
From Detroit, The Jones Girls are sisters Shirley, Brenda and Valerie who first sang professionally together in the early '70s. After establishing a reputation for their fine harmonies and releasing a debut single 'Will You Be There' for the Paramount label (1974), they found work as a concert support act for artists including **B.B.King**, **The Four Tops**, Little Richard and **The Impressions**. Through their work with The Impressions they met **Curtis Mayfield** who took them to Chicago to record a few songs for his Curtom label (including 'I Turn To You', 1975). In 1978 they sang backgrounds with **Aretha Franklin** (on the Curtis Mayfield-produced *Almighty Fire*) and **Linda Clifford** ('Runaway Love') before the sisters were given a major break by **Diana Ross**. The Jones Girls accompanied Diana on a marathon tour which took them to Philadelphia and to the attention of **Kenny Gamble**. (Through Diana they had also acquired some studio experience at Motown, but nothing was released.)

Kenny signed them to the Philadelphia International (PIR) label in 1979 where they released four albums, *The Jones Girls* (1979) including 'This Feeling's Killing Me', 'You Gonna Make Me Love Somebody Else' and 'Life Goes On'; *At Peace With Woman* (1980), including 'Dance Turned Into A Romance' and 'Let's Celebrate'; *Get As Much Love As You Can* (1981), including 'Nights Over Egypt'; and *Keep It Comin'* (1984), including 'You Can't Have My Love' and 'Ah Ah Ah Ah'. The last album was released after they had switched labels to RCA in 1983 for *On Target*. This one **Robert Wright/Fonzi Thornton**-penned/produced RCA album featured '2 Win U Back', 'On Target' and 'Knockin''.

The Jones Girls also sang backgrounds for many acts on the PIR label (including **Dexter Wansel**, **Michael Pedicin Jr**, **Lou Rawls** and **Jean Carne**), and elsewhere with **Norman Connors** (*Take It To The Limit*), **Prince Philip Mitchell**, **L.J.Reynolds**, **Glenn Jones** ('I Am Somebody'), **Margie Joseph**, **Brass Fever**, **George Duke**, **Noel Pointer**, and **Bobby Wilson** among many more. Shirley Jones later recorded one solo album for PIR, but as of 1991 the sisters are working on a new Jones Girls album.

JONES, BOBBY
(Singer)
Gospel singer Bobby Jones recorded a version of the **Glenn Jones** (no relation) anthem 'I Am Somebody' on his 1983 album *Come Together* for the Myrrh label. Bobby tours and performs with his own gospel group New Life.

JONES, BOOKER T.
(Singer/Songwriter/Organ/Producer)
Born in Memphis, Tennessee, Booker formed a band with **Maurice White** during his school days in the mid-'50s. After leaving school he turned to music professionally and formed The MGs (MGs standing for Memphis Group), the line-up of Booker T. & The MGs being Steve Cropper (guitar), Donald 'Duck' Dunn (bass) and Al Jackson (drums). Initially they became an in-house band at Stax Records, recording with acts including **Otis Redding**, **Sam & Dave**, **William Bell** and **Rufus Thomas**.

From 1962 they began to record in their own right and scored American success with 'Green Onions' (1962), 'Chinese Checkers' (1963), 'Outrage' (1965), 'Hip Hug Her' (1967) and 'Soul Limbo' (1968), the latter being their UK Top 30 chart debut. Follow-up hits in the UK were 'Time Is Tight' from the movie *Uptight* (Top 5, 1969), 'Soul Clap '69' (Top 40, 1969) and an issue of their American chart debut 'Green Onions' (Top 10, 1979). All these hits helped to establish the B-3 Hammond organ style through the '60s.

In 1972 the group split up and Booker T. moved to California where he married Priscilla Coolidge, sister of Rita Coolidge. Here he worked as arranger/producer with Rita on 'I'd Rather Leave While I'm In Love' and albums for A&M Records, later signing to the label himself as a solo artist. In the meantime he recorded a reunion album with The MGs *Universal Language* (Asylum, 1976), with Willie Hall replacing drummer Al Jackson who had earlier cultivated **The Barkays** but was shot dead by a burglar in his home in 1972. In 1975 he signed briefly to Epic ('Evergreen'), while his solo albums at A&M included *Try And Love Again* (1978), *The Best Of You* (1980) and the **Michael Stokes**-produced *I Want You*, including 'I Came To Love You'. More recently he has recorded for MCA, his albums including *The Runaway* (1989).

As a producer, he has also worked with artists including **Bill Withers** (*Just As I Am*, 1971), **The Memphis Horns** (*High On Music*, 1976), Willie Nelson and Bob Dylan.

JONES, GLENN

(Singer/Songwriter/Guitarist)

Born in Jacksonville, Florida, Glenn sang gospel music as a child and became a member of The Bivens Specials while still at school. Aged just fourteen he formed his own group The Modulations with Walter Givens and Ronnie Jones. The group impressed the Reverend James Cleveland who invited them to California where they recorded two albums, *James Cleveland Presents The Modulations* (1975) and *Feel The Fire* (1976) on the Savoy label. Both were recorded at a studio owned by **Ray Charles**.

With The Modulations Glenn toured America, landing in Washington where he met **Genobia Jeter** whose Reverend uncle suggested they worked together. The Modulations worked on Genobia's 1981 album *Things 'Have' Got To Get Better* while Glenn also recorded his first in a number of duets, 'Not Just For Today', with Genobia on the album *Genobia Jeter* later that year.

Glenn also attracted the attention of **Norman Connors**, who invited him to be a part of his next album. Excited by the opportunity to work in the secular field, Glenn accepted the invitation which lead to the release of 'Melancholy Fire', a single from Norman's 1980 *Take It To The Limit*. Glenn began touring with Norman, and worked with him further in the studio on *Mr C* ('Sing A Love Song'). A solo deal with RCA came his way in 1983, the year the company were experimenting with 'mini albums'. Glenn debuted with such an album, *Everybody Loves A Winner*, including 'I Am Somebody', 'Love Intensity' and a Genobia Jeter duet 'Keep On Doin''. Producers included **Al McKay**, **Robert Wright** and **Hubert Eaves**, while the album instantly won him support on the UK soul scene.

The follow-up was the **Leon Sylvers**-produced *Finesse* (1984) including 'Show Me' and 'Meet Me Halfway There'. In 1985 Glenn recorded the duet 'Finder Of Lost Loves' with **Dionne Warwick** (from *Without Your Love*) and sang 'Talk Me Into It' from the movie *Youngblood*. His last RCA album was *Take It From Me* (1986), including 'Stay', before he switched to Jive for *Glenn Jones* (1987), including 'That Night Mood' and 'At Last', and *All For You*, including 'Stay' (different song) and 'No Additional Love'.

JONES, GLORIA

(Singer/Songwriter/Producer)

Based in Los Angeles, Gloria worked at Motown during the early '70s as writer and producer for artists including **Junior Walker**, **Sisters Love** ('Give Me Your Love'), **Gladys Knight** ('If I Were Your Woman') and **The Commodores** ('The Zoo – Human Zoo'). Her own solo recording career, meanwhile, had begun in the late '60s where releases for the Minit label included 'Look What You Started', 'Come Go With Me', 'Finders Keepers', 'Heartbeat' and 'Tainted Love' (a UK 'Northern soul' classic many years before Soft Cell had a chart success with the song in 1982).

In 1973 she recorded *Share My Love* for Motown before moving to London where she settled down with Marc Bolan and had his child before Marc was tragically killed in a car crash in 1977. She then moved back to Los Angeles where she has recorded for labels including Capitol (*Windstorm*, 1977), AVI and Sidewalk. She also resumed her writing career and scored a UK Top 20 hit with 'Haven't Stopped Dancing Yet' for Gonzales (1979).

JONES, GRACE

(Singer)

Grace would have you believe that she was born in a log cabin in Missouri (1963) to a family of poor Russian immigrants. At the age of six she built a raft and floated down the Mississippi River to Memphis where she was discovered by saxophonist **Pharaoh Sanders**. During the '80s she was signed to Island Records where she scored with UK hits including 'Private Life' (Top 20, 1980), 'My Jamaican Guy' (Top 75, 1983), 'Slave To The Rhythm' (Top 20, 1985), 'Pull Up To The Bumper' (Top 20, 1986, a re-issue from 1981), and 'Love Is The Drug' (Top 40, 1986). She later signed to Capitol for *Bulletproof Heart* (1989).

In addition to Grace's unique mixture of soul, dance, rock music and fashion, she is an actress and has built up something of a cult following outside of the dance music scene.

JONES, KIPPER

(Singer/Songwriter/Producer)

Born in Flint, Michigan, Kipper had settled in Los Angeles by the time he was working with the group **Tease** during the early '80s. As a songwriter he co-wrote 'The Right Stuff' for **Vanessa Williams** prior to signing to Virgin

Records in 1989 where his albums have included *Ordinary Story*, including 'Footsteps In The Dark'.

JONES, LINDA
(Singer)
Born in New York in 1945, Linda worked closely with **Richard Tee** and **George Kerr** through the '60s, her biggest success being the American million-selling hit 'Hypnotised' in 1967 for Loma Records (via Warner Brothers). She briefly recorded for the **Gamble/Huff** label Neptune before switching to Turbo Records in the early '70s for 'Stay With Me Forever' and 'Your Precious Love'. She died of diabetes in 1972.

JONES, ORAN 'JUICE'
(Singer/Songwriter)
Born in Houston, raised in Harlem, Oran signed to New York's Def Jam/OBR labels (via CBS) in 1985 where his albums have been *Oran 'Juice' Jones* (1986), including 'The Rain', *G.T.O. – Gangsters Takin' Over* (1987), including 'How To Love Again' (a duet with **Alyson Williams**), and *To Be Immortal* (1989).

JONES, QUINCY
(Producer/Songwriter/Arranger/Trumpet)
Born in Chicago in 1933, Quincy Delight Jones Jr was one of ten children, and grew up in a tough neighbourhood. Aged fifteen he moved with his family to Bremerton (near Seattle), Washington, and was encouraged to take up the trumpet by his father. In 1950 he met **Ray Charles** who inspired him to take up music arranging after Ray wrote songs for a vocal group Quincy was working with. The next year he attended the Berklee School Of Music, and was later given his first big break by Lionel Hampton who employed him in his trumpet section.

During 1953 he travelled with Lionel to Europe, and fellow members of the band made some recordings for Sweden's Metronome label and France's Vogue label. With titles written and arranged by Quincy, his reputation began to grow. He left Lionel Hampton and set up home in New York working as a staff arranger for CBS Records. In 1956 he became musician, arranger and musical director for the **Dizzy Gillespie** band on a major tour, following which he recorded a big band album *That's How I Feel About Jazz* for ABC. He also began to take producing seriously, producing Dinah Washington the same year.

Next he moved to Paris to work as a staff arranger for the Disques Barclay label and studied composition during his time off. He recorded with **Sarah Vaughan**, Andy Williams and a great many French artists. He also travelled to Stockholm where he recorded *Quincy's Home Again* with the Harry Arnold Radio Studio Orchestra, released on the Metronome label (and featuring the much acclaimed 'The Midnight Sun Never Sets').

After returning to the USA in 1959, he produced a Count Basie album, then financed musicians to travel Europe with the Harold Arlen jazz opera *Free And Easy*. It flopped badly, and he had to sell his publishing companies to pay his musicians $4,800 a week on a doomed visit to Paris, the lowest point in Quincy's otherwise sparkling career.

In 1961 he signed as an artist to Mercury Records, and became vice-president of the label by 1964. During this time he worked for artists including Count Basie, **Sarah Vaughan**, Ella Fitzgerald, **Aretha Franklin** and **Johnny Mathis**, while also releasing his own albums including *Newport 1961*, *This Is How I Feel About Jazz*, *Quintessence* and *Bossa Nova* (1963), including 'Soul Bossa Nova', recently utilized by the Dream Warriors. He also arranged 'Sinatra Live In Las Vegas At The Sands' with the Count Basie Orchestra. In 1963 he moved to Hollywood and became the first black jazz musician to penetrate the American film score (a.k.a 'stopwatch symphony') industry. During this era he wrote scores for *The Pawnbroker*, *In Cold Blood* and *In The Heat Of The Night*, while for TV he composed themes to *Ironside* and *Roots*.

As a recording artist he signed to A&M Records in 1971 where his albums included *Smackwater Jack* (1971) and *Body Heat* (1974), including 'If I Ever Lose This Heaven' featuring **Minnie Riperton**, before he nearly died of an aneurysm (an artery defect) in 1975. He was saved after two dangerous operations where the odds of survival were four to one against.

His next A&M albums were *Mellow Madness* (1975), featuring **The Brothers Johnson**; *I Heard That* (1976), including 'There's A Train Leavin'; *Sounds ... And Stuff Like That* (1978), including 'Stuff Like That' (UK Top 40); and the multi-Grammy award-winning *The Dude* (1981), including 'Ai No Corrida' (UK Top 20), 'Just Once' featuring **James Ingram** (UK Top 20) and 'Razzamatazz' featuring **Patti Austin** (UK Top 75).

Elsewhere, he wrote *A Black Requiem* in honour of **Ray Charles**'s twenty-five years in the music business (1971), produced the tribute album *Duke Ellington We Love You Madly* for CBS (1973), produced the **Aretha Franklin** album *Hey Now Hey* (1973), including 'Angel', worked with **Donny Hathaway** on a soundtrack album *Come Back Charleston Blue*, co-wrote 'The New Killer Joe' with **Benny Golsen**, adapted Broadway's musical *The Wiz* for the screen, winning himself an Oscar nomination in the process (1978), before in 1979 he produced the first of three albums for **Michael Jackson**, *Off The Wall*. The others were *Thriller*, for which he co-wrote 'P.Y.T.' with **James Ingram** (1982) and *Bad* (1987).

Launching his own Qwest label in Los Angeles he signed artists including **James Ingram**, **Patti Austin**, **Deco** and **The Winans**, before releasing a new album of his own, *Back On The Block* (1989), including 'I'll Be Good To You', 'The Secret Garden' and 'Tomorrow'.

He also produced artists including **The Brothers Johnson**, **Rufus** & **Chaka Khan** ('Do You Love What You

Feel', 1979), **George Benson** (*Give Me The Night*, 1980), **Donna Summer** (*Donna Summer*, 1982, including 'State Of Independence' and his own co-written song 'Love Is In Control (Finger On The Trigger)' and in 1985 worked on the Steven Spielberg movie *The Colour Purple* (which grossed over $100m) while producing 'We Are The World' to raise funds for famine in Ethiopia the same year. He is possibly the most respected producer in the soul/r&b music field.

JONES, SHIRLEY

(Singer)

From Detroit, although now based in Atlanta, Shirley is one of **The Jones Girls**. During the early–mid-'80s the three sisters recorded for the Philadelphia International label, a company Shirley signed to herself as a solo artist in 1986. Here she recorded one album *Always In The Mood* which included 'Do You Get Enough Love' and 'She Knew About Me'. Independent of her sisters she also sang backgrounds with **Peabo Bryson**, and Z.Z.Hill ('That Ain't The Way You Make Love').

More recently she has worked on a new solo album with **Keni Burke** and Dean Gant, in addition to a reunion Jones Girls album planned for 1991.

JONES, TAMIKO

(Singer)

From West Virginia, Tamiko first established herself as a jazz singer during the '60s. She sang with **Herbie Mann** and also worked as a producer with **Soloman Burke**. In the '70s she recorded 'I'm Spellbound' for the Golden World label, later re-recording the song for the UK Contempo label (owned by John Abbey to whom she was married at the time). She also signed to Arista where she recorded **Stevie Wonder**'s 'Creepin'' and scored an American hit with **Johnny Bristol**'s 'Touch Me Baby'.

In 1979 she kept UK dancefloors buzzing with 'Can't Live Without Your Love', written and arranged by **Randy Muller**, then in 1986 re-recorded the **Marvin Gaye** hit 'I Want You' which was released in the UK on the Detail label.

JONES, THELMA

(Singer)

From Fayetteville, North Carolina, Thelma sang gospel before switching to secular r&b and recording the original version of 'The House That Jack Built' (later sung by **Aretha Franklin**). In 1976 she signed to CBS for a single 'Salty Tears', later recording *Thelma Jones* for the label (1978). This included 'How Long', a highly regarded and collectable track on the UK modern soul scene.

JORDAN, ROXANNE

(Singer)

Born in Detroit, Roxanne signed to Chance Records in the late '80s where she has worked with local producers including **Kevin McCord**. Her singles have included 'I'm So Into You', popular with UK soul fans.

JOSEPH, DAVID

(Singer/Songwriter)

Born in London, David initially shot to prominence as instigator, lead singer, principal songwriter and keyboard player with pioneering 'Brit funk' band **Hi-Tension**. In 1978 he co-wrote 'Hi-Tension', 'British Hustle' and 'Peace On Earth', and solely wrote 'Autumn Love' for the group's debut album *Hi-Tension*.

In 1982 he signed directly to Island Records as a solo artist and made immediate impact with 'You Can't Hide Your Love' (UK Top 20), which remains a British soul classic. Follow-ups included 'Let's Live It Up (Nite People)' (UK Top 30, 1983), 'Joys Of Life' (UK Top 75, 1984), and 'No Turning Back' (1987).

David also sang lead vocals on a version of 'Expansions' recorded by London disc jockey Chris Paul.

JOSEPH, MARGIE

(Singer)

From New Orleans, Margie took to singing during her days in school and church choirs. Catching the ear of New Orleans DJ Larry McKinley, she was introduced to the Okeh label who released a couple of singles in 1968 before Stax signed her in 1969. With a similar style to **Aretha Franklin**, her debut album did very well and scored an American hit single with a cover version of **The Supremes'** song 'Stop! In The Name Of Love' (1970). When a second Stax album didn't do so well she was brought to Atlantic by **Jerry Wexler**. Her first album there was *Margie Joseph* (1973), which included 'Let's Stay Together' and her most successful American single 'My Love' (a Paul McCartney song) released in 1974.

After two further Atlantic albums, *Sweet Surrender* (1974) and *Margie* (1975), including 'Stay Still', with producer **Arif Mardin**, she switched to the Cotillion subsidiary to work with **Lamont Dozier** for *Hear The Words, Feel The Feeling* (1976). This was followed in 1978 by the **Johnny Bristol**-produced *Feeling My Way* which included 'Feel His Love Getting Stronger'.

Margie's next deal was with WMOT Records in Philadelphia, but her **Dexter Wansel** album did not get released as the label went bankrupt just as it was completed. Margie resumed her career teaching elocution to elementary schoolchildren. In 1982 she signed briefly to the HcRc label (Houston Connection Recording Corporation), releasing the single 'Knockout' and an album before returning to Cotillion in 1984 for 'Ready For The Night' under the direction of **Narada Michael Walden**.

Her most recent album, *Stay* (1988), was for the Ichiban label.

JOUBERT SINGERS

(Vocal Group)

A gospel group from the Bronx, New York, The Joubert Singers are Phyllis Joubert (lead singer), sister Michelle McKoy with cousins Gwen Carter, Debra Cleavest and Douglas Miller. They perform together regularly at the Bronx Baptist Church. One song 'Stand On The Word', written by Phyllis, was released in the UK by Virgin/10 Records in 1982.

JUICY

(Group)

From North Carolina, Juicy are Jerry Barnes (bass/vocals), Katresse Barnes (keyboards/vocals), Wyatt Staton (guitar/vocals), Allison Bragdon (sax/keyboards/vocals) and John Tucker (drums). Through the faith of producer **Deodato** the group landed a deal with Arista for a debut album *Juicy* in 1982. From here they wrote songs for Deodato's *Motion* and returned in 1985 for *It Takes Two*, including 'Sugar Free', for Epic Records.

JULIA & CO

(Group)

Julia McGirt was born in Rowland, North Carolina, in 1955 where her father was a member of the Dixie Hummingbirds for five years. While taking professional singing lessons and studying opera at the North Carolina School of Arts, she met David Ylvisaker. A few years later they decided to form a group, Julia & Co, and after a brief spell in Boston moved the operation to Washington. While the group established itself Julia took the role as understudy to **Jennifer Holliday** in the stage musical *Dreamgirls* (1983), but left when Julia & Co was offered a nationwide tour with comedian Richard Pryor. When Jennifer left *Dreamgirls* Julia took over her role while still maintaining dates with Julia & Co. In 1983 the group (Julia, David, **Amy Keys** and four musicians) released a debut single 'Breaking Down' (UK Top 20, 1984) and follow-up 'I'm So Happy' (UK Top 75, 1985).

JUNIOR

(Singer/Songwriter/Producer)

Born in Clapham, London, Junior made a big impression on the UK 'Brit funk' scene in 1982 with his debut single 'Mama Used To Say' (Top 10), closely followed by 'Too Late' (Top 20), 'Let Me Know' (UK Top 75) and an album *Ji* for Mercury Records. Later singles including 'Communication Breakdown' (1983) and 'Somebody' (produced by **Arif Mardin**, 1984) didn't do so well for him in the UK, but established him in America where he became more popular.

In 1985 *Acquired Taste*, including 'Oh Louise' (UK Top 75) and 'Not Tonight', featured productions by **Dexter Wansel** and a guest appearance by **Stevie Wonder** on a single 'Do You Really Want My Love' (UK Top 50), the latter song also appearing on the soundtrack album to *Beverly Hills Cop*. Junior later sang background vocals for Stevie Wonder and moved into production on artists including **Paul Johnson** ('Half A World Away').

He continued at Mercury/Phonogram with singles including 'Come On Over' (1986) and 'Yes If You Want Me' (1987), before switching to MCA for 'Another Step Closer To You' (UK Top 10, 1987, duet with Kim Wilde), 'Stand Strong' (1990) and 'Morning Will Come' (1991).

JUVET, PATRICK

(Singer/Songwriter)

Patrick surfaced briefly on the disco scene in 1978 with *Got A Feeling* produced by Jacques Morali. The album featured 'I Love America', issued on blue vinyl 12″ in the UK and a Top 20 hit single. The title track (released by Casablanca) was also a UK Top 40 hit.

K

K.C. & THE SUNSHINE BAND
(Group)
Formed in Miami in 1973 by **Harry W.Casey** and **Rick Finch**, former stockboys at what was to be their first record label (TK), K.C. & The Sunshine Band launched immediately into a string of dance hits with songs like 'Blow Your Whistle', 'Queen Of Clubs' (UK Top 10) and 'Sound Your Funky Horn' (UK Top 20) from their debut 1974 album *Do It Good*. In 1975 came *K.C. & The Sunshine Band*, a triple platinum-selling set featuring 'That's The Way I Like It' (UK Top 5) and 'Get Down Tonight' (UK Top 25). Their remaining TK albums were *Part 3* (1976); *Who Do Ya Love* (1978); *Do You Wanna Go Party* (1979), including 'Please Don't Go' (UK Top 3) and 'I Betcha Didn't Know That'; and *Space Cadet* (1980). Then they signed to Epic and released *The Painter* (1981) and *All In A Night's Work* (1983), the latter featuring their UK No. 1 hit 'Give It Up'.

KANDIDATE
(Group)
From London, Kandidate formed in 1976 and consisted of Ferdi Morris (vocals/bass), Teeroy Morris (lead vocals/keyboards), Lloyd Phillips (drums), Bob Collins (percussion/guitar/vocals), Jascha Tambimuttu (rhythm guitar/vocals) and **Phil Fearon** (lead guitar/vocals). They were one of the UK's first Brit funk/soul groups. Signing to RAK Records in 1978 they released the singles 'Don't Wanna Say Goodnight' (UK Top 15, 1978), 'I Don't Wanna Lose You' (1979), 'Girls Girls Girls' (1979) and 'Let Me Rock You' (1980) before signing to Polydor and releasing 'I Want To Be Yours' (1981) and 'Can't Say Bye' (1982), featuring **Viscount Oliver**. Their most notable performance was as support act to **Crown Heights Affair** at London's Hammersmith Odeon.

KASHIF
(Singer/Songwriter/Producer/Keyboards)
Born in Brooklyn, New York, Kashif began his professional career in the '70s playing keyboards with **B.T.Express**. He has also played keyboards with **The Four Tops**. In the early '80s he co-founded a production company Mighty M (inspired by **Gamble/Huff**'s 'Mighty Three') with **Paul Lawrence Jones** and Morrie Brown. Here he wrote and/or co-produced 'I'm In Love' (1981), 'Love Come Down' and 'Back To Love' (1982) for **Evelyn 'Champagne' King**; 'So Fine', 'Keeping Love New' and 'Say You Wanna' (1982) for **Howard Johnson**; 'Take My Love' and 'Underlove' for **Melba Moore**; and 'Don't Stop My Love' for **Passion**. Also in 1982 he wrote 'Hold On' and 'Next To You' for **High Fashion**, co-producing the group's album with **Mike Theodore** and **Dennis Coffey**. His song 'Easier Said Than Done' was recorded by **The Average White Band** that year on *Cupid's In Fashion*.

In 1983 he signed to Arista as a solo artist and released *Kashif*. It featured the American hits 'I Just Gotta Have You', 'Stone Love', 'Help Yourself To My Love' and 'Say Something Love'. The same year he produced 'Inside Love (So Personal)' for **George Benson** (later working with George again on 1986's *Secrets In The Night*). A follow-up, *Send Me Your Love* (1984), featured **Al Jarreau** on 'Edgartown Groove', ahead of a busy 1985. It was in this year, in addition to his own *Condition Of The Heart*, that he produced 'You Give Good Love' and 'Thinking About You' (which he co-wrote with **La La**) for **Whitney Houston**, while also producing a **Kenny G** album *Gravity*, singing lead on the track 'Love On The Rise'.

In 1987 he co-wrote/produced 'One Track Mind' for **Giorge Pettus**, 'Just Another Lover' for **Johnny Kemp** and delivered a new album *Love Changes* which included duets with **Dionne Warwick** ('Reservations For Two') and **Meli'sa Morgan** ('Love Changes'). In 1988 he wrote/produced a duet 'I'm In Love' with **Melba Moore** on her album of the same name and co-wrote/produced 'Jump Into My Life' for **Stacy Lattisaw**. His last Arista album was in 1990.

KEITH, BRIAN
(Singer)
Born in Philadelphia into a large family, Brian moved to New York with a schoolmate after graduating from the Creative & Performing Arts School. As a duo they impressed **Darryl Payne** at New Image Records, but he passed on their songs at this stage. After Brian's friend left for England, Darryl began looking for a singer and

Brian was put in the studio to record 'Touch Me (Love Me Tonight)', released in the UK via Citybeat (1988).

KELLY, FRANKIE

(Singer)

Born in Washington, Frankie began a professional career as a session singer during the mid-'70s. He worked with artists including **Herbie Hancock** and **Melba Moore** while also performing hits of the day in local nightclubs. In 1985 he recorded 'Ain't That The Truth' (inspired by **Marvin Gaye**), released in the UK via Virgin/10 (UK Top 75).

KELLY, PAUL

(Singer/Songwriter/Producer)

Born in Miami in 1940, Paul was singing in local groups The Spades and The Valadeers by the time he was a teenager. His first professional break came in the early '60s when **Clarence Reid** invited him to join his group **The Del-Mires**. In 1963 he recorded with the group on a song 'Down With It Can't Quit It' on the Selma label. Turning solo artist, Paul made his debut with 'It's My Baby' (on the Lloyd label), and recorded a series of Clarence Reid songs through to the late '60s. His main success during this era was 'Chills And Fever' (1968), later recorded by Tom Jones.

The song which established Paul across America was 'Stealing In The Name Of The Lord', a controversial song which upset church groups but didn't stop the record being a hit for the Happy Tiger label. Also on the label he had success with 'Cryin' For My Baby', both these songs produced by country producer Buddy Killen prior to the demise of the label when Paul signed with Warner Brothers. Here he released an album *Dirt* (1972), which included Paul's own songs 'Poor But Proud', 'Hangin' On In There' and '509'. Next to come were *Don't Burn Me* (1973) and *Hooked, Hogtied and Collared* (1974), including 'Take It Away From Him And Put It On Me', both highly regarded in soul circles. His last Warner's album was *Stand On The Positive Side*, co-produced by **Gene Page** in 1976.

From here Paul recorded briefly with Epic ('Everybody's Got A Jones', 1978) and A&M ('I've Been To The Well Before', 1980) before forming Laurence Records in 1983. He ran the label under the pseudonym Laurence Dunbar, but recorded singles 'Livin' In A Dream', 'Children Are Listenin'' and 'I Keep Holding On' in 1984 under his real name Paul Kelly.

KEMP, JOHNNY

(Singer/Songwriter)

Born in Nassau, Barbados, Johnny Kemp was one of ten children and the son of Johnny Kemp Sr, a popular performer in the Bahamas. After performing with local band Mighty Makers he formed his own group Fire Fox which became **Kinky Foxx** after they moved to New York in the early '80s. Here Johnny also worked as a session singer with **Millie Jackson**, **Glenn Jones** and **Change** (*Sharing Your Love*) while also writing songs for **B.B.&Q.** (*All Night Long*, 1982). He also worked with **Kashif** who co-wrote his debut single 'Just Another Lover' (1986) from his debut album *Johnny Kemp* for CBS. The follow-up was *Secrets Of Flying* (1988), including 'Just Got Paid' co-produced by **Teddy Riley**.

KENDRICK, WILLIE

(Singer)

'60s Detroit vocalist recorded 'Let Me Know' for the Checker label (1963) before one release on Golden World, 'Stop This Train' (1963), and two on RCA, 'You Can't Bypass Love' (1966) and 'Change Your Ways' (1967).

KENDRICKS, EDDIE

(Singer)

Born in Birmingham, Alabama, in 1940, Eddie moved to Detroit during his teens and began work with various vocal groups in the area. Becoming close with the artists at Motown he was eventually adopted as lead vocalist with Motown group **The Temptations** for whom he sang hits including 'The Way You Do The Things You Do' and 'Just My Imagination'. In 1971 he left the group to start a solo career at Motown, and established himself with 'Keep On Truckin'' (UK Top 20) in 1973. His follow-up releases included 'Boogie Down' (UK Top 40, 1974), 'Shoeshine Boy' (1975), 'Happy' (1975) and 'He's A Friend' (1976) before he switched to Arista for an album 'Vintage '78' produced by **Jeff Lane** (1978).

His later recordings include albums for Atlantic (*Love Keys*, 1981), Ms Dixie (*I've Got My Eyes On You* – music provided by **The S.O.S. Band** – 1983) and a single 'Surprise Attack' for Corner Stone Records (1984). In 1987 he joined **David Ruffin** for *Ruffin & Kendrick* for RCA.

KERR, GEORGE

(Singer/Songwriter/Producer)

Born in West Palm Beach, Florida, George relocated to New York where he replaced **Little Anthony** as lead singer with The Imperials. After touring with the group for three years he settled in Detroit where he became an in-house songwriter for Motown.

As a producer he has worked with **The O'Jays** ('I Dig Your Act', 1967), **Linda Jones** ('Hypnotised') and **Dutch Robinson** ('Happy', 1985), while his own solo releases include '3 Minutes To Hey Girl' and the Light Records album *Love Love Love*.

KERSEY, RON

(Producer/Keyboards/Singer)

From Philadelphia, Ron became an integral part of the Philly soul scene during the '70s and works consistently today in the '90s. Initially he played piano with **The Trammps**, following which he moved into session work as musician, writer, arranger and producer. He also became known as Ron 'Have Mercy' Kersey.

As writer and/or producer he has worked with **Sweet Thunder** (*Above The Clouds*, 1976), **Salsoul Orchestra/Johnnie Taylor** ('Seconds'), **Janice McClain**, **O'Bryan** (*Doin' Alright*, 1982), **Colonel Abrams**, **Jeffrey Osborne** (*Ready For Your Love*), Howard Huntsberry, **Stephanie Mills** ('I Have Learned To Respect The Power Of Love', 1985, and 'If I Were Your Woman', 1987), **Gladys Knight** & The Pips ('You', 1987), **Stacy Lattisaw**, **Peggi Blu** ('All And All'), and **Evelyn King** ('Kisses Don't Lie'). As arranger he also worked with **Anthony White** ('Stop And Think It Over'), **First Choice** and **Gloria Gaynor** ('This Love Affair'). He has recorded keyboards with **Rockie Robbins** and **Patti Labelle** ('Kiss Away The Pain') among many more.

KEY, BELINDA
(Singer)
Born in Los Angeles in 1961 to a family of musicians, Belinda's Swiss father and Danish mother moved the family to Switzerland where Belinda spent most of her growing years. Here she developed her vocals before joining Switzerland's leading r&b group The Jungletown Band. She soon became established as one of the finest r&b singers in Switzerland and was hired by numerous artists including **Chaka Khan**, **Johnny 'Guitar' Watson** and **Mother's Finest**. In 1989 she recorded as lead singer with studio group Key III on a street soul remake of 'Ain't No Mountain High Enough', released in the UK by GTI Records.

KEYS, AMY
(Singer)
From Washington, Amy is a former Miss Maryland who competed in 1983 to be Miss America. She also auditioned for the Broadway show *Dreamgirls*, where she met Julia McGirt and was invited to join **Julia & Co.** She later returned to Washington and almost studied dentistry before Epic Records signed her on the strength of her demos. Here, in 1989, she recorded a debut album *Lover's Intuition* which included 'Has It Come To This', produced by **Dexter Wansel**.

KHAN, CHAKA
(Singer)
Born Yvette Stevens in Chicago, Chaka Khan began her singing career in local nightclubs during her teenage years in the '60s. In 1971 she joined a group American Breed, replacing their lead singer **Paulette McWilliams**. Later that year the group changed their name to **Rufus**, and Chaka was the lead voice from their debut single 'Whoever's Loving You Is Killing Me'.

In 1975 she met **Quincy Jones** on a plane which initially lead to her involvement on Quincy's 'Stuff Like That'. He later produced Rufus featuring Chaka on the dance anthem 'Do You Love What You Feel'. Shortly afterwards she launched her solo career with Warner Brothers, although continuing to work with Rufus which she continues to do periodically. **Ashford & Simpson** and **Arif Mardin** contributed to her debut album *Chaka* (1978), including 'I'm Every Woman' (UK Top 20) and 'Life Is A Dance'. By now she was living in Los Angeles, but after albums *Naughty* (1980), including 'Clouds', 'Nothing's Gonna Take You Away' and 'Papillon' (aka 'Hot Butterfly'), and *What Cha' Gonna Do For Me* (1981), including 'And The Melody Still Lingers On (Night In Tunisia)' and 'Any Old Sunday', she moved to New York.

Here her albums continued with *Chaka Khan* (1982), including 'Be Bop Medley' and 'Got To Be There', although her next big hit was 'Ain't Nobody' with **Rufus** in 1984. Directly after this she scored a solo UK No. 1 hit with 'I Feel For You', the song written and produced by **Prince** and the title track of her album that year which also included 'This Is My Night' (UK Top 20) and 'Eye To Eye' (UK Top 20). Her later albums have included *Destiny* (1986), including 'Love Of A Lifetime' (UK Top 75), and *C.K.* (1988), while 1989's *Life Is A Dance – The Remix Project* featured remixes of all her classics and produced a UK hit 'I'm Every Woman'. At this time Chaka was living in London although she worked with **Quincy Jones** again on 'I'll Be Good To You' and 'The Places You Find' from his album *Back On The Block* (1989).

Chaka also has a sister **Taka Boom** and brother **Mark Stevens**.

KHEMISTRY
(Vocal Group)
From Washington, Khemistry were Marie Council, Shirl Hayes and Kimus Knight. They were put together by writers/producers **Lester/Brown** on the back of their success with **Bobby Thurston** and **Gayle Adams**. In 1982 Lester/Brown took the group to CBS who signed them for one album *Khemistry*, including 'Can You Feel My Love', 'Walking Papers' and 'Whatever It Takes'. **Al Johnson** played keyboards on the sessions. After leaving CBS, Lester/Brown wrote/produced one single 'I Can't Win For Losing' for their own Mainline label in 1985.

KIARA
(Group)
Kiara is Gregory Charley (vocals/keyboards/drums) and John Winston (guitar/keyboards/drums). In 1988 they signed with Arista where their debut album was *To Change And/Or Make A Difference*, including 'Every Little Time'. The follow-up single 'This Time' featured guest vocals from **Shanice Wilson** (1988).

KING DREAM CHORUS
(Group)
El Debarge, **Whitney Houston**, **Stacy Lattisaw**, Lisa Lisa with **Full Force**, **Teena Marie**, Menudo, **Stephanie Mills**, **New Edition** and **James 'J.T.' Taylor** joined together as King Dream Chorus for a recording, 'King Holiday',

dedicated to the memory of Martin Luther King on Mercury Records in 1986. Also featured on the record were **Kurtis Blow**, The Fat Boys, Grandmaster Melle Mel, Run DMC and Whodini, collectively known as The Holiday Crew.

KING, ALBERT

(Singer/Guitarist/Drums)

Born in Indianola, Mississippi, in 1923, Albert gained valuable vocal experience in the church and later toured with the Harmony Kings Quartet. His first break in the secular field came after he moved to Chicago where initially he found work as a drummer for artists including **Jackie Wilson** and **Brook Benton**. His recordings include 'Bad Luck Blues' (1953), typifying his bluesy vocal and guitar skills, while during the early '70s he was responsible for putting **Shirley Jones** on the road to success by taking her on tour and ultimately landing her a deal with Stax Records.

KING, ANNA

(Singer)

Anna sang with **James Brown** before a string of solo releases for the Phillips label in the '60s including 'Make Up Your Mind' and 'I Don't Want To Cry'.

KING, B.B.

(Singer/Guitar)

Born Riley B.King in Mississippi in 1925 (and now based in Las Vegas), 'B.B.' was raised by foster parents and first made a living as a disc jockey in Greenwood on the station Radio WGRM. Here he established his taste for blues music, while also supplementing his earnings by playing blues guitar. He later became recognized as perhaps the most successful blues artist of all time.

He made his debut recording in 1949 with a single 'Miss Martha King' before signing to the RPM label and making numerous recordings in Memphis through to the early '60s. His American single success during this time included 'Three O'Clock Blues' (1950), and the million-seller 'Every Day I Have The Blues' (1955).

In 1960 he switched to Kent Records where his American chart success continued with singles including 'Let Me Love You' (1964) and 'The Thrill Is Gone' (1969) while in the '70s he recorded for ABC Records where his albums included *L.A.Midnight* (1972) and *To Know You Is To Love You* (1973).

In 1985 he sang 'Into The Night' (for MCA), the title song from a Jon Landis movie, then in 1987 he was the featured lead vocalist on a song 'Caught A Touch Of Your Love' on the **Grover Washington** album *Strawberry Moon*.

KING, BEN E.

(Singer/Songwriter)

Born Benjamin Earl King in 1938 in Henderson, North Carolina, Ben was the son of a restaurant owner, and it was in his father's restaurant that Ben launched his singing career. He later joined **The Drifters** and sang lead on many of their hits. Today there are two different line-ups of The Drifters, and Ben has alternated between the two over the years.

In the meantime he also signed to Atlantic as a solo artist (originally via the London label in the UK) where his UK hits include 'First Taste Of Love' (Top 30, 1961), 'Stand By Me' (Top 30, 1961), 'Amor Amor' (Top 40, 1961). In America he also scored with 'I (Who Have Nothing)', 'Don't Play That Song', 'Spanish Harlem', 'What Is Soul?' and 'Seven Letters'. In the late '60s he left Atlantic and recorded unsuccessfully for a series of independent labels before returning to Atlantic in 1975 for the American hit 'Supernatural Thing' (from *Supernatural*). In 1977 he recorded an album with **The Average White Band** *Benny And Us* including 'A Star In The Ghetto'. His last Atlantic album was *Street Tough*.

After the UK success of 'Stand By Me' re-released in 1987 (No. 1), Manhattan (via EMI) charted his single 'Save The Last Dance For Me' (Top 75), while 'Supernatural Thing' was remixed and reissued by East West Records (via Atlantic) in 1990.

KING, BOBBY

(Singer)

Born in Lake Charles, South Carolina, Bobby is the son of a preacher and one of nine brothers and four sisters. He moved to Los Angeles in 1968 with his brother Billy to pursue a singing career. Together they formed a group The Relations which culminated in his first break. In 1971 he was given the role of a preacher in the gospel musical *Don't Bother Me, I Can't Cope*. The production lasted three years and led to a recording contract with Warner Brothers. During his time with the musical he also sang background vocals with Boz Scaggs, George Harrison and **Billy Preston**.

He recorded two albums for Warner Brothers, and later one for Motown (*Love In The Fire*, 1984, including 'Fall In Love'), all three of which were produced by Steve Barri. He has also toured with Ry Cooder, with whom he wrote the soundtrack to the film *Streets Of Fire*.

KING, EVELYN 'CHAMPAGNE'

(Singer)

From the Bronx, New York, Evelyn was born into a family of nine. She was encouraged to sing by her father, who himself sang with The Orioles and The Harptones. Her mother also managed a group Red Quality. In 1970 the family moved to Philadelphia where Evelyn turned professional at the age of sixteen. While performing with a number of local bands, she stood in for her sister one day who had a cleaning job at the city's Sigma Sound Studios. While on duty she was overheard singing **Sam Cooke**'s 'A Change Is Gonna Come' by producer **T. Life**. He took her to RCA where her debut single 'Shame' (UK

Top 40) sold millions around the world. It came from her debut album *Smooth Talk* (1978).

In 1982 Evelyn teamed up with Mighty M Productions who had an extremely in-vogue dancefloor sound at the time. The team included **Kashif** and Morrie Brown who collaborated on *Get Loose*, which put her back in the UK chart that year with 'Love Come Down' (Top 10) and 'Back To Love' (Top 40). Also in 1982 Evelyn recorded a duet 'Can We Be Friends' with **Michael Wycoff** on his album *Love Conquers All*. Her next solo chart entry was 'Get Loose' (UK Top 50) in 1983. A 1984 album *So Romantic* (including 'Out of Control'), was followed in 1985 by *A Long Time Coming (A Change Is Gonna Come)* on which she teamed up with writers/producers **McFarlane/George** for UK hit singles 'Your Personal Touch' (Top 40) and 'High Horse' (Top 60, 1986). Then she left RCA.

In 1988 she signed with Manhattan (via EMI) for *Flirt*, including 'Kisses Don't Lie', 'When Your Heart Says Yes' and the **Leon Sylvers**-produced UK Top 50 single 'Hold On To What You've Got'; and *The Girl Next Door* (1990), including 'Cross Your Mind'.

Incidentally, between 1981 and 1983 'Champagne' was dropped from her name.

KING, JAMES

(Singer/Songwriter)

From Philadelphia, James was one of four high-school friends who became **The Futures** in 1968. Recording for Amjo, Gamble, Buddah, PIR, and United Artists through the '70s, they are possibly best remembered for 'Ain't Got Time Fa Nuthin'' in 1978. After the group disbanded, James recorded as a session singer and in 1982 co-wrote 'Let's Stay Together' with Terri Wells, recorded by **Roy Ayers** on *Feeling Good* (on which James also co-sang 'Turn Me Loose'). He also sang backgrounds with **52nd Street**.

In 1987 he made his solo recording debut with a single 'Memory', released in the UK on the Expansion label.

KING, WILL

(Singer)

From Los Angeles, Will gained his early singing experience through the church and talent shows. While at high school he formed a group Rhythm Rebellion which toured the States, Canada and Europe. He also spent some time as lead vocalist with another r&b group Redd Eye Express before taking on a solo career. Singing in a nightclub owned by his manager he gained further experience performing with members of **War** and **Rufus**. In addition he sang **Marvin Gaye** hits on the 'Tribute To Motown' roadshow, though vocally he is compared with **Al Green**.

Performing in a contest one night with the group Formula Five, he was spotted by producer Lonnie Simmons who signed him to his Total Experience label. Here he recorded one album *Backed Up Against The Wall* in 1985.

KINGDOM

(Gospel Group)

Kingdom are vocalists (including **Scott White**) from The Ministry Choir Of The Agape Christian Center. 1987's *Amazing* (for Light Records), featured **Najee** and generated interest in soul circles for the inspirational track 'Don't Be Afraid', arranged and produced by Rhani Song.

KINNEY, FERN

(Singer)

Born in Jackson, Mississippi, Fern sang with **Dorothy Moore** in a group The Poppies prior to signing as a solo artist with Atlantic. In 1977 she switched to Malaco for *Groove Me* and *Fern*, although it was back at WEA that she scored her UK No. 1 hit 'Together We Are Beautiful' in 1980.

KINSMAN DAZZ

(Group)

Originally known as Telephunk, and later **The Dazz Band**, Kinsman Dazz signed to the 20th Century label in the late '70s where they released two albums. In 1978 and 1979 they had two Top 30 American r&b hits with 'Might As Well Forget About Lovin'' and 'Catchin' Up On Love'.

KIRKLAND/DAVIS

(Singers)

Bo Kirkland (from Mississippi) and Ruth Davis (from Arkansas) both sang independently before landing a recording deal at the same independent label, Claridge Records. Label boss Frank Slay put them together for one album *Bo And Ruth*, released in the UK by EMI in 1977 and featuring the Top 20 hit single 'You're Gonna Get Next To Me'.

KIRTON, LEW

(Singer/Drummer)

From Barbados, West Indies, Lew was initially known as Jigs Kirton and acquired his vocal training in a local Anglican choir. His first professional break was in 1969 as drummer with the **Sam & Dave** revue, then in 1972 he joined the line-up of **The Invitations**. The group had a hit with 'They Say The Girl's Crazy' for Silver Blue Records.

In 1977 he recorded an album for TK, *Just Arrived* from which 'Do What You Want' was his debut single, while 'Heaven In The Afternoon' became an in-demand album track in the UK. While at TK he also recorded 'It's Where You're Coming From' as featured lead vocalist with jazz ensemble B. Baker's Chocolate Company.

In 1983, after having moved to Brooklyn, New York, he recorded one album *Talk To Me* for Believe In A Dream Records (via CBS). The title track was released as a single and remains a popular song on the UK soul scene (although it didn't make the charts here). His next release was 'Don't Wanna Wait' in 1986, issued at first on a small American label Tweedside, but later made available in the UK by MCA. It remains his last recording, although he has finished writing some new songs and toured the UK in 1989. (Songs of his have also been recorded by **Tyrone Brunson** and **Melba Moore**.)

KLEEER

(Group)

From Baltimore, **Woody Cunningham** (drums), Norman Durham (bass) and Richard Lee (keyboards) first worked together as the backing band for local vocal group **The Choice Four** in 1971. The following year they moved to New York where they joined with Paul Crutchfield (percussion) to become a heavy metal band Pipeline. In 1976 **Patrick Adams** needed a group of musicians to tour as **The Universal Robot Band**; they were prepared to give it a try, and got the job. When that job finished they found they enjoyed playing to dance audiences so much they continued, renaming themselves Kleeer (as they didn't own the name Universal Robot Band), and signed to Atlantic. They also added the services of Mic Murphy (manager)/David Frank in keyboards (**The System**) and vocalists Isabelle Coles, Melanie Moore and Yvette Flowers.

Their debut album *I Love To Dance* (1979) included 'Keep Your Body Working' (UK Top 75) and 'Tonight's The Night'. Later albums were *Winners* (1980), including 'Open Your Mind', and *License To Dream* (1982), including 'Get Tough' (UK Top 50, 1981) and 'Taste The Music'. In 1984 they switched producers from Dennis King to **Deodato** for *Intimate Connection* (1984) and *Seeekret*, including 'Take Your Heart Away' and 'Never Cry Again' (with all songs on this album written by their bass player Norman Durham).

In 1990 they returned on the Image label with a single 'Delicious' co-produced by Woody Cunningham and **Darryl Payne**. Drummer Woody Cunningham was also instrumental in **Candido** as drummer, singer and vocal arranger. He and Norman also recorded with **Two Tons Of Fun** on 1980's *Backatcha*.

KLEMMER, JOHN

(Saxophone)

Based in Los Angeles, John recorded for the ABC label in the late '70s where the title track of his 1979 album *Brazilia* (featuring drummer **Lenny White**) was popular on the UK jazz funk scene. He then switched to Elektra for *Magnificent Madness* (1980) and *Hush* (1981).

KLIQUE

(Group)

Los Angeles-based group Klique were Isaac Suthers (vocals/keyboards), Deborah Hunter (vocals/percussion) and Howard Huntsberry (vocals/drums). Signing with MCA in the early 80s, their albums included *Let's Wear It Out* (1982), including 'I Can't Get Enough', and *Love Cycles* (1985), including the **Ronnie McNeir**/**Renaldo Benson**-penned/produced 'Ain't Nothing Better'.

Howard later signed to MCA as a solo artist where in 1988 he recorded *With Love*.

KLUGH, EARL

(Guitar)

Born in Detroit, Earl picked up his first guitar at the age of three. When he was seventeen he left home to tour with **George Benson**, eventually leaving to join Chick Corea's Return To Forever. He began his solo career with Blue Note Records in the mid-'70s, early albums being *Living Inside Your Love* (1976), including 'I Heard It Through The Grapevine', and the **Grusin/Rosen**-produced *Finger Paintings* (1977).

Switching to United Artists, Earl scored with three jazz funk albums during 1980, *Dream Come True*, *One On One* with **Bob James** (for Tappan Zee Records) and the soundtrack *How To Beat The High Cost Of Living* with **Hubert Laws** (for CBS). In 1983 he returned with a further soundtrack *Marvin & Tige* (1983) for Capitol, where he also delivered *Wishful Thinking* (1984), *Key Notes* (1985) and *Two Of A Kind* with **Bob James** (1985).

In 1985 he switched to Warner Brothers where his albums have included *Soda Fountain Shuffle* (1985), *Life Stories* (1986), *Collaboration* with **George Benson** (1987), and *Midnight In San Juan* (1991).

KLYMAXX

(Group)

Formed by drummer **Bernadette Cooper** in Los Angeles, Klymaxx were originally Bernadette with the addition of Cheryl Cooley (guitar), Lorena 'Lungs' Porter (lead vocals), 'Fenderella' (bass), Lynn 'Lynnie Pies' Malsby (keyboards) and Robbin 'Space Baby' Grider (synths/guitar). In 1982 they signed to the Solar label and became the first ever group or artist to work with writers/producers **Jam/Lewis**. The team wrote and produced a song 'Wild Girls' for their debut album *Girls Will Be Girls*.

After a second Solar album *Never Underestimate The Power Of A Woman* (1983), they switched the Constellation label (via MCA) for *Meeting In The Ladies' Room* which featured the American Top 10 hit 'The Men All Pause' in 1984. Two years later their song 'Man Size Love' was featured on the soundtrack album to the movie *Running Scared*.

The group were down to six members by the end of 1988 and by 1989 they had become just Cheryl Cooley, Lorena Porter and Robbin Grider. In 1990 they returned with *The Maxx Is Back*, including 'Good Love' and 'Don't Run Away'.

Cheryl, incidentally, first took guitar lessons from **Hubert Laws** who is now married to her sister. Lorena landed a position in the group after initially auditioning to be in **Rose Royce**.

KNIGHT, FREDERICK

(Singer/Songwriter/Producer)

Born in Birmingham, Alabama, in 1944, Frederick went to New York to begin his recording career, but his early releases with Mercury and Capitol were unsuccessful. In 1972 he signed to the Stax label and scored an American hit with his debut 'I've Been Lonely For So Long' (co-written by his wife). While at Stax he remained an in-house writer and producer for many of the label's acts through to its eventual demise in the mid-'70s. Towards the end of the '70s Frederick launched his own label Juana (via TK) and worked as writer and/or producer with artists including **The Controllers** ('Somebody's Gotta Win, Somebody's Gotta Lose' and 'I Can't Turn The Boogie Loose') and **Anita Ward** ('Ring My Bell').

As an artist he recorded *Let The Sunshine In*, though he is best known for 'I've Been Lonely For So Long'. He has also written and/or produced for artists including **Gwen McCrae** ('Be For Real'), **Major Lance** ('You're Everything I Need'), **James Bradley** ('I'm In Too Deep'), **C.L.Blast** ('Lay Another Log On The Fire') and **Keisa Brown**, the latter two for his mid-'80s Park Place label.

KNIGHT, GLADYS

(Singer)

Born in Atlanta, Georgia, in 1944, Gladys was seven years old when she won $2000 on *The Ted Mack Amateur Hour*. Two years later with brother Merald and cousins William Guest and Edward Patten she became Gladys Knight & The Pips, and performed at a local function for the very first time. 'Pip', incidentally, was the nickname of Gladys's cousin James Woods who became their manager. When Gladys was twelve she and the group toured the country with **Sam Cooke** and **Jackie Wilson** before recording 'Every Beat Of My Heart' for the local Huntom label. Soon they re-recorded the song for another label, Fury, only to face competition in the charts with the reissue of the original which first established the group in the American charts in 1961.

In 1963 they switched to the Maxx label and teamed up with producer **Van McCoy** for some success with 'Giving Up' before Gladys took a year off to have a baby. In 1966 Gladys Knight & The Pips signed to Motown where their first single was 'Just A Walk In My Shoes' on the Soul subsidiary. Later in the year they scored an American hit with 'Everybody Needs Love', following which they established themselves in the UK with 'Take Me In Your Arms And Love Me' (Top 20, 1967). Further Motown hit singles included 'I Heard It Through The Grapevine' (Top 50, 1967), 'It Should Have Been Me' (1968), 'The Nitty Gritty' (1969), 'If I Were Your Woman' (1970), 'Just Walk In My Shoes' (UK Top 40, 1972), 'Help Me Make It Through The Night' (UK Top 20, 1972), 'Look Of Love' (UK Top 25, 1973) and 'Neither One Of Us' (UK Top 40, 1973).

In 1973 the group switched to the Buddah label where they felt they would get more attention. In the UK, success came first with 'The Way We Were/Try To Remember' (Top 5, 1975), followed by 'The Best Thing That Ever Happened To Me' (Top 10, 1975), 'Part Time Lover' (Top 30, 1975), 'Midnight Train To Georgia' (Top 10, 1976), 'Make Yours A Happy Home' (Top 40, 1976), 'So Sad The Song' (Top 20, 1976), 'Nobody But You' (Top 40, 1977), 'Baby Don't Change Your Mind' (Top 5, 1977), 'Home Is Where The Heart Is' (Top 40, 1977), 'The One And Only' (Top 40, 1978), 'Come Back And Finish What You Started' (Top 20, 1978) and 'It's Better Than A Good Time' (Top 75, 1978). Buddah albums included *Imagination*, *Claudine* (the **Curtis Mayfield**-produced movie soundtrack including 'The Makings Of You'), *I Feel A Song*, *Second Anniversary* and *Still Together* (1977), including 'Baby Don't Change Your Mind'.

At this point **The Pips** recorded two albums on their own for Casablanca, before reuniting with Gladys in 1980 to sign with CBS. Here they teamed up with writers/producers **Ashford & Simpson** for *About Love*, including 'Taste Of Bitter Love' (UK Top 40) and 'Bourgie, Bourgie' (UK Top 40). Also in 1980 Gladys recorded a duet album with **Johnny Mathis**, *Celebration*, including 'When A Child Is Born' (UK Top 75).

The 1983 **Leon Sylvers**-produced *Visions*, including 'Save The Overtime For Me', was followed by a final CBS album *Life* (1985) before a switch to MCA. Here in 1985 Gladys recorded the original version of 'Wind Beneath My Wings', later a hit for Bette Midler and country artist Lee Greenwood. *All Our Love* became the 25th Gladys Knight & The Pips album in 1987 and featured 'Love Overboard' (UK Top 50), 'Lovin' On Next To Nothin'', and a **Sam Dees**-penned title track. In 1989 Gladys sang the theme to the James Bond movie *License To Kill* before announcing she was to record without The Pips as of 1990. In 1991 her first solo album for MCA was released, *Good Woman*, including 'Men'.

Gladys has also recently launched a hair-care business, Knight Nutritional Hair Supplements.

KNIGHT, JEAN

(Singer)

Recording for the Memphis-based Stax label in the early '70s, Jean is best remembered for 'Mr Big Stuff', originally released by the label in 1971, and revived on the UK 'rare groove' scene during the mid-'80s.

KNIGHT, JERRY

(Singer/Songwriter/Producer/Bass)

Born in Los Angeles in 1955, Jerry played bass with the **Bill Withers** band before **Ray Parker Jr** invited him to join his group **Radio**. Here he sang lead vocals on the 1978 UK Top 20 hit 'Jack And Jill', but left the group in 1980 to sign to A&M as a solo artist. His debut solo single was 'Overnight Sensation' from *Jerry Knight* (1980). His other A&M albums included *Love's On Our Side* (1983). He then recorded for Polydor as one half of the duo **Ollie & Jerry** (1984).

As a songwriter he has written for **The Whispers** ('Tonight', 1983) and **Philip Bailey** ('Desire', 1983), while as a producer he has worked with **Howard Hewett** ('Challenge'). He has played bass with numerous artists.

KNUCKLES, FRANKIE
(DJ/Songwriter/Producer)
Originally from the South Bronx, New York, Frankie was all set to embark on a career in fashion and costume design before a chance encounter with New York's underground club scene. In 1971 he took up work as a disc jockey and secured a residency at the club Better Days. Six months later he was working in a famous New York bath house, prior to being approached by a couple of guys from Chicago who offered him his own club in the windy city, The Warehouse. Within three years he was established on the Chicago scene as a personality disc jockey and a pioneer on the 'house' music scene.

Inspired by the popularity of his own remix of 'Let No Man Put Asunder' (**First Choice**), Frankie ventured into the recording studio and worked with **Jamie Principle** on some early Principle hits (including 'Baby Wants To Ride'). On a tour of Japan he met Japanese keyboard artist **Satoshi Tomiie** with whom he teamed up for 'Tears' (1989). As a solo artist he debuted with 'You Can't Hide (From Yourself)' which featured Ricky Dillard on vocals, while more recently he signed to Virgin for 'The Whistle Song' (1991).

KOKO POP
(Group)
From Columbus, Ohio, Koko Pop were Eric O'Neal (keyboards), Matt Seward (lead vocals/guitar), Chris Powell (lead vocals/keyboards/sax), Recco Philmore (lead vocals/keyboards) and Alexandro (guitars). Chris was a former member of **Rick James**'s Punk Funk Horn Section, a situation which opened the doors to Motown. In 1984 the group signed to the label, and from their debut album *Koko Pop* the song 'I'm In Love With You' made a good impression with UK soul fans. It was issued as a single, but was not a hit.

Nothing from 1985's *Secrets Of Lonely Boys* made any impact, and the group left Motown later that year.

KOOL & THE GANG
(Group)
From New Jersey, Kool & The Gang were formed by brothers Robert 'Kool' Bell and Ronald Bell, with friends Dennis Thomas and Robert Mickens. They were originally known as The Jazziacs when they began playing at school from 1964. By 1969 the group had become Kool & The Gang and signed with De-Lite Records. The full line-up was Robert 'Kool' Bell (bass), Ronald Bell (sax/keyboards), George Brown (drums), Curtis 'Fitz' Williams (keyboards), Charles Smith (guitar), Dennis 'Dee Tee' Thomas (alto sax), Robert 'Spike' Mickens (trumpet), Clifford Adams (trombone) and Michael Ray (trumpet).

The group's recording career can be divided between two periods, the first commencing in 1973 with *Wild And Peaceful*. This first album, including 'Jungle Boogie', 'Funky Stuff' and 'Hollywood Swinging', established the group on the burgeoning UK funk scene with a style which combined earthy brass, funky bass/guitar and often chanted vocals used more for effect than to carry an actual song (much like the technique of early **Fatback**). This style carried them through to 1978, with further tracks 'Summer Madness' (1974), and 'Winter Sadness' and 'Caribbean Festival' (from 1975's *Spirit Of The Boogie*) making the most impact on the UK black music scene. 1976's *Love And Understanding* featured 'Open Sesame' which appeared on the *Saturday Night Fever* movie soundtrack. Their final album during this era was *The Force* (1977).

In 1979 the group made a clear-cut transition into mainstream dance/soul/pop by bringing in vocalist **James 'J.T.' Taylor** and utilizing the services of producer **Deodato**. The group released *Ladies' Night*, and immediately scored a UK Top 10 hit with the title track. The B side was originally 'Too Hot' (also on the album), which remains one of the group's most highly acclaimed ballads, and also charted in the UK Top 25 when issued as an A-side the following year. The group then charted every year through to 1988, their formula gradually appealing less to soul fans but more to mainstream pop fans up until the departure of James Taylor from the group. Their biggest UK hits during this period were 'Celebration' (Top 10, 1980), 'Steppin' Out' (Top 20, 1981), 'Get Down On It' (Top 5, 1981), 'Big Fun' (Top 20, 1982), 'Ooh La La La' (Top 10, 1982), 'Straight Ahead' (Top 20, 1983), 'Joanna' (Top 5, 1984), 'In The Heart' (Top 10, 1984), 'Fresh' (Top 20, 1984) and 'Cherish' (Top 5, 1985).

In 1988 'Celebration' was remixed by **Stock/Aitken/Waterman** and Jon Williams, both mixes charting Top 75 back-to-back in the UK that year.

KREAMCICLE
(Studio Group)
This studio group was put together by **Darryl Payne** and featured vocalists Barbara Harris ('Dancin' In The Street') and **Carol Williams** ('No News Is News', released in the UK by Bluebird in 1986).

KRYSTOL
(Vocal Group)
From Los Angeles, Krystol are girl group Tina, Roberta, Dee and Karon, who originally got together at high school as Krystol Blue. On a social night out, the girls met producer **Leon Sylvers** at a hamburger stall and struck up a friendship. Leon helped secure Krystol a record deal with Epic in 1984 and was brought in to produce the first album. Prior to this they had worked on individual projects, Roberta becoming a member of Alton McClain & **Destiny**.

Their debut album was *Gettin' Ready* which included

'After The Dance Through', a huge club record through 1984–5 although not a hit in the UK. The follow-up *Talk Of The Town* (1985) offered 'The Things That Men Do' and 'Passion For A Woman'. The group's third album *I Suggest U Don't Let Go* (1989) included songs and productions by **Leon Ware** (including 'Just Don't Make It Hurt') and **Craig T. Cooper**.

L

L.A./BABYFACE

(Songwriters/Producers)

Antonio 'L.A.' Reid and Kenneth 'Babyface' Edmonds were both members of the group **The Deele** prior to extending their joint songwriting/production skills to other artists from the mid-'80s. Their first production was for **Material Thangz** (1985), following which they delivered hits for numerous artists, in many cases launching their careers. Artists they have written and/or produced for include **The Whispers** ('Rock Steady'), **The Mac Band** ('Roses Are Red'), **Bobby Brown** ('Don't Be Cruel', 'My Prerogative' and 'Every Little Step'), **Karyn White** ('The Way You Love Me' and 'Superwoman'), Sheena Easton ('The Lover In Me'), **The Jacksons** ('Nothin' (That Compares To U)'), **Johnny Gill** ('My My My'), **Whitney Houston** ('I'm Your Baby Tonight'), and **Pebbles** who became 'L.A.' Reid's wife.

In 1991 they launched their La'Face label (via Arista) with artists including **Jermaine Jackson**, Damian Dane and Level 3.

L.A. BOPPERS

(Group)

Instigated by **Augie Johnson**, The L.A.Boppers included Gerry Davis (drums), Ed 'Funky Thumbs' Reddick (bass), Kenny Styles (guitar), Michael Stanton (keyboards) and Vance 'Mad Dog' Tenort (lead vocals). Augie had previously been associated with **Side Effect**, and The L.A.Boppers were for him an extension of that group. In 1980 *L.A.Boppers* was released by Mercury, including 'Be Bop Dancing' and the group's finest moment, 'Watching Life'. **Miki Howard**, another former Side Effect member, guested on the album.

L.A. MIX

(Group)

The concept of L.A.Mix was pioneered by London disc jockey **Les Adams** as an extension of his successful work as a remixer and producer for other artists during the mid-'80s. With wife Emma Freilich and multi-instrumentalist Mike Stevens, L.A.Mix signed with A&M Records and have to date enjoyed success from two albums, *On The Side* (1989), including 'Don't Stop Jammin'' (UK Top 50), 'Check This Out' (UK Top 10), 'Get Loose' and 'Love Together', and *Coming Back For More* (1990), including 'Mysteries Of Love' and 'We Shouldn't Hold Hands In The Dark'.

L.A.X.

(Studio Group)

Ralph Benatar and Galen Senogles created this studio group in 1980. A 12″ single 'Possessed' stormed UK dancefloors later that year, and the track was included on the group's one Epic album, *All My Love*.

L.L. COOL J

(Rapper/Songwriter)

Born James Todd Smith in Queens, New York, in 1969, L.L. began rapping at the age of nine after his grandfather bought him some disc jockey equipment. In 1986, he released his debut album *Radio* (a first album for Def Jam via their first liaison with CBS), and scored UK hit singles with 'I'm Bad' (Top 75, 1987), 'I Need Love' (Top 10, 1987), 'Go Cut Creator Go' (Top 75, 1987) and 'Going Back To Cali'/'Jack The Ripper' (1988). More recently he made an impact on UK dancefloors with 'Around The Way Girl' from an album *Mama Said Knock You Out* (1990).

L.R. SUPERSTARS

(Group)

Albert L.Smith Sr, Albert L.Smith Jr, Tomaro Coleman and Sid Hill worked together as the L.R.Superstars in the late '80s. In 1989 they recorded 'I Just Can't Say It' for the Budweiser label, later included on a 1990 UK-released album *Sayin' It* for the Rare Grooves label.

L.T.D.

(Group)

Formed in 1968, L.T.D. stands for Love, Togetherness and Devotion. Originally formed in North Carolina, the group moved to Los Angeles after adding the talents of lead singer **Jeffrey Osborne** (who had originally joined as a drummer). Other members are Arthur Lorenzo Carnegie (sax/guitar – player from Florida who originally played with **Sam And Dave**), Jack Riley Jr (trombone player from Florida who had also worked with Sam And Dave), Carle Vickers (trumpet/flugelhorn/sax/flute), Henry Davis (keyboards), Abraham Joseph Miller (sax player from North Carolina, also worked with Sam And Dave), Johnny McGhee (guitarist from Chicago), **Billy Osborne** (keyboards/percussion/vocals), Jimmy 'J.D.' Davis (keyboards/music director), Leslie Wilson (former vocalist with **New Birth**) and Alvino Bennet (drummer from Chicago who joined the group full-time in 1978). Their first big break came as a result of being invited to play as support act to **Merry Clayton** at the Monterey Folk Festival in 1971. The event was attended by executives from A&M Records in Los Angeles, and duly impressed they signed the group to the label that year.

Their debut album *Love, Togetherness, And Devotion* (1973) was produced by the group themselves, as was the follow-up *Gettin' Down*. For their third album *Love To The World* (1976) they worked with producer **Fonce Mizell** and scored with an American hit 'Love Ballad' (later a UK hit song for **George Benson**). Teaming up with producer **Bobby Martin** they released a fourth album *Something To Love* (1977) which featured a further American hit 'Back In Love Again', but it was in 1978 that the group scored their one UK Top 75 hit with 'Holding On', from a fifth album *Togetherness* (which also included 'We Deserve Each Other'). Their next albums were *Devotion* (1979) and *Shine On* (1980) before **Jeffrey Osborne** left the group for a solo career. **Billy Osborne** also left to form **Osborne & Giles**.

L.T.D's final A&M album was *Love Magic* released in 1981, with lead vocals shared by Leslie Wilson and Andre Ray.

LA LA

(Singer/Songwriter)

From Queens, New York, La La (real name La Forrest Cope) took up the piano at the age of five and gave a piano recital at Carnegie Hall aged nine. After leaving New York's High School Of Music And Art she formed a band Jack Sass, which played Top 40 cover versions on the club scene. As the group built a reputation, La La began introducing more of her own songs into the repertoire before she went to Juilliard to major in composition. In 1981 she was invited to tour with **Stacy Lattisaw** who opened for **The Jacksons** on a national tour. Following this she sang with **Change** (recording on their *Glow Of Love*) and further developed her songwriting skills.

She played one of her songs 'Stone Love' to neighbourhood friend **Kashif** who recorded it on his debut album in 1983. Then came songs for **Lillo Thomas** ('All Of You'), **Melba Moore** ('Living For Your Love' and 'It's Really Love'), **Glenn Jones** ('Show Me' and 'Stay'), **Giorge Pettus** ('My Night For Love') and a solo release 'Into The Night' which was featured on the *Beat Street* soundtrack album. Through Kashif she placed songs with **Whitney Houston** ('You Give Good Love' and 'Thinking About You') before signing to Arista (both Kashif and Whitney's label) as an artist. In 1987 a debut album *La La*, including 'We'll Keep Striving' (a duet with **Bernard Wright**, was released, but she left the label soon after.

La La has also written for **Carl Anderson** and **Stephanie Mills** in addition to further songs for herself, now that she is with Motown. Her debut Motown album was *La La Means I Love You* (1991).

LABELLE

(Group)

From Philadelphia, **Patti Labelle** and **Cindy Birdsong** originally sang together with The Ordettes. They became The Bluebelles when Patti and Cindy together with **Nona Hendryx** and **Sarah Dash**, who had their own group The Del Capris, signed to Bluebelle Records (from which they took their name) in 1961. The same year they had a million-selling hit in America with 'I Sold My Heart To The Junkman'. The track was also a career break for arranger/producer **Bobby Martin**.

Becoming Patti Labelle & The Bluebelles, releases continued with 'Cold Water', 'Decatur Street' and 'Down The Isle' (1963) before Cindy left to join **The Supremes**. At this point the group became simply Labelle and signed to Warner Brothers. Here they recorded *Labelle* before switching to RCA for 'Moon Shadow' and 'Pressure Cookin'' (inspired by **Gil Scott-Heron**'s poems). Their major hit came on signing to Epic with the platinum *Nightbirds* album and single 'Lady Marmalade (Voulez-Vous Coucher Avec Moi Ce Soir)', a UK Top 20 hit in 1975. Later in the '70s the group disbanded after creating a near-cult following on the rock scene.

LABELLE, PATTI

(Singer)

Born Patricia Holt in West Philadelphia (1944), Patti took to singing while in high school and became a soloist with the Beulah Baptist Church Choir. While a teenager she teamed up with **Cindy Birdsong** in The Ordettes. Their friends **Sarah Dash** and **Nona Hendryx** had a group, The Del Capris, and the two groups came together as The Bluebelles, later to become Patti Labelle And The Bluebelles, then simply **Labelle**.

In 1977 Patti became a solo artist and signed to Epic. She released two albums, *Patti Labelle* (1977) and *Tasty* (1978), before hitting the disco scene during 1979. Producer **Skip Scarborough** helped make 'Music Is My Way Of Life' a dancefloor anthem from *It's Alright With Me* released that year. Her next album *Released* returned to her earlier Labelle sound (with producer **Allen Toussaint**) before she signed to the Philadelphia International label in 1981 for *The Spirit's In It*. After recording further material for the label she decided to leave before it was released. Two further albums were issued in her absence, 1983's *I'm In Love Again* going gold in 1984 and 1985's

Patti including the highly regarded soul ballad 'I Can't Forget You'.

In the meantime Patti toured for two years in a theatre production of *Your Arms Too Short To Box With God*, including a spell with the show on Broadway with **Al Green**. She also sang lead vocals on 'The Best Is Yet To Come', the title track of **Grover Washington Jr's** 1982 album. In 1984 she sang at 'Live Aid' and recorded three duets with **Bobby Womack** on his *Poet II* album (including 'Love Has Finally Come At Last'), prior to signing with MCA. Here an album *Winner In You* (1986) included a UK Top 20 duet 'On My Own' with **Michael McDonald**, and a UK Top 30 follow-up 'Oh, People'.

These days she runs a boutique in Philadelphia. In 1988 she reunited with **Sarah Dash** for a duet 'You're All I Need To Get By', the title track of Sarah's solo album that year.

LACE

(Vocal Group)

From Washington, Lace are Vivian Ross, Lisa Frazier and Kathy Merrick who met at the Duke Ellington School of Arts. Caught live in concert by **Lionel Job** and **Preston Glass** they were signed to Wing Records (via Phonogram), which in 1987 released their debut album *Shades Of Lace*.

LAKESIDE

(Group)

From Dayton, Ohio, Lakeside are Mark Wood (vocals), Tiemeyer McCain (vocals), Thomas Oliver Shelby (vocals), Steve Shockley (lead guitar), Norman Beavers (keyboards), Fred Lewis (percussion/keyboards), Marvin Craig (bass), Fred Alexander (drums), Barrington (lead/backing vocals), and Larry Bolden (lead/backing vocals). Most of the members of the group met at school, and after forming Lakeside moved to Los Angeles. Here they signed to the Solar label in the late '70s and enjoyed a consistent run of American hit r&b singles. In the UK they first made an impact on the dance scene with 'All The Way Live' in 1978. Their album releases include *Shot Of Love*, *Rough Riders*, *Your Wish Is My Command* (1981), *Fantastic Voyage* (1982), *Untouchables* (1983), *Outrageous* (1984), *Keep On Movin' Straight Ahead* and *Party Patrol* (1990).

Unlike other acts on the Solar label, Lakeside have always maintained a distinct Ohio sound to their music, while making a visual impact with different themes on each of their album sleeves. As songwriters they also contributed to **The Whispers**' 'And The Beat Goes On' and **Shalamar**'s 'Second Time Around'.

LANCE, MAJOR

(Singer)

Chicago singer Major Lance recorded for the Okeh label during the '60s, making an impact on the soul scene with songs including 'Um, Um, Um, Um, Um, Um', 'The Monkey Time', 'Hey Little Girl' and 'The Matador'. He later recorded for labels including CBS ('Too Hot To Hold', 1965), Daker, Curtom, Contempo (a live album recorded in the UK at The Torch), Osiris ('You're Everything I Need', 1975), and Kat Family (*The Major's Back*, 1983). He also discovered the group **The Artistics**.

LANDS, LIZ

(Singer)

Born in New York in 1942, Liz developed a five-octave vocal range by the time she was seventeen. Moving to Atlanta she signed to Mercury Records and released *Untamed* (1959), including 'Plain Gold Ring'. She also worked in a bank where Martin Luther King Jr held an account. After they met, Liz began to tour as a performer alongside Dr King's speeches. While in Detroit she was approached by **Berry Gordy**, and following the tragic assassination of Dr King in 1963 Motown recorded Liz's tribute 'May What He Lived For Live', released as a single. The following year **The Temptations** sang backing vocals on her singles 'Keep Me' and 'We Shall Overcome' before she moved to Chicago to record for the One-Der-Ful label.

Here she recorded a number of singles before returning to Atlanta and working with **Hamilton Bohannon**, who produced her version of 'Baby I'm For Real' (1980). Much later, in 1989, **Ian Levine** signed her to his Motorcity label in the UK where 'Starting All Over Again' was her first single.

LANE, JEFF

(Producer)

Jeff Lane worked consistently as a producer on the New York funk scene from the mid- to late '70s. Initially he ran a management company, one of his clients being **Randy Muller**, founder of **Brass Construction**. He produced a number of Randy Muller's projects including the debut Brass Construction album in 1976, a **Mark Radice** album *Ain't Nothin' But A Party* the same year and the **Garnet Mimms** dance anthem 'What It Is' in 1978. He also worked in the capacity of producer with **Mandrill** (including 'Funkey Monkey'), **B.T.Express**, **Spiders Webb**, McGee and former Temptations vocalist **Eddie Kendricks** (*Vintage 78*).

LANIER & CO.

(Group)

Pronounced 'Lan-neer & Co.', this group were formed in Jackson, Tennessee, in 1968 by Farris Lanier Sr with Farris Lanier Jr, Lee Freeman, Fennoye Lanier and Marlon Lanier. Their debut single was 'Hook To The News' for the Way Out label, before switching to MGM Sounds Of Memphis for 'California Dreamin'' (1970), recorded under the name of The Jacksonians. Changing their name, they released a critically acclaimed album *Lanier & Co.* on the Larc label in 1983. With the addition of Arvall Wiley, Marvin Hill, Van Beard and Stephanie

Beard, the group signed to **Willie Mitchell**'s Waylo label and released 'Dancing In The Night' (1986). An album of the same name followed in 1987 and included 'I Don't Know', released by Syncopate in the UK in 1986.

LARKINS, PERCY

(Singer)

Florida-based singer Percy Larkins teamed up with **Betty Wright** in the mid-'80s for a duet 'I Need To See You Again'. It was released on Percy's debut album *Music Of Passion* on Encore Records (via Move in the UK). Percy has since recorded with **Alltrinna Grayson**.

LARSON, NEIL

(Keyboards/Producer)

Neil played keyboards with Philadelphia group **The Soul Survivors** prior to teaming up with Buzz Feiten as the Larsen-Feiten Band. Playing fusion jazz they signed to Warner Brothers in the mid-'70s and released albums including *Larsen-Feiten Band* and *Full Moon*. In 1978 Neil signed as a solo artist to Horizon Records (via A&M) and released *Jungle Fever*. It included 'Sudden Samba' which became a jazz funk classic in the UK. More recently Neil recorded *Smooth Talk* (1989) with featured guests **George Howard**, **Ernie Watts** and **Steve Ferrone**.

Neil has also recorded with **Easy Pieces**, **Brenda Russell**, **Randy Crawford** ('Rainy Night In Georgia') and **Womack & Womack** (*Love Wars*).

LARUE, D.C.

(Songwriter/Instrumentalist)

D.C.LaRue emerged in the mid-'70s with a series of heavily orchestrated, disco-orientated instrumentals with vocal refrains. From these he is best remembered for the 1976 Roulette release (Pye in the UK) 'Ca-The-Drals', although it wasn't a chart success. In 1978 a more vocal-orientated track 'Let Them Dance' was issued from *Confessions* (Pye in the UK again), and his track 'You Can Always Tell A Lady (By The Company She Keeps)' was featured in the movie *Thank God It's Friday*.

LASALLE, DENISE

(Singer)

Born Denise Craig in Greenwood, Mississippi (raised in Belzona, Mississippi), Denise moved to Chicago at the age of thirteen where she took the name Lasalle from the city's Lasalle Avenue. Her debut release was 'A Love Reputation' (1969), produced by Billy Emerson and released on the Parka label prior to a national issue on the Chess label. The following year she signed with Westbound and released a single 'Hung Up, Strung Out', produced by **Willie Mitchell** in Memphis.

In 1971 Willie Mitchell produced a follow-up, Denise's self-penned 'Trapped By A Thing Called Love' which reached gold status having made the No. 1 position in the US r&b charts and selling over a million copies. Further Mitchell productions followed with 'Now Run And Tell That', and 'Man-Sized Job'. Her Westbound albums included *Here I Am Again* (1975) and *Doin' It Right* (1976), including 'Married But Not To Each Other'. Denise moved to ABC for albums including *Second Breath* (1976), *The Bitch Is Bad* and *Under The Influence*, before ABC became MCA for *Unwrapped*, *I'm So Hot* (1980) and *Satisfaction Guaranteed* (1981).

In 1982 she was signed by Malaco after the label were impressed by a song she had written for **Z.Z.Hill**. Here she caused controversy with her 1983 single 'Come To Bed' prior to a 1984 album *Right Place, Right Time*. She also had an American hit with 'Don't Mess With My Tutu'. Her Malaco albums include *Rain And Fire* (1986) and *Still Trapped* (1990).

She now owns her own radio station WFXX in Jackson, Tennessee, with second husband James Wolfe, a DJ on the station. Her first husband was Bill Jones with whom at one point she ran a small record label, Crajon Records.

LASLEY, DAVID

(Singer/Songwriter/Arranger)

Born in Branch, Michigan, David idolized black soul singers and decided that one day he would sing like one, even though he was white! After becoming a self-taught vocalist, his first professional break came when, aged seventeen, he got a part in *Hair* and joined a local group Valentine And Rosie. Moving into the lucrative field of session work, David's reputation found him work with numerous artists including **Donna Summer**, **Aretha Franklin**, **Chaka Khan**, **Sister Sledge** ('We Are Family'), **Chic** ('Everybody Dance'), Boz Scaggs, **Debra Laws**, **Herb Alpert**, **General Johnson** and **Luther Vandross**. He also arranged vocals for **Odyssey** on their classic 'Native New Yorker'.

In 1984 he signed to the EMI America label for the Don Was-produced solo album *Raindance*, including 'Saved By Love', while through the course of the '80s he established his songwriting skills writing/co-writing for artists including **Chaka Khan** ('Roll Me Through The Rushes'), **Debra Laws** ('Meant For You' and 'All The Things I Love'), **Angela Bofill** ('Tell Me Tomorrow'), **Janice McClain** ('Last Goodbye'), **Patti Labelle** ('Come What May' and 'I See Home'), **Jennifer Holliday** ('I Am Ready Now'), **Aretha Franklin** ('There's A Star For Everyone'), and perhaps most successfully **Anita Baker** ('You Bring Me Joy', earlier recorded by **Norman Connors** for whom he also wrote 'Justify').

In 1990 a second solo album *It's Too Late* was released by the Japanese Agenda label and included his own version of 'You Bring Me Joy'.

LASO

(Sax)

New York-based sax man Laso made an impression on the UK dance scene in 1977 with *Laso* for MCA. It included a disco instrumental version of the **Stevie Wonder** song 'Another Star', produced by **Joe Bataan**.

LATIMORE

(Singer/Songwriter)

Born in Charleston, Tennessee, in 1939, Benny Latimore worked as a music arranger during the '60s before landing himself a recording deal with Glades Records (via TK) in the early '70s. Here he recorded *Latimore* (1971), *More More More Latimore* (1972), *Latimore III* (1973), *Let's Straighten It Out* (1974) and *Dig A Little Deeper* (1975), all the while developing a following in the southern states of America and among soul fans in the UK. Switching to Malaco Records where he remains to this day, his albums have included *It Ain't Where You Been* (1976), *Getting Down To Brass Tacks* (1980), *Good Time Man* (1985), *Every Way But Wrong* (1986) and *Slow Down* (1986), including 'One Man, One Woman, One Love.'

LATTISAW, STACY

(Singer)

Born in Washington in 1967, Stacy's mother went to the same school as **Marvin Gaye** where they sang together as children. Stacy became a professional singer at the age of eleven after her success at local talent shows. In 1979 she was signed to the Cotillion label (via Atlantic) after she impressed them with a demo tape. She was put to work with **Van McCoy** who produced her debut album *Young And In Love*.

Her first taste of success came in 1980 after working with producer **Narada Michael Walden** on her follow-up album *Let Me Be Your Angel* (1980), including 'Jump To The Beat' (UK Top 5) and 'Dynamite' (UK Top 75). In 1981 she supported **The Jacksons** on a national tour, for which **La La** played keyboards in her band. A further album *With You* was followed by a duet album *Perfect Combination* with **Johnny Gill** (1984) before she switched labels to Motown.

Here her albums have been *Take Me All The Way* (1986), including 'Nail It To The Wall', *Personal Attention* (1988), including 'Call Me', and *What You Need* (1989), including the duet with Johnny Gill 'Where Do We Go From Here'.

LAURENCE, LYNDA

(Singer)

Based in Los Angeles, Lynda worked as a background singer at Motown with **Stevie Wonder** in his group Wonderlove during the early '70s before replacing **Cindy Birdsong** in **The Supremes**. Lynda continues in The Supremes to this day, and also records as a solo artist for the Motorcity label in the UK.

LAURENCE, PAUL

(Singer/Songwriter/Producer)

Born in New York in 1962, Paul sang in the White Rock Baptist Church where he first met **Freddie Jackson** during the '70s. They were both to work together professionally in the '80s when Paul wrote and produced Freddie's debut hit 'Rock Me Tonight'.

In the early '80s, Paul joined forces with **Kashif** and **Morrie Brown** to form the writing/production team Mighty M and working with artists including **Howard Johnson** and **Melba Moore** ('Love's Comin' At Ya', 'Love Me Right', 'Got To Have Your Love' and 'Knack For Me'), while outside of Mighty M he has worked with **Michael Henderson** (*Fickle*), **Janice Dempsey** (*Thirsty*), **Lillo Thomas** ('Sexy Girl'), **Stephanie Mills** ('You're Puttin' A Rush On Me'), **Meli'sa Morgan** ('Do Me Baby') and **Smokey Robinson** ('Love Is The Light').

In 1985 he signed to Capitol as an artist where his albums have been *Haven't You Heard* (1985), including 'Strung Out', and *Underexposed* (1989).

LAVETTE, BETTYE

(Singer)

Born in Muskegan, Detroit, in 1946, Bettye was signed by Atlantic Records in 1962 and scored an immediate American hit with 'My Man, He's A Lovin' Man'. The song was originally intended for another singer who struggled with the words in the studio. Bettye, in the right place at the right time, stepped in and took her place. After a follow-up single 'You'll Never Change' she switched to the Detroit-based Lupine label for 'Witchcraft In The Air' before the label went out of business. Bettye continued to record for a number of other smaller labels. For Calla in 1965 she recorded 'Let Me Down Easy' (regarded as a soul classic and reissued on the Mojo label in the early '70s), 'I Feel Good All Over' (1965) and 'Only Your Love Can Save Me' (1965). After a brief spell with Big Wheel Records for 'I'm Holding On' (1966), she moved to the Karen label for 'What Condition My Condition Was In' (1968), 'A Little Help From My Friends' (1969) and 'Ticket To The Moon' (1969). At SSS International in 1969 she recorded a number of singles before one single for the TCA label, 'Never My Love' (1971), and then returned to the Atlantic family (Atco) directly after. Here she recorded such American r&b hits as 'Heart Of Gold' (1971) and 'Your Turn To Cry' for the Atco subsidiary. An album *Child Of The 70s* was recorded but, not released.

In 1975 she appeared on Epic for 'Thank You For Loving Me' and 'Behind Closed Doors' before joining the New York-based West End label and scoring a huge dance hit with 'Doing The Best That I Can', nearly charting in the UK during early 1979. In 1981 she joined Motown for a Steve Buckingham-produced album *Tell A Lie*, including the **Sam Dees**-penned 'Right In The Middle (Of Falling In Love)', and single release 'I Can't Stop' (promo'd in the UK back-to-back with **Bobby Womack**'s 'So Many Sides Of You' and High Inergy's 'First Impressions'.

She has also recorded for Street King Records ('Trance Dance'), and in the early '90s Motorcity ('Surrender').

LAWS, DEBRA

(Singer)

Born in Houston, Texas, Debra is sister to **Eloise Laws**, **Ronnie Laws** and **Hubert Laws**. In 1981 she signed to Elektra for *Very Special*, including 'On My Own', produced by brothers Ronnie and Hubert. She was also the lead vocalist on 'Family' (title track of an album for Hubert), and sang backing vocals with sister Eloise for **Aquarian Dream** on their classic 'You're A Star'.

LAWS, ELOISE

(Singer)

Born in Houston, Texas, in 1949, Eloise is sister to **Debra Laws**, **Ronnie Laws** and **Hubert Laws**. In 1969 she signed briefly to CBS but first made an impression on the soul scene after moving to Los Angeles in the early '70s. Here she worked with **Holland/Dozier/Holland** and their artists including **The Fifth Dimension** before Brian Holland produced her album *Ain't It Good Feeling Good* for the Invictus label in 1977. Also in 1977 she teamed up with **Jerry Goldstein** and his Far Out production company to record *Eloise*, including 'Baby You Lied,' 'Love Comes Easy' and 'Forever Now', for ABC Records, co-produced by **Linda Creed**. Linda produced her next album *Eloise Laws* (1980), including 'Let's Find Those Two People Again', for Liberty Records.

In 1982 **Ronnie Laws** produced her Capitol album *All In Time*, including 'Love Ain't Easy', while Eloise also worked with sister Debra as backing singers on the **Aquarian Dream** classic 'You're A Star'.

LAWS, HUBERT

(Flute)

Born in Houston, Texas, in 1939, Hubert is the brother of **Debra Laws**, **Eloise Laws** and **Ronnie Laws**. He originally studied piano, but his high-school band required a flute player so Hubert learned this instrument instead. His professional engagements began in 1954 after he joined a local jazz group. In the six years he played with them, they changed their name from The Nite Hawks to The Swingsters and then The Modern Jazz Sextet before becoming The Jazz Crusaders in 1960. Upon his departure the group became **The Crusaders**.

Hubert also studied classical flute and played as a soloist with the Houston Youth Symphony Orchestra before he moved to Los Angeles in 1958 and found work with artists including Mongo Santamaria, Lena Horne, Arthur Prysock and **Sergio Mendes**.

As a solo recording artist he spent a brief period with Blue Note Records before recording three albums for the CTI label, *The Chicago Theme* (1975), *Afro Classic* (1976), and *The San Francisco Concerts* (1977). The latter album was released just after he had signed to CBS Records where his first album was *Romeo And Juliet* (1976).

Appealing to UK jazz funk fans, his later albums include *California Suite* (a soundtrack album with composer/pianist Claude Bollins, 1978); *Say It With Silence* (1978); *Land Of Passion* (1979), including 'We're In Ecstasy'; *Family* (1980), featuring his sister **Debra Laws** on the title track; *How To Beat The High Cost Of Living* (a soundtrack album with **Earl Klugh**, 1980); and *Make It Last* (1983).

His wife is the sister of Cheryl Cooley of the group **Klymaxx**, and Hubert at one time gave Cheryl guitar lessons! Hubert has also recorded with artists including **Roberta Flack** (*Chapter Two*), **Norman Connors** (*Slew-foot*), **Alphonse Mouzon** (*Morning Sun*), **Bob James** (*Touchdown*), **Sarah Vaughan** (*Brazilian Romance*), **Patrice Rushen** (*Before The Dawn*), and **Charles Earland**.

LAWS, RONNIE

(Vocals/Saxophone/Songwriter/Producer)

Born in Houston, Texas, in 1950, Ronnie formed his own group The Lightmen while still at high school. After his college days he moved to Los Angeles where in 1970 he became the sax player with **Earth Wind & Fire**. His playing is featured on their album *Last Days In Time*. He also recorded with Doug and **Jean Carne** and Hugh Masekela during this time. In 1976 he launched a solo career with Blue Note Records and producer **Wayne Henderson**, making immediate impact on the UK jazz funk scene with his debut album *Pressure Sensitive*, including the classic instrumental 'Always There' (later recorded by numerous other artists including **Willie Bobo**, **Side Effect**, **Jeff Lorber**, **Wood Brass & Steel**, **Incognito** and the James Taylor Quartet).

For the United Artists label, he consolidated his popularity with *Fever* (1976), *Friends & Strangers* (1977), *Flame* (1978) and *Every Generation* (1980), slowly but surely introducing more of his own vocals on his songs. Vocals were predominant on his next two albums, *Solid Ground* (Liberty Records, 1981) including 'Stay Awake', and *Mr Nice Guy* (Capitol Records, 1982). A final Capitol album *Classic Masters* (1984) was a compilation featuring two new vocal songs, 'City Girl' and '(You Are) Paradise'. Switching to CBS, he continued to pursue his vocal career on *Mirror Town* (1986) and *All Day Rhythm* (1987) before switching to the independent ATA label and resuming his instrumental sax style on CD-only albums *True Spirit* (1990) and *Identity* (1990).

Ronnie has also recorded with **Alphonse Mouzon** (*The Sky Is The Limit*), **Ramsey Lewis** (*Tequila Mockingbird*), **Arthur Adams** (*Home Brew*), **Howard Hewett** ('This Time'), **Jeff Lorber**, **Sister Sledge** ('Once In Your Life'), **David Sea** and numerous others.

His brother is **Hubert Laws** while his sisters are **Eloise Laws** (for whom he wrote and produced) and **Debra Laws** (for whom he co-produced *Very Special*, writing the leading song 'On My Own').

LAWSON, RICKY
(Drummer/Songwriter)
Born in Los Angeles, Ricky has established himself as a top session drummer on the r&b music scene, and has recorded with artists including **Michael Jackson**, **Whitney Houston**, **Lionel Richie**, **Anita Baker**, **George Duke**, **The Emotions**, **Sister Sledge**, **Roy Ayers** (as part of Ubiquity) and **Helen Baylor** (co-writing 'There's No Greater Love'). He was also music director on Michael Jackson's 'Bad' tour.

LEE, LAURA
(Singer)
From Detroit, Laura recorded one single 'To Win Your Heart' for Ric Tic in 1966 before the label was bought out by Motown. Between 1967 and 1969 she recorded for Chess, many of the tracks recorded during this period only recently issued on a Chess album *That's How It Is*. When Motown's songwriters **Holland/Dozier/Holland** left Motown, they signed Laura to their Hot Wax label, projecting her as a major star. Recordings here included 'Woman's Love Rights', inspired by her work as a campaigner for black women's rights in the USA.

LEE, MARVA
(Singer)
Chicago singer Marva Lee recorded for the Atco subsidiary of Atlantic in the early '70s. Her singles include the highly collectable 'If You Can't Be True', written by **Curtis Mayfield**.

LEE, TONEY
(Singer)
Based in New York, Tony stirred dancefloors from the early to mid-'80s with songs including 'Reach Up' (Radar Records, 1982) and 'Night Lights' (Critique Records, 1985).

LEFTURNO
(Group)
Lefturno were Robin Leslie (singer/model) and Manny Dopazo (a disc jockey) from New York. The group released one single through MCA, 'Out Of Sight' (1985), which was loosely based on **War**'s song 'Galaxy'.

LEGACY
(Group)
Los Angeles-based group Legacy are Vaneta Thomas, Curtis Thompson, Richard Dixon, Marcus Williams and Larry Bolden, who met at high school and have worked together ever since. One night they met Jody Sims, the drummer with **Switch**, and impressed him with their song 'Spend My Life', which Switch later recorded. In 1984 they released their debut single 'The Groove' on the Air Wave label, following which they signed to Private I (via CBS) where they released one further single, 'Don't Waste The Night' (1985).

LEO'S SUNSHIP
(Group)
Leo's Sunship were Johnny Simone, Kenny Stover and Alvin Few, all born under the Leo star sign. In 1978 the trio recorded a self-written/produced album *We Need Each Other* for the Atlanta-based label Lyon's Record Co., Inc. The album featured numerous guest musicians and background vocals by **Susaye Greene**. To this day the album remains popular and collectable on the UK soul scene for two tracks 'Give Me The Sunshine' and 'I'm Back For More'. Both tracks were first issued back-to-back on a 12″ in the UK on the Grapevine label (via RCA) in 1980, reissued on Expansion in 1986. 'I'm Back For More' was also recorded as an **Al Johnson/Jean Carne** duet on Al's 1980 CBS album *Back For More*.

LESTER/BROWN
(Songwriters/Producers)
From Washington, Willie Lester and Rodney Brown (guitar) first emerged on the dance scene in 1980. As songwriters/producers at the Prelude label they delivered a series of albums including successful dance singles for **Bobby Thurston** ('You Got What It Takes' and 'Check Out The Groove'), **Sharon Redd** ('Can You Handle It') and **Gayle Adams** ('Stretchin' Out'). After the demise of Prelude they formed their own Mainline Records label where they continued to work with **Gayle Adams** ('I'm Warning You', 1984), **Bobby Thurston** and other artists including Marie Malloy ('I Surrender') and **Khemistry**. Elsewhere their songs have been recorded by artists including **Esther Williams** ('I'll Be Your Pleasure') and **Al Johnson**.

LESTER, SONNY
(Producer)
Sonny established himself in the early '70s as a producer with artists popular on the UK jazz funk scene including **Jimmy McGriff** (*Black Pearl*, 1971), **O'Donel Levy** (*Simba*, 1973, and *Time Has Changed*, 1977). Towards the end of the '70s he launched his own Lester Radio Corporation label via Miami-based TK Records and has produced artists including **Jimmy Ponder** and the **B.Baker Chocolate Company**.

LEVERT
(Group)
From Ohio, Levert are brothers Gerald and Sean Levert (sons of **Eddie Levert** of **The O'Jays**), together with Marc Gordon. Initially they were turned down by numerous record labels (including Philadelphia International) for sounding too much like The O'Jays, but they eventually made their recording debut in 1985 on the independent label Tempre in Philadelphia. Here they released the single 'I'm Still/I Want Too', closely followed by an album *I Get Hot*.

From here they switched to Atlantic where in 1986 they scored an American No. 1 r&b single '(Pop Pop Pop

Pop) Goes My Mind' from *Bloodline*. They have enjoyed continued success across America with *The Big Throwdown* (1987), including their one UK Top 10 hit 'Casanova', penned/produced by **Calloway**, *Just Coolin'* (1988), and *Rope A Dope Style* (1990), including 'Absolutely Positive' and 'All Season'.

As producers, Levert have worked with artists including **James Ingram** ('I Wanna Come Back'), **Eugene Wilde** ('Who's That Girl' and 'Ain't Nobody's Business'), **Miki Howard** (Gerald duetting on 'That's What Love Is'), **Millie Jackson** ('Something You Can Feel' and 'In My Dreams') and **Stephanie Mills** ('Good Girl Gone Bad').

LEVINE, IAN

(Songwriter/Producer)

Born in Blackpool, Ian worked as a disc jockey on the 'Northern soul' scene in the early '70s before turning songwriter/producer in 1975. He scored success with artists including **The Exciters** ('Reaching For The Best', UK Top 40, 1975), **Evelyn Thomas** ('Weak Spot', UK Top 30, 1976, and 'Doomsday', UK Top 50, 1976), and L.J.Johnson ('Your Magic Put A Spell On Me', UK Top 30, 1976).

In the mid-'80s he was a pioneering producer on the 'high energy' scene with songs/productions (with Fiachra Trench) for artists including Miquel Brown ('He's A Saint, He's A Sinner', UK Top 75, 1984, and 'Close To Perfection', UK Top 75, 1985), **Evelyn Thomas** ('High Energy', UK Top 5, 1984 and 'Masquerade', UK Top 75, 1984), Seventh Avenue ('Love's Gone Mad'), Barbara Pennington ('All American Boy' and 'On A Crowded Street') and Eastbound Expressway ('You're A Beat').

In 1986 Ian launched his own Nightmare label, but after the demise of the 'high energy' scene he changed the name to Motorcity and switched musical direction in an attempt to recapture the magic of '60s Motown. He began writing and/or producing numerous former Motown artists including **The Supremes**, **Martha Reeves**, **Syreeta**, **Mary Johnson**, **Kim Weston**, **Chuck Jackson** ('All Over The World'), **Johnny Bristol** ('Man Up In The Sky'), **G.C.Cameron**, **The Marvelettes**, **The Velvelettes**, **The Elgins**, **Billy Griffin**, **Edwin Starr** and many more. From the lesser-known names among the hundred-plus artists recorded, 'Footsteps Following Me' was a UK Top 20 hit for **Frances Nero** in 1991.

LEVY, O'DONEL

(Guitar)

Guitarist O'Donel Levy ventured into fusion jazz in the mid-'70s with albums including *Simba* (1973, for the Groove Merchant label), and in particular the **Sonny Lester**-produced *Time Has Changed* (1977, for TK) which included 'Sophisticated Disco' (featuring the vocals of Aleta Greene). O'Donel can also be found on albums by **Jimmy McGriff** and more recently **Norman Connors** (*Passion*) among others.

LEWIS, BARBARA

(Singer)

Born in Detroit, Barbara recorded for Atlantic in the early '60s and is perhaps best remembered for 'Hello Stranger' (1963, featuring **The Dells** on background vocals). Other fine moments include 'Someday We're Gonna Love Again' (1963), 'Baby I'm Yours' (1964), the Lou Courtney-coproduced 'Thankful For What You Got', and 'I Remember The Feeling' (1966). After leaving Atlantic she recorded *You Made Me A Woman* for the Enterprise label.

LEWIS, DEE

(Singer)

Based in London, Dee is the sister of **Linda Lewis** and **Shirley Lewis**. In addition to her work with family group The Lewis Sisters, Dee signed to Phonogram in 1987 where she enjoyed some dancefloor success with 'Stuck On Love'.

LEWIS, LINDA

(Singer/Songwriter)

Born in London, Linda initially established herself as a child actress and appeared in films including *A Taste Of Honey* and The Beatles' *Hard Day's Night*. As a singer, she signed to Bell Records in the early '70s where her debut album was *Say No More* (1971). *Lark* (1972) and *Fathoms Deep* (1974) followed, and in 1973 she scored her first hit single with 'Rock-A-Doodle-Doo' (UK Top 20).

In 1975 she switched to Arista for her most significant album *Not A Little Girl Anymore* (1975), including 'It's In His Kiss' (UK Top 10) and 'This Time I'll Be Sweeter'. *Woman Overboard* (1976), including 'Baby I'm Yours' (UK Top 40), followed before Linda switched to Ariola for 'Can't We Just Sit Down And Talk It Over' (1978) and 'I'd Be Surprisingly Good For You' (UK Top 40, 1979).

Linda's sisters are **Dee Lewis** and **Shirley Lewis**.

LEWIS, PAT

(Singer)

Born in Detroit, Pat was originally a member of **The Adorables** before becoming the fourth member of **The Andantes**, a group which recorded background vocals for over 20,000 songs at Motown Records! As a solo artist her debut single was 'Can't Shake It Loose' – later recorded by **The Supremes** (1965) for the Golden World label – following which she made a series of recordings for the Solid Hit label which became classics on the UK's 'Northern soul' scene. These included 'Look At What I Almost Missed', 'Warning', 'The Loser' and 'No One To Love'.

In 1970 she switched to Stax Records and sang with her sister Dianne in **Hot Buttered Soul**. The group was put together by **Isaac Hayes** and sang on all his hits (including 'Shaft').

In the late '70s Pat rejoined **The Andantes** to sing backgrounds which she continues to do for artists including **Aretha Franklin** and **Anita Baker**. As a solo artist she has recorded for the Motorcity label where her singles have been 'No Right Turn' and 'Separation' (both 1991).

LEWIS, RAMSEY
(Keyboards)
Born in Chicago, Ramsey was playing piano with an ensemble The Clefs by the time he was fifteen. In 1956 the group signed to the Argo label (via Chess) as The Ramsey Lewis Trio. It consisted of Ramsey (keyboards), Eldee Young (bass) and Red Holt (drums). Between 1956 and 1965 they made eighteen albums, during which time Ramsey co-wrote and recorded 'Wade In The Water' with **Marlena Shaw**. In 1965 the trio decided to cover the **Dobie Gray** song 'The In Crowd', originally planning it as an album filler. When released as a single in the USA it reached the Top 5 and went gold. Later that year the original trio broke up, Eldee Young and Red Holt moving on to form **Young-Holt Unlimited**. Ramsey's replacements were **Maurice White** (drums) and **Cleveland Eaton** (bass). Maurice remained with the trio until launching **Earth Wind & Fire** in 1970.

In 1972 Ramsey released his Chess classic 'Wade In The Water' (UK Top 40), then in 1974 Maurice White returned in the capacity of producer on Ramsey's solo album *Sun Goddess*, by which time both Earth Wind & Fire and Ramsey were signed to CBS. Maintaining a mix of jazz, jazz funk and r&b through to the present day, Ramsey's CBS albums have included *Love Notes*, part-written with **Stevie Wonder** (1977); *Tequila Mockingbird*, featuring **Ronnie Laws** (1977); *Legacy*, with a classical edge recorded with a symphony orchestra (1978); *Ramsey*, part-produced by **Wayne Henderson** (1979); *Routes*, featuring **Keni Burke** (1980); *Three Piece Suite* (1981); *Live At The Savoy*, featuring **Phil Upchurch**, Dean Gant and **Grover Washington** (1982); *Ramsey And Nancy*, a duet album with **Nancy Wilson** produced by **Stanley Clarke** (1984); *Fantasy* (1985); and *Keys To The City*, on which Maurice White returned on percussion (1987).

LEWIS, SHIRLEY
(Singer)
London-based singer Shirley Lewis is the sister of **Dee Lewis** and **Linda Lewis**, and gained her first professional experience singing backgrounds for Linda on a *Top Of The Pops* performance of 'It's In His Kiss'. She later recorded as a solo artist for CBS, EMI and A&M (where her first album *Passion In The Heart* was released in 1989). She attracted media publicity after becoming the girlfriend of Luke Goss of the group Bros.

LEWIS, TERRY
(Songwriter/Producer)
Born in Minneapolis, Terry played in a nameless group with **Jellybean** Johnson (drums) and David Eiland (sax) in his school days during the early '70s. Also at school he met **Jimmy 'Jam' Harris** whom he persuaded to join them as organist. Jimmy later left the group, leaving Terry to expand the band into an eleven-member outfit which he renamed **Flytetime**. He later became one half of the songwriting/production team **Jam/Lewis**, scoring numerous major hits during the mid-late '80s.

LEWIS, WEBSTER
(Songwriter/Producer/Keyboards)
Born in Baltimore, Webster settled in Los Angeles during the mid-'70s where he signed to Epic Records and began to make an impact on the UK jazz funk scene. His albums were *On The Town* (1976); *Touch My Love* (1978), including 'Barbara Ann'; *8 For The 80s* (1979), including 'Give Me Some Emotion' co-produced by **Herbie Hancock**; and *Let Me Be The One* (1981), including 'El Bobo'.

His most recent album was with **Barry White** and **The Love Unlimited Orchestra** for which he co-wrote/produced 'Lift Your Voice And Say (United We Can Live In Peace Today)' (1981). He has worked with **Michael Wycoff** ('Come Into My World', and producing *Love Conquers All*, 1982, and *On The Line*, 1983), and **Gwen McCrae** (producing *On My Way*, including 'Keep The Fire Burning', 1982). He also wrote two movie soundtracks (*The Hearse* and *The Sky Is Grey*). Recently he has left the record business to concentrate on a very successful career in the field of TV commercials.

LIGHT OF THE WORLD
(Group)
Formed in London in 1978, Light Of The World were a pioneering Brit funk band, their original line-up being Canute 'Kenny' Wellington (trumpet), David 'Baps' Baptiste (trumpet), Jean Paul 'Bluey' Maunick (guitar), Everton McCalla (drums), Neville 'Breeze' McKreith (guitar), Chris Etienne (percussion), Paul 'Tubbs' Williams (bass) and Peter Hinds (keyboards). In 1979 they signed with Ensign Records, and under the direction of disc jockey/label boss Chris Hill stirred UK dancefloors with their debut single 'Swingin'' (UK Top 50). After their follow-up 'Midnight Groovin'' (UK Top 75) and an album *Light Of The World*, Chris Etienne was killed in an accident when the group went on tour.

New members **Nat Augustin** and **Gee Bello** were added to the line-up (Nigel Martinez also becoming the new drummer), and the group set to work with American producer **Augie Johnson** for *Round Trip* (1979), including 'London Town' (UK Top 50, 1980), 'I Shot The Sheriff' (UK Top 40, 1981), 'I'm So Happy' (UK Top 40, 1981), 'Ride The Love Train' (UK Top 50, 1981), 'The Boys In Blue', 'This Is This', 'Time' and 'Pete's Crusade'. In 1981 the group disbanded. Kenny, Baps and Breeze became **Beggar & Co.**, although Nat, Gee and Tubbs teamed together for a reunion album *Famous Faces* for EMI in 1982. In the meantime Bluey, Tubbs and Peter Hinds formed **Incognito**.

In 1985 'London Town' was remixed and reissued by

Ensign, while in 1990 the group reformed and signed to Chrysalis for a single 'One Destination'. In between times, Pete Hinds became a prominent musician/producer on the UK r&b scene, recently co-producing 'Heaven' with **The Chimes**.

LIL LOUIS

(DJ/Keyboards/Producer/Artist)

From Chicago, Lil Louis is the son of **Bobby Sims**, and first established himself as a DJ by the age of thirteen. After learning the basics of synthesizers he met **Marshall Jefferson** with whom he co-produced a track '7 Ways To Jack' for an artist Hercules. Soon he was releasing his own singles on the US Dance Mania label. These included 'Jupiter', 'Frequency' and 'Wargames'. In 1989 he created 'French Kiss' which scored him crossover success and an album deal (Epic in the States, FFRR in the UK/Europe). His father played guitar on the album *From The Mind Of Lil Louis* which also included 'I Called You'.

THE LIMIT

(Duo)

From Holland, The Limit are Bernard Oattes and Rob Van Schaik who originally met in the mid-'70s as members of the group Steam. They released their debut single 'Desire' in 1981 as Future World Orchestra prior to their club hit 'She's So Divine' for Ariola Records in 1982 (which featured the popular B-side 'Pop'). The group moved temporarily to New York to sign with Arista but returned to Holland after an album deal fell through. On a later visit to New York they signed to Portrait Records for 'Say Yeah' which featured **David Sanborn** on sax and some guest vocals by **Gwen Guthrie**. The single became the group's only UK hit when it reached the Top 20 in 1985 from the album *The Limit*.

LIMMIE & THE FAMILY COOKING

(Group)

From Canton, Ohio, Limmie & The Family Cooking were Limmie Snell, Jimmy Thomas and Martha Stewart. Signing to Atco Records in the early '70s they scored UK hits with 'You Can Do Magic' (Top 5, 1973), 'Dreamboat' (Top 40, 1973) and 'A Walkin' Miracle' (Top 10, 1974). Limmie had previously recorded as a solo artist for labels including CBS, Mercury and Warner Brothers.

LINX

(Duo)

London Brit funk duo Linx were **David Grant** and Sketch (bass) who met in a hi-fi store where Sketch worked. Collaborating on some songs, 'You're Lying' was pressed up on their own Aves label and enthusiastically promoted to disc jockeys by the City Sounds record shop in High Holborn. On the back of this, Chrysalis signed both the group and the record in 1980, 'You're Lying' becoming a UK Top 20 single. Later in the year they released *Intuition*, while in 1981 they scored with the single 'Intuition' (UK Top 10), followed by 'Throw Away The Key' (UK Top 25), 'So This Is Romance' (UK Top 20) and 'Can't Help Myself' (UK Top 75), leading to a second album *Go Ahead*. 'Plaything' (1982) was their last UK Top 50 hit before David Grant began a solo career.

LIPPS INC.

(Group)

Lipps Inc. was the concept of Steven Greenberg from St Paul, Minnesota. Moving to Los Angeles, he formed a duo Atlas & Greenberg before moving into the disco field and forming Lipps Inc. with vocalist Cynthia Johnson (formerly with **Flytetime**). Signing to Casablanca Records, their debut single was 'Rock It' prior to their disco hit 'Funkytown' (UK Top 5) and albums *Mouth To Mouth* and *Pucker Up*, both in 1980.

LIPUMA, TOMMY

(Producer)

Through the '70s and '80s, Tommy has established himself as one of the leading producers of soul and r&b-based jazz with numerous artists (particularly for Warner Brothers) including **Seawind** (*Light The Light*), **George Benson** (including *Breezin'* and *In Flight*), **Randy Crawford** (*Secret Combination*), **Brenda Russell** (*Two Eyes*, including 'Hello People'), Barbra Streisand, **Al Jarreau**, **Peabo Bryson**, **Earl Klugh**, **Miles Davis**, **Joe Sample** and **Jennifer Holliday**.

Prior to joining Warner Brothers as a staff producer (where he was particularly instrumental in shaping a successful career for **George Benson**), he ran his own r&b/jazz label Horizon Records (via A&M), where artists included **Seawind, Neil Larsen** and **Jimmy Owens**.

LIQUID HEAT

(Group)

Liquid Heat are Linda Holland from Detroit and Leslie Cole from Ontario who met when they both moved to Los Angeles. In 1984 they became a songwriting team before forming a recording group.

LITTLE ANTHONY AND THE IMPERIALS

(Vocal Group)

From Brooklyn, New York, Anthony Gourdine originally sang lead with The Duponts before forming his own group The Chesters. In 1958 the group signed to the End label, changing their name to The Imperials and consisting of Anthony with Clarence Collins, Tracy Lord, Ernest Wright and Nat Rogers. The group scored an American Top 10 hit in the late '50s with their debut release 'Tears On My Pillow', but the original line-up broke up in 1960.

In 1964 Anthony re-formed the group with Clarence Collins and Sammy Strain. They signed to the DCP label and scored a series of American hits including 'I'm On The Outside Looking In', 'Going Out Of My Head' and

'Hurt So Bad'. From here they signed to United Artists where *Out Of Sight Out Of Mind* (1966) included 'You Take My Heart' (UK Top 40). After further releases for the Janus and Avco labels, Anthony left the group. Without him they scored a UK Top 20 hit with 'Who's Gonna Love Me' (1977) for the Power Exchange label. More recently Anthony sang backgrounds on **Nancy Wilson**'s *A Lady With A Song* (1989).

LITTLE BENNY AND THE MASTERS
(Group)
Formed by Little Benny in the mid-'80s, this Washington DC-based go-go group featured trumpeter/lead vocalist Little Benny (formerly with **Rare Essence**); Rick Wellman (drums); Rick Holmes (bass); Tommy Crosby (guitar); Lowell Tucker and Mark Lawson (keyboards); Tyrone Williams (percussion); Steve Colman, Vernon McDonald and Reggie Thomas (horns); and Diane Borg and Kim Anderson (backing vocals). Their debut single was 'Who Comes To Boogie' released by Bluebird (via Virgin) in 1985.

LITTLE MILTON
(Singer/Bass/Guitar)
Born Milton Campbell in Inverness, Mississippi, in 1934, little Milton began recording for the Sun and Meteor labels in Memphis from the early '50s. From here he moved to St Louis where he worked with Oliver Sain before settling in Chicago (where he is now based). He recorded briefly for the Bobbin label before signing with Checker (via Chess) in 1962. Here some of his most memorable soul and blues moments include 'Blind Man', 'Grits Ain't Groceries', 'We're Gonna Make It', 'Who's Cheating Who' and 'Sacrifice' (1964). Drummer on most of these sessions was **Maurice White**.

In 1971 Milton left the Chess stable to sign with Stax where his success continued with songs including 'Behind Closed Doors', 'Let Me Back In' and an album *Blues 'n' Soul*. Back in Chicago he formed his own Camil production company for whom he recorded *Me For You* and *Friend Of Mine*, later issued by the Glades label (via TK). More recently he has recorded for the Malaco label.

LITTLE SISTER
(Group)
Little Sister were a vocal group fronted by **Rose Banks**. Their recordings include the **Sly Stone**-produced 'Somebody's Watching You' for Atlantic in the early '70s. Rose was Sly's little sister!

LIVE BAND
(Group)
From New York, Live Band were Norvell Holmes (drums/vocals), Tony Gambrell (lead vocals), Paul Chevalier (guitar/vocals), Lorita Perry (lead vocals), Michael Dogan (bass), Keni Chavis (lead vocals) and Dobie Malone (lead guitar). In 1982 they attracted attention with an album *A Chance For Hope*, as the title track was in a similar vein to 'Joy and Pain' by **Maze**. It was released on the TSOB (The Sound of Brooklyn) label.

LIVING PROOF
(Group)
This Detroit group recorded the **Ivy Jo Hunter** co-written song 'Hold On To Your Dreams' in 1986 for the Marquee label.

LOCKSMITH
(Group)
Locksmith were **John Blake** (violin), Tyrone Brown (bass/vocals), Leonard 'Doc' Gibbs (percussion/vocals), James 'Sid' Simmons (keyboards), **Richard 'Lee' Steacker** (guitars/vocals) and Millard 'Pete' Vinson (drums/vocals). Individually they worked with **Bob James**, **Donny Hathaway**, **Freddie Hubbard**, **Jerry Butler**, **George Benson**, **Hank Crawford**, **Norman Connors**, **Kool & The Gang** and many more. Collectively they became the regular band for **Grover Washington**, writing and playing on Grover's albums *Reed Seed*, *Paradise* and *Live At The Bijou*.

After leaving Grover they recorded an album, *Unlock The Funk* (1980), produced by **Harvey Mason** and released by Arista. The title track became a UK Top 50 hit single, although it was the instrumental 'Blackjack' which sold the album to UK jazz funk fans.

LONG, SHORTY
(Singer/Songwriter)
Born in Alabama in 1940, Shorty signed with the Motown label in 1964. His debut release was 'Devil With A Blue Dress'. This was followed by 'Function At The Junction' and in 1968 'Here Comes The Judge', the title of his subsequent first album. The follow-up, *The Prime Of Shorty Long*, included a cover version of 'Whiter Shade Of Pale'. He died in a boating accident in 1969.

LONGMIRE, WILBERT
(Guitar)
Wilbert Longmire landed his initial recording contract through a friendship with fellow guitarist **George Benson**. George introduced him to **Bob James** who was looking for artists to record on his Tappan Zee label (via CBS). Upon signing to the label Wilbert teamed up with top session musicians including **Eric Gale**, **David Sanborn**, **Richard Tee** and **Harvey Mason** for a 1978 debut album *Sunny Side Up* featuring the UK jazz funk anthem and single release 'Black Is The Color'. A follow-up album *Champagne* was released in 1979, but it wasn't until 1980's *With All My Love* that he found favour in the UK again with another jazz fusion instrumental 'Hawkeye'.

LOOSE ENDS

(Group)

Loose Ends were originally Jane Eugene, Steve Nichol and Carl McIntosh, who first formed the group in London as Loose End in 1982. Steve met Jane at the Guildhall School of Music and Drama, and were later joined by Carl who was a top session bass player. Steve had also worked as a keyboard and trumpet player, lending both these services to The Jam on their album *The Gift*.

After taking demos round the record companies they were signed by Virgin (the first all black British group on the label). Their debut single 'In The Sky' (1981) was written by Chris and Eddie Amoo of **The Real Thing**. The follow-up 'We've Arrived' was written and produced by George Hargreaves (who wrote 'So Macho' for **Sinitta**). Changing their name to Loose Ends they released 'Don't Hold Back Your Love' (1983), written by the group themselves, before they involved the services of Philadelphia producer **Nick Martinelli**.

In 1984 they group established themselves in soul/dance circles with 'Tell Me What You Want' (UK Top 75), and a debut album *A Little Spice* which included follow-up UK singles 'Emergency Dial 999' (Top 50) and 'Choose Me' (Top 75). Retaining the services of Nick Martinelli, they continued their success in 1985 with *So Where Are You*, including UK singles 'Hangin' On A String' (Top 20), 'Magic Touch' (Top 20) and 'Golden Years' (Top 75). The album also included a **Dexter Wansel**-arranged version of 'The Sweetest Pain' (featuring **Joanna Gardner**), while establishing the group across America (via MCA).

After writing and producing 'Ain't You Had Enough Love' for **Juliet Roberts** (later recorded by **Phyllis Hyman**), the group recorded their next album *Zagora* (1986), including UK singles 'Stay A Little While, Child' (Top 75), 'Slow Down' (Top 30) and 'Nights Of Pleasure' (Top 50). Loose Ends recorded one last album as the original line-up, *The Real Chuckeeboo* (1988), including a UK Top 50 single 'Mr Bachelor' and the **Leon Ware**-co-produced 'Easier Said Than Done'. As songwriters and producers they had also worked with Five Star, **Ray Shell**, Peter Royer ('Love Is In Season') and **Cheryl Lynn**. As remixers they worked on **Lavine Hudson**'s 'Flesh Of My Flesh'.

In 1990 a new line-up included one original member, Carl McIntosh, with Linda Carriere and Sunay Suleyman. Their album *Look How Long* included 'Don't Be A Fool' and 'Love's Got Me'. Carl also ventured into productions with artists including **Caron Wheeler**.

LORBER, JEFF

(Keyboards/Songwriter/Producer)

Born in Philadelphia, Jeff took piano lessons from the age of four, and upon leaving high school studied at the Berklee School Of Music. In 1972 he moved to Portland, Oregon, and formed the Jeff Lorber Fusion, an instrumental jazz funk ensemble which included **Kenny G** on sax. In 1975 the group signed with Inner City Records and released a debut album *The Jeff Lorber Fusion*. This was followed by *Soft Space* (1978) before the group switched to Arista for *Water Sign* (1979). Further Jeff Lorber Fusion albums were *Wizard Island* (1980) and *Galaxian* (1981), his first with vocal tracks. As a solo artist Jeff recorded for Arista *It's A Fact* (1982), including 'Always There'; *In The Heat Of The Night* (1984); and *Step By Step* (1985), including 'Best Part Of The Night' featuring **Gavin Christopher**, 'Step By Step' produced by **The System** featuring **Audrey Wheeler** and 'Every Woman Needs It' featuring **James Robinson**, which was released in the UK by Club Records (via Phonogram). By now, following the break-up of his marriage, Jeff had moved to Los Angeles where in 1986 he switched to Warner Brothers for *Private Passion*, including 'Facts Of Love' featuring **Karyn White** (again released by Club Records in the UK).

From here Jeff moved into session work both as a pianist and producer. Over the years he has worked with numerous artists including **Marlon McClain** (*Changes*, 1981), **Kenny G** (*Kenny G*), **The Commodores** ('Nightshift'), **The Dazz Band**, **Debarge**, **The Fit**, **Pleasure**, **Eugene Wilde**, **Miki Howard** and **Jody Watley** ('Real Love').

LOREN, BRYAN

(Singer/Songwriter/Producer)

Born in Long Island, New York, Bryan's father had a band called Ray Hudson & The Soul Rockers. His uncle encouraged him to play drums, and soon he had mastered drums, guitar and keyboards. His first professional gig was as a synthesizer player with **Fat Larry's Band** (FLB) in Philadelphia. He later played on FLB's hit 'Zoom' (1982).

Hanging around Alpha recording studios in Philadelphia, Bryan and some friends were given a break by the in-house label, Philly World, who put them to work with producer **Nick Martinelli**. As **Cashmere** they recorded 'Do It Anyway You Wanna' before Bryan was offered a solo deal. In 1983 Philly World released his debut solo single 'Lollipop Luv' (via Virgin in the UK), the popularity of which led to an album *Bryan Loren* (1984).

From here he concentrated on writing and/or producing with artists including **Vesta Williams** ('Don't Blow A Good Thing'), **Shanice Wilson** (*Discovery*), **Barry White**, **Meli'sa Morgan** ('Getting To Know You Better'), **The Valentine Brothers** (*Picture This*) and **Whitney Houston** ('Feels So Good').

LOST GENERATION

(Vocal Group)

From Chicago, Lost Generation recorded for the Innovation II label, the single 'Your Mission (If You Decide To Accept It)' being popular with UK soul fans.

LOVE UNLIMITED

(Vocal Group)

Instigated by **Barry White**, Love Unlimited are Glodean White (Barry's wife), Linda James and Diane Taylor, who began by singing with Barry on his records and at live shows. Together with Barry's **Love Unlimited Orchestra**, their solo recording debut was the million-seller 'Walking In The Rain With The One I Love' (UK Top 20, 1972), followed by 'Under The Influence Of Love'.

After their recordings for Uni Records, Love Unlimited recorded a series of albums for the 20th Century label and in 1975 scored with another hit single 'It May Be Winter Outside (But In My Heart It's Spring)', before Barry formed the Unlimited Gold label (via CBS). Here they recorded *Love Is Back* (1979), including 'High Steppin' Hip Dressin' Fella' and 'If You Want Me, Say It', *In Heat* (1980) and *Under The Influence Of Love Unlimited* (1980).

LOVE UNLIMITED ORCHESTRA

(Orchestra)

Based in Los Angeles, this ensemble of strings, horns and rhythm players provided all the accompaniment for **Barry White**, **Love Unlimited** and many of Barry White's productions through the '70s. Arranged by **Gene Page** and produced by Barry, they had a classic instrumental hit of their own with 'Love's Theme' (UK Top 10, 1974). Their albums included *Under The Influence Of . . .*, *White Gold*, *Music Maestro Please*, *Rhapsody In White* and *My Sweet Summer Suite*, all for the 20th Century/Pye labels. When Barry launched his Unlimited Gold label via CBS, The Love Unlimited Orchestra recorded *Let 'Em Dance* (1981), including 'Jamaican Girl', and *Welcome Aboard*, including 'Lift Your Voice And Say (United We Can Live In Peace Today)' (1981) featuring **Webster Lewis**.

LOVE, RUDY

(Singer/Songwriter/Guitar)

Based in Los Angeles, Rudy Love recorded with his brothers and sisters Bob (vocals/percussion), Ace (vocals/percussion), Peggy (vocals/percussion), Shirley (vocals/percussion), Denise (vocals), Robert (vocals) and Gerald (drums), as Rudy Love & The Love Family. Their albums for the Calla label included *Rudy Love & The Love Family* (1976) and *This Song Is For You* (1978), featuring members of **Earth Wind & Fire** and **The Crusaders**, and arrangements by **Randy Muller** and **Norman Harris**.

LOVESMITH, MICHAEL

(Singer/Songwriter/Producer)

Born in St Louis, Missouri, Michael first established himself as a songwriter and musician. During the '60s he wrote for **The Isley Brothers** ('Little Girl'), and worked with **Isaac Hayes** at Stax before moving with his brothers to Los Angeles in the early '70s. Here he met **Holland/Dozier/Holland** and signed himself and his brothers as The Smith Connection to their Invictus label. Michael also moved into production for other acts on the Invictus/Hot Wax labels including **Honey Cone**. From here Michael met **Jermaine Jackson** for whom he co-wrote and produced songs for the album *My Name Is Jermaine* (1976), including 'My Touch Of Madness'. This led to a position at Motown as an engineer, pianist, music conductor and writer. In 1977 he wrote and produced a duet album for **G.C.Cameron** and **Syreeta** *Rich Love, Poor Love*, including 'Let's Make A Deal', later co-writing/producing *Jump On It* for **Ozone** (1981) and singing lead on five of the tracks.

In 1983 Motown signed Michael as an artist and released his debut album *I Can Make It Happen*, including 'Baby I Will', popular on the UK soul scene. Also that year his song 'Better Friends Than Lovers' was recorded by **Aretha Franklin** on *Get It Right*. After a second album *Diamond In The Raw* (1984), he returned in 1985 for *Rhymes Of Passion*, from which 'Break The Ice' and 'Ain't Nothin' Like It' were popular on the UK soul scene.

Michael has also written for **Gladys Knight** ('Don't Make Me Run Away'), **Patti Brooks** (producing *Patti Brooks*), **Bobby Brown** ('You Ain't Been Loved Right', which he also produced), and has sung backgrounds with **Luther Vandross**.

LOWRELL

(Singer/Songwriter)

From the States, Lowrell Simon made one major impression on the UK soul scene with the Bruce Hawes/**Eugene Record**-produced 'Mellow Mellow Right On' for AVI Records (UK Top 40, 1979).

LUCAS, CARRIE

(Singer)

Born in Los Angeles, Carrie landed a record deal with Solar after becoming the girlfriend of label boss Dick Griffey. Her albums from the early to mid-'80s include *Simply Carrie*, *Street Cornet Symphony*, including 'Tic Toc', *Carrie Lucas In Danceland*, *Still In Love* and *Portrait Of Carrie Lucas*. In 1984 she switched to the Solar subsidiary Constellation for *Horsin' Around*.

LUCAS, REGGIE

(Songwriter/Producer/Guitar)

During the early '70s Reggie worked in Philadelphia with artists including **Norman Connors** (co-writing 'Slewfoot' and 'Saturday Night Special'), while also touring with the **Miles Davis** band. Here he met **James Mtume** and became one half of the **Mtume/Lucas** writing/production team who were extremely successful in the mid to late '70s.

Independently of James Mtume, he has written and/or produced for artists including Madonna ('Lucky Star'), **Rebbie Jackson**, **Randy Crawford** ('Almaz') and **The Four Tops** ('Don't Turn Away').

LUTHER
(Group)
Before his solo career, **Luther Vandross** formed a vocal group called Luther featuring himself with G. Diane Sumler, Anthony Hinton, Theresa V.Reed and Christine Wiltshire. 1976's *Luther* included 'Everybody Rejoice', a song he wrote for *The Wiz*.

LW5
(Group)
London band LW5 were Sammy Jacobs (bass/vocals/synths), Jeffrey Durrant (percussion), Maria Bell (vocals), Mark Murfit (keyboards), Kevin Gibbs (vocals), Theodore Thunder (drums) and John Jamieson (guitar). Sammy and Jeffrey previously played with **Savanna** while Theodore is also the drummer with **I.C.Q.** After building a following on the club circuit, the group signed to Virgin in 1985 for *Get To Know You*, including 'Ripe For The Picking' and 'Kill Or Be Killed', utilizing the services of producer **Paul Hardcastle**.

LYLE, BOBBY
(Keyboards)
Bobby was playing piano by the age of eight, but didn't take it seriously until he moved to Los Angeles in 1974. His first major gig here was with **Sly & The Family Stone** before he met **Wayne Henderson**. With Wayne's At Home Productions, Bobby played keyboards on numerous albums for **Side Effect**, **Pleasure**, **Willie Bobo**, **Ronnie Laws**, **Gabor Szabo**, **Michael White**, **Ramsey Lewis**, **L.A.Boppers**, **Flora Purim**, **David Oliver**, **Hilary** and many more. He also recorded two fusion jazz/r&b albums for Capitol, *The Genie* (1977), *New Warrior* (1978) and *Night Fire* (1979). His first album was a little-known CBS *Bobby Lyle Plays The GX1*, released in Japan after Bobby won a contest showcasing that keyboard instrument.

In 1980 he re-arranged and re-recorded his composition 'The Genie' (from which is derived his nickname Bobby 'The Genie' Lyle) with **The Starship Orchestra** for their CBS album *Celestial Sky*. As the '80s progressed Bobby was taken on tour as musical director for major artists including **George Benson**, **Al Jarreau**, Bette Midler and **Anita Baker**. He also moved into production with artists including **The Valentine Brothers** (*First Take*, 1982) and **Stanley Turrentine** (*L.A.Place*, 1989). He resumed his own recording career with Atlantic for *Ivory Dreams* (1989) and *The Journey* (1990).

Elsewhere Bobby has recorded with **Benny Golson**, Blue Mitchell, **Pharaoh Sanders**, **Raul De Souza**, **Womack & Womack**, **Jeffrey Osborne**, **Norman Connors**, **Beau Williams**, **Debra Laws**, **Dee Dee Bridgewater** ('Night Moves'), **Eloise Laws**, **Phyllis Hyman**, **Paul Jackson Jr** and many others.

LYNN, BARBARA
(Singer/Songwriter/Guitar)
Born Barbara Lynn Ozen in Alabama, Barbara began her recording career in the early '60s with songs including 'You'll Lose A Good Thing' (1962) and 'Oh Baby (We Got A Good Thing Going)' (1964) for the Jamie label. In the late '60s she recorded songs including '(Until Then) I'll Suffer' and 'Take Your Love And Run' (1968) for Atlantic, while more recently she is fondly remembered for her single 'I'm Still The Same' for the Jamstone label (1984).

In 1988 she signed to the Atlanta-based Ichiban label where *Barbara Lynn* included 'Trying To Love Two' and the self-written 'You Make Me Feel So Hot'.

LYNN, CHERYL
(Singer)
Born in Los Angeles in 1957, Cheryl got her break courtesy of *The Gong Show*, a TV talent show which brought her to the attention of CBS who signed her in 1978. In her first year with the label she guested with Toto on their rendition of 'Georgy Porgy' and recorded a debut album *Cheryl Lynn* which included the dance anthem 'Got To Be Real' (selling a million copies across America). In 1981 she stirred dancefloors again with the **Mike & Brenda Sutton**-penned 'Shake It Up Tonight' before working with **Luther Vandross** on *Instant Love* (1982), including the duet 'If This World Were Mine'.

1983's *Preppie* included the **Jam/Lewis** written/produced 'Encore', released in the UK on the Streetwave label and a Top 75 hit. 'At Last You're Mine' was later a single on the American Private I label (via CBS) from the movie soundtrack *Heavenly Bodies* (1985), while later in the year she returned for a final CBS album *It's Gonna Be Right*, including 'Fade To Black' and the Jam/Lewis-produced 'Fidelity'. She then switched to the Manhattan label (via EMI) for *Start Over* (1987), including 'If You Were Mine', and sang backgrounds with **Lenny Williams**.

LYNN, TRUDY
(Singer)
From Houston, Texas, Trudy has toured with **B.B.King**, **George Benson** and **Tina Turner** while all the time building an audience of her own on the blues scene. As a solo artist in the mid-'80s she recorded 'Bring The Beef Home To Me', released in the UK on the Move label.

M

M&M

(Remixers)

M&M are **Sergio Munzabai** and **John Morales** who met at New York's WBLS radio station while Sergio worked there as a musical director. Discovering a chemistry that worked well in the recording studio, they set up M&M in the early '80s as remixes developed as an industry marketing tool. The name M&M was derived from their surnames and a mutual love for the chocolate candy of the same name. Their first official remix was 'No Stopping That Rocking' for **Instant Funk** in 1982. Later mixes included 'Rhythm Of The Night' for **Debarge**.

M, BOBBY

(Saxophonist)

Bobby M (aka Bobby Militello) was born in Buffalo, New York, where he played with various jazz ensembles in the '70s. After being Maynard Ferguson's road manager for two years, he moved into the studio and worked with **Stevie Wonder**, **Marvin Gaye** and **Sarah Vaughan** among many others. In 1982 he recorded a solo album for Motown (**Gordy**) *Blow ... Rick James Presents* which featured a rendition of 'Let's Stay Together' with vocals by **Jean Carne**.

M.C.B.

(Group)

From Washington, M.C.B. were Aaron Mills (bass/lead vocals) and Jheryl Bright (trombone/lead vocals). In 1983 they signed to Epic and released an album *M.C.B.*

M.F.S.B.

(Group)

Standing for Mother, Father, Sister, Brother, M.F.S.B. is the assembly of musicians who were the driving force behind the Philadelphia sound in the '70s. An ensemble of string, horn and rhythm players they accompanied virtually every recording on the Philadelphia International (PIR) label through to the early '80s.

Regular players included Larry Moore (bass), Lenny Pakula (keyboards), Norman Harris (guitar), James Herb Smith, Roland Chambers (guitar), Earl Young (drums), Miguel Fuentes and Quinton Joseph (drums/percussion), with strings by Albert Barone, Angelo Petrella, Charles Appollonia, Diana Barnett, Romeo Distefano, Rudy Maliazia, Joe Donofrio, and horns by Joe DeAngelis, Danny Eillions, Scott Temple, Milton Phibbs, Frederich Jainer, Ricci Genovese, Fred Linge, Rocco Bene, Robert Hartzwell and Edward Cascaralle. The orchestra was directed by either **Kenny Gamble**, **Leon Huff**, Don Renaldo, **Dexter Wansel** or **Vince Montana**.

M.F.S.B. also recorded albums in their own right at the Philadelphia International label. These were *M.F.S.B.* (1973), *Love Is The Message* (1973), *Universal Love* (1975), *Philadelphia Freedom* (1975), *Summertime* (1976), *End Of Phase One* (1977) and *M.F.S.B., The Gamble & Huff Orchestra* (1978). UK hit singles from these were 'T.S.O.P. (The Sound Of Philadelphia)', featuring **The Three Degrees** (UK Top 30, 1974), and 'Sexy' (UK Top 40, 1975). 'K-Jee' and 'Freddie Dead' became classic Philly instrumentals. In 1978 they enjoyed some success with 'Use Ta Be My Guy', but it was in 1980 under the direction of Dexter Wansel that they made an impact on the UK soul/dance scene with 'Mysteries Of The World' (UK Top 50), the title track of their last album.

Away from PIR the orchestra recorded with **Melba Moore** ('Standing Right Here'), **The Stylistics**, **The Detroit Spinners** and many others.

MAC BAND

(Vocal Group)

Formed in Los Angeles, The Mac Band are the McCampbell brothers Ray, Derrick, Charles and Kelvin, with a backing band including Ray Flippin (bass), Rodney Frazier (keyboards), Mark Harper (guitar) and Steve Fuller (drums). Their debut album *Mac Band Featuring The McCampbell Brothers* was produced by **L.A./Babyface** ('Roses Are Red', UK Top 10, 1988) and David and Wayne Lewis from **Atlantic Starr** ('Girl Your Love's So Fine', and 'Stalemate', UK Top 40, 1988). The follow-up *Luv U 2 The Limit* (1990) was essentially written and produced by **Gary Taylor**. Rodney Frazier, incidentally, also recorded with **Atlantic Starr** on *We're Movin' Up*.

MACDONALD, RALPH

(Percussion/Songwriter/Producer)

Born in Harlem, New York, in 1944, Ralph's parents were from Trinidad. As a child Ralph played congas in his father's band around Brooklyn and Queens. He also took up steel drums, later to join Harry Belafonte's band playing these and later congas. He wrote, arranged and conducted Harry Belafonte's *Calypso Carnival* album on RCA before leaving to take up residence with **Roberta Flack**. He worked with Roberta for five years, during which time he wrote 'Where Is The Love' (with Bill Salter), a hit duet for Roberta with **Donny Hathaway**. This classic song has since been recorded over 150 times in 19 different languages! He also played percussion on 'Killing Me Softly' and co-wrote/produced numerous other songs.

Launching a solo career in 1976 he played to a star-studded audience at New York's Lincoln Center before recording his first solo album *Sound Of A Drum* (including two hit singles 'Calypso Breakdown', used on the *Saturday Night Fever* soundtrack, and 'Jam On The Groove') for the Marlin label (via TK). In 1977 he released a further Marlin album *The Path* featuring **Grover Washington**, **Bob James**, **Eric Gale** and **Richard Tee**, following which he made his vocal debut on 'Discolypso', a single from his third album *Counterpoint* (1978).

From here Ralph concentrated on songwriting and production, his productions including two Epic albums for **Bobbi Humphrey**, *Part Of You* for **Eric Gale** (1979), 'Song For Jeremy' for **Spaces** (1981), 'Goodbye Sadness' for Yoko Ono and various tracks for **Sadao Watanabe** and others. He also wrote 'Trade Winds', a hit song for both Rod Stewart and **Lou Rawls**. In 1984 he signed to Polydor as a solo artist, his albums being *Universal Rhythm* (released in the UK on London Records) and *Surprise*, (1985), including 'You Need More Calypso', a vocal track featuring Dennis Collins.

He has also recorded with **Donny Hathaway** ('Love Love Love'), **Grover Washington**, **Ashford & Simpson**, **Al Jarreau**, **Pieces Of A Dream**, **Neil Larsen** ('Sudden Samba'), **General Johnson** ('Don't Walk Away'), **Aretha Franklin**, **Margie Joseph** and many more.

MAD LADS

(Vocal Group)

From Memphis, John Gary Williams, Julius Green, William Brown and Robert Phillips originally got together in 1963 and called themselves The Emeralds. In 1964 they signed to the Volt label (via Stax) and became The Mad Lads for the single 'Sidewalk Surf', followed by 'You Don't Have To Shop Around' which remained on the American charts for nine months.

In 1985 they returned as The World Famous Mad Lads for an album *New Directions*, including 'You Blew It', for the Express Records label. William's brother, incidentally, is **Randy Brown**.

MADDEN, DANNY

(Singer/Songwriter)

From Washington, John 'Danny' Madden is the son of a church minister. At the age of fourteen he sang on stage with Duke Ellington and decided from that point to make singing his career. Becoming a session singer, predominantly in New York, Danny worked with artists including **Angela Bofill** (co-writing 'Is This A Dream' and 'I Can See It In Your Eyes'), **Gwen Guthrie**, **Ashford & Simpson**, **Freddie Jackson** ('Rock Me Tonight'), **Will Downing**, **Jenny Burton** ('Bad Habits'), **Melba Moore** and **Evelyn King** prior to a trip to London. Here he met **Danny D** in a record store who hired him as lead vocalist on 'All I Do', a cover of the **Stevie Wonder** song for the **D-Mob** album *A Little Bit Of This, A Little Bit Of That*.

In 1989 he signed with Eternal Records (via WEA) and worked with Danny and Carl McIntosh (of **Loose Ends**) on a debut single 'The Facts Of Life'.

MADRID, FRANKIE

(Singer)

From Portland, Oregon, Frankie formed Madrid And The Counts and toured Washington, Northwest Canada, locally in Oregon and then Japan before returning to Oregon to record a couple of singles. Moving to Hollywood, he starred in an LA production of *Jesus Christ Superstar* and worked as an extra on a number of TV films before making a trip to San Francisco where he recorded 'Paper Back Pony', a collectable item on the soul scene. He then moved to London where he has worked on the club scene as an entertainer while involving himself on various recording projects. In 1990 he was featured vocalist on 'Understand This Groove' by U.F.I. released by Circa (via Virgin).

MAGIC LADY

(Group)

Magic Lady is the brainchild of singer/songwriter Linda Stokes, wife of **Michael Stokes**. The all-girl group first signed to Arista for *Magic Lady* (1980), including 'I Just Wanna Be Free', following which they moved on to A&M for *Hot And Sassy* (1982), including the American r&b hit 'Hot And Sassy' and a cult UK soul track 'Hold Tight'. On signing to Motown the group was reduced to just Linda Stokes and Jackie Ball. A single 'Betcha Can't Lose With My Love' and album *Magic Lady* were released in 1988.

MAGNUM FORCE

(Group)

From Chicago, Magnum Force were Rick Starr (bass/percussion/vocals), Rory Star (keyboards/drums/lead vocals), Nate Williams (lead vocals/percussion), Stan Winfield (guitar/percussion), Dwayne Liddell (lead vocals/percussion), Marc Vines (sax) and Mike Young (trap drums). In 1982 their album *Share My Love* for the

Chicago-based Kelli-Arts label was released in the UK via Bluebird Records.

MAHONEY, SKIP
(Singer)
Philadelphia vocalist Skip Mahoney recorded as Skip Mahoney & The Casuals in the mid-'70s and was one of the first acts to release a 12" single. The song was 'Running Away From Love', released on the A-Bet label in 1976, and came from *Land Of Love*, recorded in the Philly tradition of the day. As Skip Mahoney he also recorded for Salsoul Records, both the A side ('Janice') and B side ('Don't Stop Me Now') of a 1980 single being popular on the New York club scene at the time.

MAI TAI
(Group)
Formed in Amsterdam in 1983, Mai Tai were Jettie Wells, Carolien De Windt and Mildred Douglas from Guyana. Mai Tai released four singles before scoring a hit with 'History', the group's first UK release and a Top 10 hit single in 1985 on Virgin Records. Follow-ups were 'Body And Soul' (UK Top 10, 1985) and 'Female Intuition' (Top 75, 1986).

THE MAIN
(Vocal Group)
This Los Angeles-based group recorded *Universal Love* in the late 80s for Pete Moore (formerly of The Miracles) on Satellite Records. It featured a single 'All Of Me' produced by **Craig T. Cooper**.

MAIN INGREDIENT
(Group)
Formed in New York, Donald McPherson, **Tony Silvester** and Luther Simmons first sang together as The Poets in the '50s. Their initial recordings were for the Red Bird label and they scored their first American success with 'She Blew A Good Thing' in 1966. Becoming The Main Ingredient, they recorded a series of singles through to 1971, when Donald died (of leukemia) and was replaced by **Cuba Gooding**. In 1972 they signed to RCA and scored further American chart success with 'Everybody Plays The Fool'. For the next three years the group recorded a series of albums including *Tasteful Soul*; *Bitter Sweet*; *Afrodisiac* (1973), including 'Work To Do'; *Euphrates River* (1974), including 'Happiness Is Just Around The Bend' and 'California My Way'; *Shame On The World* (1975), including 'Over You'; and *Rolling Down A Mountainside* (1975), while in the UK the group scored a Top 30 hit with 'Just Don't Want To Be Lonely' (1974).

From here they took on individual projects, Tony becoming a producer with artists including **Sister Sledge**, **Ben E. King**, **Donny Hathaway**, **Bette Midler** and **Linda Lewis** ('It's In His Kiss', 1975). Cuba signed as a solo artist to Motown, and Luther became a stockbroker. In 1980 they rejoined RCA for two albums, *Ready For Love*, including 'Spoiled', and the **Patrick Adams**-produced *I Only Have Eyes For You* (1981), including 'Evening Of Love', 'Save Me' and 'Party People', before Cuba re-recorded the group's 'Happiness Is Just Around The Bend' as a solo artist for the Streetwise label.

In 1986 they reunited again and signed with the independent Edge label, and in 1989 switched to Polydor for *I Just Wanna Love You*, although by this time Luther had returned to the stock market and was replaced by Jerome Jackson.

MAJORS
(Vocal Group)
From Philadelphia, The Majors were Ricky Cordo, Ronald Gathers, Eugene Glass, Frank Troutt and Idella Morris. In 1962 they scored an American hit with 'A Wonderful Dream' on the Imperial label. Their follow-ups were 'A Little Bit Now', 'She's A Troublemaker' and 'What In The World'.

MALLORY, GERALD
(Singer/Songwriter)
Gerald's one release for Prelude Records in 1982 was 'Lay It Down On Me' before he joined **Active Force**. He also co-wrote 'I Just Wanna Be Free' for **Magic Lady** (Linda Stokes from Magic Lady co-wrote 'Lay It Down On Me').

MANCHA, STEVE
(Singer)
Born in Detroit, Steve sang as one of **Two Friends** who scored an American hit with 'Just A Little Too Much To Hope For' (**Marvin Gaye** played drums) on Motown in 1962. Solo American hits came on the Grovesville label with 'Friday Night', 'Just Keep On Loving Me' and 'Don't Make Me A Storyteller'. His producer was **Don Davis**, who later took Steve's master tapes to Stax Records where they were used to compile a shared album with **J.J.Barnes** called 'Rare Stamps'. In 1970 he sang lead with the group **100 Proof Aged In Soul**, before joining **8th Day** and later turning to gospel music. In 1986 he returned to the secular field to work with writer/producer **Ian Levine** on 'It's All Over The Grapevine' for EMI in the UK.

MANDELL, MIKE
(Keyboards)
This New York-based blind pianist created interest on the UK jazz funk scene with his 1978 album for Vanguard Records *Sky Music*, including 'Peg', featuring **David Sanborn** and Chris Hills (from **Players Association**). His follow-up was *Utopia Parkway* (1980). He also recorded with **Hubert Laws**.

MANDRILL

(Group)

Originally from New York, Mandrill were Carlos D. Wilson (trombone/flute/guitar/percussion), Louis Wilson (trumpet/congas/percussion/vocals), Neftali Santiago (drums/percussion/vocals), Wilfredo 'Wolf' Wilson (bass/congas/percussion/vocals), Ric Wilson (sax/percussion/vocals) Juaquin Jessup (lead guitar/percussion/vocals) and Claude 'Coffee' Cave II (keyboards/percussion/vocals). The group were formed initially in the early '70s by the Wilson brothers who found other members by advertising in local New York music papers. Shortly after settling on a line-up they signed with Polydor and cut *Mandrill Is*. Building a following for their earthy funk sound they recorded a further Polydor album *Consummate Truth* (1973) before moving to Los Angeles and switching labels to United Artists. Here they released *Solid* (1975).

In the UK their popularity began to take off in 1977 upon signing with Arista. Their first album for the label, *We Are One*, featured 'Funkey Monkey' and 'Can You Dig It', produced by **Jeff Lane**. The following year they self-produced a second Arista album *New Worlds* from which 'It's So Easy Lovin' You' and 'Mean Streets' became in-demand 'rare grooves' in the late 1980s.

MANGIONE, CHUCK

(Flugelhorn/Keyboards)

Born in Rochester, New York, in 1940, Charles Frank Mangione began his career as a trumpeter in the mid-'60s with Maynard Ferguson and Art Blakey. As one of Art Blakey's Jazz Messengers he was also joined by his pianist brother **Gap Mangione**. He and brother Gap also recorded as The Jazz Brothers for Riverside Records before they both signed solo deals with the Mercury label. Here Chuck's albums included *Land Of Make Believe* before he switched to A&M for *Bellavia* (1976). In 1977 he created interest on the UK jazz funk scene with the instrumental 'Feels So Good' before he became a teacher at the Eastman School Of Music, where one of his protégés was **Jeff Tyzik**. Further albums including *Fun And Games* (1980) were released at A&M before he switched to CBS in 1982 for *Love Notes*.

MANGIONE, GAP

(Keyboards)

From Upstate New York, Gap and his brother **Chuck Mangione** formed an accordion and trumpet duet The Jazz Brothers when they were both in their teens. For Riverside Records they recorded *The Jazz Brothers* (1960), *Hey Baby* (1961) and *Spring Fever* (1961). Gap also recorded a solo album *Diana In The Autumn Wind* for the GRC label (1968), and later a Mercury album *Sing-A-Long Junk* before he signed with A&M. Here he released *She And I*, produced by brother Chuck. Still with A&M, he brought in **Larry Carlton** to produce *Suite Lady*, which in 1978 brought Gap to the attention of UK jazz funk fans with the instrumentals 'Time Of The Season' and 'Mellow Out'. Larry was also on hand for the follow-up *Dancin' Is Makin' Love* (1979), a less subtle disco jazz album which didn't have the same impact.

MANHATTANS

(Vocal Group)

Formed in the early '60s by Edward 'Sonny' Bivins (originally a member of The Dulcets who released one single, 'Pork Chops'), The Manhattans were originally Sonny Bivens, Richard Taylor, Blue Lovett, Kenny Kelley and lead singer George 'Smitty' Smith. They chose the name Manhattans from their days singing on 116th Street in Harlem. In 1964 they won third prize at an Apollo Theater talent show and were immediately signed by the local Carnival label where they released 'For The Very First Time' and 'There Goes A Fool'. In 1965 they had an American r&b hit with 'I Wanna Be (Your Everything)', and through to 1968 they scored further American success with 'Searching For My Baby', 'Follow Your Heart', 'Baby I Need You' and 'I Call It Love'.

In 1969 they switched to the Deluxe label (a subsidiary of King Records), and success continued with 'The Picture Became Quite Clear', 'It's Gonna Take A Lot To Bring Me Back', 'From Atlanta To Georgia' and 'Let Them Talk'. They also recorded an album for the label, *One Life To Live*, including 'A Million To One'. In 1970, following the departure of Smitty (who later died), **Gerald Alston** took over as lead singer, and in 1972 the group signed to CBS. Here they scored major American success with the million-seller 'There's No Me Without You', taken from the album of the same name (1973). The following year they recorded a disco album with Philly musicians/producers **Norman Harris/Alan Felder**, before entering their most successful period.

In the UK, their hits began to role from an album *Manhattans* (1975) which included 'Kiss And Say Goodbye' (Top 5) and 'Hurt' (Top 5). They continued with singles 'It's You' (Top 50, 1977), 'Shining Star' (Top 50, 1980) and 'Crazy' (UK Top 75, 1983), while their albums included *After Midnight* (1980), including 'Girl Of My Dream'; *Black Tie* (1981); *Forever By Your Side* (1983), including 'Just The Lonely Talking' and 'Locked Up In Your Love'; *Too Hot To Stop It* (1985), including 'C'est La Vie'; and *Back To Basics* (1986), featuring **Bobby Womack** songs/productions including 'Where Did We Go Wrong' with guest vocals by **Regina Belle**.

In 1988 **Gerald Alston** left the group to commence a solo career and was replaced by Roger Harris. Switching to the Valley Vue label, they worked with producers including **Gary Taylor** on *We're Back* (1989), including 'Why You Wanna Love Me Like That'.

MANIQUIN

(Group)

From Washington, Maniquin were Kenny Lattimore (lead vocals), Dal Romeo Lowe (keyboards/vocals), Brian

Stanley Jones (keyboards/vocals), David News (guitar/lead and backing vocals) and Ray Richards (bass/lead and backing vocals). Their debut album *Maniquin* was released by Epic in 1989, producers including the Wilson brothers from **The Gap Band** and **Charlie Singleton**.

MANTRONIX

(Duo/Writers/Producers)

From New York, Mantronix were originally Mantronik and M.C.Tee, who made their debut with 'Needle To The Groove'. Blending hip hop with soul and dance music, they signed to Sleeping Bag Records in 1985, releasing a debut *The Album*, including 'Bassline' and 'Ladies' (via Virgin/10 Records in the UK).

In between albums, Mantronik established himself as a remixer and worked with artists including **Joyce Sims**, **Dhar Braxton** and **Hanson & Davis** before the second Mantronix album *Music Madness* in 1986. They switched to Capitol for *This Should Move Ya* (1990), including 'Got To Have Your Love'.

In 1991, the Mantronix line-up was Mantronik, Jade Trini and Bryce Luvah for 'Don't Go Messin' With My Heart'.

MARCUS, WADE

(Arranger/Producer)

In addition to recording his own album *Metamorphosis* (featuring **Joe Sample**) for ABC Records in 1976, Wade has worked in the capacity of music arranger over the years for an array of artists including **Creative Source** (*Pass The Feeling On*, 1975), **Brass Fever** (*Brass Fever*, 1975), **Johnny Hammond** (*Forever Taurus*, which he also produced), **The Emotions** ('Tricks Were Made For Kids'), **Bobby Womack**, **Donald Byrd**, **The Blackbyrds** ('Rock Creek Park'), **Keni Burke** ('Never Stop Loving Me'), **Stevie Wonder**, **Rena Scott** ('If I Had A Chance') and **Tavares**.

MARDIN, ARIF

(Producer/Songwriter)

Based in New York, Arif Mardin has been prolific on the r&b scene from the '60s to the present day. As an artist he had limited releases in the '60s (including a single 'Glass Onion'), but he is most famous for his work as a producer for Atlantic with artists including **Aretha Franklin**, **Donny Hathaway** ('The Ghetto', 'Someday We'll All Be Free' and 'Love, Love, Love'), **Margie Joseph**, **Miki Howard** ('You've Changed'), **Roberta Flack**, **Average White Band** ('Pick Up The Pieces' and 'Queen Of My Soul'). Within the WEA group he has worked with **Chaka Khan** ('Life Is A Dance', and cowriting the words for Chaka's vocal version of 'A Night In Tunisia') among many others.

MARIA, TANIA

(Singer/Keyboards)

From São Luis, Brazil, Tania's father was a metalworker who encouraged his daughter to take piano lessons from the age of seven. Aged twelve she was playing keyboards for local dance bands, and at seventeen she formed her own group. Her vocal debut came later when her group's singer failed to make it for a gig. Taking to vocals naturally, she was soon singing on a regular basis, although by day she studied law before deciding to take her music more seriously. In the mid-'70s she was invited to Paris for a three-month club residency. She ended up staying in Europe for seven years where she cut five albums.

In 1981 she signed to the American-based Concord label, releasing *Piquant* and four further albums for the label including the popular *Come With Me*. Wishing to branch out and appeal to a wider audience she switched to Manhattan/EMI in 1985, and released *Made In New York*, co-produced by **Deodato**. She has also recorded with **Dave Valentin** ('Very Nice Indeed').

MARIE, TEENA

(Singer/Songwriter)

Born Mary Christine Brocker in Santa Monica, California, Teena Marie began her music career as a teenager, forming a school band with her brother and cousin. It was through wanting to become an actress that, in the mid-'70s, Teena met **Berry Gordy** who was was looking for new faces for a TV programme. Although the project didn't come to fruition, Berry signed Teena to his Gordy label (via Motown) and was put in the studio with **Rick James**.

In 1979 Rick produced her debut album *Wild And Peaceful*, including 'I'm A Sucker For Your Love' (UK Top 50). Her follow-up albums were *Lady T* (1980), including 'Behind The Groove' (UK Top 10); *Irons In The Fire* (1980), including 'I Need Your Lovin'' (UK Top 30) and 'You Make Love Like Springtime'; and *It Must Be Magic* (1981), including 'Square Biz' and 'Portuguese Love'.

In 1982 she sang the duet 'Happy' with Rick James on his album *Throwin' Down* and worked as writer/arranger on the album *A.W.O.L. (Absence Without Love)* for **Carl Anderson** at Epic Records. The following year she switched to Epic herself where her albums were *Robbery* (1983); *Starchild* (1984) including 'Lovergirl', 'My Dear Mr Gaye' and the **Ronnie McNeir** duet 'We've Got To Stop'; *Emerald City* (1986); and *Naked To The World* (1988), including 'Ooh La La La' (UK Top 75). On tour in Texas she broke several ribs and couldn't work for six months. Once recovered she began work on her most recent album *Ivory* (1990), including 'Since Day One' (co-penned/produced by **Jazzie B**), 'Cupid Is A Real Straight Shooter' and 'Just Us Two'. Also at Epic she secured a recording deal for her protégé group **Q.T.Hush**, producing and performing on their debut album in 1985.

Teena is one of the few white singers to have been

totally accepted on the black music scene through the '70s and '80s. In 1991 she is no longer with Epic Records and is looking for a new label.

MARTIN, BOBBY

(Singer)

Born in Cincinnati, Bobby originally wanted to be a jazz pianist after being inspired by a Lionel Hampton concert. In 1950 he joined a jazz ensemble led by sax man Billy Lynn Hope and made his recording debut playing on 'Tenderly', an American r&b hit on the Premium label. Also with Billy Lynn Hope he learned the basics of arranging, writing the charts for the group. In 1961 he moved to Philadelphia where he was hired as an arranger by Harold Robinson at Newtown Records. He soon moved into production at the label, arranging and producing 'I Sold My Heart To The Junk Man' for both The Four Sportsmen and **Patti Labelle** & The Bluebelles, the latter version being an American million-seller.

Throughout the '70s he was employed by Philadelphia International Records and arranged such classics as 'I'll Always Love My Mama' (**The Intruders**), 'Me and Mrs Jones' (**Billy Paul**), 'For The Love Of Money' and 'Darlin' Darlin' Baby' (**The O'Jays**), 'The Whole Town's Laughing At Me' (**Teddy Pendergrass**), 'When Will I See You Again' and 'Dirty Ol' Man' (**The Three Degrees**), 'Free Love' (**Jean Carne**), 'Show You The Way To Go' (**The Jacksons**) and many more. Bobby has also arranged and/or produced for artists including **The Manhattans** ('There's No Me Without You'), **Monk Montgomery** (*Reality*), **L.T.D.**, **Rockie Robbins** ('You And Me') and **Tavares** ('Never Had A Love Like This Before').

MARTINELLI, NICK

(Producer)

Born in Philadelphia, Nick worked on the local club scene as a disc jockey with partner David Todd before they moved into production and mixing in the early '80s. Nick first came to prominence in the UK through his work with **Loose Ends**, establishing the style of the 808 drum machine with songs including 'Hangin' On A String' in 1984, and producing albums for the group. He also produced *Children Of The Night* (1986) for another British group **52nd Street**.

Elsewhere Nick has produced artists including **Brandi Wells** (*Watch Out*, 1981), **Sybil Thomas** ('Rescue Me'), **F.L.B.** ('Zoom'), **Harold Melvin & The Blue Notes**, **Joanna Gardner** ('Special Feelings'), **Phyllis Hyman** ('Ain't You Had Enough Love'), **Janice McClain** ('Passion And Pain'), **Terri Wells** ('You Make It Heaven' and 'I'll Be Around'), **Peggi Blu** ('Tender Moments'), **Stephanie Mills** ('Stand Back', 'I Feel Good All Over' and 'Home'), **Regina Belle** ('Show Me The Way'), **Gladys Knight & The Pips** ('Let Me Be The One'), **Kiara** ('This Time'), **Billy Preston** ('It Don't Get Better Than This'), Leata Galloway (*The Naked Truth*, 1988), **Jean Carne** ('You're A Part Of Me'), **Miki Howard** ('Baby Be Mine', 'Reasons' and 'Love Under New Management'), **Christopher Williams** and **Peabo Bryson/D'Atra Hicks** ('Palm Of Your Hand').

MARVELETTES

(Vocal Group)

The Marvelettes were originally five high-school friends from Inkster, Michigan, Gladys Horton, Katherine Anderson, Georginna Gordon, Georgia Dobbins and Juanita Cowart. They formed in 1960 to compete in a talent show, the three finalists from which were to win auditions at Motown. The Marvellettes actually came fourth but a schoolteacher persuaded Motown to listen to them too. The audition went well and the group were advised to write some songs. Georgia came up with the idea for 'Please Mr Postman' which impressed Motown chief **Berry Gordy**. After completion of the song by staff songwriters (including **Robert Bateman** and **Freddie Gorman**) it was recorded and released in 1961, becoming both the group's first success and Motown's first American No. 1 national hit. The average age of the group at the time was seventeen!

For family reasons Georgia and Juanita left the group, and Wanda Rogers joined the remaining line-up. With Wanda and Gladys sharing lead vocals, further American hits followed with 'Used To Be A Playboy' and 'Beachwood 45789'. Georginna then left (though she remained at Motown as a secretary). As a trio The Marvelettes continued to have hits with 'Too Many Fish In The Sea', 'Don't Mess With Bill' and 'The Hunter Gets Captured By The Game'. Their only UK success was 'When You're Young And In Love' which reached the UK Top 20 in 1967. Gladys Horton was next to leave the group (to have her first child) and was replaced by Anne Bogan who later fronted the group **New Birth**. With Anne the group had one last American hit with 'My Baby Must Be A Magician'.

The Marvelettes officially split up in 1971 when they left Motown, but more recently Gladys Horton has reformed the group with two new members, Echo Johnson and Jean McClain. They have been performing together since the mid-'80s. In 1989 they signed with the UK Motorcity label, at which point Wanda Rogers rejoined for recording purposes, but does not tour live. Their first single release on Motorcity was 'Holding On With Both Hands', produced by **Ian Levine**.

Former member Katherine Shaffner now runs a crime-prevention programme in Detroit after the tragic death of her son.

MARY JANE GIRLS

(Vocal Group)

From Los Angeles, The Mary Jane Girls were originally Joanne 'Jojo' McDuffie, Candice 'Candi' Ghant, Kim 'Maxi' Wuletich and Cherri Wells. The group was formed by writer/producer **Rick James** in 1983 and signed to the Gordy label (via Motown) the same year. A debut album *Mary Jane Girls* (1983) featured UK singles 'Candy Man'

(Top 60), 'All Night Long' (Top 20) and 'Boys' (Top 75), before Cherri was replaced by Yvette 'Corvette' Marine for a second Rick James-produced album *Only For You* (1985), including 'In My House'.

MASON

(Group)

From Tulsa, Oklahoma, brothers Tre Mason (guitar/synths), Gary Mason (bass/vocals) and Tony Mason (lead vocals/guitar) teamed up with producer **Kae Williams** in 1987 for *Livin' On The Edge*, released by Elektra. 'Pour It On' from the album was released as a single.

MASON, BARBARA

(Singer/Songwriter)

Born in Philadelphia in 1949, Barbara formed a vocal group while at high school. Her next-door neighbour was Bill Oxydine from the group The Larks who let Barbara's group sing occasionally at their shows. Through this work she met producer Welson McDougal who produced her debut single 'Trouble Child' for the Crusader label (featuring The Larks on backgrounds) in 1965.

Later that year Barbara switched to Artic Records and scored her first American Top 30 hit with 'Girls Have Feelings Too', the follow-up being the even more successful 'Yes I'm Ready', which she co-wrote. She recorded briefly for the National General label before settling at Buddah where she scored further American hits with 'We Got Each Other' (a duet with **The Futures**), and 'From His Woman To You' (1974), a Top 3 answer record to 'Woman To Woman' by **Shirley Brown**. Her Buddah albums include *If You Knew Him Like I Do*, *Lady Love* (1973), *Transition* (1974) and *Barbara Mason* (1975), before she recorded 'I Am Your Woman, She Is Your Wife', a US Top 20 hit for Prelude Records in 1978.

Following this she faced hard financial times and was supported by **Norman Harris** before her fortunes changed in 1980 when K.C. (of **K.C. & The Sunshine Band**) recorded her song 'Yes I'm Ready' as a duet with Terri Deasrio. The record sold more than a million copies and put her back on the road to success. The same year she signed to the WMOT/Fantasy label for singles 'Let Me Give You Love' (1981) and 'She's Got The Papers (But I Got The Man)', before a move to West End Records where 'Another Man' became Barbara's one UK Top 50 chart entry (1983). The song later featured on *Tied Up*, produced by **Butch Ingram**.

MASON, HARVEY

(Drummer/Producer/Songwriter)

Born in Atlantic City, New Jersey, in 1947, Harvey took naturally to drums and percussion as a young child and by 1970 he had begun to build his reputation as a top session musician. By the mid-'70s he was playing regularly with **Herbie Hancock**'s group **The Headhunters**, a situation which led to him signing to Arista Records as a solo artist in 1975.

Through Herbie's influence Harvey's music became a fusion of jazz and funk, greatly appealing to the UK 'jazz funk' scene of the mid–late '70s. His albums were *Marching In The Street* (1975), *Earth Mover* (1976), *Funk In A Mason Jar* (1977), including 'Till You Take My Love' and 'What's Going On', *Groovin' You* (1979) and *M.V.P.* (1980), including 'How Does It Feel'. His albums by this time had progressed from instrumental fusion to vocal-orientated dance music.

As a songwriter and/or producer he worked with artists including **Shirley Brown** ('I Need Somebody To Love Me'), **Locksmith** (*Unlock The Funk*), **Seawind** ('He Loves You' and two albums), and **Esther Phillips**, while he has recorded drums with numerous artists including **Johnny Hammond** (*Gears*), **Bob James** (*Three*), **Dave Grusin** ('Mountain Dance'), **Rockie Robbins** ('Time To Think'), **George Benson**, **Grover Washington**, **Aretha Franklin**, **Raul de Souza**, **Sadao Watanabe**, **Debarge**, **Bobbi Humphrey**, **Carmen McCrae**, **Patrice Rushen**, **Charles Earland**, **Donald Byrd**, **Mark Soskin** ('Walk Tall'), **Patti Austin** (*Love Is Gonna Getcha*) and **Jean Carne**.

MASQUERADERS

(Vocal Group)

Based in Memphis, this '70s vocal group was instigated by **Isaac Hayes** who produced all their releases including *Everybody Wanna Love On* (1975) and *Love Anonymous* (1977) for his Hot Buttered Soul label (via ABC).

MASS PRODUCTION

(Group)

Originally from Richmond, Virginia, '70s funk group Mass Production were Larry Marshall (vocals/percussion), Coy Bryant (guitar), Tiny Kelly (vocals), Gregory McCoy (sax), Kevin Douglas (bass), Rodney Phelps (guitar), Emanual Redding (congas), Tyrone Williams (keyboards), Otis Drumgole (trumpet), Ricardo Williams (vocals) and Samuel Williams (drums). In the mid-'70s the group set off for New York signed to the Cotillion label (via Atlantic). Their debut album was *Welcome To Our World* (1976), the title track being a UK Top 50 single. However it was the follow-up *Believe* (1977) that truly established them on the UK jazz, funk and soul scene with 'Cosmic Lust'.

Their other Cotillion albums were *In The Purest Form* (1979), including 'Strollin'', *Masterpiece* (1980), including 'Shante', and *Turn Up The Music* (1981). A further single 'Time Bomb' was released in 1983, following which they signed to the Paran label for 'Come Get Some Of This' (1984). While the group were essentially vocal-orientated, it was their instrumentals 'Cosmic Lust', 'Shante' (a UK Top 60 single) and 'Strollin'' which won them their greatest acclaim on the dancefloors.

MASSER, MICHAEL

(Songwriter/Producer)

Based in Los Angeles, Michael wrote numerous songs in the '70s and '80s, his ballads being particularly popular at the more commercial end of the soul music scene. Songs he has written, co-written and/or produced include 'Touch Me In The Morning', 'Theme From Mahogany', 'It's My Turn' and 'Last Time I Saw Him' (**Diana Ross**); 'A New Way To Say I Love You' (**Billy Preston/Syreeta**); 'Greatest Love Of All' (**George Benson/Whitney Houston**); 'Hold Me' (**Teddy Pendergrass/Whitney Houston**); 'Saving All My Love For You', 'All At Once', 'Didn't We Almost Have It All' and 'You're Still My Man' (**Whitney Houston**); 'In Your Eyes' (**George Benson**); 'Miss You Like Crazy' and 'Someone That I Used To Love' (**Natalie Cole**); 'Tonight I Celebrate My Love' (**Peabo Bryson/Roberta Flack**), and numerous others.

MATHIS, JOHNNY

(Singer)

Born in San Francisco in 1935, Johnny Mathis has been scoring hits since the late '50s. While his music does appeal to an r&b audience, it has been more geared towards middle-of-the-road pop, where it has been extremely successful.

Originally recording for Fontana Records, his early UK success came with 'Teacher Teacher' (Top 30, 1958), 'A Certain Smile' (Top 5, 1958), 'Winter Wonderland' (Top 20, 1958), 'Someone' (Top 10, 1959) and 'The Best Of Everything' (Top 30, 1959). When Fontana released these songs on *Johnny's Greatest Hits*, it stayed in the American charts for 490 weeks!

Further UK single success came with 'Misty' (Top 20, 1960), 'You Are Beautiful' (Top 50, 1960), 'Starbright' (Top 50, 1960) and 'My Love For You' (Top 10, 1960), before he switched labels to CBS. The hits followed with 'What Will My Mary Say' (Top 50, 1963), 'I'm Stone In Love With You' (Top 10, 1975), 'When A Child Is Born' (No. 1, 1976), 'Too Much Too Little Too Late' – a duet with **Deniece Williams** (Top 5, 1978), 'You're All I Need To Get By' – also with **Deniece Williams** (Top 50, 1978), and a disco single 'Gone Gone Gone' (Top 20, 1979). In 1981 he returned to the charts with a duet version of 'When A Child Is Born' with **Gladys Knight** (Top 75).

MATTHEW, ERIC

(Songwriter/Producer)

Based in New York, Eric was particularly productive on the early '80s dance scene with his songs and/or productions for artists including **Gary's Gang** ('Knock Me Out'), **Elektric Funk** ('On A Journey'), **Toney Lee** ('Reach Up'), **Arnie's Love** ('I'm Out Of Your Life'), **Sharon Redd** ('Never Give You Up' and 'Love How You Feel'), and **Sinnamon** ('Thanks To You'). He also instigated the studio group Status IV for whom he wrote and produced songs including 'You Ain't Really Down'.

MAUPIN, BENNIE

(Sax/Flute/Percussion)

Through the '60s Bennie worked on the fusion jazz scene with **Sonny Rollins**, Horace Silver, **McCoy Tyner**, **Freddie Hubbard**, **Miles Davis** and Chick Corea (among others). In the '70s he worked closely with **Herbie Hancock** as a member of **Headhunters**. As a solo artist he recorded for ECM (*The Jewel In The Lotus*) and Mercury (*Slow Traffic To The Right*, featuring **Patrice Rushen**, 1977).

MAYFIELD, CURTIS

(Singer/Songwriter/Producer)

Born in Chicago in 1942, Curtis was leading his own group The Alphatones before his teens. In 1956 he met **Jerry Butler** who sang in his grandmother's choir. Together they formed The Roosters which were later to become **The Impressions**. When the group scored with 'For Your Precious Love' the lead singer was Jerry Butler, and the hit launched Jerry's solo career.

Initially, Curtis continued to work with Jerry both writing songs (including 'He Will Break Your Heart') and touring as his guitarist. In 1961 he returned to The Impressions and became their lead singer on their recordings through to 1970.

In 1968 he launched his own Curtom label, his debut solo release for the label being 'Move On Up' (1970). Through the remainder of the '70s he released a series of his own singles/albums for the label, while also writing and/or producing with a number of artists he signed to Curtom including **Leroy Hutson**, **Linda Clifford**, **Natural Four** and **Mystique**. His own albums on the label include *Curtis* (1970); *Roots* (1971); *Superfly* (1972); *Back To The World* (1973), including 'Future Shock'; *Sweet Exorcist* (1974), including 'Kung Fu'; *There's No Place Like America Today* (1975); *Give, Get, Take And Have* (1976), including 'Soul Music'; *Do It All Night* (1978), including 'No Goodbyes'; and *Something To Believe In* (1980).

A number of these albums were soundtracks to movies, an area where Curtis scored success as both writer and producer for himself and other artists including **The Staple Singers** (*Let's Do It Again*), **Gladys Knight** (*Claudine*), **Aretha Franklin** (*Sparkle*) and **Mavis Staples** (*A Piece Of The Action*). Also during this time he wrote and/or produced with artists including **M.F.S.B.** ('Freddie's Dead'), **Marva Lee** ('If You Can't Be True'), **Aretha Franklin** (*Almighty Fire*) and **Keni Burke** ('Never Stop Loving Me').

In 1982 Curtis signed to the Broadwalk label (via Epic in the UK) where he recorded *Honesty*, including 'Hey Baby, Give It All To Me', before the liaison was cut short due to the death of label boss Neil Bogart. From here he moved to the CRC label for *We Come In Peace With A Message Of Love*, including 'Baby It's You', before rejuvenating the Curtom label via Ichiban Records in Atlanta.

In 1990 he teamed up with rapper Ice-T for 'Superfly 1990' on Capitol Records (the single release remixed by

Mantronix), but later in the year he was involved in an accident in New York which left him paralysed. A lighting rig fell on him during a concert, and he is still recovering in hospital.

MAZARATI

(Group)

From Minneapolis, Mazarati were begun by **Brownmark** and Sir Casey in 1982. They are Sir Casey (lead singer), Romeo (bass), Marr Starr (keyboards), Aaron 'Ace' Keith (keyboards), Tony Christian (rhythm guitar), Craig 'Screamer' Powell (lead guitar) and Kevin 'Blondie' Patricks (drums/percussion), who first worked together during their school days. Brownmark managed to sign them to **Prince**'s Paisley Park label after Brownmark himself became bass player with Prince. *Mazarati* was released in 1986, following which the group signed to Motown.

MAZE

(Group)

From Philadelphia, Maze were formed by **Frankie Beverly** in 1971, and were originally known **Raw Soul**. After local success Frankie took the group to San Francisco where they created a new style and changed their name. Upon signing to Capitol Records in 1976, Maze were **Frankie Beverly** (lead vocals), Roame 'Roame' Lowry (congas/vocals), McKinley 'Bug' Williams (percussion/vocals), Robin Duhe (bass), **Philip Woo** (keyboards), Sam Porter (keyboards), Wayne 'Ziggy' Lindsay (keyboards), Wayne Thomas (guitar), Ahaguna G. Sun (drums), and former **Patti Labelle** band members Ron Smith (lead guitar) and Billy 'Shoes' Johnson (drums). At Capitol they released a string of albums, *Maze Featuring Frankie Beverly* (1977), *Golden Time Of Day* (1978), *Inspiration* (1979), including 'Feel That You're Feelin'', and *Joy And Pain* (1980), including 'Southern Girl' and 'The Look In Your Eyes', all the while building a cult following on the UK soul scene.

Their next album was recorded live at the Saenger Theatre in New Orleans, with 15 November declared 'Maze Day' in the city. The album featured a live version of 'Joy And Pain' which made a major impact on the UK soul scene and won them a larger fan base. On 22 March 1981 Maze made their London stage debut at the Hammersmith Odeon, an event which goes down as one of the most electrifying live performances of all time. Frankie was so overcome he needed medical attention after coming off stage! Live recordings of 'Before I Let You Go' and 'Golden Time Of Day' were later released in the UK.

From here their albums were *We Are One* (1983), including 'Love Is The Key'; *Can't Stop The Love* (1985), including 'Too Many Games' (UK Top 40: B side of the single, 'Twilight', was 'instrumental of the year') and 'Back In Stride'; and *Live In Los Angeles* (1986), featuring the studio cut 'I Wanna Be With You' (UK Top 75). Reports of unrest within the group led to various changes, following which they switched to Warner Brothers. Here 1989's *Silky Soul* included 'Can't Get Over You'. The same year Capitol released an album of Maze remixes as a greatest hits collection.

MAZELLE, KYM

(Singer)

Born in Gary, Indiana, Kym lived in a house around the corner from **The Jacksons**, often calling in to sing them songs she had written. By the time she moved to Chicago in 1985 she was an accomplished gospel singer, and soon established herself on the city's underground 'house' music scene too. In 1987 she was approached by producer **Marshall Jefferson** to sing lead vocals with group House To House on recordings 'Taste My Love' and 'I'm A Lover' (1988), released by Police/Lower Level Records. While performing at a house music night in London, Kym was approached by Syncopate Records (via EMI) who signed her worldwide. Teaming her once again with Marshall Jefferson, her solo debut 'Useless (I Don't Need You Now)' reached the UK Top 75 in 1988.

Shortly afterwards she teamed up with Dr Robert of UK group The Blow Monkeys to record 'Wait' (1989), a Top 20 duet (for RCA Records) which firmly established Kym in the UK. She has since released 'Got To Get You Back' (UK Top 30, 1989), 'Love Strain' (1989), 'Was That All It Was' (1990), an album *Crazy* (1990) and a further single 'No One Can Love You More Than Me' (1991). These singles later featured on her album *Brilliant* (1991).

Kym has also worked closely with **Soul II Soul** and was the voice on their hit single 'Missing You' (1990).

McBRIDE, GEOFF

(Singer)

Born in North Carolina in 1963, Geoff sang gospel in his local Baptist church before turning to secular r&b music. Aged sixteen he sent a demo of his voice to Arista Records, the label which eventually signed him as a solo artist ten years later in 1989. In between times he toured clubs along the East Coast of America signing Top 40 songs. His debut album *Geoff McBride* was released in 1990.

McCLAIN, ALTON

(Singer)

Based in Los Angeles, Alton McClain sang with D'Marie and Robyrta as Alton McClain & Destiny for Polydor Records during the late '70s/early '80s. Appealing to the disco scene, she initially scored with 'It Must Be Love', the title track of her debut album (1979), following which she recorded a further two albums, *More Of You* (1980), including 'Hang On In There Baby' – dubbing on the voice of **Johnny Bristol** to make a duet, and *Gonna Tell The World* (1981), including 'My Destiny'. Much of her music was produced by **Skip Scarbrough**, whom she later married.

McCLAIN, JANICE
(Singer)
Born in Philadelphia, Janice decided to make singing her career while at elementary school. By her teens she was signed to Warner Brothers where in 1980 she recorded her first single 'Smack Dab In The Middle' produced by her uncle Milton Tennant. In 1982 Janice went to see **Patti LaBelle** perform at Jonesy's, a club in New Jersey. Patti picked her from the audience to sing acappella, Janice's rendition of 'Evergreen' being so impressive that Patti told MCA about her. The label signed Janice in 1986 and she released *Janice McClain* including 'Passion And Pain', a song produced by **Nick Martinelli**.

McCLAIN, MARLON
(Producer/Guitar)
Marlon McClain played guitar with Portland group **Pleasure** in the late '70s/early '80s, in addition to working as musician and producer for a number of artists for Fantasy Records. In 1981 he recorded his one solo album *Changes*, which featured **Jeff Lorber** with whom he later recorded again. In 1986 he joined **The Dazz Band** as guitarist and songwriter.

McCLARY, THOMAS
(Singer/Songwriter/Guitarist/Producer)
From Tuskegee, Alabama, Thomas was an original member of **The Commodores** when the group formed in 1969. Thomas played guitar and was one of the vocalists. In 1984 he left The Commodores and signed to Motown as a solo artist. A single 'Thin Walls' (featuring **Lionel Richie** on background vocals) and album *Thomas McClary* were released that year.

Thomas has also written and produced songs for **Michael Henderson** (*Fickle*, 1983) and **Klique** (*Love Cycles*, 1985).

McCLENDON, DAVID
(Singer)
The son of Revd Walter McClendon from California, David recorded one soul album *Better Make Sure* for the G.M.L.P. label in 1988.

McCLURE, BOBBY
(Singer)
Born in Chicago, the youngest of three brothers, Bobby moved with his family to East St Louis, Illinois, by the time he was old enough to go to school. Developing vocal skills in church, he sang with a vocal group The Spirit Of Illinois by the age of nine. At one performance with the group in a Chicago church, he was joined by **Sam Cooke** for an impromptu performance. From school he joined Big Daddy Jenkins & The Rhythm Kings as lead vocalist before touring with the *Oliver Sain* revue and eventually signing to Chess Records. Here he worked with **Fontella Bass** and had success with the duets 'You Gonna Mess Up A Good Thing' and 'Don't Jump (Out Of The Skillet Into The Fire)'. As a solo artist he recorded 'I Want To Reach The Peak Of Love' and 'You Don't Love Me' for the label.

When Chess folded and domestic problems arose, he took time off from the business to work as a correction officer inside an Illinois penitentiary. He quit in 1982 after deciding at the last minute not to take a test to become a lieutenant. Giving his singing career another chance he took to the club circuit again, two years later hooking up with drummer/producer **James Gadson**.

In 1986 a demo tape landed on the desk of **Al Bell** who had just started Edge Records in Los Angeles. Impressed by Bobby's voice, Al flew him to the city to sign a record deal. He released a single, 'You Never Miss Your Water'/'It Feels So Good (To Be Back Home)', arranged and produced by James Gadson, in 1987.

McCOO, MARILYN & BILLY DAVIS JR
(Vocal Duo)
Marilyn McCoo and Billy Davis Jr were members of **The Fifth Dimension** before becoming a vocal duo in the late '70s. Recording for ABC Records, they are best remembered for the **Don Davis**-produced 'You Don't Have To Be A Star (To Be In My Show)' (UK Top 10, 1977), followed by the Frank Wilson-produced album *The Two Of Us* (1977), including 'Look What You've Done To My Heart'. In 1978 they recorded the original version of 'Saving All My Love For You', later a huge international hit for **Whitney Houston**.

McCORD, KEVIN
(Singer/Songwriter/Producer)
Born in Detroit, Kevin Duane McCord was one of the three founder members of **One Way** (for whom he wrote songs including 'Lady You Are'). While the group were signed to MCA Records he wrote and produced for label mates **Alicia Myers** ('You Get The Best From Me' and 'Appreciation') and **Oliver Cheatham** (cowriting 'Get Down Saturday Night') before forming his own label Chance in Detroit.

His other productions include 'You Hit My Love' (**Hari Parris**), 'Say That You Will' (**Cortez**), 'Play Your Cards Right' (**Vicki Harvey**), 'Loved Right' (**Plush**) and 'I Want You' (Reel Touch). His wife is recording artist Candye Edwards (now Candy McCord) for whom he has written and produced; he also produced a single 'True Love' for his brother Snooky McCord.

McCOY, VAN
(Producer/Songwriter)
Born in Washington DC in 1940, Van McCoy initially worked with his brother in a group called The Starlighters. They recorded three singles for the End label before going their separate ways in 1961. Moving into song-writing and production Van worked with artists for the Wand label, including **Chuck Jackson** and **The Shirelles**,

and other artists including **Ruby & The Romantics**, ('When You're Young And In Love'), **The Marvelettes** (another recording of 'When You're Young And In Love'), **Jackie Wilson** ('I Get The Sweetest Feeling') and The Presidents ('5–10–15–20'). He also ran a couple of small labels, including Vando (artists including Chris Bartley) and Share (artists including The Ad-Libs), during the '60s.

In the early '70s he formed the group **Faith, Hope & Charity** before becoming a solo artist and signing with the Avco label. Here he scored with a series of instrumentals with backing vocal refrains: 'The Hustle' (UK Top 5, 1975), 'Change With The Times' (UK Top 40, 1975), 'Soul Cha Cha' (UK Top 40, 1977) and 'The Shuffle' (UK Top 5, 1977). His albums included *Disco Baby* (1975), *The Disco Kid* (1975), *The Real McCoy* and *Lonely Dancer*.

In the meantime he worked consistently as a songwriter and/or producer for artists including **Gladys Knight & The Pips** ('Baby Don't Change Your Mind'), **Aretha Franklin** ('Walk Softly', 'You Brought Me Back To Life', 'The Feeling' and most of *La Diva*; **Linda Clifford** ('You Gotta Tell Her'), **Stacy Lattisaw** ('Young And In Love'), **Melba Moore** and **Barbara Lewis**. He died in the late '70s.

McCRAE, GEORGE

(Singer)

Born in West Palm Beach, Florida, in 1944, George formed a vocal group The Jivin' Jets before serving in the Navy. Upon his return he married **Gwen McCrae** and the couple performed in local Florida clubs before their recording debut with 'Three Hearts In A Tangle' for Alston Records (via TK) in the early '70s.

Deciding to record as independent solo artists, George signed to United Artists while Gwen signed with CBS where she was initially more successful. Because of this, George worked as her road manager until his own success with 'Rock Your Baby' (UK No. 1, 1974) reversed the roles. George followed up (via Jayboy Records in the UK) with hits 'I Can't Leave You Alone' (Top 10, 1974), 'You Can Have It All' (Top 30, 1974), 'Sing A Happy Song' (Top 40, 1975), 'It's Been So Long' (Top 5, 1975), 'I Ain't Lying' (Top 20, 1975) and 'Honey I' (Top 40, 1974). His popularity put a strain on his marriage to Gwen and the couple split up.

Moving to Canada, George resumed his career in 1984 after signing to President Records for 'One Step Closer To Love' (UK Top 75, 1984) and 'Let's Dance' (1985), although it was only recently that he returned once again for 'Breathless', released by Tam Tam Records in 1991.

McCRAE, GWEN

(Singer)

Born in Pensacola, Florida, in 1943, Gwen began a recording career with her husband **George McCrae** shortly after their marriage. Deciding on solo recording careers, Gwen signed to CBS and was more successful until George scored with 'Rock Your Baby' (a song that was originally written by H. Cassey for Gwen) and a string of hits.

Switching to the Cat label (via TK) she recorded a series of singles/albums during the mid-'70s which became popular on the UK 'rare groove' scene during the mid-'80s. These include '90% Of Me Is You' (from 1975's *Rockin' Chair*), and 'All This Love That I'm Giving' (re-issued on Flame Records/Rhythm King and a UK Top 75 hit in 1988). Cat albums included *Gwen McCrae*, *Melody Of Life* and *Let's Straighten It Out* (1978).

In the early 80s she switched to Atlantic where she recorded the dance classic 'Funky Sensation' (1981) prior to working with producer **Webster Lewis** on *On My Way* (1982), including the **Willie Hutch**-penned 'Keep The Fire Burning'.

McCRARYS

(Vocal Group)

Based in Los Angeles, family group The McCrarys are best remembered for the **Wayne Henderson**-produced *All Night Music* (1982), including 'Love On A Summer Night', for Capitol Records. The group featured Howard McCrary who later recorded a solo gospel album *So Good* for the Good News label (via A&M) in 1985.

McCULLER, ARNOLD

(Singer)

Based in Los Angeles, Arnold has sung backgrounds for artists including **General Johnson**, **Debra Laws** and **Brenda Russell**, in addition to being the featured lead vocalist on 'It's A Fact' for **Jeff Lorber**.

McCULLOUGH, ULLANDA

(Singer)

Based in New York, Ullanda worked consistently through the '70s and early '80s as a backing singer, particularly with **Ashford & Simpson** who produced her solo album *Ullanda McCullough* for Atlantic in 1981. Elsewhere she recorded backing vocals with **Lou Rawls**, **Teddy Pendergrass**, **Z.Z.Hill**, **Lonnie Liston Smith**, **Cliff Dawson**, **Melba Moore**, **Roberta Flack**, **Hi-Gloss** and **Charles Earland** among many more.

McDANIELS, EUGENE

(Singer/Songwriter/Producer)

Born in Kansas City, 'Gene' McDaniels grew up in a gospel environment before scoring in the American charts with 'A Hundred Pounds Of Clay' (1961). His follow-ups included 'Tower Of Strength', 'Chip Chip', 'Point Of No Return' and 'Another Tear Falls' (from the film *It's Trad, Dad* in which he also appeared, 1962).

In the mid-'60s he recorded for Liberty Records (including 'Walk With A Winner', 1965), before switching to Atlantic in the early '70s for *Outlaw* and *Headless Horseman Of The Apocalypse*. He is perhaps best known for writing the classic 'Feel Like Making Love' for **Roberta**

Flack, while he also built a reputation as a producer for artists including **Merry Clayton**.

McDONALD, MICHAEL

(Singer/Songwriter/Keyboards)

Based in Los Angeles, Michael originally played keyboards and sang with The Doobie Brothers in the mid-'70s. As (white falsetto) lead vocalist he is featured on their American hits 'Takin' It To The Streets' (1976), 'It Keeps You Runnin'' (1976) and 'What A Fool Believes' (UK Top 40, 1979), which he also co-wrote.

Elsewhere he co-wrote songs including 'Hello People' (**Brenda Russell**), 'That's How You Start Over' (**Diana Ross**), 'Any Way You Can' (**Patti Austin**) and 'Yah Mo B There' (**James Ingram**) on which he sang prior to signing to Warner Brothers as a solo artist in 1985. Here he recorded *No Looking Back* (1986), including 'I Keep Forgettin'' (UK Top 50), although he scored greater success at MCA with 'Sweet Freedom' from the movie soundtrack *Running Scared* (UK Top 20, 1986) and 'On My Own' – a duet with **Patti Labelle** (UK Top 5, 1986).

He has also sung backgrounds with artists including **Sergio Mendes**, **El Debarge**, **Diana Ross** and **The Winans** (lead on 'Love Has No Colour', 1987). His most recent album was *Take It To Heart* (1990).

McDOWELL, CARRIE

(Singer)

From Des Moines, Iowa, Carrie appeared on Johnny Carson's *The Tonight Show* at the age of ten singing 'Somewhere Over The Rainbow'. Moving to Los Angeles she auditioned for **Willie Hutch** with whom she worked on an album for the Motown label. In the meanwhile **Berry Gordy** employed her as his personal manager. Back in the studio, her debut release for Motown was an anti-AIDS record 'Uh Uh, No No Casual Sex' (also an antidote to George Michael's 'I Want Your Sex'), produced by Willie Hutch.

McFADDEN & WHITEHEAD

(Singers/Songwriters/Producers)

From Philadelphia, Gene McFadden and **John Whitehead** first met at school during the '60s. Here they formed a group The Epsilons with Lloyd Parkes (who later joined **Harold Melvin & The Blue Notes**). When **Otis Redding** came to Philadelphia, The Epsilons were invited to become part of his revue, an opportunity which led to a small record deal with Stax. Here the group had an r&b hit in 1970 with 'The Echo'.

After the departure of Lloyd Parkes, Gene and John changed the name of their group to Talk Of The Town, and worked with **Gamble/Huff** who groomed them on their North Bay label. Discovering their talent for writing and producing, Kenny Gamble and Leon Huff employed McFadden & Whitehead at their Philadelphia International (PIR) label through the '70s, collaborating with them at first on 'I'll Always Love My Mama' for **The Intruders**. While at the label their songs and/or productions were utilised by **Archie Bell** & The Drells ('Let's Groove', 'Soul City Walk', 'Strategy' and 'Don't Let Love Get You Down'), **The O'Jays** ('Backstabbers'), **Harold Melvin & The Blue Notes** ('Bad Luck', 'Wake Up Everybody' and 'Prayin'') – the latter for the Source label and **Carolyn Crawford** ('Just Got To Be More Careful'), a number of these songs written in collaboration with their associate Victor Carstaphen.

In 1979 they recorded their own album *McFadden & Whitehead*, from which 'Ain't No Stoppin' Us Now' became a dancefloor anthem and a UK Top 5 hit. (Two more versions of the song were released back to back in 1981 – The Philadelphia Phillies version and The Philadelphia Eagles version, on the label's T.S.O.P. subsidiary.) After leaving PIR they re-recorded 'Ain't No Stoppin' Us Now' as 'Ain't No Stoppin' (Ain't No Way)' for the Sutra label in New York (1984), and worked on some individual projects.

Away from PIR they also worked with **Melba Moore** ('Standing Right Here', 'Pick Me Up I'll Dance' and 'Let's Stand Together'), **Gloria Gaynor** ('Let's Mend What's Been Broken'), **Freddie Jackson** ('I Don't Want To Lose Your Love'), **Willie Collins** ('Determination') and **Beau Williams**.

McFADDEN, RUTH

(Singer)

This Philadelphia-based singer worked with **Kenny Gamble** during the early '70s and recorded 'Ghetto Woman' on his Gamble label in 1973.

McFARLANE/GEORGE

(Songwriters/Producers)

Based in New York, Fred McFarlane and Allen George emerged on the dance scene from the mid-'80s with songs and/or productions for artists including **Jocelyn Brown** ('Somebody Else's Guy' and 'I Wish You Would'), **Intrigue** ('Fly Girl'), **Jenny Burton** ('Bad Habits'), **Evelyn 'Champagne' King** ('Your Personal Touch' and 'High Horse') and **Alton 'Wokie' Stewart** (*All Our Love*). They have their own company Terrible Two Productions. Independently, Fred McFarlane played keyboards on the **Fatback** classic 'I Found Lovin'' (1983).

McFERRIN, BOBBY

(Singer/Songwriter)

Based in San Francisco, Bobby first began writing and performing professionally in the mid-'70s, eventually landing a recording deal with the Elektra Musician label in 1980 (the year he was the featured lead vocalist with **Pharaoh Sanders** on 'You've Got To Have Freedom'). His debut album *Bobby McFerrin* (1982), including 'Dance With Me' (a duet with **Phoebe Snow**) and 'Moondance', appealed to both soul and jazz fans, although subsequent albums have been voice only, in his own unique style. A second album *The Voice* was released by

Elektra Musician in 1984, following which he switched to Manhattan/EMI where *Spontaneous Inventions* (1986) included the hit 'Thinkin' About Your Body' and *Simple Pleasures* (1988) included 'Don't Worry Be Happy' (UK Top 5). *Medicine Music* was released in 1991.

In 1990 he recorded with **Quincy Jones** on 'Wee B. Dooinit' from Quincy's *Back On The Block* and was the voice on the TV adverts for Cadbury's Flake with a song 'Chocolate' (illegally remixed with a dance beat and later issued as a bootleg single!).

McGEE
(Singer)
Tommy McGee teamed up with producers including **Jeff Lane** to cut his single 'Now That I Have You' for the American Dream Records label in 1984. The strings arrangement was by **Norman Harris**.

McGEE, FRANCINE
(Singer/Songwriter/Keyboards)
Very little is known about Francine McGee except for the one 12" single 'Delirium' for RCA in 1978. An instrumental jazz funk classic, it was in fact the B-side to a vocal 'Feelin' Good' which had no impact whatsoever.

McGEE, JAY W.
(Singer)
Born in Lumberton, North Carolina, Jay performed with groups including Salongon and Crack Of Dawn prior to his solo single debut 'When We Party' (1984) for Scorpio Records (later on an album *Over And Over*). By this time he had moved to Toronto, Canada, where he worked in a record shop and sang with a group The Executives.

McGRIFF, JIMMY
(Organ)
Born in Philadelphia in 1936, Jimmy originally played bass before **Jimmy Smith** inspired him to take up the organ. Forming a trio in 1962, he recorded 'I Got A Woman' (the **Ray Charles** song) originally released on the Jell label (later Sue Records). He stayed on at Sue for 'All About My Girl' (1963) and 'The Last Minute' (1964), before recording for Solid State, Capital and Groove Merchant, where he recorded with fellow organist Richard 'Groove' Holmes. During the '70s he recorded for the Blue Note label, albums including *Black Pearl* (1971) and *Electric Funk* prior to a further switch to Milestone for albums including *Skywalk* (1984). It was Jimmy who encouraged **Charles Earland** to switch from sax to organ.

McKAY, AL
(Guitar/Producer)
Born in Los Angeles, Albert Philip McKay became guitarist with **Earth Wind & Fire** once the group had moved from Chicago and signed with CBS. He remains with the group to this day, and co-produced 'Boogie Wonderland', while elsewhere he has produced for artists including **A Taste Of Honey**, **Carl Anderson** ('Can't Stop This Feeling'), **Finis Henderson** ('Skip To My Lou'), **Caldera**, **Glenn Jones** ('Keep On Doin''), **The Temptations** (*Truly For You*, including 'Treat Her Like A Lady') and **Durell Coleman** ('Do You Love Me').

McLEAN, JACKIE
(Singer/Saxophone)
Signed to RCA in the late '70s, Jackie is best remembered for 'Doctor Jackal And Mister Funk', popular on the UK dance scene and taken from *Monuments* (1979).

McLEOD, MARILYN
(Singer/Songwriter/Producer)
Based in Los Angeles, Marilyn recorded for Fantasy Records in the late '70s (including 'I Got Love On My Mind', 1979), but is best remembered for her songs and/or productions for artists including **Diana Ross** ('Love Hangover'), **Junior Walker** ('Walk In The Night'), High Inergy ('You Can't Turn Me Off In The Middle Of Turning Me On'), **Mighty Fire** (*No Time For Masquerading*), **The Four Tops** ('Back Where I Belong'), **Anita Baker** ('Same Ole Love') and **Jean Carne** ('Don't Let Me Slip Away' and 'Super Explosion').

More recently she has recorded again as a solo artist, this time for the UK Motorcity label, where her songs have been 'Straight On The Line' and 'Wish You Were Here' (1990).

McLOYD, EDDIE
(Singer)
Eddie emerged during the pre-disco era in 1975 with 'Baby Get Down', but is more fondly remembered for the single's B-side, 'Once You Fall In Love'.

McNAIR, BARBARA
(Singer)
Based in Los Angeles, Barbara established herself on the '60s jazz scene before signing with Motown for the r&b-based *The Real Barbara McNair* (1968), including 'It Happens Every Time'. Also at Motown she recorded the original version of 'For Once In My Life', later a classic hit for **Stevie Wonder**.

Barbara was also a national American beauty queen, starred in her own TV show, gave tips on makeup in numerous women's magazines and appeared nude in Playboy! More recently she has recorded with songwriter/producer **Ian Levine** at the UK Motorcity label, her songs including 'Face To Face With Love' (1990).

McNEIR, RONNIE
(Singer/Songwriter/Producer)
Born in Camden, Alabama, in 1951, Ronnie was raised in Pontiac, Michigan, where he was mesmerized by the Motown sound of Detroit. As a child, however, most of his energy was directed at basketball until a car accident

left him with a minor leg injury which forced him to give the game up. Playing the piano became an obsession, and by the age of fourteen he was an accomplished musician and writer. In 1966 he won $250 in a talent show, an award which led to his debut single 'Sitting In My Class', later regarded as a Northern soul classic.

In 1971 he moved to Los Angeles where he met **Rene Moore** (of **Rene & Angela**) and joined his church choir. Here he met **Kim Weston** who gave him a job as her musical director. While on tour he wrote Kim some songs, 'What Kind Of Man' and 'Gonna Be All Right', in return for which she helped him secure a record deal with RCA. Here an album *Ronnie McNeir*, produced by Mickey Stevenson (Kim's husband), was released in 1972.

In 1975 he was with Prodigal Records, which gave him his first taste of success with an American hit 'Wendy Is Gone'. This was followed up by a Prodigal album *Ronnie McNeir* before the company was acquired by Motown. The following year Motown released *Love's Comin' Down*, including 'You're All I Need To Survive' and 'It Won't Be Long (When We're All Gone)'. He recorded a further four albums at Motown which were not released.

Ronnie then recorded for a number of small labels before joining Capitol and working with **Rene & Angela** on a mini-album *The Ronnie McNeir Experience* (1984). In the UK this project was released as a 12" EP and featured all four tracks, 'Come Be With Me', 'Light My Fire', 'Is This What Happens To A Love' and 'Keep Giving Me Love'.

In 1987 *Love Suspect*, including 'Lately', 'Everybody's In A Hurry' and 'Follow Your Heart', was released on his own Setting Sun label, and licensed in the UK by Expansion. Its popularity here led to Expansion signing him for a second album *Life And Love* (1989), including 'Hold On' and 'Simply Ridiculous'. (In between, a single 'My Baby' was released on Setting Sun.) In the UK Ronnie recorded a number of sides for the Motorcity label as part of its Detroit reunion project in 1989–90 (songs including 'Wholeheartedly', 'You're My Lucky Number' and 'No More Confusion'). He is also the featured vocalist on 'Magic In The City', a tribute to Detroit by Dan Yessian on the Stardisc label (1989).

Elsewhere Ronnie has worked as writer and/or producer with **Smokey Robinson** (movie soundtrack *Big Time*, 1977), **Teena Marie** ('Love Just Wouldn't Be Right' and the duet 'We've Got To Stop'), **Sandra Feva**, **David Ruffin/Eddie Kendricks**, **Rance Allen** ('Feeling Like Going On'), **Bobby Womack** ('Caught Up In The Middle'), **T.W.Bankston**, **Klique** ('Ain't Nothing Better') and The Dramatics ('Live Your Life'). He has also toured with **The Four Tops**, the group's Renaldo Benson being Ronnie's co-writer/producer over the last few years.

McPHATTER, CLYDE

(Singer)

Born in 1933, Clyde McPhatter joined The Dominoes as pianist, arranger and songwriter in 1950. After building a following for himself Clyde let **Jackie Wilson** take over as lead singer while he formed his own group **The Drifters** in 1953 and later scored solo hits in his own right. In the States he recorded for the Atlantic and Amy labels (including 'Lonely People Can't Afford To Cry'), while in the UK 'Treasure Of Love' was a Top 30 hit for the London label in 1956.

McWILLIAMS, PAULETTE

(Singer)

Born in Chicago, Paulette sang gospel from the age of three and appeared several times on TV's *The Amateur Hour* during her childhood. In the '60s she sang lead vocals with local group American Breed which scored an American r&b hit with 'Bend Me Shape Me' before she was replaced by **Chaka Khan** and the group changed their name to **Rufus** in 1970.

Paulette established herself as a top session singer, recording with **Quincy Jones** on his *Mellow Madness* album (1975) prior to her own solo record deal with Fantasy. Here she recorded *Never Been Here Before* (1977), including 'Main Squeeze'. Settling in Los Angeles, she moved into the lucrative world of singing on TV commercials, while building a relationship with **Luther Vandross** as one of his key backing singers.

In 1985 she teamed up with Toi Overton to record an album as co-lead vocalist of **Fire Fox**, following which she resumed her work with Luther alongside backing vocal duties for **Aretha Franklin**, **Carl Anderson**, **Stephanie Mills**, **Dennis Edwards** and **Millie Scott**.

MECO

(Arranger/Producer/Multi-instrumentalist)

Meco Monardo is perhaps best remembered for his disco version of the 'Star Wars Theme', released by RCA in 1977 and a UK Top 10 hit. His credits can also be found as arranger and/or producer for artists including **Gloria Gaynor** ('Never Can Say Goodbye' and 'I've Got You', 1976), **Kenny G** (*Kenny G*) and **Don Downing**.

MEL & TIM

(Duo)

Mel Hardin and Tim McPherson were cousins from Mississippi. In 1969 they were signed to the Bamboo label (owned by **Gene Chandler**) and released 'Blackfield In Motion'. The song was a million-seller across America before they signed to Stax for a series of singles and a 1972 album *Starting All Over Again*.

MELLA

(Group)

This little-known group from Los Angeles recorded just one single 'Makin' Love In The Fast Lane' in 1982. It was released by the Larc label (prior to it becoming Private I), and generated interest in the UK for the B side 'Free', which remains popular among UK soul fans.

MELVIN, HAROLD

(Singer)

Born in Philadelphia, Harold decided to form a vocal group with some friends with whom he sang doo-wop on Philly street corners in the mid-'50s. Calling themselves Harold Melvin & The Blue Notes they first put their voices to vinyl in 1956 with a single debut 'If You Love Me' released by the local Josie label. During the '60s they built up a professional reputation on the local club scene, recording 'My Hero' for the Value label (1960), 'Get Out' (1964) and 'This Time Will Be Different' for the Uni label (1969). Harold worked during this period as the group's songwriter, arranger and choreographer.

In the early to mid-'70s they were groomed into international stars by **Gamble/Huff** who signed them to their Philadelphia International (PIR) label in 1972. However it was **Teddy Pendergrass** who was the powerful lead singer on their UK hits including 'If You Don't Know Me By Now' (Top 10, 1973), 'The Love I Lost' (Top 25, 1973), 'Satisfaction Guaranteed (Or Take Your Love Back)' (Top 40, 1974), 'Wake Up Everybody' (Top 25, 1976) and 'Don't Leave Me This Way' (Top 5, 1977). Their PIR albums to this point had included *Harold Melvin & The Blue Notes* (1972), *Black And Blue* (1973), *To Be True* (1975), *Wake Up Everybody* (1975) and *Collector's Items* (1976).

When Teddy took up a solo career in 1977, Harold replaced him with David Ebo who had a remarkably similar voice. Leaving PIR **Harold Melvin & The Blue Notes** signed to ABC where the title track from *Reaching For The World* was a UK Top 50 single. A move to the Source label (one album *1980*, including 'Praying', 1979) was followed by a further switch to MCA where *All Things Happen In Time* included 'Hang On In There'. Other MCA albums were *Now Is The Time* and *The Blue Album*.

In 1984 they signed to Philly World who were rejuvenating the city's r&b scene during the mid-'80s. *Talk It Up* was released (via London in the UK), and singles 'Don't Give Me Up' and 'Today's Your Lucky Day' (co-produced by **Nick Martinelli**) reached the UK Top 75 that year.

MEMPHIS HORNS

(Horn section)

The Memphis Horns were a group of brass and reed players who were integral to the Memphis sound during the '60s and '70s, particularly at the Stax label. When they came to record in their own right, Wayne Jackson (trumpet), Andrew Love (tenor sax), Ed Logan (tenor sax), Lewis Collins, Jack Hale (trombone) and James Mitchell (baritone sax) signed to RCA for albums including *High On Music* (produced by **Booker T. Jones**) and *Get Up And Dance* (1977). They can also be found on recordings by **King Curtis** (*Live At Fillmore West*, 1971) and **Aretha Franklin** (including *With Everything I Feel In Me*, 1974), among many more.

MENDES, SERGIO

(Keyboards/Bandleader)

Born in Niteroi, Brazil, in 1941, Sergio took up classical piano at the age of seven. During his teens he discovered jazz and was leading his own band by the age of sixteen. He soon gained international recognition composing bossa nova, a fusion of Brazilian music with soul and jazz. In 1965 he and his band moved to Los Angeles, and in 1966 they toured as opening act for **Herb Alpert** & The Tijuana Brass. The following year Herb signed him to his A&M label and produced his debut album *Sergio Mendes 66*.

Continuing to record on and off for A&M over the years, his hits include 'The Look Of Love' (US Top 10), 'Scarborough Fair', 'The Fool On The Hill' (Lennon/McCartney song), and 'Never Gonna Let You Go' featuring **Leza Miller** (1983). He also recorded for the Riverside, Philips, Atlantic, Capitol, Elektra and Bell labels. In 1986 an A&M album *Brasil '86* featured lead vocals from **Siedah Garrett**, and in 1987 Sergio produced the **Sarah Vaughan** album *Brazilian Romance*. His most famous release is 'Mas Que Nada', originally released in the '60s and remixed in 1989 by Justin Strauss for A&M.

He has also worked with **Jeffrey Osborne**, **James Ingram**, Lani Hall and **Michael McDonald**.

MERC AND MONK

(Duo)

Merc and Monk are **Thelonius Monk III** and **Eric Mercury**, who teamed up in 1983 after first working together in **T.S. Monk**. Signing to Manhattan Records in 1985 they released the single 'Baby Face' and one album.

MERCER, BARBRA

(Singer)

From Detroit, Barbra recorded with Golden World Records in the mid-'60s delivering r&b songs like 'Hey' and 'Can't Stop Loving You Baby' (back-to-back in 1965). In 1967 Sidra Records released 'So Real'/'Call On Me' (later issued by Capitol).

MERCURY, ERIC

(Singer/Producer)

Born and raised in Toronto, Eric was the youngest of seven children and the son of a Methodist minister. After developing his vocal skills in church, he worked on the Toronto club scene, becoming resident at the Blue Note. His first solo recording was *Electric Black Man* for the Avco Embassy label. He later cut albums for Enterprise, Mercury, Columbia and Capitol.

As a producer he has worked with **Roberta Flack** and **Donny Hathaway**, co-producing 'Don't Make Me Wait Too Long' and 'Back Together Again', also co-writing 'You Are My Heaven' with **Stevie Wonder** from the same 1979 album, *Roberta Flack Featuring Donny Hathaway*.

METERS
(Group)
From New Orleans, The Meters were Art Neville (keyboards), Leo Nocentelli (guitar), Joseph 'Zig' Modeliste (drums) and George Porter (bass), originally known as The Hawkettes. Initially hired as a backing band, they toured and/or recorded with Fats Domino, Lee Dorsey and Art's brother Aaron Neville (both later forming The Neville Brothers). In 1969 they began recording in their own right, scoring with tracks like 'Sophisticated Cissy' and 'Cissy Strut' for the Josie label. In 1970 the group switched to Reprise, moving in the direction of rock.

METROPOLIS
(Studio Group)
In 1977 Salsoul Records put their in-house string and horn sections together with a bunch of other New York session musicians and girl singers to record as Metropolis. A 1978 release 'I Love New York' created a brief stir on the disco scene that year.

MIAMI
(Group)
Instigated by Willie Clarke, and featuring Robert Moore, Florida group Miami recorded for the Drive label (via TK) in the mid-'70s. In 1974 they stirred dancefloors with 'Party Freaks' but it was in 1976 that they delivered 'Kill That Roach' which remains a classic dance track and 'rare groove'.

MIDNIGHT STAR
(Group)
Formed in 1976 at Kentucky State University, Midnight Star were originally fellow students **Reggie Calloway** (trumpet/flute/percussion), Vincent Calloway (trombone/trumpet/percussion), Belinda Lipscomb (lead vocals), Melvin Watson (lead vocals), Boaz 'Bo' Watson (lead vocals/keyboards), Jeffrey Cooper (lead guitar/keyboards), Kenneth Gant (bass/vocals), Bobby Lovelace (drums) and William Simmons (sax/keyboards/percussion). After their university days they relocated to Cincinnati, then eventually landed a recording deal with Solar Records in Los Angeles. Early albums included *Midnight Star, The Beginning* (1981) and *Victory* (1982), before the group first made an impact across America and on the UK dance scene with *No Parking On The Dancefloor* (1983). The album included 'Electricity', 'Wet My Whistle' and 'Freak-A-Zoid'.

Planetary Invasion was released in 1984 from which 'Operator' marked the group's first UK commercial success when it reached the Top 75 in 1985. The album also included 'Curious', popular with UK soul fans. The pinnacle of the group's UK success came in 1986 when *Headlines* included the hit singles 'Headlines' (Top 20), 'Midas Touch' (Top 10) and 'Engine No. 9' (Top 75).

At this point the Calloway brothers left the group to form **Calloway** while the remaining members stayed on at Solar for *Midnight Star* (1988) and *Work It Out* (1990) including 'Money Can't Buy You Love'.

MIDNITE EXPRESS
(Group)
Based in the UK, Midnite Express featured the lead vocals of **Patrick Boothe** and recorded for GTO Records in the early '80s. The group were forerunners of the Brit funk scene and are best remembered for their live work supporting visiting American artists.

MIGHTY FIRE
(Group)
Based in Los Angeles, Mighty Fire were Darryl K. Roberts (keyboards/bass/vocals), Perry Payton (lead vocals/drums), Mel Bolton (guitar/producer/vocals), D'Laine McQuaig (lead vocals/guitar) and Harry Kim (trumpet/vocals). For Elektra Records they made an impact on the UK soul scene with *No Time For Masquerading* (1981), including 'Sweet Fire'.

MILES, ARTHUR
(Singer/Guitarist)
Born in the state of Indiana, Arthur is the nephew of the late Wes Montgomery. By the age of sixteen he was a professional guitarist and worked with artists including **Edwin Starr** during the '70s. After a number of years touring with various artists he settled in Italy where in 1990 he recorded a solo debut 'Helping Hand', released in the UK by London Records.

MILES, BUDDY
(Singer/Drummer)
Buddy Miles recorded for CBS from the mid to late '70s and is most fondly remembered for the **Johnny Bristol**-penned/produced 'Just A Kiss Away' (1974). As The Buddy Miles Express, his albums included *Booger Bear.*

MILIRA
(Singer)
From Hollis, New York, Milira Jones was born into a musical family. Her mother and aunt had sung with **Jackie Wilson** as members of The Wilsonettes. In 1990 she became the first artist to record on the Apollo Theatre label (via Motown), her debut single being a version of 'Mercy Mercy Me' from her debut album *Milira.*

MILLER, BYRON
(Bass/Keyboards/Vocals)
Byron established himself as a bass player in the early '70s, joining **Roy Ayers** in Ubiquity during 1975 (playing bass on 'Mystic Voyage' and 'Evolution'). During the mid-'80s he performed with **The Crusaders** while much later in 1990 he teamed up with a star cast including **Stanley Clarke**, **George Duke**, **George Howard** and **Rodney Franklin** for *Git Wit Me*, including 'Gotta Get It Right' and 'You That I Need', for Nova Records in Los Angeles.

MILLER, CAT

(Singer)

Born in North Carolina, Cat Miller took her vocal training from her local church choir before joining the group **Chanson** in 1979. Later she sang with Carnival, before touring with **The Brothers Johnson** and **War** as a solo artist. Following this she toured Europe with her own show.

As a session singer she has worked with **Stacy Lattisaw**, **Hiroshima** and scored a solo deal with Solar Records after originally auditioning to be **Jody Watley**'s replacement in **Shalamar**. A solo single 'Ready Or Not' was released by ARS Records in Belgium (1985).

MILLER, MARCUS

(Bass/Songwriter/Producer/Singer)

Born in Brooklyn, New York, in 1960, Marcus has built himself a reputation as one of the finest jazz/r&b bass players in the business. He was initially discovered in the mid-'70s by **Lonnie Liston Smith**, who employed him at various gigs. In 1978 Lonnie recorded a Marcus Miller composition 'Space Princess', a UK jazz funk anthem.

In 1979 Marcus wrote 'Love When I'm In Your Arms' for **Bobbi Humphrey** before teaming up with **Dave Grusin** as bass player on his 1980 album *Mountain Dance*. From here Marcus embarked on a string of session work with artists including **Bernard Wright**, **Tom Browne** ('Funkin' For Jamaica'), **The Brecker Brothers**, **Bob James** (for whom he has also written), **Charles Earland** and eventually **Luther Vandross**. With Luther, Marcus developed a songwriting/production partnership which remains to this day. Songs they have co-written to date include 'You're The Sweetest One', 'I Wanted Your Love', 'Busy Body', 'The Night I Fell In Love' and 'See Me' for Luther's own albums. They have also written, produced and recorded for **Aretha Franklin** ('Jump To It' and 'It's Just Your Love'), **Dionne Warwick** ('Got A Date') and **The Temptations** ('Do You Really Love Your Baby').

In 1983 Marcus recorded the first of two solo albums for Warner Brothers, *Suddenly* (including 'Much Too Much'). His second album *Marcus Miller* was released in 1984.

In 1988 he produced/co-wrote 'Da 'Butt', a go-go anthem for **E.U.** taken from the movie soundtrack *School Daze*. He has also written and/or produced for **David Sanborn**, **Bernard Wright**, **Steven Dante**, **Roberta Flack**, **Grover Washington** ('Summer Nights') and most recently **Joe Sample** ('Strike Two'). His bass sessions include recordings with **Marc Sadane**, **Peggi Blu**, **Miles Davis** and **Roberta Flack** among many others.

MILLER, RONALD DEAN

(Songwriter/Producer)

Based in New York, Ronald worked on the '80s dance scene writing and/or producing for artists including **Raw Silk**, a group he formed ('Do It To The Music' and 'Just In Time'), **Nuance** ('Loverride'), Vikki Love ('Stop Playing On Me') and **Oran 'Juice' Jones** ('Never Say Goodbye').

MILLS, ELEANOR

(Singer)

Based in New York, Eleanor worked with **Norman Connors** during the late '70s and was featured vocalist on *Romantic Journey*, including 'You Are Everything', and *This Is Your Life*, including 'You Make Me Feel Brand New'. She also sang backgrounds with artists including **Roberta Flack**.

In 1986 she recorded a single 'Mr Right', originally released in New York on the Vinylmania label (via Debut Records in the UK). In the early '90s her acappella vocal on the song was utilized by groups including Those Guys ('Tonight') and Bassheads.

MILLS, STEPHANIE

(Singer)

Born in New York in 1957, Stephanie's first professional success was to land a role in the Broadway show *Maggie Flynn* when she was just nine years old. Following this she entered a talent contest at Harlem's Apollo Theatre where she won for six consecutive weeks. This led to a professional touring engagement with **The Isley Brothers**. Back on Broadway she landed the role of Dorothy in *The Wiz* when she was seventeen. She was invited to audition after the producer of the show heard her debut single 'I Knew It Was Love', released on the Paramount label in 1974. Stephanie remained in the role for four years while pursuing a recording career at the same time.

After an album for Motown (produced by **Bacharach/David**), Stephanie signed to the 20th Century label and worked on three albums with writers/producers **Mtume/Lucas**. *Whatcha Gonna Do With My Lovin'* (1979) featured the club hit 'Put Your Body In It' and her solo version of 'Feel The Fire'. The title track of the album, also regarded as a classic, was later a hit for Detroit group **Inner City** in 1989. In 1980 Stephanie reached No. 4 in the UK charts with 'Never Knew Love Like This Before' from *Sweet Sensation*. She also married **Jeffrey Daniel**, although this only lasted for just over a year.

During 1981 she worked closely with **Teddy Pendergrass**, recording a duet of 'Feel The Fire' for his album *T.P.* and touring as his opening act. In the UK, their live duets on this tour are regarded as among the most electrifying and intense ever witnessed! Later in the year Teddy guested with Stephanie on a duet 'Two Hearts' from her album *Stephanie*. The duet reached the UK Top 50.

Her next label was Casablanca, for which she released *Tantalizingly Hot* (1982) and *Merciless* (1983), including 'Pilot Error'. From 1983 she presented her own daytime TV special on NBC for two years, and then made history as Dorothy in the revival of *The Wiz*, making her the youngest actress ever to return to an originally created role. Her next Casablanca album was *I've Got The Cure* (1984), jointly produced by **George Duke** and **David**

'Hawk' Wolinski. It featured 'The Medicine Song', which put Stephanie back in the UK Top 30 that year.

In 1985 she moved to MCA and *Stephanie Mills* included the popular 'Stand Back'. It marked the start of an association with **Nick Martinelli** who produced 'I Feel Good All Over' from 1987's *If I Were Your Woman*. Also on the album was '(You're Puttin') A Rush On Me', a UK Top 75 hit covered by Technomania in 1991. Her next album *Home* (1989) included 'Something In The Way (You Make Me Feel)' (later remixed by Marley Marl), and the American hit 'Comfort Of A Man'.

Stephanie has also recorded two duets with **Robert Brookins**, 'In The Night (Making Love)' (1986) and 'Where Is The Love' (1988). She also co-wrote and produced songs for Robert's 1988 *Let It Be Me*. Her manager is sister Cassandra Mills who also looks after the interests of Robert Brookins and **Christopher Williams**.

MIMMS, GARNET

(Singer)

Born in West Virginia in 1933 but raised in Philadelphia, Garnet comes from a religious family. By 1954 he was singing in local gospel groups including the Evening Stars and the Norfolk Four (who recorded for Savoy Records). In 1958 he formed **The Gainors**, following which he fronted **Garnet Mimms & The Enchanters** before going solo in 1964. On Loma Records (via United Artists) he had American hits 'One Girl' (1954), 'A Quiet Place' (1964), 'A Little Bit Of Soap' (1965), 'I'll Take Good Care Of You' (1966) and 'Looking For You' (1966), the latter issued as a B side. His two albums during this era were *It Was Easier To Hurt Her* and *I'll Take Good Care Of You*, produced by **Jerry Ragavoy**.

While touring the UK he recorded a live album with a band from Scotland called Senate before returning to the States and signing with Arista. Here, in 1977, *Garnet Mimms Has It All* was produced by **Jeff Lane** and featured 'What It Is' (a **Brass Construction**-style dance UK Top 50 hit co-written by **Randy Muller**) and the popular soul track 'Right Here In The Palm Of My Hand'.

MIRACLES

(Vocal Group)

From Detroit, The Miracles were formed in 1955 by **Smokey Robinson** and his high-school friends Ronnie White and Pete Moore. In 1957 Smokey's songs attracted the attention of **Berry Gordy** who secured a debut release for the group, 'Bad Girl' with the Chess label. By 1959 Bobby Rogers joined the group, while Marv Tarplin (Smokey's co-writer) and Emerson Rogers had also become an integral part of their line-up (Emerson was later replaced by Claudette who became Smokey's wife.) In 1959 the group signed with Tamla (via Motown) and scored immediately in America with a Top 10 hit 'Shop Around'. Follow-ups included 'What's So Good About Goodbye' (1961), 'You Really Got A Hold On Me' (1962), and 'Mickey's Monkey' (1964) before they hit the UK with 'Going To A Go-Go' (Top 50, 1966), '(Come 'Round Here) I'm The One You Need' (Top 50, 1966), 'I Second That Emotion' (Top 30, 1967), 'If You Can Want' (Top 50, 1968), 'Tracks Of My Tears' (Top 10, 1970), 'Tears Of A Clown' (No. 1, 1970) and 'I Don't Blame You At All' (Top 20, 1971).

When Smokey left the group in 1971, he was replaced as lead singer by twenty-year-old **Billy Griffin**. After *Do It Baby* (1974), many thought the group wouldn't survive, but 1975's 'Love Machine' (co-written by Billy) was a multi-million international seller and UK Top 5 (1976) from a highly successful album *City Of Angels*. *Power To The Music* (1976) was their last for Motown before they switched to CBS for one album *Love Crazy* (1976). It included the single 'Spy For The Brotherhood', withdrawn from sale following complaints from the FBI! From here The Miracles split up and Billy Griffin became a solo artist.

In the late '80s Bobby Rogers formed The New Miracles, while endorsing a Miracles reunion project for the UK Motorcity label which included a remake of 'Love Machine' (with Billy Griffin and Claudette Robinson) in 1990.

MIRAGE

(Group)

Formed in 1978, Mirage were Bernard Michael (lead vocals), Morris Michael (vocals/guitar), John McKenzie (bass), Joey Blake (drums), Carl Clark (percussion), Dave Eytle (guitar) and Zandy Gordon (keyboards). They originally performed as Star Syndicate. They toured West Africa in 1979 and released two singles, 'Summer Groove' on Flamingo Records (1980) and 'As From Now' on Copasetic. In concert they were the most soulful of any British band around and extremely underrated.

MISSION

(Group)

From Philadelphia, Mission were Russell 'P-nut' Weekley (drums/percussion/vocals), Curtis Ronell Dowd Jr (keyboards), Curt Campbell (lead vocals), John Martin (bass), Sidney Weston (lead vocals), Randy Bowland (guitar/synths) and Bobby Lovett (lead vocals). The group were officially formed in 1985 after various members had previously worked together as Eastbound. Signing to CBS, their debut album *Mission* was produced in London by **Roy Carter**. A second album *Search*, including 'Show A Little Love', was produced by **Nick Martinelli** in Philadelphia.

MITCHELL, BARBARA

(Singer)

Based in Atlanta, Barbara originally sang lead vocals with the Motown group High Inergy in Los Angeles. She later signed as a solo artist to Capitol for *Get Me Through The Night* (1984), following which she sang a duet with **Larry Blackmon**, 'I'll Never Look For Love', for his Cameo album *Single Life* (1985). Larry later produced her album *High On Love* (Atlanta Artists, 1986).

MITCHELL, PRINCE PHILLIP
(Singer/Songwriter/Producer)
Born in Louisville, Kentucky, in 1945, Philip recorded for numerous labels including Shout, Smash ('Keep On Talking', 1960, and 'Lollipop', 1961), Hi, Event ('There's Another In My Life', 'We Get Caught' and 'I'll See You In Hell First') before being the featured vocalist with **Norman Connors** on 'Once I've Been There' and 'Destination Moon' from *Romantic Journey* (1977). He signed to Atlantic Records for *Make It Good* (1978) including 'One On One' and 'If I Can't Be Your Man', and *Top Of The Line* (1979) before retiring from recording (not wanting to compete with disco). In 1986 he returned for *Devastation*, released by the Ichiban label.

MITCHELL, WILLIE
(Producer/Trumpet)
Born in Ashland, Mississippi, in 1928, Willie was two years old when his family moved to Memphis, Tennessee. After graduating from Melrose High School (where he learned the trumpet) and majoring in music at Rust College in Holly Spring, Mississippi, he served in the US Army between 1950 and 1952. In 1955 he formed a jazz/blues band in the Memphis area, and recorded a single 'That Driving Beat' with his trumpet. The first acts he worked with as producer were The Five Royals and Roy Brown before he joined Hi Records, initially as an artist in 1960. By 1965 he had become exclusively a producer and was working with **Al Green**, **O.V.Wright**, **Ann Peebles**, **Syl Johnson**, **Rufus Thomas**, **Denise Lasalle**, **Otis Clay**, **Dionne Warwick**, **Detroit Emeralds**, Rod Stewart, Elvis Presley, Bobby Blue Band, and **Ike & Tina Turner**. For Al Green alone he produced twenty-two gold and platinum records, and a gold for Denise Lasalle with 'Trapped By A Thing Called Love' (1971).

He became vice president of Hi Records from 1970 to 1977 before working at Bearsville Records between 1977 and 1980. At this point he formed Waylo Records, launching it with his production of 'Didn't We Do It' for **Billy Always**. Other artists he produced at Waylo include Lynn White, **Lanier & Co**, **Otis Clay**, Joyce Cobb, and **David Hudson**.

Away from Waylo he won a Grammy for producing Al Green's 'Going Away' (1987), and produced UK pop group Wet Wet Wet who lived with him for four months. Willie also has a brother James Mitchell, who was a studio musician at Muscle Shoals studios during the '60s.

MIZELL, CINDY
(Singer)
Based in New York, Cindy is one of the city's top session singers and has recorded backgrounds (often alongside **Audrey Wheeler** with artists including **Najee**, **Freddie Jackson**, **James 'D-Train' Williams**, Lisa Fischer and numerous others. In 1984 her solo 'This Could Be The Night' was included on the movie soundtrack *Beat Street* for Atlantic. More recently she has signed to East West Records.

MIZELL, FONCE
(Producer/Percussion/Keyboards)
After brother **Larry Mizell** was given a professional break by **Donald Byrd**, both Larry and Fonce Mizell developed a unique style of fusion jazz with their songs and/or productions during the mid-'70s for artists including **Gary Bartz** ('The Shadow Do'), **Johnny Hammond** (*Gears*), **Roger Glenn** (*Reachin'*, 1976), and albums for **Bobbi Humphrey**. In a more soulful/dance direction they worked with **A Taste Of Honey** ('Boogie Oogie Oogie'), **The Blackbyrds**, **L.T.D.** ('Love Ballad') and also co-produced 'Farewell My Summer Love' for **Michael Jackson**.

MIZELL, LARRY
(Songwriter/Producer/Keyboards)
A student of **Donald Byrd** at Howard University, Larry got his first professional break in the early '70s by writing and producing Donald's *Blackbyrd* album. With brother **Fonce Mizell** he created a unique style of fusion jazz, popular on the UK 'jazz funk' scene through the '70s and early '80s. As a writer, his solo credits include 'Change (Makes You Want To Hustle)' (**Donald Byrd/Blow**), 'Life Styles' (**Blackbyrds**) and 'Harlem River Drive' (**Bobbi Humphrey**).

MODERN-NIQUE
(Group)
Formed by New York session musicians **Larry Woo** and Gordon Worthy, Modern-Nique featured the vocals of Grindle and Monique on their debut release 'Love's Gonna Get You' (via Virgin/10 Records in the UK, 1986) and an album for Sire Records *Modern-nique* (1987).

MODULATIONS
(Vocal Group)
Formed in Philadelphia, The Modulations worked with the mainstay of the city's 'Philly sound' musicians/arrangers/producers including **Norman Harris** and **M.F.S.B.** during the mid-'70s. Their recordings include *It's Rough Out Here* for the Buddah label (1975).

MOHAWKS
(Group)
In 1968 organ-led instrumental group The Mohawks recorded 'The Champ', released on the Pama label. From the late '80s through to the '90s the familiar organ riff has been sampled and copied on what has become a countless number of hip hop and dance records.

MOIR, MONTE

(Songwriter/Producer)

Monte Moir has worked closely with writers/producers **Jam/Lewis** as part of their Flytetime production company from the mid-'80s. His own songs and/or productions have been utilized by **Alexander O'Neal** ('If You Were Here Tonight'), **Cheryl Lynn** ('Love's Been Here Before'), **Ruby Turner** ('In My Life It's Better To Be In Love'), **Deniece Williams** ('All I Need'), **Patti Austin** ('Only A Breath Away'), **Thelma Houston** ('Fantasy And Heartbreak'), **Steven Dante** ('It's Only Love') and **Centerfold**.

MOMENTS

(Vocal Group)

From Baltimore, Harry Ray, Al Goodman and Billy Brown came together as The Moments and recorded hits for the All-Platinum label including 'Girls' (UK Top 5, 1975, with The Whatnauts), 'Dolly My Love' (UK Top 10, 1975), 'Look At Me I'm In Love' (UK Top 50, 1975) and 'Jack In The Box' (UK Top 10, 1976) before changing their name to **Ray, Goodman & Brown** in 1978.

MONITORS

(Vocal Group)

Detroit group The Monitors recorded for Motown during the '60s and scored an American hit with 'Greetings (This Is Uncle Sam)'. Their original line-up featured Richard Street (who later joined **The Temptations**), while more recently the group has comprised Warren Harris, Maurice Fagin, Laeh Harris, Hershell Hunter and Darrell Littlejohn. Recording in the UK for the Motorcity label with producer **Ian Levine**, 1990's *Grazing In The Grass* included the popular 'Standing Still'.

MONK III, THELONIUS

(Producer/Drummer/Songwriter)

Son of the great jazz pianist Thelonius Monk II, Thelonius III took up the drums at the age of seven after being given a set by family friend Art Blakey. In 1973 he formed **Natural Essence**, following which he teamed up with Yvonne Fletcher and his sister Boo to form **T.S.Monk**. The group's 1982 album *Human* was produced by **Eric Mercury**, and when T.S.Monk disbanded Thelonius and Eric teamed together to form **Merc & Monk**.

MONTANA, VINCE

(Vibes/Songwriter/Producer)

Having grown up in Philadelphia, Vince Montana established himself on the East Coast r&b scene as a vibes player in the mid-'60s. By the late '60s he was fully acquainted with the burgeoning Philly music scene. His early sessions include 'At The Top Of The Stairs' for The Formations, a song co-written by **Leon Huff**. From vibes he moved into arrangements (including songs for **The Delfonics** and **First Choice**), and ultimately orchestrations at the peak of the disco symphony, directing **The Salsoul Orchestra** in New York and **M.F.S.B.** in Philadelphia. He also wrote and produced for the Salsoul Orchestra, including such disco hits as 'Ooh I Love It', and produced 'Dance A Little Bit Closer' for the Salsoul label in 1977. Other production work in 1977 included Astrud Gilberto's 'The Girl From Ipanema', while he also co-wrote 'Runaway' (originally sung by **Loleatta Holloway** and later by **Urban High**).

In 1978 he signed as an artist to Atlantic, releasing *I Love Music*. The title track was a rousing disco rendition of the **Gamble/Huff O'Jays** classic, but the album was also acclaimed for the brassy big-band instrumental 'You Know How Good It Is'. Also in 1978 he wrote and produced an Atlantic album for **Goody Goody**, including the disco hit 'No. 1 Dee Jay'.

His greatest solo success came in 1982 when as front man for the Montana Sextet he recorded a single 'Heavy Vibes' on his own Philly Sound Works label. The track became a UK Top 60 hit in 1983 (via Virgin), and various dance hits have utilized either the bass line or riffs from his vibes lead instrumental.

In 1983 the PSW label resurrected **The Trammps** for whom Vince co-wrote 'What Happened To The Music', following which both Vince and The Trammps have been quiet on the music scene.

Vince has also played on session for artists including **Keni Burke** ('Rising To The Top') and **Touch of Class**.

MONTGOMERY, MONK

(Bass)

Born in Indianapolis, Monk is the brother of Wes Montgomery and while playing with Lionel Hampton in the '50s took up the electric bass, having settled in Las Vegas. In 1974 he recorded one solo **Bobby Martin**-produced album, *Reality*, including 'Me & Mrs Jones', for the Philadelphia International label.

MONYAKA

(Group)

Meaning 'good luck' in Swahili, Monyaka are the six Jamaican-born members Errol Moore (lead guitar), Beres Barnet (guitar/vocals), Paul Henton (bass/vocals), William Brown and John Allen (keyboards), and Richard Bertram (drums/percussion). They currently live in New York. Formed in 1974 they toured and supported acts including Black Uhuru and Burning Spear before releasing a single 'Go De Yaka' on New York's Easy Street label in 1983. The track was a UK Top 20 hit (via Polydor) the same year. They later released 'Street People' on the A&M label.

MOODY/BELL

(Songwriters/Producers)

New York writers/producers Alvin Moody and Vincent Bell emerged in the late '80s with their tough street soul productions for artists including **Kym Mazelle** ('Love Strain'), **Alyson Williams** ('Sleep Talk'), **Blue Magic**

('Romeo & Juliet), **Oran 'Juice' Jones** (*G.T.O. – Gangsters Takin' Over*) and Neneh Cherry.

MOONGLOWS

(Group)

This early-'60s group from Chicago was put together by **Harvey Fuqua** and consisted of three members of The Marquis, one of whom was **Marvin Gaye**. They recorded two singles for the Chess label.

MOORE, DOROTHY

(Singer)

Born in Jackson, Mississippi, in 1947, Dorothy studied music at university before singing in local group The Poppies (with **Fern Kinney**). In 1976 she recorded the song she is best remembered for, 'Misty Blue', released in the UK on the Contempo label and a Top 5 hit. Her follow-up on the label was 'Funny How Time Slips Away' (UK Top 40, 1976) before she switched to Epic for *Dorothy Moore* (1977), including 'I Believe You' (UK Top 20), and *Talk To Me* (1978).

In 1984 she returned with 'Just Another Broken Heart' for the Street King label.

MOORE, JACKIE

(Singer)

Born in Jacksonville, Florida, Jackie scored initial American success with 'Dear John' and 'Precious Precious' (1971) for the Scepter label before switching to Atlantic for the **Phil Hurtt/Bunny Sigler**-produced *Sweet Charlie Babe* (1973), recorded in Philadelphia. In 1975 she signed to the Kayvette label for 'Make Me Feel Like A Woman', the first of seven singles for the label and the title track of her one album for the label before a further move to CBS. Here Philly producer **Bobby Eli** delivered her most commercially successful release 'This Time Baby' (UK Top 50, 1979), a dance classic taken from *I'm On My Way* (1979).

In 1985 she returned on the Sunnyview label with 'Love Is The Answer'.

MOORE, LEE

(Singer)

Lee Moore recorded just one single, 'Reachin' Out (For Your Love)' for the Source label, popular on the UK dance scene in 1979.

MOORE, MELBA

(Singer)

Born in New York, Melba first broke into show business by performing in the Broadway production *Hair*. As a solo recording artist she initially worked in Philadelphia where writers/producers **McFadden & Whitehead** played an integral role in her career. In 1976 she signed with Buddah Records where her debut album *This Is It* included a UK Top 10 hit in the title track. After a further Buddah album *A Portrait Of Melba*, including the McFadden & Whitehead-penned/produced 'Standing Right Here', she switched to Epic Records for *Melba*, including 'Pick Me Up, I'll Dance' (UK Top 50, 1978), and *Closer* (1980), including 'Something On Your Mind', before a final switch to the Capitol/EMI family of labels where she remains to this day.

Here her albums have been *What A Woman Needs* (1981), including 'Let's Stand Together', her particularly successful *The Other Side Of The Rainbow* (1982), including 'Love's Comin' At Ya' (UK Top 20), 'Mind Up Tonight' (UK Top 25) and 'Underlove' (UK Top 75); *Never Say Never* (1983), including 'Love Me Right', 'Keepin' My Lover Satisfied' and 'Livin' For Your Love'; *Read My Lips* (1985), including 'When You Love Me Like This' and 'King Of My Heart'; *A Lot Of Love* (1986); *I'm In Love* (1988), including 'Love And Kisses' and featuring duets with **Freddie Jackson** and **Kashif**; and *Soul Exposed* (1990), including 'Do You Really Want My Love'.

Melba played an integral role in discovering **Freddie Jackson** and signing him to Hush Productions run by her husband Beau Higgins.

MOORE, RENE

(Singer/Songwriter/Producer/Keyboards)

From Los Angeles, Rene Moore worked with the Los Angeles Philharmonic Orchestra and Leon Russell before meeting **Angela Winbush** in the mid-'70s. As **Rene & Angela** they worked as writers, producers and ultimately artists after signing to Capitol in 1980.

After falling out with Angela and the publicity of a court case, Rene signed as a solo artist to Mercury Records where his debut album was the self-written/produced *Destination Love* (1988).

MORALI, JACQUES

(Producer)

New York producer scored success with his Can't Stop Productions company during the late '70s disco era. He was primarily responsible for **The Village People** and also worked with artists including, **Patrick Juvet** ('I Love America'). He also scored in the early '80s with a run of UK hits for the group Break Machine (including 'Street Dance').

MORGAN, MELI'SA

(Singer/Songwriter/Producer)

Born in New York, Meli'sa began her career as a backing singer before joining the group **High Fashion** in 1982. Here she sang lead vocals on *Feelin' Lucky* and co-wrote 'You're The Winner'. The group were signed to Capitol, the label Meli'sa signed to as a solo artist in 1986.

Teaming up with co-writer/producer **Lesette Wilson**, her debut album *Do Me Baby*, including 'Fool's Paradise' (UK Top 50) and 'Do You Still Love Me', was released in 1986. It was followed by *Good Love* (1987), including 'If You Can Do It, I Can Too', 'Here Comes The Night', 'Love Changes', a duet with **Kashif** and 'I Still Think About

You'. The title track was later remixed and reached the UK Top 75 in 1988, while the Mastermix label in the UK issued an earlier unreleased recording 'With Coffee, Tea Or Me' on the back of its popularity.

Also with Lesette Wilson, Meli'sa wrote and produced 'All Of My Love' for **Genobia Jeter**, before a change to producer **Attala Zane Giles** on her third album *The Lady In Me* (1990). Meli'sa has also sung backgrounds with **Kleeer** ('Taste The Music') and **Glenn Jones** ('You're The Only One I Love').

MORNING, NOON & NIGHT

(Group)

This six-piece self-contained group worked with producer **Michael Stokes** on *Morning, Noon & Night* for the Roadshow label division of United Artists in 1977.

MORODER, GIORGIO

(Songwriter/Producer)

Giorgio emerged on the New York disco scene of the late '70s co-writing songs including 'I Feel Love' with **Donna Summer**. He also scored in the UK as a solo artist with 'From Here To Eternity' (Top 20, Oasis, 1977) and 'Chase' (Top 50, Casablanca, 1979), while as a producer he worked with Donna on 1977's *Four Seasons Of Love* and with other artists including **The Three Degrees** ('Giving Up, Giving In'), **Debarge** ('Single Heart'), **Janet Jackson** ('Two To The Power') and **Irene Cara** ('Flashdance').

He later scored two duet hits in the UK with Phil Oakey, 'Together In Electric Dreams' (Top 5, 1984) and 'Goodbye Bad Times' (Top 50, 1985) on Virgin Records.

MORRIS, GEE

(Singer)

London singer Gee Morris recorded a version of the **Isley Brothers** classic 'This Old Heart Of Mine' (1988) with producer **Ian Levine** for the Nightmare label before becoming the lead vocalist with **Innocence** created by writers/producers **Jolley/Harris/Jolley**.

MORRISSEY MULLEN

(Duo)

Comprising a nucleus of UK musicians **Dick Morrissey** and **Jim Mullen**, Morrissey Mullen were formed in the late '70s after meeting in New York while working with **The Average White Band**. Their first album, *Up*, was recorded for Atlantic and featured the Average White Band. Back in the UK they released *Cape Wrath* for EMI before switching to the Beggars Banquet label and establishing themselves on the UK 'jazz funk' scene with the Chris Palmer-produced *Badness* (1981), including 'Slipstream'. From here they introduced vocalists on *Life On The Wire*, including 'Stay A While' (featuring **Linda Taylor**), and *It's About Time*, featuring **Carol Kenyon** and **Tessa Niles**.

As a live group, they were particularly prolific on the UK club scene in the late '80s.

MORRISSEY, DICK

(Saxophone)

English musician Dick Morrissey formed a jazz ensemble and recorded seven jazz albums in four years before meeting **Jim Mullen** in New York. Here he formed **Morrissey Mullen**, although the duo made their most impact back in the UK after signing with Beggars Banquet Records.

Independently Dick has toured with Cannonball Adderley and recorded with Jimmy Witherspoon and **The UK Players**. His solo album *After Dark* was released by Coda Records in 1983.

MOSLEY & JOHNSON

(Duo)

From Jackson, Mississippi, vocal duo Sam Ray Mosley and Robert A. Johnson recorded *Mosley & Johnson* (1987) and *Premium* (1988) for the MSS label out of Muscle Shoals Studios.

MOTEN, PATRICK

(Songwriter/Producer/Keyboards)

Based in Los Angeles, Patrick has developed somewhat of a cult following on the soul scene of the late '80s with his rich songs and/or productions with artists including **Bobby Womack** ('How Could You Break My Heart', *Poet 1* and *Poet 2*), **Johnnie Taylor** ('What About My Love'), **Anita Baker** (*Songstress*), **Rosie Gaines** ('Crazy') and **Mica Paris** ('Where Are The Children').

MOTHER'S FINEST

(Group)

Originally from Chicago, Mother's Finest were formed in the late '60s by Jean ('Joyce') Kennedy and Glenn Murdoch (both vocalists, later husband and wife). Playing dates in Dayton, Ohio they met Gary James 'Moses' Moore (guitar) who joined the duo and travelled with them to Miami where they joined up with Jerry 'Wizzard' Sey (bass) and Harold Sey (drums) before settling down in Atlanta, Georgia. After one album for RCA they signed with Epic in 1976, releasing *Mother Factor* (1978), including 'Love Changes', *Another Mother Further* and *From One Mother To Another* (1983), then Capitol in the late '80s for *Looks Could Kill* (1989). In 1984 Joyce recorded a solo album *Lookin' For Trouble* for A&M Records.

MOTIVATION

(Group)

From Los Angeles, Motivation were Larry Blaylock (drums), Rick Davenport (guitar), Anthony Scott (congas/percussion), Gregory Roberson (bass), Charles Lavender (guitar), Avery H.Scott (keyboards), Anthony Ray West (drums), Greg Ray Pickens (vocals), Lonnie Garner (vocals) and Michael L.Rucker (vocals). In 1980 they released *Steppin' Into Now* on the local Ham-Sem label prior to signing with De-Lite Records (via Phonogram).

Here they achieved some UK dancefloor/soul scene support with 1983's *Motivation*, which included 'Crazy Daze'.

MOUZON, ALPHONSE

(Drummer/Songwriter/Producer)

Born in Charleston, South Carolina, in 1948, Alphonse took to the drums as a child and played for a local society orchestra. His first real job, however, was as a laboratory technician after studying at medical school. At the age of 21 he toured with **Roy Ayers** (later recording with Roy on his debut Polydor album *Ubiquity*), and worked on the Broadway show *Promises, Promises* before tours with Gil Evans, **George Benson**, Chubby Checker, **Weather Report**, **McCoy Tyner**, **Donald Byrd** and Larry Coryell.

With Larry Coryell he formed a fusion jazz ensemble 11th House prior to signing as a solo artist to the Blue Note label in 1972 where he cultivated a unique style of writing and playing. He recorded four albums of an r&b/dance nature, including *The Essence Of Mystery*, *Funky Snakefoot* and *The Man Incognito* (1976), including 'Take Your Troubles Away'. 1980's *By All Means* featured **Herbie Hancock**, **Hubert Laws**, **Michael Brecker** and **Freddie Hubbard**. Such was its impact on the UK jazz funk scene that Alphonse was brought in to appear at London's Horseshoe Hotel in 1981. A follow-up *Morning Sun* was also released that year, both on the Pausa label.

Alphonse also recorded fusion jazz/r&b albums for the MPS and High Rise (*Distant Lover*, 1983) labels and a 12" 'Our Love Is Hot' (1984) for Private I (via CBS). In 1985 he returned to Pausa for *The Sky Is The Limit* prior to moving to Optimism for 1988's *Early Spring*.

He has recorded with **Stevie Wonder**, **Roberta Flack**, **McCoy Tyner** and **Freddie Hubbard** among many other artists.

MOY, SYLVIA

(Songwriter/Singer)

From Detroit, Sylvia thought she'd find success with her songs in New York, but after a brief stay in the city returned to Detroit where her services were hired by Motown. She had auditioned by performing her songs 'I'm Still Loving You' and 'Little More Love', both of which were later recorded by **Kim Weston**. She was soon to save the recording career of Little **Stevie Wonder**. His voice had just broken and the label felt he might have had his day. Nobody wanted to write or produce for him and he was nearly dropped. Sylvia volunteered to work with him and was told that if she could write him a hit he could stay. Together they came up with 'Uptight', which was an international hit, and a UK chart debut for Stevie in 1966 when it reached the Top 20.

Her songwriting collaborations with Stevie continued with hits including 'My Cherie Amour', 'I Was Made To Love Her' and 'Thank You Love', while she also wrote for other Motown acts including **Martha Reeves**, **Gladys Knight**, **The Isley Brothers**, **Michael Jackson**, **The Temptations** and **Diana Ross**. Sylvia was the first woman producer at Motown, although she was not given credits.

When Motown moved to Los Angeles in 1972, Sylvia decided to stay in Detroit where she got involved with local talent and held music seminars. She formed her own record company Michigan Satellite Records, where in 1985 she produced and co-wrote *Person To Person* for **Ortheia Barnes**. She also recorded for the 20th Century label and continued her songwriting, co-writing 'My Baby Loves Me' (**Jean Carne**) and others.

More recently Sylvia has worked closely with **Ian Levine**, writing for over a hundred former Motown artists for the Motorcity label. She has also recorded as a solo artist for the company, 'Major Investment' being a debut single in 1989.

MTUME

(Group)

An extension of **James Mtume** the singer/songwriter/producer is Mtume the group (pronounced 'emtoomay'). The line up has included **Tawatha Agee** (vocals), Raymond Jackson (bass), Ed Moore, Howard King, Vincent Henry (sax), Gerry Cooper and Roger Parker. Mtume were signed to Epic in 1980 while James was still writing and producing with Reggie Lucas. **Mtume/Lucas** wrote and produced the 1980 Mtume album *In Search Of Rainbow Seekers*.

In the mid-'80s James moved away from the full string and horn sound towards what he called 'sophisti-funk', a much sparser formula utilized on 'Juicy Fruit' (UK Top 40, 1983) and 'Prime Time' (Top 75, 1984). Albums included *Juicy Fruit* (1983), *You, Me And He* (1984) and *Theatre Of The Mind* (1986).

Group member Howard King more recently worked as a producer for **Smokey Robinson**.

MTUME/LUCAS

(Songwriters/Producers)

James Mtume and **Reggie Lucas** met during their days as members of the **Miles Davis** band during the early '70s. As songwriters and/or producers they became prolific at the quality end of the late '70s disco/soul scene with their work for artists including **Roberta Flack/Donny Hathaway** ('The Closer I Get To You' and 'Back Together Again'), **Phyllis Hyman** ('You Know How To Love Me' and 'Under Your Spell'), **Gary Bartz**, **Marc Sadane** ('One Minute From Love'), **Lou Rawls** ('Now Is The Time For Love'), **Rena Scott** ('If I Had A Chance'), **Stephanie Mills** ('What Cha Gonna Do With My Lovin'' later recorded by **Inner City**, 'Put Your Body In It' and 'Never Knew Love Like This Before') and **Eddie Henderson** ('Say You Will').

In 1980 when the group **Mtume** signed with Epic Records, Mtume/Lucas worked together on the debut *In Search Of Rainbow Seekers* before going their separate ways.

MTUME, JAMES

(Singer/Guitarist/Songwriter/Producer/Percussionist)

Born in Philadelphia, James was brought up in a musical family where his father and uncles played professionally as **The Heath Brothers**. Taking to music himself in the '60s, James was first inspired by the sound of African drums which he heard through the music of Hugh Masekela. After developing his skills in percussion he took up the guitar as a profession and worked with **Herbie Hancock** and **Sonny Rollins** before moving to Newark and performing with Joe Henderson and **Freddie Hubbard**. Through Freddie he met **Miles Davis** who hired him as his group's percussionist. Also in Miles's band at the time was guitarist **Reggie Lucas** with whom James developed a songwriting/production partnership (see **Mtume/Lucas**).

Through the early 70s James released two African music-orientated albums, *Kawaida* and *Alkebu-Lan*, before moving closer to r&b with *Rebirth Cycle* (1974), featuring **Reggie Lucas**, **Jean Carne**, **Dee Dee Bridgewater**, **Tawatha**, Jimmy Heath, Azar Lawrence, Stanley Cowell and **Michael Henderson** (1974), issued by Third Street Records (a division of an r&b record store in Philadelphia).

In addition to his work with Mtume/Lucas he formed a group **Mtume** who toured as musicians for **Roberta Flack** before signing to Epic Records in 1980. As writer and/or producer (outside of Mtume/Lucas), James has also worked with artists including Nu Romance Crew ('Tonight'), **Levert**, **Tease** (*Remember*), **Tyrone Brunson** (*Love Triangle*), **Sue Ann** ('Love Dies Hard'), **Roy Ayers** ('Hot'), and **Eddie Henderson** ('Prance On').

MUHAMMAD, IDRIS

(Drummer)

Born Leo Morris in New Orleans in 1939, Idris (taking this name from an Islamic prophet) established himself as a top-class session drummer/percussionist during the '50s. During this time he performed with rock & roll singer Larry Williams while also recording on hits including 'Raindrops' (Dee Clark) and 'Chapel Of Love' (The Dixie Cups). In 1961 he became the drummer personally requested by **Sam Cooke**, and worked in both New York and Chicago, hooking up with **Curtis Mayfield** to be the drummer on 'People Get Ready' (**The Impressions**) and 'Keep On Pushing' (**Jerry Butler**) among others.

He later played drums with Emerson Lake & Palmer and **Roberta Flack** while taking on session work for the CTI label in New Jersey. The company's subsidiary label Kudu signed him as a solo artist, his debut album being *Power Of Soul* (1974), featuring **Bob James** and **Grover Washington Jr**. In 1977 he made his greatest impact on the UK jazz funk scene with a Kudu album *Turn This Mutha Out*, including 'Could Heaven Ever Be Like This', while he later recorded albums including *Make It Count*, *Boogie To The Top*, *House Of The Rising Sun* and *For Your Love* (1980) for the Prestige/Fantasy labels.

As a session drummer, Idris recorded with artists including **Bob James** (*Touchdown*, *Lucky Seven* and *The Genie*), **Pharaoh Sanders**, **Charles Earland** and **Dexter Wansel**.

His son is Idris Muhammad Jr who is a member of the group **A.R.B.**

MULLEN, JIM

(Guitar/Bass)

Originally a double bass player, UK musician Jim Mullen was hired by **The Average White Band** and went to work in New York where he performed with fellow artists on the Atlantic label including **Herbie Mann** and **Ben E.King**. Through AWB he met **Dick Morrissey**, with whom he formed **Morrissey Mullen** in the late '70s. As a solo artist he recorded *Thumbs Up* for the Coda label in 1983.

MULLER, RANDY

(Singer/Songwriter/Producer)

Born in Guyana, Randy moved to Brooklyn, New York, where he first took up music at Thomas Jefferson High School. Here he became friends with **Solomon Roberts Jr** and **Jeff Lane**. After Randy arranged some songs for Jeff's group **B.T.Express**, Jeff became Randy's manager and produced early material for his group **Brass Construction**. Through the '70s and early '80s Randy became the brain behind New York-based funk groups **New York Skyy**, **Funk Deluxe**, **First Circle** and the aforementioned **Brass Construction**, for which he writes, produces and sings lead vocals.

As a writer and/or producer, he has also worked with **Garnet Mimms** ('What It Is', co-written with Jeff Lane, 1977), **Charles Earland** (*Perception*, including 'Let The Music Play', 1978), **Tamiko Jones** ('Can't Live Without Your Love', 1978) and **Rafael Cameron** ('All That's Good To Me' and the Muller instrumental 'Boogie's Gonna Get Ya', 1981).

In 1988 he launched his own Plaza label, while more recently he has put together a new group BC Underground.

MUNZABAI, SERGIO

(Mix Engineer/Industry)

One half of the production team **M&M**, Sergio was a junior high school teacher before becoming a disc jockey on the New York club scene. He worked at The Roxy, Studio 54 and Flamingo before landing a midday radio show on the city's black music station WBLS. He later became music director at the station and met **John Morales** with whom he formed M&M.

When Motown temporarily opened a New York office in 1985, fifteen years after moving to Los Angeles, Sergio was hired to run it.

MURDOCH, SHIRLEY

(Singer)

Born in Toledo, Ohio, Shirley was the youngest of six children and was determined to be a singer. In the late '70s she gave a demo of her voice to her cousin who worked for **Roger Troutman**. Duly impressed, Roger hired her as a backing singer for his productions on artists including **Zapp**, **Human Body** and **Bobby Glover**. She also toured as a backing singer before Roger secured her a recording deal with Elektra where he wrote/produced (with Zapp) *Shirley Murdoch* (1985), including 'Truth Or Dare' and 'The One I Need', and *A Woman's Point Of View* (1988) including 'Husband' and 'I Still Love You'.

MURPHY, WALTER

(Songwriter/Arranger/Producer/Keyboards)

Based in New York, Walter capitalized on the disco scene of the mid-'70s and made an impact on dancefloors with 'A Fifth Of Beethoven' as Walter Murphy & The Big Apple Band on Private Stock Records in 1976. A solo Walter Murphy album *Rhapsody In Blue* followed in 1977, while he also produced and co-wrote *Uncle Louie's Here* for **Uncle Louis**.

MUSIQUE

(Studio Group)

Musique was the concept of writer/producer **Patrick Adams** who formed the group at the peak of the disco era in 1978. Featuring the vocals of Chris Wiltshire (who also sang with **Class Action**), one album *Keep On Jumpin'* was released and featured 'Summer Love' and 'In The Bush' (UK Top 20, 1978).

MYERS, ALICIA

(Singer)

Born in Detroit into a family of nine, Alicia found her confidence to sing the same year Motown closed up in the city and moved to Los Angeles (1972). Hence she did not audition for the label whose artists had greatly inspired her.

Her brother is Jackie Myers with whom she won a major talent contest. Jackie became a member of **Chairman Of The Board**, while Alicia joined forces with **Al Hudson** & The Soul Partners, later to become **One Way**. Alicia co-wrote and recorded lead vocals on One Way's 1979 dance anthem 'You Can Do It', following which she began a solo career with MCA. From 1980 she released four albums for the label, produced by Al Perkins with One Way's **Al Hudson** and **Kevin McCord**. 'You Get The Best From Me (Say Say Say)' reached the UK Top 60 in 1984 from *Appreciation* (which also included 'I Appreciate').

MYSTIC MERLIN

(Group)

From New York, Mystic Merlin were Clyde Bullard, Jerry Anderson (guitar), Keith Gonzales (vocals), Sly Randolph (drums) and Barry Strutt (sax/keyboards). They were originally a novelty act incorporating magic into their live shows before being taken seriously on the soul/dance scene. In 1980 they signed with Capitol and delivered *Mystic Merlin*. It featured the dance classic 'Just Can't Give You Up', a UK Top 20 single (the a cappella from which was recently utilized by UK group Life On Earth on their single 'Can't Give You Up'). After a second album *Sixty Thrills A Minute* (1981) they added **Freddie Jackson** to the group, and he sang on their third album *Full Moon*. It included 'Mr Magician', popular among UK soul/dance fans.

MYSTIQUE

(Vocal Group)

From Chicago, Mystique were Ralph Johnson (lead), Larry Brownlee, Fred Simon and Charles Fowler. Ralph Johnson was a former lead singer of **The Impressions**. Signed to the Curtom label, their one album *Mystique* (1977) featured the single 'If You're In Need', the **Grey Hanks** song made successful by **Lenny Williams**. The track was produced by **Jerry Butler**, other producers on the album including **Eugene Daniels** and **Bunny Sigler**.

N

NAJEE
(Saxophone)
Born in New York, Najee's father was a professional cellist. His mother bought him a saxophone when he was fourteen and as a teenager he played with a group Area Code, hired as musicians for a Miss Black America Tour in 1976. He later toured with **Chaka Khan** whose backing singer **Meli'sa Morgan** employed him to play on her own solo album. From here he was signed to Hush Productions who secured a solo recording deal with EMI-America, his debut album *Najee's Theme* (1986) earning him a Grammy nomination for Best R&B Instrumental Performance.

His other albums are *Sweet Love* (1987) and *Day By Day* (1988), while he has also recorded with **Milira**, **Omar Hakim** and **Freddie Jackson**. His brother is producer Fareed.

NATURAL ESSENCE
(Group)
Natural Essence were formed in 1973 by drummer **Thelonius Monk III** and featured vocalist Yvonne Fletcher, who later became an integral part of **T.S.Monk**. They released one single, 'Out Of Darkness', produced by **Billy Cobham**.

NATURAL FOUR
(Vocal Group)
Chicago-based vocal quartet Delmos Whitley, Chris James, Steve Striplin and Darryl Cannady recorded for ABC Records ('I Thought You Were Mine'), before recording the songs and productions of **Leroy Hutson** at Curtom Records from 1973. Their Curtom albums include *Natural Four* (1974), including 'You Bring Out The Best In Me'; *Heaven Right Here On Earth* (1975), including 'Love's So Wonderful'; and *Night Chaser* (1976), including 'Get It Over With', with producers Leroy Hutson, **Jackson/Yancy**, Lowrell Simon and **Richard Evans**.

NATURAL HIGH
(Group)
From Mississippi, Natural High were Taji Shahid (guitar/vocals), Willie James Hatten (bass/vocals), Ameen Rasheid (drums/percussion/vocals), Charles Gilliam (sax) and Henry Rhodes (lead vocals). 1979's *Natural High 1* on the Chimneyville label (via Malaco) generated interest on the UK soul scene for 'Trust In Me'.

NATURE'S DIVINE
(Group)
Based in Los Angeles, Nature's Divine were Keith Fondren (bass), Duane Mitchell (guitar), Lynn Smith (lead vocals/percussion), Charles Woods (synths), Marvin Jones (keyboards/vocals), Charles Green (horns), Opelton Parker (horns), Robert Carter (lead vocals/percussion), Mark Mitchell (drums) and Robert Johnson (percussion). In 1979 they signed to the Infinity label (via MCA) for *In The Beginning* produced by **Michael Stokes**.

NAYOBE
(Singer)
Born in the Bronx, New York, Nayobe began her career as a backing singer, recording with artists including Love Bug Starski ('You've Gotta Believe'), The Fat Boys ('Can You Feel It') and **Kurtis Blow** ('8 Million Stories'). In 1985 she signed to the Fever label where her debut single was 'Please Don't Go'. More recently she has worked with producers including **Teddy Riley** on *Promise Me* (1990), including 'I'll Be Around', for Wig Records (via CBS).

NDUGU
(Drummer/Songwriter/Producer)
Leon 'Ndugu' Chancler went to his first **Crusaders** concert in 1966, not thinking that in 1983 he would replace **Stix Hooper** as drummer in the group. Leon began his career with the Harold Johnson Sextet before touring with **Willie Bobo**. Establishing himself as a top class jazz drummer, he proceeded to work with **Miles Davis**, **Freddie Hubbard**, Santana, **Flora Purim**, **Ramsey Lewis**, **Stanley Turrentine** and **George Duke** during the '70s/early '80s.

As a producer he took charge of 'Straight To The Bank', a dance anthem for **Bill Summers** in 1978, prior to forming the Chocolate Jam Co. for two albums (the first of which featured the much sought after 'Come Into My Life Again').

In 1983 he replaced **Stix Hooper** in **The Crusaders** for *New Moves*, although the move turned out to be more on a freelance basis. He continued drum sessions with artists including **Michael Jackson**, **Tina Turner**, Frank Sinatra, **Donna Summer** ('State Of Independence'), **George Howard, Raul De Souza**, **Debarge**, **Patrice Rushen, Keni Burke, Beau Williams** and **Phyllis Hyman**. As a songwriter his contributions include 'Let It Whip' (**Dazz Band**), 'Reach For It' (**George Duke**) and 'Night Ladies' (**The Crusaders**).

In 1990 he recorded a solo MCA album *Old Friends, New Friends* with guest artists including Alphonso Johnson, **Patrice Rushen** and Ronnie Foster.

NELSON, TYKA

(Singer)

Born in Minneapolis, Tyka Nelson is the sister of **Prince**. In 1988 she signed as a solo artist to Chrysalis Records and released *Royal Blue*.

NERO, FRANCES

(Singer)

Born in Detroit, Frances began her singing career as a teenager, winning a 1965 talent show at the age of 14 (**Ronnie McNeir** came second in the same contest). Her prize was a year's contract with Motown, but although she ended up recording with them for three years, only one single was released. It was the double-header 'Keep On Loving Me' and 'Fight Fire With Fire' on Motown's 'Soul' subsidiary label.

From here she recorded briefly with **Gino Parks** on the Crazy Horse label. She didn't record again until 1989, when she signed with the UK label Motorcity and teamed up with Gino again for a duet 'Your Precious Love'. In 1990 Motorcity released her first single for the label, 'Footsteps Following Me', which was highly acclaimed on the soul scene and remains one of the label's most successful singles (later remixed and re-released by Debut Records). She also released an album *Out On The Floor* for Motorcity and is currently working on new songs.

NEVILLE BROTHERS

(Group)

From New Orleans, The Neville Brothers are Aaron (vocals), Cyril (vocals), Art (keyboards) and Charles (sax), who first worked together professionally as a group in 1977. Art had solo hits in the '50s before forming local groups The Hawkettes and later (in the '60s) The Meters; in 1966 he had an American solo hit with 'Tell It Like It Is'. Charles played sax with **Bobby Bland** and **B.B.King** and Cyril formed his own band Soul Machine before teaming up with Art in The Meters.

Their albums include *The Neville Brothers*, *Fiyo On The Bayou*, *Uptown*, *Treacherous* (a two-record retrospective released by Rhino Records) and *Yellow Moon*.

NEW BIRTH

(Group)

New Birth were instigated by **Harvey Fuqua** in the late '60s. They were the combination of three groups: **The Nite-Lighters** (instrumentalists), The Mint Juleps (female vocalists) and The New Sound (male vocalists). A super-group prior to the days of **Earth Wind & Fire**, New Birth first recorded for RCA. Initially they recorded a string of cover versions including 'Never Can Say Goodbye', 'It's Impossible' and 'Make It With You'. Their early albums were *New Birth* (1970), *Ain't No Big Thing But It's Growing* (1971) and *Coming Together* (1972), including 'I Don't Want To Be Wrong', by which time The Mint Juleps had been replaced by Ann Bogan (a former member of **The Marvelettes**) and Londee Loren.

In 1973 the group scored their first major American chart success with the **Bobby Womack** song 'I Can Understand It', which came from their fourth album *Birth Day*. A fifth, *It's Been A Long Time*, including 'Wild Flower', was released the following year, the same year as *Coming From All Ends*.

In 1975 the group switched to the Buddah label, parting company with **Harvey Fuqua** and releasing *Blind Baby* which included the American No. 1 r&b hit 'Dream Merchant'. On the move again, this time to Warner Brothers, their next two albums were *Love Potion* (1976) and *Behold The Mighty Army* (1977), the latter produced by **Frank Wilson**. From here, Leslie Wilson (original male vocalist from The New Sound) left the group to join **L.T.D.**, and New Birth's 1979 *Platinum City* was released by Ariola.

In 1982 the group returned for one final album with RCA, *I'm Back*.

NEW EDITION

(Vocal Group)

Formed in Boston during the early '80s, New Edition were originally **Bobby Brown**, Ricky Bell, Michael Bivins, Ronnie De Voe and **Ralph Tresvant**. Bobby, Ricky and Michael had been school friends since 1978, and it was in 1980 that they met Ronnie and Ralph. Their professional career began in 1981 following an appearance at a talent show held in Boston at the Strand Theater. Their performance attracted the attention of songwriter/producer **Maurice Starr** who took them to Streetwise Records and worked with them on their debut single 'Candy Girl' (UK No. 1, 1983) and 'Popcorn Love' (UK Top 50, 1983).

They were adopted by the youth of America as a major new teen group and signed to MCA Records. Here they worked with producers including **Ray Parker Jr** and **Richard Rudolph** on *New Edition* (1985), including 'Mr Telephone Man' (UK Top 20). From this album until the departure of **Bobby Brown** (who was replaced by **Johnny**

Gill, the group's popularity grew across America while it declined in the UK. Their albums during this time included *All My Love* (1985) and *Under The Blue Moon* (1986).

Their UK popularity was revived in 1988 with the **Jam/Lewis**-produced single 'If It Isn't Love' and album *Heartbreak* (1989), before **Johnny Gill** and **Ralph Tresvant** pursued solo careers, and the remaining members found new success as Bell Biv Devoe with songs including 'Poison' and 'Do Me' (1990).

NEW EXPERIENCE
(Group)
The eight-strong Guinn family group from Philadelphia performed as support act for **Harold Melvin**, **Major Harris** and **Blue Magic** in the Philly area and recorded 'Prove It To Me' for Philly World. Following the demise of the label they changed their name to **Guinn** and recorded an album for Motown.

NEW JERSEY CONNECTION
(Group)
Based in New Jersey, this group are best remembered for 'Love Don't Come Easy' (featuring vocalist Kenny Bristol) (Carnival Records, 1981).

NEW YORK CITY
(Group)
John Brown, Tim McQueen, Edward Schell and Claude Johnson came together as New York City in the early '70s. With producer **Thom Bell** they scored with 'I'm Doin' Fine Now' (UK Top 20, 1973) from their debut album of the same name. Musicians on the album were the Big Apple Band featuring **Nile Rodgers** and **Bernard Edwards**. Recording for the Chelsea label, their second album was *Soulful Road*.

NEW YORK CITY BAND
(Studio Group)
Top session musicians including Eddie Daniels (sax), Will Lee (bass), Hiram Bullock (guitar), Jimmy Maelin (percussion) with the vocals of **Luther Vandross** recorded as the New York City Band. The group recorded one album, *New York City Band*, in 1979 on the American International Pictures label; it was the soundtrack to the movie *Sunnyside*.

NEW YORK PORT AUTHORITY
(Group)
New York Port Authority are best remembered for *Three Thousand Miles From Home* (1967) and the **Brian Holland**-produced dance classic 'I Got It' (1977), released on the Invictus label owned by **Holland/Dozier/Holland**.

NEW YORK SKYY
(Group)
Formed in Brooklyn, New York Skyy (known as just Skyy in America) was formed by **Solomon Roberts Jr** and featured **Randy Muller** (principal songwriter/mentor), Gerald Le Bon (bass), Anibal Anthony (guitar), Tommy McConnel (drums) and Larry Greenberg (keyboards), and sisters Denise Dunning-Crawford (vocals), Delores Dunning-Milligan (vocals) and Bonnie Dunning (vocals). In 1978 they provided the instrumentation and vocals for **Charles Earland** on his album *Perception*, including 'Let The Music Play', before signing to the Salsoul label later in the year where their debut album *Skyy* brought them to the attention of UK dance fans with the single release 'First Time Around'. Later albums were *Skyway* (1979) including 'High' (a B-side single with 'Skyzoo' as a C side!); *Skyline* (1980), featuring 'Let's Celebrate' and 'Call Me'; *Skyjammer* (1982), including 'Let Love Shine'; *Skyylight* (1983), including 'Show Me The Way'; and *Inner City* (1984).

Also at Salsoul they provided the instrumentation for **Rafael Cameron** on his album *Cameron*. In 1986 they switched to Capitol for *From The Left Side*, including 'Givin' It (To You)', before a further move to Atlantic for *Start Of A Romance* (1988).

NEWBERRY III, BOOKER T
(Singer/Songwriter)
Born in Youngstown, Ohio, Booker was born into a musical family where his parents were members of the Wings Over Jordan gospel choir. He was inspired to make music his own career after watching an Ohio Players concert at the age of fourteen. In 1975 he put together **Sweet Thunder**, with himself as the lead singer and keyboard-player. When the group disbanded, Booker played with lounge bands until he recorded a demo of 'Love Town'. The song was released by the US Broadwalk label (1983) and later by Polydor in the UK where it became a Top 10 hit. An album of the same name was subsequently released in the UK by Malaco.

Booker also recorded the duet with **Jean Carne**, 'It Must Be Love'.

NEWMAN, DAVID 'FATHEAD'
(Flute/Saxophone)
Born in Dallas, Texas, David began his professional career in the mid-'50s playing saxophone for **Ray Charles**. He worked with Ray for twelve years, also occasionally playing with artists including T-Bone Walker and Lowell Fulson.

As a solo artist he made his debut with *Hard Times* in 1968, followed by *House Of David* and *The Weapon*, before appealing to UK jazz funk fans with *Newmanism* (1974), including 'Sweet Tears' featuring **Roy Ayers**. In 1976 he switched from Atlantic to Warner Brothers for *Mr Fathead* (1976) and *Front Money* (1977), the latter marking David's debut as a vocalist. In 1978 he switched to the Prestige label where he is best remembered for the title track of *Keep The Dream Alive*. He also released *Concrete Jungle* that year.

More recently he has recorded with **Hank Crawford** on his album *Night Beat* (1989).

NEXT MOVEMENT
(Group)
From Chicago, Next Movement were a dance group signed to Prelude Records in the early eighties. Their single 'Let's Work It Out' was co-written and produced by **Leroy Hutson**.

NICOLE
(Singer)
Born in Rochester, New York, in 1960, Nicole McCloud moved to Miami, Florida, when she was sixteen, having already gained experience as a club singer. In 1983 one of her shows caught the ear of an investor who put her in a recording studio. The results impressed the Portrait label (via CBS) who released *What About Me* in 1985. It included a duet with **Timmy Thomas**, 'New York Eyes' (UK Top 50).

A second album, *Jam Packed* (1988), including 'Everlasting Love', was released by Epic.

NIGHTINGALE, MAXINE
(Singer)
Born in the UK, Maxine is best remembered for 'Right Back Where We Started From' (UK Top 10, 1975) for United Artists Records. She returned to the charts with 'Love Hit Me' (Top 20, 1977), while in the early '80s she recorded *It's A Beautiful Thing* in America (Highrise, 1982).

NIGHTS
(Group)
The Nights were Ira Clark (lead vocals/trumpet/timbales), Dennis Hagger (lead vocals/sax), Joey L. Mingo (lead vocals/congas/percussion), Anthony Brahum (vocals/guitar), Vincent Rocto (vocals/drums), Anthony Williams (bass/vocals) and Rickey Blain (vocals/alto sax). In 1976 they worked with producer **H.B.Barnum** on *The Nights*, released by ABC Records.

NIGHTWIND
(Group)
From Chicago, Nightwind are essentially songwriter/arranger/producer Charles M.Lawrence and singer/songwriter Angela Charles. Musicians on their 1988 Wind Song album, *Nightwind Featuring Angela Charles*, including 'Love Me Baby' and 'You're Someone Special', were session players.

NIGHTWRITERS
(Group)
Chicago house music duo Henry Watson and Alan Walker scored a dance hit with the **Frankie Knuckles**-produced anthem 'Let The Music (Use You)' in 1988, featuring vocals by **Ricky Dillard**. The follow-up was 'Over You', released later the same year.

9.9
(Vocal Group)
From Boston, vocal trio 9.9 first sang at school and were voted best female group in the city by their local radio station WILD. They were given their first recording break by the boxer Joe Frazier who was making a record and needed some backing singers. Lead singer Margo Thunder also recorded a solo single for Capitol Records, 'Expressway To Your Heart', when she was eleven years old.

A few years later **Richard 'Dimples' Fields** came to Boston to perform. The group offered to be his backing singers, and soon he signed them to his production company. In 1985 Richard produced their debut album *9.9*, including 'All Of Me For All Of You', released by RCA. They later recorded backing vocals on Richard's *Dimples* album (1990).

94 EAST
(Group)
From Minneapolis, 94 East were **Prince** (keyboards/guitar), Pepe Willie (keyboards/songwriter), **Andre Cymone** (bass) and Alvin Moody (guitar) with vocalists including Marcy Ingvoldstad, Kristie Lazenberry and **Colonel Abrams**. In 1977 they recorded *Minneapolis Genius* including 'If You Feel Like Dancing', made more available by Hot Pink Records in 1985.

NITEFLYTE
(Group)
Formed in Miami, Niteflyte were **Sandy Torano** and **Howard Johnson**, both of whom recorded as solo artists after two albums for the Ariola label. From these the song 'If You Want It' (1979) was popular on the UK soul scene.

NITE-LIGHTERS
(Instrumental Group)
From Louisville, Kentucky, The Nite-Lighters were a group of instrumentalists. From 1970 they became the backbone of **New Birth**. Their own recordings for RCA included a popular cover version of the Philly classic 'K-Jee' (1972).

NOBLE, IKE
(Singer)
Born in Forrest City, Arkansas, in 1948, Ike moved to Toledo in 1967 where he started performing with small local bands. After recording a track or two for the Ali label in 1968 he retired from the recording scene until

1978, when he recorded *Fresh Start* and started touring again. Between times he had a job as an iron-welder. His next album was *Angie* (1984) for the Connowil label, the title track from which generated interest on the UK soul scene.

NOLEN & CROSSLEY

(Duo)

From Los Angeles, Curtis Anthony Nolen (guitar/vocals) and Raymond A. Crossley (keyboards/vocals) recorded with **Louis Johnson**'s gospel group **Passage** (1981) before signing to Gordy (via Motown). Here they released their *Ambience* (1982), including 'Salsa Boogie', and wrote 'Can't Stop' for **Debarge**.

Individually, Curtis co-produced *Captured* for **Rockwell** (1985) and five tracks on the **Chico Debarge** debut solo album *Chico Debarge* (1986). Raymond more recently co-produced *3 For 3* by 3 For 3 on Kerry Gordy's Song label.

NOMAD

(Duo)

Nomad are writer/producer/keyboard player Damon Rochefort (from Cardiff) and singer **Sharon Dee Clarke** (from North London). They first worked together in 1986 when Damon took Sharon to Arista Records and instigated her debut solo release 'Dance Your Way Out Of The Door'.

In 1990 Damon formed Nomad ('Damon' in reverse) with Sharon as the group's lead vocalist. Signing to Rumour Records, their debut single was '(I Wanna Give You) Devotion' – featuring rapper MC Mikee Freedom – (UK Top 5) which became one of the most significant dance records of 1991. The follow-up was 'Just A Groove' (UK Top 20, 1991), after which came the release of their album *Changing Cabins* (1991), including 'Something Special.'

As producer, Damon has worked with artists including **LaToya Jackson**, Junior Gee, Mr E and Tracie Ackerman.

NORWOOD

(Singer/Songwriter)

Born in Philadelphia, Norwood recorded a solo album *I Can't Let You Go* for the Magnolia label (via MCA) in 1987 before becoming the lead singer of **Pieces Of A Dream**.

NOTATIONS

(Group)

This '70s group is best remembered for 'Super People' and 'It's All Right (This Feeling)', the latter taken from *Notations* (1975).

NU SHOOZ

(Group)

From Portland, Oregon, Nu Shooz are husband and wife John Smith and Valerie Day. They formed in 1980, initially playing rock though both were into r&b/soul music. Eventually they signed with Atlantic and released 'I Can't Wait' (UK Top 5, 1986), followed by 'Point Of No Return' (UK Top 50, 1986).

NUNN, BOBBY

(Singer/Songwriter/Producer)

Based in Los Angeles during the early '80s, Bobby is best remembered for Motown singles 'She's Just A Groupie' (1982) and 'Don't Knock It Until You Try It' (1983), the latter taken from *Private Party* and featuring the instrumentals of **Ozone**.

O

O'BRYAN
(Singer)
Born in Sneads Ferry, North Carolina, in 1961, O'Bryan Burnette II took up piano at the age of six, and was writing songs by the time he was eighteen. In 1973 the family moved to Santa Ana, California, and O'Bryan was singing in local clubs by the time he was seventeen. While his name means little to UK soul audiences, O'Bryan built a healthy live following in America, and recorded steadily for Capitol from 1982 to 1986. His albums were *Doin' Alright* (1982), including 'Still Water', *You and I* (1983), *O'Bryan* (1984), including 'Lovelite', and *Surrender* (1986).

One of his regular backing singers on tour was **Karyn White** who later gained greater solo recognition in her own right.

OCEAN, BILLY
(Singer/Songwriter/Producer)
Born Les Charles in Trinidad in 1950, Billy Ocean moved with his family to Stepney, East London, in 1968. With a love for singing he joined a local group called Shades Of Midnight which played local pubs and clubs during the early '70s. In 1976 Billy signed as a solo artist to GTO (via CBS), scoring an immediate UK No. 2 hit with 'Love Really Hurts Without You', a song he had written four years earlier (remixed/re-released by Supreme Records in 1986). His follow-up UK hits with GTO were 'L.O.D.' (Top 20, 1976), 'Stop Me' (Top 20, 1976), 'Red Light Spells Danger' (No. 2, 1977), and 'American Hearts' (Top 60, 1979).

In 1980, 'Are You Ready' made the UK Top 50 and his final GTO album *City Limit* was released. However it was the single 'Nights (Feel Like Getting Down)' which firmly established Billy on UK dancefloors and across the USA, where it hit Top 5 in the r&b charts. The song remains a UK club classic, although it has never been a chart hit here (having been re-released on a number of occasions).

In 1982 he signed to Epic, self-producing his next album, *Inner Feelings*, before a deal with Jive Records put him on the road to fortune in 1984. His debut release for the label was 'European Queen' which was initially ignored in the UK. In the States, however, it was re-titled 'Caribbean Queen', and when re-issued under that name in the UK it hit the Top 10 later that year. Extremely successful on both sides of the Atlantic, Billy's UK hits continued with 'Loverboy' (Top 20, 1985), 'Suddenly' (Top 5, 1985), 'Mystery Lady' (Top 50, 1985), 'When The Going Gets Tough, The Tough Get Going' (No. 1, 1986, from movie *The Jewel Of The Nile*), 'There'll Be Sad Songs' (Top 20, 1986); 'Love Zone' (Top 50, 1986) and his second biggest hit 'Get Outta My Dreams Get Into My Car' (No. 3, 1988). By this time Billy had become a major 'pop' act.

As a writer, Billy has had songs recorded by **Lenny Williams**, **The Dells** and **LaToya Jackson** among others. He also produced **Ruby Turner**'s 1985 remake of 'If You're Ready (Come Go With Me)'.

OCTAVIA
(Singer)
Born in Brooklyn, New York, Octavia made her professional stage debut in America playing Doris Winter (a portrayal of **Doris Troy**) in the musical *Mama I Want To Sing*. Her acclaim in this role brought her to the attention of writer/producer **Kenny Beck** who produced her debut 'To The Limit', released on Cooltempo Records in 1986.

ODYSSEY
(Vocal Group)
The Odyssey story begins in New York, in 1968 when three sisters, Lillian, Louis and Carmen Lopez, won rave reviews for their local stage show as The Lopez Sisters. This led to a tour of Europe, following which Carmen left the group and the remaining sisters recruited Tony Reynolds. Changing their name to Odyssey the trio signed with RCA and scored immediately with the dance anthem 'Native New Yorker' (UK Top 5) from their debut album *Odyssey* (1977).

At this point Tony Reynolds left the group to be replaced by Bill McEachern (formerly with **We The People**) before the group returned with *Hollywood Party Tonight* (1979). In 1980 they regained their dancefloor and chart success with *Hang Together*, including 'Use It Up And Wear It Out' (UK No. 1), 'If You're Lookin' For A Way Out' (UK Top 10), the title track single (UK Top 40) and 'Don't Tell Me, Tell Her' (also recorded by **Phyllis Hyman**). *I've Got The Melody* (1981) included 'Going Back To My Roots' (UK Top 5) and 'It Will Be Alright' (UK Top 50), before they teamed up with **Jimmy Douglass** for the UK Top 5 hit 'Inside Out' and UK Top 50 'Magic Touch' (1982). From here they switched to Priority Records to work with **Butch Ingram** on the UK Top 75 single '(Joy) I Know It' in 1985.

OHIO PLAYERS

(Group)

From Hamilton, Ohio, The Ohio Players were formed by **Sugarfoot** (vocals/guitar) in 1968. Other members were Marvin 'Merv' Pierce (horns), Ralph 'Pee-Wee' Middlebrook (sax), Marshall 'Rock' Jones (bass), David Johnson (keyboards), Vincent 'Vennie' Thomas (percussion) and Jimmy Sampson (drums). Together they created one of the most influential funk sounds of the '70s.

Originally calling themselves The Ohio Untouchables, the group played as session musicians on songs including 'I Found A Love' for The Falcons featuring **Wilson Pickett** (1962). As The Untouchables they also recorded a single 'I'm Tired' for the Lupine label. In 1967 they were with the TRC label, and then Compass Records with 'It's A Crying Shame', before signing with Capitol in 1968 for *Observations In Time*.

After a period at Westbound Records (albums including *Pain*, 1972), they switched to Mercury where they released a string of albums including *Skin Tight* (1974), *Fire* (1975), *Contradiction* (1976), including 'Who'd She Coo?' (UK Top 50), *Honey*, *Jazz-Ay-Lay-Dee* and the soundtrack *Mr Mean* (1977), before officially splitting up after their third world tour. From these albums they scored American single success with 'Fire' (later utilized by **Sly & Robbie**), 'Love Rollercoaster', 'Sweet Sticky Thing', 'O-H-I-O', 'Jive Turkey' and 'Rattlesnake'.

In 1979 they reformed for *Everybody Up* on Arista Records, and again in 1981 for *Tenderness* on the Broadwalk label. In 1982 they teamed up with **Richard 'Dimples' Fields** for *Ouch*, and released *Graduation* for the Air City label in 1984. In 1985 various members of the group worked together again on a solo album for lead member **Sugarfoot**.

OHLSON, CURTIS

(Bass/Songwriter/Producer)

From Oakland, California, Curtis has played bass for a variety of fusion groups/acts including **Rodney Franklin** and **Sheila E**. In 1987 he cut a solo album *So Fast* for US Intima Records, which featured the lead vocals of **Rosie Gaines** on the title song.

O'JAYS

(Group)

From Canton, Ohio, Eddie Levert, Walter Williams, Bobby Massey, William Powell and Bill Isles were fellow high-school students who first sang together as The Mascots. Performing at a nightclub they impressed Cleveland DJ Eddie O'Jay, who helped train them and secured their debut release with the Imperial label in the early '60s. They changed their name to The O'Jays, and their first release was 'Do The Wiggle'. By now Bill Isles had left the group. In 1963 they stirred r&b interest with 'Lonely Drifter' followed by 'Lipstick Traces', prior to 'I Dig Your Act' (Stateside, 1967) and 'Look Over Your Shoulder' (Bell, 1968) both latter singles with the services of writer/producer **George Kerr**.

Their next move was to Neptune Records in Philadelphia where they met writers/producers **Gamble/Huff**. 1970's *The O'Jays In Philadelphia* included popular r&b singles 'One Night Affair' and 'Looky, Looky'. Bobby Massey soon left the group, and in 1971 Gamble/Huff took The O'Jays to their Philadelphia International (PIR) label, immediately scoring a gold record with 'Backstabbers' (UK Top 20, 1972). From here their UK hits flowed with 'Love Train' (Top 10, 1973), 'I Love Music' (Top 20, 1976), 'Darlin' Darlin' Baby (Sweet, Tender Love)' (Top 30, 1977), 'Used Ta Be My Girl' (Top 20, 1978), 'Brandy' (Top 25, 1978), 'Sing A Happy Song' (Top 40, 1979) and 'Put Our Heads Together' (Top 50, 1983). In 1975 William Powell was replaced by Sammy Strain due to ill health, and died from cancer two years later.

Albums during this classic Philly era included *Backstabbers* (1972); *Ship Ahoy* (1973), including 'For The Love Of Money' and 'Now That We Found Love'; *Survival* (1975); *Message In The Music* (1976); *Travellin' At The Speed Of Thought* (1977); *So Full Of Love* (1978); *Identify Yourself* (1979); *The Year 2000* (1980); *My Favourite Person* (1982), including 'I Just Want To Satisfy You'; *When Will I See You Again* (1983); and *Love And More*, including 'Summer Fling' (1984) and 'Love Fever' (1985). (An album *The O'Jays* can also be found on the Springboard/DJM label, released in 1975.)

When PIR changed distribution from CBS to EMI, The O'Jays were the only group which remained with the label. From here albums *Love Fever* (1985), including 'Just Another Lonely Night' and 'I Love America', and *Let Me Touch You* (1987), including 'Lovin' You', were released before the group signed directly to EMI for *Serious* (1989), including 'Fading', and *Emotionally Yours* (1991).

Eddie Levert is father to Gerald Levert (lead singer with **Levert**) and also co-wrote/produced 'My Love Don't Come Easy' for **Jean Carne**.

OLIVER

(Group)

Oliver were known as **Round Trip** before changing their name and releasing one album for MCA. The group's lead singer, **Oliver Cheatham**, then recorded as a solo artist.

OLIVER, DAVID
(Singer/Songwriter)
Born in Jamaica, David Oliver established his singing career in America after moving to Los Angeles. While signed to Mercury Records he worked with producer **Wayne Henderson** on *American Man* (1977), *Mind Magic* (1978), including 'Southern Comfort', *Rain Fire* (1979) and *Here's To You* (1980). He died in 1981.

OLIVER, MONDEE
(Singer)
Based in Chicago, Mondee duetted with **Roy Ayers** on 'Don't Stop The Feeling' before signing to the Gherkin label. Here she recorded with Galifre and as a solo artist on singles including 'Newsy Neighbours' (1990) and 'Make Me Want You' (1991).

OLIVER, VISCOUNT
(Singer)
Viscount Oliver Miller worked as a train guard on London's Underground network and was overheard singing by the group **Kandidate** at a bus stop! The group featured him as lead vocalist on their single 'Can't Say Bye' (1982).

OLLIE & JERRY
(Duo/Songwriters/Producers)
Drummer **Ollie Brown** and vocalist **Jerry Knight** first worked together in Los Angeles as members of **Ray Parker**'s group **Raydio** in 1978. From here Ollie played drums with **Michael Henderson**, **Rene & Angela**, **Lenny Williams** and **Lamont Dozier**, while Jerry sang background vocals and recorded two solo albums for A&M Records.

Ollie also recorded as **Ollie Baba** before forming a production company, signing **Tease** and Black Diamond. He then rejoined Jerry and the duo recorded as Ollie & Jerry, with songs including 'Breakin' Ain't No Stopping Us' (UK Top 5, 1984) for the movie soundtrack *Breakdance*. Their follow-up single was 'Electric Boogaloo' (UK Top 75, 1985).

OLYMPIC RUNNERS
(Group)
Pioneers of the Brit funk scene in the late '70s, The Olympic Runners were British-born DeLisle Harber (bass), Glen LeFleur (drums) and Pete Wingfield (keyboards), and two Americans Joe Jammer (guitar) and **George Chandler** (vocals). They recorded for RCA ('Keep It Up', 1977) before switching to Polydor for 'Sir Dancealot' (1978).

OMAR
(Singer/Songwriter/Multi-instrumentalist)
Born in Canterbury, Kent, in 1969, Omar Hammer was sixteen when he sent a demo of his song 'Mr Postman' to DJ Dave Pearce at Radio London. Dave played it on the air and featured Omar live on the station's 'soul nights out'. After a spell as drummer with the Kent Youth Percussion Ensemble/Orchestra, Omar signed with the Kongo label which in 1990 released his debut album *There's Nothing Like This*. Its subsequent popularity in the UK led to a major recording deal with Talkin' Loud Records (via Phonogram) where the song was re-released in 1991.

Omar has also worked with **Mica Paris**, producing the song 'I Should've Known Better' (1990).

OMARI
(Singer)
Based in Miami, Omari made one single 'After Loving You' for the Bound Sound label in 1983. When the song became a hit in Belgium, Omari was not keen on travelling there to promote it. Instead, Brian O'Connor from a British-based promotion company went there as Omari!

ONE WAY
(Group)
From Detroit, One Way was founded by **Al Hudson** (vocals/percussion), **Kevin McCord** (bass/keyboards) and Dave Roberson (lead guitar). Other members of the group included **Candye Edwards** (now Candye McCord, Kevin's wife), **Cortez Harris** (guitar), **Alicia Myers** (vocals), Brenda Wiley (vocals), Leroy Hyter (sax/keyboards), Gregg Gregg (drums) and more recently Jeanette Mack (vocals), Lorrie Tice (vocals), Valdez Brantley (keyboards) and Jonathan 'Corky' Meadows (keyboards).

The group began life as Al Hudson & The Soul Partners, scoring popularity with songs including 'Spread Love', prior to becoming One Way Featuring Al Hudson in 1979. Switching from ABC to MCA (essentially the same company), the group delivered a series of albums: *One Way* (1979), including 'You Can Do It' 'Music' (UK Top 75) and 'I Am Under Your Spell'; *One Way* (again, 1980), including 'Let's Go Out Tonight'; *Shine On Me* (1983); *Lady* (1984), including 'Lady You Are'; *Wrap Your Body* (1985), including 'Let's Talk About Sex' (UK Top 75) and 'Serving It'; and *IX* (1986), including 'Don't Think About It' and the **Deodato**-produced 'You Better Quit'. In 1987 they recorded 'Turn Up The Music' for Extra Records prior to signing with Capitol for *A New Beginning* (1988), including 'Driving Me Crazy'.

ONE WORLD
(Group)
One World are Mike Percy and Tim Lever, who first made an impression on the dance scene with an illegal remix of **Soul II Soul**'s 'Back To Life' in 1990. Approved by **Jazzie B**, the remix was made available and launched the duo's career. Later in the year they released 'Can't Stop' for **After 7** before signing to the FFRR label (via Phonogram). Adding London blues vocalist Sheilah, One

World made a single debut in 1991 with 'Come Into My Heart'.

101 NORTH

(Group)

West Coast session musicians assembled by **George Duke**, the group released a debut album *101 North* on Valley Vue Records in 1988. Its featured vocalists were **Josie James**, Carl Carwell and **Ellis Hall**. All songs were written and produced by George himself. In 1991 the group returned with *Forever Yours*.

100% PROOF AGED IN SOUL

(Vocal Group)

Formed in 1970 by **Holland/Dozier/Holland**, this group featured the lead vocals of **Steve Mancha**. From the first of their two albums for the Hot Wax label, 'Somebody's Been Sleeping In My Bed' became a No. 1 hit in America. They also provided backgrounds for **Eloise Laws** on her Invictus recording 'Love Goes Deeper Than That' (1977).

O'NEAL, ALEXANDER

(Singer)

Born in Natchez, Mississippi, in 1953, Alexander moved to Chicago for a number of years before joining his cousin in Minneapolis. Initially he worked as a petrol-pump attendant and was a keen football-player before venturing into singing. Realizing his own vocal capabilities he sang with local group The Philadelphia Stories, before forming his own groups The Black Market Band and then The Mystics. In 1983 he made his recording debut with the single 'Do You Dare', released by the Erect label in Chicago. His next single was 'Attitude' (featuring **Jesse Johnson** on guitar) for the Rich Records label. He also spent a brief time as lead singer with **Flytetime**, though he left when the group amalgamated with **Morris Day**'s group Enterprise to become **The Time**.

Writers/producers **Jam/Lewis** took Alex to Tabu Records in 1985 and have worked with him through to the present day on *Alexander O'Neal* (1985), including 'If You Were Here Tonight' (UK Top 20), 'A Broken Heart Can Mend' (UK Top 75) and 'What's Missing'; *Hearsay* (1987), including 'Fake' (UK Top 40), 'Criticize' (UK Top 5), 'Never Knew Love Like This' (UK Top 30), 'The Lovers' (UK Top 30), 'What Can I Say To Make You Love Me' (UK Top 30) and 'Sunshine'; *My Gift To You* (1988) a Christmas album including 'Christmas Song' (UK Top 30); and *All True Man* (1991).

He also sang the duet 'Saturday Love' (UK Top 10) with **Cherrelle** on her album *High Priority* (1985).

ONENESS OF JUJU

(Group)

Based in New York, Oneness Of Juju were Plunky Nkabinde (horns/percussion), Muzi Nkabinde (bass/percussion), Ras Mel Glover (guitar), Virtania 'Cookie' Tillery (vocals), Kevin Davis (drums/percussion), Weldon Hill (keyboards), Marcus Macklin (guitar), Lady Eka-Ete (vocals), O. Asante (drums), Ronnie Toler (drums), Tony Green (drums), Judy Spears (backing vocals), Veronica 'Nilaja' Jones (backing vocals) and William 'Bill' Joyner (piano/clavinet). Signing to the Sutra label, they made an impact on the UK dance scene with 'Every Way But Loose' (1981).

THE ONES

(Group)

Signed to Motown in Detroit during the late '60s, The Ones featured the Hispanic lead singer Danny Hernandez on their three singles 'You Haven't Seen My Love', 'Don't Let Me Lose This Dream' and 'As Long As I've Got You'.

OPUS 7

(Group)

Recording for the Source label (via MCA) in the late '70s, Opus 7 were Sam Hamlin Jr (lead vocals/keyboards), Gary Hairston (drums/percussion), Daniel Edwards (bass), Abdul Rahiim Jamal Amiyr (trumpet/guitar), Galvin Crisp (sax/flute/keyboards), Charles Burns (guitar/trombone/vocals) and Victor Burks (lead vocals/keyboards/principal songwriter). Their albums included *Thoughts* (1979).

ORIGINALS

(Vocal Group)

Formed in Detroit, The Originals were formed by **C.P.Spencer**, Walter Gaines and Hank Dixon in 1965. They were soon joined by singer/songwriter **Freddie Gorman** and through C.P.'s friend **Lamont Dozier** they landed a job as backing singers at Motown. In 1966 they were given an opportunity to record as The Originals, their debut single being 'Goodnight Irene'. However it was three years later that **Marvin Gaye** and Anna Gordy wrote their million-selling American hit 'Baby I'm For Real'. The song was also the title track of their debut album (also including 'The Bells'), followed by 'Portrait Of The Originals', 'Naturally Together', 'Definition', 'Game Called Love', 'California Sunset', 'Communique' and 'Down To Love Town'.

By 1972 the group had settled in Los Angeles with the Motown company, but in 1977 they switched to Fantasy Records, releasing 'Another Time, Another Place' in 1978, and *Come Away With Me* in 1979. More recently, the group have recorded for the UK Motorcity label with writer/producer **Ian Levine**.

OSBORNE & GILES

(Duo/Songwriters/Producers)

Billy Osborne and **Atalla Zane Giles** first emerged as a duo in 1985 and signed to the Chicago-based Red label company for *Stranger In The Night*. Since then they have worked as writers and/or producers for artists including **The Reddings**, **Bert Robinson**, **The Emotions** ('You're

The One' and 'You're The Best'), **Linda Clifford** ('We've Got Our Chance'), **Shirley Jones** and **Vesta Williams** (*Vesta 4 U*).

OSBORNE, BILLY
(Keyboards/Percussion/Vocals)
Born in Providence, Rhode Island, Billy is the brother of **Jeffrey Osborne**. He also worked as musical director with **Friends Of Distinction** before joining his brother in **L.T.D**. As songwriter and/or producer, he has worked with artists including **The Emotions** (*If I Only Knew*, 1985) and **Con Funk Shun** (*Burnin' Love*, 1986), in addition to being one half of **Osborne & Giles**.

OSBORNE, JEFFREY
(Singer/Songwriter/Producer)
Born in Providence, Rhode Island, in 1951, Jeffrey was the youngest of twelve children and was encouraged to sing by his mother who made him entertain her friends with renditions of Johnny Mathis songs. By the age of fifteen he had taught himself to play drums, the instrument on which he first found professional work before joining the group **L.T.D.** as lead vocalist. The year was 1970, and he was already married with two children!

While with L.T.D. he continued session work for artists including **Smokey Robinson** and **The Sylvers** before signing to A&M as a solo artist in 1982. Here he worked predominantly with producer **George Duke** on *Jeffrey Osborne* (1982), including 'On The Wings Of Love' and 'I Really Don't Need No Light'; *Stay With Me Tonight* (1983), including 'Don't You Get So Mad' (UK Top 75); *Don't Stop* (1984); *Emotional* (1986), including 'Soweto' (UK Top 50); and the self-produced *One Love – One Dream* (1988). In 1990 he switched to Arista Records, having already recorded a duet 'Love Power' with **Dionne Warwick** for the label in 1987. Here he recorded *Only Human* (1990), including 'If My Brother's In Trouble'.

As a producer he has worked with **Joyce Kennedy** ('Lookin' For Trouble') and **Johnny Gil**, and as a songwriter he co-wrote 'All At Once' with **Michael Masser** for **Whitney Houston**. He also appears in the video to Frank Sinatra's 'L.A. Is My Lady', during which he gets served a hamburger by **Donna Summer**! He has recorded with **Sister Sledge** ('Thank You For The Party'), and has a brother, **Billy Osborne** of **Osborne & Giles**.

OSIBISA
(Group)
Teddy Osei (sax/percussion), Sol Amarifio (drums), Mac Tontoh (bass), all from Ghana, and Wendell Richardson (guitar) from the West Indies came to the UK in the early '70s where they formed Osibisa. After three albums for MCA, *Osibisa* (1973), *Woyaya* (1974) and *Heads* (1975), they signed with Bronze Records where they scored UK chart success from *Welcome Home* (1976), including 'Sunshine Day' (Top 20) and *Ojah Awake* (1976), including 'Dance The Body Music' (Top 40). Four years later they recorded one more album, *Mystic Energy*, this time for the Pye label.

OSKAR, LEE
(Harmonica)
Born in Copenhagen, Denmark, Lee was given his first harmonica by a visiting American friend. Instantly addicted, he mastered the instrument before moving to the United States when he was eighteen. After a brief spell in New York he relocated to Los Angeles where he met producer **Jerry Goldstein** who was looking for a harmonica player to complete some tracks for a group he was working with called **War**. Lee became an integral part of the group as well as recording a solo project for MCA Records.

He also has a harmonica business, 'Lee Oskar's Harmonicas', and commutes between the States (where he continues to live) and Japan (where his harmonica factory is based!).

OTIS, JOHNNY
(Vibes/Drums/Keyboards)
Born in Vallejo, California, in 1921, Johnny was inspired by the big band jazz bands of the 1930s and had his own by the mid-'40s. In Los Angeles the band played regularly at the Barrelhouse club where Johnny built a reputation for discovering talented vocalists. These included **Esther Phillips**, Amos Milburn and **Etta James**.

During the late '50s and '60s Johnny and his band were signed to Capitol, and scored two UK hits with 'Ma He's Making Eyes At Me' (Top 5, 1957) and 'Bye Bye Baby' (Top 20, 1958). In America his success continued with 'Willie & The Hand Jive' (Top 10, 1958) and much later 'Country Girl' (1969). In 1974 he launched his own label Blues Spectrum, but without much success.

OWENS, JIMMY
(Trumpet)
Born in New York, Jimmy Owens studied trumpet with **Donald Byrd** and at the age of twenty-six played with Newport Youth Jazz Band. In 1969 he formed the Jimmy Owens Quartet. In 1976 he signed to the Horizon label (via A&M) where *Jimmy Owens* attracted interest on the UK jazz funk scene for 'Do It To It'.

OZONE
(Group)
Los Angeles-based group Ozone were Herman Brown (guitar/lead vocals), Thomas Bumpass (sax/trumpet/vocals), Darren Durst (guitar/vocals), Joseph Foxworth (keyboards/vocals), Charles Glenn Jr (bass/vocals), Paul Hines (drums/vocals), James Stewart (keyboards/vocals), Benny Wallace (guitar/vocals), William White (sax/vocals) and Ray Woodard (sax/vocals). In 1980 they signed to Motown and released *Walk On*, although it was from their second album *Jump On*

It (1982) that they stirred UK dancefloors with the track 'Come On In', featuring the vocals of **Michael Lovesmith** who also co-wrote the song and produced the album.

Their final Motown album was the **Michael Stokes**-produced *Glasses* (1983), including 'Our Hearts Will Always Shine'. Later in the year they provided the instrumentation for **Bobby Nunn**'s *Private Party*.

P-FUNK ALL STARS
(Group)
Instigated by **George Clinton**, this particular line-up of P-funkers included Jerry Jones (drums), David Lee Chong (keyboards), Gary Shider (guitar), Robert Johnson (vocals), Jeannette McGruder (vocals), Tony Thomas (guitar) and Norma Jean Bell (sax/vocals). Their one 1983 CBS-associated album *Urban Dancefloor Guerrillas* included the popular 'Acupuncture' and featured guest appearances by **Fred Wesley**, **Sly Stone** and **Maceo Parker**.

PACIFIC EARDRUM
(Group)
This unusual white group from the UK consisted of Joy Yates (vocals), Isaac Guillory (vocals/guitar), Brian Smith (sax/flute/percussion), Billy Kristian (bass/vocals/percussion), Dave MacRae (keyboards), Jeff Seopardie (drums/vocals) and Simon Morton (percussion). Musically they were a cross between fusion jazz, soul and rock, and made two albums, *Pacific Eardrum* (1977) and *Beyond Panic* (1978) for Charisma Records (via Phonogram). From the latter the instrumental 'Inner Circles' was a popular Latin jazz item in the late '70s.

PAGE, GENE
(String Arranger)
Born in Los Angeles, Gene was taught piano by his father and went on to win a four-year scholarship to the Brooklyn Conservatory. Back in Los Angeles he found work arranging demo tapes, and in 1962 was hired by Reprise Records as their arranger. His early successes included 'You've Lost That Lovin' Feelin'' for The Righteous Brothers and 'The In Crowd' for **Dobie Gray**, alongside hits for **The Drifters**, The Mamas & The Papas and Barbra Streisand. He also arranged numerous records for the Motown label.

On meeting **Barry White** he was hired to work with **Love Unlimited**, his first collaboration with them being 'Walking In The Rain With The One I Love'. Gene went on to co-arrange the strings on every Barry White hit in the '70s, while also showcasing his own arranging skills through **Love Unlimited** and **The Love Unlimited Orchestra**, and eventually his own albums *Hot City* (1975) and *Lovelock* (1976) featuring **Merry Clayton** and **Augie Johnson**, for Atlantic Records.

From 1977 to 1980 he recorded as a solo artist for Arista (including a disco single 'Close Encounters Of The Third Kind', 1977, and 'Love Starts After Dark', 1980). He has arranged strings on an impressive number of hits and classic recordings for artists including **Diana Ross** ('Touch Me In The Morning'), **Diana Ross/Lionel Richie** ('Endless Love'), **Aretha Franklin** ('It Only Happens When I Look At You'), **Johnnie Taylor** ('What About My Love' and 'Just Ain't Good Enough'), **Johnny Mathis**, **The Four Tops**, **The Jones Girls**, **Deniece Williams** ('I Found Love'), **Jackson Sisters** ('I Believe In Miracles'), **Nancy Wilson**, **Natalie Cole**, **Eloise Laws** ('Baby You Lied'), **Dionne Warwick**, **The Gap Band**, **Carrie Lucas**, **Carl Anderson**, **Gerald Alston** ('Take Me Where You Want To'), Kiki Dee, Randy Edelman, **Lamont Dozier**, **Anita Baker** (*Songstress*), **The Mac Band**, **Shalamar** ('High On Life' and 'Take That To The Bank'), **The Whispers**, **Peabo Bryson/Roberta Flack** ('Tonight I Celebrate My Love'), **Whitney Houston** ('You're Still My Man') and Elton John ('Philadelphia Freedom').

He has also written and/or produced for **Stanley Turrentine** ('Midnight And You', 1974), **Paul Kelly** (*Stand On The Positive Side*, 1976) and Maxi Anderson (*Maxi*, 1977), among others.

PAGODA
(Group)
British funk band Pagoda were Erica Harold (vocals), Greg Knowles (drums), Mark Glentworth (percussion), Isobel Ward (vocals), Chris Gregord (bass) and John Palmer (guitar). A single 'Finders Keepers' with 'We're Alright Tonight' on the B-side was released by Chrysalis in 1983.

PANDY, DARRYL
(Singer)
Born in Chicago, Darryl studied operatic singing before bursting on the 'house music' scene in 1986 as featured vocalist on 'Love Can't Turn Around' by Farley

'Jackmaster' Funk on the DJ International label (UK Top 10 via London Records). Later in the year he came to London where he worked with writer/producer **Ian Levine** on a solo release 'Animal Magnetism' for the Nightmare label. It was followed by 'Put My Love On The Line' (1987). More recently he has recorded for the Eternal label (via WEA), where a version of 'I Love Music' was a single in 1990.

PARADISE

(Group)

Paradise were originally David Aiyeola (guitar), Philip Edwards (keyboards), **Paul Johnson** (lead singer), Doug Williams (vocals), Junior Edwards (bass/vocals) and Bobby Clarke (drums). They first worked together as instrumentalists at their local Pentecostal church in Camberwell, London, during the late '70s. Touring with Andre Crouch they met producer Barry Evans and recorded two gospel albums, *Paradise* and *Worlds Midnight* (scoring success in the States), before creating a stir in UK soul circles in 1983 with the Top 50 single 'One Mind, Two Hearts' on the Priority label.

Paul Powell, later to become bass player with The Style Council, played with the group at one point.

PARIS

(Singer)

From Illinois, Paris is the son of a former bandleader for Billie Holliday. He released a single 'I Choose You', much acclaimed on the UK soul scene in the mid-'80s. The song was produced by Carl Davis in Chicago and originally released on the city's Kelli-Arts label prior to a UK release on Bluebird Records.

PARIS, HARI

(Singer)

Born in Detroit, Hari Paris is the daughter of former Chess Records artist Lena Gordon. In addition to performing on the local club scene, Hari recorded one single 'You Hit My Love', produced by **Kevin McCord** and released on the Caredaja label in 1986.

PARIS, MICA

(Singer)

Born in South London in 1970, Mica (pronounced Meesha) developed her vocal skills on the London gospel circuit. After performing with numerous choirs she became the lead voice in the Spirit Of Watts gospel quintet. In the hope of securing a contract she recorded some demos, during which time she met Mark Rogers from the group Hollywood Beyond. For a year between August 1986 and July 1987 she toured with the group, and also recorded with them.

While on the gospel circuit she had met Paul Powell, bass player with The Style Council. Paul worked with Mica on some more demos before she was signed to 4th & Broadway Records (via Island) for *So Good* (1988), including 'My One Temptation' (UK Top 10), 'Like Dreamers Do' (UK Top 30), 'Breathe Life Into Me' (UK Top 30), 'Don't Give Me Up' and 'Words Into Action', a duet with **Paul Johnson**. In 1989 she joined **Will Downing** for a duet 'Where Is The Love', and returned in 1990 with *Contribution*. UK soul fans preferred the **Omar**-produced 'I Should've Known Better' and the **Patrick Moten**-produced 'Where Are The Children', both featured only on the B-side to a single 'South Of The River'.

PARKER, MACEO

(Sax)

Maceo was closely involved in the music of **James Brown** in the '70s as the Godfather of Soul's saxophone player. In addition to playing on his numerous recordings, Maceo also recorded as a solo artist for Polydor where James produced his most memorable album *Us* (1974), including 'Soul Power '74'. In 1975 he recorded 'Cross The Tracks', written by James Brown, and released as by Maceo & The Macks. Ten years later it became an anthem on the UK 'rare groove' scene, prompting its re-release in 1987.

Maceo has also recorded with **George Clinton**, and in the Horny Horns as part of **Bootsy Collins**' Rubber Band. More recently he signed to the 4th & Broadway label where a Bill Laswell/**Bootsy Collins**-produced single 'Let 'Em Out' with 'Sax Machine' on the B-side of the record was released in 1990.

PARKER JR, RAY

(Singer/Songwriter/Guitarist/Producer)

Born in Detroit in 1954, Ray first took to the guitar as a result of a leg injury which confined him to home. Aged thirteen he formed a group The Stingrays with **Ollie Brown** and Nathan Watts. Joining forces with other young talent, Ray and his band became road musicians for Motown artists including **The Temptations**, **Stevie Wonder** and **Gladys Knight & The Pips**. During the early '70s he became an in-demand session guitarist, spending extensive time on the road with Stevie Wonder. In 1972 he toured with Stevie on a support tour with The Rolling Stones, following which Ray toured and recorded with the Stones between 1975 and 1977. (He appears on their first platinum album *Black And Blue*.) He also worked with **Gene Page**, recording numerous sessions for **Barry White** after moving to Los Angeles.

In 1977 he formed a group **Raydio**, signing to Arista and scoring with a debut single 'Jack And Jill' in 1978 (although Ray wasn't the vocalist). He had by now moved into songwriting, production and had opened his own recording facility, Ameraycan Studios, in LA. In 1979 he co-produced the **Deniece Williams** album *When Love Comes Calling* (including 'I Found Love') and soon his songs were being recorded by **Bobby Womack**, **Pockets** ('You And Only You') and **Herbie Hancock** ('Doin' It', a co-written song which won a Grammy).

While recording a new Raydio album *A Woman Needs*

Love in 1981, the group suggested they keep Ray's lead vocal which had only been recorded as a guide. The song became an American hit single, released as a solo Ray Parker record at the suggestion of Arista. Also in 1981 he produced 'Shake It Up Tonight' for **Cheryl Lynn** before returning to the studio to record his own solo follow-up 'The Other Woman' which hit the American Top 10 in 1982. In 1983 he co-wrote songs and produced *Jr Tucker* for **Jr Tucker**, while also working as writer and producer on **Diana Ross**'s *Ross*.

His greatest solo commercial success came in 1984 when he was assigned by Columbia Pictures to write the lead song for the movie *Ghostbusters*. In two days he came up with the title song which was an international hit, reaching No. 2 in the UK charts. Also in 1984 he produced a debut album *I Belong To You* for **Randy Hall**. In 1985 he played jazz guitar on **Alphonse Mouzon**'s *The Sky Is The Limit* and released his next solo album *Sex And The Single Man*. In the UK 'Girls Are More Fun' reached the Top 50 early in 1986.

From here Ray switched labels to Geffen, and in 1987 returned with a highly regarded soul album *After Dark*. It included 'I Don't Think That Man Should Sleep Alone', a UK Top 20 hit. Also with Geffen, 'Over You' reached the UK Top 75 early in 1988.

Ray has also recorded with **Marvin Gaye**, **Aretha Franklin**, **Barry White**, **Greg Perry**, **Paul Kelly**, **Ronnie McNeir**, **Z.Z.Hill**, **Side Effect**, **Benny Golson**, **Fire Fox**, and **New Edition** (whose debut MCA album he produced).

In 1991 he switched to MCA for *I Love You Like You Are*, including 'She Needs To Get Some'.

PARKS, GINO

(Singer)

This Detroit blues vocalist signed to Motown in the early '60s where 'Same Thing (Will Happen To You)' and 'For This I Thank You' were released on the Tamla label. In 1962 he left Tamla, later to emerge on Golden World Records in 1966, and later again with 'Nerves Of Steel' and 'Help Me Somebody' on Crazy Horse Records in 1968. At Crazy Horse he recorded duets with **Frances Nero**, with whom he reunited in 1989 for 'Your Precious Love' on the UK Motorcity label.

PARLIAMENT

(Group)

Formed by **George Clinton** in Detroit during the mid-'50s, Parliament were a group of singers and musicians whose debut release was 'Poor Willie' for the ABC label in 1956. Their follow-up was 'Lonely Island', before they switched to Motown (although nothing was ever released). As The Parliaments they also recorded 'Heart Trouble' for the Golden World label. In the mid-'60s the group signed to the Revilot label and scored an American r&b hit with '(I Wanna) Testify' (1967), though the label went out of business soon after. Atlantic bought the rights to the Revilot catalogue and issued an album of unreleased Parliament material.

At this point George lost the right to use the name Parliament, so he formed a new group **Funkadelic** with the same members and signed them to Westbound Records. When he won the Parliament name back, he signed the same group to 20th Century Records and for a while had one set of musicians recording under two different names for two different labels!

In 1974 Parliament scored a major American hit with 'Up For The Down Stroke', and in the mid to late '70s had further success from albums including *Chocolate City*, *Mothership Connection*, *Give Up The Funk (Tear The Roof Off Sucker)* and *The Clones Of Funkenstein*. In 1978 they scored two American r&b No. 1 hits with 'Flashlight' and 'Aqua Boogie'.

The group later signed to Casablanca Records and released *Gloryhallastoopid* (1980), but when the label was taken over by Polygram George Clinton's empire was involved in legal hassles and the group got lost in the reshuffle.

PASSAGE

(Group)

Passage were a gospel group comprising **Louis Johnson**, wife Valerie Johnson and Richard Heath. In 1981 they released one A&M album *Passage* which included 'Have You Heard The Word'. Participating in the project were **Ricky Lawson** (drums), **Nolen & Crosby** and **Rene Moore**.

PASSION

(Studio Group)

Featuring **Dr York**, Passion were a studio concept who created a stir on dancefloors both sides of the Atlantic in 1982 with a **Kashif** song 'Don't Stop My Love'. It was released on the Prelude label (via CBS).

PASSIONETTES

(Group)

The Passionettes were Bonnie and Marjorie Guinn from Philadelphia, who later joined their brothers and changed their name to **Guinn**. As The Passionettes, the sisters performed locally and recorded 'Memories', a song written by Wilbert Hart of **The Delfonics**.

PATRICK, KEITH

(Singer)

Philadelphia singer Keith Patrick signed to Omni Records (via Atlantic) in 1986. He worked with producer Kenny Copeland from **Rose Royce** on a debut single 'Night To Remember' and album *Keith Patrick*.

PATRICK, RIKKI

(Singer/Guitar/Sax)

From Manchester, Rikki played guitar and saxophone in his first group Masterpiece at the age of fifteen. He then spent three years as lead singer on the club circuit with Sweet Sensation following their hits 'Sad Sweet Dreamer' and 'Purely By Coincidence', replacing original lead singer Marcel King. Next he moved to Canada before returning to the UK and appearing on a David Essex TV showcase. In 1982 he signed to CBS and released 'Night Moves', produced by **Talkback**. His other singles were 'I Never Thought It Would Come To This' (1984) and 'Clear The Way' (1985), before 'Night Moves' was remixed and released again on the DMC label via Arista (1987).

PATTERSON, BOBBY

(Singer/Songwriter/Producer)

Born in Dallas, in 1944, Bobby formed The Royal Rockers as a teenager, and soon recorded as a solo artist for the local Jetstar label (including 'If I Didn't Have You', 'Long Ago' and 'Let Them Talk'). Through the '60s his regular backing band was The Mustangs, who accompanied him on songs including 'Sock Some Lovin' At Me', 'The Knockout Power Of Love' and 'My Baby's Coming Back To Me', later popular in the UK on the 'Northern soul' scene. During the '70s he recorded for a number of labels including Paula (*It's Just A Matter Of Time*, 1971), Proud ('I Can Help You Get Even With Him', 1976), Granite and All Platinum ('Right Place Wrong Time' and 'Groove Me', 1983).

As a producer he worked with **Chuck Jackson** ('I Fell Asleep'), **Fontella Bass** ('Homewrecker', 1983), **Ted Taylor**, Roscoe Robison and Eddie Giles ('Losing Boy').

PAUL, BILLY

(Singer)

From Philadelphia, Billy (real name Paul Williams) began his music career at the age of twelve. After formal jazz training he worked with Charlie Parker, **Dinah Washington**, **Miles Davis** and **Roberta Flack** (among others) before putting a trio together and recording 'Why Am I' for the Jubilee label. In 1959 he recorded 'Ebony Woman' for the New Dawn label before he became one of **Gamble/Huff**'s first signings to their Philadelphia International (PIR) label in 1971. Here he first made an impression with the classic/platinum hit 'Me & Mrs Jones' (UK Top 20, 1973 – some years later the song was re-recorded by a female singer, Sarah Jane Morris and banned on Radio One after anti-lesbian protests). UK single success followed with 'Thanks For Saving My Life' (Top 40, 1974), 'Let's Make A Baby' (Top 30, 1976), 'Let 'Em In' (Top 30, 1977), 'Your Song' (Top 40, 1977), 'Only The Strong Survive' (Top 40, 1977), and the classic dance anthem 'Bring The Family Back' (Top 75, 1979).

His first album for PIR was *Feelin' Good At The Cadillac Club*, essentially a jazz album, but this wasn't released until 1973. His first official album was *Going East* (1971), followed by *360 Degrees Of Billy Paul* (1972); *Ebony Woman* (1973), the title track being a re-recording of his 1959 single release; *War Of The Gods* (1973); *Got My Head On Straight* (1975); *When Love Is New* (1976); *Let 'Em In* (1976); *Only The Strong Survive* (1977); and *First Class* (1979).

From here Billy switched to the Total Experience label for *Lately* (1985), including 'Hot Date', before a brief spell at Ichiban Records. In 1989 he announced on stage at the Dominion in London that he was quitting the business, but he can still be seen at various cabaret dates.

PAUL, CHRIS

(Keyboards/Producer)

DJ turned recording artist from Harrow, Middlesex, Chris broke onto the recording scene in 1986 with a cover version of the **Lonnie Liston Smith** classic 'Expansions' on 4th & Broadway (featuring vocals by **David Joseph**). The following year he became the first signing to EMI's new dance label, Syncopate, for which he released the single 'Back In My Arms', co-written by **Total Contrast** who were also the featured vocalists on the track.

PAUL, CLARENCE

(Songwriter/Producer)

Currently based in Los Angeles, Clarence worked closely with **Stevie Wonder** during the '60s co-writing (sometimes producing) songs including 'I Call It Pretty Music, But The Old People Call It The Blues', 'Until You Come Back To Me (That's What I'm Gonna Do)', 'Ain't That Asking For Trouble', 'Fingertips' and 'Kiss Me Baby'. He has also worked with a number of other artists including **Ronnie McNeir**.

PAYNE, DARRYL

(Songwriter/Producer)

Based in New York, Darryl worked consistently on the dance scene through the '80s writing and/or producing for artists including **Sharon Redd** ('Beat The Street' and 'Never Gonna Give You Up'), **France Joli** ('Your Good Lovin''), **Sinnamon** ('Thanks To You' and 'I Need You Now'), **Brian Keith** ('Touch Me'), **Richard Jon Smith** ('She's The Master Of The Game' and 'Baby's Got Another'), **Carol Williams** ('Can't Get Away', 'You've Reached The Bottom Line' and 'What's The Deal?'), **Katie Kisson** ('You're The One'), **Carol Douglas** ('When Love Goes Wrong') and **Electrik Funk** ('On A Journey'). More recently he co-produced the **Kleeer** single 'Delicious' (1990).

As a solo artist he recorded 'I Can't Believe It's Over' in 1983 with guest vocals by **Will Downing**. It was released in 1988 by Graphic Records in the UK on an album showcasing Darryl's work called *Past, Present & Future*.

PAYNE, FREDA

(Singer)

Born in Detroit, Michigan, Freda is the sister of former **Supremes** member **Scherrie Payne**. Her own career began when she sang with the Pearl Bailey Revue, regularly performing with Duke Ellington. Her next break came when **Quincy Jones** invited her to perform as a soloist with his orchestra one night at the Apollo in Harlem, New York.

In 1965 she signed with ABC Records and sang strictly jazz until 1969 when she was signed by the Invictus label owned by writers/producers **Holland/Dozier/Holland**. Here she made an impact on the American r&b scene with 'Unhooked Generation', followed by her biggest hit 'Band Of Gold' (UK No. 1, 1970). In the UK this success was followed by 'Deeper And Deeper' (Top 40, 1970) and 'Cherish What Is Dear To You' (Top 50, 1971), while in America her anti-Vietnam song 'Bring The Boys Home' was a million-seller before she diverted her attention to TV and the theatre.

She returned to the ABC label for *Payne And Pleasure* (1974), including 'Don't Wanna Be Left Out', and *Out Of Payne Comes Love* (1975), including 'You', before a switch to Capitol for *Supernatural High* (1976). In 1982 she made a single 'In Motion' for the Sutra label (via Buddah in the UK), while more recently she re-recorded 'Band Of Gold' for the UK Motorcity label (1990). She is married to **Gregory Abbott**.

PAYNE, SCHERRIE

(Singer)

Born in Detroit, Scherrie (sister of **Freda Payne**) began her career in the '60s as a member of vocal group **Glass House**. In 1969 she took over from **Jean Terrell** as lead singer of **The Supremes**, remaining with the group until 1977 on songs including 'He's My Man', 'I'm Gonna Let My Heart Do The Walking' and 'You're My Driving Wheel'. When **Mary Wilson** left The Supremes, Scherrie recorded one last Motown album *Partners* (1979) with **Susaye Greene** as Scherrie & Susaye, and also had a solo single release 'Fly'.

From here Scherrie joined a group D'llegance and worked with producer **Ian Levine** on a popular American dance record 'Chasing Me Into Somebody Else's Arms'. In 1982 Scherrie became the first artist to sign with the Record Shack label in the UK, and recorded a 'high energy' version of the 10CC hit 'I'm Not In Love'.

Back in Los Angeles she recorded 'One Night Only' for the Megatone label before joining a reformed line-up of **The Supremes** in 1986 with **Susaye Green** and **Jean Terrell**. They called themselves FLOS ('Former Ladies Of The Supremes'), and released 'We're Back'. More recently Scherrie has recorded with a 'Supremes' line-up known as Jean, Scherrie & Lynda Of The Supremes for Motorcity Records, as well as solo releases for the label including 'Pure Energy' (1989).

PEACHES & HERB

(Duo)

Peaches & Herb were originally Francine Barker and Herb Fame from Washington. Herb was a sales assistant in a local record store and was given his first break by **Van McCoy** who agreed to audition the young hopeful in the store's stockroom in 1965. Van put Herb together with Francine and created the partnership Peaches & Herb which recorded for Epic until Francine got married and Herb joined the Washington police force. During this time they recorded the **Gamble/Huff** song 'United'.

In 1975 Van McCoy persuaded Herb to re-form the duo and put him in touch with a new 'Peaches', Linda Green (formerly vocalist with the Rondells). Signing to Polydor they scored UK chart hits with 'Shake Your Groove Thing' (Top 30, 1979) and 'Reunited' (Top 5, 1979). Their mid to late '70s albums were *Twice The Five*, *Worth The Wait*, *Sayin' Something* and *2 Hot*.

PEARSON, DANNY

(Singer)

Los Angeles-based singer Danny Pearson was signed by **Barry White** to the Unlimited Gold label (via CBS) in 1978. Here he released one album *Barry White Presents Mr Danny Pearson*, including 'Say It Again'.

PEASTON, DAVID

(Singer)

Born in St Louis, David Peaston's mother is Martha Bass, one of The Clara Ward Singers. His older sister is **Fontella Bass**. David initially began a career as a schoolteacher, but after a staff layoff in 1981 he moved to New York where he took up session work as a singer and auditioned for a gospel musical *Don't Get God Started*. Alongside four hundred hopefuls, he also auditioned for the infamous talent contest at the Apollo in Harlem. He sang thirty seconds of 'God Bless The Child' (which he first sang at a funeral) and instantly qualified. In 1988 he began winning TV audiences on the televised *Showtime At The Apollo*. The result was a deal with Geffen Records and his 1989 album *Introducing David Peaston*, including 'Two Wrongs (Don't Make It Right)', 'Don't Say No' and 'Can I?'. The same year he made his London concert debut supported by **Gerald Alston**, and also toured in the USA with **Gladys Knight**.

PEBBLES

(Singer/Songwriter)

Born Perri McKissack in Oakland, California, in 1964, Pebbles originally studied opera and classical ballet. Her vocal potential was first recognized by **Bill Summers** who signed her to his production company when she was sixteen. She sang on his albums before teaming up with **Con Funk Shun** for whom she sang, produced and wrote 'Bodylovers'. At the age of twenty-three she signed with MCA as a solo artist and teamed up with producers **L.A./Babyface** for *Pebbles* (1987). The album included the UK Top 10 single 'Girlfriend', and UK Top 50 follow-up 'Mercedes Boy' (both hits in 1988) together with a popular soul track 'Do Me Right'.

She then married Antonio 'L.A.' Reid (of L.A./Babyface), with whom she worked on her second MCA album *Always*, including 'Giving You The Benefit', in 1990.

PEDICIN JR, MICHAEL

(Saxophone)

Born in Philadelphia, Michael was inspired to take a musical career by his father who had an American million-selling single 'Shake A Hand' in the mid-'50s. After leaving music college he performed with artists including **Nancy Wilson**, David Bowie, **Michael Henderson**, Cannonball Adderley, Buddy Rich, Johnny Mathis, **Donald Byrd**, **George Duke** and **Dionne Warwick** before signing as a solo artist with Philadelphia International Records.

Here he recorded one album, *Michael Pedicin Jr* (1979), including 'That's A Good One' (featuring vocals by **The Jones Girls**) and 'Soncere (The Infinite Hour Glass)'. As a session player he has recorded with artists including **Geraldine Hunt** ('Can't Fake The Feeling'), while more recently he returned for a single 'Just West Of The East Side' on Billy/Gene label (1985).

PEEBLES, ANN

(Singer)

Born in East St Louis in 1947, Ann was one of eleven children born into a gospel music family. Her father was Perry Peebles, under whom she was performing at the First Baptist Church by the time she was nine. Inspired by **Aretha Franklin** she progressed into local club work, eventually travelling to Memphis where she was offered work with **Willie Mitchell**. Willie took her to Hi Records where her debut single 'Walk Away' was an American hit in 1969.

Her follow-ups during this era included 'Give Me Some Credit' (1969), 'Generation Gap Between Us' (1970), 'Part-Time Lover' (1970), 'I Pity The Fool' (1971) and 'Slipped Tripped & Fell In Love' (1971). Also at Hi she wrote songs with label mate **Don Bryant** whom she eventually married. Together they wrote for artists including Quiet Elegance and **Otis Clay**.

Her own albums at Hi included *I Can't Stand The Rain* (1974), including 'You Keep Me Hangin' On' and 'A Love Vibration'. The title track of the album became Ann's one UK Top 50 hit (via London Records), and was later re-recorded by artists including **Eruption** and **Tina Turner**. Further albums at Hi through to 1981 were *Tellin' It*, including 'Beware' and 'Come To Mama'; *If This Is Heaven; Part Time Love*; and *The Handwriting Is On The Wall*.

PEECH BOYS

(Group)

Featuring the vocals of **Bernard Fowler**, The Peech Boys signed to Island Records in New York in 1982 where they released a pioneering record on the 'electro' music scene 'Don't Make Me Wait' (UK Top 50). Follow-ups included the Larry Levan-co-penned/produced 'Life Is Something Special' (1983).

PEELES, NIA

(Singer)

Based in Los Angeles, Nia is the wife of **Howard Hewett**, who produced songs on her debut album for Mercury Records *Nia Peeples* (1988), including 'Star Crossed Lovers', alongside **Monte Moir** and **Steve Harvey**.

PENDERGRASS, TEDDY

(Singer/Drummer)

Born in Philadelphia in 1950 to a deeply religious family, Teddy's early singing was in church. In his teens he was ordained as a priest while his first professional gig was as a drummer with The Cadillacs. In 1969 the group was hired to support **Harold Melvin & The Blue Notes** the group he was soon to join as lead singer. After fronting the group on hits including 'If You Don't Know Me By Now', 'The Love I Lost', 'Wake Up Everybody' and 'Don't Leave Me This Way', Teddy left in 1976 to concentrate on a solo career. He remained with the same label (Philadelphia International), and immediately scored a UK Top 50 hit with 'The Whole Town's Laughing At Me' from his debut solo album *Teddy Pendergrass* (1977).

In 1978 came the double platinum-selling album *Life Is A Song Worth Singing*, which spawned the double-header 'Close The Door'/'Only You', his biggest solo hit in the UK at No. 41. His other Philadelphia International albums were *Teddy* (1979), including 'Come Go With Me' and 'Turn Off The Lights'; *T.P.* (1980), including 'Love TKO', 'Is it Still Good To Ya' and a **Stephanie Mills** duet 'Feel The Fire'; *Ready For Teddy* (1980); and *It's Time For Love* (1981), including 'I Can't Live Without Your Love', before he came to the UK for some spectacular shows with Stephanie Mills. He recorded again with Stephanie on 'Two Hearts' for her album *Stephanie* (1981), before tragedy struck in 1982. A car crash left him paralysed from the waist down.

In the meantime Philadelphia International released two albums of previously unissued songs, *This One's For You* (1982) and *Heaven Only Knows* (1983), before the label began to wind down. It was two years before Teddy could record again, *Love Language* (1984) being his ninth solo album and his debut for Elektra. It featured a duet with **Whitney Houston**, 'Hold Me' (also on Whitney's 1985 debut album), and a **Luther Vandross** song/production 'You're My Choice Tonight (Choose Me)'. The album lacked the vocal depth of his earlier recordings, although that has improved with subsequent releases.

In 1985 came *Workin' It Back*, following which *Joy* (1988) featured a UK Top 60 hit 'Joy' (his last UK chart entry to date). *Joy* also featured '2 a.m.', acclaimed by UK soul fans. Teddy is still recording, his most recent album being *Truly Blessed* (1991).

In the meantime he has started a company, Teddy Bear Productions, which launched a line of designer jeans, not to mention introducing **Miles Jaye** to the soul world.

PENNINGTON, BARBARA
(Singer)
From Chicago, Barbara first put her voice to vinyl in the mid-'70s when she met **Ian Levine**, producer of her debut single 'Run In The Other Direction' (1975) for Island Records. Remaining with Ian she moved to United Artists in 1976 for the follow-up 'Twenty-Four Hours A Day', a No. 1 American dance record in 1977. Her United Artists album *Midnight Rider* included further singles 'You Are The Music Within Me', 'Spend A Little Time With Me' and 'All Time Loser', before she retired for a quieter life.

In 1984 she met Ian Levine again and was prompted to record 'All American Boy' which became a classic on the 'high energy' scene when released in 1984 by Record Shack. From here she recorded *Out Of The Darkest Night* which included the UK Top 75 hits 'Fan The Flame' and 'On A Crowded Street'. She later recorded 'Don't Stop The World', 'There Are Brighter Days', and 'I've Been A Bad Girl' for Ian Levine's Nightmare label.

PEOPLE'S CHOICE
(Group)
Formed by **Frank Brunson** (vocals/keyboards) in Philadelphia during the early '70s, People's Choice were David Thompson (drums/percussion), Valerie Brown and Marc Reed (vocals), Darnell Jordan and Johnnie Hightower (guitars), Clifton Gamble (keyboards), Bill Rodgers (keyboards) and Stanley Thomas (bass/vocals). Signing to Philadelphia International Records (PIR), they worked with writer/producer **Leon Huff** (without **Kenny Gamble** on this occasion) on 'Do It Any Way You Wanna' (UK Top 40, 1975), a Philly dance classic. The song was taken from *Do It Any Way You Wanna* (1975). Further PIR albums were *We Got Rhythm* (1976) and *Turn Me Loose* (1978), including 'Jam Jam Jam' (UK Top 40).

In 1982 the group were with the TPC label for 'You Got It', before signing briefly to Mercury Records for *Strikin'* in 1984.

PERKINS, AL
(Producer)
Born in Detroit, Al established himself as a disc jockey before turning to record producing. Working closely with ABC Records (later MCA where he ran the r&b department), he worked with artists including **Round Trip**, **The Dells**, **Alicia Myers** and to a greater extent **One Way**. He was shot dead in 1984.

PERREN, FREDDIE
(Songwriter/Producer)
Based in Los Angeles, Freddie was particularly prolific as a writer and/or producer in the '70s when he worked with artists including **Gloria Gaynor** ('I Will Survive'), **Tavares** (*Sky High*, including 'Don't Take Away The Music' and 'Heaven Must Be Missing An Angel'), **The Miracles** (*City Of Angels*, including 'Love Machine'), **Minnie Riperton** ('Young Willing And Able'), **Peaches & Herb** ('Shake Your Groove Thing' and 'Reunited'), and even **Demis Roussos** ('L.O.V.E. Got A Hold Of Me').

PERRI
(Group)
The Perri sisters (Lori, Carol, Sharon and Darlene) first started performing in their high-school days, proceeding from high school events to the local club circuit. At the time they sang Top 40 material which they found boring, resulting ultimately in the group splitting up for a number of years. In 1982 they were inspired to sing together again after attending a Pat Metheny concert. The sisters put together a tape featuring cover versions of Pat's songs, and two days later Pat invited them to join him for a recording session. Following live appearances with Metheny in 1983 and 1985, they signed with Zebra Records (via MCA) and recorded a debut album *Celebrate* (1986), featuring two Metheny numbers, 'Airstream Two' and 'Jaco Two'.

Through a fortunate meeting at a doctor's office, **Anita Baker** invited Perri to back her in concert for a week in Los Angeles during 1986, then extended her invitation for a year-long world tour. They also appeared on Joe Zawinul's album *The Immigrant* and teamed up with Anita's producer **Michael Powell** for *The Flight* in 1988 (which included 'I'm The One', co-written by Michael Powell, Dean Gant and **Keni Burke**).

In 1989 they hooked up with Spike Lee for the soundtrack album to his film *Do The Right Thing*. This included the songs 'Prove To Me', 'Feels So Good' (released as a single) and a duet by Lori Perri and **Gerald Alston**, 'Hard To Say'. That year they signed directly to MCA where to date they have released one album *Tradewinds* (1990), which includes 'Someone Like You'. Also at MCA, Lori Perri co-wrote 'Touch Me Up' for the group **Body**.

PERRIN, SUE
(Singer)
First signing to Detroit's Golden World label (with 'I Wonder' in 1962), Sue cut such discs as 'You Are My Love', 'Ring Bells Ring', 'Candy Store Man' (written and produced by **Marv Johnson**) and 'Can't Let Go', ending in 1964.

PERRY, GREG
(Singer/Songwriter/Producer)
Based in Los Angeles, Greg had four brothers, Dennis, Zachary, Leonard and **Jeff Perry** his musical family. As a solo artist his albums include *One For The Road* (Casablanca, 1975), and *Smokin'* (RCA, 1977), the latter including 'How's Your Love Life Baby', for which he is perhaps best remembered.

PERRY, JEFF
(Singer/Songwriter/Producer)
Born into a musical environment, Jeff's brothers include **Greg Perry** and his manager Leonard Perry. In 1975 he

signed to Arista where his debut single was 'Love Don't Come No Stronger', something of a cult record on the UK soul scene. The follow-up was 'Honest Baby (You're My Perfect Lady)' (1976), although he left Arista directly afterwards.

In 1979 he signed to MCA where he recorded one album *Jeffrey*, including 'Love's Gonna Last'.

PERRY, RICHARD
(Producer)
Based in Los Angeles, Richard has been prolific on the r&b scene as a producer throughout the '70s and '80s in addition to running one of LA's leading nightclubs, Studio 55. He has produced for artists including **Martha Reeves** (*Martha Reeves*), **Diana Ross** (*Baby It's Me*, including 'The Same Love That Made Me Laugh'), **The Pointer Sisters** ('Jump'), **Greg Phillinganes** (*Pulse*), **Jeffrey Osborne** ('Emotional'), **Donna Summer** ('Dinner With Gershwin'), **Thelma Houston/The Winans** ('Lean On Me'), **Debarge** ('Rhythm Of The Night'), Carly Simon ('Nobody Does It Better'), Leo Sayer ('You Make Me Feel Like Dancing') and **Patti Labelle** ('Oh People').

PERSON, HOUSTON
(Sax)
This New York-based saxophonist recorded for Mercury in the mid-'70s where his fusion jazz-orientated albums included *Pure Pleasure* (1976), featuring **Patti Austin** and **Gwen Guthrie** and *Harmony* (1977). He also recorded with artists including **Mike Mandell** (*Utopia Parkway*, 1980), **Charles Earland** and **Reuben Wilson**.

PERSUADERS
(Vocal Group)
From New Jersey, The Persuaders are best remembered for their one American hit 'Thin Line Between Love And Hate' for Atlantic Records (1971). This was re-recorded by The Pretenders. Their other recordings from the same era include 'Some Guys Have All The Luck' and 'Win Lose Or Draw'.

PETERS, JERRY
(Producer/Arranger/Keyboards)
Jerry Peters has worked consistently on the American soul and jazz scene from the '70s to the present day. As a producer he has worked with artists including **Brainstorm** ('Wake Up And Be Somebody'), **The Waters**, **Lamont Johnson** ('Music Of The Sun'), **Rockie Robbins** (*I Believe In Love*, with **Skip Scarbrough**), **Ronnie Foster** (*Love Satellite* and *Delight*), **Manfredo Fest** ('Jungle Kitten'), **Phyllis Hyman** ('No One Can Love You More') and **Gladys Knight** ('Love Is Always On Your Mind').

He has arranged music for artists including **Lenny Williams** ('Changes'), **Philip Bailey** (*The Wonders Of His Love*), **Norman Connors** (writing 'For You Everything') and **Starship Orchestra**. He has recorded keyboard sessions with **Marvin Gaye**, **Bobbi Humphrey**, **The Temptations**, **Arthur Adams**, **Donald Byrd**, **Side Effect** and many more.

PETRUS, JACQUES FRED
(Producer)
Based in New York, Frenchman Jacques Fred Petrus masterminded groups including **Change**, **High Fashion** and **B.B.&Q.** during the early '80s. He was later shot dead.

PETTUS, GIORGE
(Singer)
Based in New York, Giorge signed to MCA Records in 1987 where **La La** wrote and produced his debut single 'My Night For Love' taken from an album *Giorge Pettus* released later that year.

PHASE II
(Group)
From New Jersey, Phase II are Vincent Herbert, Sean Sims and Kevin Washington. Recording for the Republic label, their debut release was 'Reachin'' (1988), followed by 'It's A Mystery', produced by **Blaze**.

PHILADELPHIA ALL STARS
(Group)
'Let's Clean Up The Ghetto' by the Philadelphia All Stars was the spearhead record for a campaign by **Kenny Gamble** to raise money for ghetto committees across America. It was the brainchild of Kenny Gamble, and was originally written for **Lou Rawls** who recorded the opening line in 1975. As it sounded out of context with the rest of his album that year it was held over to 1977 when the voices of **Archie Bell**, **The O'Jays**, **Billy Paul**, **Teddy Pendergrass**, **The Three Degrees**, **Harold Melvin** and **Dee Dee Sharp** were added. The song reached the UK Top 40 (1977) when released by Philadelphia International.

PHILLINGANES, GREG
(Keyboards/Songwriter/Singer)
Originally from Detroit, now resident in Los Angeles, Greg is one of the West Coast's top session keyboard players. His credits include recordings and/or tours with **Michael Jackson**, **Lionel Richie**, **George Benson**, **Aretha Franklin**, Paul McCartney and **Quincy Jones**.

Stevie Wonder gave Greg his first break in 1975 having heard Greg's instrumental renditions of Stevie songs on a cassette passed his way by **Ricky Lawson**. Greg joined Wonderlove, following which he met Quincy Jones and worked with him on a song 'The Best Thing' for **Billy Eckstine** (1976). This led to work with Michael Jackson for whom Greg has played on all three Epic albums. At the time of the *Thriller* album, Michael wrote a song called 'Behind The Mask' which was left off at the last minute. Greg asked if he could use it himself, and a positive reply led to Greg's own version being released on his *Pulse* album in 1984. (The song was a UK Top 20 hit for Eric Clapton in 1987.) Earlier Greg had released his debut solo album *Significant Gains* (1981). Both solo albums were released on the Planet label (via RCA).

As a songwriter Greg has written/co-written 'Love Till The End Of Time' (**Paulino Da Costa**), 'Smilin' On Ya' (**Brothers Johnson**), 'Love Will Find A Way' and 'Se La' (**Lionel Richie**), while he has also recorded keyboards with **Atlantic Starr**, **Debarge**, **Donald Byrd**, **Patti Austin**, **Diana Ross**, **Patti Labelle** and many others.

PHILLIPS, ESTHER

(Singer)

Born Esther Nay Jones in Galveston, Texas, in 1935, Esther was discovered by vibes man/bandleader **Johnny Otis** at a talent contest in 1949. She made her debut as Little Esther by recording for the Savoy label in 1950. That year 'Double-Crossing Blues' was an American r&b No.1. Under the musical direction of Johnny Otis she continued to record through to 1954 (though for King Records from 1951), when she retired from the music scene for six years.

In 1960 she signed to the Lenox label for a Top 10 hit 'Release Me' (later recorded by Englebert Humperdinck) before switching to Atlantic in 1963, where she remained through to 1970 (except for one album on Roulette in 1969). While at Atlantic she did well with the Lennon/McCartney song 'And I Love Him' (1964) and 'When A Woman Loves A Man' (1966), an answer record to Percy Sledge's 'When A Man Loves A Woman'. In 1971 she signed with Kudu for a string of notable releases: *From A Whisper To A Scream* (1974), including 'Home Is Where The Hatred Is'; *What A Difference A Day Makes* (1975); *Mr Magic* (1975); *Fever* (1976); *Capricorn Princess*, *Performance* and *For All We Know*. The single 'What A Difference A Day Makes' was an international hit and reached the UK Top 10 in 1975.

From here she switched to Mercury in 1979 for *You've Come A Long Way Baby* (1979), *All About Esther Phillips* (1981) and *Good Black I Hard To Crack* (1982).

Down to earth and sharp-tongued, Esther suffered most of her life from an addiction to drunk and drugs, which led to her death in 1984.

PHILLY CREAM

(Studio Group)

Philly Cream was the concept of Larry James, a.k.a. Fat Larry of **Fat Larry's Band**. During the late '70s Philly-disco era, the group scored on the dancefloors with 'Sexy Cream' and 'Sly-Hi' (1978). They also released a medley 'Motown Revue' which featured **The Jones Girls**, **Butch Ingram** and a star Philly line-up.

PHILLY DEVOTIONS

(Vocal Group)

Formed in Philadelphia during the early '70s, The Philly Devotions scored with a local hit 'I Just Can't Say Goodbye' on the Dondee label in 1973. Its popularity prompted CBS to sign the group and reissue the single along with follow-ups including 'Hurt So Bad'.

PICKETT, WILSON

(Singer)

Born in Prattville, Alabama, in 1942, Wilson grew up with his family in Detroit. Here he sang gospel in church before joining **The Falcons** and later releasing his first solo single 'My Heart Belongs To You' on the US Correc-Tone label.

His first American hit was 'If You Need Me' (1963) on the US Double-L label following which he signed with Atlantic. Here he established himself internationally with a string of classic hits, 'In The Midnight Hour' (UK Top 20, 1965), 'Don't Fight It' (UK Top 30, 1965), '634–5789' (Top 40, 1966), 'Land Of 1000 Dances' (Top 30, 1966), 'Mustang Sally' (Top 30, 1966), 'Funky Broadway' (Top 50, 1967), 'I'm A Midnight Mover' (Top 40, 1968), and 'Hey Jude' (Top 20, 1969).

He later recorded for RCA (*Pickett In The Pocket*), EMI America (*I Want You*, 1979) and Motown, where he re-recorded 'In The Midnight Hour' for *American Soul Man* (1987).

PIECES OF A DREAM

(Group)

Formed in Philadelphia during the early '80s, Pieces Of A Dream was formed by James K.Lloyd (keyboards), Cedric Napoleon (bass), and Curtis Harmon (drums). Over the years the group has also included Lance Webb (lead vocals), Randall Bowland (guitar), Vincent Davis (synths) and **Norwood** (vocals). Launched as protégés of **Grover Washington** (who wrote and produced for the group on early albums), the group signed to Elektra where their albums – *Pieces Of A Dream* (1981), including 'Warm Weather' featuring the vocals of Barbara Walker, *We Are One* (1982) and *Imagine This* (1983), including 'Fo-Fi-Fo' – were a fusion of jazz, funk and soul.

They continued this formula following their switch to Manhattan (via EMI) with *Joyride* (1986), *Makes You Wanna* (1988), including 'We Belong To Each Other', and the **Gene Griffin**-co-produced *Bout Dat Time* (1989).

PIPS

(Vocal Group)

From Atlanta, Georgia, The Pips are Edward Patten, William Guest and Bubba Knight. They first sang together in the early '50s with **Gladys Knight**, and then on their own when Gladys took a year off to have a baby (1964–5). When Gladys Knight & The Pips left Buddah Records in 1977, The Pips signed on their own to Casablanca Records. Here they recorded two albums, *At Last* (1977) and *Callin'* (1978), produced by **Bunny Sigler** with music by **Instant Funk**.

PLAYERS ASSOCIATION

(Group)

From New York, Players Association was masterminded by Chris Hills (vocals/keyboards/drums/guitar) and producer Danny Weiss. Originally a studio band further comprising **Joe Farrell** (sax) and Jon Faddis (trumpet), they signed with Vanguard Records for *Born To Dance* (1977), including 'I Like It', 'Love Hangover' and 'Goin' To The Disco; *Turn The Music Up*, (1979) including the title track UK Top 10 dance classic and 'Ride The Groove' (UK Top 50); and *We Got The Groove* (1980).

Chris Hill also played percussion with **Mike Mandell**, while in 1987 Danny Weiss produced a jazz album for Members Only (*Members Only*) released by Muse Records and featuring former members of Players Association.

PLEASURE

(Group)

Formed in Portland, Oregon, Pleasure blended soul, funk and jazz with a tough street edge and became a cult group on the underground black music scene of the late '70s. They were Bruce Carter (drums), Tony Collins (trumpet/flugelhorn), Sherman Davis (vocals), Donald Hepburn (keyboards), Michael Hepburn (keyboards), Marlon McClain (guitars), Nathaniel Phillips (bass), Bruce Smith (percussion/vocals) and Dennis Springer (sax). Working closely with producer **Wayne Henderson** in Los Angeles, they signed to Fantasy Records for *Dust Yourself Off* (1975), including 'Midnight At The Oasis'; *Accept No Substitutes* (1976), including 'Ghettos Of The Mind'; *Joyous* (1977), including 'Sassafras Girl'; and *Get To The Feeling* (1978), including 'Ladies Night Out'; before themselves producing *Future Now* (1979), including 'Glide'. They later recorded an album for RCA.

In 1976 they recorded with label mate **Side Effect** on their version of 'Always There'.

PLUM, JEAN

(Singer)

Based in Memphis, Jean worked with producer **Willie Mitchell** at Hi Records at the time **Al Green** was scoring all his best-known hits. Jean is best remembered for her Hi singles 'Look At The Boy' and 'Pour On The Loving' during the early '70s.

PLUSH

(Group)

Based in Los Angeles, this two-guy/one-girl group worked with writers/producers **Rene & Angela** on their one album for RCA, *Plush* (1981), including 'We've Got The Love'. In 1986 **Kevin McCord** and his wife **Candye Edwards** wrote a song 'Loved Right', which Kevin produced for a different group called Plush on the Presents label.

POCKETS

(Group)

Based in Los Angeles, Pockets were protégés of **Earth Wind & Fire**. The group consisted of Albert McKinney (keyboards/vocals), Gary Grainger (bass/vocals), Larry Jacobs (vocals/percussion), Charles Williams (trumpet/vocals/percussion), Irving Madison (sax/vocals/percussion), Kevin Barnes (trombone/vocals/percussion), Jacob Sheffer (guitar/percussion) and George Gray (drums/vocals/percussion).

Signed to **Maurice White**'s label ARC (via CBS), their albums included the Maurice White-produced *Take It On Up* (1978), including 'Heaven Only Knows' (later recorded by **Teddy Pendergrass**), 'Tell Me Why' (written by **Keni Burke**) and 'You And Only You' (written by **Ray Parker Jr**); and the Verdine White/**Robert Wright**-produced *So Delicious* (1979).

POINTER SISTERS

(Vocal Group)

From Oakland, California, the Pointer Sisters are four of the six children of Elton and Sarah Pointer, both church ministers. Growing up in a gospel music environment, Ruth, Anita, June and Bonnie were originally only allowed to sing non-secular music. Bonnie and June first sang together in Dorothy Morrison's California State Youth Choir until it disbanded. Eventually turning to secular music, the two sisters worked in a number of San Francisco nightclubs before they were joined by Anita and Ruth when they officially formed The Pointer Sisters. At first they sang in cabaret and as background singers with artists including **Elvin Bishop** and **Esther Phillips**. After establishing a reputation of their own through regular appearances at the Troubadour club in Los Angeles, the sisters made their recording debut in 1973 with 'Yes We Can Can', and after a couple of singles for Atlantic signed with Blue Thumb (via ABC).

Here they delivered 'Fairy Tale' (written by Anita and Bonnie) which became a country music smash, later winning a Grammy award for Best Country Song Of The Year (1974). In 1977 a final album for Blue Thumb, *Having A Party*, including 'Bring Your Sweet Stuff Home To Me' (co-written with **Stevie Wonder**), was released, following which **Bonnie Pointer** signed directly to Motown as a solo artist.

The remaining three sisters signed to the Planet label (via RCA) and enjoyed a string of international hit singles. In the UK, these included 'Fire' (Top 40, 1979), 'Slowhand' (Top 10, 1981), 'Automatic' (Top 5, 1984), 'Jump (For My Love)' (Top 10, 1984), 'I'm So Excited' (Top 20, 1984), and 'Neutron Dance' (Top 40, 1985). During this time they worked with **Richard Perry** who in 1985 produced their one RCA album *Contact*, including 'Dare Me' (UK Top 20). In 1987 Anita delivered a solo album 'Love For What It Is' (produced by **Preston Glass**) before rejoining her sisters and signing to the Motown label where *Right Rhythm* was released in 1990.

POINTER, BONNIE
(Singer)
Born in Oakland, California, Bonnie sang with her family group **The Pointer Sisters** from 1973. She began a solo career in 1978 with Motown, where her two albums were *Bonnie Pointer* (1978), including 'Free Me From My Freedom', and *Bonnie Pointer 2* (1979), including 'Heaven Must Have Sent You'. Due to contractual disputes with Motown she could not record again until 1984, at which point she signed with Private I (via CBS) for *If The Price Is Right*.

POINTER, NOEL
(Violin/Singer)
Born in New York in 1957, Noel studied classical violin before signing to Blue Note as a jazz instrumentalist in the mid-'70s. Here he recorded a series of albums incorporating a mixture of jazz and soul styles and featuring guest musicians/singers. His debut album was *Phantazia*.

In 1978 he took his formula to United Artists where he worked with producers **Grusin/Rosen** on *Hold On*, featuring vocals by **Patti Austin**. The follow-ups were *Feel It* (1979), featuring **The Jones Girls** and **Patrice Rushen**, *Calling* (1980), and the **Richard Evans**-produced *All My Reasons* for Liberty Records (1981).

Noel also recorded with **Norman Connors** and numerous other artists. He recently contributed a violin solo on the debut single for **Milira**, 'Mercy Mercy Me' (1990).

POLLARD, RAY
(Singer)
Born in New York, Ray was lead singer of a 'doo-wop' group The Wanderers prior to heading south to Washington to record for **Eddie Singleton**'s Shrine label in the mid-'60s. He is best remembered for the 'Northern soul' anthems 'The Drifter' and 'This Time' (1965).

POLO, JIMI
(Singer)
From Chicago, Jimi established himself on the city's 'house' music scene with groups Libra Libra and Revelation. He then moved to London and released 'Free Yourself' (1989) as a solo on Urban/Polydor.

PONDER, JIMMY
(Guitar)
Born in Pittsburgh in 1946, Jimmy played guitar with various r&b/jazz groups at school before joining the **Charles Earland** band where he played from 1965–68. He made his first recordings with Charles prior to sessions with artists including **Stanley Turrentine**, **Donald Byrd**, **Jimmy McGriff** and Richard 'Groove' Holmes.

His solo recordings have been for labels including Chess, ABC/Impulse, LRC (*Chasing the Face*, produced by **Sonny Lester**) and Milestone (*Down Here On The Ground*, 1983).

PONSAR, SERGE
(Singer)
French artist Serge Ponsar made an impression on the UK dance scene with 'Out In The Night'. It was taken from his one album *Back To The Light* (WEA, 1983).

PORTER, DAVID
(Singer/Songwriter)
From Memphis, David is best known for his songwriting collaborations with **Isaac Hayes** during the '60s, including 'Hold On I'm Coming' (**Sam & Dave**), 'I Got To Love Somebody's Baby' (**Johnnie Taylor**), 'B-A-B-Y' (**Carla Thomas**) and 'The Sweeter He Is' (**Soul Children** – a group he put together with **Isaac Hayes**). As a solo artist for the Enterprise label (via Stax) his albums included *Gritty, Groovy & Gettin' It*, *Into A Real Thing*, *Victim Of The Joke? – An Opera* and *Sweet And Love* (1973).

POSITIVE FORCE
(Studio Group)
Positive Force's one contribution to the dance scene was 'We Got The Funk' (1979), originally released by the Turbo label in New York, later by Streetwave Records in the UK.

POWELL, DOC
(Guitar)
This top American session guitarist has worked with artists including **Luther Vandross**, **Ronnie Dyson** and **Aretha Franklin**. In 1987 he signed to Phonogram where his one album was *Give It Up*.

POWELL, MICHAEL J.
(Songwriter/Producer/Guitar)
Born in Detroit, Michael is an original member of **Chapter 8** which at one point featured the vocals of **Anita Baker**. When Anita launched her solo career, Michael became her principal songwriter and producer, and was in demand by other artists following the success of Anita's *Rapture* album in 1985.

He has written and/or produced for numerous artists including **Regina Belle** ('Please Be Mine', 'After The Love Has Lost Its Shine' and 'Take Your Love Away', 1987), **Mini Curry** ('I Think I'm Over You', 1987), **Peabo Bryson** (songs on *Positive*, 1988), **Brick** ('Too Tuff', 1988), **Randy Crawford** ('Knockin' On Heaven's Door', 1989), **James Ingram** ('You Make Me Feel Like A Natural Man', 1989), **David Peaston** (*Introducing* ..., 1989) and **The Winans** (songs on *Return*, 1990).

He also continued to play guitar and produce **Chapter 8**, writing songs for the group including 'How Is It Possible', 'Don't Stop Loving Me' and 'So In Love'.

PRESSURE
(Group)
Pressure were a group of musicians and singers instigated by **Ronnie Laws** in the late '70s. They were

musicians Ronnie Laws (sax), Melvin Robinson (guitar), Barnaby Finch (keyboards), Bobby Vega (bass), Pat Kelly (guitar) and Art Rodriguez (drums), together with singers Melvin Robinson, Betty Jo Miller, Samuel Moore, Reggie Alexander, Sandra, Johnny Laws and Pat Kelly. Ronnie produced their one album *Pressure* (1980) for MCA, and took them on his tours.

PRESSURE POINT
(Group)
This British soul/jazz group consisted of Lydia Gayle (vocals), Anthony Longden (bass), Sean Maher (guitar), Matthew Best (drums) and Steve Young (percussion). Signed to Viceroy Records, their singles were 'Mellow Moods' (1985) and 'Dreaming' (1986).

PRESTON, BILLY
(Singer/Keyboards/Songwriter/Producer)
Born in Houston, Texas, in 1946, Billy grew up in Los Angeles where he developed his piano-playing skills as a child. Aged ten he appeared in the film *St Louis Blues*, and as a session player during the '60s his duties included work with Mahalia Jackson, **Sam Cooke** and Little Richard.

His early recordings were for the Derby and Vee-Jay labels, the popularity of an instrumental 'Billy's Bag' leading him to a deal with Capitol in the mid-'60s. He then met **Ray Charles** who employed him as a musician. During a UK TV appearance with Ray he caught the attention of The Beatles who signed him as an artist to their Apple label. Here he recorded 'That's The Way God Planned It' (UK Top 20, 1969) and featured on Beatles hits 'Get Back' (UK No. 1, 1969) and 'Let It Be' (UK Top 5, 1970). This led to his nickname of 'The Fifth Beatle'.

Relocating to Los Angeles (where he now lives), Billy continued his solo career with A&M Records, scoring hits including 'I Wrote A Simple Song', 'Outta Space' (UK Top 50, 1972), 'Space Race' (1973) and 'Will It Go Round In Circles', while continuing his session work with a diverse selection of artists from **Sly & The Family Stone** to The Rolling Stones (with whom he toured the States in 1975). Through his association with George Harrison of The Beatles, Billy secured a record deal for **Keni Burke** and his group **The Stairsteps** with George's label Dark Horse Records in 1976. Here he produced the group's album *2nd Resurrection*, while his manager (then **Diana Ross**'s husband) signed Billy as an artist to Motown.

In 1979 he recorded a solo album *Fast Break*, generating some disco interest with 'Go For It', but his greatest commercial success came when he recorded 'With You I'm Born Again', a UK Top 5 hit duet with **Syreeta** the same year. 'It Will Come In Time' (UK Top 50, 1980) was the follow-up prior to an album *Billy Preston & Syreeta* (1981), including the **Michael Masser**-produced 'A New Way To Say I Love You'. He had also recorded a further solo album *Late At Night* in 1980.

He later recorded sessions with **Luther Vandross** ('Til My Baby Comes Home', 1985) and **Al Green** ('You've Got A Friend', 1987), and a solo single 'Kick It' for the independent ERC label prior to working with **Ian Levine** at his UK-based Motorcity label. Here a duet with **Syreeta** 'Watching The Hands Of Time' was released in 1991.

PRICE, LOUIS
(Singer/Songwriter)
Born in Chicago, Louis began his singing career after moving to Los Angeles where he was discovered by **Berry Gordy**. Before making his recording debut he starred in the TV series *L.A. Law* and also appeared on the Motown 30th Anniversary TV special singing a version of of 'Ribbon In The Sky', the **Stevie Wonder** song.

After signing with Motown as a solo artist, he worked with producers **Michael Powell** and **Michael Stokes** on a debut album *Louis Price* (1991), including 'Heart's Devotion' and 'Flesh & Blood'.

PRIDE, LOU
(Singer/Songwriter)
Born in Chicago, in 1950, Lou gained his initial singing experience in church, where his pastor was the Reverend E.J.Cole, father of Nat King Cole. Inspired by **B.B.King** he experimented in blues, and after National Service settled in Texas to team up with JLC as JC & Lou. Also in Texas he landed a small solo recording contract with the Suemi label resulting in his debut single 'I'm Com'un Home In The Morn'un'.

Moving to Memphis, he recorded 'Lonely Road' (also for Suemi). Through the '70s he recorded for labels Albatross (including 'Look Out Love' and 'You've Got To Work For Love'), Gemco ('We're Only Fooling Ourselves') and Onyx ('Been Such A Long Time'). In 1980 he recorded an album *Very Special* for the Black Gold label, while more recently he has worked with **Curtis Mayfield** for the relaunched Curtom label.

PRIME TIME
(Group)
Formed in 1972, Prime Time are a Los Angeles-based group consisting of Jimmy Hamilton (vocals/keyboards, formerly of the Jimmy Hamilton Trio), Frankie 'Babe' Moore (vocals/drums), Dale Hightower (vocals/percussion) and Maurice Hayes (bass/lead vocals). It took the group twelve years to land a record deal, eventually signing to Total Experience for a 1984 single 'Love Talk' and album *Flying High*. In 1985 there was a second album *Confess It Baby* prior to the demise of the label.

PRIMETTES
(Vocal Group)
From Detroit, The Primettes were **Diana Ross**, **Mary Wilson**, Florence Ballard and Barbara Martin, prior to becoming **The Supremes**. As The Primettes they recorded for the Lupin label, and one album with Al Garner.

PRINCE

(Singer/Songwriter/Producer)

Born Prince Rogers Nelson in north Minneapolis in 1958, the name Prince was inspired by The Prince Rogers Jazz Trio, led by his father. Prince took naturally to music as a young child, and by the time he was fifteen was proficient on the piano, bass, guitar and drums, playing in local schools and hotels with a group Champagne.

He made some early recordings in a studio that gave him work after leaving school, also performing with another group **94 East** (featuring **Colonel Abrams**). His demos later won him a contract with Warner Brothers where his albums include *For You* (1978); *Prince* (1979), including 'I Wanna Be Your Lover' (UK Top 50) and 'I Feel For You' (later recorded by **Chaka Khan**); *Dirty Mind* (1980); *Controversy* (1981); *1999* (1983), including the title track (UK Top 25) and 'Little Red Corvette' (UK Top 40); *Purple Rain* (1984), including 'When Doves Cry' (UK Top 5) the title track (UK Top 10) and 'I Would Die For You' (UK Top 75); *Around The World In A Day* (1985), including 'Let's Go Crazy' (UK Top 10), 'Paisley Park' (UK Top 20), 'Raspberry Beret' (UK Top 25) and 'Pop Life' (UK Top 75); *Parade* (1986), including 'Kiss' (UK Top 10), 'Mountains' (UK Top 50) and 'Girls And Boys' (UK Top 20); *Sign Of The Times* (1986), including a single of the same name (UK Top 20, 1986), 'If I Was Your Girlfriend' (UK Top 20, 1987), 'U Got The Look' (UK Top 15, 1987) and 'I Could Never Take The Place Of Your Man' (UK Top 30, 1987); *Love Sexy* (1988), including 'Alphabet Street' (UK Top 10, 1988), 'Glam Slam' (UK Top 30, 1988) and 'I Wish You Heaven' (UK Top 30, 1988); and *Batman* (1989), including 'Batdance' (UK Top 5, 1989), 'Partyman' (UK Top 15, 1989) and 'Arms Of Orion' (UK Top 30, 1989).

In 1987 he launched his own Paisley Park label (via Warner Brothers) where he has worked as writer and/or producer with artists including **The Family** ('Nothing Compares 2 U', later a hit for Sinead O'Connor), **Sheila E.** ('A Love Bizarre'), **Mavis Staples** and **The Time**. Elsewhere his songs and/or productions have been utilized by artists including **Andre Cymone**, **Meli'sa Morgan** ('Do Me Baby') and **Mica Paris** ('If I Love U 2 Nite').

PRINCE CHARLES

(Singer)

Based in New York, Prince Charles & The City Beat Band emerged in the early '80s with 'Cash (Cash Money)', released in the UK by PRT Records. *Gang War* was issued by the Greyhound label in 1983, then in 1985 they returned with 'We Can Make It Happen' on Solid Platinum Records.

PRINCESS

(Singer)

Princess sang with **Osibisa** prior to touring as a backing singer with artists including **Evelyn Thomas** and **Precious Wilson**. Teaming up with writers/producers **Stock/Aitken/Waterman** she signed to the Supreme label and had a string of UK hits including 'Say I'm You're No. 1' (Top 10, 1985), 'After The Love Has Gone' (Top 30, 1985), 'I'll Keep On Loving You' (Top 20, 1986), 'Tell Me Tomorrow' (Top 40, 1986), and 'In The Heat Of A Passionate Moment' (Top 75, 1986). She later switched to Polydor and scored with 'Red Hot' (UK Top 75, 1987).

PRINCIPLE, JAMIE

(Singer/Songwriter/Producer)

Born in Chicago, Jamie was the son of a Baptist deacon and studied the clarinet at school in addition to singing in church. His family wanted him to stick with gospel singing, so he left home and established himself on the local 'house' music scene with singles including 'Waiting On My Angel' and 'Your Love' for the Persona label. In 1988 'Baby Wants To Ride' made a major impact on the UK 'house' scene (via FFRR). More recently he recorded a version of the **Eddie Kendricks** song 'Date With The Rain' for Atlantic (1990).

PROCESS AND THE DOO-RAGS

(Vocal Group)

From Buffalo, New York, Process And The Doo-Rags were James 'Bunty' Hawkins (aka 'Process'), Stacey 'Wave' Lattimore, Richard 'Gumps' Graham, Michael 'Smoothie' Gibson and Dennis 'Shorty' Andrews. In 1983 James Hawkins was invited to sing backing vocals on tour with **Rick James**, following which he sang on Rick's *Reflections* album. Impressed, Rick created the group around James, writing and producing some songs which he took to CBS. Their debut album was *Too Sharp* (1985).

Their image was that of a '50s doo-wop group, while musically they reflected mid-'80s street funk.

PURIFY, JAMES AND BOBBY

(Singers)

From Florida, cousins James and Bobby Purify are best remembered for their one hit 'I'm Your Puppet' (UK Top 15, 1976), originally recorded and released in 1966. Their mid-'70s success with the song on Mercury Records was followed by 'Morning Glory' (Top 30, 1976).

PURIM, FLORA

(Singer)

The wife of **Airto**, Flora is a jazz singer whose Latin-flavoured albums had great appeal on the UK jazz funk scene of the '70s and '80s. Her albums for Milestone Records during the early '70s included *Butterfly Dreams*, featuring **George Duke** and **Stanley Clarke**, *Open Your Eyes You Can Fly* and *Stories To Tell*. She has also recorded for labels including Warner Brothers (*Carry On*, 1979), Crossover (*The Magicians*, with **Airto**, 1986) and Virgin (*The Midnight Sun*, 1988). She was the lead vocalist with **Joe Sample** on 'Shadows' from his album *Voices In The Rain* (1980).

PUSH

(Group)

This British funk group consisted of **Kevin Henry** (lead vocals), Frank Abrams (sax/flugelhorn), Andrew Whitmore (keyboards) and Kwaku 'Reg' Dzidzornu (percussion). Recording for the Excalibur label (via PRT), their single releases included 'Midnight' (1983).

Q

Q-FEEL
(Group)
Based in the UK, Q-Feel were Martin Page and Brian Fairweather (two songwriters whose credits include four tracks on **Earth Wind & Fire**'s *Magnetic*), together with Chris Richardson and Trevor Thornton. Signing to the Jive label in the mid-'80s, they recorded a debut single 'Heroes Never Die'.

Q.T. HUSH
(Group)
Protégés of **Teena Marie**, Q.T.Hush are London Carmichael (vocals/keyboards), Nikki Slikk (vocals/guitar), Allen McGrier (bass/vocals/keyboards/drums), Wyman Brown (keyboards/synths/vocals) and Cocoa La Boy (percussion/vocals). Their debut Epic album *Q.T.Hush* (1985) was produced by Teena Marie, who also helped out on lead vocals.

QUADRAPHONICS
(Vocal Group)
Chicago vocal group The Quadraphonics generated some interest on the UK soul scene in 1974 with a single 'Betcha If You Check It Out' for the Innovation II label (via Warner Brothers). It was released on the UK Contempo label in 1975.

QUALLS, SYDNEY JOE
(Singer)
Chicago singer Sydney Joe Qualls recorded for the Dakar label (including 'Run To Me') before signing to 20th Century Records in 1979. Here the **Sonny Sanders**-arranged/produced *So Sexy* included 'I Don't Do This', popular on the UK soul scene.

QUIET ELEGANCE
(Vocal Group)
Formed in Detroit by **Millie Scott**, Lois Reeves (sister of **Martha Reeves**) and Frankie Gearing, Quiet Elegance toured with **The Temptations** before **Willie Mitchell** signed them to the Hi label in the early '70s. Here they recorded four singles and toured as backing singers with **Al Green** before splitting up.

R

RADICE, MARK
(Singer/Songwriter)
New York-based singer Mark Radice recorded for United Artists in the mid-'70s, where *Ain't Nothin' But A Party* featured the music of **Brass Construction** and was produced by **Jeff Lane** (1976). Mark's songs included 'The Answer Is You', recorded by **Phyllis Hyman**.

RAE, FONDA
(Singer)
This New York-based singer was the voice on several dance records of the early '80s. Under her own name she recorded for labels including Vanguard (including the **Leroy Burgess**-co-written 'Over Like A Fat Rat', 1982) and Telescope ('Tuch Me', 1984). The latter was released in the UK by Streetwave Records where it reached the Top 50.

RAGOVOY, JERRY
(Songwriter/Producer)
Based in Philadelphia, Jerry became an influential songwriter/producer during the '60s and early '70s with his work for artists including **The Majors**, **Garnet Mimms**, **Erma Franklin** ('Piece Of My Heart'), **Irma Thomas** ('Time Is On My Side'), **Lou Courtney** (on his own Rags label via Epic), **Lorraine Ellison** ('Stay With Me'), **Howard Tate**, **Dionne Warwick** ('Sure Thing'), **Major Harris** (*How Do You Take Your Love*) and **Peggi Blu** ('I Got Love').

RAGTYME
(Group)
Formed in Chicago, Ragtyme featured T.C.Roper and recorded 'Fix It Man' for the Bright Star label during 1987. The group later became far more successful under their new name **Ten City**.

RAH BAND
(Group)
The brainchild of Londoner Richard A.Hewson, who gave The RAH Band his initials, the band's UK single success on the soul/dance and pop scene came with 'The Crunch' (Top 10, 1977) on Good Earth Records. Switching to DJM, success continued with 'Falcon' (Top 40, 1980), 'Riding On A Fantasy' (1981) and 'Slide' (Top 50, 1981), before a further move to KR Records for 'Perfumed Garden' (Top 50, 1982), 'Tears And Rain' (1982) and 'Messages From The Stars' (Top 50, 1983).

Later in 1983 they released 'Questions (What You Gonna Do)' (1983) on the Sound Recordings label, before RCA brought them further chart success with 'Are You Satisfied' (Top 75, 1985) and 'Clouds Across The Moon' (Top 10, 1985).

RAHMLEE
(Trumpet)
Rahmlee Michael Davis is best known as one of The Phoenix Horns, resident brass section with **Earth Wind & Fire**. As a solo artist he recorded *Rise Of The Phoenix* (1981), including 'Think', for the Headfirst label, produced by **Dean Gant**.

RALLO, TONY
(Singer/Songwriter)
Tony made one major impression on the disco scene with 'Holding On', released in the UK on the Calibre label from an album *Burnin' Alive* (1979).

RANCE ALLEN GROUP
(Group)
Formed in Detroit, The Rance Allen Group were brothers Rance, Steve, Tom and Esau Allen, who were later joined by cousins Annie, Linda and Judy Mendez on r&b-flavoured gospel recordings for labels including Gospel Truth (via Stax) and Capitol.

RANDOLPH, BARBARA
(Singer)
From Detroit, Barbara toured briefly with **Marvin Gaye**, replacing **Tammi Terrell** in the '60s. As an artist, she recorded 'I Got A Feeling', regarded as a classic among Motown fans (and an American hit) before marrying Eddie Singleton. Eddie's first wife had been Raynoma Gordy (**Berry Gordy**'s second wife!). Barbara and Eddie formed a production company and retired from the limelight, although Barbara re-recorded 'I Got A Feeling' for the UK Nightmare label in 1989.

RARE EARTH

(Group)

Formed in Detroit by Gil Bridges in 1969, Rare Earth were the first major signing of a white group to Motown Records. Formerly known as The Sunliners, the group changed their name to Rare Earth which was also the name of the new Motown subsidiary label which released their singles including 'Generation Light Up The Sky' and their first American hit 'Get Ready' (a version of the **Temptations** song). Original lead singer with the group was Pete Hoorelbeke, who brought the group further success with early '70s singles including 'I Know I'm Losing You' and their American No. 1 'I Just Want To Celebrate', before the Rare Earth label folded in 1976.

The group then switched to the Prodigal label for a number of recordings before Wayne Baraks took over as lead singer. He remains with them today on their singles for Motorcity Records including 'Love Is Here And Now You're Gone' (1990). Pete Hoorelbeke has recorded solo singles for Motorcity including 'Talk To The World' (1990).

RARE ESSENCE

(Group)

Formed in Washington during the late '70s, Rare Essence were pioneers of the city's 'go-go' live music scene and featured **Little Benny**. In the mid-'80s they were signed to Mercury where **Patrick Adams** produced their single 'Flipside' (1986).

RARE MOODS

(Group)

From East London, Rare Moods were Dave Stevens (keyboards), Treva Green (vocals) and Jayne Plues (vocals). Their recordings included 'Dancing Through The Night' (1986).

RAW SILK

(Studio Group)

Instigated by **Ronald Dean Miller** in New York during the early '80s, Raw Silk were signed to the West End label where they stirred dancefloors with 'Do It To The Music' (UK Top 20, 1982) and 'Just In Time' (UK Top 50, 1983).

RAW SOUL

(Group)

Forerunner of the group **Maze**, Raw Soul were formed by **Frankie Beverly** in Philadelphia (1971) and featured Roame Lowry, McKinley Williams and Sam Porter. They recorded 'Colour Blind', 'Tomorrow May Not Be Your Day' and 'While I'm Alone' for the Gregar label (via RCA), and toured with **Kool & The Gang**, **Isaac Hayes** and **Mandrill**.

RAWLS, LOU

(Singer)

Born in Chicago in 1937, Lou sang gospel with the Greater Mount Olive Baptist Church from the age of seven. In 1957, after army service (82nd Airborne Division) he joined gospel group The Pilgrim Travellers, although they split up in 1959 after a serious car accident in which Lou nearly died. He was in a coma for five and a half days and lost his memory for three months.

As a solo artist he began recording for the Shardee and Candix labels and sang with **Sam Cooke** on 'Bring It On Home To Me' (1962). Also in 1962 he signed with Capitol and worked with musicians (led by Les McCann) on his major label debut 'Stormy Monday'. This was followed by albums including *Black And Blue* (1963), *Tobacco Road* (1963), *Nobody But Lou*, *Carryin' On*, including 'On Broadway', *The Way It Was, The Way It Is* and *Soulin'* (1966), including 'Love Is A Hurtin' Thing'. In 1967 his recording 'Dead End Street' won a Grammy. In 1971 he switched to MGM Records where his song 'A Natural Man' won him a second Grammy. His albums there included *Silk And Soul* (1972) before he joined forces with writers/producers **Gamble/Huff** at their Philadelphia International (PIR) label in 1976. Here he scored his one UK national chart entry (UK Top 10) with 'You'll Never Find Another Love Like Mine' from the album *All Things In Time*, also including 'Groovy People'. His other PIR albums were *Unmistakably Lou*, including 'See You When I Get There', *When You Hear Lou, You've Heard It All (1977)*, including 'Lady Love', *Let Lou Be Good To You*, *Sit Down And Talk To Me* (1979) and *Shades Of Blue* (1981). Also at PIR he sang the intro to the UK Top 40 hit for **The Philadelphia All-Stars**, 'Let's Clean Up The Ghetto' (1977).

In 1982 he switched to Epic for albums including the **Mtume/Lucas**-produced *Now Is The Time* (1982), **Thom Bell**-produced *When The Night Comes* (1983), **Dexter Wansel**-produced *Close Company* (1984), *Here Comes Garfield* (a children's album), and *Love All Your Blues Away* (1986), including 'Stop Me From Starting This Feeling', produced by **Jay Graydon**.

In 1987 he returned to work with **Gamble/Huff** on *Family Reunion* for their new label before signing to Blue Note Records in 1989. Here his albums have been *At Last*, featuring **Dianne Reeves**, **George Benson**, **Ray Charles** and **Stanley Turrentine**, and *It's Supposed To Be Fun* (1990), featuring producer **Narada Michael Walden**.

RAY, GOODMAN & BROWN

(Vocal Group)

Formerly known as **The Moments**, **Harry Ray**, Al Goodman and Billy Brown changed their group name to Ray, Goodman & Brown in 1978. Signing to Polygram they recorded *Ray, Goodman & Brown* (1979), including 'Special Lady' and 'Inside Of You', *Ray, Goodman & Brown II* (1980), including 'My Prayer' and 'Happy Anniversary', and *Stay* (1981). They later switched to Manhattan/EMI for *Take It To The Limit* (1987), including 'Where Did You Get That Body (Baby)', and sang backgrounds for **Sarah Dash** on 'Don't Make Me Wait' for her album *You're All I Need* (1988).

RAY, HARRY

(Singer)

From New Jersey, Harry Ray was a featured vocalist with **The Moments**, who later became known as **Ray, Goodman & Brown**. As a solo artist he recorded briefly for the Sugarhill label where he is best remembered for 'Love Is A Game' (1982) from *It's Good To Be Home*. In 1985 he returned with 'My Baby Loves Me' for the Panoramic label.

RAYDIO

(Group)

Instigated by **Ray Parker Jr** in 1977, Raydio featured the vocals of Arnell Carmichael and **Jerry Knight** on the group's 1978 UK hits 'Jack And Jill' (Top 20) and 'Is This A Love Thing' (Top 30) through to 'Two Places At The Same Time' in 1980, all for the Arista label. In 1981 Ray Parker decided to sing lead vocals himself, and, remaining with Arista, dissolved Raydio to record under his own name.

READY FOR THE WORLD

(Group)

Formed in Flint, Michigan, Ready For The World are Melvin Riley (lead vocals), Greg Potts, Gordon Strozier, John Eaton, Gerald Valentine and Willie Triplet. Initially they recorded for their own Blue Lake label, their single 'Tonight' becoming a local hit before MCA signed the group and re-released it nationally. In the UK their hits have been 'Oh Sheila' (Top 50) and 'Love You Down' (Top 75) from their debut album *Ready For The World* (1985).

REAL THING

(Group)

From Liverpool, The Real Thing were vocalists Chris Ammo, Ray Lake, Dave Smith and Kenny Davis. After two years on the cabaret circuit they appeared on the UK TV show *Opportunity Knocks*, following which they signed to Bell Records.

After a series of unsuccessful releases for Bell they switched to Pye Records in 1976 to work with writers/producers Ken Gold and Mickey Denne. About that time Kenny Davis was replaced by Eddie Amoo, and they toured with David Essex while scoring on vinyl that year with 'You To Me Are Everything' (UK No. 1) and 'Can't Get By Without You' (UK No. 2), both songs establishing them on the soul/disco scene. Further UK hits came with 'You'll Never Know What You're Missing' (Top 20, 1977), 'Love's Such A Wonderful Thing' (Top 40, 1977), 'Whenever You Want My Love' (Top 20, 1978), 'Let's Go Disco' – which the group performed in the movie *The Stud* (Top 40, 1978), 'Can You Feel The Force' with 'Children Of The Ghetto' on the B-side (Top 5, 1979), and 'Boogie Down (Get Funky Now)' (Top 40, 1979).

Switching to the Calibre label they had a UK Top 60 hit 'She's A Groovy Freak' (1980) and worked with **Johnny Bristol** on 'Love Takes Tears' (1982), before moving to RCA. Here they worked with producer **Nick Martinelli** on 'We Got Love' (1984).

In 1986 the group enjoyed a re-run of UK hits from their Pye days when a series of their early recordings was remixed and released. These were 'You To Me Are Everything' (Top 5), 'Can't Get By Without You' (Top 10) and 'Can You Feel The Force' (Top 25). Also in 1984 the group signed with Jive and a new single 'Straight To The Heart' made the Top 75.

Chris and Eddie also wrote 'In The Sky', the debut single release for **Loose Ends**.

REAL TO REEL

(Group)

Formed in 1980 in Los Angeles, Real To Reel are brothers Matthew (lead vocals), Dominic (guitar) and Peter Leslie (guitar) with additional members including Daniel Morgan (drums) and Billy Smith (bass). They were groomed in the early days by producer **Leon Sylvers**. The Sylvers and Leslie families met at a local gym through a mutual interest in keep-fit!

Real To Reel's early gigs were as concert support to **The Sylvers**, after which Leon produced their debut single 'Love Me Like This', (Arista, 1983). They also recorded an album, *Real To Reel*, which included one of the first ever songs written by **Jam/Lewis**, 'Can You Treat Me', but the album was never released.

Leon also involved members of the group in his productions for Solar Records, primarily 'Dead Giveaway' and 'Over And Over' for Shalamar. Incidentally, this group should not be confused with another group called **Reel to Real**.

REAVES, PAULETTE

(Singer)

Based in Miami, Paulette Reaves made one major impression with the **Clarence Reid**-penned/produced 'Jazz Freak', released on the Blue Candle label (via TK) in 1977. It was taken from *All About Love*, released later the same year.

RECORD, EUGENE

(Singer/Songwriter/Producer)

Born in Chicago, Eugene is best remembered as lead singer with **The Chi-Lites**. Away from the group he recorded for Warner Brothers, *The Eugene Record* (1977), including 'Overdose Of Joy', *Trying To Get To You* (1978) and *Welcome To My Fantasy* (1979), including 'Magnetism'.

He wrote and/or produced for artists including **Barbara Acklin** ('Love Makes A Woman'), **Young–Holt Unlimited** ('Soulful Strut'), Wales Wallace ('Somebody I

Know'), **The Dells** ('All About The Paper', 'Happy Song' and 'I Touched A Dream'), and **Lowrell** ('Mellow Mellow Right On').

REDD, JEFF
(Singer)
Born in New York, Jeff first began singing professionally as a seventeen-year-old with The Sophisticated Gents. He was later signed as a solo artist by the Uptown label (via MCA), where his debut album was *A Quiet Storm* (1990), including 'Love High', 'Surrender' and 'What Goes Around, Comes Around'.

REDD, SHARON
(Singer)
Born in Norfolk, Virginia, Sharon's father worked at King Records (which signed **James Brown**), her stepfather was a member of Benny Goodman's band, her brother Gene Redd wrote and produced for **Kool & The Gang** and **BMP**, while her sister **Pennye Ford** also has a successful singing career. During her childhood Sharon had an operatic training, although she initially worked as an actress. After landing the lead role in an Australian production of *Hair* she starred in her own TV special before coming to London in 1974 with an American production of *The Wedding Of Iphigenia* in which she performed at the Old Vic.

When Shaffer Beer were looking for a 'Shaffer Beer Girl' for an advertising campaign, Sharon found herself elected and returned to America. Through this lucky break she was hired by Bette Midler to be an outrageous Harlette. In concert one night, Sir Laurence Olivier singled her out as the real star and sent roses to her dressing room. As a backing singer she recorded with artists including **Norman Connors** ('You Are My Starship').

In 1980 she landed a solo recording contract with Prelude Records after her voice was featured on a Top 3 dance hit 'Love Insurance'. Making a major impact on UK dancefloors, her Prelude albums were *Sharon Redd* (1980), including 'Can You Handle It' (UK Top 40) and 'Love Is Gonna Get Ya'; *Redd Hott* (1982), including 'Never Gonna Give You Up' (UK Top 20), 'In The Name Of Love' (UK Top 40) and 'Beat The Street'; and *Love How You Feel* (1983), from which the title track was a UK Top 40 hit.

In 1991 she returned with a new single 'All The Way To Love' after a long break from the recording scene.

REDDING, OTIS
(Singer/Songwriter/Producer)
Born in Dawson, Georgia, in 1941, Otis grew up and sang in a gospel environment before he was old enough to sing in local clubs around his hometown. Moving with his family to Macon, Georgia, Otis first got a break with established singer Johnny Jenkins who put him in his group The Pinetoppers. When Johnny scored a recording deal with Atlantic, Otis joined him in the studio and was invited to take advantage of some spare studio time at the end of a session. He used it to record his own composition 'These Arms Of Mine', which was immediately snapped up for release by Volt (via Stax/Atlantic) in 1962. It was followed by the release of 'Pain In My Heart' (1964), also the title of his debut album which included 'Security' (later recorded by **Etta James**) and 'That's What My Heart Needs'. Future American hits followed with 'That's How Strong My Love Is', 'I've Been Loving You Too Long', 'Respect' (later recorded by **Aretha Franklin**, and more recently **Adeva**), before Otis first charted in the UK.

In 1965 he made his UK chart debut (via Atlantic) with 'My Girl' (Top 20) and proceeded with hits in 1966, 'Satisfaction' (Top 40), 'My Lover's Prayer' (Top 40), 'I Can't Turn You Loose' (Top 30), 'Fa Fa Fa Fa (Sad Song)' (Top 25), and then in 1967 'Try A Little Tenderness' (Top 50), 'Day Tripper' (Top 50), 'Let Me Come On Home' (Top 50), 'Shake' (Top 30) and the classic '(Sittin' On) The Dock Of The Bay' released a year after he was tragically killed when his private jet crashed into a lake in Wisconsin (along with members of **The Barkays**) in 1967. It was an American No. 1 and UK Top 5 in 1968.

His albums included *The Great Otis Redding Sings Soul Ballads*, *For Your Precious Love*, *The Soul Album*, *Dictionary of Soul*, *Otis Blue*, and in 1967 *King & Queen*, a duet album with **Carla Thomas** which included 'Tramp' (UK Top 20) and 'Knock On Wood' (UK Top 40).

Otis also ran his own label Jotis Records (where he had produced 'Sweet Soul Music' for **Arthur Conley**). His sons later recorded together as **The Reddings**.

REDDINGS
(Group)
From Macon, Georgia, The Reddings are two sons of the late **Otis Redding**, Dexter Redding (vocals/bass) and Otis Redding III (guitar), together with cousin Mark Locket (keyboards/drums/vocals). They recorded one album *The Awakening* (1981) for Believe In A Dream Records (via CBS), and two for Polydor, *If Looks Could Kill* (1985) and *The Reddings* (1988).

Otis Redding III also wrote 'The Smurf' for **Tyrone Brunson**.

REEL TO REAL
(Group)
Not to be confused with former Arista group **Real To Reel**, this group of musicians and singers consisted of Diane Organ, Ken Harris, Jamie Bruce and Nathan Webb from Ohio. Their one album *Cycles* was released on the US Silhouette label in 1988.

REEVES, DIANNE
(Singer/Keyboards)
Born in Detroit but raised in Denver, Dianne's music (and three-and-a-half-octave vocal range) has appealed to both soul and jazz fans. On the PAJ (Palo Alto Jazz)

label her albums included *For Every Heart* (1984), before she switched to Blue Note for *Dianne Reeves* (1987) and *The Nearness Of You* (1988).

Elsewhere Dianne has recorded with **George Duke** (lead on 'You And Me' and 'Broken Dreams', 1977), **Caldera** (lead on 'Ancient Source', 1977), **Sergio Mendes**, Harry Belafonte, **Stanley Turrentine** (lead on 'Only You And Me', 1981), **Alphonso Johnson**, **David Diggs** ('Dancing With His Shadow', 1985) and **Lou Rawls** (duets 'Fine Brown Frame' and 'At Last', 1989).

REEVES, MARTHA
(Singer)
Born in Eufaula, Alabama, Martha Reeves is the daughter of a Methodist minister and the eldest of eleven children in her family. Before her first birthday her family moved to Detroit, which remains her home today. By the age of six she was singing in church with her brothers Benny and Thomas. Her first recording was Bach's 'Allelujah' which she had sung at her college graduation. From here she began singing blues in clubs using the name Martha Laverne. She also sang with The Fascinations (with **Curtis Mayfield**), before joining The Delphis (which initially included **J.J.Barnes**) and recording 'Won't You Let Me Know' for Chess Records, although Martha was not lead singer.

Determined to land a recording deal with Motown, she took a secretarial job at the company. She moved into singing by laying down guide vocals on demo tapes for other Motown artists. Later, when **Mary Wells** failed to turn up for a session, Martha and her group The Delphis were asked to stand in. They recorded 'There He Is At My Door', and the song was released under the name The Velvs. Again, however, Martha did not sing lead vocals. The record didn't do well and the lead singer left the group. When Mary Wells failed again to show for a session, the group once again stood in, only this time the record was released as Martha Reeves & The Vandellas.

Under the wing of Motown A&R director/songwriter William Stevenson, their debut was 'I'll Have To Let Him Go' (1962) before they, teamed up with **Holland/Dozier/Holland** for a string of hits commencing with 'Come And Get These Memories' in 1963. The same year 'Heatwave' was a major American hit before Martha & The Vandellas cracked the UK charts in 1964 with 'Dancing In The Streets' (Top 30), initially issued here on the Stateside label.

Other UK Motown hits included 'Nowhere To Run' (Top 30, 1965), 'I'm Ready For Love' (Top 30, 1966), 'Jimmy Mack' (Top 25, 1967) and 'Honey Chile' (Top 30, 1968). 'Dancing In The Street', 'Jimmy Mack' and 'Nowhere To Run' re-entered the UK charts in later years. Her other American hits included 'Quicksand', 'In My Lonely Room', 'My Baby Loves Me', 'Love Bug' and 'I Can't Dance To That Music You're Playing'.

Towards the end of the '60s the relationship between Martha and **The Vandellas** became strained, and Martha decided to pursue a solo career. In 1970 she recorded 'No One There' (co-written/produced by **Johnny Bristol**), following which she left Motown, although her UK chart success continued with 'Forget Me Not' (Top 20, 1971) and 'Bless You' (Top 40, 1972), subsequently released by the label. Martha recorded four solo albums after leaving Motown. These were *Martha Reeves* (1974), produced by **Richard Perry** for MCA; *The Rest Of My Life* (1976), including 'Higher And Higher' and 'Thank You', for Arista; *We Meet Again* (1979) for Fantasy; and *Gotta Keep Movin'* (1980), including a follow-up to 'Dancin' In The Street' called 'Skatin' In The Street', also for Fantasy.

In 1989 Martha reunited with The Vandellas and maintained an extensive schedule of live tours while turning down a number of recording opportunities. In 1989, however, Martha and the original Vandellas (Rosalind Holmes and Annette Beard) recorded a number of new songs with **Ian Levine** for the Motorcity label. 'Step Into My Shoes' was the first of these, released that year as a single.

The Motorcity label also recorded solo songs by Martha's sister Lois Reeves (a temporary member of The Vandellas) and brother Benny Reeves.

REID
(Vocal Group)
Reid are brothers Tony, Ivor and Mark Reid from Luton, Bedfordshire. In 1987 they signed with Syncopate Records (via EMI), emerging the following year with a debut single 'One Way Out', written and produced by **Jolley/Harris/Jolley**. Follow-up singles included 'Real Emotion' (also written/produced by J/H/J).

REID, CLARENCE
(Singer/Songwriter/Producer)
Born in Miami, Clarence sang with The Del-Mires during the '60s, the group at one point including **Paul Kelly** for whom Clarence wrote a series of solo songs including 'Chills And Fever' (later recorded by **Tom Jones**). As a solo artist he was signed by **Henry Stone** to the Alston label (via Atlantic) where 'Nobody But You Babe' proved popular in 1969. In the early '70s Stone signed Clarence to his own TK label where he worked primarily as songwriter and producer, initially scoring success with **Betty Wright** for whom he co-wrote 'Clean Up Woman' in 1971. Also at TK he wrote and produced 'Jazz Freak' (1977) for **Paulette Reaves**.

As a solo artist, his popularity didn't pick up until he recorded under the pseudonym of Blowfly, delivering rude versions of other people's hits and developing a big cult following.

RENE & ANGELA
(Group/Songwriters/Producers)
Rene Moore and **Angela Winbush** met through a mutual friend in the mid-'70s in Los Angeles, and first worked

together as songwriters. Their early work was with **Lenny Williams** ('Changes'), **Alton McClain** ('I Have Learned To Respect The Power Of Love') and **Lamont Dozier**, following which they landed their own record deal with Capitol Records in 1980. Their debut album release was *Rene & Angela*, including 'Free And Easy', 'Do You Really Love Me' and 'Everything We Do', followed by *Wall To Wall* (1981), from which 'Secret Rendezvous' first made an impression as a 'rare groove' in 1985. After a release here on the Champion label it reached the Top 75.

Switching to Mercury in 1985, their first single for the label 'Save Your Love (For No. 1)' (UK Top 75) featured **Kurtis Blow** and came from an album *Street Called Desire* which also included 'I'll Be Good' (UK Top 30) and 'Your Smile'.

As writers and/or producers they also worked with **Janet Jackson** (two American hit singles), **Plush** (including 'We've Got The Love'), **Ronnie McNeir** (four-track *Ronnie McNeir Experience* EP), **Evelyn 'Champagne' King** ('Spellbound') and **Odyssey** ('Love's Alright'). They also recorded with **Rufus** and **Chaka Khan** on *Camouflage* (1981).

More recently, Rene Moore and Angela Winbush have been involved in legal proceedings against each other. Rene was recently awarded $200,000 to be paid by Angela's management/production company (for loss of income on production work), while Angela is taking action over an alleged assault by Rene. In the meantime they both have solo recording careers.

REYNOLDS, L.J.

(Singer)

Born in Detroit, L.J.Reynolds first recorded as Larry 'Chubby' Reynolds for the Tri-Spin label during the early '60s. Here his singles included 'The Bells Of My Heart', 'Please Don't Leave Me' and 'Searching And Looking' before he switched to the Mainstream label in 1969 for 'Intruder' and 'Call On Me'.

From here he became lead singer of The Relations whose singles for the Monique label included 'We're In The Middle' (1970). He also made solo recordings for a number of small labels including Lawton ('Let One Hurt Do' and 'What's A Matter Baby Is It Hurting You', both 1971) and Lady ('All I Need', 1972) before replacing William Howard as lead singer of **The Dramatics** in 1973.

L.J. sang with The Dramatics until 1980, from which point he recorded as a solo artist for Capitol (including 'Key To The World', 1981, and *Travelin'*, 1982) and Mercury (*Lovin' Man*, including 'Love Me All Over' featuring **The Jones Girls**, 1984), before rejoining **The Dramatics** in 1986 where he remains today.

RHYTHM MAKERS

(Group)

From New York, The Rhythm Makers were Rahiem LeBlanc (lead vocals/guitar), Sabu Crier (bass/vocals), Kenny Banks (drums/vocals) and Herb Lane (keyboards/vocals). They recorded one album *Soul On Your Side* (1976), including 'Zone', for the Vigor label before becoming better known as **G.Q.**

RHYZE

(Group)

Formed in the late '70s, Rhyze were Roscoe Taylor (lead vocals/trumpet), Ellsworth 'El-T' Anderson (bass/lead vocals), Vince Jackson (guitar/lead vocals), Charles Holmes (drums), Joseph 'Jo Jo' McKnight (congas/percussion), Kevin Barbee (keyboards), Richard Menter (trumpet) and Kenneth Hicks (sax). Their debut release 'Just How Sweet Is Your Love' was issued by the Sam label in 1980 before they signed to 20th Century. Here their album *Rhyze To The Top* (1981) featured 'Bizarre', popular with the UK soul fraternity for its Detroit Spinners flavour!

RICHIE, LIONEL

(Singer/Songwriter)

Born in Tuskegee, Alabama, Lionel was first introduced to music by his grandmother who taught him classical piano. During his college days he and some friends formed **The Commodores** and he remained as lead singer with the group for fifteen years.

In 1980 country singer Kenny Rogers asked him for a song, 'Lady' stayed at No. 1 in the American charts for six weeks. Lionel then produced Kenny's next album *Share Your Love*, and wrote 'Endless Love' which Lionel and **Diana Ross** recorded as a duet in 1981 (UK Top 10). This was followed by the launch of his solo career at Motown in 1982 with the album *Lionel Richie*, including 'Truly' (UK Top 10), 'You Are' (UK Top 50) and 'My Love' (UK Top 75, 1973). Later in 1983 came *Can't Slow Down*, including 'All Night Long' (UK Top 5), 'Running With The Night' (UK Top 10), 'Hello' (UK No. 1, 1984), 'Stuck On You' (UK Top 20, 1984), 'Penny Lover' (UK Top 20, 1984) and 'Say You, Say Me' (UK Top 10, 1985).

In 1984 he wrote and co-produced 'Missing You' (a tribute to **Marvin Gaye**) for **Diana Ross**, and in 1985 co-wrote 'We Are The World' with **Michael Jackson** (USA For Africa) before recording his third album *Dancing On The Ceiling* (1986), including the title track (UK Top 10), 'Love Will Conquer All' (UK Top 50), 'Ballerina Girl' (UK Top 20) and 'Sela' (UK Top 50).

RIDLEY, SHARON

(Singer)

Sharon recorded for the Sussex label in the '70s, including the **Van McCoy** penned/produced 'Where Did You Learn To Make Love The Way You Do', popular with soul fans.

RIFF

(Vocal Group)

Based in Los Angeles, Riff are Dwayne Jones, Kenny Kelly, Anthony Fuller, Michael Best and Steven E.Capers.

Working with West Coast musicians, the group made their recording debut in 1991 with an album *Riff* for the SBK label.

RIGHT CHOICE

(Group)

From Memphis, Right Choice are Archie Love (lead vocals), Tony Black (keyboards) and Eric Shotwell (lead vocals). Signing to Motown in the late '80s, their debut album was *The Right Choice* (1989), including 'Tired Of Being Alone'.

RILEY, CHERYL 'PEPSII'

(Singer)

Born in New York, Cheryl was inspired to make singing her career by **Patti Labelle**. Signing to CBS, her debut album was the **Full Force**-penned/produced *Me Myself And I* (1988), including 'Thanks For My Child'.

RILEY, TEDDY

(Songwriter/Producer/Singer)

Born in New York, Teddy performed as a singer with **Omar Chandler** and the group Kids At Work before establishing himself as a writer and producer in the mid-'80s. From this point he has worked with artists including **Keith Sweat**, Kool Moe Dee ('How Ya Like Me Now'), **The Jacksons** ('2300 Jackson Street'), **Starpoint**, **The Winans** (*Return*), and **Nayobe** (*Promise Me*). He is also a member of the group **Guy**.

RINDER/LEWIS

(Songwriters/Producers)

Based in Los Angeles, Laurin Rinder and W. Michael Lewis formed Rinlew Productions in the late '70s. They have written and/or produced for artists including **David Benoit** ('Life Is Like A Samba' and *Stages*), Eloise Whitaker (*Eloise Whitaker*, including 'Fallin' In Love') and **El Coco** ('Let's Get It Together' and 'Cocomotion').

RIPERTON, MINNIE

(Singer/Songwriter)

Born in Chicago in 1947, Minnie was the youngest of eight children. While studying classical music as a child she developed a five-octave vocal range and originally intended to become an opera singer. In the meantime she sang with a local group The Gems, their debut recording 'That's What They Put Erasers On Pencils For' (on Chess Records) building them a strong local reputation.

The group also worked as in-house backing vocalists for Chess artists including **Ramsey Lewis**, **Etta James**, **The Dells** and **Fontella Bass** before breaking up and going their separate ways. From here Minnie worked as a secretary at Chess, recording some solo singles using the name Andrea Davis, and working with a group Rotary Connection.

Janus Records signed her in the early '70s, and she recorded a solo album *Come To My Garden* before meeting **Richard Rudolph** and marrying him. Together they wrote a series of songs which led to a recording deal for Minnie with Epic. Here she worked with **Stevie Wonder** on *Perfect Angel*, including her one major hit 'Lovin' You' (UK Top 5, 1975).

Later in 1975 she returned with *Adventures In Paradise*, having been attacked by the lion which appears on the front of the album sleeve (although she escaped serious injury). Her final Epic album was *Stay In Love* (1977), including 'Can You Feel What I'm Saying?' and 'Young Willing And Able'. By this time she had realized she was suffering from malignant breast cancer and in 1978 became chairman of the American Cancer Society. She also signed to Capitol for *Minnie* (1978) and *Love Lives Forever* (1980), the latter released after her death on 12 July 1979.

Minnie also recorded with **Deniece Williams**, **The Jackson 5**, **Stevie Wonder** (*Fulfillingness First Finale*, 1974, and 'Ordinary Pain', 1975) and **Quincy Jones** (lead on 'If I Ever Lose This Heaven' from *Body Heat*, 1975).

RIPPLE

(Group)

Based in New York, Ripple were Simon Kenneth Carter (vocals/bass), Walter Carter (lead vocals/percussion), Brian Sheerer (vocals/drums), Victor Burks (vocals/keyboards) and Barry Lee (guitar). After initially working with writer/producer **Big Dee Irvin** and recording 'I Don't Know What It Is But It Sure Is Funky' (1975, but popular on the UK 'rare groove' scene ten years later), the group switched to Salsoul where *Sons Of The Gods* (1977) included their **Floyd Smith**-produced disco classic 'The Beat Goes On'.

RISER, PAUL

(Arranger/Producer/Songwriter)

Based in Detroit, Paul has written some of the finest musical arrangements (mainly strings) over the years for artists including **Stevie Wonder** ('Yester-Me, Yester-You, Yesterday' and 'Signed Sealed Delivered'), **Diana Ross** ('Reach Out And Touch Somebody's Hand'), **Luther Vandross** ('At Christmas Time'), **The Supremes** ('Automatically Sunshine'), **Ashford & Simpson**, **Chapter 8**, **Creative Source**, **David Ruffin**, **Greg Perry**, **Lamont Dozier**, **Randy Brown**, **Gladys Knight & The Pips**, **Anita Baker**, **Norman Connors** ('Take It To The Limit'), **Teena Marie** ('Portuguese Love') and most recently **Keith Washington**.

As co-writer his credits include the classic 'What Becomes Of The Broken Hearted' for **Jimmy Ruffin**, while as producer he was responsible for songs including 'Give Me Your Love' for **Sisters Love**.

RITCHIE FAMILY

(Vocal Group)

Instigated by New York songwriter/producer **Jacques Morali** (also responsible for **The Village People**), The

Ritchie Family was fronted by **Richie Rome** who had already signed to the Polydor label and recorded an album *Brazil* (1975), with 'family' singers Cheryl Mason Jacks, Cassandra Ann Wooten and Gwendolyn Oliver. The line-up shortly changed to Jacqueline Smith-Lee, Theodosia (Dodie) Draher and Edna Holt, and they scored major success on the disco scene with 'The Best Disco In Town' (UK Top 10) in 1976. After Polydor albums *Arabian Nights* (1976) and *African Queens* (1977), the group switched to Casablanca/Mercury for 'American Generation' (UK Top 50, 1979) and 'Put Your Feet To The Beat' (1979).

RITENOUR, LEE

(Guitar)

Born in Los Angeles in 1952, Lee Ritenour has become one of the West Coast's most in-demand session guitarists. He can be found on recordings by **Aretha Franklin**, **Diana Ross**, **George Benson**, **Stanley Clarke**, Barbra Streisand, **Norman Connors**, **Patti Austin**, **Herbie Hancock**, **The Brothers Johnson**, **George Duke**, Leo Sayer, **Patrice Rushen** and **Dan Siegel**.

As a solo artist he has recorded a number of r&b/rock-edged albums for various labels including Epic (*First Course* and *Captain Fingers*), Elektra (*Rit*, *Rit 2*, *The Captain's Journey* and *Feel The Night*) and GRP (*Rio*, *Harlequin* with **Dave Grusin** in 1985, and *Portrait*, 1987).

ROBBINS, ROCKIE

(Singer/Songwriter)

Born in Minneapolis, Rockie's uncle owned a record shop where he discovered his love for music. By the time he was eleven he had collected over 10,000 singles and had decided to be a performer. As a teenager he sang with a group The Mystics, during which time he sent a demo of his voice to A&M Records in Los Angeles. He was signed immediately and released a debut album *Rockie Robbins* (1979), including 'I Can Hardly Wait', 'When I Think Of You' and 'Be Ever Wonderful'. The following year the title track of *You And Me* was an American r&b hit and established him with UK soul fans. By now he had moved to Los Angeles where he remains today.

His next album was *I Believe In Love*, including 'Time To Think', 'Give Our Love A Chance', 'Talk To Me' and 'An Act Of Love', produced by **Skip Scarbrough** and **Jerry Peters**. It was his last for A&M before he switched to MCA for *Rockie Robbins*, including 'I've Got Your Number', 'We Belong Together' and 'Goodbye Don't Last Forever'. Also at MCA he recorded 'Emergency' for the soundtrack of the movie *Beverly Hills Cop*. In 1989 he signed to the Respect label in the UK, initially for a single 'Serious', later an album *Are You Ready* (1991), including 'You Hit My Love' and 'I'll Always Love You'.

ROBERTS, JULIE

(Singer/Keyboards)

Not to be confused with **Juliet Roberts**, Julie made an impact on the early '80s UK latin jazz/'jazz funk' scene with albums including *The Other World* (1980) and *Nights In Brazil* (1981), including 'I Can't Help It' and 'Ole', for the American jazz label Inner City.

ROBERTS, JULIET

(Singer)

From Harrow Road, London (although her parents come from the Caribbean), Juliet's father was in a calypso band Nightingale, while her own first venture into music was via reggae and a group called Black Jade. The group were featured on a TV series *Reggae In Schools*. When her local record shop, Bluebird Records (Church Street, W2) ventured into the recording business and wanted artists, Juliet persuaded them she could sing and passed an audition. Her first single, 'The Bed's Too Big Without You', was later released on the Red Bus label.

Soon London band **The Funk Masters** informed the record shop that they needed a new singer, and impressed by Juliet they featured her as lead singer on the hit single 'It's Over'. Bluebird (via Virgin/10 Records) then released Juliet's solo singles 'Fool For You' (1983) and 'Ain't You Had Enough Love', written/produced by **Loose Ends** (1985), before Juliet became the lead singer with **Working Week**.

Elsewhere she worked as a sports tutor and co-presented the UK TV programme *Soul Train* during the mid-'80s. She also sang lead vocals on 'Just Waiting' for **L.A. Mix** before signing to the Eternal label (via WEA) in 1990 where to date her single releases include a version of Nat King Cole's 'Again'.

ROBERTS JR, SOLOMON

(Singer/Songwriter/Guitar/Producer)

From Brooklyn, New York, Solomon attended Thomas Jefferson High School with **Randy Muller** in the late '60s, following which he built his own basement recording studio (called 'Hole In The Ground Studios'). Early clients were Randy Muller's group **Brass Construction** (with whom Solomon sang backgrounds) and Jeff Lane's group **B.T. Express**. Inspired by the success of these groups, Solomon formed **New York Skyy**.

ROBIE, JOHN

(Songwriter/Producer)

From New York, John became an integral part of the early '80s 'electro' dance scene and worked as writer and/or producer with artists including Soulsonic Force ('Planet Rock'), **Freeez** ('I.O.U'), **Arthur Baker** and **Jenny Burton** (using her as vocalist on his own production 'One More Shot').

ROBINSON, BERT

(Singer)

New York-based singer Bert Robinson first appeared on Capitol Records in 1987 on a duet 'All The Way With You' with **Peggi Blu** from her album *Blu Blowin'* (1987). In 1989 he returned on Capitol with a solo album *I Promise You Love*, featuring productions by **Osborne & Giles**, **Craig T. Cooper** and **Al Hudson**, among others.

ROBINSON, DUTCH

(Singer)

Dutch briefly sang with **The Ohio Players** before recording a solo album *Nothing's Got Me* for United Artists in 1977. Through the '80s he worked in New York as a member of Elbow Bones & The Racketeers and sang backgrounds with artists including **Melba Moore** in addition to recording solo singles 'Happy' (1985) and 'Low Down' (released by Expansion Records in the UK in 1990). He has also toured in a stage musical 'Through The Grapevine', portraying **Marvin Gaye**.

ROBINSON, JAMES

(Singer/Guitar/Songwriter)

Based in New York, James sang guest lead vocals with artists including **Norman Connors** ('Stella' and 'Listen') and **Lonnie Liston Smith** ('Song For The Children' and 'Love Is The Answer') before replacing **Luther Vandross** in **Change** and singing lead with the group on songs including 'The Very Best In You' (1982).

As a solo artist he signed to Tabu Records in 1987 where his one album was *Guilty*. Other artists he has recorded with include **Jeff Lorber** ('Every Woman Needs It'), **Lenny White** (*Attitude*) and **Bob Baldwin**. While with **Lonnie Liston Smith**, incidentally, James wrote 'Speak About It' on which he also played guitar.

ROBINSON, SYLVIA

(Singer/Songwriter/Producer/Arranger)

Born in New Jersey, Sylvia first recorded as one half of Mickey & Sylvia, scoring a million-seller across America in the '50s with 'Love Is Strange'. As a solo artist she is best remembered for 'Pillow Talk' (1973), while in between times she was a co-founder of All-Platinum Records where she worked as a writer and/or producer with artists including **The Moments**, **Brook Benton** and **Chuck Jackson**.

In 1978 she founded Sugarhill Records and discovered three rappers who she signed and called **The Sugarhill Gang**. Their debut single 'Rappers Delight' (1979) was one of the first rap records. She was also responsible for signing Grandmaster Flash, **Candi Staton** and **Harry Ray** to the label.

ROBINSON, WILLIAM 'SMOKEY'

(Singer/Songwriter)

Born in Detroit in 1940, Smokey wrote his first song at the age of six. It was for a school play, *Uncle Remus*, in which he took the lead role. As a teenager he and his friends **The Miracles** impressed **Berry Gordy** who instigated their first single 'Bad Girl' for Chess Records in 1957. After 'Got A Job' for the End label, Berry signed the group to Tamla (via Motown) where *Way Over There* was their first release including their American hit 'Shop Around'.

With The Miracles, Smokey sang lead vocals and wrote/co-wrote most of their hits including 'Going To A Go Go', 'I Second That Emotion', 'You Really Got A Hold On Me', 'Ooh Baby Baby', 'The Tracks Of My Tears' and 'Tears Of A Clown'. He also wrote numerous other Motown classics, including 'My Guy' and 'Two Lovers' (**Mary Wells**), 'The Way You Do The Things You Do', 'My Girl' and 'Get Ready' (**The Temptations**), 'Ain't That Peculiar' (**Marvin Gaye**), 'Don't Mess With Bill' (**The Marvelettes**), 'Floy Joy' and 'Automatically Sunshine' (**The Supremes**).

In 1971 Smokey launched a solo career with his first album being *Smokey* (1973), followed by a UK hit single 'Just My Soul Responding' (Top 40, 1974). Then came albums including *Deep In My Soul* (1977), *Pure Soul* (1978) and *Cruisin'* (1979) before the UK No. 1 hit single, the self-penned 'Being With You' (1981). Then came *Touch The Sky* (1982), including 'I've Made Love To You A Thousand Times'; *Yes It's You Lady* (1982), including 'Tell Me Tomorrow'; *Essar* (1984), including 'Gone Forever' from the film *Cry Of The City*; *Smoke Signals* (1986), including 'Sleepless Nights'; *One Heartbeat* (1987), including 'Just To See Her'; and *Love Smokey* (1990). He also became vice-president at Motown.

Smokey sang a duet, 'Ebony Eyes', with **Rick James** (on Rick's *Cold Blooded*), sang lead on 'We've Saved The Best For Last' for **Kenny G** (on *Silhouettes*) and joined **The Four Tops** on 'Indestructible'.

Smokey's former wife Claudette Robinson sang with The Miracles, his daughter Tamla is the voice on numerous American TV commercials, while his nephews Keith and Darryl are also recording artists. Smokey also has his own perfume, 'Smoke'.

ROCCA, JOHN

(Singer)

Based in London, John Rocca instigated the Brit funk band **Freeez** in the early '80s before working as a producer with artists including **Juliet Roberts** ('Fool For You', 1983). He later recorded as a solo artist on the City Beat label where *Extra Extra*, including 'I Want It To Be Real', was released in 1987.

ROCHELLE

(Singer)

Born in Hamilton, Bermuda, Rochelle sang in local gospel choirs before forming a group The Mellotones. From here she moved to New York and established herself on the local club scene before producer Ted Currier picked her to record 'My Magic Man'. Released by Warner Brothers, it was a UK Top 30 hit in 1986.

RODGERS/EDWARDS

(Songwriters/Producers)

Nile Rodgers and **Bernard Edwards** first met in New York during the early '70s. As members of The Big Apple Band they played on recordings including 'I'm Doing Fine Now' for **New York City** (1972) before coming up with an idea for their own group **Chic** in 1977.

After establishing their writing/production style with **Chic** on songs including 'Dance Dance Dance', 'Everybody Dance' and 'Good Times', they used it with other artists during the late '70s including **Sister Sledge** ('We Are Family', 'He's The Greatest Dancer', etc.), **Diana Ross** ('I'm Coming Out', 'Upside Down', 'My Old Piano', etc.), and Carly Simon ('Why'). In the '80s they ventured into their own separate writing and production projects.

RODGERS, NILE

(Singer/Songwriter/Guitar/Producer)

From New York, Nile studied classical music and jazz before taking his skills to the Apollo Theater in Harlem where he joined the house band. In 1972 he joined the Big Apple Band where he met **Bernard Edwards**. The band recorded with **New York City** on their hit 'I'm Doin' Fine Now'. **Rodgers/Edwards** worked together as writers and producers to create a sound which led to international hits for **Chic** and **Sister Sledge** in the mid- to late '70s. Independently Nile began working as producer for an array of artists including David Bowie ('Let's Dance'), Madonna, Peter Gabriel, Brian Ferry and Mick Jagger.

In 1985 he took time to record a solo album *B-Movie Matinee* for Warner Brothers. It included 'Stay Out Of The Light' and 'State Your Mind', which received strong reactions from UK dance audiences. He then returned to production projects for artists including **Al Jarreau** (*L Is For Love*), **Philip Bailey** ('State Of The Heart'), **Sister Sledge** ('Frankie') and **Diana Ross** ('Workin' Overtime').

ROGERS, CE CE

(Singer/Songwriter/Producer)

From Cleveland, Ohio, Ce Ce's real name is Kenny Rogers but it was changed so he would not be confused with the country singer of the same name. 'Ce Ce' was a nickname given to him by **James Brown** when he saw young Kenny dance like a mini-Chubby Checker. Studying music in Boston, he ended up in the same classroom as jazz trumpeter Branford Marsalis, who suggested Ce Ce should develop his vocal skills. Moving to New Jersey he formed the group Ce Ce & Company, singing with **Sybil**. Producer **Marshall Jefferson** saw a show and invited Ce Ce to be the vocalist on a song he had written called 'Someday'. The American success of this, his debut single on the Atlantic label (1987), opened the doors for him to sign direct to the label in 1988.

In 1989 his debut album *Forever* was released, while a single 'All Join Hands' stirred dancefloor interest in 1990. As a songwriter, Ce Ce's credits include 'Got To Get You Back' for **Kym Mazelle**.

ROGERS, D.J.

(Singer/Songwriter/Producer/Keyboards)

Born in Los Angeles, D.J. Rogers worked with Rev. James Cleveland during his teens and recorded five albums with the Los Angeles Community Choir. In the '60s he worked as a session musician for artists including **Bobby Womack**, Helen Reddy and **Billy Preston**, prior to signing with the Shelter label for a debut solo album *D.J.Rogers* in 1970. Switching to RCA in 1975, he recorded *It's Good To Be Alive*, *On The Road Again* and *Love, Music And Life*, before working with producer **Maurice White** on his one CBS album *Love Brought Me Back*.

ROGERS, EVAN

(Singer/Songwriter/Producer)

The son of Italian parents, Evan grew up in Connecticut, where he first found work as a session singer. He also worked with a group Too Much Too Soon before joining **Dayton** in the early '80s and recording with them on *Hot Fun In The Summertime*. From here he spent a period with **Heatwave** as lead singer before he recorded his debut solo release 'Every Breath You Take' (the Police song) on the Emergency label under the pseudonym of Otis Liggett (1983), due to contractual disputes with Heatwave.

In 1984 he signed with RCA where 'Secret Love' and 'Stay Here With Me' were popular on the UK dance scene. He and Carl Sturk established themselves as writers/producers for artists including Brother Beyond ('Girl I Used To Know'), **Giorge Pettus** ('Trouble In Paradise'), **St Paul** ('Stranger To Love'), **Pauli Carman**, **Stephanie Mills** ('Stand Back'), **Evelyn 'Champagne' King** ('When Your Heart Says Yes' and 'Kisses Don't Lie'), **Cheryl Lynn** ('If You Were Mine') and many more. In 1991 Evan and Carl formed a group Rhythm Syndicate and released *Rhythm Syndicate* for the Impact label. Also recently Evan signed as a solo artist with Capitol.

ROGERS, RICHARD

(Singer)

Born in Chicago, Richard actually quit his music course in favour of one in business studies during his teens. After leaving college he sold advertising for the *Chicago Tribune* before some friends persuaded him to perform with them on a talent show. A talent scout in the audience found him a recording deal with Sam Records. Here he worked with producer John Davis on *Can't Stop* (1990), including 'I'll Be Your Dream Lover', 'Can't Stop Loving You' and 'Spread A Little Love'.

ROKOTTO

(Group)

This little-known funk band hit the UK Top 40 in 1977 with a dance/disco release 'Boogie On Up' released by State Records. They had a UK Top 50 hit the following year with 'Funk Theory' before disappearing from the music scene.

ROMAN, LYN

(Singer)

From Washington DC, Lyn originally sang gospel music and toured with the Heavenly Brooklyn Stars. During this time she performed with **Sam Cooke** and Roy Hamilton before attracting the attention of **Smokey Robinson** who signed her to Motown under her real name Linda Griner. Her brief spell in Detroit included a Motown single 'Goodbye Cruel Love' written by Smokey, before she became Lyn Roman once again and signed to Dot Records (1968), a subsidiary of Paramount Pictures. Here she did soundtrack recordings for movies *Taste Of Love* and *The Brotherhood*. She recorded two further albums for the Dot label, *The Greatest Roman Of Them All* and *Girl For All Reasons*, before returning to film work. She recorded songs for *The Penthouse*, and with John Williams (of *E.T./Indiana Jones* fame) on *Daddy Going Hunting*.

Her next label was Brunswick in Chicago where she worked with Carl Davis on 'Stop I Don't Need No Sympathy'. She moved to CBS for *The Many Faces Of Lyn Roman*, while more recently she began her own label, Lanai, and released a single 'A Different Kind Of Sweet'. She also recorded a number of songs for the UK Motorcity label in 1990.

ROME, RITCHIE

(Arranger/Producer)

Born in Philadelphia, Ritchie established himself on the local soul scene during the '60s, one of his early arrangements being a medley of 'Green Apples' and 'Something' for **The O'Jays** on their Neptune album *The O'Jays In Philadelphia*. In the early 70s he put together a group **The Ritchie Family** with three female backing singers he had worked with at Sigma Sound Studios. Also at Sigma he arranged 'Nights Over Egypt' for **The Jones Girls** and produced 'Fallin' In Love With You' for **Jimmy Ruffin**. He co-wrote 'Giving It Back' for **Phil Hurtt** (who wrote The Ritchie Family's 'Best Disco In Town') and 'Disco Dancing' for **Stanley Turrentine**.

ROMEOS

(Group)

The Romeos were formed in Philadelphia by **Kenny Gamble** and **Thom Bell** in 1960. The duo had previously released a single 'Someday' as Kenny & Tommy, but were soon joined by Roland Chambers (guitar), Karl Chambers (drums) and Winnie Walford (bass). In 1964 they became staff singers/musicians at Cameo Records before signing to the Arctic label where they recorded 'Down By The Sea Shore' and 'Ain't It Baby' as Kenny and The Romeos. They also toured with **Little Anthony** & The Imperials, at which point **Thom Bell** left to get married.

ROSE ROYCE

(Group)

From Los Angeles, Rose Royce were originally known as Total Concept Unlimited (themselves the remnants of two other local groups). They were originally founder member Kenny Copeland (lead vocal/trumpet), Michael Moore (sax), Freddie Dunn (trumpet), Lequeint 'Duke' Jobe (bass/vocals), Walter McKinney (guitar), Michael Nash (keyboards), Terral Santiel (percussion) and Henry Garner (drums/vocals). In 1973, while working as a support band to **Edwin Starr**, they were approached by **Norman Whitfield** who was looking for a young band to record. In the meantime another of Norman's bands **Undisputed Truth** had discovered **Gwen Dickey** singing in a Miami group The Jewels. They persuaded her to join Total Concept Unlimited, which was then renamed Rose Royce. Under Norman's direction they had numerous hits in the '70s.

Norman had just launched his Whitfield label (via MCA) and had been commissioned to prepare a soundtrack album for the movie *Car Wash* (1976). Rose Royce stepped in with the title song which became a UK Top 10 hit that year. An album *Car Wash* featured follow-up UK hits 'Put Your Money Where Your Mouth Is' (Top 50), 'I Wanna Get Next To You' (Top 20) and 'Do Your Dance' (Top 30). A second album *In Full Bloom* (1977) featured further hits 'Wishing On A Star' (Top 5), 'It Makes You Feel Like Dancin'' (Top 20) and the group's biggest ever hit 'Love Don't Live Here Anymore', which reached the No. 2 position in 1978.

1979 delivered the Top 20 hit and dance classic 'Is It Love You're After', the brass intro from which was later utilized by S-Express on their smash hit 'Theme From S-Express' in 1988 (resulting in a re-issue of the track which made the Top 20 as a double A side with 'Car Wash'). A final Whitfield album *Jump Street* followed in 1981 before the group signed with Epic.

Gwen Dickey left to be replaced by Ricci Benson. *Stronger Than Ever* (1982) was highly acclaimed for 'Best Love' and 'Still In Love', although there were no hits from this album in the UK. In 1984 Rose Royce recorded for the independent Montage label, and *Music Magic* delivered a UK Top 60 hit 'Magic Touch', released in the UK by Streetwave Records. Also via Streetwave in the UK, 'Love Me Right Now' hit the UK Top 60 from the **Michael Stokes**-produced *The Show Must Go On*. Next they signed with Omni (via Atlantic) for *Fresh Cut* (1986), which included 'Lonely Road', before Ricci Benson left to be replaced by Lisa Taylor.

In 1989 an Atlantic album *Perfect Lover* created interest among UK soul fans for the tracks 'All I Want To Do' and 'Wish I Could Love You Back'. The group return regularly to the UK for cabaret dates.

ROSS, DIANA

(Singer)

Born in Detroit, Michigan, Diana first sang duets with Paul Williams (who later became a member of **The Temptations**). Her debut release was the duet 'Tears Of Sorrow' released on the Lu-Pine label. She was invited by Florence Ballard and Mary Wilson to join their group **The Supremes**, who were originally turned down by Motown but eventually hired as background singers. With The Supremes, Diana's first recording was 'I Want A Guy' (1961) before the group broke internationally in 1964 with 'Where Did Our Love Go'. As the hits went by, Diana became more and more the focal point of the group, and in 1967 they became known as Diana Ross & The Supremes. Soon the friction within the group became too much and Diana left to become a solo artist in 1969.

In 1970 she made her solo debut at Motown with 'Reach Out And Touch (Somebody's Hand)' (UK Top 40), and an album *Diana Ross* written and produced by **Ashford & Simpson**. She remained with Motown until 1981, her UK single hits being 'Ain't No Mountain High Enough' (Top 10, 1970), 'Remember Me' (Top 10, 1971), 'I'm Still Waiting' (No. 1, 1971), 'Surrender' (Top 10, 1971), 'Doobedood'ndoobe Doobedood'ndoobe' (Top 20, 1972), 'Touch Me In The Morning' (Top 10, 1973), 'All Of My Life' (Top 10, 1974), 'You Are Everything' with **Marvin Gaye** (Top 5, 1974), 'Last Time I Saw Him' (Top 40, 1974), 'Stop Look Listen (To Your Heart)' with **Marvin Gaye** (Top 25, 1974), 'Love Me' (Top 40, 1974), 'Sorry Doesn't Always Make It Right' (Top 25, 1975), 'Theme From Mahogany' (Top 5, 1976), 'Love Hangover' (Top 10, 1976), 'I Thought It Took A Little Time' (Top 40, 1976), 'Gettin' Ready For Love' (Top 25, 1977), 'Lovin', Livin' And Givin'' (Top 75, 1978), 'The Boss' (Top 40, 1979), 'No One Gets The Prize' (Top 60, 1979), 'It's My House' (Top 40, 1979), 'Upside Down' (Top 5, 1980), 'My Old Piano' (Top 5, 1980), 'I'm Coming Out' (Top 20, 1980), 'It's My Turn' (Top 20, 1981), 'One More Chance' (Top 50, 1981) and 'Cryin' My Heart Out For You' (Top 60, 1981). Her albums during this period were *Surrender*, *Lady Sings The Blues* (1972), *Touch Me In The Morning*, *Last Time I Saw Him* (1973), *Diana & Marvin* (1973), *Mahogany* (1975), *Diana Ross*, *Baby It's Me* (1977), *The Boss* (1979), *Diana* (1980) and *To Love Again* (1981). She made her acting debut portraying Billie Holliday in *Lady Sings The Blues* (1972), later returning to the screen as fashion designer Tracey Chambers in *Mahogany* (1975), and as Dorothy in *The Wiz* (1977).

In 1981 she scored one last Motown hit 'Endless Love' (a duet with **Lionel Richie** from the movie of the same name) before switching to RCA (Capitol in the UK). Here she scored immediately with 'Why Do Fools Fall In Love' (UK Top 5, 1981). She also charted with 'It's Never Too Late' (Top 50, 1982), 'Muscles' (Top 20, 1982), 'So Close' (Top 50, 1983), 'Pieces Of Ice' (Top 50, 1983), 'Touch By Touch' (Top 50, 1984), 'Eaten Alive' (Top 75, 1985), 'Chain Reaction' (No. 1, 1986), 'Experience' (Top 50, 1986), 'Dirty Looks' (Top 50, 1987) and 'Mr Lee' (Top 60, 1988). Her Capitol albums were *Why Do Fools Fall In Love* (1981), *Silk Electric* (1982), *Ross* (1983), *Swept Away* (1984), including 'Missing You', *Eaten Alive* (1985) and *Red Hot Rhythm & Blues* (1987), including 'Cross My Heart' and the **Luther Vandross**-co-penned/produced 'It's Hard For Me To Say'.

Back at Motown 'Love Hangover' and 'I'm Still Waiting' were remixed (in 1988 and 1990 respectively) and charted in the UK while Diana negotiated a new contract with the label in America. *Workin' Overtime* was then released (still on Capitol in the UK). Later in 1990 she teamed up with **Al B. Sure** on a duet 'No Matter What You Do' for his album *Private Times . . . And The Whole 9*.

Diana also has a string of her own companies including Ross Records (her own label), RTC Management Corporation (headquarters for her production companies), Diana Ross Productions (parent company for all recording activities), Rosstown Music and Rossville Music (her two publishing companies), Chondee Inc. (which handles her concert appearances), Anaid Film Productions (TV specials and films), Diana Ross Enterprises Inc. (which oversees all overseas business) and JFF Enterprises which researches and develops fashion, cosmetics and merchandising lines. Incidentally, at one time she hand-made all The Supremes' costumes.

ROSS, JACKIE

(Singer)

Born in Chicago, '60s singer Jackie Ross is best remembered for her 1964 recording for Chess, 'Selfish One' (via Pye in the UK). Also in the '60s she recorded for labels including Scepter, Brunswick ('Keep Your Chin Up', 1967) and Fountain ('Don't Change Your Mind', 1969), while more recently she signed to the Memphis-based Waylo label for a single 'I'm Gonna Make It Without You' (1989).

ROSS, JAMES

(Singer/Songwriter)

James instigated the group **UK Players** in the late '70s, after which he signed direct to A&M Records for the single 'Slow Down' 1983.

ROUND TRIP

(Group)

From Detroit, Round Trip featured lead vocalist **Oliver Cheatham** and were originally known as Sins Of Satan. After one album for MCA they changed their name to **Oliver** for one further MCA album before Oliver himself went solo.

ROUSSOS, DEMIS

(Singer)

Greek singer Demis Roussos has very little to do with the soul scene, except for one venture into dance music with the **Freddie Perren**-co-penned/produced 'L.O.V.E. Got A Hold Of Me' from *Demis Roussos* (Mercury 1978).

ROY, BARBARA

(Singer/Songwriter)

Born Barbara Jean Haskins in North Carolina, Barbara was the youngest of nine brothers and three sisters. She began her recording career by moving to New York in 1964 and recording with her niece as Barbara and Brenda for the Avanti label. Brenda later left the music business to get married.

In 1973 Barbara formed **Ecstasy, Passion And Pain**, for which she wrote 'Don't Burn Your Bridges Behind You', 'Ask Me', 'I Wouldn't Give You Up' and many of their popular songs. In 1984 she met producer Roy Be and signed to his Roy Be Records label. Her solo single debut was 'With All My Love', which created a stir on dancefloors and was released by Arista in the UK. **Paul Simpson** later produced a single 'Gonna Put Up A Fight' released by RCA in 1987.

Barbara's niece is **La-Rita Gaskin**.

ROYSTER, VERMETTYA

(Singer)

Born in Jacksonville, Florida, Vermettya was sixteen years old when she joined The Clara Ward Singers as a lead soloist. Moving to Los Angeles she joined the group **Sisters Love** where as lead vocalist she scored success with songs including 'Are You Lonely?', 'Mr Fix It Man', 'The Bigger You Love', 'Gimme Your Love' and 'Forget It, I've Got It'. She also sang backgrounds with artists including **Diana Ross**, **The Jackson 5**, **Billy Preston**, **Tina Turner** and Elvis Presley.

More recently she re-recorded 'Gimme Me Your Love' as a solo artist with producer **Ian Levine** on the UK Motorcity label (1991).

RUBY & THE ROMANTICS

(Group)

From America's East Coast, Ruby and her four male Romantics made an impression on the soul scene between 1963 and 1966. 'Our Day Will Come' was both an American hit and a UK Top 20 hit when released here on the London label in 1963. 'Baby Come Home' was also an American hit (1964), while the group also did well with a version of **Van McCoy**'s 'When You're Young And In Love'. 'Our Day Will Come' was a 1991 duet release for **Edwin Starr** and **Chaka Khan**.

RUDOLPH, RICHARD

(Songwriter/Producer)

Richard Rudolph was the husband of **Minnie Riperton**, for whom he co-wrote 'Lovin' You' and 'Can You Feel What I'm Saying'. Elsewhere he has produced artists including Manhattan Transfer, **Jermaine Jackson**, **Carl Anderson**, **New Edition** (with **Michael Sembello**), **Gladys Knight**, **Teena Marie** (co-writing 'Behind The Groove'), **Janice McClain**, **Stephanie Mills** and **Sheree Brown** ('You'll Be Dancing All Night' and 'It's A Pleasure').

RUFFIN, DAVID

(Singer/Drummer)

Born in 1941 in Meridian, Mississippi, David recorded solo records for the Chess label in Chicago before joining Detroit group **The Temptations** as their drummer in the early '60s. He became lead vocalist after the departure of Elbridge Bryant and scored a series of hits with them including 'My Girl' (UK Top 50, 1965) and 'Ain't Too Proud To Beg' (UK Top 50, 1966). After trying to make Motown change the group name to David Ruffin & The Temptations, he was removed in 1968 to be replaced by **Dennis Edwards**.

Remaining at Motown, David became a solo recording artist and soon scored an American hit with 'My Whole World Ended The Moment You Left Me'. In 1970 he recorded the duets 'He Ain't Heavy, He's My Brother' and 'Stand By Me' with brother **Jimmy Ruffin**, and worked with producers including **Norman Whitfield** on albums including *Me 'N'Rock & Roll Are Here To Stay* (1974), and *Who Am I* (1976), including his one UK solo hit 'Walk Away From Love' (Top 10).

With producers including **Don Davis**, further Motown albums followed with *Everything's Coming Up Love* and *Mellow Mood*, including 'What Now My Love', 'Somewhere' and 'The Impossible Dream', before he switched to Warner Brothers for *So Soon We Change* (1979), including 'I Get Excited', and *Gentleman Ruffin* (1980).

More recently he recorded with **Eddie Kendricks** (*Ruffin & Kendrick*, including 'Don't Know Why You're Dreaming', RCA, 1987); and Ruffin, Kendricks and **Dennis Edwards** worked together as former lead vocalists with **The Temptations**. David's last solo release was the **Ronnie McNeir**-co-written/produced 'Hurt The One You Love' on the Motorcity label (1990).

In 1991 after returning to Detroit from a tour of the UK he died of a drug overdose. Foul play in connection with his death, however, was not ruled out.

RUFFIN, JIMMY

(Singer)

Born in Colinsville, Mississippi, in 1939, Jimmy and brother **David Ruffin** moved to Detroit in 1960. Here they found work as session singers at Motown, although Jimmy's first solo record was for the Golden World label (before it was bought by Motown). In 1961 he recorded 'Don't Feel Sorry For Me' on Motown's small Miracle subsidiary. Jimmy then spent a couple of years away from full-time employment in the music business and worked for the Ford Motor Company in the foundry.

Burns he acquired from the blast furnace remain as scars to this day. He also spent some time in the army.

In 1964 Jimmy recorded 'Since I've Lost You' for Motown's Soul label subsidiary. He was also offered the job of lead with **The Temptations**, but passed on the offer leaving his brother to take on the position. Instead Jimmy continued his solo career with Motown, scoring major success in 1966 with 'What Becomes Of The Broken-Hearted' (a song originally intended for **The Detroit Spinners**), a UK Top 10 hit. His UK success continued with 'I've Passed This Way Before' (Top 30, 1967), 'Gonna Give Her All The Love I Got' (Top 30, 1967), 'Farewell Is A Lonely Sound' (Top 10, 1970), 'I'll Say Forever My Love' (Top 10, 1970) and 'It's Wonderful' (Top 10, 1970). In 1970 he recorded an album of duets, *I Am My Brother's Keeper*, with David Ruffin.

Despite this run of hits in the UK, Jimmy's success back in the USA had not been great, which led him to leave Detroit and settle in London where he lives today. During 1974 'What Becomes Of The Broken-Hearted' and 'Farewell Is A Lonely Sound' were UK hits for a second time, by which time Jimmy had left Motown and signed to Polydor (Atlantic in the USA). In 1974 he released 'Tell Me What You Want', a record which is regarded as instrumental in shaping the disco sound which took off in New York during the mid-'70s. In the UK it made the Top 40, but this was his last '70s hit.

In 1977 Jimmy recorded 'Fallin' In Love With You' (produced by **Richie Rome**) during a brief spell with Epic prior to returning to the Polydor family for 'Hold On To My Love', a UK Top 10 single on the RSO label in 1980. During 1984 Jimmy was a voice on the UK Top 25 Council Collective hit 'Soul Deep' and teamed up with **Jackson Moore** for a 'hi-energy' duet 'I'm Gonna Love You Forever' (1984), released by ERC prior to his recording deal with EMI in 1985. Here he recorded 'There Will Never Be Another You', his last UK Top 75 chart entry to date.

More recently Jimmy has recorded for the Nightmare label, including 'Wake Me Up When It's Over' (1988) and a duet with **Brenda Holloway** 'On The Rebound' (1989), both co-written and produced by **Ian Levine**.

RUFUS

(Group)

Formed in Chicago in 1970, Rufus were originally the nucleus of a local group American Breed (who charted in the late '60s with 'Bend Me Shape Me'), featuring vocalist **Paulette McWilliams**, who was then replaced by **Chaka Khan**. When Rufus signed to ABC Records in 1973 the line-up was Chaka Khan (vocals), Al Ciner (vocals/guitar – later Tony Maiden), **Andre Fisher** (drums – later John Robinson), Kevin Murphy (keyboards), Bobby Watson (bass), **David 'Hawk' Wolinski** (keyboards), and David Williams (guitar). Their debut album was *Rufus* (1973).

In 1974 the group were at work on *Rags To Rufus* when **Stevie Wonder** called by the studio and wrote them 'Tell Me Something Good' on the spot. The song established the group across America (where they have remained more popular than in the UK) and the album (which also included 'You Got The Love') was their first gold-seller. Further albums were *Rufusized* (1974), including 'Once You Get Started', 'Stop On By' and 'Please Pardon Me'; *Rufus Featuring Chaka Khan* (1975), including 'Sweet Thing', 'Fool's Paradise' and 'Little Boy Blue'; *Ask Rufus* (1977), including 'Hollywood' and 'At Midnight'; *Street Player* (1978), including 'Best Of Your Heart', 'Stranger To Love' and 'Destiny'; *Masterjam* (1979), including 'Do You Love What You Feel', 'Any Love' and 'Heaven Bound'; and *Camouflage* (1981), including 'True Love' and also featuring **Rene & Angela**.

By now **Chaka Khan** had begun a solo career, and although she continued to record with them, Rufus recorded *Numbers* (1978) and *Party 'Til You're Broke* (1981) without her. The group had also switched to Warner Brothers where 1983's *Live-Stompin' At The Savoy* included new studio cuts featuring Chaka Khan on songs including 'Ain't Nobody' (UK Top 10) and 'One Million Kisses'.

Through Chaka Khan meeting **Quincy Jones** in 1975, John Robinson, Bobby Watson and Hawk Wolinski recorded on the **Michael Jackson** album *Off The Wall*, while Quincy also produced the group's *Masterjam* album.

RUMPLE-STILT-SKIN

(Group)

Brothers Sam, Leroy, James and Chris McCant performed with the Chicago Gangsters from the early '70s, recording the **Willie Hutch** song 'I Choose You' for the Red Coach label in 1974. The follow-up was 'Blind Over You', an American chart success before they switched to RCA for 'What's Goin' On'. The Gangsters then switched to Heat and recorded *Life Is Not Easy* before becoming Rumple-Stilt-Skin for 'I Think I Want To Dance With You', a UK Top 75 hit released by Polydor in 1983. They later changed their name to **Ivy**.

RUSHEN, PATRICE

(Singer/Songwriter/Keyboards/Producer)

Born in Los Angeles in 1954, Patrice enrolled at a special music school at the age of three and was giving classical piano recitals from the age of six. In 1972 she entered and won a competition at the Monterey Jazz Festival, shortly after which she was signed as an artist by the jazz label prestige Records. Here she was the first woman to emerge on the jazz and r&b scene as a self-contained recording artist writing, playing and singing her own music. She released three albums, *Traverse* (1974), *Before The Dawn* (1975) and *Shout It Out* (1977), including 'Let Your Heart Be Free', 'The Hump' and 'Roll With The Punches', by which time she was also adding her vocals. Switching to Elektra Records, her music became more dance/vocal-oriented commencing with a single 'Hang It Up' (1978) and an album *Patrice*.

With *Pizzazz* (1979), Patrice began to notch up a series of dance hits and UK chart singles with 'Haven't You Heard' (Top 75, 1980) and 'Never Gonna Give You Up (Won't Let You)' (Top 75, 1981, from *Posh*), establishing a popular writing/production style with partner Charles Minns Jr. Her most successful album in the UK was *Straight From The Heart* (1982), including 'Forget Me Nots' (UK Top 10, 1982, and later a hit for **Tongue 'N' Cheek**), 'I Was Tired Of Being Alone' (UK Top 40, 1982) and 'Number One'. *Now* (1984), including 'Feels So Real (Won't Let Go)' (UK Top 75) was her last for Elektra. In 1987 she switched to Arista for the single/album *Watch Out*, including 'Come Back To Me'. Now she records with fusion jazz ensemble The Meeting for GRP Records.

As a session keyboard player she has recorded with numerous artists including **Lalo Schifrin**, **Noel Pointer**, **Raul De Souza**, **The Blackbyrds**, **Donald Byrd**, **Lenny Williams**, **Urban Ensemble**, **Beau Williams**, **Teena Marie**, **Sheree Brown**, **Active Force**, **Gary Taylor**, **Minnie Riperton**, **Peabo Bryson**, **The Sylvers** and **Prince**. As an arranger she has worked with **Ramsey Lewis** (*Three Piece Suite*, 1981). She sang lead vocals on 'Heaven Is Waiting' for pianist **Tom Grant** on his album *You Hardly Know Me*, and toured with **Soul II Soul** as music director.

RUSS, EDDIE

(Keyboards)

From Pittsburgh, Eddie played keyboards on the jazz scene with artists including **Sarah Vaughan**, **Benny Golson**, Stan Getz and **Dizzie Gillespie** during the '60s and '70s. He also formed his own group The Mixed Bag, with whom in the early '70s he recorded *Fresh Out* for the Jazz Masters label. Also at Jazz Masters he recorded two albums with **Sonny Stitt**, *Tornado* and *The Best Of Two Worlds*. In 1976 he switched to Monument (via CBS) where *See The Light* included 'Zaius', a classic instrumental on the UK jazz funk scene (1976). His follow-up album, also for Monument, was *Take A Look At Yourself* (1978).

RUSSELL, BRENDA

(Singer/Songwriter)

Born in Brooklyn, New York, Brenda is the daughter of two singers; her father was a member of The Ink Spots. Moving to Toronto at the age of twelve, Brenda took to performing in local bands (including The Tiaras) three years later. After a brief spell back in New York to launch her singing/songwriting career, she returned to Toronto to join the cast of the hit musical *Hair*. Here she met her husband Brian Russell and moved to Los Angeles where they worked as session singers. One TV engagement with Neil Sedaka was watched by Elton John who was immediately impressed. Brian & Brenda Russell recorded two albums for Elton's Rocket label in 1976/77 (including songs 'Highly Prized Possession' and 'That's All Right Too'). Elsewhere their songs were recorded by **Paulette McWilliams** ('Don't Let Go'), **Tata Vega** ('Gonna Do My Best To Love You'), **Jermaine Jackson** and **Rufus**. Brian and Brenda separated in 1978.

In 1979 Brenda signed to A&M and her debut solo album *Brenda Russell* included 'In The Thick Of It' (UK Top 75, 1980, as double A side). Her next album was *Love Life* (1981), before she switched to Warner Brothers for *Two Eyes* (1983), including 'Hello People' and 'It's Something'. She also resumed her session work with artists including Barbra Streisand and Bette Midler.

Her next move was to Sweden, originally to appear in a TV special, but she loved the place so much she settled there. In 1984 she returned to Los Angeles and signed once again to A&M. In 1985 she sang lead on **Herb Alpert**'s *Wild Romance* and co-wrote 'Men And Women' with **Sadao Watanabe** (singing lead on 'Maisha' for him). In 1986 she sang lead on 'Look What's Showing Through' for **Rodney Franklin** on his album *It Takes Two*, while in 1987 she wrote 'Dinner With Gershwin' for **Donna Summer**.

Brenda's own *Get Here* was released in 1988 and included the UK Top 30 hit 'Piano In The Dark'. The title track was later recorded by **Oleta Adams**, while elsewhere her songs were recorded by **Luther Vandross** ('If Only For One Night'), **Roberta Flack** ('My Love For You'), **Earth Wind & Fire** ('I've Had Enough' and 'You'), and **Leslie Smith/ Lalah Hathaway** ('It's Something'). In 1990 she returned with *Kiss Me With The Wind*, recorded duets with **Gerald Alston** and **Carl Anderson**, and produced an album for **Marilyn Scott**.

RYAN, ROZ

(Singer)

Based in Philadelphia, Roz appeared in the musical *Dreamgirls*, recorded with **Skipworth & Turner**, and worked with **Butch Ingram** while signed to the Mirage label (via Atlantic).

S

S.O.S. BAND
(Group)
From Atlanta, Georgia, **Mary Davis** (lead vocals), Jason Bryant (keyboards/lead vocals), Abdul Raoof (trumpet/vocals), Billy Ellis (sax), John Simpson (bass/vocals), Bruno Speight (guitar/vocals), Jerome 'JT' Thomas (drums) and Willie 'Sonny' Killebrew (sax) first worked together under the group name Santa Monica during the '70s. In 1980 they became The S.O.S. Band and signed to the Tabu label (via CBS) for *S.O.S.* (1980), including 'Take Your Time Do It Right' (UK Top 75) and *S.O.S. II* (1981), before their 'High Hopes' became the the first commercially released song by **Jam/Lewis**. It was taken from *S.O.S. III* (1983), which also included the song 'Groovin', That's What We're Doin'' (UK Top 75).

Jam/Lewis later wrote and produced the group's albums *On The Rise* (1983), including 'Just Be Good To Me' (UK Top 20) and 'Tell Me If You Still Care'; *Just The Way You Like It* (1984), including the title track single (UK Top 40), 'Weekend Girl' (UK Top 75) and 'No One's Gonna Love You'; and *Sands Of Time* (1986), including 'The Finest' (UK Top 20) and 'Borrowed Love' (UK Top 50). Singer Mary Davis then signed to Tabu as a solo artist.

The group also provided the instrumentation for **Eddie Kendricks**'s *I Got My Eyes On You* (1983), Jason Bryant writing songs for the project which he also co-produced for the Atlanta-based Ms Dixie label.

SADANE, MARC
(Singer)
Born in Savannah, Georgia, Marc Sadane gained his vocal experience from the church and became musical director for his local choir before moving into off-Broadway acting/singing in New York. From here he joined a group Tungsten Steele and was lead singer for three years prior to his departure in 1977.

Launching a solo singing career, he sang in a number of New Jersey clubs before coming to the attention of writers/producers **Mtume/Lucas**. In 1981 they signed Marc to Warner Brothers and worked with him on two albums, *One Way Love Affair* (1981) and *Exciting* (1982), including 'One Minute From Love'. Marc then opted out of the music business until 1988 when he recorded 'Why Can't You Believe In Me' (featuring **Will Downing** on backing vocals), produced by **Darryl Payne**, for Darryl's showcase album *Past Present & Future*.

SADE
(Singer/Songwriter)
Born in Nigeria to an African father and British mother, Sade Adu moved to North London during her early teens. She studied fashion and designed men's clothing from a shop in Chalk Farm. Her move to music was through local band Pride who took her on as a backing singer in the early '80s. Here she developed confidence as a performer and took to songwriting. Soon she was signed to Epic, although 'Sade' is in fact a group comprising Sade Adu (vocals), Stuart Matthewman (sax/guitar), Andrew Hale (keyboards) and Paul S. Denman (bass).

In 1984 they rose to immediate international acclaim with a debut album *Diamond Life* which included UK hits 'Your Love Is King' (Top 10), 'When Am I Gonna Make A Living' (Top 40) and 'Smooth Operator' (Top 20). *Promise* (1985) carried the hits 'The Sweetest Taboo' (Top 40) and 'It's A Crime' (Top 50).

Sade's last album to date, *Stronger Than Pride* (1988), included 'Love Is Stronger Than Pride' (Top 50) and 'Paradise' (Top 30), while 'Keep Looking' also kept dance-floors busy that year.

SAE, KELLI
(Singer)
Born in South Bronx, New York, in 1966, Kelli began her career performing in an off-Broadway play *Don't Tell Mama* and with several local bands. Impressing producer Russell Booker, she recorded a debut single 'To Take A Chance', released on the Emergency label in 1986. From here she recorded 'Forever' for the Midnight Sun label (1987) before joining the group J.J. Jumpers in 1988. Her next solo release, 'It's Too Late', was on the Easy Street label in 1989.

SAIN, OLIVER

(Sax)

Born in St Louis, Oliver established himself as a top bandleader and worked with numerous singers and musicians during their formative years, including **Fontella Bass**. As a solo recording artist he is best remembered on the disco scene for the instrumental 'Bus Stop' (1974), issued by Abet Records in America and Contempo in the UK.

SAINT & STEPHANIE

(Duo)

Roger Kenerly-Saint (drums/vocals) and **Stephanie Spruill** (vocals) teamed up to make one album *Saint & Stephanie* produced by **Michael Zager** for Arista in 1979. Prior to this album, and indeed after it, Stephanie worked as a top American session singer.

ST JAMES, PHYLLIS

(Singer/Songwriter/Percussion)

Based in Los Angeles, Phyllis wrote songs for a number of artists during the '80s including **Norman Connors** ('Take It To The Limit'), **Jean Carne** ('Mystic Stranger' and 'Bet Your Lucky Star'), **Rodney Franklin** ('You'll Never Know', 'Parkay Man', 'Endless Flight' and 'Return To The Source'), and **The Jones Girls** ('The World Will Sing Our Song').

As a solo singer she signed to Motown in 1984 where her one album was *Ain't No Turning Back*, including 'Candlelight Afternoon' and 'Phonemate'. She has also sung backgrounds with artists including **Rodney Franklin** (lead on 'Windy City'), **Randy Crawford** and **Atlantic Starr**.

ST PAUL

(Singer/Songwriter/Guitar/Producer)

Taking his name from his home town in Minnesota, St Paul wrote songs and recorded as a member of **The Family** prior to signing as a solo artist with MCA. Here he recorded *St Paul* (1987), but is best remembered for his single 'Intimacy' (1988). He later switched to Atlantic for *Down To The Wire* (1990) and played guitar with **Joe Sample** on his album *Ashes To Ashes* (1990).

SALSOUL ORCHESTRA

(Group)

What **M.F.S.B.** was to the Philadelphia International Records label, The Salsoul Orchestra was to Salsoul Records, a number of musicians playing in both groups of top East Coast instrumentalists. It was predominantly **Vince Montana** who wrote, conducted and produced the orchestra from the mid-'70s to the mid-'80s, their finer moments including 'Ooh I Love It (Love Break)' (1975), 'You're Just The Right Size' (1976), 'Salsoul 3001' (1976), 'Runaway' (1977), 'Christmas Time Medley' (1981), 'Take Some Time Out' (1982) and the **Patrick Adams**-produced 'Seconds' featuring **Loleatta Holloway** (1982). The orchestra also played on numerous recordings for the label's other groups and artists such as **Charo**'s *Charo And The Salsoul Orchestra* (1977), including 'Dance A Little Bit Closer'.

SALSOUL STRINGS

(String Section)

In addition to working as **The Salsoul Orchestra**, New York and Philly's Salsoul musicians recorded a few releases as The Salsoul Strings. These include 'Sun After The Rain' (1979), a disco instrumental with girlie vocals produced by Tom Moulton.

SAM AND DAVE

(Duo)

Sam Moore (from Florida) and Dave Prater (from Georgia) performed individually before Sam called Dave on stage at one of his gigs in 1958. It turned out so well that they teamed up professionally and initially scored a record deal with the Roulette label.

In 1965 they switched to the Stax label (via Atlantic) and were put to work with Booker T. and the MGs (see **Booker T. Jones**)and writers/producers **Isaac Hayes** and **David Porter**. Establishing themselves as a top soul duo of the mid-'60s, they scored numerous hits which in the UK included 'Soothe Me' (Top 50, 1967), 'Soul Man' (Top 30, 1967), 'I Thank You' (Top 40, 1968) and 'Soul Sister Brown Sugar' (Top 20, 1969). They are also fondly remembered for 'You Don't Know Like I Know', 'I Take What I Want', 'Hold On I'm Comin'' and 'When Something Is Wrong With My Baby'.

After the demise of Stax, the group continued to work directly for Atlantic but without the same success. Sam Moore recorded a solo album, then in 1971 the duo reunited for United Artists and later Contempo in the UK.

SAMPLE, JOE

(Keyboards/Songwriter)

Born in Houston, Texas, in 1939, Joe and fellow musicians at high school formed a group The Jazz Crusaders, later to become **The Crusaders**. After majoring in music at Texas State University, Joe began playing with The Crusaders professionally, while embarking on his own ventures too.

In 1969 he recorded a debut solo album *Try Us* (via Sonet Records in the UK) and numerous sessions before an ABC album *Rainbow Seeker* (1978), including 'There Are Many Stops Along The Way', established him as a solo artist on the 'jazz funk' scene. His follow-up was *Carmel* (1979) before his label became MCA for *Voices In The Rain* (1980), including *'Burnin' Up The Carnival'*, *The Hunter* (1983), *Oasis* (1985), featuring **Phyllis Hyman**, and *Roles* (1987). In 1989 he switched to Warner Brothers and worked with producer **Tommy LiPuma** for a more adult, sophisticated jazz/r&b approach on *Spellbound*, including 'Seven Years Of Good Luck' and also featuring **Al Jarreau**, **Take 6** and **Michael Franks**; and *Ashes To Ashes* (1990).

Elsewhere he has recorded keyboards with artists including **The Supremes** (*High Energy* 1976), **Gene Page** ('Lovelock'), **Mark Winkler** ('Ebony Rain' and his co-written 'Night Flight'), **Al Jarreau** ('Glow'), **Ronnie Laws**, **Martha Reeves**, **Jermaine Jackson**, **The Main Ingredient**, **Pleasure**, **Rufus**, **Minnie Riperton** (co-writing 'Adventures In Paradise'), Lea Roberts and many others.

As a songwriter he has worked with Will Jennings – Will writing the words to Joe's melodies – on 'Streetlife' (**The Crusaders**), and 'Last Night In Danceland' and 'One Day I'll Fly Away' (**Randy Crawford**).

SANBORN, DAVID

(Saxophone)

From St Louis, David took up the saxophone at school, influenced by **Hank Crawford** and the **Ray Charles** band. A visit to San Francisco in 1967 led to a place in the Paul Butterfield Blues Band, playing a solo on Paul's *In My Own Dream*. David then spent two years with **Stevie Wonder** (playing on *Talking Book*), and later recorded with David Bowie (*Young Americans*), **James Brown**, **Phoebe Snow** and **The Brecker Brothers**. By the late '70s he had signed to Warner Brothers and was delivering fusion jazz-orientated albums including *Taking Off*, *Sanborn*, *Promise Me The Moon*, *Heart To Heart* (1978) and then *Hideaway*, including 'The Seduction', the theme to the movie *American Gigolo* and a single which enjoyed 57 consecutive weeks on the American charts in 1980.

On the UK jazz funk scene, David's most well known recording became 'Let's Just Say Goodbye', an instrumental from 1981's *Voyeur*. In 1982 David performed the theme to 'Love Is Not Enough' live at Montreux, Switzerland. He had originally recorded this piece on *Heart To Heart*, but this live version proved to be the highlight of *Casino Lights*, released by Warner Brothers, that year. His later albums are *Backstreet* (1983), featuring **Marcus Miller** and **Luther Vandross**, *Straight To The Heart* (1984), *Double Vision* with **Bob James** (1986), featuring **Al Jarreau**, *As We Speak* (1986) and *A Change Of Heart* (1987).

David has also recorded with Mike Mandell, **Fatback**, **Chaka Khan** and Brenda Russell ('Le Restaurant') among many others. More recently he has presented a Saturday jazz show on London's Jazz FM radio station.

SANDERS, PHARAOH

(Saxophone)

Sax player Pharaoh Sanders first established himself on the San Francisco jazz scene in the early '60s. His nickname at the time was 'Little Rock'. By the mid-'60s he was working with John Coltrane and had his own jazz ensembles which gave artists like **Norman Connors** early career breaks. (He later recorded on many albums for Norman, who recorded one of his compositions 'Thembi'.) He has recorded numerous albums over the years, many fusing his rasping style with funky rhythms and vocal guests. His early albums included *Black Unity*, *Live At The East*, *Wisdom Through Music*, *Village Of The Pharaohs* and *Love In Us All*, prior to a recording deal with Arista.

Here, in 1978, he recorded *Love Will Find A Way*. His most r&b set to date, it included a rendition of **Marvin Gaye**'s 'Got To Give It Up' and featured **Phyllis Hyman**, **Lenny White**, **David T. Walker**, **Bobby Lyle** and The Waters, among a star cast. It was produced by **Norman Connors**. 1980's *Journey To The One* (Thresa Records) featured **Eddie Henderson**, **Idris Muhammad** and vocals from **Bobby McFerrin** on the star cut 'You've Got To Have Freedom'.

SANDERS, STEPHAN

(Singer)

Philadelphia-based vocalist Stephan Sanders recorded a single 'All The Women In The World' written and produced by **Dexter Wansel** and released on the Magnum label in 1983.

SANDERS, WILLIAM 'SONNY'

(Singer/Songwriter/Arranger/Producer)

Born in Detroit, Sonny sang in the late '50s with The Satintones, who became the first group to have a release on the Tamla label (via Motown). After six singles the group split up and Sonny moved to Chicago where he established himself as a songwriter and producer with numerous artists including **Aretha Franklin** ('Angel'), **Young-Holt Unlimited** ('Soulful Strut'), Sue Perrin, **Sydney Joe Qualls** ('I Don't Do This') and **Margie Alexander** ('Gotta Get A Hold On Me'). He has also arranged songs for artists including **The Dells**, **Leon Bryant** ('Are You Ready (Until Tonight)') and **Gene Chandler** ('I'll Make The Living If You Make The Loving Worthwhile').

More recently he rejoined The Satintones and recorded for the UK Motorcity label where his voice can be heard on songs including 'Perfect Combination' (1991).

SANDRIDGE, SHAWN

(Guitarist/Songwriter)

Apart from being a top Ohio session musician, Shawn played guitar with the group **Sun** for three years. He and fellow Sun member Chris Jones left to form their own group Magnum, shortly changing the name to **Dayton**.

SAPPHIRES

(Vocal Group)

Recording for the KMV label in the mid-'60s, Philly soul group The Sapphires released a single 'Gotta Have Your Love' in 1965. The B-side was 'Gee I'm Sorry Baby', one of the first songs written by **Gamble/Huff**.

SASSS
(Group)
From Philadelphia, Sasss are a self-contained soul/funk/rock group who formed in the early '80s. In 1984 their three female vocalists worked with producer **Dexter Wansel** on 'Baby Talk' and 'I Didn't Mean It At All', both featuring **Grover Washington Jr** and released in the UK by Virgin. The girls also sang backgrounds on *You Got What It Takes* and *The Main Attraction* for **Bobby Thurston**.

SATURDAY NIGHT BAND
(Studio Group)
The epitome of late '70s disco, The Saturday Night Band was instigated by New York producer Jesse Boyce. An ensemble of session musicians, Jesse wrote and produced their one album *Saturday Night Band* which included the UK Top 20 hit 'Come On And Dance, Dance' (1978).

SAULSBERRY, RODNEY
(Singer/Songwriter)
Born in Detroit in 1958, Rodney's father sang with Motown group The Downbeats. While developing his own vocals in the church, Rodney also trained as an actor, performing in local shows. A production of *Your Arm's Too Short To Box With God* took him to Los Angeles where he landed a role in *Taxi*. Following this he worked on *M.A.S.H.* and *Dynasty*, then between July 1982 and August 1983 he played FBI agent Jeff Johnson in the TV drama *Capitol*.

With an appetite for a recording career, he wrote eight songs with **Peter Brown** and sent the demos to **Stanley Clarke**. Stanley called the next day, resulting in a collaboration on his debut single 'I Wonder' and album *Rodney Saulsberry* for the Allegiance label (1984). A further single 'Who Do You Love' was released on the Ryan Records label, while more recently his song 'Love's Not Coming In' (co-written with Peter Brown) won first prize for r&b in *Billboard* magazine's 1990 song contest.

SCALES, HARVEY
(Singer/Songwriter/Producer)
Over the years Harvey worked as a writer for a number of Detroit artists including **Johnnie Taylor** (including 'Disco Lady' and 'Did He Make Love To You') and **The Dramatics** ('Blame It On New York City'). Elsewhere he co-wrote/produced 'I Can Do Bad By Myself' for **Jesse James** in addition to recording as a solo artist for labels including Casablanca (*Rock Your Body*, 1979) and Earthtone (various releases from the late '80s including 'Spend The Night Forever' and *All In A Night's Work*).

SCARBROUGH, SKIP
(Songwriter/Producer)
Based in Los Angeles, Skip wrote/co-wrote numerous soul classics through the '70s and '80s. These include 'Love Ballad' (**L.T.D.** and **George Benson**), 'No One Can Love You More' (**Bill Summers** and **Phyllis Hyman**), 'Living Inside Your Love' (**Phyllis Hyman**), 'I Just Can't See Myself Without You' (**Creative Source**), 'Love Changes' (**Mothers Finest** and **Kashif/Meli'sa Morgan**), 'Can't Hide Love' (Carmen McCrae, **Dionne Warwick** and **Jimmy Smith**), 'Reasons Why' (**Aretha Franklin** and **The Emotions**), 'Lovely Day' (**Bill Withers**), 'He Don't Lie' (**Philip Bailey**) and 'Don't Ask My Neighbours' (**The Emotions** and **Nancy Wilson**).

He also produced/co-produced albums for artists including **Bill Summers** (*Feel The Heat*), **Patti Labelle** (*It's Alright With Me*), **Rockie Robbins** (*I Believe In Love*), **Alton McClain** (now Skip's wife Alton McLain Scarbrough!), and **Chuck Cissel** (*Cisselin' Hot*). His cousin is singer/songwriter/producer **Gary Taylor**, who was greatly inspired by Skip's success.

SCHIFRIN, LALO
(Composer)
Born in Argentina, Lalo's father was leader of the Buenos Aires Philharmonic Orchestra, and his uncle was a cellist. After taking up the piano, he discovered his talent for composition and went to study in Paris. Here he was influenced by jazz music and later returned to Argentina with an ambition to be a jazz pianist.

In 1958 **Dizzy Gillespie** came to Buenos Aires and gave Lalo a place in his quintet. Relocating to Hollywood after a brief spell in New York, he established himself in the movie business as a premier composer for themes and soundtracks. Examples of his work include film/TV themes for *Bullitt*, *The Cincinnati Kid*, *Cool Hand Luke*, *Starsky & Hutch* and *Mission Impossible*.

As a recording artist he signed to the CTI label in 1976 and made a name for himself on the fusion jazz scene with *Black Widow* (1976), including 'Jaws'. In 1977 he wrote and arranged *Free Ride*, including 'Ozone Madness', for **Dizzy Gillespie** before switching to Tabu (via CBS) for *No One Home* (1979), including 'Memory Of Love' and the **Minnie Riperton/Richard Rudolph/Freddie Perren**-penned 'Oh Darlin' ... Life Goes On'.

He is currently the musical director of the Glendale Symphony Orchestra in Los Angeles.

SCOTT, GLORIA
(Singer)
Barry White discovered Gloria Scott and produced her one album *What Am I Gonna Do*, including 'A Case Of Too Much Love Makin'', for Casablanca Records in 1974. The album was largely ignored until a brief revival on the UK soul scene during the late '80s.

SCOTT, JIMMY
(Singer)
Born in Detroit, Jimmy recorded for the Fee and Eastbound labels between 1973 and 1975, before signing to Westbound Records and scoring American chart

success with his own song 'Backbone' (1975). He also became a touring member with **The Detroit Emeralds**, later replacing their lead singer.

In 1980 he recorded briefly with the Earwax and The New Sound Of Detroit labels before forming Backbone Productions. Here he recorded 'The Hunt', released only in the UK by Move Records. In the late '80s he recorded a solo **Michael Powell**-produced song 'Games' with the nucleus of **Chapter 8**.

SCOTT, MARILYN
(Singer)
Born in Los Angeles, Marilyn began her career as a backing singer with artists including **George Duke**, **Bobby Womack**, **Etta James** and a number of rock acts. In 1979 she signed to the Atco label (via Atlantic) and delivered a soul/jazz album *Dreams Of Tomorrow*. In 1983 she switched to Mercury where she worked with producer **Michael Sembello** on *Without Warning*, including 'You Can Do It'. More recently she has worked with **Brenda Russell** on her 1991 album for GRP Records.

SCOTT, MILLIE
(Singer)
Born in Savannah, Georgia, Millie sang in gospel groups The Pilgrim Gospel Singers and The Sermonettes before moving into jazz. After a spell with Bobby Dilworth & The Blazers she moved to New York and began working on the session scene. Soon she formed a group The Glories which released one single 'I Stand Accused' for the local Date label.

When **The Temptations** came to New York they tempted Millie to move to Detroit, where she remains to this day. She formed a new group **Quiet Elegance** and toured with The Temptations and **The Detroit Spinners** before **Willie Mitchell** signed Quiet Elegance to the Hi label down in Memphis.

After touring as a backing singer with **Al Green**, Millie formed **Cut Glass** with **Ortheia Barnes** (1976), and worked with the group for three years. In 1986 she signed as a solo artist to Island Records and released a debut single 'Prisoner Of Love' (UK Top 75). It was followed by an album *Love Me Right*, including 'Automatic' (UK Top 75) and 'Every Little Bit' (UK Top 75). Her second Island album, *I Can Make It Good For You*, (1988), included 'A Love Of Your Own' and 'To The Letter'.

SCOTT, RENA
(Singer)
Rena worked with writers/producers **Mtume/Lucas** in the late '70s on her album for Buddah/Arista *Come On Inside* (1979), including 'If I Had A Chance'. In 1988 she returned with *Love Zone* on the Sedona label.

SCOTT, TOM
(Saxophone)
Born in Los Angeles in 1948, Tom established himself on the fusion jazz scene during the '70s. From the early '70s he worked with his group L.A.Express, and recorded as a solo artist for Ode Records (via A&M), where his albums included *Rear* (1974), including 'Spindrift', before he switched to CBS. Here his albums include *Blow It Out*, *Intimate Strangers* (1978) and *Street Beat* (1979). He has also recorded for labels including Elektra Musician (*Desire*, 1982), Atlantic (*Target*, 1983) and Soundwings (*One Night/One Day*, 1986). As a session player he has also recorded with **Sarah Vaughan**, **T-Connection**, **Whitney Houston** (solo on 'Saving All My Love For You'), **Al Jarreau**, **Aretha Franklin** (solo on 'Without You'), Carole King, Paul McCartney, Joni Mitchell, **Minnie Riperton** and many others.

SCOTT-HERON, GIL
(Singer/Songwriter)
Born in Chicago in 1949, Gil was raised by his grandmother in Jackson, Tennessee. During his teens he wrote detective stories before switching to black politics following the death of his grandmother. Moving to New York, he studied composition at university before writing a series of novels (including *The Vulture* and *The Nigger Factory*) and later putting his radical stories to music with the help of **Brian Jackson**. As Gil Scott-Heron & Brian Jackson, the duo signed with the Flying Dutchman label in the early '70s, initially for an album *The Revolution Will Not Be Televised*. In 1974 they delivered *Winter In America* for the Strata-East label. It included 'The Bottle', which remains to this day a dancefloor classic, having been reissued in the UK on various occasions.

Switching to Arista in 1975 they recorded *From South Africa To South Carolina* (1975), including 'Johannesburg'; *It's Your World* (1976), including 'Home Is Where The Hatred Is', earlier recorded by **Esther Phillips**; *Bridges*; and *Secrets*. By the end of the '70s Gil was recording his political poems as a solo artist, further albums being *Real Eyes* (1980), *Reflections* (1981), including 'Is That Jazz', and *Re-Ron* (1984). In 1990 he signed to the Castle Communications label in the UK.

SEA LEVEL
(Group)
In 1977 top session musicians Chuck Leavell (keyboards), Jamie and Lamar Williams (of The Allman Brothers), George Weaver (drums) and Jimmy Nalls (guitar) experimented with a fusion of funk and jazz on an album *Sea Level*. Later that year they added Randall Bramblett (sax) and Davis Causey (guitar). In 1978 they released *Cats On The Coast*, including 'That's Your Secret', and toured both America and Europe. At the end of the tour George Weaver left the group to be replaced by Joe English who had played drums for Paul McCartney in

Wings (recording on *Venus And Mars*, *At The Speed Of Sound*, *Wings Over London* and *London Town*).

Also in 1978 they recorded *On The Edge*, stirring UK dancefloors with the **Stewart Levine**-produced instrumental 'Fifty Four' (UK Top 75) released on the Capricorn label (via Polydor). In 1979 they moved towards rock with *Long Walk On A Short Pier*, and further still with *Ball Room* (Arista, 1980).

SEA, DAVID

(Singer)

From Birmingham, Alabama, David became lead singer with his family's gospel group before forming David Sea & The Question Marks in 1970. Later they changed their name to David Sea & The Uptown Movement, basically a rock & roll group. As solo soul singer he initially recorded for the Hy-Tyde label, releasing singles including 'Angel' and 'Destiny' in the early '80s.

In 1984 he switched to the Crown Limited label for the **Roscoe Robinson**-produced 'Do It Right Now' and 'Who's Been Warming My Oven' before coming close to replacing **Dennis Edwards** in **The Temptations**. Opting to remain with his solo career, his releases for Magic City Records continued with 'Night After Night' and albums *David Sea* (1986), including 'I'm In The Mood' and 'Love C.O.D', and *An Ocean Apart* (1990).

SEAWIND

(Group/Horn Section)

The history of Seawind dates back to 1972 when Kim Hutchcroft (flute/sax) met Larry Williams (flute/sax) at university in Hawaii. Kim later met Kenn Wild (bass) at a Honolulu recording studio, and Bob Wilson (drums) soon joined to complete the rhythm section. Bob and Larry later discovered singer Pauline playing with another local band; Pauline Wilson became lead singer (and Bob's wife). During the remainder of 1972 the group toured Alaska and Canada using the name Ox, and soon acquired an additional member Bob Nuanez (guitar). Returning to Hawaii they built a solid reputation on the jazz scene and worked as opening act for visiting artists including **Herbie Mann**, **Billy Cobham** and **Herbie Hancock**.

In 1976 they moved to Los Angeles, acquired Jerry Hey (trumpet/flugelhorn), changed their name to Seawind and signed to CTI Records where their debut album *Seawind* included the **Harvey Mason**-produced 'cult' jazz/soul track 'He Loves You'. Harvey also co-produced the follow-up *Window Of A Child* (1977), before the group switched to Horizon Records (via A&M) and worked with producers **Tommy LiPuma** (*Light The Light*, including 'Free', 1979) and **George Duke** (*Seawind*, 1980).

Outside of their own recordings, the horn section of the group worked consistently through the late '70s and '80s with numerous artists including **Michael Jackson** (*Off The Wall*), **Stacy Lattisaw** ('Jump To The Beat'), **Aretha Franklin**, **Alphonse Mouzon**, **Marlon McClain**, **The Blackbyrds**, **The Commodores**, **Flora Purim**, **The Temptations**, **Rufus** and **Sister Sledge**.

SECOND IMAGE

(Group)

From North London, Second Image were one of the early 'Brit funk' bands, and consisted of Junior Bromfield (bass/guitar), George Bromfield (percussion), Rem Fiori (keyboards), Weston Foster (guitar), Ozie Selcuck (guitar), Frank Burke (trumpet), Simon Eyre (guitar) and Tom 'Zoot' Heritage (sax/flute). Signing to Polydor, their debut single 'Dance Dance Dance' was followed by 'Pinpoint The Feeling', 'Special Lady', 'Can't Keep Holding On' (1981), 'What's Happening' (1982), 'Star' (Top 75, 1982), 'Better Take Time' (Top 75, 1983) and a Polydor album *Dance* (1983).

From here they switched to MCA for singles 'Don't You' (1983), 'Sing And Shout' (1984), and 'Starting Again' (1985), all of which made the UK Top 75 without giving them the major breakthrough they had strived for over the years. Their manager, incidentally, was London disc jockey Robbie Vincent, while Junior and Frank also designed their own skateboards after being members of a successful British skateboard team.

SEMBELLO, MICHAEL

(Producer/Songwriter/Guitar)

Born in Philadelphia, Michael was influenced by his brother who was a guitar teacher and rock musician. By the time he was fourteen Michael was using a fake ID card to obtain work in local jazz clubs. Aged eighteen, **Stevie Wonder** accepted him as guitarist for his group Wonderlove where he stayed for seven years, working on albums including *Fulfillingness First Finale, Songs In The Key Of Life* (co-writing 'Saturn') and *The Secret Life Of Plants*.

From here he signed to Warner Brothers as a solo artist, and recorded 'Maniac', a song used in the film *Flashdance*. In 1985 he contributed 'Gravity' to the film soundtrack of *Cocoon*, a song later used on his A&M Records debut album *Without Walls*, featuring **Stevie Wonder** on 'Funkabilly Swing'.

As writer and/or producer he has worked with artists including **Diana Ross** ('Mirror Mirror'), **New Edition** (with **Richard Rudolph**), **Jeffrey Osborne** ('Don't You Get So Mad' and 'Eenie Meenie'), **Chaka Khan** ('Eye To Eye'), **Cheryl Lynn** ('Look Before You Leap'), **Stephanie Mills** ('Merciless') and **Marilyn Scott** (*Without Warning*), and has arranged for **Jermaine Jackson**.

SERIOUS INTENTION

(Studio Group)

New York group Serious Intention featured the lead vocals of **Anthony Malloy** and made an impression on the mid-'80s 'garage' music scene with 'Serious', written by **Paul Simpson** and released on the Pow Wow label (via Phonogram in the UK).

SHABAZZ

(Group)

From Long Island, New York, Shabazz are Paul Stewart (lead vocals), Marc Poussaint (drums), Wesley Walker (keyboards) and Dennis Brown (guitars). In 1986 they signed with the local Coslit label and made waves on UK dancefloors with a debut single 'Unified' with 'Open Your Heart' on the B-side. Follow-ups were 'Respect' and 'Takes Me Higher', before they switched to RCA for 'Glad You're In My Life' (1990).

SHAKATAK

(Group)

Formed in London in 1980, Shakatak are Bill Sharpe (keyboards), Jill Saward (vocals), Keith Winter (guitars), George Anderson (bass), Roger Odell (drums) and initially Nigel Wright (keyboards), who later retired from the band while remaining as the group's producer. Their debut single was 'Steppin'', an instrumental which created interest on the Brit funk scene when released on the Record Shack label in 1980. In fact the name Shakatak was derived from the former Soho record shop/label's name.

From here they switched to Polydor where through the '80s they scored a string of UK hits: 'Feels Like The Right Time' (Top 50, 1980), 'Living In The UK' (Top 75, 1981), 'Brazilian Dawn' (Top 50, 1981), 'Easier Said Than Done' (Top 20, 1981), 'Night Birds' (Top 10, 1982), 'Streetwalkin'' (Top 40, 1982), 'Invitations' (Top 30, 1982), 'Stranger' (Top 50, 1982), 'Dark Is The Night' (Top 20, 1983), 'If You Could See Me Now' (Top 50, 1983), 'Down On The Street' (Top 10, 1984), 'Don't Blame It On Love' (Top 75, 1984), 'Day By Day' featuring **Al Jarreau** (Top 75, 1985), and 'Mr Manic And Sister Cool' (Top 75, 1987).

More recently the group have scored success abroad, particularly in Japan and America.

SHALAMAR

(Group)

The concept of Shalamar was that of Dick Griffey, president of Soul Train Records in Los Angeles. In 1977 the label released a song 'Uptown Festival' which became an international hit (UK Top 30). It was followed by an album of the same name (which also included 'High On Life', later popular on the UK 'rare groove' scene). The success of the single prompted Dick Griffey to form an official group, the line-up being former dancers from the *Soul Train* TV show (in LA) **Howard Hewett, Jody Watley** and **Jeffrey Daniel**. In 1978 the Soul Train label changed its name to Solar (Sound Of Los Angeles Records), and the group worked with writer/producer **Leon Sylvers** on an album *Disco Gardens*, including 'Take That To The Bank' (UK Top 20). Continuing their work with Leon Sylvers, and epitomizing the 'Solar' sound, follow-up UK hits were 'The Second Time Around' (Top 50, 1979), 'Right In The Socket' (Top 50, 1980), 'I Owe You One' (Top 20, 1980), 'Make That Move' (Top 30, 1981), 'I Can Make You Feel Good' (Top 10, 1982), 'A Night To Remember' (Top 5, 1982), 'There It Is' (Top 5, 1982) and 'Friends' (Top 20, 1982). *Friends* was also the title of their most popular album, which included the latter four hits.

In 1983 the group took on a more commercial 'pop' direction, commencing with *The Look*, including 'Dead Giveaway' (UK Top 10), 'Disappearing Act' (UK Top 20) and 'Over And Over' (UK Top 30). In 1984 Jeffrey and Jody left the group and moved to the UK where they both recorded briefly for the Phonogram label. Jeffrey, who had also just divorced **Stephanie Mills** (having been married for one year), also took a stage role in *Starlight Express*. Back in Los Angeles, **Howard Hewett** formed a new line-up of Shalamar with Micki Free and former Miss Tennessee Delissa Davis. Commencing with an album *Heart Break*, UK hits followed with 'Dancing In The Sheets' (Top 50, 1984), 'Deadline USA' (Top 75, 1984), 'Amnesia' (Top 75, 1984) and 'My Girl Loves Me' (1985).

At this point Howard Hewett left for a solo career, while Solar Records continue to release new Shalamar albums (Sid Justin replacing Howard) but without UK chart success.

SHANNON

(Singer)

Born in New York, Brenda 'Shannon' Green first sang professionally in 1978 when she joined the New York Jazz Ensemble as featured vocalist. Through this experience she met **Lenny White** and a local soul group Brownstone with whom she worked in the early '80s.

Moving into session work, she recorded 'Let The Music Play' (1983), not expecting to see her name credited on the label! When the song became a hit (UK Top 20), she signed directly to the Mirage label (initially via Phonogram in the UK) and released *Let The Music Play* (1984), including 'Give Me Tonight' (UK Top 30) and 'Sweet Somebody' (UK Top 30); *Do You Wanna Get Away* (1985), including 'Stronger Together' (UK Top 50); and *Love Goes All The Way* (1986).

SHARP, DEE

(Singer)

London-based Dee Sharp was the lead singer of Buzzz during the late '70s while also recording as a reggae artist on the Fashion label. Following the demise of Buzzz he signed as a solo artist to RCA where a version of Nat King Cole's 'Straighten Up And Fly Right' was his debut solo release. From here he joined the JB All Stars, recording with the 2 Tone label before rapping on Nick Heywood's single 'Warning Sign' (UK Top 30, 1984). In 1987 he recorded a version of Van Morrison's 'Moondance', released by Syncopate/EMI Records.

SHARP, DEE DEE

(Singer)

Born Dione LaRue in Philadelphia in 1945, Dee Dee began singing in church as a member of her grandfather's choir. In 1961 she was hired as a background singer by the city's Cameo Parkway label. Here she met Chubby Checker with whom she recorded 'Slow Twistin'' (1962). The same year she signed as an artist with the label, scoring with three American dance hits 'Mashed Potato Time', 'Gravy' and 'Ride!'. In the UK 'Do The Bird' reached the Top 50 in 1963.

After a final 'dance' record 'Let's Twine' (1965), Dee Dee settled into soul/r&b, releasing 'Standing In The Need Of Love' (1965) and 'I Really Love You' (1966). In 1967 she married **Kenny Gamble**, and in 1975 signed to the Philadelphia International label as Dee Dee Sharp Gamble. Here her albums were *Happy 'Bout The Whole Thing* (1975), including 'Ooh Child' and 'Touch My Life'; *What Colour Is Love* (1977), including 'I Believe In Love' and 'I Wanna Be Your Woman'; and *Dee Dee* (1980), including 'I Love You Anyway' and 'Easy Money'. She later divorced Kenny Gamble.

SHAW, MARLENA

(Singer/Songwriter)

Born in New Rochelle, New York, Marlena first appeared on stage at the age of ten at New York's Apollo Theater. In 1960 she co-wrote 'Wade In The Water' with **Ramsey Lewis** and began to establish herself as a club singer prior to signing to the Cadet label in 1966. Here her albums were *Out Of Different Bags* (1966) and *Spice Of Life* (1967), including 'Mercy Mercy Mercy', before she joined Count Basie's band in 1968 and stayed for five years singing jazz. In 1972 she became the first female artist to sign with the Blue Note label and released 'It's Better Than Walking Out' (1976), 'I'm Back For More' and 'Loving You' which established her on the r&b scene.

After performing 'Go Away Little Boy' in a nightclub, she was approached by a record executive who signed her to CBS where she re-recorded the song for an album *Sweet Beginnings* (1977). She also recorded *Take A Bite* for CBS, had a huge New York disco hit with her rendition of 'Touch Me In The Morning' and became the first artist to record a **Gary Taylor** song ('Without You In My Life').

In 1983 Marlena was vocalist on 'Could It Be You' from **Phil Upchurch**'s *Name Of The Game*, while in 1988 she signed to Polydor for *Love Is In Flight*.

SHELL, RAY

(Singer/Songwriter/Producer)

Born in Saratoga County, North Carolina in 1951, Ray Lancaster Shell grew up in New York and developed an interest in acting. From 1971 he toured America in various shows and eventually landed in London in 1978.

After work in films and stage musicals Ray made his debut single 'Night Of Bliss' for the Lagos International label in 1980. He then recorded briefly for EMI (releasing 'Them Heavy People', 1981), and formed **The Street Angels** (as writer/producer).

He has continued to work in stage, film, TV and other music-orientated ventures.

SHERRICK

(Singer)

Los Angeles-based singer Sherrick was given his professional break by Raynoma Gordy, former wife of Motown founder **Berry Gordy**. Raynoma secured Sherrick a recording deal with Warner Brothers where his **Michael Stokes**-produced debut album *Sherrick* (1987), included 'Just Call' (UK Top 30) and 'Let's Be Lovers Tonight' (UK Top 75).

SHINETTE, CAROL

(Singer)

Born in Lake Charles, Louisiana, Carol recorded locally on the Zadar and Zilko labels and performed regularly around the Southern states of the USA. She also worked with **Bobby Womack** and **Bobby Bland**. Her solo single releases include 'Cyanide Love' (Zilko, 1984).

SHIRELLES

(Vocal Group)

Formed in New Jersey in 1958, The Shirelles were Shirley Alston (aunt of **Gerald Alston** and **Johnetta Alston**), Beverley Lee, Addie Harris and Dorris Kenner, who met at their local high school. Their initial recordings were for the Tiara label before Decca signed them and they scored an American hit with 'I Met Him On Sunday' (1959). Later in 1959 they signed to Scepter Records where they scored hits (via various labels in the UK) including 'Will You Love Me Tomorrow' (UK Top 5, 1961), 'Soldier Boy' (UK Top 25, 1962) and 'Foolish Little Girl' (UK Top 40, 1963). Much later they recorded *Happy And In Love* for RCA and starred in a movie *Let The Good Times Roll*.

SHOCK

(Group)

Like **Pleasure** and **Side Effect**, Shock were a late '70s/early '80s funk group signed to Fantasy Records. In 1982 they worked with producer **Marlon McClain** on one of their few UK releases, 'That's A Lady'.

SHOKK

(Group)

British soul group recorded 'Lock Me Out', produced by Ian Prince (Polydor, 1987).

SHO-NUFF

(Group)

Memphis group Sho-Nuff were Lyn Chambers (bass/keyboards), James Lewis (keyboards/brass), Lawrence Lewis (guitar), Bruce Means (drums) and Freddie Young (keyboards/lead vocals). In the late '70s they recorded briefly for the Stax label (including 'I Live Across The Street', 1978), following which they signed to Malaco where their first single 'It's Alright' was issued in the UK by Ensign Records. They later released a Malaco album *Stand Up For Love* (1982).

SIDE EFFECT
(Group)
From Los Angeles, Side Effect were originally **Augie Johnson**, Greg Matta, Louis Patton and Sylvia Nabors who began playing an earthy mix of funk, soul and jazz in the mid-'70s. Under the direction of producer **Wayne Henderson** they signed to Fantasy Records where their debut album *Side Effect* was released in 1975.

By their next album, *What You Need* (1976), Sylvia had been replaced by Helen Lowe, vocalist on the group's rendition of 'Always There', who later recorded as **Helen Baylor**. The album also featured 'Keep That Same Old Feeling', a song Wayne Henderson had originally recorded with **The Crusaders**.

Helen left Side Effect in 1977 and was replaced by Sylvia St James on *Goin' Bananas* (1977), which included 'Keep On Keepin' On'. Although they were shortly to stop recording as a group, they took on **Miki Howard** as lead singer for club dates, recording sessions as backing musicians/singers for **Roy Ayers**, **Billy Cobham** and **Stanley Turrentine** together with Augie's other projects including **The L.A. Boppers**.

SIEGEL, DAN
(Keyboards)
Dan is a fusion jazz pianist who recorded albums for the Inner City label including *Nite Ride* (1980), featuring **John Klemmer** and **Lee Ritenour**, *The Hot Shot* (1980) and *Oasis* (1981).

SIGLER, BUNNY
(Singer/Songwriter/Producer)
Walter 'Bunny' Sigler was born in Philadelphia in 1941 two days before Easter, hence his nickname. After singing in church as a child he formed a vocal group The Opals with his brother and two friends. In 1959 he recorded a debut single 'Promise Me' for the local Hilo label, and later re-recorded it with local group The Cruisers on the V-Tone label. Local disc jockey Cannonball later signed him to the Craig label where he recorded 'Come On Home' (1964) and earned the name 'Mr Emotions' as he cried while singing love songs in concert. He first met **Gamble/Huff** in 1965, initially working with **Leon Huff** in 1967 on a single for the Cameo Parkway label 'Girl Don't Make Me Wait'. Leon also co-wrote and produced Bunny's Cameo Parkway album *Let The Good Times Roll*.

From here he teamed up with Gamble/Huff as staff writer/producer for the Neptune label, later to join them in the same capacity at the Philadelphia International (PIR) label. His songs and/or productions were used by artists including **Patti Labelle** ('I'm In Love Again' and 'Living Double'), **The Whitehead Brothers**, **Lou Rawls** and **Shirley Jones** ('Do You Get Enough Love'). Also at PIR he recorded his own albums *That's How Long I'll Be Loving You*, shortly reissued as *Keep Smilin'* (1974), the title cut being one of three different versions, and *My Music* (1976), including 'Come On And Dance Dance Dance'.

While continuing his writing/production services at PIR, Bunny as an artist signed to Gold Mind/Salsoul in the late '70s and released *I've Always Wanted To Sing* (1979), *Let It Snow* (1980) and *Let Me Party With You*. Most of this material was in a disco/'high energy' style in contrast to his slick/soulful recordings at PIR.

Bunny has also written and/or produced for **Jackie Moore** ('Sweet Charlie Babe', 1973), **Joe Simon** (*Drowning In The Sea Of Love*), **The Whispers** ('Bingo', 1974), **Force of Nature** ('Simba', 1974), The Vibrations ('Shake It Up', 1974), **Linda Clifford** ('From Now On', 1977), **Philippe Wynne**, **The Pips** (without **Gladys Knight**), **Gabor Szabo** (*Nightflight*, including an instrumental version of 'Keep Smilin''), **First Choice**, **Double Exposure**, **Chaka Khan** (co-writing 'Tearin' It Up') and **Eugene Wilde** ('Rainbow', 1984).

His most recent solo release was the single 'What Would You Do Without Love', released on the Star Island label in 1986.

SILAS, ALFIE
(Singer)
This Los Angeles-based singer signed to Motown in 1986 for *That Look*, produced by **Norman Whitfield** and **Willie Hutch**. It included a version of **Gary Taylor**'s 'Just Gets Better With Time', and three further songs which were featured in the movie soundtrack *The Last Dragon*.

Alfie also recorded backgrounds with **Quincy Jones** and **Morris Day**.

SILK
(Group)
Formerly known as **Anglo Saxon Brown**, Melvin Watson, **Debra Henry**, Dwight Smith, Alvin Brown, Tyrone Durham, Clemente Burnette and Charles Mann became Silk for one album *Midnight Dancer* (1979). It included the Philly soul 'rare groove' 'I Can't Stop Turning You On' and was released on the Philadelphia International label.

This group should not be confused with vocal trio Silk (Marlena Jeter, Maxi Anderson and Gwen Machu), a top background vocal session trio from Los Angeles who recorded an RCA album *Smooth As Silk* (1977).

SILVESTER, TONY
(Singer/Songwriter/Producer)
Born Enrique Antonio Silvester in Panama in 1941, Tony settled in New York during the '50s where he became part of a vocal group The Poets. This group later became **The Main Ingredient** with whom Tony has sung and recorded through to this day.

In the mid-'70s he took time away from the group to concentrate on producing, including albums and singles for Ben Vereen, **Linda Lewis**, **The Imperials** and **Marlena Shaw**.

SIMMONS, DAVID
(Singer)
From Philadelphia, David went to the same high school as **Bunny Sigler**, and first sang with local friends in a group The Exzels. He gained his first studio experience when the group recorded a single 'Hit Talk' with producer **Bobby Martin**. In 1975 he formed a group Neo Experience and recorded two singles, 'Human' and 'Eternal Sunshine'. The group included Vera Brown (who later joined **The Richie Family**) and Venson Unto (later the lead singer of Executive Suite).

In 1978 David signed as a solo artist to the WMOT/Fantasy label for a debut album *Hear Me Out*, including 'Will You Miss Me When I'm Gone'. The following year *The World Belongs To Me* included the US r&b hit 'Holdin' Back' and a **Butch Ingram**-penned/produced ballad 'Hooked On You'. In 1981 David worked with **Sister Sledge** on a duet with Kathy Sledge 'All The Man I Need', and toured with the group that year. Through a recording date with **Damaris** he met producers George Guess and Eugene Curry with whom he recorded 'Love Tonight'. The song was initially issued on the Pearl Harbor label in Philadelphia before its major release on Atlantic in 1984.

David's voice is very similar to that of **Teddy Pendergrass**, which has done him few favours over the years. While Teddy has been incredibly successful, David has been seen as a carbon copy rather than a fine singer in his own right.

SIMMS, JOHN & ARTHUR
(Duo)
For the Casablanca label, *John & Arthur Simms* was an album for this duo in 1980, popular on the UK soul scene for the track 'Love Will Getcha'.

SIMON, JOE
(Singer/Songwriter)
Born in Louisiana in 1943, Joe grew up in Oakland, California where he initially sang with The Goldentones. He later moved to Nashville where he pioneered a fusion of soul and country music after signing to the Sound Stage 7 label. From 1964 he had a succession of American hits commencing with 'Teenager's Prayer' and including 'The Chokin' Kind', 'Hangin' On', 'No Sad Songs', 'Misty Blue', 'Message From Maria' and 'My Special Prayer'. In 1970 he switched to the Spring label, initially working with producers **Gamble/Huff** on *Drowning In The Sea Of Love*. His other albums for Spring were *Mood Heart & Soul*, *Simon Country* and *Get Down*, while his one UK single hit was 'Step By Step' for Mojo Records (Top 20, 1973).

More recently he has recorded for the Compleat label where his albums have included *Mr Right* (1985).

SIMONE, NINA
(Singer)
Born Eunice Waymon in North Carolina in 1933, Nina took to both singing and playing the piano by the age of seven. After studying music, she and her family moved to Philadelphia where she established herself on the local nightclub scene.

Her debut single was 'I Loves Porgy' (1959), an American hit on the Bethlehem label before she switched to Phillips where 'I Put A Spell On You' was a UK Top 50 hit in 1965. From here she signed to RCA for further UK hits including 'To Love Somebody' (Top 5, 1969). Her RCA albums during the late '60s were *Nina Simone Plays The Blues*, *Silk And Soul*, *Here Comes The Sun* and *It Is Finished*.

In 1978 Nina recorded *Baltimore* for the CTI label, while her next UK hit was an issue of 'My Baby Just Cares For Me' (Top 50, 1987).

SIMPLICIOUS
(Group)
From Miami, this family group first worked together as La Voyage before changing their name to Tight Connection and recording one single 'Does Anybody Really Know' for the Taurus label (via TK). In 1984 they recorded one single 'Let Her Feel It' for the Philly World label (via 4th & Broadway in the UK) and could have recorded an album had they wanted to move from their Miami base to Philadelphia. With the exception of Ron Eugene Broomfield (aka, **Eugene Wilde**), the group decided they didn't want to leave Miami.

SIMPSON, PAUL
(Producer/Songwriter/Arranger/Musician)
Born in New York, Paul initially established himself as a disc jockey on the city's radio stations MGR, Kiss and WBLS. In the early '80s he settled in Philadelphia where he got acquainted with **Vince Montana**, **Norman Harris** and the Philly soul community. Here he worked as arranger/musician with artists including **M.F.S.B.**, **First Choice**, **The Trammps** and Montana himself ('Heavy Vibes'). He also produced artists including **The Main Ingredient** and **The Detroit Spinners**.

In 1985 he formed The Paul Simpson Connection and signed to Easy Street Records back in New York. His debut single was 'Treat Her Sweeter' (released via 10 Records in the UK). Also at Easy Street he co-wrote and produced 'Serious' for **Serious Intention** (1986), his other productions being for artists including **Barbara Roy** ('Gonna Put Up A Fight'), Rozlyn Sorrell ('Sucker For Candy') and Simphonia ('Can't Get Over Your Love').

He later signed to the Cooltempo label in the UK where his singles 'Musical Freedom' (featuring **Adeva**, **Carmen Marie** and **Candi Staton** over various versions) and 'Walk Away From Love' (featuring **Anthony White**) were featured on his album *One* (1989).

SIMPSON, RAY

(Singer)

Brother of **Valerie Simpson** of **Ashford & Simpson**, Ray recorded one album *Tiger Love*, produced by the duo, and later became a member of **The Village People**. He also sang backgrounds on **Noel Pointer's** *Feel It* (1979).

SIMPSON, VALERIE

(Singer/Songwriter/Producer)

One half of the husband & wife duo **Ashford & Simpson**, Valerie was born in 1946 and had a gospel group The Followers before she met Nick Ashford during her days with the White Rock Baptist Choir in Harlem. When the duo were signed as songwriters at Motown, Valerie recorded three albums for the Tamla label, *Exposed* (1971), *Valerie Simpson* (1972) and *Keep It Comin'* (1977), which was a compilation of the previous two.

SIMS, BOBBY

(Guitarist)

From Chicago, Bobby played blues and jazz guitar with artists including **B.B.King** and **Bobby Bland**. His son is **Lil Louis**, for whose recent album he played guitar on three tracks.

SIMS, JOHN AND ARTHUR

(Duo)

Brothers John and Arthur Sims recorded one self-titled album for the Casablanca label in 1980. It included 'Love Will Getcha' and 'Somebody New', popular on the UK soul scene.

SIMS, JOYCE

(Singer/Songwriter)

Born in Rochester, New York, in 1959, Joyce studied music at college where she learned a number of musical instruments. Unable to play professionally at first, she took a job in a hamburger bar and wrote songs in her spare time. One of her songs was overheard by an agent who introduced her to Ron Resnick at Sleeping Bag Records, the label she signed to in 1986. Working with producer Mantronik (of **Mantronix**), her debut single 'All And All' (UK Top 20) was followed by 'Lifetime Love' (UK Top 40, 1987) and the title track of her first album *Come Into My Life* (UK Top 10, 1987). The follow-up was *All About Love* (1989), including 'Walk Away' (UK Top 30) and 'Looking For A Love'.

SINCLAIR, LORETTA

(Singer)

From Bristol, Loretta sang in reggae bands before moving to London where she met **Phil Fearon**. She recorded one single for City Beat Records, 'Every Time We Touch' (1985).

SINE

(Studio Group)

Sine was one of numerous studio groups conceived during the '70s disco boom. This one was instigated by **Patrick Adams** and consisted of vocalists Craig Derry, Venus Dobson (who later recorded a solo album) and Kenny Simmons, with a host of New York session musicians. One album *Happy Is The Only Way* was released on Prelude (via CBS) in 1977, the album's leading dance track 'Just Let Me Do My Thing' being a UK Top 40 hit in 1978.

SINGLETON, CHARLIE

(Singer/Songwriter/Guitar/Producer)

Born in New Orleans in 1954, Charlie became a professional guitarist during the '70s and originally toured with **Billy Cobham**, Dizzy Gillespie and Cannonball Adderley. He later formed his own group Star Gazum before he joined **Cameo** in 1980.

After five years as an integral part of Cameo he signed to Arista as a solo artist, while initially continuing to record with the group. After a debut album *Modern Man* (1985) he switched to Epic Records for a follow-up *Nothing Ventured, Nothing Gained*, which featured his former Cameo teammates together with **Kathy Mathis** and **Peabo Bryson**.

As songwriter and/or producer he has also worked with **Kiara** ('This Time'), **Chaka Khan** ('Earth To Mickey'), **Maniquin** and **Billy Always**.

SINNAMON

(Studio Group)

A **Darryl Payne** and **Eric Matthew** instigated group, Sinnamon was put together in 1982 and featured vocalists Barbara Fowler, Bernard Fowler and **Toni Smith**. Initially recording for the New York Becket label (later Jive), their dance records included 'Thanks To You' (1982), 'He's Gonna Take You Home (To His House)' (1982), 'I Need You Now' (1983), 'Say It Again' – later a hit for **Jermaine Stewart**, 'Thin Line' and 'Send It C.O.D.'

SISTERS LOVE

(Vocal Group)

Based in Los Angeles, Sisters Love were originally Vermettya Royster (lead vocals), Jeanne Long, Lillie Fort, Gwen Berry and founder member **Merry Clayton**. In the mid-'60s the group signed with A&M and scored a series of American r&b hits with songs including 'Forget It, I've Got It' before they switched to the Mowest label (via Motown) following the departure of Merry Clayton.

Here they scored further American success in the early '70s with songs including 'Mr Fix It Man' (written and produced by **Willie Hutch**, 1972), 'I'm Learning To Trust My Man' (1972) and the **Curtis Mayfield** song 'Give Me Your Love' (1973), originally recorded by Curtis on his *Superfly* album, and produced for Sisters Love by **Gloria Jones** and **Paul Riser**. Also in 1973 they played cameo roles in the film *The Mack*, the soundtrack becoming a solo album for their regular producer **Willie Hutch**.

'Gimme Your Love' became in demand on the UK 'rare groove' scene in the mid-'80s, prompting its re-release on Motown, while Vermettya re-recorded the song as a solo artist on the UK Motorcity label in 1991.

SKIPWORTH & TURNER

(Vocal Duo)

Rodney Skipworth and Phil Turner met through being lead singers in rival bands in their home town of Syracuse, New York. Rodney sang lead with New Sound Express, the longest surviving local band in Syracuse history (1972–83), while Phil was lead singer with Sunrise.

While Rodney was from Syracuse, Phil was born in Memphis and began a singing career with a group called The Fames after moving to Buffalo. The Fames played gigs supporting **The Manhattans** and **The O'Jays**. Rodney worked in a fast-food restaurant during the day, and when Phil came in as a customer on one occasion they talked about a joint venture.

Signing to 4th & Broadway in 1985 they released 'Thinking About Your Love', a song Rodney had originally sung with New Sound Express. It reached the UK Top 25, and was followed by a single 'Hot Pursuit' and a **Patrick Adams**-produced album *Skipworth & Turner*. From here they signed to Warner Brothers for a brief spell before a return to 4th & Broadway for singles 'Cash', 'Make It Last' (both 1989) and a 1990 **Paul Simpson** remix of 'Thinking About Your Love'.

SKOOL BOYZ

(Group)

The Skool Boyz were Stan Shepherd, Billy Shepherd and Chauncey Matthews, all natives of Chicago who grew up in Los Angeles. Stan had previously been with **Triple 'S' Connection** prior to forming The Skool Boyz in 1980 while all three were indeed still at school. In 1981 an album *Skool Boyz* was released on the US Destiny label, following which they signed to CBS and released a second self-titled album in 1984 (which included 'Slip Away' and 'Before You Go'). 1985's *This Is The Real Thing* included 'You Are My Love' (featuring **Jeanie Tracy**) and 'Superfine (From Behind)', before Billy left to become guitarist with **By All Means** (with Stan working as a producer with the new group).

SKWARES

(Group)

A six-piece funk ensemble from New York, Skwares formed at high school and were encouraged to take their music seriously after winning a number of local talent shows. After investing their savings in demo recordings, they sent their tapes to the record companies and were signed by Cotillion.

They were put in the studio with **Slave** producer Jimmy Douglass, and one album *Skwares* (including 'Step By Step') was released in 1984.

SLAVE

(Group)

From Ohio, Slave were originally formed in 1975 from members of two local groups, The Young Mystics (Floyd Miller, vocals/horns; Mark Adams, bass; Tom Lockett Jr, sax) and Black Satin Soul (**Steve Washington**, trumpet; Mark Hicks, guitar; Tim Dozier, drums). **Steve Arrington** had also played with The Young Mystics (drums) but had left Ohio for San Francisco when Steve Washington formed Slave. The original line-up became complete with the addition of Orion Wilhoite (sax), Charles Bradley (keyboards) and Danny Webster (guitar/percussion/vocals).

Signing to Cotillion Records (via Atlantic) in 1977, the group's debut album *Slave* established them immediately with 'Slide'. Their follow-up was *Hardness Of The World* (1977) before **Steve Arrington**, Curt Jones and **Starleana Young** joined the group as regular background singers beginning with *The Concept* (1978), including 'Stellar Funk'. With producer **Jimmy Douglass**, the group scored their one UK chart entry in 1979 with the dance anthem 'Just A Touch Of Love' (UK Top 75) featuring **Steve Arrington** as lead vocalist. The song came from an album of the same name, following which Steve Washington, Tom Lockett, Curt Jones and Starleana Young left the group to form **Aurra**.

With new members Keith Nash (vocals/drums), Wayne Foote (vocals) and Eugene Jackson (vocals), the group continued with *Stone Jam* (1980), including 'Watching You', and *Show Time* (1981), including 'Wait For Me', before **Steve Arrington** took on a solo career. Two further Cotillion albums, *Bad Enuff* (1983), including 'Steppin' Out', and *New Plateau* (1984), were released before the group switched to Ichiban Records for *Unchained At Last* (1985), including 'Jazzy Lady', *Make Believe* (1986) and *Slave '88* (1988).

SLEDGE, PERCY

(Singer)

Born in Leighton, Alabama, in 1941, Percy began his singing career in church and on the gospel circuit. He later joined The Esquires before breaking away in 1966 to make his solo recording debut for Atlantic Records. The song was 'When A Man Loves A Woman', which sold millions of copies around the world and reached No. 4 in the UK charts that year. Later in 1966 he returned to the UK Top 40 with 'Warm And Tender Love', but it wasn't until 'When A Man Loves A Woman' was reissued in 1987 that he charted in the UK again. The song reached No.2 on the back of a Levi 501's jeans commercial.

Percy's other Atlantic recordings in the late '60s/early '70s included 'It Tears Me Up', 'Out Of Left Field', 'Love Me Tender' (the Elvis Presley song), 'Take Time To Know Her' and 'Sudden Stop'. In 1973, he switched to the

Capricorn label where his recordings include 'I'll Be Your Everything'.

SLEEQUE

(Studio Group)

Sleeque were New York vocalists Adrienne Garrett and **Inez Brown**, put together by Don Casale in 1985. They recorded one single, 'One For The Money', released by Easy Street in America and Malaco Dance in the UK.

SLICK

(Studio Group)

Slick were essentially the musicians from **F.L.B**. (Fat Larry's Band) under a different name. Instigated by Larry James and his wife Doris James, the group stormed the UK dancefloors in 1979 with 'Space Bass' Top 20, co-written and produced by Larry. Lead vocalist was **Brandi Wells**. Later in 1979 they hit the UK Top 50 with 'Sexy Cream', but were never heard from again.

SLY & ROBBIE

(Duo)

Noel 'Sly' Charles Dunbar (drums) and Robbie Shakespear (bass) first met while working together in Jamaican band The Aggrovators. Sly got his nickname from his emulation of **Sly Stone** as a teenager.

As arrangers/producers, Sly & Robbie first established their reputation in the reggae world where they worked with artists including The Mighty Diamonds (*The Right Time*), Dennis Brown, Bunny Wailer and Gregory Isaacs during the '70s. They later broadened their horizons to work with artists including **Grace Jones** (*Nightclubbing*) and **Gwen Guthrie**.

As recording artists they signed to 4th & Broadway Records in the mid-'80s where they made *Language Barrier* (1985) and scored UK hits with 'Boops' (Top 20, 1987) and 'Fire' (Top 75, 1987).

SLY & THE FAMILY STONE

(Group)

Sly & The Family Stone was the concept of Sly Stone, born Sylvester Stewart in Dallas, Texas, in 1944, who made his recording debut at the age of four! The song was 'Oh My Battlefield For My Lord', following which he broadened his gospel base to encompass doo-wop. During his teens he recorded again, this time as lead singer with The Viscanes on 'Yellow Moon'. From here he moved to San Francisco where he worked as a disc jockey on a local radio station before becoming a record producer in the mid-'60s. Working for the Autumn label he produced Bobby Freeman, the Beau Brummels and one single of his own 'Buttermilk'.

From here he performed with a group, The Stoners, who were signed by CBS and become Sly & The Family Stone. Initially they recorded as a rock group, their debut *A Whole New Thing* being very much a rock album. In 1968 the group switched direction to funk/soul and delivered 'Dance To The Music', a UK Top 10 hit that year (via Direction Records in the UK). They further established themselves with 'M'Lady' (UK Top 40) and 'Everyday People' (UK Top 40) prior to an album *Stand* (1969), also including 'I Want To Take You Higher'. Also in 1969 *Hot Fun In The Summertime* proved popular before they returned to the studio for *There's A Riot Going On* (1971). Now via Epic Records in the UK, further hits followed with 'Family Affair' (UK Top 20, 1972) and 'Runnin' Away' (UK Top 20, 1972) while albums included *Fresh* and *Small Talk*.

Switching to Warner Brothers, Sly's albums included *On The Right Track* (1979), including 'Remember Who You Are', and *Ain't But The One Way* (1983), including 'Who In The Funk Do You Think You Are'. A drug problem interfered with his career and led to his withdrawal from the recording scene until very recently.

SMITH, FLOYD

(Songwriter/Producer)

Floyd Smith is best remembered for his work with **Loleatta Holloway** (whom he married), from 'Cry To Me' in the mid-'70s to 'Sweet Thing' in the mid-'80s just prior to his death. He also wrote and/or produced for artists around New York and Chicago including **John Edwards** (*John Edwards*, including 'Messing Up A Good Thing'), **Tyrone Davis** and **Ripple** ('The Beat Goes On').

SMITH, JIMMY

(Organ)

Born in Norristown, Pennsylvania, in 1925, Jimmy was a pioneer of the jazz organ scene in the late '50s/early '60s, inspiring other artists including **Jimmy McGriff** and **Johnny Hammond**. He formed The Jimmy Smith Trio in 1956, and played frequently in New York before signing with the Blue Note label where his recordings included *Sermon*, *Home Cooking*, *Prayer Meeting*, *Plays Pretty For You*, *Midnight Special* and *Back At The Chicken Shack* during the early '60s.

In 1962 he signed to Verve Records where he worked with the **Lalo Schifrin** orchestra for an American hit single version of 'Walk On The Wild Side'. His popularity as an instrumentalist grew until 1966 when he lost credibility for introducing his vocals on new recordings 'Got My Mojo Working' and 'I'm Your Hoochie Coochie Man'.

While recording for Mercury during the mid-'70s, *Unfinished Business* and *Sit On It* (1977), including 'Can't Hide Love', proved popular on the UK jazz funk scene. In 1982 he switched to the Elektra Musician label for *Off The Top* featuring **George Benson** and **Stanley Turrentine**.

SMITH, LESLIE

(Singer)

Based in Los Angeles, Leslie is best remembered for his one solo album *Heartache*, released by Elektra in 1982. It included 'It's Something' (the **Brenda Russell** song later recorded by **Lalah Hathaway**) and the duet with **Merry Clayton** 'Before The Night Is Over'.

SMITH, LONNIE LISTON

(Keyboards)

Born in Richmond, Virginia, to a musical family, Lonnie was influenced by his father who was a member of the gospel quartet the Harmonizing Four. At school he learned how to play piano, tuba and trumpet, and later went to work in the house band at the Royal Theater in Baltimore (accompanying visiting acts like **The Supremes**). Concentrating on keyboards, he toured with Art Blakey (1966–7), Joe Williams (1967–8), **Pharaoh Sanders**, Leon Thomas (1969–71), **Gato Barbieri** and **Miles Davis**, following which he formed his own group The Cosmic Echoes.

With the group he progressed to fusion jazz and recorded albums for the Flying Dutchman label including *Cosmic Funk*, *Astro Travelling*, *Expansions* (1975), *Visions Of A New World*, *Reflections Of A Golden Dream* and *Renaissance* before switching to CBS. Here his albums were *Loveland* (1978), including 'Sunburst'; *Exotic Mysteries* (1978) including 'Space Princess'; *Song For The Children* (1979), featuring **James Robinson**; and *Love Is The Answer* (1980), including 'Give Peace A Chance (Make Love Not War)'. Throughout this time 'Space Princess' was an anthem, although superseded by his 1975 recording 'Expansions' (via RCA in the UK), which was re-released numerous times and remains an all-time classic.

In 1984 a rather out-of-character single 'Say You Love Me' appeared on the Other End label, then after a three-year break Lonnie signed to the Doctor Jazz label (PRT in UK) and released the **Marcus Miller**-produced *Dreams Of Tomorrow*, including 'A Lonely Way To Be' and 'Never Too Late', which featured his brother Donald on vocals (he also sang 'Expansions'). Further albums were *Silhouettes* (1984), *Rejuvenation* (1985) and the straight jazz-orientated *Make Someone Happy* (1986), before a switch to the Startrak label (via Ichiban) for *Love Goddess*, featuring **Grover Washington**, **Phyllis Hyman**, **Jean Carne**, **Najee** and **Norman Connors** (Lonnie had previously recorded with Norman on his *Slewfoot* album).

SMITH, O.C.

(Singer)

Born Ocie Lee in Mansfield, Louisiana, in 1936, O.C.'s first professional break came when he was hired to replace Joe Williams in Count Basie's band. Here he stayed for two years singing jazz before touring as a solo artist and eventually settling in Los Angeles, where he landed a recording deal with CBS Records.

In 1965 he broadened into country music and scored a hit single with 'Son Of Hickory Holler's Tramp' (UK Top 5, 1968). His follow-ups included 'Little Green Apples' and 'Honey' released the same year. In 1973 he moved into soul music and worked with producer **Johnny Bristol** on 'La La Peace Song' (1973). His next hit was 'Together' (UK Top 25, 1977).

SMITH, RICHARD JON

(Singer/Songwriter/Producer)

Born in Cape Town, South Africa, Richard Jon Smith was brought up in the American-based music scene in Johannesburg. Here he won several talent shows before becoming a popular artist in South Africa. When Percy Sledge toured the country, Richard supported him, having just scored local success with his debut single release 'Candlelight'. After recording two albums and taking his career as far as he could in South Africa, he moved to London. He had earlier met a co-owner of Jive Records, and it was Jive that he signed to upon reaching the UK in 1980. His debut UK release was 'Don't Go Walkin' Out That Door' (1982), followed by 'Stay With Me Tonight' the same year.

In 1983 'Baby's Got Another' (co-written with **Darryl Payne**) reached the Top 20 in the US dance charts, and Richard's song 'There's No Easy Way' was recorded by **Michael Wycoff** on his *On The Line*. Later that year *Richard Jon Smith* was released, from which 'She's The Master Of The Game' made the UK Top 75. The following year Richard spent some time in New York writing with **Keith Diamond** who produced his next single release 'In The Night'. This was followed by 'Dance With Me' before Richard concentrated on songwriting and production projects at Jive for artists including Warren Mills and Hugh Masakela.

SMITH, TONI

(Singer)

Born in New York, Toni first established herself in 1980 as co-writer and featured vocalist on 'Funkin' For Jamaica', a UK Top 10 hit for trumpeter **Tom Browne**. As a solo recording artist her singles include 'Ooh, I Like The Way It Feels' for Malaco (1983), and 'Can't Stop This Feelin'' for Lisson Records (1986). Her solo 'I've Got The Hots For You' was later utilized by S-Express on their UK No. 1 hit 'Theme From S-Express' (1988).

SMITH, WILLIAM D.

(Singer/Songwriter/Keyboards)

Based in Los Angeles, William has worked as a session musician over the years in addition to recording as a solo artist for labels including A&M (*Smitty*, 1979). He has played keyboards with artists including **Randy Crawford** ('Endlessly'), and he co-wrote 'My Love For You' with **Brenda Russell**, recorded by **Roberta Flack**.

SMOKE

(Group)

Smoke were Michael Fisher (guitar/vocals), Anthony Fisher (bass/vocals), Arnold N. Riggs (lead vocals), Rodney Thompson (keyboards), Bradford Henry Thoelke (bass trombone/vocals), Clifford Ervin (trumpet/vocals),

Buddy McDaniel (sax/flute/vocals) and Raymond Genovese (drums), who worked with Los Angeles-based producer **Wayne Henderson** on albums including *Smoke* (1976).

SNOW, PHOEBE
(Singer/Songwriter)
Born in America in 1951, Phoebe Snow has won support from soul, jazz and rock fans over the years. She recorded 'Shaky Ground' (the **Temptations** song), 'Gone At Last' (a duet with Paul Simon), and 'Poetry Man' (1975) before scoring a UK Top 40 hit with 'Every Night' on the CBS label in 1979. Switching to Elektra she released *Rock Away* (1981), including 'Games' and 'Mercy Mercy Mercy', following which she retired from recording to take care of her mentally handicapped child. Her next album was *Something Real* (1989), while she also sang with **Dave Grusin** on his *Night Lines*.

SOCCIO, GINO
(Singer/Songwriter/Producer)
Best remembered for his disco single 'Dancer' (1979), Gino recorded for the WEA family of labels for a number of years. 'Turn It Around' was popular on UK dancefloors in 1984.

SOFTONES
(Vocal Group)
From Baltimore, The Softones established themselves on the R&B scene with a number of ballads during the late '60s and early '70s before hitting the disco scene with 'This Old Black Magic' for Avco Records during the mid-'70s.

SOSKIN, MARK
(Keyboards/Songwriter)
Recording for Prestige Records in California, Mark is best remembered for his jazz funk instruments 'Walk Tall' and 'Colossus' taken from *Rhythm Vision* (1980). Elsewhere he recorded with artists including **Bill Summers** (*Brazilian Skies*), Pete And Sheila Escovedo (see **Sheila E**) and **Roger Glenn**.

SOUL BROTHERS SIX
(Group)
From Rochester, New York, the Soul Brothers Six were **Willie John Ellison** (lead singer/songwriter/guitarist/producer), Benny Vonell Benjamin (bass), Lester Peleman (vocals/congas), and three brothers Sam Armstrong (drums), Mo Armstrong (guitar) and Charles Armstrong (vocals). Coming together in the mid-'60s, they initially recorded for the Philly-based Lyndell label (releases including 'I Need You Yes'), but are best remembered for the American hit 'Some Kind Of Wonderful' (1967). Their follow-ups were not so successful and the original line-up broke up in 1969. In 1972, Willie put a new line-up together which toured in Canada until the final demise of the group in 1977.

SOUL CHILDREN
(Vocal Group)
Instigated by songwriters/producers **Isaac Hayes** and **David Porter** in Memphis in 1968, The Soul Children were Anita Louis, Shelbra Bennett, John Colbert and Norman West. Signed to the Stax label, they worked closely with Hayes and Porter, recording *Soul Children* (1969), *Best of Two Worlds* (1971) and *Genesis*, including 'I Want To Be Loved' and 'Heresay', which established the group in 1972. Follow-up albums were *Friction* (1974), including 'Don't Take My Kindness For Weakness' and 'I'll Be The Other Woman', and *Open Door Policy* before they switched to Epic and eventually split up. Lead singer John Colbert began a solo career under his nickname **J. Blackfoot**.

SOUL SURVIVORS
(Group)
The Soul Survivors were, a white soul/pop group who met **Gamble/Huff** in the mid-'60s and recorded with them on the Crimson label. They later signed to the T.S.O.P. subsidiary of Philadelphia International Records for an album *Soul Survivors* in 1974. The group featured keyboard player **Neil Larsen**.

SOUL II SOUL
(Group)
The brainchild of **Jazzie B** from London, Soul II Soul began as a roadshow of disc jockeys and rappers in 1983. Playing at warehouses and clubs up and down the country, they eventually settled in at the Africa Centre in Covent Garden, calling their weekly night 'The Sweat-down Party'. After building a solid following they were moved out, and Jazzie B and his crew spent some time in Japan. Upon their return to the UK they expanded their empire with record and clothes shops under the umbrella of Soul II Soul. A natural extension was making records themselves, and Jazzie teamed up with Nellee Hooper of The Wild Bunch. Together they produced a song 'Fairplay' featuring the vocals of Rose Windross (who co-wrote the song) in 1988 for 10 Records.

Through 1989 Soul II Soul established themselves and their 'sound' internationally with a debut album *Club Classics Vol. 1*, including 'Keep On Movin'' and 'Back To Life', both showcasing the vocals of **Caron Wheeler** who then launched a solo career.

The follow-up, *Vol II: 1990 A New Decade* (1990) included 'A Dream's A Dream' (featuring **Victoria Wilson James**) and 'Missing You' (featuring **Kym Mazelle**).

SOUTHSIDE MOVEMENT
(Group)
A mid-'70s soul group instigated by James R. Vanleer,

they signed to the 20th Century label in Los Angeles for an album *Moving South* (1975), including 'Do It To Me'.

SOUZA, RAUL DE

(Trombone)

Brazilan trombone/'Souzabone' (trombone with valves) player made an impact on the UK jazz funk scene from the mid- to late '70s, his debut album being *Colors*, produced by **Airto** for the Milestone label in 1975. Switching to Capitol and moving to Los Angeles, he utilized the services of pianist/producer **George Duke** on albums *Sweet Lucy* (1977), featuring **Patrice Rushen**, **Freddie Hubbard** and **Airto**; *Don't Ask My Neighbours* (1978), including 'Daisy Mae' and featuring **Harvey Mason**, **Bobby Lyle**, **Ndugu** and **Josie James**; and *Till Tomorrow Comes* (1979).

SPACES

(Group)

Philadelphia musicians Scott Clancy (vocals/guitar), Steve Dubin (drums), Marc Goodman (keyboards), Don Eaton (sax) and Michael Schlesinger came together as Spaces for one album *Spaces* (Arista, 1981). Produced by **Ralph Macdonald**, the album included the popular jazz fusion instrumental 'Song For Jeremy'.

SPANK

(Group)

From New York, Spank were Eddie Greene (lead vocals), Johnny Davis (guitar/vocals), Bernie Croha (keyboards), Frank Mobus (guitar), Steve Falc (drums), Ralph Larman (drums), Ian Urbank (percussion), Jack Dyler (trumpet), Rik Dyler (trombone) and Mike Prince (sax). Their one album *Spank You* generated healthy interest on the UK soul/funk scene in 1985. It was released in the States on the US Metrovinyl label that year.

SPECIAL DELIVERY

(Group)

From Washington, **Special Delivery** featured the lead vocals of **Mick Jessup**, who later became an integral personality on the Washington 'go-go' scene. Prior to this, however, the group released an album *Special Delivery* for the Shield label (via TK) in 1978, the track 'This Kind Of Love' becoming a 'cult' song on the UK soul scene in the early '80s.

SPENCER, C.P.

(Singer)

From Detroit, Crafman Plato Spencer inherited his musical interests from his parents who were both musicians. His mother was also a cousin of **The Winans**. C.P. was a co-founding member of **The Detroit Spinners** in 1955 before joining the Five Jets in 1957. Here he recorded 'Mattie' and 'I'm In Love', co-written and produced by **Berry Gordy**. He also recorded for the Big Top and Audrey ('I Wish You Were Mine') labels as Spencer Stirling in the early '60s prior to joining the line-up of **The Originals** as a lead singer, and recording with Motown between 1965 and 1975.

In 1988 he recorded *Love Swept* which included a solo version of 'Baby I'm For Real' and was released on the A-Zone label. From here he recorded both as a solo artist and as a member of the re-formed Originals on the Motorcity label, where he remains today.

SPIDER'S WEBB

(Duo)

Husband and wife duo Spider's Webb were Kenneth Rice and Carol Kaye. Prior to their own recordings, Kenneth played drums and Carol played bass on a number of Motown records during the '60s as well as working in backing bands for artists including Frank Sinatra. Signing to Fantasy, they released one album featuring 'I Don't Know What's On Your Mind (You Don't Know What's On Mine)' in 1976, produced by **Jeff Lane**.

SPIRITUAL CONCEPT

(Group)

From Philadelphia, Spiritual Concept were fronted by **T-Life** and were a self-contained group whose music was a fusion of soul, gospel and rock. Their one album *Spiritual Concept* was released on the Philadelphia International label in 1973.

SPLENDOR

(Vocal Group)

Splendor were a vocal group consisting of Sascha Meeks, Robert Nunn, Richard Shaw and Carl Carwell. Their one CBS album *Splendor* was produced by **Philip Bailey** in 1979.

SPRUILL, STEPHANIE

(Singer/Percussion)

Stephanie Spruill was one half of **Saint & Stephanie**. She has also sung backgrounds with **Aretha Franklin**, **Bobby Womack**, **Bobby Lyle**, **Donald Byrd**, **Rockie Robbins**, **Carl Anderson** and **Rufus**, while playing percussion for artists including **David Ruffin** and **Donald Byrd**.

SPYRO GYRA

(Group)

Formed in Buffalo, New York, in 1975, Spyro Gyra are jazz fusion players Jay Beckenstein (sax), Jeremy Wall (keyboards), Jim Kurzdorfer (bass), Tom Schuman (piano), Chet Catallo (guitar), Ed Konikoff (drums) and Richard Calandra (percussion). Their debut album *Spyro Gyra* (1977), including 'Shaker Song', was originally released on their own Crosseyed Bear label but was licensed by Amherst Records (1978) and sold over 200,000 within twelve months. Its success led to a deal with Infinity Records where they scored a UK Top 20 hit with the title track of *Morning Dance* (1979). Their follow-up Infinity album was *Catching The Sun* (1980) before they switched to MCA for *Carnival* (1980), *Freetime* (1981), *City Kids* (1983) and *Alternating Current* (1985).

STAIRSTEPS
(Group)
From Chicago, The Stairsteps are a family group consisting of brothers **Keni Burke** (bass), **Clarence Burke**, James Burke and Dennis Burke, sister **Aloha Burke** and their father 'Papa Stairstep'. They were given their name by their father who thought they looked like a staircase when they stood next to each other. After winning a number of local talent shows they got talking to their next-door neighbour, Fred Cash of **The Impressions**. Fred took them to see **Curtis Mayfield** who signed them to his Windy City label (via Buddah) in the late '60s. In 1970 they were joined by younger brother Cubie and released *Stairsteps* including 'Ooh Child', and *Step By Step By Step* (1970).

The group travelled across America and later split up and worked at nine-to-five jobs. In the meantime they did occasional session work with artists including **Stevie Wonder**, **Quincy Jones** and then **Billy Preston**, who took them to see George Harrison (of The Beatles) who signed the group for a reunion album *2nd Resurrection* (1975), including 'From Us To You', 'Tell Me Why' – later recorded by **Pockets** – and 'Time', **Billy Preston** co-producing the album.

Keni Burke later launched a solo career while Clarence Burke formed **The Invisible Man's Band**.

STANLEY, CHUCK
(Singer)
Signed to the New York-based Def Jam Records (via CBS), Chuck made his debut in 1987 with *The Finer Things In Life*, including the duet with **Alyson Williams** 'Make You Mine Tonight'. In 1989 he teamed up with Alyson again for 'I'm So Glad' on her album *Raw* (1989).

STANSFIELD, LISA
(Singer/Songwriter)
Born in Rochdale, UK, Lisa Stansfield hosted the TV show *Razzamatazz* during her teens before signing to Polydor as a singer in the early '80s. She later became the lead singer of **Blue Zone**, who signed to the Rocking Horse label in 1985. After one release 'Dirty Talk', the Rocking Horse label was acquired by Arista where Blue Zone was signed directly in 1986.

In 1989 Lisa was the featured lead vocalist with Coldcut on their hit 'People Hold On', following which she returned to Arista as a solo artist for songs including 'This Is The Right Time', 'All Around The World' and 'Live Together' (1991). Her debut album was *Affection*.

STAPLES, MAVIS
(Singer)
Born in Chicago in 1940, Mavis joined her family gospel group **The Staples Singers** as lead singer, a role she maintains to this day. As a solo artist her debut album was *Only For The Lonely* for the Volt label (1976), following which **Curtis Mayfield** wrote and produced her Curtom album *A Piece Of The Action* (1977), in fact a soundtrack album of songs originally intended for **Roberta Flack**. She also recorded a number of duets with **Eddie Floyd** for the Stax label.

In 1979 she signed to Warner Brothers for *Oh What A Feeling*, although its lack of success discouraged her from pursuing a solo career at this stage and she concentrated on **The Staples Singers**. In 1983, however, she was approached by a company of tax-shelter lawyers who were keen to start a label for financial reasons. A song called 'Love's Gone Bad' was recorded in Detroit and has subsequently become a collector's item on the UK soul scene.

Meanwhile a TV programme featuring Mavis with The Staples Singers caught the eye of **Prince** who was so impressed he signed her to his Paisley Park label. In 1989 she released her first solo album for ten years, the **Prince/Al Bell**-produced *Time Waits For No One*. Mavis has since toured with Prince as well.

STAPLES SINGERS
(Group)
The Staples Singers are a family gospel group begun by Roebuck 'Pops' Staples who was born in Winoma, Mississippi, in 1915. After beginning a career as a blues guitarist he married Oceola, and their first daughter Cleotha was born in 1935. Yvonne was born in 1939 before the family moved to Chicago prior to the birth of third daughter **Mavis Staples** in 1940. As the daughters grew up, Pops encouraged their singing at home while he sang and played guitar as one means of making money. By the early '50s he realized he had the roots of a group within his family, and together they began to perform in their local Baptist church. Encouraged by the reaction the family turned professional. In 1955 they recorded a debut single 'Sit Down Servant' for United Records, prior to signing with the Vee-Jay label where they remained until 1960. With the chart success of songs like 'Cloudy Day' they became America's most successful gospel group.

From here the group switched to Riverside and then Epic (in 1961) where in 1967 they did well in the American charts with 'Why Am I Treated So Bad'. By now Mavis had established herself as the prominent voice within the group. Leaning more towards a secular music group, The Staples Singers changed labels to Stax in 1968 and released an album *Soul Folk In Action*. Under the direction of producer **Al Bell**, American chart success came their way with 'Heavy Makes You Happy' (1971) and 'Respect Yourself' (1972). Also in 1972, 'I'll Take You There' sold two million copies across America and reached the UK Top 30 to become the group's biggest hit in this country. A follow-up 'If You're Ready (Come Go With Me)' hit the UK Top 40 in 1974, from *Be What*

You Are. Later in 1974 *City In The Sky* sold well across the USA before the demise of the Stax label.

In 1976 The Staples returned with a soundtrack album *Let's Do It Again*, written and produced by **Curtis Mayfield**. The title track single sold a million copies across America but was not a hit in the UK. In 1981 the group were with 20th Century for *Hold On To Your Dream* prior to liaising with Private I (via CBS) for *The Turning Point* (1984) which included the dance hit 'Slippery People' (also recorded by Talking Heads).

STARGUARD

(Vocal Group)

Formed in Los Angeles during the late '70s, Starguard was instigated by producer **Norman Whitfield** and comprised Rochelle Runnells, Debra Anderson and Janice Williams. In 1978 they scored a UK Top 20 hit with the theme from *Which Way Is Up* (a Richard Pryor movie), taken from their debut album *Starguard*, also including 'Love Is So Easy' (UK Top 50). Their follow-up was *What You Waiting For* (the title track being a UK Top 40) before they switched to Warner Brothers for *Changing Of The Guard* (1980) and *Back 2 Back* (1981).

STARPOINT

(Group)

Formed in New York in 1969, Starpoint consisted of brothers Ernesto, George, Orlando and Gregory Phillips with the addition of lead singer Renee Diggs and Hayode Adeyemo. Originally they called themselves Licyndiana (made up from the first few letters of each of the group's sister's Christian names!), but soon changed it because no one could understand or pronounce it.

After building a reputation on the club scene, they were signed by Casablanca in 1982 for *All Night Long*, including 'Bring Your Sweet Lovin' Back' and 'Get Your Body Up'. Their follow-up was *It's So Delicious* for the Broadwalk label in 1983. From here they switched to Elektra where they have scored chart success in America without making a major impression in the UK. Their Elektra albums have been *It's All Yours* (1984), *Restless* (1985), including 'Objects Of My Desire' and 'Emotions', *Sensational* (1987) and *Have You Got What It Takes* (1990).

Renee Diggs has also worked as a backing singer with artists including **James Ingram** and **Bob James**.

STARR, EDWIN

(Singer/Songwriter)

Born in Detroit, Edwin got his first break by making an appearance on American TV's *The Uncle Jake Show*, performing with Billie Holliday. In the mid-'60s he signed to the local Ric Tic label and scored (via Polydor in the UK) with hits 'Agent OO Soul' (US Top 30), 'S.O.S. Stop Her On Sight' (UK Top 40, 1966), 'Headline News' (UK Top 40, 1966), as well as 'Girls Are Getting Prettier' and 'You're My Mellow' for Golden World Records before Edwin found himself at Motown.

Here he re-recorded 'Stop Her On Sight' with different lyrics and called it 'Scotts On Swingers' in praise of local Detroit disc jockey Scott Regan on station WKNR. It was only issued on a promotional 7" single and is very rare. His success at Motown came with his co-written song '25 Miles' (UK Top 40, 1969), which was also recorded by **Michael Jackson**, 'War' (UK Top 5, 1970) and 'Stop The War Now' (UK Top 40, 1971). His backing singers during this time were Total Concept Unlimited, who later became **Rose Royce**.

After moving to Los Angeles he continued his work as an entertainer and later signed to 20th Century Records where he enjoyed further chart success from *Clean*, including 'Contact' (UK Top 10, 1979), 'H.A.P.P.Y. Radio' (UK Top 10, 1979, for RCA), and 'Stronger Than You Think I Am' (1980).

In 1984 he recorded a tribute to **Marvin Gaye**, 'Marvin', for the UK Streetwave label, by which time he had moved to the UK and settled in Warwickshire. From here he signed to the Hippodrome label, a division of Peter Stringfellow's nightclub the Hippodrome, and released 'It Ain't Fair' (UK Top 75, 1985) and 'Soul Singer' (1986) before a brief spell at Virgin Records under the direction of **Stock/Aitken/Waterman**.

More recently he has recorded for the UK Motorcity label (including 'Let's Fall In Love') while being signed to WEA in Germany for whom he has recorded with **Chaka Khan** (including the duet 'Our Day Will Come', 1991). Edwin also recorded songs for a gold-selling Walt Disney album, *Mousersize*.

STARR, MAURICE

(Songwriter/Producer)

Maurice Starr was responsible for discovering **New Edition** in Boston (1981), and writing/producing their debut hit 'Candy Girl' (UK No. 1, 1983). He has also produced for artists including **Jean Carne** and **Tom Browne** ('Secret Fantasy', 1984).

STARSHIP ORCHESTRA

(Group)

From Philadelphia, The Starship Orchestra was instigated by drummer/producer **Norman Connors** who utilized them on his own albums in addition to securing them a record deal with CBS in 1980. Lead members were Ralph Jones (sax), Billy McCoy (keyboards) and Darryl Munyungo Jackson (percussion). Their 1980 album *Celestial Sky* featured an acoustic piano lead version of 'The Genie', played by its composer **Bobby Lyle**.

STARVUE

(Group)

A late '70s Chicago group, Starvue remain popular on the Northwest England soul scene with 'Body Fusion', a

Judy Davis song from their *Upward Bound* album (MR Chicago Sound, 1980).

STATON, CANDI

(Singer)

Born in Hanceville, Alabama, Candi Staton was performing with an all-girl vocal quartet at the age of five. By the time she was ten she was touring with the Jewel Gospel Trio. In 1968 she secured some work at a nightclub in Birmingham, Alabama, where on her first professional night she supported **Clarence Carter** whom she later married. Clarence also took her to the Fame label where she was given her first recording contract in 1968. Her debut single was 'I'd Rather Be An Old Man's Sweetheart', taken from 1970's *I'm Just A Prisoner* (later issued by Capitol). Her other Fame albums included *Stand By Your Man* (1970) and *Candi Staton* (1972) before the label became affiliated to United Artists. Here she continued with the American hit single 'In The Ghetto' before divorcing Clarence Carter and signing with Warner Brothers.

In 1976 she released *Young Hearts Run Free*, the title track becoming a UK Top 5 hit. Follow-up UK hits included 'Destiny' (UK Top 50, 1976), 'Nights On Broadway' (Top 10, 1977), and 'Honest I Do Love You' (Top 50, 1978). Her albums included *Music Speaks Louder Than Words*, *House Of Love*, *Chance* and *Candi Staton*. In 1978 she also sang with **Bobby Womack** on 'Stop Before We Start'. For Sugarhill Records she scored a UK Top 40 hit with 'Suspicious Minds' (1982), before returning to her gospel roots and signing to her own Beracah label. In 1986, however, she was the featured vocalist on 'You Got The Love' for a group The Source. The song was for a video about weight problems and Candi never expected it to be released. The acappella vocal however, was later utilized by **Paul Simpson** on 'Musical Freedom' (1989) and remixed in 1991 (released by The Total Record Co. in the UK).

Candi's Beracah albums include *Sing A Song*, *The Anointing* and more recently *Love Lifted Me* (1989).

STATUS IV

(Studio Group)

Instigated by writer/producer **Eric Matthew** in New York, Status IV enjoyed some UK dancefloor success with 'Lovin' You' on the Radar label (1983) before hitting the UK Top 75 later that year with 'You Ain't Really Down' for the TMT label (reissued in 1985 by Domino Records).

STEACKER, RICHARD

(Singer/Guitar/Songwriter)

From Philadelphia, Richard was musical director for **Eddie Holman** on a UK tour in 1973. He wrote songs for Chubby Checker and recorded with **Stevie Wonder**. While back in Philadelphia he met **Grover Washington** and joined his band, which later recorded independently as **Locksmith**.

STENNETT, ANDY

(Singer/Keyboards/Producer)

Founder member of **Freeez** with Johnny Rocca, Andy also contributed keyboards and arrangements for **Princess**, **O'Chi Brown** and **Arthur Baker** before forming Hard Times Productions. Here he created The Gangsters (originally calling themselves Gangsters Of House), Scram, The Bootleggers, Black Jack and Rough Club.

STEVENS, KENI

(Singer/Songwriter)

British-born singer Keni Stevens is the son of a US serviceman and began his career as lead singer of the group Raw Energy in the mid-'70s. He also worked as a session singer with artists including Marianne Faithfull and Eddy Grant before signing to the Elite label as a solo artist in 1985. He recorded *Night Moves* (1985) and *Blue Moods* (1987) before a switch to Debut Records for *You* (1988) and *Living On The Edge* (1989).

STEWART, ALTON 'WOKIE'

(Singer/Songwriter/Producer)

Born in New York, Alton sang gospel as a nine-year-old with the Harlem Boys' Choir before joining The Ecstatics, voted top gospel quartet in the New York area for five consecutive years. In 1989 he signed to Epic as a solo artist and **Fred McFarlane/Allen George** produced his debut album *All Our Love* (1989). He later wrote and produced (with **Timmy Gatling**) 'When Will I See You Smile Again' for Bell Biv Devoe.

STEWART, AMII

(Singer)

From Washington DC, Amii began her career as an actress when she was sixteen. After plenty of theatre and film work she created a cabaret act. While on tour with her show she recorded 'Knock On Wood', a version of the 1967 **Eddie Floyd** hit. Amii's version hit the Top 10 in 1979 after she signed with the Hansa label (via Atlantic). During the peak of the disco era, she continued a run of Euro-flavoured disco hits with 'Light My Fire'/'137 Disco Heaven' (UK Top 5), 'Jealousy' (UK Top 60, 1979), 'Paradise Bird'/'The Letter' (UK Top 40, 1980), and a **Johnny Bristol** duet 'My Guy–My Girl' (UK Top 40, 1980). By this time Amii had settled in Italy, which remains her home to this day. She continued her work on the cabaret circuit before returning to the UK charts in 1984 with 'Friends' (Top 20) from an RCA album *Try Love*.

In 1985 both 'Knock On Wood' and 'Light My Fire' were remixed, released back to back and made the UK Top 10 on the Sedition label. RCA released a new album *Love Ain't No Toy* in 1986, the same year Sedition took Amii and Deon Estus to the UK Top 75 with their duet version of 'My Guy–My Girl'.

STEWART, BILLY
(Singer/Keyboards)
Born in Washington DC in 1937, Billy grew up in a gospel music environment before turning to doo-wop in the '50s and joining The Rainbows with **Marvin Gaye** and **Don Covay**. Due to his weight he was nicknamed 'The Fat Boy'.

From the mid-'50s to the mid-'60s he recorded as a solo artist, predominantly for the Chess label on songs including 'Billy's Blues' (1956), 'Billy's Heartaches' (Okeh label, 1957), 'Reap What You Sow' (1962), 'I Do Love You' (1966), 'Sitting In The Park' (1966) and 'Summertime' (UK Top 40, 1966). He was killed in a car crash in 1970.

STEWART, JERMAINE
(Singer/Dancer)
Born in Ohio, Jermaine was one of the first and most prominent dancers in the Los Angeles-based TV show *Soul Train* during its formative years in the late '70s. His dancing partners were **Jeffrey Daniels** and **Jody Watley** who later formed **Shalamar**, taking Jermaine with them as a backing singer.

He later toured as a backing singer with **Millie Jackson**, **Tavares**, **The Temptations** and **Gladys Knight** before landing a solo deal with Arista (via Virgin in the UK), where his UK hits were 'We Don't Have To Take Our Clothes Off' (Top 5, 1986), 'Jody' (Top 50, 1986), 'Say It Again' (Top 10, 1988), 'Get Lucky' (Top 20, 1988) and 'Don't Talk Dirty To Me' (Top 75, 1988).

STIKKI STUFF
(Group)
From Luton, Bedfordshire, Stikki Stuff were an early '80s Brit funk group consisting of I.Nicholls, E.Poole, K.Jones, A.Culley and D.Ellis. Released on their own Floppy Discs label, recordings included 'The Wiggle' (1981).

STITT, SONNY
(Sax)
Sonny Stitt established himself on the American jazz scene in the '60s before making an impact on the UK jazz funk scene during the mid-'70s. After recording for the Jazz Masters label (albums including *Tornado*, featuring **Eddie Russ**) he switched to Cadet Records for *Satan* (1974) and the most sought-after *Never Can Say Goodbye* (1975), including 'Slick Eddie'. He then moved to Roulette Records for *Stardust* (1976).

STOCK/AITKEN/WATERMAN
(Group/Songwriters/Producers)
Mike Stock, Matt Aitken and Pete Waterman first came together in 1984, initially as a songwriting and production team. Pete had previously worked as a disc jockey and employee of Magnet Records, while Mike and Matt were session musicians. Their first production to reach No.1 in the UK charts was 'You Spin Me Round' for Dead or Alive (1984), following which they established themselves on the UK dance scene with songs and/or productions for artists including **Princess** ('Say I'm Your Number One' and 'After The Love Has Gone'), Bananarama ('Venus'), Mel & Kim ('Showin' Out', 'Respectable' and 'FLM'), Rick Astley ('Never Gonna Give You Up') and **Donna Summer** ('This Time I Know It's For Real' and 'Love's About To Change My Heart').

In 1987 they released their own record on A&M, 'Roadblock' (UK Top 20), initially disguised as a 'rare groove'. Their follow-up 'Packjammed (With The Party Posse)' reached the UK Top 50, while in between London Records issued their instrumental 'Mr Sleaze' which reached the UK Top 5 as a B-side to 'Love In The First Degree' by Bananarama.

Between March 1986 and October 1990 Stock/Aitken/Waterman had at least one of their songs/productions in the UK Top 100 every week on numerous labels including their own PWL, where artists include Kylie Minogue and Jason Donovan.

STOKES, MICHAEL
(Producer/Songwriter)
Based in Los Angeles, Michael has worked consistently as a producer through the '70s and '80s with artists including **Creative Source** (*Creative Source*, 1973, and *Pass The Feeling On*, 1975), **Morning Noon And Night** (*Morning Noon & Night*, 1977), Shirley Caesar (*From The Heart*, 1978), **Keith Barrow** ('Turn Me Up', 1978), Nature's Divine ('In The Beginning', 1979), **Booker T. Jones** (*I Want You*, 1981), **Rose Royce** ('Love Me Right Now', 1984), **Gerald Mallory** ('Lay It Down On Me', 1982), **Active Force** ('Give Me Your Love', 1983), **Sherrick** ('Just Call', 1987) and **Smokey Robinson**. His wife is Linda Stokes, a member of the group **Magic Lady** for whom Michael has produced their three albums.

STONE
(Studio Group)
From New York, Auvil Gilchrist, Daniel Terry, Roland Nembhard and Don Howard recorded as Stone for West End Records during the early '80s. On UK dancefloors they created interest with their singles 'Time' (1981) and 'Girl I Like The Way That You Move' (1982).

STONE CITY BAND
(Group)
The Stone City Band were a conglomerate of musicians instigated by **Rick James** for use on his own albums and tours. Rick wrote and produced songs for their two Gordy (via Motown) albums, *In 'N' Out* (1980) and *Out From The Shadow* (1983), including 'Bad Lady' and 'Ladies Choice'.

STONE, HENRY
(Industry)
Based in Miami during the '70s, Henry worked at Alston Records (via Atlantic) signing artists including **Beginning**

Of The End and **Clarence Reid** before forming his own TK label which worked with numerous artists on the disco scene including **Anita Ward**, **T-Connection**, **The Controllers**, **Foxy** and at one point **James Brown**.

STONE, SLY

(Singer/Songwriter/Producer)

Born Sylvester Stewart in Dallas, Texas, in 1944, Sly made his recording debut as a child prodigy at the age of four on 'On My Battlefield For My Lord'. In high school he sang with The Viscannes on 'Yellow Moon', following which he settled in San Francisco and became a disc jockey.

By the mid-'60s Sly had moved into production and worked on songs for **Bobby Freeman** including 'C'Mon And Swim', 'S-W-I-M' and 'The Duck'. He also formed a group The Stoners who in 1966 were signed by CBS and became **Sly & The Family Stone** (which included his sister **Rose Banks**).

An inventive blend of rock and soul, Sly & The Family Stone made their debut in 1968 with 'Dance To The Music' (UK Top 10), follow-ups including 'M'Lady' (UK Top 40, 1968), 'Everyday People' (UK Top 40, 1969), 'Stand' (1969) (all singles via Direction Records in the UK thus far), 'Family Affair' (UK Top 20, 1972) and 'Runnin' Away' (UK Top 20, 1972).

His albums included *Dance To The Music*, *Stand*, including 'I Want To Take You Higher', *There's A Riot Going On*, *Fresh*, *Smalltalk* and *Ten Years Too Soon*, before he signed with A&M Records where his recordings included the single 'Echobostic Automatic (Tell Me Where The Funk You Been)' (1986). More recently he has been working on new songs with **Jerry Goldstein** for release in 1992 on the Avenue label.

STORY, BOBBY

(Singer/Songwriter/Producer)

Born in Dallas, Texas, Bobby Patterson wrote songs and recorded as Bobby Story on his one album for the Proud label *Bobby Story* (1982), including 'Let's Do Something Different'.

STRANGERS

(Group)

Based in New York, The Strangers recorded for Salsoul Records in the early '80s and are best remembered for 'Step Out Of My Dream', taken from *The Strangers* (1983).

STRICK, BILLY

(Singer)

From Newark, New Jersey, Billy was given a break in 1988 by **Darryl Payne**, who produced his debut release 'Can You Love Me'.

STRIKERS

(Group)

New York-based group The Strikers were **Milton 'Boe' Brown** (drums/vocals), Willie 'Skip' Slaughter (bass/vocals), Robert Gilliom (guitar/vocals), Howie Young (keyboards/vocals), Robert Rodriguez (guitar/vocals), Ruben Faison (lead vocals) and Darryl Gibbs (sax/vocals). In 1981 they signed with Prelude Records where their debut single 'Body Music' (Top 50) became one of the big UK floor-fillers of the early '80s. Their follow-up 'Inch By Inch' was equally popular (without charting), both songs coming from *The Strikers* (1981). In 1982 they returned with a new single 'Contagious'. Milton 'Boe' Brown later became lead vocalist with **Warp 9**.

STRIPLIN, SYLVIA

(Singer)

Based in New York, Sylvia sang with groups including **Aquarian Dream** ('You're A Star', 1978), before **Roy Ayers** signed her to his Uno Melodic label in 1980. Here she sang with **Eighties Ladies** in addition to stirring UK dancefloors with her one solo single 'Give Me Your Love' (via Champagne/DJM, 1980).

STRONG, BARRETT

(Singer/Songwriter)

Born in Mississippi in 1941, Barrett moved to Detroit where he was instrumental in the early success of the Motown label in the '60s. A close friend of **Berry Gordy**, he wrote, played piano and sang on many early singles released by the company. Berry also wrote (with **Janie Bradford**) 'Money' for Barrett to record, a hit later covered by The Beatles.

He is best remembered for his songwriting collaborations at Motown in the late '60s/early '70s with **Norman Whitfield**. These include 'I Heard It Through The Grapevine' and 'Too Busy Thinking About My Baby' (**Marvin Gaye**), 'Just My Imagination', 'Take A Look Around', 'Cloud Nine', 'Ball Of Confusion', 'Papa Was A Rollin' Stone' and 'I Can't Get Next To You' (**The Temptations**), and 'War' (**Edwin Starr**). He also co-wrote 'Take Me In Your Arms And Love Me' (**Gladys Knight & The Pips**).

When Motown settled in Los Angeles in 1972, Barrett withdrew his services and in 1975 he signed to Capitol for an album *Stronghold*. While working on it he met **Billy Always** with whom he wrote songs for both this album and the 1976 follow-up *Live & Love*. The latter album featured the Strong/Always composition 'Man Up In The Sky', a '70s soul classic for Barrett made popular again in the late '80s by **Johnny Bristol**.

In 1981 a single 'Rock It Easy' was a small independent release while more recently he worked with **The Dells** writing and arranging 'You Can Depend On Me' for the group's *The Second Time* (1988).

STUFF

(Group)

Consisting of Cornell Dupree (guitar), Gordon Edwards (bass), Steve Gadd (drums), **Eric Gale** (guitar), Chris Parker (drums) and **Richard Tee** (keyboards), Stuff were top session musicians who came together for a Warner Brothers album *Stuff It* (1979).

STYLISTICS

(Vocal Group)

From Philadelphia, The Stylistics formed in 1968 from the remnants of two local groups, The Monarchs and The Percussions. They met while competing in a talent show at Benjamin Franklin High School. The group were Russell Thomkins (lead vocals), Aaron Love, James Smith, Herbie Murrell and James Dunn (who left in 1980). After two years of playing in local clubs and theatres they recorded their debut single 'You're A Big Girl Now' which became a US Top 10 r&b hit in early 1971. Recording for the Avco label under the guidance of producer **Thom Bell** (and later **Van McCoy**) they scored a run of UK hits: 'Betcha By Golly Wow' (Top 20, 1972), 'I'm Stone In Love With You' (Top 10, 1972), 'Break Up To Make Up' (Top 40, 1973), 'Peek-A-Boo' (Top 40, 1973), 'Rockin' Roll Baby' (Top 10, 1974), 'You Make Me Feel Brand New' (Top 5, 1974), 'Let's Put It All Together' (Top 10, 1974), 'Star On A TV Show' (Top 20, 1975), 'Sing Baby Sing' (Top 5, 1975), 'Can't Give You Anything (But My Love)' (No. 1, 1975), 'Na Na Is The Saddest Word' (Top 5, 1975), 'Funky Weekend' (Top 10, 1976), 'Can't Help Falling In Love' (Top 5, 1976), '16 Bars' (Top 10, 1976), 'You'll Never Get To Heaven' (Top 30, 1976) and '7000 Dollars And You' (Top 30, 1977). Incidentally, the group's American success with 'People Make The World Go Around' prevented **Lenny Williams** from having a hit with the same song and subsequently halted his solo career for a number of years.

From Avco, The Stylistics switched to the Philadelphia International label for three albums, *Hurry Up This Way Again* (1980), *Closer Than Close* (1981), including 'What's Your Name', and *1982* (1982). In 1984 they signed to **Arthur Baker**'s Streetwise label in New York for *Some Things Never Change*. Released in the UK by Virgin it featured a single 'Love Is Not The Answer' written and produced by **Maurice Starr** and Michael Jonzun. Streetwise also released *A Special Style* (1986).

SUGARFOOT

(Singer/Songwriter/Guitar)

Born in Hamilton, Ohio, Sugarfoot was the eldest of fourteen children and in 1968 formed a group as a means of earning much-needed money for his less than wealthy family. This group which he wrote, sang and played guitar for became the internationally famed **The Ohio Players**. After the group disbanded in 1977, Sugarfoot became highly in demand as a session guitarist, working with **Ray Charles**, **Gladys Knight** and **Earth Wind & Fire**. Throughout his career he had also been friends with **Roger Troutman** of **Zapp**, and Roger offered Sugarfoot the use of his studio to experiment on a solo album.

The project included former members of The Ohio Players and was produced by Roger Troutman who took the project to Warner Brothers. In 1985 *Sugar Kiss* was released by the label.

SUGARHILL GANG

(Vocal Group)

From New Jersey, The Sugarhill Gang were Master Gee, Wonder Mike and Big Bang Hank. One of the first exponents of rap music, they scored a UK Top 5 hit single in 1979 with 'Rappers Delight', which was essentially the rhythm track to 'Good Times' by **Chic** with a wordy rap overlay. In 1982 they reached the UK Top 75 with the more soulful melodic 'The Lover In You', while maintaining their rap style for 'Kick It Live From 9 To 5' (1983).

SUMMER, DONNA

(Singer/Songwriter)

Born in Boston in 1950, Donna was one of six children and grew up in a strict church environment. Leaving the security of home as a teenager she became vocalist for a rock group Crow before moving to New York and auditioning to replace **Melba Moore** in the Broadway production of *Hair*. She missed out on the part, but landed a role in the German production of the show. She settled in Germany and after *Hair* had run its course moved on to further musicals including *Godspell*, *The Me Nobody Knows* and *Porgy And Bess*.

In 1975 she met producers **Giorgio Moroder** and Pete Belotte, and the three worked together on what was to be a controversial record, 'Love To Love You Baby'. Vocally very sexually suggestive, this early disco record was banned by numerous radio stations around the world, but still became a huge hit for her in 1976 (UK Top 5). By now she was signed to GTO Records (via CBS) for whom the hits continued with 'Could It Be Magic' (1976), 'Winter Melody' (1976), 'I Feel Love' (a UK No. 1 platinum-selling hit in 1977), 'I Remember Yesterday' (1977) and 'Love's Unkind' (1977).

During 1977 she also recorded for Casablanca, resulting in an unusual situation where both GTO and Casablanca were releasing singles by Donna at the same time. Her first hit for Casablanca was 'Down Deep Inside', which was a hit only four weeks before 'I Remember Yesterday' on GTO, and four weeks after 'I Feel Love' on GTO. She remained with Casablanca exclusively from 1978–80, scoring further hit singles including 'Last Dance' (1978), 'Macarthur Park' (1978), 'Bad Girls' (1979), 'No More Tears (Enough Is Enough)' (a duet with Barbra Streisand, 1979), 'On The Radio' (1980) and 'Sunset People' (1980).

Having established herself successfully on the gay-orientated USA disco scene, her fortunes changed when she was alleged to have criticized the gay community over the spread of AIDS. While she has always denied this (and was forgiven in later years), there were widely reported 'mass burning' sessions of all her records, and her name was taboo on the gay scene.

In 1980 she changed labels to Geffen/Warner Brothers, with which she has retained an affiliation to this day. Working in a number of styles, her early hit singles for the label have included 'Love Is In Control (Finger On The Trigger)' (1982), and 'State Of Independence' (produced by **Quincy Jones** in 1982, and remixed in 1990 for further chart success). Also in 1982 Patrick Cowley remixed 'I Feel Love' for Casablanca, taking it to 15 minutes in length (and into the UK Top 25), before Donna began a brief flirtation with the Mercury label for 'She Works Hard For The Money' and 'Unconditional Love' (1983) before returning to the Warner Brothers family in 1984 for *Cats Without Claws*. Also with Warners she reached the UK Top 20 with 'Dinner With Gershwin' (1987), written by **Brenda Russell**. She then teamed up with London hitmakers **Stock/Aitken/Waterman** who began writing and producing for her in 1988. Her success with the trio has included the hit singles 'This Time I Know It's For Real' and 'Love's About To Change My Heart', and an album containing these and others.

While generally regarded as a disco artist, Donna is highly regarded by the industry and music connoisseurs as a finer singer than she is often given credit for.

SUMMERS, BILL
(Percussion)
After studying the piano for ten years at The Detroit Conservatory, Bill found his vocation as a top percussionist after making San Francisco his home. Through playing percussion as a member of **Herbie Hancock**'s group **Headhunters** he was invited to Los Angeles to record with **Quincy Jones** on the soundtrack to the TV series *Roots*. In 1977 he signed to the Prestige label as an artist and released a debut album *Feel The Heat*, produced by **Skip Scarbrough**. It featured guest performances by Mikki Morris, **Diane Reeves** and **Pete Escovedo** (father of **Sheila E**). On the UK dance/jazz funk scene Bill made an impact in 1978 with a single 'Straight To The Bank', followed by a further single 'Feel The Heat' (1979 – not featured on the 1977 album of the same name).

In addition to recording with **Johnny Hammond**, **Patrice Rushen** and **Carl Anderson**, Bill was also first to discover **Pebbles**, whom he signed to his production company and featured on his own albums seven years before Pebbles began a successful solo career with MCA.

SUN
(Group)
Formed in Ohio during the mid-'70s, Sun recorded a number of funk albums for Capitol before founder members **Shawn Sandridge** (lead vocals/guitar) and Chris Jones (lead vocals/keyboards/trumpet) left to form a new group **Dayton**. In 1985 an amended line-up recorded 'Legs' for the Air City label.

SUNFIRE
(Group)
Based in New York, Sunfire were Kevin Moore (guitar), Michael King (keyboards), Scott Lipsker (bass), **Bruce Fisher** (guitar), Holden Raphael (percussion) and Jeff Holman (drums). They are best remembered for 'Step In The Light', written by **Brian Jackson**, produced by **Mtume/Lucas** and released by Warner Brothers in 1982. The group also provided the instrumentation for the **Leon Ware** album *Inside Is Love* (1979).

SUNRISE
(Group)
New York group Sunrise featured the lead vocals of Ronnie Scruggs and recorded *Sunrise* for the Broadwalk label in 1982. It was arranged and produced by **The Isley Brothers**.

SUPREMES
(Vocal Group)
The Supremes story begins when **Mary Wilson** and Florence Ballard met at a junior high school talent contest in Detroit in 1959. They decided they wanted to form The Primettes, inspired by a male vocal group The Primes (who later became **The Temptations**), who liked the idea of a sister group. Mary and Florence became The Primettes along with neighbourhood friend **Diana Ross** (who became lead singer) and Betty Travis, an older girl who soon left the group. Determined to get a record deal they auditioned for Motown, but were told they were too young. The average age of the girls was fourteen!

Diana's neighbour (by four or five doors) was **Smokey Robinson** whose group **The Miracles** she overheard rehearsing in the basement. Smokey was impressed by The Primettes and set up a second audition with Motown. This time they were employed as backing singers, and Betty was replaced by Barbara Martin. Eventually they were signed to the label on the condition they change their name. Florence came up with 'The Supremes' while Barbara left the group as her mother wanted her to get a proper job! In 1963 they scored a local hit with 'When The Lovelight Starts Shining Through His Eyes', and a debut album *Meet The Supremes* featured follow-up singles which hadn't done so well.

In 1964 their fortunes changed upon teaming up with writers/producers **Holland/Dozier/Holland**. Their first collaboration was 'Where Did Our Love Go' which was an American No.1 and UK Top 5 single. An album of the same name featured 'Baby Love' (UK No.1) and 'Come See About Me' (Top 30) prior to a string of Motown single hits through to 1969. In the UK these included 'Stop! In The Name Of Love' (Top 10, 1965), 'Back In My Arms Again' (Top 40, 1965), 'I Hear A Symphony' (Top 50, 1965), 'You Can't Hurry Love' (Top 5, 1966), 'You Keep

Me Hangin' On' (Top 10, 1966), 'Love Is Here And Now You're Gone' (Top 20, 1967), 'The Happening' (Top 10, 1967), 'Reflections' (Top 5, 1967), 'In And Out Of Love' (Top 20, 1967), 'Forever Came Today' (Top 30, 1968), 'Some Things You Never Get Used To' (Top 40, 1968), 'Love Child' (Top 20, 1968), 'I'm Living In Shame' (Top 20, 1969), 'No Matter What Sign You Are' (Top 40, 1969) and 'Someday We'll Be Together' (Top 20, 1969).

In 1967 Florence Ballard had been replaced by **Cindy Birdsong** following a rift between Florence and Motown over special attention **Diana Ross** was getting (Florence died in 1976). From August 1967 the group had become known as Diana Ross & The Supremes, although in 1969 (following 'Someday We'll Be Together') Diana left to launch her solo career.

Jean Terrell joined the group as lead singer, replacing Diana, and The Supremes continued their run of hits which (in the UK) included 'Up The Ladder To The Roof' (Top 10, 1970), 'Stoned Love' (Top 5, 1971), 'Nathan Jones' (Top 5, 1971), 'Floy Joy' (Top 10, 1972), 'Automatically Sunshine' (Top 10, 1972) and 'Bad Weather' (Top 40, 1973).

There were further changes in the group when Jean left to be replaced by **Scherrie Payne**, and **Susaye Greene** replaced **Cindy Birdsong**. With this new line-up two albums, *High Energy* (including 'I'm Gonna Let My Heart Do The Walking') and *Mary, Scherrie & Susaye* (including 'You Are The Heart Of Me' and 'You're My Driving Wheel') were released in 1976. Lynda Laurence also spent some time with the group before Motown put a lid on The Supremes in 1977. At this point Mary Wilson entered into a legal battle with Motown over who owned the group name The Supremes. The matter has not been resolved to this day.

In 1986 Jean Terrell, Scherrie Payne and Susaye Greene reunited as F.L.O.S. (Former Ladies Of The Supremes) and recorded 'We're Back', following which Susaye was replaced by Lynda Laurence and the Motorcity label signed the group as Jean, Scherrie & Lynda Of The Supremes. Single releases to date have been 'Crazy 'Bout The Guy' and a re-recording of 'Stoned Love' (1990).

SURE, AL B.
(Singer/Songwriter/Producer)

Born in New York, Al didn't think about a music career while he was growing up. However he did write a number of songs and spent time recording them with his cousin Kyle West. These were entered into various songwriting contests. In 1988 Al won the Sony Innovators Award by one deciding vote from **Quincy Jones** and was plucked from obscurity into the limelight. Signing to Warner Brothers, he delivered his debut album *In Effect Mode*, from which 'Nite And Day' was the most successful UK single (Top 50) while 'Off On Your Own' (Top 75) remains the classic.

Through 1989 Al worked with Kyle on a number of outside writing/producing/mixing projects for artists including Rod Stewart and **Tevin Campbell**. Al also joined **El Debarge**, **Barry White** and **James Ingram** as featured vocalist on a single 'The Secret Garden' from the **Quincy Jones** album *Back On The Block*.

A second album *Private Times ... And The Whole 9!* was released in 1990. It included 'Touch You' (which Al refers to as 'The Secret Garden Part 2'), and a duet with **Diana Ross**, 'No Matter What You Do'.

SURFACE
(Group)

New York-based group Surface are **David 'Pic' Conley** (sax), David Townsend (guitar) and Bernard Jackson (lead vocals). In the early '80s they signed with Salsoul Records and scored with 'Falling In Love' (UK Top 75, 1983) and 'When Your Ex Wants You Back' (UK Top 75, 1984) before switching to CBS. Here they established themselves on the 'quiet storm' scene with *Surface* (1986), including 'Happy' (UK Top 75); *2nd Wave* (1988), including 'I Missed', 'Hold On To Love' (featuring **Regina Belle**) and 'You Are My Everything'; and *3 Deep* (1990).

SURFACE NOISE
(Group)

From London, Surface Noise was the brainchild of songwriter/producer Chris Palmer in 1980. Chris's mother founded Groove Records record shop in Greek Street, Soho, while brother Tim Palmer runs the dance label City Beat Records. Surface Noise appealed to the 'Brit funk' scene with 'The Scratch' (UK Top 30, 1980) and 'Dancin' On A Wire' (UK Top 60, 1980) on Chris's own Groove Productions label.

Chris later produced albums for **Morrissey Mullen** and **Linda Taylor** before starting a computer software company for the music industry, Musicalc Systems Ltd.

SURRETT, ALFONZO
(Singer)

This Chicago vocalist recorded one album *Comin' Out* for MCA in 1980, featuring 'Gimme Your Love', popular on the UK soul scene. As a backing singer Alfonzo also recorded with **Leroy Hutson** (*Feel The Spirit* and *Closer To The Source*) and **Aretha Franklin** (*Almighty Fire*).

SUTTON, MIKE & BRENDA
(Singers/Songwriters)

From Los Angeles, the husband and wife team of Mike and Brenda Sutton first worked together as staff writers and singers for the Motown label in the early '70s. During this time they wrote for **Michael Jackson**, **Jermaine Jackson** ('Stay With Me'), **Three Ounces Of Love** and **Thelma** (Houston) **& Jerry** (Butler). While at Motown Brenda sang backgrounds on 'Don't Leave Me This Way' for **Thelma Houston**, while both Mike and Brenda wrote and performed as part of the group **Finished Touch** in 1979.

Away from Motown they wrote and/or produced for **The Detroit Spinners**, Anita **Pointer** ('Overnight Success'), **Cheryl Lynn** ('Shake It Up Tonight') and **Jr Tucker** ('Treat Me Right'). As artists in their own right they wrote and produced 'We'll Make It' (1981) for Sam Records (via Virgin in the UK), followed up by 'Don't Let Go Of Me' (1982), again on Sam (via Silvertown in the UK). They later released an album *So Good* for the Rocshire label as The Suttons (1984).

More recently they recorded 'No Other Love' for the UK Motorcity label, once again as Mike & Brenda Sutton.

SWANN, BETTYE

(Singer/Songwriter)

Born Betty Jean Champion in Shreveport, Louisiana, in 1944, Betty began her recording career in her teens after moving to Los Angeles. Here she joined a group The Fawns before making her solo debut with 'Don't Wait Too Long' on the Money label (1964). In 1965 she scored an American Top 10 hit with 'Make Me Yours' before she switched to Capitol in 1968. Here her albums included *Don't Touch Me* and *Don't You Ever Get Tired (Of Hurting Me)*, including 'Today I Started Loving You Again'. By this time she had become established as queen of the deep soul ballad.

In the UK 'Make Me Yours' is her most fondly remembered recording on the soul scene, originally appearing on the Mojo label before CBS re-released it in 1967. Bettye also recorded a number of duets with **Sam Dees** for the Big Tree label.

SWEAT, KEITH

(Singer/Songwriter/Producer)

New York singer Keith Sweat played an integral role in the group **G.Q.** before signing to the Vintertainment label (via Warner Brothers) in 1987. Here he worked with **Teddy Riley** on a debut album *Make It Last Forever* (1988), including 'I Want Her' (UK Top 30), 'Something Just Ain't Right' (UK Top 75) and 'Don't Stop Your Love'. His follow-up was the self-produced *I'll Give All My Love To You* (1990), including 'Make You Sweat', while elsewhere he has worked as a writer and/or producer with artists including **Roberta Gilliam** ('All I Want Is My Baby', 1985) and **Omar Chandler** ('Giving You Every Drop').

SWEET INSPIRATIONS

(Vocal Group)

The Sweet Inspirations featured the lead vocals of **Cissy Houston**, mother of **Whitney Houston**. As backing singers they recorded frequently with **Dionne Warwick** and **Aretha Franklin** (among others) during the '60s as well as making an impact as a group with their release 'Sweet Inspirations'.

SWEET TALKS

(Group)

Four young ladies from Los Angeles assembled as Sweet Talks for one self-titled album for Mercury in 1979 (which included the popular dance track 'Do The Beat'). It was produced by **McKinley Jackson** for **Wayne Henderson**'s At Home Productions.

SWEET THUNDER

(Group)

From Philadelphia, Sweet Thunder were formed in 1975 by **Booker T. Newberry III** (keyboards/lead vocals), and further consisted of John Aaron (drums/vocals), Rudell Alexander (bass/vocals) and Charles Buie (guitar/lead vocals). In 1976 the group recorded their debut album *Above The Clouds* (produced by **Ron Kersey**), but their golden moment came in 1978 when 'Everybody's Singin' Love Songs' (produced by **Larry James**) became an anthem on the UK soul scene, though it was not released here as a single. The song came from the group's WMOT/Fantasy album *Sweet Thunder*, following which Booker Newberry took on a solo career.

SWEETHEARTS

(Vocal Group)

From Philadelphia, The Sweethearts were top female session singers Carla Benson and Yvette Benton, and **Barbara Ingram**. The trio toured briefly as Flower And The Sweethearts, and in 1985 recorded 'You're Wearing Me Out' for the Society Hill label. It was produced by James Ingram of the **Ingram** family.

SWITCH

(Group)

From Ohio, Switch were originally **Philip Ingram** (vocals), Jody Sims (drums), Gregory Williams (keyboards/vocals), Eddie Fluellen (keyboards/trombone/vocals), with brothers Bobby and Tommy Debarge. Part of the group were formerly known as White Heat, and released an album produced by **Barry White**. They later became First Class before they met **Jermaine Jackson** and were taken to Motown to become Switch. Under the wing of Jermaine they recorded five Motown albums, and between 1978 and 1980 scored US Top 10 singles with 'There'll Never Be', 'I Call Your Name' and 'Love Over And Over Again'.

In 1980 **Philip Ingram** left to pursue solo activities while Bobby and Tommy joined other members of their family to form **Debarge**. Their replacements were Renard Gallo (percussion/vocals), Gonzales Ozen (percussion/vocals) and **Attala Zane Giles** (keyboards). In 1984 the group switched to The Total Experience for an album *Am I Still Your Boyfriend*, which won UK soul scene recognition for a track 'Keeping Secrets' (UK Top 50). Drummer Jody Sims also gave the group **Legacy** a break by getting Switch to record one of their songs 'Spend My Life' for the album.

SYBIL

(Singer)

From New Jersey, Sybil initially gained recognition by working with **Ce Ce Rogers** in a group called Ce Ce & Company. The group were based at a New Jersey nightclub before Sybil secured a solo recording deal with Next Plateau Records in 1986.

Licensed by Champion Records in the UK dancefloor and chart success came with 'Falling In Love' (Top 70, 1986), 'Let Yourself Go' (Top 40, 1987) and 'My Love Is Guaranteed' (Top 50, 1987), and the international hit 'Don't Make Me Over' (1989), a remake of the **Bacharach/David** song originally recorded by **Dionne Warwick**. In 1990 Sybil signed with PWL Records in the UK, working with **Stock/Aitken/Waterman** on 'Make It Easy On Me'.

SYLVERS

(Group)

The Sylvers were family group Leon Frank III, Olympia-Ann, Charmaine, Jonathan, Edmund, Ricky, Angie, Pat and Foster, who initially recorded for the Pride label in the early '70s. **Jerry Butler** produced their debut album *The Sylvers* in 1972. Switching to Capitol, their hits included 'Any Way You Want Me' (1977), but while the teen group were popular in the USA they had no impact in the UK. In 1981 the group signed with Solar Records, where **Leon Sylvers** wrote and produced the group's *Concept* before going onto greater things as an in-house writer/producer.

In the meantime Edmund Sylvers penned and produced 'In Motion' for **Freda Payne**, and **Foster Sylvers** enjoyed some solo success. They also released a single 'Out One Love And In The Other' and an album *Bizarre* for the Geffen label in 1984.

SYLVERS, FOSTER

(Singer/Producer)

Foster Sylvers was a lead singer with his family group **The Sylvers** in the early '70s. His brother is **Leon Sylvers III** who wrote and produced 'Misdemeanor', a solo release for Foster in 1973 (on MGM) regarded in the mid-'80s as a 'rare groove'. In 1984, in conjunction with Jerry Weaver, he co-produced a number of songs on the debut solo album by **Janet Jackson** *Dream Street*. He then formed a group Foster Sylvers & Hy Tech, releasing *Flavour* (EMI America, 1987).

SYLVERS III, LEON

(Songwriter/Producer)

Leon began his career with his family group **The Sylvers**, his early songs including 'Misdemeanor' for brother **Foster Sylvers** in 1973. From here he became an integral part of the Los Angeles dance music scene, his production epitomizing the 'Solar' sound at Solar Records (Sound Of Los Angeles Records). With label boss Dick Griffey he instigated groups like **Dynasty** (producing 'I Don't Want To Be A Freak') and wrote/produced for label mates **Shalamar** ('Take That To The Bank', 'Second Time Around' and 'Night To Remember') and **The Whispers** ('And The Beat Goes On' and 'Tonight').

Elsewhere he wrote and/or produced for artists including **Gladys Knight & The Pips** ('Save The Overtime For Me'), **Evelyn 'Champagne' King** ('Hold On To What You've Got'), **Stacy Lattisaw** ('You Ain't Leavin''), **The Detroit Spinners** ('Right Or Wrong'), **Gina Foster** ('Love Is A House'), **The Brothers Johnson** ('You Keep Me Coming Back'), **Krystol** ('After The Dance Is Through'), **Glenn Jones** (*Finesse*), **Howard Hewett**, **Gene Page** ('Love Starts After Dark') and **Real To Reel** ('Love Me Like This'), among many others.

As an artist he also recorded a solo album *Leon Sylvers III* (Motown, 1989).

SYLVESTER

(Singer/Songwriter)

Born in Los Angeles in 1946, Sylvester established himself as a child gospel star before he moved to San Francisco and fronted The Cockettes. Here he cross-dressed and sang vocal jazz classics, eventually taking the group and this unusual show to New York. The group became Sylvester & The Hot Band, and while touring with **Billy Preston**, he met **Martha Wash** and Izora Rhodes who became his backing singers **Two Tons of Fun**. By now Sylvester had recorded a debut album *Lights Out San Francisco*, released by Blue Thumb (via ABC) in 1973.

In 1977 he switched labels to Fantasy for *Sylvester* (including 'Over And Over' written by **Ashford & Simpson**), produced by **Harvey Fuqua**. This was just prior to his major assault on the disco scene with the high energy anthem 'You Make Me Feel (Mighty Real)', a UK Top 10 single in 1978. This classic dance record came from *Step Two*, which also included the UK Top 30 follow-up 'Dance Disco Heat'. UK hit singles on Fantasy continued with 'I (Who Have Nothing)' (Top 50, 1979) and 'Stars' (Top 50, 1979), prior to 1981's *Too Hot To Sleep*, which showcased a mellower side to his music. Included was a duet with **Jeanie Tracy** 'Here Is My Love' which remains a popular soul track. His other Fantasy albums were *Mighty Real*, *Living Proof* and *Sell My Soul*. During this time Sylvester also wrote and worked closely with **Two Tons Of Fun** (later to become **The Weather Girls**) on their own Fantasy recordings.

In 1982 Sylvester switched to the Megatone label (via London in the UK) for a duet with Patrick Cowley 'Do You Wanna Funk' which reached the UK Top 40. The next year 'Band Of Gold' reached the UK Top 75, to be followed by 'Don't Stop'. 1984's *M 1015* was released by Chrysalis/Cooltempo in the UK and featured a single 'Rock The Box'. While in the UK he teamed up with Earlene Bentley for a duet 'Stargazing', released by Record Shack. His vocal on this duet was later utilized on a single release 'Your Love Is Amazing' (1991), after his death from AIDS. In the meantime *Mutual Attraction* had been released by Warner Brothers (1986).

SYREETA
(Singer/Songwriter)
Born in Detroit, Syreeta Wright began her career as Rita Wright after being told that her real name was too awkward. In 1967 she signed with Motown and recorded 'I Can't Give Back The Love I Feel For You' under that name, but the hits didn't start to roll until she changed her name back to Syreeta.

In 1970 she married **Stevie Wonder**, and although they only lived together for eight months, they worked together through the first half of the '70s and remain friends to this day. Syreeta was also coached as a songwriter by Stevie who had hits with their songs 'Signed, Sealed, Delivered I'm Yours' (UK Top 20, 1970) and 'If You Really Love Me' (UK Top 20, 1972) before he produced her hits 'Spinning & Spinning' (UK Top 50, 1974), 'Your Kiss Is Sweet' (UK Top 20, 1975) and 'I'm Going Left'.

Another hit song Syreeta and Stevie had co-written was 'It's A Shame' for **The Detroit Spinners** (UK Top 20, 1970), whose lead singer (**G.C.Cameron**) Syreeta teamed up with for a duet album *Rich Love, Poor Love* in 1977. From here she had a couple of American solo hits ('Love Fire' and 'Quick Slick') before teaming up with **Billy Preston** for 'With You I'm Born Again' (UK No. 2) in 1979. Their follow-up was 'It Will Come In Time' (UK Top 50, 1980). Her next solo albums were *Set My Love In Motion* (1981), including 'I Must Be In Love', and *The Spell* (1983), including 'Forever Is Not Enough', before she was a guest vocalist on 'The Glow' for **Willie Hutch** (from the movie *The Last Dragon*).

Today she lives in Los Angeles, her current recordings being for the Motorcity label. In 1989 she re-recorded 'With You I'm Born Again' followed by a number of new songs including the UK single 'If The Shoe Fits' and a duet with **Billy Preston** 'Watching The Hands Of Time' (1990).

Outside of Motown she has written and/or recorded with **George Duke**, **Gary Bartz**, **Patrice Rushen**, **Jeffrey Osborne**, **Wayne Henderson**, **Donald Byrd** (lead vocal on 'Sunning In Your Loveshine'), **Sheree Brown** (co-writing 'Everything You Do'), **The Stairsteps** (co-writing 'Time'), **Quincy Jones** (*The Dude* and *Back On The Block*), and **George Howard** (lead vocal on 'Fakin' The Feelin'').

SYSTEM
(Group)
The System's two members Mic Murphy and David Frank first met while working with the group **Kleeer**. Here they discovered a mutual interest in what they called 'emotio electro', the fusion of soul music with technology. While still with Kleeer they formed The System and wrote/produced their debut single 'It's Passion'. When they heard it on the radio of Kleeer's tour bus it provided the encouragement to leave and concentrate on The System full-time. At this point (1981) they also formed their own company, Science Lab Productions.

In 1982, after a brief spell under the pseudonym Sass for the 25 West label, they signed to Mirage (via Polydor) and a single 'You Are In My System' established them on US/UK dancefloors. The song came from a debut album *Sweat* released in 1983.

In between this and their second album *I Wanna Make You Feel Good* (1984) the group embarked on a number of writing and/or production projects for other artists including **Howard Johnson** (*Doin' It My Way*) and Attitude. After their second album they continued with artists including **Jeff Lorber** ('Step By Step'), **Angela Bofill** (*Let Me Be The One*), **Evelyn 'Champagne' King** ('I'm So Romantic' and 'So In Love'), **Chaka Khan** ('This Is My Night'), **Pauli Carmen** ('Dial My Number') and the UK's Person To Person, a group fronted by ABC's former drummer David Palmer.

Their other Mirage albums (now via Atlantic) are *The Pleasure Seekers* (1985), including 'This Is For You', *Don't Disturb This Groove* (1987) and *Rhythm And Romance* (1989).

SZABO, GABOR
(Guitar)
Fusion guitarist Gabor Szabo made an impression on the UK jazz funk scene with two albums recorded for Mercury Records in the mid-'70s. These were *Nightflight* (1976), including 'Keep Smilin'' produced by **Bunny Sigler**, and *Faces* (1977), produced by **Wayne Henderson**.

T

T-CONNECTION

(Group)

Formed by T-Coakley (vocals/keyboards/guitar/percussion), T-Connection's further members were brother Kirkwood Coakley (bass/drums/percussion), Anthony Flowers (drums/percussion) and David Mackey (guitar). T-Coakley commenced his music career in 1965 playing maracas in a calypso band in the Bahama Islands. In 1975 he left to form T-Connection which fast became the most popular group in the Grand Bahamas. A year later they went to Miami and signed to TK Records. Here their debut album *Magic* featured 'Do What You Wanna Do' (UK Top 20, 1977), one of the first records to be released in 12" single format and a classic record of the disco era.

Follow-up UK singles were 'On Fire' (Top 20) and 'Let Yourself Go' (Top 60), prior to a 1979 album *T-Connection* and further Top 75 UK hits 'At Midnight' and 'Saturday Night'. *Totally Connected* (1980) followed before the group switched to Capitol. Here they released *Everything Is Cool* (1981), *Pure & Natural* (1982), *The Game Of Life* (1983) and *Take It To The Limit* (1984).

T.H.P.

(Group)

T.H.P. were a New York disco group/orchestra featuring Joyce Cobb (vocals), Brian Russell (guitar), Michael Toles (guitar), Carl Marsh (keyboards), Errol Thomas (bass), Barry Keane (drums), Dick Smith (percussion) and assorted horn and string players. Recordings include *Good To Me* (Atlantic, 1977).

T.H.S. (THE HORNE SECTION)

(Duo)

T.H.S. were Henry Horne (multi-instrumentalist) and Roger Garnett (vocals) from Philadelphia. Henry began writing songs in 1978 and worked on the session circuit (with **F.L.B.** and **Captain Sky**) before working with Roger in 1984. Through 4th & Broadway, T.H.S. had one release, 'Lady Shine', which hit the UK Top 60 in 1984.

T. LIFE

(Singer/Songwriter/Producer)

From Philadelphia, T. Life put together a group **Spiritual Concept** in the '70s prior to becoming a freelance writer and producer with groups including **Instant Funk** (co-writing 'Philly Jump'). While working in Sigma Sound Studios he discovered **Evelyn 'Champagne' King** whose debut hit 'Shame' he produced in 1978. He also wrote and produced 'Kiss You All Over' for **Phyllis Hyman**.

In 1981 he signed as an artist to Arista and scored some dancefloor success with 'Something That You Do To Me (Keeps Turning Me On)'.

T.S. MONK

(Group)

Formed in the late '70s, T.S.Monk were **Thelonius Monk III**, Boo Monk and Yvonne Fletcher. Thelonius and Yvonne had previously been in a group **Natural Essence**. Signing to Mirage (via WEA) in 1980, the group released *House Of Music*. 'Bon Bon Vie' was a US Top 40 hit, while in the UK 'Candidate For Love' was a dance anthem. The follow-up was 'More Of The Good Life', after which they teamed up with producer **Eric Mercury** for 1982's *Human*. Tragically both Boo and Yvonne passed away in 1983, leaving Thelonius and Eric to team together as **Merc and Monk**.

TA MARA & THE SEEN

(Group)

Born in Morocco, Ta Mara (real name Margaret) is the daughter of a baroque music singer. When she was five her family moved to Minneapolis, and it was here she later began performing in clubs before meeting **Jesse Johnson** from **The Time**. Through Jesse, Ta Mara and her group The Seen were introduced to A&M Records in Los Angeles, and Jesse produced her debut album *Blueberry Gossip* in 1988. In the USA singles 'Everybody Dance' and 'Affection' were successful in the charts, while UK soul fans were also impressed by a soul ballad 'True Ecstasy'.

TAFURI

(Singer)

Born to Italian parents in New York, Tafuri spent three years auditioning for bands in Manhattan prior to working on some demos with the group Vertical Hold. Sleeping Bag Records signed her in 1988 and a debut soul/dance single 'What Am I Gonna Do' was released in 1990.

TAMS

(Vocal Group)

From Atlanta, Georgia, The Tams were Charles Pope, Joseph Pope, Robert Lee Smith, Floyd Ashton and Horace Kay. After singing together on their local club scene they recorded a debut single 'Untie Me' for the Arlen label in 1962.

Albert Cottle replaced Floyd Ashton when the group signed with ABC, following which they scored '60s American hits, 'What Kind Of Fool (Do You Think I Am)' and 'You Lied To Your Daddy', and '70s UK hits 'Be Young Be Foolish Be Happy' (Top 40, 1970), and 'Hey Girl Don't Bother Me' (No. 1, 1971). On the '80s 'beach music' revival scene, the group scored a UK Top 30 hit with 'There Ain't Nothing Like Shaggin'' (1983) ('shag' being the name of a dance).

TAPESTRY

(Group)

From Philadelphia, Tapestry signed to Capitol and worked with producer **Norman Harris** on 'It's Not The World That's Messed Up'.

TASHAN

(Singer/Songwriter/Producer)

Born in New York in 1963, the musical roots of Tashan (pronounced Tay-Shon) Rasheed are in hip hop and rap. In 1983 he made his professional debut by writing and producing 'Yours For A Night' for rap ensemble Whodini. Developing as a singer, he landed himself a recording deal with Def Jam Records (via CBS) in 1985 and set to work on *Chasing A Dream*, released in 1986. Among his own solo recordings, the album included two duets, 'You've Got The Right Attitude' and 'Love Is', with **Alyson Williams**. Tashan teamed up with Alyson again for the duet 'Do You Wanna Know' on *On The Horizon* (1989), following which the two singers toured the UK together. This second album also featured 'I'm A Black Man' and 'Keep Movin' On', the latter of which was remixed in the UK (1990) to good reactions.

TATE, HOWARD

(Singer)

Born in Macon, Georgia, Howard moved with his family to Philadelphia by the time he was seven. Here he sang gospel and joined a local group **The Gainors**. In 1966 he signed to the Verve label and released a debut album *Get It While You Can* the following year. It included the American hit 'Ain't Nobody Home', written by **Ragovoy** who also wrote his follow-up singles including 'Look At Granny Run Run' (1966), 'Half A Man' (1967) and 'Stop' (1968). He later signed to Atlantic.

TATE, TOMMY

(Singer)

Born in Homestead, Florida, in 1944, Tommy recorded his debut for the Rise label (1964), prior to releases over the next six years with Okeh, Verve and Big Ten. In 1970 he joined Stax group The Nightingales, though in 1972 resumed his solo career with 'School Of Life' released by the Koho label. The song was an American Top 30 hit. His follow-ups weren't so successful, and after moving to Jackson, Mississippi, he worked on the local club scene. In 1980 he recorded 'If I Gave You My Heart' and 'What Gives You The Right' for Sundance Records, released in the UK on the Move label.

TAVARES

(Group)

The Tavares brothers Ralph, Arthur, Antone, Feliciano and Perry were the sons of a Massachusetts musician, and originally performed together as the Del Rios. By the mid-'60s they turned professional and changed their name to Chubby and The Turnpikes before becoming Tavares while on a European tour.

In 1973 the group signed with Capitol and worked with producer **Johnny Bristol** for their debut single 'Check It Out', an American r&b hit from an album of the same name. In the UK the group had a run of dance/disco hits with 'It Only Takes A Minute' (1975), 'Heaven Must Be Missing An Angel' (Top 5, 1976), 'Don't Take Away The Music' (Top 5, 1976), 'Mighty Power Of Love' (Top 25, 1977), 'Whodunit' (Top 5, 1977), 'One Step Away' (Top 20, 1977), 'The Ghost Of Love' (Top 30, 1978), and 'More Than A Woman' from the *Saturday Night Fever* soundtrack (Top 10, 1978). Their albums during this era were *Sky High* (1976), *Love Storm* (1977), *Future Bound* (1978) and *Madam Butterfly* (1979), including 'Never Had A Love Like This Before', but not the popular B side instrumental on the single.

In 1983 Tavares signed with RCA for a single 'Deeper In Love' and album *Words And Music*, but it was when Ben Liebrand remixed 'Heaven Must Be Missing An Angel' that the group were back in the UK Top 20 (1985).

TAYLOR, BOBBY

(Singer/Songwriter/Producer)

Initially a solo nightclub performer, Canadian singer Bobby Taylor formed a group The Vancouvers with Tommy Chong (of Cheech & Chong) while working in San Francisco. Performing in Vancouver, Bobby Taylor & The Vancouvers were spotted by **Mary Wilson** and Florence Ballard of **The Supremes** who flew **Berry Gordy** in the next evening to catch the show live. The group signed to the Motown label in Detroit.

During the mid-'60s the group built up a cult following with their singles including 'Does Your Mother Know About Me', 'Malinda' and 'I Am Your Man'. After one Bobby Taylor & The Vancouvers album on Motown, Bobby recorded two solo albums for the company's subsidiary VIP and Mo-West labels as well as discovering **The Jackson 5**. While performing in Gary, Indiana, Bobby's opening act was The Little Jackson Brothers. Impressed, he took them to Motown where he wrote and produced early Jackson 5 hits 'A.B.C.', 'I Want You Back' and 'The Love You Save'.

Following his departure from Motown he recorded for numerous labels including Epic, Playboy and Philadelphia International (where he recorded with producer **Thom Bell** as BT & TB). He later co-wrote and produced 'I Believe In Miracles' for **The Jackson Sisters** (1976), and wrote 'I Can't Quit Your Love' for **The Four Tops**. Through the late '70s and '80s he pursued an acting career before hooking up with the Nightmare/Motorcity label in the UK as an artist and songwriter. His debut single for the label was 'Do Unto Others' (1989). *Find My Way Back* (with The Vancouvers) was released in 1990.

TAYLOR, BRENDA
(Singer)
Based in New York, Brenda is best remembered for her solo single 'You Can't Have Your Cake And Eat It Too' for West End Records in 1982.

TAYLOR, CREED
(Producer)
Born in Lynchburg, Virginia, in 1929, Creed worked as producer at the Verve label where his work includes Astrud Gilberto's original recording of 'The Girl From Ipanema' in 1967. In 1969 he launched his own CTI label in New Jersey, a label which greatly contributed to the pioneering jazz fusion movement during the '70s. Producing most of the label's releases himself, his artists included **George Benson**, **Esther Phillips**, **Grover Washington**, **Bob James**, **Deodato**, **Hubert Laws**, **Idris Muhammad**, **Hank Crawford**, **Stanley Turrentine** and **Fuse One**.

After the demise of CTI, Creed continued his work as producer, recent projects including *Red On Red* for trumpeter Claudio Roditi.

TAYLOR, DEBBIE
(Singer)
Debbie Taylor first made an impression on the soul scene in 1973 when she recorded 'I Have Learned To Do Without You' in Philadelphia with the strings of **M.F.S.B.** It was released by Polydor, following which she signed to Arista in 1976 for a further single 'Just Don't Pay'/'I Don't Wanna Lose You'. She released just one album, *Love's Coming Down*, for the Today label.

TAYLOR, FELICE
(Singer)
Felice was one of the first singers to be produced by **Barry White** with her hit single 'I Feel Love Coming On' (UK Top 20, 1967). She also recorded the original version of 'It May Be Winter Outside'.

TAYLOR, GARY
(Singer/Songwriter/Producer)
Born in Los Angeles, Gary studied psychology and began a career in supermarket management. He first started writing songs in the late '70s after a friend needed some material for a musical comedy. Finding a good reaction to his work he taught himself keyboards and invested in his own recordings. He had also composed a theme for a local radio programme, and the station got repeated calls asking if they could buy it (the track later became the song 'Tease Me'). In the meantime he witnessed his cousin **Skip Scarbrough** succeed as a songwriter, a further incentive for Gary to make this his new career.

By 1983 his songs had been recorded by **Marlena Shaw** ('Without You In My Life') and **Michael Wycoff** ('On The Line'). Gary recorded the latter song himself upon signing to A&M and releasing an album *G.T.* (1983), also including 'Just What I Have In Mind', 'This Time,' 'Special' and 'Don't Fight It', winning him support on the UK soul scene. He then wrote and/or produced **The Whispers** ('Just Gets Better With Time'), **Anita Baker** ('Good Love'), **Vesta Williams** ('I'm Coming Back'), **Chico Debarge** ('I Like My Body'), **Grover Washington/The Controllers** ('Keep In Touch'), **Carl Anderson** ('Let's Talk'), **Beau Williams** ('Don't Say No' and 'Slave') and **The Dazz Band** ('If Only You Were In My Shoes'), before he switched to Virgin as an artist. Here he released *Compassion* (1988) including 'Tease Me' and 'Love To The Limit'.

His songs and/or productions were utilised by **The Manhattans**, **The Mac Band** and **Lalah Hathaway** before Gary signed to the Expansion label in the UK for *Take Control* (1990) including 'Don't Be So Distant', 'Time After Time', 'Whatever' and 'I Live 4 U'.

TAYLOR, JOHNNIE
(Singer)
Born in Crawford, Arkansas, in 1938, Johnnie's first singing engagement was at church on an Easter Sunday when he was eight years old. From here he sang in various choirs around Memphis and Kansas City before moving to Chicago. Here, aged fourteen, he sang with gospel group The Highway Q.C.s and met **Sam Cooke**. Johnnie later replaced Sam as lead singer with The Soul Stirrers (recording 'Stand By Me Father'), but when Sam formed his Sar label, Johnnie signed as a solo artist and established himself with singles including 'Rome Wasn't Built In A Day' (1963).

In 1966 he signed to Stax and in 1968 collaborated with producer **Don Davis** on his American hits 'Who's Making Love To Your Old Lady' (from 1969's *Who's*

Making Love), 'I Ain't Particular', 'I Believe In You' (1973), 'Cheaper To Keep Her' (1973), 'Testify (I Wanna)', 'Mr Nobody Is Somebody' and 'Somebody's Sleeping In My Bed'. He also recorded a series of duets with **Carla Thomas**. In 1976 he signed to CBS and scored his greatest commercial success that year with 'Disco Lady' (UK Top 25) from *Eargasm*. His other CBS albums included *Rated Extraordinaire* (1977), including 'Your Love Is Rated X', *Ever Ready* and *Super Taylor*.

In 1984 he worked with the Beverly Glen label on 'What About My Love', 'Seconds Of Your Love' (both issued as singles), 'I'm So Proud' and 'Just Ain't Good Enough' (on *Best Of The Old And New*), before signing with Malaco. Here his albums include *This Is Your Night* (1984) and *Wall To Wall* (1985).

TAYLOR, LINDA

(Singer)

Born in the UK, Linda has worked as a top session singer and featured singer with **Gonzales** and **The Street Angels**. In 1981 she guested with **Morrisey Mullen** ('Stay Awhile'), and **Cayenne** ('Roberta Who ...?') before signing with the Groove Productions label. Here she recorded one dance/soul album *Taylor Made* (1982), including 'You And Me Just Started' (via Prelude in America), '(You're) In The Pocket' and 'Do You Know Who I Am?'. She later recorded 'Every Waking Hour' for the Nightmare label.

TAYLOR, LITTLE JOHNNY

(Singer)

Born in Memphis, Little Johnny Taylor (not to be confused with **Johnnie Taylor**) sang with gospel group Mighty Clouds Of Joy before signing to Galaxy Records as a solo artist in 1963. Here he recorded a series of blues-orientated singles before 'Zig Zag Lightning' and 'Big Blue Diamond' in 1966, both popular on the UK 'Northern soul' scene. In 1970 he signed to the Ronn label and scored with 'Everybody Knows About My Good Thing' (1972), while more recently he has recorded for the Atlanta-based Ichiban label.

TAYLOR, TED

(Singer)

Born in Okmulgee, Oklahoma (1938), Ted began his singing career in California where he joined The Cadets. During the early '50s he moved to Los Angeles where he became an original member of the gospel group Mighty Clouds Of Joy. In the late '50s he went solo and made his recording debut for the Ebb label with 'Keep Walking On' (1958). Also at the Ebb label he recorded 'Wrapped Up In A Dream' (1959) before he switched to the Duke label where he is best remembered for 'Be Ever Wonderful' (1960).

From here he recorded for labels Top Rank ('I Need You So' and 'Look Out', in 1961), and Golden Eagle before settling at Okeh Records (via Epic) where his American hits were 'I'll Release You' (1963), 'Stay Away From Me' (1965) and the critically acclaimed '(Love is Like A) Ramblin' Rose' (1965). Recording in Nashville, much of his music appealed to country fans as well as r&b audiences.

He later recorded for labels including Atco, Ronn ('Strangest Feeling', 1968), Alarm (single 'Steal Away', 1976) and MCA.

TEAM

(Group)

The Team were former members of British funk groups **Light Of The World**, **Beggar & Co**, **Incognito** and Onward International. Members were Gee Bello (vocals/percussion), Paul 'Tubbs' Williams (vocals/bass), Mel 'Hothead' Gaynor (drums), David 'Baps' Baptiste (sax/vocals), Breeze (rhythm guitar), Rick Taylor (trombone), Don 'Dish' Doobay (piano) and Paul Spong (trumpet). In 1985 they recorded a medley of **The Fatback Band**'s 'Wicky Wacky' with Fred Wesley's 'Houseparty', released by EMI (UK Top 75).

TEAM WORK

(Group)

Duane Patton, Gary Mackey and Danny McLane recorded as Team Work for **Holland/Dozier/Holland**'s Music Merchant label in 1989. A single release 'Spotlight' was produced by **Edward Holland**.

TEASE

(Group)

From Southern California, Tease were **Kipper Jones** (lead vocals), Derek Organ (drums), Thomas Organ Jr (guitar), Rex Salas (keyboards) and Jay Shanklin (bass). They originally formed in 1979 to try and win a talent show on Los Angeles radio station KACE. This experience led to a record deal with RCA where one album was released before Rex was replaced by **Chuckii Booker**. Switching to Epic, *Tease* (1986) and *Remember* (1988) were released, produced by **James Mtume**.

In 1989 Kipper Jones left the group and signed to Virgin Records as a solo artist.

TEE, RICHARD

(Keyboards/Arranger)

One of New York's top session musicians, Richard established himself during the early '70s. While working with **Aretha Franklin** he met **Eric Gale** with whom he has recorded numerous sessions over the years in addition to their playing together in a group **Stuff**. He used to write a double guitar part for Eric to compensate for the fact he didn't know how to arrange strings!

Richard also worked as a staff arranger at Motown before **Grover Washington** and **Hank Crawford** employed him to work with them at CTI Records. Here he met **Bob James** who signed him to the Tappan Zee label (via CBS) where he recorded solo albums including

Strokin' (1979). Elsewhere his sessions have been with artists including **Roberta Flack**, **Chaka Khan** ('I'm Every Woman'), **Margie Joseph**, **Jennifer Holliday** and **The O'Jays**.

TEMPERTON, ROD

(Songwriter/Keyboards)

This British songwriter began his career as keyboard player with **Heatwave**, also writing their hits including 'Boogie Nights', 'The Groove Line' and 'Always & Forever'. His songwriting skills were soon noticed by **Quincy Jones** who hired him to write for an album he was producing for **Michael Jackson**. Rod ended up writing 'Rock With You', 'Baby Be Mine', 'The Lady In My Life' and the title track of Michael's *Off The Wall* (1979), together with the title song 'Thriller' of his follow-up!

Also through **Quincy Jones** he wrote for **Rufus** ('Masterjam'), **The Brothers Johnson** ('Treasure'), **Donna Summer** ('Love Is In Control (Finger On The Trigger)', 'Livin' In America' and 'Love Is Just A Breath Away') and Quincy himself ('The Dude,' 'Razzamatazz', 'Somethin' Special', 'Turn On The Action', 'The Secret Garden' and 'Back On The Block'). Elsewhere his songs have been recorded by **Herbie Hancock** ('Lite Me Up'), **Aretha Franklin** ('Livin' In The Streets'), **Jeffrey Osborne** ('We Belong To Love', which Rod also produced), **Bob James** ('Sign Of The Times' and 'The Steamin' Feelin'), Manhattan Transfer/**Anita Baker** ('Mystery'), **Michael McDonald** ('Sweet Freedom') and **Stephanie Mills** ('Time Of Your Life' and 'Hold On To Midnight').

Rod also wrote and produced a complete solo album for Karen Carpenter of The Carpenters, but to date none of the songs have been released.

TEMPTATIONS

(Vocal Group)

From Detroit, this group began in the '60s as The Primes before becoming The Elgins (not to be confused with **The Elgins**), The Pirates, The Distants, The Voicemasters and ultimately The Temptations. Original members were Paul Williams, Otis Williams (from Texas), Melvin Franklin (from Montgomery, Alabama), **Eddie Kendricks** and Elbridge Bryant. After signing with Motown they worked with high-school friend **Smokey Robinson** who produced an early regional hit 'I Want A Love I Can See' prior to their American chart debut with 'Dream Come True' in 1962. Two years later they released their first classic 'The Way You Do The Things You Do', another American chart hit.

By 1964 Elbridge Bryant had been replaced by **David Ruffin** who had formerly played drums for the group. Brother **Jimmy Ruffin** was offered the role first, but turned it down, leaving David to take the group on to international stardom with **Smokey Robinson**-penned hits including 'My Girl' (UK Top 50 issued by Stateside, 1965), 'Ain't Too Proud To Beg' (UK Top 25, 1966) and 'Beauty Is Only Skin Deep' (UK Top 20, 1966). Further UK hits followed: '(I Know) I'm Losing You' (Top 20, 1966), 'You're My Everything' (Top 30, 1967) and 'I Wish It Would Rain' (Top 50, 1968), and in the USA, the group had No. 1 r&b hits with 'It's Growing' and 'Since I Lost My Baby'. At this point David wanted the group renamed David Ruffin & The Temptations, much like Diana Ross & The Supremes. This idea didn't go down well with Motown, resulting in his removal from the group. David's replacement was **Dennis Edwards**, who was lead singer on 'Cloud Nine' (UK Top 20), a Grammy award-winning record which was released hot on the heels of their classic 'Get Ready' (UK Top 10, 1969).

In 1969 **Diana Ross & The Supremes** recorded a joint album with The Temptations, *T.C.B.*. The two groups had worked together on a TV special *Taking Care Of Business*, and from this spin-off UK hits flowed with 'I'm Gonna Make You Love Me' (Top 5), 'I Second That Emotion' (Top 20) and 'Why (Must We Fall In Love)' (Top 40). Solo Temptations hits in the UK followed: 'I Can't Get Next To You' (Top 20, 1970), 'Psychedelic Shack' (Top 40, 1970) and 'Ball Of Confusion' (Top 10, 1970).

Now various replacements were made in the group. Paul Williams was forced to quit touring for health reasons and was replaced by Richard Street, a cousin of Melvin Franklin who had previously sung with **The Monitors** and pre-Temps group The Distants. Paul, however, continued to record with the group although he took his own life in 1973. The spotlight was taken over by **Eddie Kendricks** and the group were back in the UK Top 10 with the Grammy award-winning 'Just My Imagination' in 1971. When Eddie left, his replacement for the 1973 *All Directions* was **Damon Harris**. In between times the group scored with 'Superstar' (UK Top 40) and 'Take A Look Around' (UK Top 20).

In 1973 The Temptations scored again with the classic 'Papa Was A Rollin' Stone' (UK Top 20). They were now working with producer **Norman Whitfield** who continued their success with 'Law Of The Land' later that year (UK Top 50), following which (in 1975) Damon Harris left the group to be replaced by Glenn Leonard. They then switched to Atlantic for *Hear To Tempt You* (1977). The majority of the songs were written by Ron Tyson, who joined the group as a full-time singer in 1983. In 1978 the group were still with Atlantic for 'Bare Back', with Louis Price now singing lead.

In 1980 the group were back at Motown for *Power*, before 1981's *The Temptations* included the popular 'Aiming At Your Heart' produced by **Thom Bell**. It was followed in 1982 by *Reunion* and a tour, reuniting **David Ruffin** and **Eddie Kendricks** with the group. The album featured the **Rick James** song/production/performance 'Standing On The Top' (UK Top 60), but a clash of egos on the tour made the reunion itself short-lived. Also in 1982 The Temps teamed up with **Jean Carne** for a rendition of 'If You Don't Know Me By Now' for her Motown album *Trust Me*. In 1983 the group reunited with producer **Norman Whitfield** for *Back To Basics*, but this was not a commercial success. It was 1984's *Truly For You* which put the group back in the UK Top 20 with 'Treat Her Like A Lady'. Lead vocalist with the group now was Ollie Woodson, who stayed in that role for a 1985 album *Touch Me*, which included the **Marcus Miller**-produced, **Luther Vandross**-co-written song 'Do You Really Love Your Baby'.

In between times **Dennis Edwards** had left the group to record two solo albums, but was back as lead singer for the group's album *Together Again* (1987). The album featured 'Look What You Started' which made the UK Top 75 after 'Papa Was A Rollin' Stone' had been remixed by Freddie Bastone and made the UK Top 40. For *Special* (1989), Ollie Woodson was back in the role of lead singer.

Incidentally, former lead vocalists **David Ruffin**, **Eddie Kendricks** and **Dennis Edwards** have regularly performed together as Ruffin, Kendricks & Edwards, while Ruffin and Kendricks recorded an album *Ruffin & Kendricks* for RCA (1987). Also, **Beau Williams** nearly became a Temptation but was turned down as he was too short.

TEN CITY
(Group)

Originally known as **Ragtyme**, Ten City are Byron Stingily (vocals), Herb Lawson (guitar/bass) and Byron Burke (keyboards) from Chicago. Under the direction of arranger/producer **Marshall Jefferson** they signed to Atlantic where they have recorded *Foundation* (1989), including 'Devotion', 'That's The Way Love Is' and 'Right Back To You', and *State Of Mind*, including 'Whatever Makes You Happy', 'Superficial People', 'Destiny' and 'Nothing's Changed'.

TERRELL, DINO
(Singer)

Born in New York, Dino sang lead vocals with **New Horizon** and **Intrigue** ('Fly Girl') from the early to mid-'80s. He also worked as a session singer and recorded one solo release 'You Can Do It (It's So Easy)' just prior to his death in 1985.

TERRELL, JEAN
(Singer)

Based in Los Angeles, Jean originally sang with brother Ernie Terrell in a group Ernie Terrell & The Knockouts before replacing **Diana Ross** as lead singer of **The Supremes** in 1969. Here she sang on a string of hits including 'Up The Ladder To The Roof' (UK Top 10, 1970), 'Stoned Love' (UK Top 5, 1971) and 'Nathan Jones' (UK Top 5, 1971).

In 1976 she recorded briefly for A&M Records as a solo artist, while more recently she has performed and recorded in a group Jean, Scherrie & Lynda Of The Supremes for the UK Motorcity label.

TERRELL, TAMMI
(Singer)

Born Tammi Montgomery in Philadelphia in 1946, Tammi was the cousin of **Lynda Laurence**, and sang in local talent shows as a child. She was first approached to record by Luther Dixon who signed her to Wand Records in 1961. From here she recorded briefly for the Try Me label, and following her work with Steve Gibson and **James Brown**, she signed to Motown where her solo singles included 'Come On And See Me', 'I Don't Believe You Love Me' and 'I Can't Believe You Love Me' in the mid-'60s.

In 1967 Motown's **Harvey Fuqua** paired her with **Marvin Gaye** which led to a string of hits with 'If I Could Build My Whole World Around You' (UK Top 50, 1968), 'Ain't Nothing Like The Real Thing' (UK Top 40, 1968), 'You're All I Need To Get By' (UK Top 20, 1968), 'You Ain't Livin' Till You're Lovin'' (UK Top 25, 1969), 'Good Lovin' Ain't Easy To Come By' (UK Top 30, 1969) and the classic 'Onion Song' (UK Top 10, 1969).

In 1968, quite unexpectedly, Tammi collapsed on stage while performing with Marvin in Cleveland. She died from a brain tumor just prior to her twenty-fifth birthday.

TERRY, TODD
(Songwriter/Producer/Musician)

Based in New York, Todd signed to Sleeping Bag Records in 1988 where he made a major impact on the UK dance scene with his debut single 'Back To The Beat' with 'Bango (To The Batmobile)' on the B-side. His follow-up single was the UK Top 75 hit 'Weekend'. Both singles were later featured on *To The Batmobile Let's Go* (1988).

TERRY, TONY
(Singer/Songwriter)

Born in Pinehurst, North Carolina, Tony was born into a musical family where all sang gospel. Aged six he and his family moved to Washington where Tony sang in a gospel group The Freedom Gospel Singers with his sister and two cousins. Wanting to sing secular r&b music, he enrolled at the Duke Ellington School for The Performing Arts and later auditioned for Duke Ellington with whom he also trained. After this experience he left for New York and landed a stage role in *Black Nativity* before joining the choir in *Mom, I Want To Sing* (one of the longest-running off-Broadway musicals). He eventually took over the lead after the original singer failed to show up one night.

Through a chance social night out at New York's Danceteria, Tony met producer Ted Currier. Together they worked on what was to become his debut solo album *Forever Yours* (1987), including 'Lovey Dovey' (UK Top 50) and 'She's Fly', for Epic Records. He continued working with Ted for *Tony Terry* (1990).

TEX, JOE

(Singer/Songwriter)

Born Joseph Arrington Jr in Baytown, Texas, in 1933, Joe won a local talent show during the early '50s which led to an appearance at New York's Apollo Theater. Here he was so well received that he was booked to appear for the following week. King Records were the first label to sign him, his debut single being 'Davy, You Upset My Home' in 1955 before he switched to Ace in 1958 and landed at Anna Records (via Motown) in 1960 for 'All I Could Do Was Cry'.

In 1961 he so impressed Nashville country music producer Buddy Killen that Buddy set up Dial Records (via Atlantic) especially for Joe's music. In 1965 Joe scored an American hit with 'Hold What You've Got', although Dial issued it against his wishes after he and Buddy fell out. Resolving the situation, Dial brought Joe further American success with singles 'A Woman Can Change A Man', 'I Want To Do (Everything For You)', 'Detroit City', 'The Love You Save (May Be Your Own)', 'Don't Let Your Left Hand Know (What Your Right Hand Is Doing)', and albums including *I've Got To Do A Little Bit Better* (1966) and *Bring A Book* (1969).

In 1972 Dial switched distributors from Atlantic to Mercury (Joe scoring another American hit with 'I Gotcha'), and then again to Epic/CBS where Joe scored the biggest hit of his career with 'Ain't Gonna Bump No More (With No Big Fat Woman)' (UK Top 5) from *Bumps And Bruises* (1977). His next albums were *Rub Down* (1978), including 'You Might Be Digging The Garden But Somebody's Picking Your Plums', and *He Who Is Without Funk (Cast The First Stone)* (1978), including 'Loose Caboose' and 'Who Gave Birth To The Funk'. He died of a heart attack in 1982.

As a songwriter he wrote for artists including **Jerry Butler** and **James Brown** ('Baby You're Right').

THEODORE, MIKE

(Arranger/Producer)

String arranger and producer Mike Theodore came to prominence as an artist during the disco era of the late '70s and early '80s. Having produced albums for **Caesar Frazier** (*Another Life*) and **C..J & Co.** (*Devil's Gun*, 1977), The Mike Theodore Orchestra signed to the Westbound label (via Atlantic) for *Cosmic Wind* (1977), including 'The Bull'.

In 1982 he co-produced the **High Fashion** album *Feelin' Lucky* with **Dennis Coffey** and **Kashif** prior to the release of his 12" disco single 'Hell Fire' for the Reelin N Rockin label in 1983. More recently he has worked with **Blue Moderne** and **Millie Scott** (arranging 'A Love Of Your Own').

THIRD WORLD

(Group)

Formed by **Michael 'Ibo' Cooper** and Stephen Coore in Kingston, Jamaica, in 1973, Third World also features William 'Rugs' Clarke, Stephen 'Cat' Coore, Richard 'Rochie' Daley, Irving 'Carrot' Jarrett and William 'Willy' Stewart. Signing to Island Records, their *Journey To Addis* (1978), included the hits 'Now That We've Found Love' (UK Top 10,) 'Cool Meditation' (UK Top 20) and 'Talk To Me' (UK Top 75). From here they switched to CBS for albums including *Rock The World* (1981), including 'Dancing On The Floor (Hooked On Love)' (UK Top 10), the **Stevie Wonder**-produced *You've Got The Power* (1982), including 'Try Jah Love' (UK Top 50), and *Sense Of Purpose* (1985), including 'One More Time'.

THOMAS & TAYLOR

(Duo/Producers)

Based in New York, **Lamar Thomas** and Judy Taylor first made an impression on the UK soul scene with 'You Can't Blame Love' on their own Thom/Tay label. Co-arranged/produced by **Patrick Adams**, the song later featured on *True Love* (1988). Earlier Lamar had recorded as a solo artist for Epic Records ('Chained To Your Love', 1979).

As producers, Thomas & Taylor have worked with artists including **Ronnie Dyson** and **Johnny Bristol**.

THOMAS, CARLA

(Singer)

The daughter of **Rufus Thomas**, Carla made her recording debut on the duet with her father ''Cause I Love You' (1959) on the Satellite label (which later became Stax Records). On 1960 she scored a million-seller across America with 'Gee Whiz (Look At His Eyes)' on the Atlantic label where she recorded through to the mid-'60s (including 'I've Got No Time To Lose', 1964, and a duet album with **Otis Redding**, *King & Queen*, including 'Tramp').

Back at Stax she scored an American Top 20 hit with 'B-A-B-Y' (1966) and recorded duets with **Johnnie Taylor** and **William Bell** plus solo albums including *Memphis Queen* (1968).

THOMAS, EVELYN

(Singer)

Born on the south side of Chicago in 1953, Evelyn took up singing at the age of seven. She made her recording debut in 1972 when invited to sing backgrounds on Annie Crockett-Ford's gospel album *Something Special*.

In 1975 she met producers **Ian Levine** and Danny Leake who produced her debut solo single 'Weak Spot' (UK Top 30, 1976) for 20th Century Records. Her follow-up was 'Doomsday' (UK Top 50, 1976). After further singles for 20th Century, Casablanca and AVI Records, Evelyn signed to the British-based Record Shack label, where she reunited with producer **Ian Levine** for 'High Energy' (UK Top 5, 1984) and 'Masquerade' (UK Top 75, 1984) together with other songs including 'Cold Shoulder', 'Reflections' and 'Heartless'. She later recorded for Ian's Nightmare label.

THOMAS, IRMA
(Singer)
Born in Pontachoula, Louisiana, in 1941, Irma was discovered in a New Orleans nightclub where aged seventeen she worked as a waitress. One evening bandleader Tommy Ridgley invited her on stage and she later toured with him as the opening act. Tommy also arranged a recording deal with Ronn Records where in 1958 she made her solo debut with 'You Can Have My Husband (But Please Don't Mess With My Man)'.

In 1961 she switched to the Minit label where she worked with producer **Allen Toussaint** on songs including 'It's Raining', 'I Did My Part', 'Cry On', 'Ruler Of My Heart' and 'Pain In My Heart' (later recorded by **Otis Redding**), before switching to the Imperial label. Here she scored greater success with 'Take A Look', 'Wish Someone Would Care' (American Top 20) and 'Time Is On My Side' (later a hit for The Rolling Stones), all in 1964.

She later recorded for Liberty ('What Are You Trying To Do', 1965) and Chess ('Good To Me', 1967), before recording for a number of smaller labels without a great deal of success. In 1970 she moved to Los Angeles and recorded one album with Swam Dogg before returning to New Orleans in 1975.

In 1979 she recorded a disco-orientated album for RCS Records before signing to Rounder Records in 1984. Here her albums include *The New Rules* (1985), while her local reputation on the live music scene over twenty-five years has earned her the title of 'The Soul Queen Of New Orleans'.

THOMAS, JOE
(Flute)
Joe recorded as a solo artist for the Miami-based TK label during the late '70s where with producer **Sonny Lester** his albums were *Get In The Wind* (1978), including 'Plato's Retreat', and *Make Your Move* (1979), both albums having appeal on both the UK disco and jazz funk scenes.

THOMAS, LEON
(Singer)
Born in East St Louis in 1937, Leon is highly regarded in jazz circles. He has recorded vocals with numerous musicians in the jazz funk field, including **Hank Crawford** and **Lonnie Liston Smith**.

THOMAS, LILLO
(Singer/Songwriter)
From Brooklyn, New York, Lillo has a sporting career alongside his music. At the age of sixteen he set a world record for the 200 meters (20.8 seconds). He still runs eight to nine miles a day.

He landed a solo recording deal at Capitol Records via his session singing with **Evelyn King**, **Kashif**, **Howard Johnson**, **James Ingram**, **George Benson** and **Melba Moore** (for whom he wrote 'Mind Up Tonight'). His debut album *Let Me Be Yours* (1983) included '(You're A) Good Girl' and 'Trust Me'. The follow-up was *All Of You* (1984) from which 'Settle Down' was a UK Top 75 hit in 1985, the same year he recorded with **Melba Moore** on 'When You Love Me Like This'. His biggest solo success came in 1987 when 'Sexy Girl' hit the UK Top 25 from an album *Lillo* (which also included the UK Top 60 'I'm In Love').

Outside of his music and sports career Lillo has a talent for drawing. At a Manhattan exhibition, one of his drawings caused controversy as it depicted a guy melting away while sitting on a chair. He called it 'Beginning Of The End' and wouldn't sell it when offered $500!

He also once played himself in *Champaign*, a Brazilian soap opera, during which he sang 'Just My Imagination'.

THOMAS, PHILIP MICHAEL
(Singer)
Better known for his acting role in the TV series *Miami Vice*, Philip also recorded as a solo artist for Atlantic where *Somebody* included the highly regarded 'Don't Make Promises' and productions by **Ashford & Simpson** and **Preston Glass**.

THOMAS, RUFUS
(Singer)
Born in Collierville, Tennessee, in 1917, Rufus initially began his career as a comedian in the mid-'30s. In the '40s he became a disc jockey on a Memphis radio station, and promoted talent shows which helped discover **B.B.King** and **Isaac Hayes**.

His early recordings were for the Star Talent and Sun labels (including 'Bearcat', 1953), before he signed with his daughter **Carla Thomas** to Stax Records. They scored with an American hit duet ''Cause I Love You' (1959), before in 1963 he had American solo hits with novelty dance records 'Walking The Dog' and 'The Dog', then through the '70s scored with further novelties 'Can Your Monkey Do The Dog', 'Do The Funky Chicken' (UK Top 20, 1970), 'Do The Funky Penguin' and 'Do The Push And Pull'. His Stax albums during this time were *Walking The Dog*, *Do The Funky Chicken*, *Did You Hear Me* and *Crown Prince Of Dance*.

His son is Marvell Thomas, a staff musician for Muscle Shoals, and his other daughter is **Sybil Thomas**.

THOMAS, SYBIL
(Singer/Songwriter)
Born in Memphis, Tennessee, Sybil is the daughter of **Rufus Thomas** and sister of **Carla Thomas**. Taking to singing during her college days, she began her professional career in the field of TV advertising for companies including Levis, the *National Enquirer* and Max Factor. Through this she found work singing background vocals with artists including **George Duke**, **Roberta Flack**, **Luther Vandross**, **Lou Rawls**, **Bernard Wright**, **Pieces Of A Dream**, **Bobby M** and **Kashif**.

For West End Records in New York she sang lead for **Raw Silk** on 'Do It To The Music' (UK Top 20, 1982), the success of which prompted the label to release her solo single debut 'Rescue Me' (1983), produced by **Nick Martinelli**.

As a writer she has contributed jazz instrumentals for artists including Manolo Adrina (percussion artist for A&M Records), Azar Lawrence (sax artist for Elektra/Asylum) and John Stubblefield (sax player for Buddah Records).

THOMAS, TASHA
(Singer)
Based in New York, Tasha recorded during the late '70s disco era, making her greatest impression in 1978 with her single 'Shoot Me (With Your Love)' for Orbit Records (via Atlantic in the UK, Top 75). She also recorded backgrounds with artists including **Norman Connors** ('You Are My Starship').

THOMAS, TIMMY
(Singer/Songwriter/Keyboards)
Born in Evansville, Indiana, in 1944, Timmy studied music locally before moving to Memphis and making his recording debut with 'Have Some Boogaloo'. He became a session organist for the Gold Wax label before moving to Texas where he took up a career as a teacher.

After a further move to Florida he became a singer on the Miami club scene and eventually signed to TK Records where he recorded his classic 'Why Can't We Live Together' (UK Top 20) in 1973. He remained with TK until the late '70s, his single 'Freak In, Freak Out' making an impact on the disco scene in 1978. He also played keyboards with **Willie 'Little Beaver' Hale**.

He later switched to the Gold Mountain label (via A&M) for *Gotta Give A Little Love (Ten Years After)* (1984), the year before he wrote the duet 'New York Eyes' (UK Top 50) which he recorded with **Nicole** on her album *What About Me?* (1985). He also recorded a single 'You're The Song (I've Always Wanted To Sing)' for Polydor.

THOMAS, VANEESE
(Singer/Songwriter/Producer)
Based in New York, Vaneese established herself as a solo artist in 1987 after signing to Geffen Records for *Vaneese Thomas*, including 'Let's Talk It Over' and 'New Love'. As a session singer she has recorded with **Bob James** (*Obsession*, on which she co-wrote 'Gone Hollywood' with **Lenny White**), **Lenny White** (*Attitude*), **Montana** (*I Love Music*), **Carl Anderson** (duet on 'It's The Love' from his *On And On*, 1984), **Freddie Jackson** (*Just Like The First Time*), **Beau Williams** (writing/producing 'I Found A Love'), **Melba Moore** ('I'll Never Find Another You' and 'Stay') and **Sarah Dash** (writing 'To Tell You The Truth').

THOMPSON, CARROLL
(Singer)
Born in Letchworth, Hertfordshire, Carroll originally sang with the New Testament Church choir in Luton, Bedfordshire, before establishing herself on the reggae scene. In 1981 she was voted Best Reggae Female Vocalist by *Echoes* magazine and her debut single 'I'm So Sorry' was voted Reggae Single Of The Year.

Signing to Red Bus she released 'Just A Little Bit' (1982), before concentrating on session work.

THORNTON, FONZI
(Singer/Songwriter/Producer)
New York-based singer Fonzi Thornton established himself as a top session singer on the r&b scene of the late '70s and '80s. His vocal credits are frequently found on albums by artists including **B.B.&Q.**, **Chic**, **High Fashion**, **Luther Vandross**, **Howard Johnson**, **Aretha Franklin**, **Al Jarreau**, Roxy Music and **The O'Jays**. In 1983 he signed to RCA as a solo artist where he worked with producer **Robert White** on *The Leader* (1983), including 'Beverly', and *Pumpin'* (1984), including 'A Natural (Yesiree)'. Fonzi and Robert also wrote and produced *On Target* for **The Jones Girls** at RCA (1983).

THREE DEGREES
(Vocal Group)
From Philadelphia, The Three Degrees were originally Fayette Pinkney, Shirley Porter and Linda Turner, who sang together in their childhood days for fun. A chance meeting with producer **Richard Barrett** led to a debut single 'Gee Baby (I'm Sorry)' for Swan Records in 1965. In the meantime Richard had discovered singer **Sheila Ferguson** and put her in the group for 1966 singles 'Tales Are True' and 'Love Of My Life', also for the Swan label. From here the line-up became Sheila (lead vocals), Fayette and Valerie Thompson. Switching to the Roulette label Richard produced a series of American r&b hits including 'Maybe', 'You're The One' and 'Ebb Tide'. They also appeared in the movie *The French Connection*.

In 1973 the group signed with the Philadelphia International label (PIR), where they were first utilized on 'T.S.O.P. (The Sound Of Philadelphia)', a recording for **M.F.S.B.** used as a theme to *Soul Train* in America and a Top 25 hit in the UK (1974). Their solo hits in the UK were 'Year Of Decision' (Top 20, 1974), 'When Will I See You Again' (No.1, 1974), 'Get Your Love Back' (Top 40, 1974), 'Take Good Care Of Yourself' (Top 10, 1975) and 'Long Lost Lover' (Top 40, 1975), by which time Prince Charles acknowledged them as his favourite group. Albums during this era were *The Three Degrees* (1973), including 'Dirty Ol' Man', and *Three Degrees International* (1975).

In 1978 the group switched to the Ariola label and released an album *3D* produced by **Giorgio Moroder**. 'Giving Up, Giving In' was popular on the disco scene, and their UK chart success continued with 'Woman In

Love' (Top 5, 1979), 'The Runner' (Top 10, 1979) and 'My Simple Heart' (Top 10, 1979).

Teaming up with writers/producers **Stock/Aitken/Waterman** in the UK, the group scored a UK Top 50 on the Supreme label with 'The Heaven I Need' prior to the departure of Sheila Ferguson (who was replaced by Victoria Wallace) and a switch to Ichiban Records. In 1989 Sheila Ferguson's *Soul Food* was published.

THREE OUNCES OF LOVE
(Vocal Group)
Formed in Detroit, Three Ounces Of Love are sisters Anne, Elaine and Regina Alexander. After evolving through church choirs and local talent shows they made their recording debut in the mid-'70s for the Pameline label where they worked with producer **Richard 'Popcorn' Wylie**. They were brought to the attention of Bennie Ashburn, manager of **The Commodores**, who were looking for an opening act for their 1978–79 tour. Impressed, he both took them on tour and secured them a recording deal at Motown. Here they worked with producers Eddie and Brian Holland (of **Holland/Dozier/Holland**) and **Mike & Brenda Sutton** on *Three Ounces Of Love* (1978), including 'Star Love' and 'Betcha Come Runnin''.

From here they switched to the Music Merchant label where they recorded 'Cruise Control' under the name Lipstick. In 1989 they became Three Ounces Of Love again. Their single for the UK Motorcity label was 'Newsy Neighbours' (1991).

THREE PIECES
(Group)
In addition to **The Blackbyrds**, producer/trumpeter **Donald Byrd** also worked with a group Three Pieces at Fantasy Records during the mid-'70s. Their one UK release was 'I Need You Girl' (1975).

THURSTON, BOBBY
(Singer)
From Washington DC, Bobby originally sang backing vocals and played congas with the group Spectrum Ltd while at high school. Eventually he took over as lead singer while maintaining a job at the State Department. Performing one night he met producers **Lester/Brown** who took him to the Prelude label. Here Lester/Brown wrote/produced his debut album *You Got What It Takes*, from which 'Check Out The Groove' was a UK Top 10 in 1980. *The Main Attraction* (1981) featured the popular 'Very Last Drop' before Bobby moved directly to Lester/Brown's own label Mainline for one album, *Sweetest Piece Of The Pie*, including 'Just Ask Me', eventually released in the UK on the Hi Hut label in 1988.

TILLERY, LINDA
(Singer)
Linda's one contribution to the UK soul scene was *Secrets*, released by the independent American-based Redwood label in 1985. The title track of the album was particularly popular.

THE TIME
(Group)
From Minneapolis, The Time was the amalgamation of two local groups **Flytetime**, featuring **Jam/Lewis**, and Enterprise, led by **Morris Day**. Original members were Jimmy 'Jam' Harris (keyboards), Terry Lewis (guitar/bass), Morris Day (lead vocals), **Jellybean** Johnson (drums), **Monte Moir** (keyboards) and **Jesse Johnson** (guitar).

From 1981 they toured extensively with **Prince** who secured them a recording deal at Warner Brothers where their albums were *The Time* (1981), *What Time Is It* (1982) and *Ice Cream Castles* (1983). They also appeared with Prince in the movie *Purple Rain*. Shortly after Jam/Lewis began their successful songwriting/production career, the group disbanded and each member began solo careers. In 1990, however, they reunited for *Pandemonium*, including 'Jerk Out', for **Prince**'s Paisley Park label.

TITUS, MARSHALL
(Singer)
Originally a member of the group **Champaign**, Marshall signed to Ardent Records in 1989, releasing a single 'Naturally' on their Zing subsidiary.

TODAY
(Vocal Group)
From Englewood, New Jersey, Today are Lee 'Bubba' Drakeford, Larry 'Chief' Singletary, Wesley 'Wes' Adams and Larry 'Love' McCain. Originally Larry ('Chief') and Wesley had formed the Supreme Clientele MCs, following which they added Lee and became The Gents (releasing a single 'For You My Baby Love'). Through a chance meeting with **Teddy Riley** the group signed to Motown via Teddy's production deal with the label. By now they had added Larry McCain and had become **Today**. To date they have released two albums, *Today* (1989), including 'Girl I Got My Eyes On You', and *The New Formula*, including 'I Wanna Come Back Home'.

TODAY, TOMORROW, FOREVER
(Group)
Alton Hudson, Ronald Broomfield (aka **Eugene Wilde**), Allison Brunson Jr, Alfredo Ramos, Deborah Peevy, Darwin Brett Brown and Willie Brown Jr recorded one album together, *TTF*, released on the Curtom label (via RSO/Polydor) in 1979.

TOMIE, SATOSHI
(Keyboards/Producer)
Born in Tokyo, Satoshi took up keyboards at the age of thirteen, originally to study jazz and classical music. However the infiltration of American 'house' music into Japan inspired Satoshi to become both a disc jockey and producer in addition to recording with his own high school band.

In 1988 he was commissioned too write a theme for a promotional campaign to launch a line of cosmetics. The advertising agency also hired **Frankie Knuckles** to be the disc jockey at the launch parties, and impressed by Satoshi's music, Frankie and Satoshi collaborated on 'Tears', later released as a single by Frankie Knuckles.

Via this collaboration Satoshi landed his own recording deal with FFRR in London, his solo debut being 'And I Love You', featuring the vocals of **Arnold Jarvis**.

TOMORROW'S EDITION
(Vocal Group)
Based in New Jersey, Tomorrow's Edition were William Jones (lead vocals), Aaron Mathis, Wesley Thomas and Jerome Gourdine. In 1981 they recorded a debut single 'U Turn Me On' for the Mel-O label, popular on the UK dance scene following its release here by CBS. In 1982 they switched to Atlantic for *A Song For Everyone*.

TONEY, KEVIN
(Keyboards)
Kevin was pianist and songwriter with **The Blackbyrds** prior to recording as a solo artist for the Fantasy label. He also played keyboards for **Bobby Thurston** ('You Got What It Takes'), **Ray Parker Jr**, **Two Tons Of Fun** and **Gayle Adams**.

TORANO, SANDY
(Singer/Guitar)
From Cuba, Sandy left school at sixteen to play guitar with Edgar Winter, following which he played with **Larry Young**, **The Brecker Brothers**, **Phyllis Hyman** and **Narada Michael Walden** before meeting **Howard Johnson** and forming **Niteflyte** at the age of 27.

He later recorded a solo single 'Shame' (Atlantic, 1987).

TOTAL CONTRAST
(Group)
Total Contrast are Robin Achampong from Clapham, London (bass/vocals), and Delroy Murray from Hackney, London (keyboards/vocals). Robin released 'Special Loving' as Mystic, while Delroy recorded as Speedy on his own Clearview label before they met and formed Total Contrast in 1983. Teaming up with producer **Steve Harvey** they recorded 'Be With Me Tonight' which was released on their own Total Contrast label. Its popularity led to a deal with London Records and subsequent releases 'Takes A Little Time' (UK Top 20), 'Hit And Run' (UK Top 50), 'The River' (UK Top 50) and 'What You Gonna Do About It' (UK Top 75) from their album *Total Contrast* (1985).

Turning to writing and production they worked with **Carroll Thompson** ('The Apple Of My Eye', 1984) and **Chris Paul** ('Back In My Arms', 1987) before returning with *Beat To Beat* (1987). They then sponsored the group **Tongue 'N' Cheek** whom they began producing and managing. In fact, with the exception of two cover versions, they wrote and produced all the tracks on the debut album *This Is Tongue 'N' Cheek* (1990).

TOUCH OF CLASS
(Group)
From Philadelphia, Pete Jackson, Gerald Jackson, Herbert Brevard and Michael Hailstock became Touch Of Class. Pete and Gerald wrote the American hit 'Turn The Beat Around' for Vicki Sue Robinson prior to 'I Love You Pretty Baby', the stand-out song from the group's one album *I'm In Heaven* for the Midland International label (via RCA) in 1976, produced by **John Davis**.

In 1985 they returned on the Atlantic label with a single 'Let Me Be Your Everything'.

TOUCHDOWN
(Group)
From Hertfordshire, Brit funk band Touchdown was formed by Alan Braithwaite (percussion) and Stephen Vincent (bass) in 1979. Their one single was 'Ease Your Mind' (1982), released first by Record Shack and then by Streetwise in New York, where the song was remixed by **Arthur Baker**.

Stephen Vincent later became Stevie V, and scored solo hits with songs including 'Dirty Cash' and 'Body Language'.

TOUSSAINT, ALLEN
(Songwriter/Producer/Pianist)
Born in New Orleans in 1938, Allen began his professional career in the mid-'50s as a pianist, recording an album of piano instrumentals as Al Tousan for RCA Records in 1958. Through the '60s and '70s he established a somewhat legendary reputation as a producer on the soul scene, writing and/or producing for artists including **Irma Thomas** ('Ruler Of My Heart'), **Lee Dorsey** ('Ride Your Pony'), **Chocolate Milk** ('Action Speaks Louder Than Words'), and **General Johnson** (his first hit, as Norman Johnson & The Showman, 'It Will Stand').

Signed as a solo artist to Warner Brothers during the early '70s, his albums included *Life, Love and Faith*, *Motion* and *Southern Nights*.

TOWER OF POWER
(Group/Horn Section)
Formed in Oakland, California, in 1967, Tower of Power were originally Lenny Pickett (sax), Emilio Castillo (sax/vocals), Steve Kupka (sax/horn/vocals), Greg Adams (trumpet/flugelhorn/vocals), Mic Gillette (trumpet/

flugelhorn/trombone/vocals), Bruce Conte (guitar/backing vocals), Chester Thompson (keyboards/vocals) and Rick Stevens (lead vocals), although until 1969 they were called The Motowns. After creating an impression on the West Coast club scene, they signed to the San Francisco label (via Atlantic) for their debut album *East Bay Grease* (1970). In 1972 they switched to Warner Brothers and went to Memphis to record *Bump City*, including 'Down To The Nightclub'. Further Warner Brothers albums were *Tower Of Power* (1973) and *Back To Oakland* (1974) before they switched to CBS.

Here their recordings included 'Ain't Nothin' Stoppin' Us Now' (1976) and 'We Came To Play' (1977), by which time lead singer Rick Stevens had been convicted of murder and had been replaced by **Lenny Williams**. In the mid-80s the group returned to Warner Brothers for albums including *Back To Oakland* (1984), while more recently **Ellis Hall** has taken over as lead vocalist and they have recorded for the independent Cypress Records label, albums including *Power* (1987).

As a horn section they have recorded with artists including **Rufus** Featuring **Chaka Khan** ('Sweet Thing') and Elton John. Musicians who have been part of the group over the years include Francis 'Rocco' Prestia (bass), Willie Fulton (guitar/vocals), Lee Thornburg (trumpet/fluegelhorn/vocals), Richard Elliot (sax) and Mick Mastek (drums).

TOWNSENDS

(Group)

From Michigan, Timothy and Eltoa Townsend first called themselves Young Blood. Changing their name to Dateline and moving to Los Angeles, they released one single with Elektra Records, a ballad called 'Earth Angel'. After working the club circuit extensively with their own brand of **Rufus**-style music they changed their name to The Townsends and released one single for the Private 1 label, 'Temporary Insanity', a song featured in the soundtrack to *Police Academy II*.

TOWNSON, RON

(Singer)

An original member of **The Fifth Dimension**, Ron formed a group Wild Honey before taking on a solo career. During his solo days, he was the first artist to hire **Vesta Williams** as a backing singer.

TOYS

(Group)

Featuring vocalist Barbara Harris, this group are best remembered for their '60s hit 'Lover's Concerto'.

TRACY, JEANIE

(Singer/Songwriter/Producer)

From Houston, Texas, Jeanie grew up in Fresno, California, where she sang in the church choir, took opera training and learned the piano. Just prior to moving to San Francisco she produced her own debut single 'Making New Friends', released on the US Brown Door label.

In 1970 she played the lead in Oscar Brown Jr's production of *Slave Driver* before being discovered by **Harvey Fuqua** in 1976. Initially she worked as songwriter and producer for the gospel group Voices Of Harmony, signed to Harvey's Milk And Honey label (via Fantasy). In 1979 Jeanie's vocals were used on the soundtrack to Francis Ford Coppola's film *Apocalypse Now*, before Harvey persuaded her to audition for **Sylvester** who was looking for a new backing singer.

Impressing Sylvester, she not only sang backgrounds but recorded a duet with him 'Here Is My Love' in 1981. This led to Jeanie's own recording deal at Fantasy commencing with the Harvey Fuqua-produced *Me And You* (1982). Also at Fantasy she was featured vocalist on **Freddie Hubbard**'s *Splash*. She sang backgrounds with **Jeffrey Osborne**, **Narada Michael Walden**, **Peabo Bryson**, **Aretha Franklin**/George Michael ('I Knew You Were Waiting'), **Two Tons of Fun**, **Herbie Hancock** (*Magic Number*) and was a featured vocalist with **Skool Boyz** on 'You Are My Love' from their album *This Is The Real Thing* (1985).

More recently she has recorded 'high energy' singles for the Megatone Records label.

TRAMAINE

(Singer)

Born in Los Angeles Tramaine began her career as a gospel singer at the age of seven. She joined The Heavenly Tones with whom she made her recording debut on the single 'He's Alright'. Two years later the group recorded a gospel album with James Cleveland on the Savoy label, called *Heavenly Tones*. From here she worked with Andrae Crouch and The Disciples (singing lead on his release 'I'm Coming Home') before leaving Berkeley High School to join the Edwin Hawkins Singers. While with the Singers she married Edwin's younger brother Walter Hawkins. The husband and wife team worked together until 1981 when Tramaine took on a solo career.

She recorded two gospel albums, *Tramaine* and *Determined* (1983), including 'Rescue Me', before switching to secular soul and signing to A&M. Here she made an impact on the soul and dance scene with 'Fall Down' (1985). The parent album *The Search Is Over* (produced by **Robert Wright**) also featured the follow-up single 'In The Morning Time'. Then she returned to gospel music and signed to Sparrow for *The Joy That Floods My Soul* (1989). Additionally, she has recorded background vocals with artists including **Jeffrey Osborne** and **The Blackbyrds**.

TRAMMPS

(Group)

From Philadelphia, the nucleus of The Trammps originated from The Volcanos, a group which briefly became The Moods following the departure of lead vocalist Gene Faith. Their replacement was Jimmy Ellis who had previously sung with The Exceptions (on 'Down By The Sea', 1965) prior to fronting The Moods on their two singles 'Rain Maker' and 'King Hustler'.

In both early groups the drummer was **Earl Young**, who came up with the concept of The Trammps, taking the name from their general appearance! With Jimmy remaining on lead vocals, and Earl as part bass, drummer and vocalist, the remaining Trammps were Dennis Harris (guitar), Michael Thompson (drums), Doc Wade (guitar/vocals), Stan Wade (bass/vocals), John Hart (organ/vocals), **Ron Kersey** (piano/vocals), Roger Stevens (trumpet), John Davis (sax) and Fred Jointer (trombone). They were officially launched in 1972 under the production guidance of **Baker/Harris/Young** and signed to the Buddah label for a debut single 'Zing Went The Strings Of My Heart', (UK Top 30, 1974). Their Buddah hits continued with 'Sixty Minute Man' (Top 40, 1975) and 'Hold Back The Night' (Top 5, 1975).

In 1975 the group recorded an album *Trammps*, released on the Golden Fleece label (via CBS) and including 'Stop And Think' which became a cult track on the UK 'rare groove' scene of the mid-'80s. Also on the album were singles 'Where Do We Go From Here', 'Shout' and 'Love Epidemic', although these were not released in the UK. At Atlantic their UK success continued with 'That's Where The Happy People Go' (Top 40, 1976), 'Soul Searchin' Time' (Top 50, 1976) and the dance anthem 'Disco Inferno' (Top 20, 1977), taken from the *Saturday Night Fever* movie soundtrack. Atlantic albums included *Disco Inferno* and *Mixin' It Up* (1980).

Vince Montana later rekindled the group with 'Whatever Happened To The Music', released on his Philly Sound Works label in 1983.

TRESVANT, RALPH

(Singer)

Born in Boston, Ralph joined **New Edition** in 1980, and remains close with the group to this day. In the late '80s he moved to Los Angeles and signed to MCA as a solo artist. His debut album *Ralph Tresvant* featured the **Jam/Lewis**-penned/produced single 'Sensitivity' (1990).

TRIPLE 'S' CONNECTION

(Vocal Group)

Triple 'S' Connection were Stan, Sterling and Steven, a Los Angeles-based vocal trio instigated by Stan Sheppard. In 1979 they delivered an album *Triple 'S' Connection* on the 20th Century label. Stan left to join **The Skool Boyz** (and eventually **By All Means**), while the others recorded an album as Sterling & Steven for RCA.

TROOP

(Group)

Based in Pasadena, California, Troop were formed in 1984 by one of the mothers of the male quintet. Entering a TV talent show, they won $1000 lip syncing to **New Edition's** 'Cool It Now' before signing to Atlantic in 1987. Here they worked with producers **Levert** on their debut single 'Mamacita' which reached No. 1 in the American r&b charts (1989).

Independently, the group's Steve Russell has since moved into production where he has worked with artists including **The Whispers**.

TROUBLE FUNK

(Group)

Formed in Washington DC in 1978, Trouble Funk consisted of Robert Reed (multi-instrumentalist/vocals), Timothy Davis (percussion), Tony Fisher (bass/vocals), James Avery (guitar/vocals) and Taylor Reed (keyboards/trumpet/vocals). Pioneers of the city's 'go-go' music scene, the group recorded for the local DETT label (including *In Times Of Trouble*, 1983), before switching to Island Records in 1987 for *Trouble Over There*, featuring **Bootsy Collins** and **Kurtis Blow**. The album also included 'Woman Of Principle' (UK Top 75).

TROUTMAN, ROGER

(Singer/Songwriter/Producer)

Born in Hamilton, Ohio, Roger has recorded as a solo artist on Warner Brothers Records in addition to his work with his group **Zapp**. Solo albums include *The Many Facets Of* (1981) and *The Saga Continues* (1984). Elsewhere he has worked as writer and/or producer with artists including **Dayton** ('Love You Anyway'), **Bobby Glover**, New Horizons, ('Gonna Have Big Fun'), **Sugarfoot** and Lynch.

TROY, DORIS

(Singer/Songwriter)

Born Doris Payne in New York in 1937, Doris first sang in the church before writing 'How About That', a hit for Dee Clark. Working as an usherette at The Apollo Theater in Harlem she became acquainted with **James Brown** who took her to Atlantic where in 1963 she scored an American hit with 'Just One Look'. In the UK her hit was 'Whatcha Gonna Do About It' (Top 40, 1964). Impressing The Beatles, she was signed by the group's Apple label, but did not score any chart success. She later recorded for Capitol (including 'Face Up To The Truth').

TRUSSEL

(Group)

Trussel were Michael Spratley (vocals), Michael Gray (guitar), H.Lorenzo Maclin (bass), Larry O.Tynes (keyboards), Hannon D.Lane (guitar), Ronald Leon Smith (drums), Lynwood Jones (sax) and William F.McGee (flugelhorn). Under the direction of Philadelphia-based producer Allen Richardson and former **James Brown** side man **Fred Wesley**, they recorded one classic dance record 'Love Injection' (also the title of their album for Elektra Records) in 1979 (UK Top 50, 1980).

TUCKER, JUNIOR
(Singer)
Based in Los Angeles, Junior Tucker made his recording debut in 1983 after signing to Geffen Records and working with producer **Ray Parker Jr** on *Junior Tucker*, including 'Take A Message (From My Body)'. After a long absence from the recording scene, he returned in 1990 to sign with 10 Records where his first single was '16 (Into The Night)'.

TURNER, IKE & TINA
(Duo)
Born in Clarksdale, Mississippi, in 1931, Ike Turner worked as a local disc jockey before forming a group Kings Of Rhythm and moving to St Louis. Here he met Annie Mae Bullock who married him, changed her name to Tina Turner and joined the group as lead vocalist.

In 1960 as Ike & Tina Turner they signed to the Sue label and established themselves across America with 'A Fool In Love' (American Top 30) and 'It's Gonna Work Out Fine' (American Top 20, 1961). From here they recorded for labels including Sonja, Innis, Kent ('I Can't Believe What You Say', 1964), Loma, Tangerine, Cenco, Philles ('River Deep Mountain High', UK Top 5 via London Records, 1966, and 'A Love Like Yours', UK Top 20, 1966), Warner Brothers ('Tell Her I'm Not Home', UK Top 50, 1966), Blue Thumb and Minit ('Come Together', 1970).

Minit was acquired by Liberty Records, which shortly became United Artists where Ike & Tina Turner scored with their classic hit 'Nutbush City Limits' (UK Top 5) in 1973. During this time they developed a breathtaking stage show complete with their own backing group The Ikettes. Soon after 'Nutbush City Limits', however, they got divorced and Tina commenced a solo career which didn't really take off until ten years later when her rendition of **Al Green**'s 'Let's Stay Together' was a UK Top 10 hit in 1983. From here her solo success (for Capitol Records) continued with songs including 'What's Love Got To Do With It' (UK Top 5, 1984), 'Private Dancer' (UK Top 30, 1984), 'We Don't Need Another Hero' (UK Top 5, 1985), and most recently 'It Takes Two', the **Marvin Gaye/Kim Weston** duet, with Rod Stewart (UK Top 40, 1990).

TURNER, RUBY
(Singer)
From Handsworth, Birmingham (UK), Ruby first took her singing seriously at the age of sixteen, eventually forming her own band with drummer Bob Lamb (UB 40's first producer), sax man Billy Paul (formerly of Wizzard), and bass player Geoff Pearse. In 1984 they toured with **Womack & Womack** and Culture Club, and started their own label, Sunflower, releasing two singles and an EP.

In 1985 Ruby signed with Jive Records and worked with **Jonathan Butler** on a version of 'If You're Ready (Come Go With Me)' produced by **Billy Ocean** (UK Top 30, 1986). Follow-ups were 'I'm In Love' (Top 75, 1986), 'Bye Baby' (Top 75, 1986), 'In My Life (It's Better To Be In Love)' produced by **Monte Moir** (1986), 'I'd Rather Go Blind' (Top 30, 1987) and 'I'm In Love' (Top 75, 1987). Her debut album was *Women Hold Up Half The Sky* (1986). Further Jive albums have been *It's Gonna Be Alright* (1989), including 'Sexy' produced by **Womack & Womack**, and *Paradise* (1990), including 'It's Gonna Be Alright'.

TURRENTINE, STANLEY
(Saxophone/Producer)
Born in Pittsburgh in 1934, Stanley has been playing professional saxophone since the early '50s. During the '60s he worked with his organist wife Shirley Scott (and at one time with **Ray Charles**) before signing to the CTI label in the '70s. Here he became a pioneer in the field of jazz funk, fusing jazz with dance rhythms (the direction of CTI). He recorded *Sugar* before switching to Fantasy in 1974.

His albums here included *Pieces Of Dreams* (1974), produced by **Gene Page**, *Have You Ever Seen The Rain*, *Everybody Come On Out*, *In The Pocket*, *Use The Stairs*, and in 1978 he moved into the disco field with *Who Are You*, featuring the single 'Disco Dancing'. Other albums in a similar style were *West Side Highway* (1978) and *Betcha* (1979), by which time he had switched labels to Elektra for *Inflation* (1980).

Moving back to jazz funk, *Tender Togetherness* (1981) introduced more vocal elements to his music and featured **Dianne Reeves** as lead singer on 'Only You And Me', produced by **Larry Dunn**. *Home Again* (1982) included a vocal-refrained dancer 'I'll Be There' which proved popular on the UK soul scene at the time of release. Then in 1989 Stanley signed with Blue Note and released *L.A. Place* produced by **Bobby Lyle**, featuring vocals by **Jean Carne**.

As a session player he can be found on tracks by **Lou Rawls** (*At Last*) and **Freddie Jackson** ('Good Morning Heartache') among others.

TWILIGHT 22
(Group)
Twilight 22 was the brainchild of Gordon Bahary with some help from lead singer and co-songwriter Joseph Saulter. Gordon created the group initially through a love of computers and synthesizers. At the age of 16 he sat in with **Stevie Wonder** during the recording of *Songs In The Key Of Life*. Impressed by his suggestions, Stevie invited Gordon to produce and program synthesizers on

his next album, *Journey Through The Secret Life Of Plants*.

Gordon met Joseph Saulter through **Herbie Hancock** (Gordon also worked on Herbie's *Feets Don't Fail Me Now*). Joseph had been the drummer with LA-based band Rhythm Ignition. After the group just missed out on a recording deal with Motown, Joseph and Gordon hooked up to work as Twilight 22. On Vanguard Records, the duo recorded *Twilight 22* (1985) from which 'Electric Kingdom' appealed to electro fans, 'Mysterious' to soul fans, and 'In The Night' to fusion jazz fans.

TWO MAN SOUND

(Group)

This group from Brussels recorded 'Que Tal America' for RKM Records in 1977, and slowly but surely took off on the UK dance scene. Pete Waterman (of **Stock/Aitken/Waterman**) was responsible for its release in the UK on Miracle Records (via Pye), the record being a Top 50 hit in 1979.

TWO TONS OF FUN

(Vocal Duo)

From San Francisco, Two Tons Of Fun were **Martha Wash** and Izora Redman, who later became **The Weather Girls**. They first sang together in gospel groups and choirs around the Bay Area before becoming a backing vocal force for **Sylvester**. They toured and recorded with him on hits such as 'Dance (Disco Heat)' and '(You Make Me Feel) Mighty Real'.

Their own recordings first came care of **Harvey Fuqua**, who signed them to his Honey label via Fantasy Records. Harvey produced the duo's two albums, *Two Tons* including 'Taking Away Your Space', and *Backatcha* (1980).

TYMES

(Vocal Group)

Originally from Virginia, Norman Burnett and George Hilliard first met and formed a vocal duo in 1956. They later teamed up with Donald Banks and Albert 'Caesar' Berry to work as The Latineers in Philadelphia. Here they were joined by George Williams and in 1960 they became The Tymes. Signing to the Cameo Parkway label they scored hits with 'So Much Love' (UK Top 25, 1963), and 'Wonderful Wonderful'. Their later recordings were with MGM, Winchester, Direction (UK Top 20 with 'People', 1969) and RCA where they scored UK hits with 'You Little Trust Maker' (Top 20, 1974), 'Ms Grace' (No. 1, 1974) and 'God's Gonna Punish You' (Top 50, 1976). They also added two female members for *Diggin' Their Roots*.

George Williams later recorded with mid-'80s UK jazz group The Chosen 3.

TYNER, McCOY

(Piano)

Born in Philadelphia in 1938, McCoy was encouraged to take up piano by his mother who also played the instrument. By the age of 17 he had his own group but in 1959 was invited to join Jazztet, a group led by **Benny Golson**. In 1960 he joined a quintet let by John Coltrane before becoming a solo artist in 1963. Between 1965 and 1970 he recorded for the Blue Note label before venturing into fusion jazz at Milestone Records until 1980 with albums including *Sahara*, *Song For My Lady*, *Atlantis*, *Trident*, *Fly With The Wind*, *Songs Of The New World*, *Echoes Of A Friend*, *Sama Layuca* and *Horizon*.

Over at CBS, his 1982 album *Looking Out* featured vocals by **Phyllis Hyman**.

TYZIK, JEFF

(Trumpeter/Songwriter/Producer)

Born in Hyde Park, New York, Tyzik attended the prestigious Eastman School of Music in 1979 and became close friends with fellow trumpeter Al Vizzutti. When Al left to be lead player with Woody Herman, Tyzik began playing alongside **Chuck Mangione** (who also taught at the school). While working with Chuck between 1975 and 1980, Jeff was also employed by 'Doc' Severinsen who in 1978 took him to London to work on two albums with the Royal Philharmonic Orchestra.

With an interest in broader-based soul and r&b music, Jeff began composing songs for himself and self-financed his first solo album *Prophecy* which included 'Florentine', a UK jazz funk favourite. The album was licensed by Capitol in 1981, and the label released a follow-up, *Radiance* (including 'Sweet Nothings') in 1982. Switching labels to Polydor in 1984, Jeff released *Jammin' In Manhattan*, introducing an electronic element to his music. Polydor issued *Smile* in 1985, Jeff's last solo album to date.

In 1990 he produced *Harlem Nocturne* for pianist Kofi, released by Warlock Records.

U

UK PLAYERS
(Group)
From Stevenage, Hertfordshire, The UK Players were one of the forerunners of the 'Brit funk' movement. They were **James Ross** (vocals/guitar/percussion/sax), Phil Bishop (guitars), Sedley Francis (bass), Rusty Jones (drums) and Patrick Seymour (keyboards/flute). Signing to A&M Records in 1980, their debut single 'Everybody Get Up' stirred UK dancefloors, the B-side 'Rivers' being a popular 'jazz funk' instrumental. *No Way Out* was released in 1982, following which they switched to RCA for a UK Top 75 single 'Love's Gonna Get You' in 1983.

UJIMA
(Group)
Signed to Epic Records in the early '70s, Ujima are best remembered for the soul classic 'I'm Gettin' Hip (To Your Ways And Actions)', released in 1973.

ULTRA HIGH FREQUENCY
(Vocal Group)
This Philadelphia-based group's recordings include 'The Saddest Smile In Town' written by **Norman Harris**, **Bunny Sigler** and **Al Felder** and released on the Wand label

UNCLE LOUIE
(Group)
Frank T.Dillard (vocals/bass) and Eddie Dillard (vocals/guitar) teamed together for one album *Uncle Louie's Here*, including 'Full-Tilt Boogie', for Marlin Records (via TK) in 1979. It was produced by **Walter Murphy** who also co-wrote all the songs with Gene Pistilli. Guest artists included **Angela Winbush**, **Wah Wah Watson** and **Stephanie Spruill**.

UNDERWOOD, VERONICA
(Singer)
Philadelphia singer Veronica recorded one album *Veronica Underwood* for the Philly World label in 1985.

UNDISPUTED TRUTH
(Vocal Group)
Instigated by songwriter/producer **Norman Whitfield**, The Undisputed Truth were formed in 1970 with a line-up originally consisting of Joe Harris, **Billie Calvin** and Brenda Joyce Evans. Signed to Motown, their debut album was *The Undisputed Truth* (1970), including 'Smiling Faces Sometimes', a song earlier recorded by **The Temptations** which became an American Top 5 hit. They continued with *Face To Face With Truth* (1971) and then *Law Of The Land* (1972) which introduced a new line-up of Tyrone Berkley, Tyrone Douglas, Calvin Stevens, and Virginia McDonald with original member Joe Harris. Albums continued with *Down To Earth* (1973), *Cosmic Truth* (1974) and *Higher Than High* (1975). **Taka Boom** (**Chaka Khan**'s sister) joined the group in 1975, the year Norman formed his own Whitfield label and took both the label and the group to Warner Brothers. Here Taka Boom was the lead singer on the group's one UK chart hit 'You + Me = Love' (UK Top 50, 1977), from *Method To The Madness*.

More recently Joe Harris signed a line-up of the group to the UK Motorcity label and worked on a number of recordings including a remake of 'Law Of The Land' (1990).

UNIQUE
(Studio Group)
Put together in New York in 1982, Unique recorded for Prelude Records where their single 'What I Got Is What You Need' was a UK Top 30 hit in 1983.

UNIVERSAL ROBOT BAND
(Group)
A studio concept created by **Patrick Adams** and **Greg Carmichael** in 1976, an official line-up of The Universal Robot Band was only created after the American success of the debut single 'Dance And Shake Your Tambourine' (for the Red Greg label) and there was demand for live appearances.

The musicians and singers worked together so well that they formed their own group **Kleeer**, while Patrick and Greg maintained the original group's name and in

1984 released 'Barely Breaking Even' with some New York session musicians.

UNLIMITED TOUCH
(Group)
Raymond Reid and William Anderson from New York-based band **Crown Heights Affair** instigated Unlimited Touch in the early '80s. Featuring vocalists **Audrey Wheeler** and Stephanie James, the group was signed to Prelude (via Epic in the UK) where they stirred UK dancefloors with the Reid/Anderson songs 'I Hear Music In The Streets' (1980) and 'Searching To Find The One' (1981). They later released *Yes We're Ready* (1983) and a further single 'Reach Out (Everlasting Love)' in 1984.

UPCHURCH, PHIL
(Guitar)
Born in Chicago in 1939, Phil was a professional guitarist by the mid-'50s. After session work with artists including **Jerry Butler**, he was hired as a house guitarist by Chess Records, where he recorded with **The Dells** and The Soulful Strings as backing for many of the label's acts. He also formed the Phil Upchurch Combo which in 1961 scored a million-seller across America with 'You Can't Sit Down' (UK Top 40, 1966, via Sue Records).

From the '70s to the present day Phil has worked consistently as a session guitarist, also putting out his own occasional solo release. These include 'Strawberry Letter 23' (1978) at TK Records, and for Jam Records *Revelation* (1982), *Name Of The Game* (1983), including 'Could It Be You' featuring **Marlena Shaw**, and *Companions* (1984). Artists he has recorded with include **The Crusaders**, **Chaka Khan**, **Booker T. Jones**, **Leroy Hutson** and **Michael Jackson**.

URBAN ENSEMBLE
(Group)
Under the direction of Roland Vazquez, **Dave Grusin**, **Patrice Rushen**, Larry Williams (from **Seawind**) and a host of top musicians recorded one album *Urban Ensemble* for the GRP label (via Arista) in 1979, much acclaimed by UK fusion jazz fans.

URBAN HIGH
(Group)
Instigated by London disc jockeys/producers Guy Wingate and Jay Strongman, Urban High recreated the 'Salsoul sound' in a modern fashion featuring vocalist **Dee Dee Wilde** on a 1989 remake of the disco classic 'Runaway' for 4th & Broadway Records (via Island).

USRY, JOHNNY
(Arranger/Musician)
Based in Philadelphia, Johnny arranged numerous Philly classics on Philadelphia International Records for artists including **Teddy Pendergrass** and **The Jones Girls** ('You're Gonna Make Me Love Somebody Else'). In 1989 he made a debut solo album *Healing* for the Atlanta-based Ichiban label, inspired by his days in Vietnam.

V

VALADIERS
(Group)
Formed in Detroit in the early '60s, The Valadiers featured the lead vocals of Stewart Avig and were the first official 'white' group to be signed to the Motown label (on the Miracle subsidiary). Here they are best remembered for their debut 'Greetings, This Is Uncle Sam' (1961), which was followed up by 'Because I Love Her' (1962) and 'I Found A Girl' (1963), both for the Gordy label. In 1963 they left Motown and recorded for a number of local labels as The Latin Counts, before Motorcity Records in London signed them as The Valadiers in 1990 for 'Truth Hurts'.

VALENTIN, DAVE
(Flute/Songwriter/Percussion)
Born in New York, Dave was influenced by Latin and Cuban music brought into the family by his father, who was in the merchant marine. Initially taking to percussion, he enrolled at music school where he made friends with **Noel Pointer** (who later recorded his composition 'Rainstorm'). Switching to flute, he impressed **Grusin/Rosen** who signed him to their GRP label in 1978. They produced his early albums, all of which made an impression on the UK 'jazz funk' scene. Recording with GRP to this day, Dave's albums have included *Legends* (1978); *The Hawk* (1979), featuring **Angela Bofill**; *Land Of The Third Eye* (1980), including 'Sidra's Dream' and 'Fantasy'; *Flute Juice* (1983); *Kalahari* (1984); *Jungle Garden* (1985), featuring **Tania Maria**; *Light Struck* (1986), featuring **Angela Bofill**; and *Mind Time* (1987).

VALENTINE BROTHERS
(Duo)
From Columbus, Ohio, brothers John and William 'Billy' Valentine first recorded together as The Valentine Brothers in the late '70s, their debut album being the **Richard Evans**-produced *The Valentine Brothers* for the Source label in 1979.

In 1982 they worked with producer **Bobby Lyle** on *First Take*, including 'Money's Too Tight' (later a hit for Simply Red), 'Just Let Me Be Close To You' and 'This Kind Of Love', a release on the Bridge label and somewhat of a cult album on the UK soul scene. Their later albums have been *Have A Good Time* for A&M Records (1984) and *Picture This* (1987), featuring 'No Better Love' and 'Starship', for EMI America.

Billy Valentine also co-wrote/produced 'You Make Me Want To Love Again' with **Leon Ware** for **Con Funk Shun** (also recorded by **Vesta Williams**).

VALENTINOS
(Group)
Formed in the early 1950s, The Valentinos were the Womack brothers **Bobby Womack**, **Cecil Womack**, Curtis, Harry and Friendly. Bobby was the group's principal songwriter and lead singer, and the group were renowned as pioneers of soul music. Towards the end of the '50s they were taken under the wing of **Sam Cooke** who signed them to his label Sar Records. Here they delivered songs including 'Looking For A Love' and 'It's All Over Now' (later a hit for The Rolling Stones).

Switching to Chess, they cut songs including 'What About Me' and 'I Found A True Love' before Bobby began a solo career. Cecil later formed **Womack & Womack**; both he and Curtis have been married to **Mary Wells**.

VANDELLAS
(Vocal Duo)
From Detroit, The Vandellas were originally Annette Sterling and Rosalind Ashford, backing singers with **Martha Reeves** from the early '60s. Betty Kelly replaced Annette, Sandra Tilley replaced Rosalind, and Martha's sister Lois later replaced Betty, but the group reverted back to the original line-up in the '80s.

Signing to the UK Motorcity label, Rosalind and Annette recorded both with Martha Reeves on 'Step Into My Shoes' (1990) and songs of their own due for 1991 release.

VANDROSS, LUTHER
(Singer/Songwriter/Producer)
Born in the Bronx, New York, in 1951, Luther was musically inspired by his family. His sister sang with The Crests who had a '50s hit with 'Sixteen Candles', and his mother encouraged him to take to piano and work with his sister

after the death of his father in 1959. As he grew older, Luther became more passionate about his music and was greatly inspired by the female singers of the day, in particular **Aretha Franklin**, **Dionne Warwick** and **Diana Ross**. In fact when Diana left **The Supremes** he was so upset that his college grades suffered!

In 1972 he met Ken Harper who was staging *The Wiz* on Broadway. Luther offered three songs of which 'Everybody Rejoice (A Brand New Day)' was used in both the stage and film versions. In the meantime a neighborhood friend Carlos Alomar had become David Bowie's guitarist. During 1974 Carlos invited Luther to a recording studio in Philadelphia where he met Bowie and impressed him with some improvised vocal arrangements. Luther was invited to arrange vocals on Bowie's *Young Americans* (on which he also contributed a song 'Fascination') and later toured with him as a backing singer. Through this he met Bette Midler who hired him to sing backgrounds on *New Depression*, produced by **Arif Mardin**. Arif then utilized him on numerous sessions and before long he was working with artists including Todd Rundgren, Cat Stevens, **Chaka Khan**, Ringo Starr, Gary Glitter and Carly Simon.

Luther also moved into the lucrative world of TV advertising and became the voice on numerous ads for Kentucky Fried Chicken. In 1975 he formed his own group **Luther** which performed live as opening act for **Marvin Gaye**, **James Brown**, **Average White Band** and **Grover Washington** in addition to signing with Cotillion Records for a single 'At Christmas Time' (1976) and albums *Luther* (1976) and *This Close To You* (1977). He later bought back the rights to both these albums so that the label could never reissue them, which is why they are so rare!

Luther returned to session singing and worked with artists including **Quincy Jones** ('Sounds And Stuff Like That') **Chic** ('Le Freak'), **Sister Sledge** ('We Are Family'), **Michael Zager** ('Don't Sneak On Me' and 'Your Love') **Peabo Bryson**, **Bob James** ('Sign Of The Times'), **David Sanborn**, **Hi Gloss** (*Hi-Gloss*), **Lou Rawls**, **Z.Z.Hill**, **Melba Moore** (*Closer*), Round Tree, **Charme** ('Georgy Porgy'), **Kleeer** and **The New York City Band** ('Got To Have Your Body'). As a featured vocalist he began to establish himself with Bionic Boogie ('Hot Butterfly', 1978), and in particular **Change** ('Glow Of Love' and 'Searchin''). He could have toured with Change, but decided instead to tour with **Roberta Flack** who had just recorded his song 'You Stopped Lovin' Me' (on the movie soundtrack album *Bustin' Loose*).

In 1981 he signed to Epic as a solo artist and has scored a multi-platinum album with each release so far. These are *Never Too Much* (1981), including 'A House Is Not A Home'; *Forever, For Always, For Love* (1982), including 'You're The Sweetest One' and 'Since I Lost My Baby'; *Busy Body* (1983), including 'I Wanted Your Love', 'Superstar', 'Until You Come Back To Me' and the **Dionne Warwick** duet 'How Many Times Can We Say Goodbye'; *The Night I Fell In Love* (1985), including 'It's Over Now'; *Give Me The Reason* (1986), including 'Stop To Love', 'See Me' and 'Because It's Really Love'; *Any Love* (1988), including 'I Wonder', 'Come Back' and 'For You To Love'; and *The Power Of Love* (1991).

Throughout this period he realized his ambitions to work as writer/co-writer (with **Marcus Miller**)/producer with artists **Aretha Franklin** (*Jump To It* and *Get It Right*), **Dionne Warwick** (*So Amazing*) and **Diana Ross** ('It's Hard For Me To Say'). He also worked as writer and/or producer with **Cheryl Lynn** (*Instant Love*, including the duet 'If This World Were Mine'), **Teddy Pendergrass** ('You're My Choice Tonight'), **The Temptations** ('Do You Really Love Your Baby'), **The Main Ingredient** ('Party People'), **Gregory Hines** (*There's Nothing Better Than Love*) and **Whitney Houston** ('Who Do You Love'). He arranged the vocals on 'No More Tears (Enough Is Enough)' for Barbra Streisand/**Donna Summer** and was a featured vocalist on **Stevie Wonder**'s 'Part Time Lover'.

VANITY

(Singer)

From Niagara Falls, Ontario, Vanity originally pursued a career as a model, getting her first break at the age of seventeen when she was hired by Pearl Drops Tooth Polish in Toronto. On a visit to Los Angeles she approached the William Morris Agency in the hope they would take her on as a singer. She was told she would never be a success, but as a consolation she was given two tickets for the American Music Awards. Backstage she met **Prince** who asked her if she would like to start her own singing group.

From here she went to Minneapolis where she and two other singers became Vanity 6. A solo album *Wild Animal* followed on Motown (with producer Bill Wolfer), prior to her starring role in *The Last Dragon*. A second solo album *Skin On Skin*, including 'Under The Influence', followed in 1986.

VAUGHN, CARLA

(Singer)

Carla made her most significant contribution to the soul scene during the late '70s as a featured vocalist with **Roy Ayers** both in the studio and on tour. She co-sang the majority of songs on Roy's *You Send Me* (1978), and the follow-up *Fever* (1979).

Carla was also a member of the **Lenny White** group Twennynine, and sang backgrounds with **Bobby M**, **Wax**, **Narada Michael Walden** and **Stacy Lattisaw** ('Jump To The Beat').

VAUGHN, WILLIAM DE

(Singer)

William's one contribution to the soul scene was 'Creme De Creme', originally released by the Texas-based HcRc label in 1982. In the UK it was issued by Excaliber Records.

VEAL, CHARLES
(Violin/Arranger)
Charles worked consistently in the '70s and '80s as a concert-master, arranging and conducting strings on albums for numerous r&b artists, including **Creative Source** (*Pass The Feeling On*), **George Duke**, **Webster Lewis** and **Be Be & Ce Ce Winans**.

He also recorded two solo albums for Capitol, *Only The Best* (1980) and *Believe It!*, including 'New Found Love' (1981).

VEGA, TATA
(Singer)
Born Carmen Rosa Vega in 1951, 'Tata' was a nickname given to her by her parents while she was growing up in Long Island, New York. In 1976, after she had moved to Los Angeles, **Berry Gordy** signed her to the Tamla label (via Motown) where her albums were *Full Speed Ahead* (1976), *Totally Tata* (1977), *Try My Love* (1978), including 'Get It Up For Love' (UK Top 75) penned by **Ned Doheny**, and *Givin' All My Love* (1979).

More recently she has sung backgrounds for **Carl Anderson** and gospel with André Crouch (featured lead vocalist on 'Oh, It Is Jesus', 1987).

VELVELETTES
(Vocal Group)
From Detroit, The Velvelettes are Carolyn Gil, Mildred Gill-Arbour, Bertha Barbee-McNeil and Norma Barbee-Fairhurst who first recorded together in 1962. Their debut single was 'There He Is' for the IPG label, following which they were signed to Motown. Here they scored American success with the classic 'Needle In A Haystack' and 'He Was Really Saying Something', both in 1964. Their other Motown singles include 'Lonely, Lonely Girl Am I', 'A Bird In The Hand Is Worth Two In The Bush' and 'These Things Will Keep Me Loving You' (UK Top 40, 1971).

In 1987 they re-recorded 'Needle In A Haystack' for the UK Nightmare/Motorcity label, with subsequent singles 'Running Out Of Luck', 'Pull My Heartstrings' and album *One Door Closes* (1990).

VILLAGE PEOPLE
(Group)
A product of the '70s disco boom, The Village People was instigated by producer **Jacques Morali** and initially appealed to audiences on the New York/San Francisco gay scenes with their stereotype camp images. In the UK 'San Francisco (You've Got Me)' was a Top 50 hit for the DJM label (1977) before 'YMCA' hit No. 1 in 1978 for Mercury Records. Their other hits were 'In The Navy' (Top 5, 1978), 'Go West' (Top 20, 1979) and 'Can't Stop The Music' (Top 20, 1980). The latter song came from the group's movie of the same name, by which time gay audiences had practically abandoned them. Lead vocalist on all their hits was Victor Wills. Also in the group was **Ray Simpson**, brother of **Ashford & Simpson**'s **Valerie Simpson**.

In 1985 they signed with Record Shack and had a UK Top 60 hit with 'Sex Over The Phone'. A temporary member of the group during this era was **Miles Jaye**, the only heterosexual among them, he was told!

VISION
(Group)
From Atlanta, Georgia, Vision are Leni Law (vocals/drums/bass/percussion) and Brandon McLaughlin (vocals/keyboards/bass). Recording for **William Bell**'s label WRC they recorded an album *Exposed* in 1986.

VISIONS
(Group)
From Cincinnati, Ohio, Visions are Tara Davis (lead vocals), Terry Gibson (guitar/keyboards/vocals), Tim Moore (lead vocals/keyboards/trumpet), Donald Stewart (bass/keyboards/vocals) and David Stewart (keyboards/vocals). A debut album *Visions* was released by Polydor in 1988.

VOICES OF EAST HARLEM
(Vocal Group)
The Voices Of East Harlem were Gerri Griffin (lead), Monica Burress (lead), Bernard Graham, Wayne Garfield, Jerome Mack, Elaine Clark, Cynthia Sessions, Kevin Griffin and Claudia Moore. Formed in the early '70s, they worked with producers **Leroy Hutson** and **Curtis Mayfield** on their recordings for the Just Sunshine Records label. They are best remembered for Leroy Hutson's song/production 'Cashing In' from a 1973 album *The Voices Of East Harlem*. Also on the album was 'Wanted Dead Or Alive', a single released in the UK by the Low Fat Vinyl label in 1988.

VOYAGE
(Group)
French musicians Marc Chantereau (keyboards/percussion/vocals), Pierre Alain Dahan (drums/percussion/vocals), Slim Pezin (guitar/percussion/vocals) and Sauveur Mallia (bass) came together as Voyage for one album *Voyage* for the GTO label in 1978. With a Euro-disco feel, the album delivered the UK Top 20 single 'From East To West', and later returned to the UK singles charts with 'Souvenirs' (1978) and 'Let's Fly Away' (1979).

W

WADE, ADAM
(Singer)
One solo album, *Adam Wade*, was released by the Kirshner label, Don Kirshner's company (via CBS) in 1977. It featured many of Philly's top session people including **Earl Young**, **Bobby Eli** and **Vince Montana**, and was produced by Gene Allan/Gary Knight at Sigma Sound Studios.

WALDEN, NARADA MICHAEL
(Singer/Producer/Songwriter/Drums)
Born Michael Anthony Walden in Kalamazoo, Michigan, in 1952, the eldest of six children, his early musical leanings were towards rock music, and after leaving college (where he was voted 'best-dressed student') he moved to Miami where he played with a rock group the New McGuire Sisters. Discovering the music of the Mahavishnu Orchestra, he met their leader John McLaughlin and became fascinated by the teachings of guru Sri Chinmoy. When he later met Sri Chinmoy, he was given the name 'Narada', an Indian word from Sanskrit (the oldest language in the world) meaning 'supreme musician'. His best friends call him Spike!

In 1973 he joined a new line-up of the Mahavishnu Orchestra as drummer (replacing **Billy Cobham** who had greatly inspired him) and recorded with them on the album *Visions Of The Emerald Beyond*. After a further album with the group, *Inner Worlds* (1975), he left to work with Jeff Beck as musician and producer on *Wired*.

In 1975 he signed to Atlantic as a solo artist and recorded a debut album *Garden Of Love Light*. Then came *I Cry, I Smile* (1976) and *Awakening* (1977) before his most commercially successful release in the UK, *The Dance Of Life* (1979), which included the dance anthems 'Tonight I'm Alright' (Top 40) and 'I Shoulda Loved Ya' (Top 10). This was followed by *Victory* (1980), *Confidence* (1982), including 'Summer Lady', and *Looking At You, Looking At Me* (1983), including a version of 'Reach Out (I'll Be There)' featuring **Maze**. He switched to the Reprise label for *Divine Emotions*, the title track from which was a UK Top 10 hit in 1988.

As writer and/or producer he has worked consistently on the r&b scene from the early '80s with artists including **Stacy Lattisaw** ('Jump To The Beat'), **Angela Bofill** ('Tropical Love' and 'Too Tough'), **Phyllis Hyman** ('Goddess Of Love', 'Riding The Tiger' and 'Why Did You Turn Me On'), **Aretha Franklin** ('Freeway Of Love' and 'Who's Zooming Who'), **Whitney Houston** ('I Wanna Dance With Somebody'), **George Benson** ('Shiver'), **Sister Sledge** ('All American Girls'), **Herbie Hancock**, **Patti Austin** ('Hot! In The Flames Of Love' and 'Starstruck'), **Margie Joseph** ('Ready For The Night'), **The Four Tops**, **Regina Belle** ('Baby Come To Me'), **Brenda Russell** ('Kiss Me With The Wind'), **Lou Rawls** ('It's Supposed To Be Fun') and **The O'Jays** ('Emotionally Yours'). He also played drums with **Rick James** and **Teena Marie**.

His most embarrassing moment was being mistaken for **Al Jarreau** at Stringfellows nightclub in London. His sister-in-law, incidentally, is Wanda Walden who recorded for Elektra in the early '80s.

WALKER, DAVID T.
(Guitar)
David is one of America's leading session guitarists who has worked consistently through the '70s and '80s with artists including **Marvin Gaye**, **Pharaoh Sanders**, **Bloodstone**, **The Brothers Johnson**, **Levert**, **Bobbi Humphrey**, **Barry White**, **Bobby Womack**, **Booker T. Jones**, **Brenton Wood**, **Johnny Bristol**, **Leon Ware**, **Aretha Franklin**, **Stephanie Mills**, **Phyllis Hyman** and **The Crusaders**.

Joe Sample and **Wilton Felder** (of The Crusaders) played on David's album for Ode Records, *On Love* (1976).

WALKER, JUNIOR
(Sax)
Born in Detroit, sax player Junior Walker brought a new dimension to the Motown sound after signing to the label in the mid-'60s. From then until the mid-'70s he scored with a series of singles. In the UK, these were 'How Sweet It Is' (Top 30, 1966), '(I'm A) Road Runner' (Top 20, 1969), 'What Does It Take (To Win Your Love)' (Top 20, 1969), 'Walk In The Night' (Top 20, 1972), 'Take Me Girl I'm Ready' (Top 20, 1973) and 'Way Back Home' (Top 40, 1973). During this time his music mellowed from gritty instruments to vocal soul records. During the early days

of disco he delivered two upbeat dance albums *Whopper Bopper Show Stopper* and *Hot Shot* before leaving Motown.

Through to the present day Junior has worked consistently on the live cabaret circuit, releasing occasional recordings for labels including Washington Hit Makers.

WALLY JUMP JR & THE CRIMINAL ELEMENT

(Group)

Born in Brooklyn, New York, Wally played in numerous local groups before forming Wally Jump Jr & The Criminal Element with a bunch of local session musicians in 1985. The following year they recorded a cover version of the **Dhar Braxton** hit 'Jump Back' which **Arthur Baker** produced and released on his new Criminal label. Arthur also extended the line-up which now comprised Jeff Smith (sax), Rick Sher (of **Warp 9**), Craig Derry (formerly of **The Moments** and **The Sugarhill Gang**), **Will Downing** (vocals), Michigan and Smiley (toasters), and Donny Calvin and Dwight Hawkes (of **Rockers Revenge**).

Further singles were 'Ain't Gonna Pay You One Red Cent' (1986) and 'Turn Me Loose' (UK Top 75, 1987) before Arthur signed them to A&M Records in the UK for *Don't Push Your Luck* (1988), including 'Tighten Up,' 'I Just Can't Stop Dancing' (UK Top 30) and 'Private Party' (UK Top 75).

WALTON, CEDAR

(Keyboards)

Born in Dallas, Texas, Cedar went to university in Denver before moving to New York. Here, in 1965, he joined Art Blakey's group The Jazz Messengers with whom he played through to the mid-'70s. Touring as a solo artist from 1975, he has played Ronnie Scott's jazz club in London every year since 1975.

Recording for CBS, his albums include *Animation* (1978) and *Soundscapes* (1980), the latter including 'Latin America', a latin fusion favourite on the UK jazz funk scene.

WANSEL, DEXTER

(Keyboards/Songwriter/Producer/Singer)

Dexter played keyboards with Philadelphia group **Yellow Sunshine**, prior to becoming a key figure on the Philly music scene from the mid-'70s to the early '80s. During the late '60s he served in the Vietnam War, an experience which has left him in constant fear of the impact of bullets. His involvement with Yellow Sunshine initially led to session work at the Philadelphia International label (PIR) where **The Ebonys** were the first group he recorded with. In 1976 he signed to the label as an artist and released *Life On Mars*, the title track from which established him on the jazz funk dance scene during the mid-'70s. From here he went on to work with most of the leading artists at PIR, ultimately becoming president of A&R for the label.

As an artist he slickly packaged soul, dance, disco, jazz and funk across his further albums *What The World Is Coming To* (1977), *Voyager* (1978) and *Time Is Slipping Away* (1979), including 'The Sweetest Pain' featuring **Terri Wells**. From this era he had one UK Top 75, 'All Night Long' (1978). He worked closely with **M.F.S.B.** as writer, producer, conductor and music director. The orchestra's *Mysteries Of The World* (1980) is often regarded as a Dexter Wansel album, his last before signing to Virgin in 1986. Here *Captured* marked a distinct change in style (although it featured Indian vocalist Meeta Gajjar, **The Jones Girls**, **Bunny Sigler**, his regular songwriting partner Cynthia Biggs, and Dexter himself on vocals).

As writer and/or producer, his American credits include work with **Billy Paul**, **Jean Carne**, **The Jacksons**, **The Jones Girls** ('Night Over Egypt'), **Patti Labelle** ('If Only You Knew' and 'I Can't Forget You'), **Pieces Of A Dream** (co-writing 'Warm Weather'), **Brandi Wells** (co-writing 'I Hate To See You Go'), **Jerry Butler**, **Dee Dee Sharp Gamble** ('I Love You Anyway' and 'I Believe In Love'), **Amy Keys** ('Has It Come To This'), **Teddy Pendergrass** ('Take Me In Your Arms Tonight'), **Grover Washington**, **Joanna Gardner** ('We Can Make It'), **Anthony White**, **The Stylistics** ('What's Your Name'), **Lou Rawls** (*Close Company*), **Miles Jaye** ('I've Been A Fool For You'), **Phyllis Hyman** ('Living All Alone'), **Marilyn Scott** ('Dreams Of Tomorrow' and 'You Are All I Need') and **Sasss**. He also worked with **Stevie Wonder** on 'Let's Get Serious' for **Jermaine Jackson**.

In the UK he has worked with **Junior** ('Not Tonight'), **Nat Augustin** ('That Girl'), **Peter Royer** ('Love Is In Season') and **Loose Ends** (*So Where Are You*, which included a version of 'The Sweetest Pain').

WAR

(Group)

War is Papa Dee Allen (percussion) from Wilmington, Delaware; Harold Brown (drums) from Long Beach, California; B.B. Dickerson (bass) from Torrance, California; Lonnie Jordan (piano); Charles Miller (sax) from Olathe, Kansas; **Lee Oskar** (harmonica) from Copenhagen, Denmark; and Howard Scott from San Pedro, California. In 1959 Charles overheard Harold playing drums in a garage and went in to see if he wanted to be in a group. The pair joined up with Howard and his nephew B.B.Dickerson. Lonnie whom Harold had met at elementary school, was the next to join. The line-up was almost complete, and the original name was Night Shift. By the late sixties the group were playing in a small club on the pier at San Pedro, California, at which point B.B. left to be replaced by Peter Rosen on bass.

At a later gig in Los Angeles, Peter invited producer **Jerry Goldstein** to a rehearsal. Impressed, he told Steve Gold at Far Out Productions about the group, and Jerry, Steve and Eric Burdon (formerly of The Animals) went to see them play at a club called Rag Doll. Jerry also took along Lee Oskar who was out of work and sleeping on

Jerry's couch. Lee joined the group on stage and the result was explosive. Immediately afterwards, Lee joined the group and Eric gave them a funkier sound while becoming a member and focal point of the group. Steve Gold then signed them to his production company, renamed them War and put them in the studio with Jerry. The year was 1969.

Sadly Peter Rosen died soon afterwards from a drugs overdose, but B.B. agreed to rejoin the line-up on a full-time basis. In 1970 the group released a debut single 'Spill The Wine', closely followed by an album *Eric Burdon Declares War*. Eric remained with the group for a second album, *Black Man's Burdon*, and toured with the group, even appearing at Ronnie Scott's jazz club in London where Jimi Hendrix joined them on stage for a jam. During 1971 Eric Burdon and War toured together again, but as two separate acts.

War signed to United Artists and released *War*, then toured with **Isaac Hayes**. Their US albums were *All Day Music*; *The World Is A Ghetto* (1972), including 'The Cisco Kid'; *Deliver The Word* (1973), including 'Me And Baby Brother'; *War Love* (platinum, 1974); and *Why Can't We Be Friends* (1975), including 'Low Rider'. While the group never found the same cult status in the UK that they had built in the USA, 'Low Rider' was a UK chart debut for the group at No. 12 when issued here by Island Records in 1976. Following this 1973's 'Me And Baby Brother' was issued by Island and a Top 25 hit (1976).

At the peak of the disco boom in 1978, War returned on MCA with *Galaxy*, the title track of which became a dancefloor anthem and a UK Top 20 hit. *The Music Band 2* (1979) included a new instrumental version of 'The World Is A Ghetto' which became a jazz funk classic. After a break, War signed to RCA in 1982 for *Outlaw*, which included a UK Top 60 hit 'You Got The Power'. The follow-up was *Life (Is So Strange)* (1983), and in the same year MCA issued *The Music Band – Jazz*, a selection of previously unreleased jazz instrumentals. Following their departure from RCA, War formed their own label Coco Plum in Florida. The first release was 'Groovin'' in 1985, a remake of The Young Rascals hit. Released by Bluebird (via Virgin) in the UK it reached the Top 50.

Outside of the group Lee Oskar has his own harmonica business and was the art director for the **Eloise Laws** album sleeve *Eloise* (1977). The group have been working on an album for 1991 release.

WARD, ANITA

(Singer)

Born in Memphis, Tennessee, in 1957, Anita sang in a local church choir prior to her one international hit in the late '70s. Her only album, *Songs Of Love*, was released by Juana (via TK) in 1979, and featured the UK No. 1 hit 'Ring My Bell', written and produced by **Frederick Knight**. **Sam Dees** and **Tommy Tate** were among the writers on the album. Anita's voice is regarded by some as being a lot finer than the one disco hit gives her credit for.

WARE, LEON

(Singer/Songwriter/Producer)

Born in Detroit, Leon initially established himself as a songwriter, early success coming his way in 1965 with 'Got To Have You Back' for **The Isley Brothers**. During the early '70s he married **Susaye Greene** for whom he produced a solo album for Motown, although it was never released. He also made a few solo recordings for the Gordy subsidiary of Motown, singles including 'Comfort' achieving only a very limited release.

In 1972 he signed as a solo artist to United Artists Records and delivered his debut album *Leon Ware*, before returning to Motown where he co-wrote and produced a number of songs for **Marvin Gaye** that became *I Want You* in 1976.

Leon's own recording career resumed in 1979 with *Inside Is Love*, including 'Inside Your Love' (co-written with **Minnie Riperton**) for the Fabulous label. In 1981 he switched to Elektra Records for *Rockin' You Eternally* and *Leon Ware* (1982), including 'Why I Came To California', before the release of his most recent album *Undercover* (1987) for the Sling Shot label. He is currently at work on new material.

As a songwriter, his work includes 'Everything Inside Of Me' (**Norman Connors**), 'I Wanna Be Where You Are' (**Michael Jackson**), 'If I Ever Lose This Heaven' (**Quincy Jones** and **Average White Band**), 'You Make Me Want To (Love Again)' (**Vesta Williams** and **Con Funk Shun**), 'The Roots In Me' (**Bobby Womack**), 'Rolling Down A Mountainside' (**The Main Ingredient**), 'Body Heat' (**Quincy Jones** and **Rufus**), 'I Know It's You' (**Donny Hathaway**), 'Can You Feel What I'm Saying' (**Minnie Riperton**), 'Easier Said Than Done' (**Loose Ends**), 'Systematic' (**Billy Griffin**) and 'Just Don't Make It Hurt' (**Krystol**). He also produced many of these acts.

Leon's wife is Carol Ware, who since 1973 has been a major figure in the world of r&b music publishing, more recently at MCA Music where she is Vice President of Creative Services.

WARP 9

(Group)

After the demise of **The Strikers** in 1983, drummer **Milton 'Boe' Brown** became the lead singer with Warp 9, initially a studio group on Prism Records catering for the burgeoning 'electro' scene. When 'Boe' left the group Katherine Joyce & Chuck Wansley became the nucleus of Warp 9 and switched to Motown where they took a more soulful direction on *Fade In, Fade out* (1986).

WARWICK, DEE DEE

(Singer)

Dee Dee Warwick is the younger sister of **Dionne Warwick**, and sang with Dionne in gospel group The Drinkyard Singers and as a backing singer. In her own right she recorded for Atco and then Mercury where she is best remembered for her singles 'Do It With All Of Your

Heart' (1965), 'I'm Gonna Make You Love Me' (1966), 'Monday Monday' (1968), 'I Haven't Got Anything Better To Do' (1973) and 'I Wanna Be With You' (1974).

WARWICK, DIONNE

(Singer)

Born Marie Dionne Warwick in East Orange, New Jersey, in 1941, Dionne was part of a musical family; her mother managed a gospel group The Drinkard Singers which included her cousin **Cissy Houston**. Dionne (and her sister **Dee Dee Warwick**) joined the group as a child before forming her own vocal trio The Gospelaires in the late '50s.

In between her studies at the Hartt College Of Music in Connecticut (1960), she spent some time in New York where she made some money as a backing singer. During a session with **The Drifters**, she came to the attention of **Burt Bacharach** who in 1962 signed her to the Scepter label. Here **Bacharach/David** wrote and produced her debut single 'Don't Make Me Over', an American Top 10 hit.

Dionne's collaboration with Bacharach/David originated soft soul music through the early '60s, making black music popular among white audiences for the first time. They worked together on numerous songs (many classics) including 'This Empty Place', 'Wishin' And Hopin'', 'Make The Music Play', 'Anyone Who Had A Heart' (UK Top 50, 1964), 'Walk On By' (Top 10, 1964), 'You'll Never Get To Heaven' (Top 20, 1964), 'Reach Out For Me' (Top 25, 1964), 'A House Is Not A Home' (1964), 'You Can Have Him' (Top 40, 1965), 'Valley Of The Dolls' (Top 30, 1968), 'I Say A Little Prayer For You', 'Do You Know The Way To San Jose' (Top 10, 1968) and 'This Girl's In Love With You' (1969). In the UK these releases were for the Pye label, contributing to her twelve million record sales worldwide during this period.

In 1972 Dionne switched to Warner Brothers where she initially teamed up with **Holland/Dozier/Holland** for 'Just Being Myself' prior to working with producers including **Thom Bell**, Steve Barri and Michael Omartian. In 1974 she recorded with **The Detroit Spinners** on the American No. 1 hit 'Then Came You' and went on the road with **Isaac Hayes** for a tour entitled 'A Man And A Woman'.

After further solo Warner Brothers albums (including *Love At First Sight*, 1977), Dionne signed with Arista in 1979 for *Dionne*, produced by Barry Manilow. Further albums were *No Night So Long* (1980); *Friends In Love* (1982), including 'For You' produced by **Jay Graydon**; *Heartbreaker* (1982); including UK Top 10 hits 'Heartbreaker' and 'All The Love In The World' produced by **Barry Gibb**; and *How Many Times Can We Say Goodbye* (1983), retitled *So Amazing* in the UK, and produced by **Luther Vandross**. She also sang two duets, 'Moments Aren't Moments' and 'Weakness', on the **Stevie Wonder** soundtrack album *The Woman In Red* (1984).

In 1985 Dionne joined Elton John, **Stevie Wonder**, **Gladys Knight** and an array of artists as Dionne Warwick And Friends to record the UK Top 20 hit 'That's What Friends Are For' (and *Friends* album) for AIDS charities, and reunited with producers **Burt Bacharach** and Barry Manilow for *Without Your Love*. It included duets 'It's You' and 'Weakness' with **Stevie Wonder** and 'Finder Of Lost Loves' with **Glenn Jones**. In 1987 she recorded further duets, this time with **Kashif** ('Reservations For Two') and **Jeffrey Osborne** ('Love Power').

On film she had a cameo role in *Rent-A-Cop*, while she also has her own perfume called 'Dionne'.

WAS NOT WAS

(Group)

Originally from Detroit, brothers Don and David Was formed Was Not Was after moving to Los Angeles in the late '70s. David moved there first, and the brothers used to write songs together over the phone. The group also includes vocalists Donald Ray Mitchell (discovered by **Ray Parker Jr**), Sweet Pea Atkinson and Harry Bowens. While their music isn't always strictly soul/r&b, it appeals to the soul audience. In the UK their hits for Geffen/Phonogram have been 'Out Come The Freaks' (UK Top 50, 1984), 'Spy In The House Of Love' (UK Top 75, 1987), 'Walk The Dinosaur' (UK Top 10, 1987), 'Out Come The Freaks Again' (Top 50, 1988), 'Anything Can Happen' (Top 75, 1988) and 'Papa Was A Rolling Stone' (Top 50, 1990). Their most recent album *Are You OK* also includes 'I Blew Up The United States', 'In K-Mart Wardrobes' and 'Elvis' Rolls Royce' (1990).

The Was brothers have also worked with Bonnie Raitt, The B-52s and Bob Dylan.

WASH, MARTHA

(Singer)

Born in San Francisco, Martha originally worked in a singing duo with Izora Redman. Known as **Two Tons Of Fun**, they worked with **Sylvester** and recorded for Fantasy Records prior to changing their name to **The Weather Girls** and recording for CBS.

Martha later worked as a session singer, anonymously contributing lead vocals to such major dance hits as 'Everybody Everybody' for Black Box and 'Everybody Dance Now' for C&C Music Factory. In 1991 she signed to BMG Records as a solo artist.

WASHINGTON, GENO

(Singer)

Geno first established himself in the UK during the mid-'60s as lead singer of The Ram Jam Band. In Detroit he recorded 'Gino Is A Coward' for the Ric Tic label (1964), but didn't pursue his singing career back home in America until the late '70s. The UK gave him somewhat of a cult status and he recorded here until the late '70s on labels including DJM. In 1980 the group Dexy's Midnight Runners paid tribute to him in their hit single 'Geno'.

WASHINGTON JR, GROVER
(Saxophone/Producer/Songwriter)
Born in Buffalo, New York, in 1943, Grover was given his first saxophone by his father (also a sax player) and was playing professionally by the age of twelve. After forming a group at the age of fourteen and establishing himself on the local jazz circuit, he made his recording debut in 1970 on **Charles Earland**'s *Living Black*. By now he had moved to Philadelphia and built a demand for his playing at the Prestige label where he worked with a number of artists including **Johnny Hammond**. He eventually attracted the attention of producer **Creed Taylor** who signed him to the Kudu subsidiary of the CTI label.

Grover's first solo album was *Inner City Blues* (allegedly an album of material originally intended for **Hank Crawford** who missed the session!). Its success enabled him to give up his other career as a record salesman. Further CTI albums included *Mister Magic* (1975), *Soul Box*, *Feels So Good* and *A Secret Place*, all of which established him on the UK 'jazz funk' scene.

In 1978 he switched to Motown for *Reed Seed*, and although he moved labels again (to Elektra) in 1979, Motown issued *Baddest* and *Skylarkin'* in 1980 with a set *Live At The Bijou* which was written and recorded with a group of musicians he put together in Philadelphia who later became **Locksmith**. In 1979 a debut Elektra album *Paradise*, including 'Tell Me About It Now', was released ahead of his 1980 Grammy award-winning *Winelight*, including the UK Top 40 hit 'Just The Two Of Us' (featuring vocals by **Bill Withers**), which sold over two million copies across America.

Follow-up Elektra albums were *Come Morning* (1981), *The Best Is Yet To Come* (featuring **Patti Labelle** and **Bobby McFerrin**, 1982), and *Inside Moves* (1984) before he teamed up with guitarist Kenny Burrell for *Togethering* on the Blue Note label (1985). He then settled at CBS where his albums have been *Strawberry Moon* (1987), including 'The Look of Love' and 'Keep In Touch' (featuring **Jean Carne**); and *Time Out Of Mind* (1989), including 'Sacred Kind Of Love' (featuring **Phyllis Hyman**). As a session player he has recorded with artists including **Sasss** ('I Didn't Mean It At All', 1984), **Bob James**, **Charles Earland** ('Milestones'), **Rose Royce** ('Lonely Road'), **Miles Jaye** ('Irresistible') and **Roy Ayers** ('Sexy Sexy Sexy'), while he has also produced **Pieces of A Dream** (their first three albums, while also playing sax/writing songs for the group) and **Jean Carne** ('Closer Than Close', 'Flame of Love' and 'Heartache').

WASHINGTON, KEITH
(Singer)
Born in Detroit, Keith sang his own versions of soul hits in nightclubs during his early teens. After an invitation to sing backing vocals with **The Dramatics** he met producer **Don Davis** who in turn introduced him to **George Clinton** for whom he also sang backing vocals in the early '70s.

In the mid-'80s he moved to Los Angeles where he eventually signed with Qwest Records who released his debut album *Make Time For Love*, including 'Kissing You', in 1991.

WASHINGTON, STEVE
(Singer/Songwriter/Producer/Trumpet)
Born in Newark, New Jersey, Steve Washington is the nephew of **Ralph 'Pee Wee' Middlebrook** of **The Ohio Players**. While at school in Ohio, Steve formed a band Black Satin Soul, which later merged with another Ohio group Young Mystics to become **Slave**.

In 1979 following Slave's success with 'Just A Touch Of Love', Steve left the group with three fellow members to form a new group **Aurra**. After a series of recordings here (including 'Make Up Your Mind' which he co-wrote/produced) he recorded 'Please Don't Go' (1984) for the Salsoul label as a solo artist.

WATANABE, SADAO
(Sax)
Born in Utsunomiya, Japan, in 1933, Sadao took up the clarinet at the age of fifteen. He studied music in Boston, USA, where he also recorded, but he built his reputation as a saxophonist back in Japan. From the mid-'70s he recorded a series of albums for the Inner City label including *Autumn Blow*, *My Dear Life* and *California Shower*, before he switched to CBS.

Here his popularity broadened to America and the UK jazz funk scene with *All About Love* (1980) and later that year *How's Everything*, including 'Nice Shot' and 'No Problem' recorded live in Japan featuring The Tokyo Philharmonic Orchestra (arranged and conducted by **Dave Grusin**). His following CBS albums included *Orange Express* (1981) before a switch to Elektra where his albums have included *Rendezvous* (1984), including 'If I'm Still Around Tomorrow' (featuring vocals by **Roberta Flack**), and *Maisha* (1985), featuring vocals by **Brenda Russell**.

WATER AND POWER
(Vocal Group)
Rachel Sanders, Warren Sams and Christine Adams Tripp recorded as Water And Power under the direction of producer **Harvey Fuqua** on his Honey Records label via Fantasy. 1975's *Water And Power* was arranged by **Wade Marcus**.

WATERS
(Vocal Group)
Based in Los Angeles, The Waters are family group Luther, Julia, Oren and Maxine Waters who have recorded/toured as backing vocalists with countless soul, jazz and rock artists through the '70s, '80s and '90s. These include **Bobby Womack**, **Pharaoh Sanders**, **Herbie Hancock**, **Alphonse Mouzon**, **Benny Golson**, **Blue Mitchell**, **Gene Harris**, **Gene Dunlap**, **Billy Paul**, **Will Downing** and **Glenn Jones**. Outside of the r&b

field they have sung with artists including Bon Jovi, Rod Stewart and Bruce Springsteen on more than 200 gold and platinum albums.

As a group they have recorded their own albums for labels including Blue Note (*Waters*, 1975), Warner Brothers (*What's On Your Mind*, 1979) and Arista (*Water Colours*, 1980). More recently they have been involved in setting up their own label.

WATLEY, JODY
(Singer/Dancer/Songwriter)
Born in Chicago, Jody's mother was a singer and pianist while her father was a travelling evangelist and friend of singers including **Sam Cooke**, **Johnnie Taylor** and **Jackie Wilson** (who was Jody's godfather), Jody made her stage debut at the age of eight when Jackie Wilson pulled her on stage during one of his shows!

At the age of fifteen she moved with her family to Los Angeles where she became a dancer on the TV show *Soul Train*. Here she met **Jeffrey Daniels** with whom she teamed up to become **Shalamar** with **Howard Hewett**. In 1984 she left the group and moved to London where she worked as a model, recorded sessions with Art Of Noise and Musical Youth, and had a brief career as a solo artist for Phonogram (joining the line-up of Live Aid on 'Do They Know It's Christmas').

From here she returned to Los Angeles for the start of a more rewarding period in her career after signing with MCA Records. She scored solo success with songs from *Jody Watley* (1987), including 'Looking For A New Love' produced/co-written by **Andre Cymone** (UK Top 20) and 'Don't You Want Me' (UK Top 75), and *Larger Than Life* (1989), including 'Real Love', 'Friends' (with Eric B and Rakim) and 'Precious Love'.

WATSON, ANTHONY
(Singer/Songwriter)
Born in Mobile, Alabama, Anthony sang in Europe with a group Return Ticket, and in Alabama with a group Praze (recording 'Solid Love Affair'), before settling in Dallas, Texas. As a session singer he recorded with **The Manhattans**, **Millie Jackson** and **L.J.Reynolds** before the Amherst label signed him as a solo artist in 1985. Here he recorded *Anthony Watson*, before joining **The Chi-Lites**, replacing **Eugene Record** as lead singer and principal songwriter.

Away from The Chi-Lites, he continued to record as a solo artist. *9 Days Of October*, including 'Do What You Want', was released on the Miami-based label Tashamba in 1991.

WATSON, JOHNNY 'GUITAR'
(Singer/Guitar/Keyboards/Songwriter)
Born in Houston, Texas, in 1935, Johnny was in his early teens when he moved to Los Angeles with a guitar he inherited from his grandfather. Initially he found work as a pianist/organist, playing on early recordings for **Herb Alpert** during the '60s. He also developed his own style of playing electric guitar, with Jimi Hendrix later crediting Johnny as a major influence. It was bandleader Johnny Otis who helped him land his first record deal as a solo artist, *Gangster Of Love*, including 'Space Guitar', being his debut album for King Records in 1952.

On RPM Records he scored American success with 'Those Lonely Lonely Nights' (1955) before touring with artists including **Sam Cooke**, **Jackie Wilson** and **Ruth Brown**. In 1965 he toured the UK with Larry Williams and was billed as Elvis Presley's private guitar player! The following year he broadened into jazz and wrote words to Cannonball Adderley's 'Mercy Mercy Mercy'. He also signed to the Okeh label and delivered *Two For The Price Of One* with Larry Williams (1967), and his tribute to pianist Fats Waller *In A Fats Bag* (1968).

During the early '70s he recorded for the Fantasy label and just fell short of a UK pop hit with 'I Don't Want To Be A Lone Ranger' (1975), also writing/co-producing for **Betty Everett** ('Sweet Dan', 1973). In 1976 he switched to DJM where his albums were *Ain't That A Bitch* (1976), including 'I Need It' (UK Top 40), *A Real Mother For Ya* (1977), including title track hit (UK Top 50), *Family Clone* (1979) and *Love Jones* (1980).

He reunited with **Herb Alpert**, recording with Herb on *Rise* (1979) and signing to his A&M label for *That's What Time It Is* (1982), co-produced with Herb and **Michael Zager**, *Giant* and *What The Hell Is This?* He then switched to the independent Valley Vue label for a single 'Strike On Computers' (1984).

WATSON, STAN 'THE MAN'
(Songwriter/Producer)
From Louisiana, Stan Watson first established himself during the '40s in the retail world with his own business Stan's Record Shack. In 1960 he launched a series of labels, Jewel, Paula and Ronn, while as a songwriter he wrote 'La La Means I Love You' (**The Delfonics**) and 'Armed And Extremely Dangerous' (**First Choice**). He in fact discovered The Delfonics whom he produced (and managed) alongside First Choice.

WATSON, WAH WAH
(Guitar/Songwriter/Producer)
'Wah Wah' Watson is one of America's top session guitarists and has played with numerous artists including **Michael Jackson**, **Pharaoh Sanders**, **Uncle Louie** and **Donald Byrd** ('Loving You'). As a songwriter and/or producer he has worked with **Herbie Hancock** ('Doin' It'), **Billy Preston** ('Since I Held You Close') and **Evelyn 'Champagne' King** ('Stop It').

WATTS, ERNIE
(Sax)
From Los Angeles, Ernie Watts has established himself as one of the top session saxophone players on the r&b scene, as well as recording in his own right. Through the

'70s and '80s he has recorded with artists including **Quincy Jones**, **Sarah Vaughan**, **Barry White**, **The Temptations**, **The Four Tops**, **Love Unlimited Orchestra**, **Neil Larsen**, **Pharaoh Sanders**, **The Blackbyrds**, **Donald Byrd**, **James Ingram**, **Margie Joseph**, **Donna Summer**, ('State Of Independence'), **Randy Crawford**, **Jean Carne** ('Trust Me') and **Teena Marie** ('My Dear Mr Gaye').

His own recordings include *Musician* (Qwest, 1985) and *Look In Your Heart* (Elektra, 1980). He is now a member of **The Meeting**, a quartet of musicians signed to GRP.

WAX
(Group)
Wax were Joe Lattisaw Jr (guitar), Bennie Melton Jr (lead vocals), James 'Chan' Claggett Jr (keyboards), David Gregory Searles (percussion), Ronnie Kidd (bass), Steve Wagner (drums), and Chuck Moritt (sax/flute). Their albums include *Do You Believe In Magic* including 'When And If I Fall In Love', produced by **Lenny White** for RCA in 1981.

WE THE PEOPLE
(Vocal Group)
Instigated by Landy McNeal in the '60s, New York group We The People featured the vocals of Bill McEachern who after seven years with the group left to replace Tony Reynolds in **Odyssey**. In the early '70s the group recorded for the Lion label (via Polydor) where 'Making My Daydream Real' (later recorded by **Frances Nero**) became in demand on the UK soul scene. Originally released in 1973, the song was written and produced by Landy McNeal who also scored on the 'Northern soul' scene with 'Counting On You' as a solo artist.

WEATHER GIRLS
(Vocal Duo)
Vocalists **Martha Wash** and Izora Redman-Armstead were formerly known as **Two Tons Of Fun** before signing to CBS as The Weather Girls in 1982. Here they scored with 'It's Raining Men', which in the UK charted Top 75 in 1983 and Top 5 in 1984. They also created interest with a cover version of Rogers/Hammerstein's 'I'm Gonna Wash That Man Right Outta My Hair' (1983), and left CBS in 1985 after *Big Girls Don't Cry*.

WEATHER REPORT
(Group)
Josef Zawinul (keyboards) and Wayne Shorter (sax) formed Weather Report in the early '70s. The line-up changed over the years, members at various times including Miroslav Vitous (bass), Jaco Pastorius (bass) and **Billy Cobham** (drums). With their own style of fusion jazz, their albums for CBS include *Weather Report*, *I Sing The Body Electric*, *Mr Gone* (1976), *Heavy Weather* (1977), including 'Birdland', and *Night Passage*. Joe Zawinul later recorded a solo album *The Immigrant* featuring the vocals of **Perri**.

WEATHERS, BARBARA
(Singer)
Barbara Weathers sang as lead vocalist with **Atlantic Starr** on songs including 'Silver Shadow' and 'One Love' before signing to the Reprise label (via WEA) as a solo artist. Here she delivered *Barbara Weathers* (1990) including the **Maurice White** co-written/produced 'Anywhere'.

WEBB, RICK
(Singer)
Born in Virginia, Rick moved to Washington DC at the age of 15. Here he sang backing vocals with The Dominoes, later fronting The Raw Band for five years, releasing 'Don't Keep Me Waiting' on the Universal Creations label (1988). In 1989 he released a solo single 'Sitting On Your Doorstep', and worked on an album with **Al Johnson** and Willie Lester for the Washington Hit Makers label.

WEBB, SPIDER
(Drummer)
'Spider' Webb worked as a session drummer for the San Francisco label Fantasy during the '70s, also recording a solo album. Among the many artists he recorded with at Fantasy were **Side Effect**.

WEEKS & CO.
(Studio Group)
Instigated by **Richie Weeks**, New York-based group Weeks & Co. delivered a series of dance singles during the early '80s on labels including Chazro ('Rock Your World', 1981), Prelude ('Go With The Flow', 1982) and Salsoul ('If You're Looking For Fun,' 1983).

WEEKS, RICHIE
(Singer/Songwriter/Producer)
From New York, Richie sang with his own group **Weeks & Co.** in the early '80s in addition to being involved in numerous dance records during the remainder of the '80s and through to this day. Under his own name, Richie Weeks & Centerfold released a single 'Forbidden Fruit' in 1985, while more recently Agape Sounds Featuring Richie Weeks released 'Your Love Never Fails' (1991).

WEISS, SAM
(Label boss)
Sam Weiss is a New York businessman who in the early '80s launched his own Sam label at the end of the disco era. Initially the label scored dancefloor success for artists including **John Davis** & The Monster Orchestra, **Mike & Brenda Sutton** and Vicky D.More. Recently the label launched the career of **Richard Rogers**.

WELLS, BRANDI

(Singer)

From Philadelphia, Brandi was given the nickname 'Peaches' during her years as a Philly backing singer with **Larry James** and his groups including **F.L.B.** and **Slick** (for whom she was lead singer). In 1981 her debut album *Watch Out* was released by the WMOT/Fantasy label (Virgin in the UK) and included 'What Goes Around Comes Around', 'When You Get Right Down To It' and 'Fantasy' produced by **Nick Martinelli**. A second album *S* was released on the Omni label in 1985.

WELLS, JAMES

(Singer)

Born in Chicago in 1956, James sang gospel before turning to secular music with his sister Sue. Performing as Sue and James, they were shortly joined by Shirley King (daughter of **B.B.King**) to become Shirley, James and Sue before signing to Stax in 1972 (although nothing was released).

From here James joined a new group 100% Pure Poison before meeting songwriter/producer **Ian Levine** who put him in the studio to record 'Baby I'm Still The Same Man', released by Polydor in 1976. Ian later wrote/produced his *My Claim To Fame*, including 'I Guess That's Life', for the AVI label in 1978.

WELLS, MARY

(Singer)

Born in Detroit, Mary was singing gospel in church by the age of four. She had ambitions of being a performer while she and her brothers were raised by her mother. Mary later discovered that her father had connections with the Mafia, a fact she discovered after he died which devastated her in later life.

In 1961 she was introduced to **Berry Gordy** at Motown by her husband **Herman Griffin** who was already recording for the label. Her debut single was 'Bye Bye Baby', a song originally recorded by **Jackie Wilson**, but Berry Gordy made Mary record it after hearing her perform it live. She became the first artist to have a release on the official Motown label, and scored American hits with 'Two Lovers', 'Your Old Standby', 'You Beat Me To The Punch', 'The One Who Really Loves You', 'What's Easy For Two Is So Hard For One', and her one classic international hit 'My Guy' (1964), a Top 5 hit when released in the UK on the Stateside label. The song also firmly established **Smokey Robinson** as a songwriter at Motown.

During this time she was known as 'Little Miss Hit-maker', and was the first Motown artist to wear elegant gowns on stage. She also toured with The Beatles, and in 1964 recorded a duet album *Together* with **Marvin Gaye** from which 'Once Upon A Time' was a UK Top 50 hit single. Under the direction of her husband she left Motown later in the year to record for the 20th Century, Warner Brothers, Jubilee and Reprise labels, although hits eluded her. She divorced Herman Griffin and married **Cecil Womack**. In 1983 **Wayne Henderson** produced a remake of 'My Guy', while **Ian Levine** produced yet another version for Mary in 1990. In the meantime she divorced Cecil Womack and married his brother Curtis Womack, a former member of **The Valentinos**.

In 1987 she began working with writer/producer **Ian Levine** and released a single 'Don't Burn Your Bridges' on his Nightmare label. Switching to Motorcity, an album *Keeping My Mind On Love* was released in 1990, the year it was announced she had cancer of the throat.

WELLS, TERRI

(Singer/Songwriter)

Born in Philadelphia, Terri sang in church before being old enough to sing in clubs. She and some local friends formed **City Limits**, who signed briefly to Philadelphia International Records (PIR) in the mid-'70s. When the group disbanded **Dexter Wansel** hired her as a session singer at PIR, and for the next few years she both toured and recorded with artists including **Lou Rawls**, **M.F.S.B.**, **Leon Huff**, **Jean Carne** and Dexter (singing on 'Love Is Everywhere', 'Life On Mars' and lead on 'The Sweetest Pain').

In 1979 Dexter retired from live performances, and Terri was hired by **Roy Ayers**. She toured in his band and co-wrote 'Let's Stay Together' for Roy on his *Feelin' Good* album. She was a featured lead vocalist on Roy's 'Turn Me Loose', and was signed by Roy to his Uno Melodic label, although nothing was released.

When **Nick Martinelli** was hired by the Philly World label as a staff producer, he recommended they sign Terri. This led to her debut solo release 'You Make It Heaven' (UK Top 75) in 1983. Her follow-up 'I'll Be Around' (UK Top 20, 1984) was a remake of the **Detroit Spinners** classic on which she had been one of the original background singers! *Terri Wells*, also including 'Who's That Stranger', was released later in 1984.

Terri co-wrote 'I Can't Forget You' (**Patti Labelle**) and 'Closer Than Close' (**Jean Carne**), and sang backgrounds with **52nd Street** and **Joanna Gardner**.

WESLEY, FRED

(Producer/Songwriter/Trombone)

Born in Mobile, Alabama, in 1944, Fred first joined the **James Brown** band The JBs as trombone player in 1968 (after he had left the army), but only stayed for two weeks. In 1971, after **Maceo Parker** had left James (taking the original JBs with him), **Bootsy Collins** was brought in to form a new line-up and Fred rejoined.

After recording on songs including 'Hot Pants' (which he co-wrote) and 'Good Foot', Fred left James in 1975, but continued his association with **Bootsy Collins** as a member of his Rubber Band. Through Bootsy's association with **George Clinton**, Fred also played as a member of The Horny Horns, while elsewhere he worked with artists including **The S.O.S. Band** (arranging 'Take Your Time, Do It Right'), **Trussel** (co-producing 'Love Injection'), **Grady Harrell** (producing *Mwana*), **Bobby Womack**, **Michael Wycoff**, **The Gap Band** and **Terry Callier**, before moving to Denver in 1988.

As a solo artist he recorded briefly for the Curtom/RSO label (including 'House Party' in 1980), then in Denver he formed the Fred Wesley Quartet. He has recorded for the Antilles label (while also appearing with the **James Taylor Quartet** on their rendition of the theme from *Starsky & Hutch* released by Polydor, 1990).

WESTON, KIM

(Singer)

Born Agatha Nathalie Weston, in Detroit, Kim first took to singing at the suggestion of her swimming coach! She felt it would improve Kim's breath control. After becoming an expert swimmer she decided she liked singing better. During the early '60s she began to sing in church and initially set her heart on being a top gospel singer. While recording some demos to make extra pocket money she attracted the attention of songwriter **Eddie Holland** (of **Holland/Dozier/Holland**) who introduced her to **Berry Gordy** at Motown.

Here she initially recorded on Motown's Divinity label with gospel group The Wright Specials before meeting Motown songwriter/A&R manager Mickey Stevenson, whom she married. Her most notable moments were 'Take Me In Your Arms', 'It Should Have Been Me', 'A Thrill A Moment', 'Love Me All The Way' and 'Helpless' (1966), and her duet with **Marvin Gaye** 'It Takes Two' (UK Top 20, 1967) from their duet album *Take Two*.

Later in 1967 Kim moved to Los Angeles where she signed to MGM for two albums. These included the highly regarded soul cut 'You're Just The Kind Of Guy' and the Northern soul classic 'I Got What You Need'. On tour she employed the services of **Ronnie McNeir**, for whom she secured a record deal with RCA in 1972. Kim later recorded with Ronnie on 'Extra Extra' (1972) and 'Spirit Of Love' (1985). She also recorded for Stax and husband Mickey's label Banyan Tree before returning to Detroit and recording for a number of independent local labels. Through the '80s Kim has also run a workshop to encourage and help young black talent to be successful in the music business (**Body** is one of her protégés).

More recently she has recorded for the UK Nightmare/Motorcity label, commencing with a single 'Signal Your Intention' (1987) and more recently an album *Investigate* (1990).

WHATNAUTS

(Group)

Formed in Baltimore, The Whatnauts recorded with **The Moments** as The Moments And Whatnauts on songs including 'Girls' (UK Top 5, 1975) before going their separate ways. In 1981 they made an impact on the UK dance scene with 'Help Is On The Way', released on the Harlem International label out of New York.

WHEELER, AUDREY

(Singer)

A top New York-based session singer, Audrey has recorded backing vocals for numerous artists through the '80s including **Najee**, **Atlantic Starr**, **Eric Gable**, **Freddie Jackson**, **Glenn Jones**, **James 'D-Train' Williams** and many more. Between 1981–3 she sang as lead vocalist with **Unlimited Touch**, and in 1985 was the featured vocalist on 'Step By Step' by **Jeff Lorber**. In 1987 she signed to Capitol and released *Let It Be Me*, including 'Irresistible' produced by **Preston Glass**. More recently she recorded the duet 'This Must Be Heaven' with **Omar Chandler** on *Omar Chandler* (1991).

WHEELER, CARON

(Singer)

London-based singer Caron Wheeler began to take her singing seriously from the age of twelve. She sang in reggae bands Brown Sugar and Afrodiziak before establishing herself as a top session singer with artists including Phil Collins, Elvis Costello and Erasure.

She was later taken on by **Soul II Soul** as lead vocalist on 'Keep On Moving' and 'Back To Life' (1989), following which she signed to RCA as a solo artist for *UK Black*, featuring 'Living In The Light' and 'Blue'.

WHISPERS

(Vocal Group)

The Whispers were originally formed by brothers Wallace and Walter Scott in the mid-'60s. Born in Texas, the brothers formed the group after moving to Los Angeles where they were joined by Nicholas Caldwell, Marcus Hutson and Gordy Hamilton. Leaveil Degree later replaced Gordy Hamilton. Across America, the group began to score hits with songs including 'Seems Like I Gotta Do Wrong' (1970) and 'I Only Meant To Wet My Feet' (1971). Recording for the Janus label their albums included *Planets Of Life* (1973) and *Whispers Gettin' Louder* (1974), including 'Where There Is Love' and 'Bingo', produced in Philadelphia utilizing the services of **BHY** and **Bunny Sigler**, before they switched to Soul Train Records (via RCA) in 1975. Here their albums included the **Norman Harris**-produced *One For The Money* (1976), while their remake of the Bread hit 'Make It With You' was popular in 1977, before the Soul Train label became known as SOLAR (Sound Of Los Angeles Records).

Their albums continued with *Headlights* (1978), including '(Let's Go) All The Way'; *The Whispers* (1979), including the **Leon Sylvers**-penned/produced 'And The Beat Goes On' (UK Top 5), 'Lady' (UK Top 75) and 'My Girl' (UK Top 30); *Imagination* (1980), including 'It's A Love Thing' (UK Top 10) and 'I Can Make It Better' (UK Top 50); *Love Is Where You Find It* (1981), including 'In The Raw' – they were one of the first groups to use the idea of dance side/ballad side with this album; *Love For Love* (1983), including the **Jerry Knight**-penned 'Tonight';

So Good (1984), including 'Some Kinda Lover' and 'Contagious' (UK Top 75); *Just Gets Better With Time* (1987), including the **L.A./Babyface**-penned/produced 'Rock Steady' (UK Top 40), 'Special F/X' (UK Top 75) and the **Gary Taylor**-penned/produced title track; and *More Of The Night* (1990), their debut for Capitol.

Independently Nicholas Caldwell arranged vocals, played keyboards and produced Solar label mates **Collage** and **Carrie Lucas**, while elsewhere he co-arranged/produced **Leroy Hutson**'s *Paradise* (1982).

WHITE, ANTHONY
(Singer)
Born in Philadelphia, Anthony White signed to the Philadelphia International label in 1975 and released a debut 'Hey Baby'. The song was not featured on his 1976 album *Could It Be Magic* which stirred interest among UK soul fans with 'Stop And Think It Over'. In 1977 Anthony recorded 'I Can't Turn You Loose' for the Salsoul label. The B side was the instrumental 'Block Party', popular on New York disco scene. This was his last release until he teamed up with **Paul Simpson** as his featured vocalist on 'Walk Away From Love' (a song first recorded by **David Ruffin**) released in 1989.

WHITE, BARRY
(Singer/Songwriter/Producer/Keyboards)
Born in Galveston, Texas, in 1944, Barry grew up in Los Angeles where he was taught the piano and sang in a high school group The Upfronts. He began his professional music career as an arranger and then producer/road manager for **Bob & Earl**, at which point he met **Gene Page** who arranged Bob & Earl's '60s hit 'Harlem Shuffle'. From here he built a friendship and working relationship with Gene which continues to this day.

Also during the mid-'60s he worked as an A&R man for Bronco Records where he produced **Viola Wills** and **Felice Taylor** ('I Feel Love Coming On') before forming **Love Unlimited** in the early 70s. Signing them to Uni Records, the group scored with 1972's 'Walking In The Rain (With The One I Love)'. This success led to a recording contract at 20th Century for both Barry as a solo artist and **The Love Unlimited Orchestra** in 1973.

Barry established himself internationally with a string of hits which in the UK (via Pye) were 'I'm Gonna Love You Just A Little Bit More Baby' (Top 30, 1973), 'Never Never Gonna Give You Up' (Top 20, 1974), 'Can't Get Enough Of Your Love Babe' (Top 10, 1974), 'You're The First, The Last, My Everything' (No.1, 1974), 'What Am I Gonna Do With You' (Top 5, 1975), 'I'll Do Anything You Want Me To' (Top 20, 1975), 'Let The Music Play' (Top 10, 1975), 'You See The Trouble With Me' (Top 5, 1975), 'Baby We Better Try And Get It Together' (Top 20, 1976), 'Don't Make Me Wait Too Long' (Top 20, 1976), 'I'm Qualified To Satisfy You' (Top 40, 1977), 'It's Ecstasy When You Lay Down Next To Me' (Top 40, 1977), 'Just The Way You Are' (Top 20, 1978), and 'Sha La La Means I Love You' (Top 75, 1979). His albums included *Can't Get Enough, Just Another Way To Say I Love You, Let The Music Play, I've Got So Much To Give, Barry White Sings For Someone You Love* and *Stone Gone*. Barry also continued his work as a writer/producer with **Love Unlimited** (featuring his wife Glodean) and **The Love Unlimited Orchestra** together with other artists for 20th Century Records.

Having earned 100 gold albums and 40 platinum albums around the world, Barry built a recording studio at his home in Sherman Oaks, California, which he calls R.I.S.E. (Research In Sound Excellence). He also formed his own label Unlimited Gold (via CBS) where he continued to record, including *Sheet Music* (1980) and *Changes* (1982), but without the same degree of success. Also at Unlimited Gold he instigated albums for artists including **Danny Pearson**, and the **Love Unlimited Orchestra** featuring **Webster Lewis**.

Disappointed by his liaison with CBS, he did not resume his solo career until 1987, signing to A&M where his albums have been *The Right Night & Barry White* (1987), including 'Sho' You Right' (Top 20) and 'For Your Love (I'll Do Most Anything)', and *The Man Is Back* (1989), including 'Follow That And See Where It Leads Y'all'. Also in 1989 he was a featured vocalist for **Quincy Jones** on 'The Secret Garden' from Quincy's *Back On The Block*. Barry's godson, incidentally, is **Chuckii Booker**.

WHITE, JOHN
(Singer)
John White made an impression on the soul scene following the release of *Night People* for Orpheus Records (via Capitol) in 1987.

WHITE, KARYN
(Singer)
Born in Los Angeles, Karyn gained early professional experience as a backing singer with **O'Bryan**. She later met vocalist **Michael Jeffries** who was working with **Jeff Lorber** on a debut album for Warner Brothers. Jeff was looking for a female singer, and Karyn became the lead vocalist on his club hit 'Facts Of Love' (1986). The popularity of this track led to a solo deal for Karyn at Warner Brothers where she worked with writers/producers **L.A./Babyface** on her debut *Karyn White* (1988), including 'The Way You Love Me' (UK Top 50), 'Superwoman' and a duet with **Babyface** 'Love Saw It'. She recorded the duet 'Not Thru Being With You' with **Michael Jeffries** (1989) and sang backgrounds with **Bobby Brown**, **Howard Hewett**, **Ray Parker Jr** and **Johnny Gill**.

WHITE, LENNY
(Songwriter/Producer/Drummer)
Born in New York in 1949, Lenny began his career as a drummer, initially playing in local groups. In the early '70s he played with **Miles Davis** (*Bitches Brew*) before joining

Return To Forever. When the group split up in 1976 he signed directly to the Nemperor label (via Atlantic) for *Venusian Summer* (1976), *Big City* (1976) and *Streamline* (1977).

In 1978 he switched to Elektra for *Best Of Friends*, before forming a group Twennynine with **Carla Vaughn** (vocals), Jocelyn Smith (vocals), Skip Anderson (keyboards), Barry Johnson (bass) and Eddy Martinez (guitar) in 1979. Recording as featured artist with the group, further Elektra albums included *Attitude* (1983), including 'Didn't Know About Love (Till I Found You)'. He later became one of the Jamaica Boys, a group also comprising of **Marcus Miller** (bass) and Dinky Bingham (vocals).

As a drummer he has recorded sessions with artists including **John Klemmer**, Miroslav Vitous, **Pharaoh Sanders**, Santana and **Bob James**, while he has also produced for **Zuice** ('I'm A Survivor'), **Wax** (*Do You Believe In Magic*), **Pieces Of A Dream** and more recently Nicki Richards (*Naked To The World*) among many more.

WHITE, LYNN

(Singer)

Based in Memphis, Lynn records for **Willie Mitchell**'s label Waylo where her albums have included *Love & Happiness* (1987), including 'If You Think You're Lonely Now'.

WHITE, MAURICE

(Singer/Songwriter/Producer/Drummer)

Born in Memphis, Tennessee, in 1944, Maurice was singing gospel by the age of six. At the age of eleven he took up drums and formed a band with schoolmate **Booker T. Jones**. In 1960 he moved to Chicago and studied music composition and percussion at Roosevelt University with a view to becoming a music teacher.

Between 1963 and 1965 Maurice became a house drummer at Chess Records, playing on sessions with Chuck Berry, **Etta James**, **Billy Stewart** ('Summertime'), **Jackie Wilson**, **Fontella Bass** ('Rescue Me'), The Radiants ('Voice Your Choice'), **Curtis Mayfield** & The Impressions and **The Dells**. At 22 he joined **Ramsey Lewis** as drummer, playing on ten of his albums during a four-year period (including the hit 'Wade In The Water'). During this time he discovered the kalimba, a small finger keyboard from Africa. In 1969 he formed his own group, The Salty Peppers, who had two hits in the Chicago area, 'La La Time' and 'Love Is Life'. The following year he changed the name to **Earth Wind & Fire**, which became one of the super groups of the '70s.

In 1976 Maurice formed Kalimba Productions, a division of Earth Wind & Fire which wrote and/or produced for artists including **Deniece Williams** (including 'Free' and *This Is Niecy*), **The Emotions** (including 'Best Of My Love' and 'Flowers'), **The Pockets** and **Ramsey Lewis**. As a natural extension of Kalimba Productions, Maurice formed a record label ARC (American Recording Company), in 1979 via CBS. The company signed the above-named artists alongside **Weather Report** and **D.J. Rogers**.

When the Earth Wind & Fire bubble burst in the early '80s, Maurice closed the ARC label but maintained his Kalimba Productions. Artists he continued to produce included **Jennifer Holliday** (debut album *Feel My Soul*, 1983), Barbra Streisand ('Time Machine', 1984), **Pieces Of A Dream** (five tracks on *Joyride*, 1986), **Atlantic Starr** ('Armed And Dangerous', 1986), and **Barbara Weathers** (debut solo album on which Maurice co-wrote 'Anywhere', 1990).

In 1985 he produced his own solo album *Maurice White* in between his outside productions. He maintains his recordings and tours with Earth Wind & Fire through to this day.

WHITE, MICHAEL

(Violin)

String player Michael White stepped out as a solo recording artist in 1972 for *Spirit Dancer* on ABC Records. In 1979 he attracted the attention of UK jazz funk fans with the **Wayne Henderson**-produced *White Night*, featuring **Miki Howard**, for Elektra.

WHITE, ROBERT

(Singer)

From St Louis, Robert first established himself on the gospel scene where in 1979 his album *The Word* hit gold status in the USA. In the UK he stirred dancefloors with 'Hold Me Tight', a 1984 import on the Paris label issued in the UK by Calibre. It was co-written and produced by Ralph Johnson of **Earth Wind & Fire**.

WHITEHEAD BROTHERS

(Duo)

Kenny and Johnny Whitehead, sons of **John Whitehead** (of **McFadden & Whitehead**), and godchildren of **Kenny Gamble**, recorded one album *The Whitehead Brothers* for the Philadelphia International label in 1986. Writers and producers on the album included **Keni Burke** and **Bunny Sigler**.

WHITEHEAD, JOHN

(Singer/Songwriter/Producer)

Born in Philadelphia, John Whitehead is one half of **McFadden & Whitehead**, the duo who delivered the dance classic 'Ain't No Stoppin' Us Now'. In 1988 he recorded a solo album *I Need Money Bad*, including 'Best Of Both Worlds', produced by Gene McFadden and released on the Mercury label.

John also has two sons who recorded for the Philadelphia International label as **The Whitehead Brothers**.

WHITFIELD, NORMAN
(Songwriter/Producer)
Born in New York in 1943, Norman became a staff writer at Motown in the early '60s. Here his early songwriting success came with **Marvin Gaye** ('Pride And Joy'), **The Marvelettes** ('Too Many Fish In The Sea') and **The Velvelettes** ('He Was Really Saying Something' and 'Needle In A Haystack'). With **Barrett Strong** he also wrote and/or produced Motown classics for **Jimmy Ruffin**, **Gladys Knight & The Pips**, **Marvin Gaye** ('I Heard It Through The Grapevine'), **David Ruffin** (*Me 'N Rock 'N Roll Are Here To Stay*) and **The Temptations** ('Cloud Nine', 'I Can't Get Next To You', 'Just My Imagination' and 'Papa Was A Rollin' Stone').

In 1970 he formed a group **Undisputed Truth**, writing and recording for the group at Motown through to 1976. This work led to a temporary fall-out with **The Temptations** when 'Smiling Faces Sometimes' was an American hit for Undisputed Truth at a time **The Temptations**' version was scheduled to be released as a single.

While producing **The Temptations** in 1973 he went to an **Edwin Starr** concert where he was impressed by the backing band Total Concept Unlimited. Under his wing, the group became **Rose Royce**, and Norman wrote and produced gold and platinum hits for them on his own Whitfield label (via Warner Brothers) following his departure from Motown. Undisputed Truth later joined the Whitfield label alongside **Starguard** and **Willie Hutch**.

WHITFIELD, ROBERT 'GOODIE'
(Singer/Musician)
From Dallas, Texas, Robert grew up with Cavin Yarbrough and Alisa Peoples (**Yarbrough & Peoples**) and attended the same high school as **Bobbi Humphrey**. He took up the saxophone professionally as a teenager, joining his father and uncle in a band. In 1973 he sang backgrounds and played sax on a tour with Leon Russell and **The Gap Band**. In 1977 he moved to Los Angeles, toured with **Natalie Cole**, and wrote 'Messin' With My Mind' for **The Gap Band** prior to impressing Gap Band producer Lonnie Simmons with his vocals. This led to a record deal with the Total Experience label for *Call Me Goodie* and *I Wanna Be Your Man* (1985), including 'Ready Or Not'.

WILDE, DEE DEE
(Singer)
Born in Miami, a member of the Broomfield family, her brothers are **Eugene Wilde** (from who she borrowed the surname) and **Al Broomfield**. She made her recording debut with family group **Simplicious** before working as a session singer with artists including **James Brown** and **Donna Allen**. Her debut solo single release was 'I Found You' for the 4th & Broadway label in the UK. She also recorded a debut album *No Way Out* (1989), including 'Lap Of Luxury'. She then teamed up with both Lenny Henry and **Urban High** for a remake of the **Loleatta Holloway** dance record 'Run Away' (1989).

WILDE, EUGENE
(Singer/Songwriter)
Born Ron Broomfield in Miami, Eugene is part of an eight-strong musical family, and he took to singing at the age of five. After growing a bit older he joined his family group La Voyage playing Top 40 songs in local clubs. During the disco boom in the mid-'70s the group became Tight Connection and released one single 'Does Anybody Really Know' on the TK-owned Taurus label. In 1979 he recorded an album with Curtom Records as a member of **Today, Tomorrow, Forever**. He became Eugene Wilde after seeing an ad in a newspaper for a nightclub called Wilde Flowers.

A few years later his family group changed their name to **Simplicious** and struck a deal with the Philadelphia-based Philly World label. Eugene soon signed a solo deal with the label and was inspired to write his debut single 'Gotta Get You Home Tonight' (1984) after a trip to England with his writing associate Micky Horton. The song was a UK Top 20 hit when released here by 4th & Broadway. The same year saw the release of *Eugene Wilde* from which 'Personality' made the UK Top 40 in 1985. He also made an appearance in the film *Rappin*, performing a duet 'First Love Never Dies' with **Joanna Gardner**.

Later in 1985 came 'Don't Say No Tonight' before Philly World closed down and Eugene switched to MCA. In 1987 he sang two lead vocals with the group **Cabo Frio** on their Zebra/MCA album *Cabo Frio* prior to his own MCA album *I Choose You (Tonight)* (1989).

WILDER, JOHNNIE
(Singer/Songwriter)
Born in Dayton, Ohio, Johnnie sang in high school choirs and stage productions before joining the army in 1969. While in West Germany he began performing with club bands, later joining the group Noblemen as lead singer. Here he remained until 1972 when he was discharged by the army. After a brief visit home he returned to Germany where he formed a group **Heatwave** with Tommy Harris. At the height of the group's success, Johnnie was involved in a car accident (February 1979) which left him paralyzed from the neck down. He was not able to continue as a singer with the group, but worked as co-producer with Barry Blue.

In 1988 he recorded a solo gospel album *My Goal*, including 'In The Garden', an acappella recording released two years later on the Light label.

WILLIAMS, ALYSON
(Singer)
Born in New York, Alyson is the daughter of bandleader/trumpeter Bobby Booker. As a background singer she recorded with artists including **Curtis**

Hairston, **Melba Moore** ('Love's Comin' At Ya'), **B.B.&Q.**, **Cashflow**, **Unlimited Touch**, **Bobby Brown** and **Barbara Mitchell** before joining the group **High Fashion** in 1982.

She later sang with **The Affair** before making a solo recording debut with the single 'Yes We Can Can' in 1986 for the Profile label. In 1987 she established herself as a vocalist on the Def Jam label (via CBS) recording duets with **Chuck Stanley** on 'Make You Mine Tonight' (for his *The Finer Things In Life*) and **Oran 'Juice' Jones** on 'How To Love Again' (for his *G.T.O. Gangsters Takin' Over*). Signing to Def Jam herself she released *Raw* (1989), including 'Sweet Talk', 'My Love Is So Raw' and 'I Need Your Lovin''. She also recorded a duet with **Tashan** that year, 'Do You Wanna Know', from his *On The Horizon*, and toured the UK with him too.

WILLIAMS, BEAU

(Singer/Songwriter)

Born in Houston, Texas, Beau nearly became a member of **The Temptations** prior to launching his solo career. He auditioned in Los Angeles but as he was only 5' 8" they decided he was too short! (The Temps can be heard as backgrounds on Beau's 1983 album track 'You've Been'.) Beau formed a group Solar Heat with his brothers and signed to ABC just prior to the demise of the label. Alas their album wasn't released. It was **George Benson** who put up some backing for Beau to record demos which were produced by **Wayne Henderson**. Via these sessions Beau was signed as a solo artist to Capitol in 1982.

Beau's debut album *Beau Williams* (1982) included 'If You're Ready' and a rendition of Leon Russell's 'A Song For You', which established him among UK soul fans. It was followed by *Stay With Me* (1983), including 'You've Been'; *Bodacious* (1984), including 'Dark And Lonely Knights'; and *No More Tears* (1986), including 'All Because Of You' and 'Been Too Long'. More recently Beau has turned to gospel music, recording a couple of albums for the Light label.

WILLIAMS, CAROL

(Singer)

Based in New York, Carol recorded a solo single 'Mr Fixit' for the Sire label before teaming up with **Darryl Payne** to become lead singer on 'No News Is News' for **Kreamcicle** (1986).

WILLIAMS, CHRISTOPHER

(Singer)

Under the direction of manager Cassandra Mills, sister of **Stephanie Mills**, Christopher signed to Geffen Records in 1989 and delivered a solo debut *Adventures In Paradise*. In 1991 his recording 'I'm Dreaming' was featured in the motion picture soundtrack *New Jack City*.

WILLIAMS, DENIECE

(Singer/Songwriter)

Born June Deniece Chandler in Gary, Indiana, Deniece was a member of a strict religious family and grew up in an environment of gospel music. She sang gospel in church until her teen years when she first acquired a taste for secular r&b music. During her high-school days she took a part-time job at a record store where she couldn't help but sing along with the records. The shop's manager told his friends at the Toddlin Town label who shortly signed her as Deniece Chandler.

Her debut single release was 'Love Is Tears' with 'Walking Away' on the B-side, following which she enrolled at Baltimore's Morgan State College to become a nursing major. She also sang in local nightclubs before returning to Indiana to study, marry and have two sons (Ken and Kevin). In 1971 **Stevie Wonder** heard her debut single and invited her to Detroit to audition for his group Wonderlove. She passed and joined full-time in 1972, her first professional engagement being when Stevie opened for The Rolling Stones in 1972.

When Stevie moved with the Motown organization to Los Angeles, so too did Deniece and her family. She toured as a backing singer with **Roberta Flack**, and continuing her services with Wonderlove worked with **Minnie Riperton** on Stevie's hit album *Fulfillingness First Finale* (1974). In the meantime she pursued her own record deal by sending demos of her songs to various record companies. She met **Maurice White** who signed her to his Kalimba Productions in 1976.

Maurice took her to CBS and produced her debut album *This Is Niecy* from which 'Free' was a UK No.1 hit and 'That's What Friends Are For' reached the UK Top 10 in 1977. The album went gold and Deniece toured extensively with **Earth Wind & Fire** on the back of this success. Maurice remained her producer on *Songbird* (1977), which included 'Baby Baby, My Love Is All For You' (UK Top 40), 'The Paper' and 'God Is Amazing'. In 1978 she recorded with **Johnny Mathis**, their duet hits being 'Too Much, Too Little, Too Late' (UK Top 5) and a version of 'You're All I Need To Get By' (UK Top 50). Her next solo album was *When Love Comes Calling* (1979), including 'I Found Love', 'I've Got The Next Dance' and 'Touch Me Again'. In 1980 she was the featured lead vocalist on 'Time Heals Every Wound' for **Michael Zager** (which she co-wrote) before she teamed up with producer **Thom Bell** for *My Melody* (1981), including 'It's Your Conscience', 'Strangers' and 'Silly' and *Niecy* (1982), including 'It's Gonna Take A Miracle', 'Waiting' and 'A Part Of Love'. **George Duke** produced her next two albums, *I'm So Proud* (1983), including 'Do What You Feel' and 'They Say', and *Let's Hear It For The Boy* (1984), including 'Black Butterfly', 'Don't Tell Me We Have Nothing' and the title track (UK Top 5).

Further albums were *Hot On The Trail* (1986), including 'We're Together' and 'Healing'; *Water Under The Bridge* (1987), including 'Not By Chance' and 'I Believe In You';

and *As Good As It Gets* (1988), including 'I Can't Wait' and 'It's You I'm After', before she switched to the Sparrow label to record a gospel album *Special Love* (1989), including 'I'm Free' and a second version of 'Healing', produced by her husband Brad Westering and later released by MCA.

Deniece has also sung backgrounds with **Gene Harris**, **George Duke** and **Howard Hewett**, while her song 'Special Part' was recorded by **The Emotions**.

WILLIAMS, GEOFFREY

(Singer/Songwriter/Producer)

Born in London in 1963, the son of West Indian parents, Geoffrey joined his first band at the age of 16 and wrote his first song at 17. In 1983 he became lead singer with club band Caleche (popular on the Scottish pub circuit), but left to concentrate on his own songwriting. Via a publishing/management deal he was signed to Polygram in 1987 and released a debut album, *Heroes, Spies & Gypsies*. 'Cinderella' was a Top 10 single in Germany following which he switched to Atlantic and released *Prisoner Of Love* (1989), including the **Chuckii Booker**-produced 'The World Is Full Of Other People'. As a writer/producer he also worked with Dusty Springfield.

WILLIAMS, JAMES

(Singer)

Born in Brooklyn, New York, James was singing by the age of three. Gaining early experience in the church, he was recognized as an outstanding member of the Erasmus High School Choral Club. In 1979 he earned the nickname **D-Train** for his defensive tackle tactics in the year's division and city championship football team. Also while at school he met bass player/drummer **Hubert Eaves**, who with his father worked with James on the debut D-Train dance classic 'You're The One For Me'.

In 1986 he signed to CBS as James 'D-Train' Williams and took a more soulful approach to his music on *Miracles Of The Heart* (1986) and *In Your Eyes* (1988) including 'Shadow Of Another Love'. Most recently he sang backgrounds with **Patti Austin** on 'Through The Test Of Time' (1990).

WILLIAMS, JESSICA

(Singer)

Born in Tyler, Texas, Jessica Williams was one of ten children who began singing gospel with her family as soon as she could talk. Moving to Los Angeles in the early '70s she was employed by **H.B. Barnum** at Motown, and sang backgrounds with artists including **Diana Ross** ('Love Hangover'), **Thelma Houston** ('Don't Leave Me This Way'), **Marvin Gaye** and **Smokey Robinson**. Through producer Simon Soussan she signed with Harem Records (via Polydor), initially as lead singer with the group Arpeggio. The group scored with 'Love And Desire' and 'Let The Music Play' before Jessica signed direct to Harem as a solo artist. Her two albums for the label included popular disco tracks 'Queen Of Fools', 'Limelight' and 'Love Hostage'.

In 1984 she recorded with **The Crusaders** on 'Night Ladies' and 'Gotta Lotta Shakalada', while more recently she has worked with her husband John Williams on *The Arsenio Hall Show*, where John is a bass player and Jessica sings backgrounds and hires other backing singers for the show.

WILLIAMS, KAE

(Songwriter/Keyboards/Producer)

Born and raised in Philadelphia, Kae is the son of Kae Williams Sr (known as 'Daddy' Kae), a Philadelphia DJ who also wrote a song for local group The Silhouettes called 'Get A Job'. While at school he formed a group **Breakwater** which split up after two albums released by Arista.

Next Kae moved to New York and took up session work, an early project being 'Rescue Me' for **Sybil Thomas**. He also met **Jacques Fred Petrus** who offered him session keyboard work with **Change**, **The Richie Family** (co-writing 'I'll Do My Best For You') and **B.B.&Q.** (writing 'Imagination'). In 1981 he joined Timmy Allen from the group **Change** and other top session players to record an album as **Hi-Gloss** for the Prelude label. He also wrote, arranged and produced all the songs on **B.B.&Q.** (*Genie*), albums for Mason (*Mason*), and then half a solo album for **Curtis Hairston**, *Curtis Hairston* (1986) who sang lead.

He then moved back to Philadelphia where to date he has worked with artists including **Mason**, **Ian Foster**, **Phyllis Hyman**, **George Howard**, **Miki Howard** and other local acts.

WILLIAMS, LENNY

(Singer)

Born Leonard Charles Williams in Little Rock, Arkansas, in 1945, Lenny moved to Oakland with his family when he was a year old. Growing up in a strict gospel environment, Lenny's uncle was Bishop Charles Henderson Mason, founder of the Church of God in Christ (America's leading black Pentecostal church). At school he studied trumpet, sang in gospel groups and planned on being a minister. He later developed a taste for secular music and entered numerous talent contests, eventually landing a record deal with Fantasy in 1968. Here his early singles were 'Lisa's Gone' and 'Feelin' Blue' before he left Fantasy to write songs with **Larry Graham**.

In 1972 Jerry Wexler signed him to Atlantic Records and one single, 'People Make The World Go Around', was recorded. Unfortunately just before it was released another version by **The Stylistics** came out and was an instant hit. Lenny was soon dropped by the label. Returning to Oakland he was invited to replace Rick Stevens as lead singer with **Tower Of Power**. He recorded three albums with the group and scored with 'So Very Hard To Go', 'What Is Hip?' and 'Don't Change Horses (In

The Middle Of The Stream)' on Warner Brothers Records between 1972 and 1974.

Desiring a solo career again he left the group and recorded two albums for Warner Brothers and one for Motown before major success came his way in 1977 with *Choosing You*, including 'Shoo Doo Fu Fu Ohh' (UK Top 40), for ABC Records. Both this and the gold-selling follow-up *Spark Of Love* (1978), including 'You Got Me Running' (UK Top 75), were produced by **Frank Wilson**. After ABC became integrated into MCA, Lenny's albums included *Love Current* (1979), including 'If You're In Need', and *Let's Do It Today*, before he released *Changing* for the Rockshire label (1984) and *New Episode* (1986), including 'Ten Ways Of Loving You', for the Knobhill label (via Fantasy) in 1986. More recently he has recorded for the Krush Groove label where *Layin' In Wait* (1990) included 'Gotta Lotta Luv'.

WILLIAMS, LINDA
(Songwriter/Arranger/Singer/Pianist)

Linda worked for four years as arranger, pianist and music director with **Natalie Cole**. As a singer she recorded 'Burning Spear' and 'Capricorn Rising' for **Richard Evans** on *Richard Evans* (1979), while Richard produced Linda's solo album *City Living* (1979), including 'Elevate Our Minds', for Arista.

Linda also wrote 'La Costa' with **Natalie Cole**, recorded both by Natalie and **Ahmad Jamal**.

WILLIAMS, VANESSA
(Singer)

Vanessa Williams had a successful career as a model before becoming an American beauty queen during the early '80s. In 1988 she signed to Wing Records (via Polygram) and delivered a debut album *The Right Stuff*, including 'Dreamin''.

WILLIAMS, VESTA
(Singer)

Born in Coshocton in 1963, Ohio, Vesta is the daughter of a disc jockey who moved his family to Los Angeles where he worked for station KGFJ. When Vesta was eight, she and her three sisters had an ambition to be a female **Jackson 5** and appeared on the American TV variety show *Jack And Jill* as The Williams Sisters.

Six years later in 1977 she moved to Ohio where she sang in her cousin's band in Dayton, but headed back to Los Angeles when she was twenty-one to launch a professional singing career. Initially she was hired by Ron Townsend (formerly of **Fifth Dimension**) who put her in his group **Wild Honey**, although she also sang sessions and/or toured with artists including **Bobby Womack**, **Chaka Khan**, **The Commodores**, **Jermaine Jackson**, **Ray Parker Jr**, **Anita Baker**, **Stephanie Mills**, **Fire Fox** and **Jeffrey Osborne**.

Vesta sang the original vocal on 'The Survivor' for **Joe Sample**, although she was replaced by **Phyllis Hyman** for the actual release as Phyllis was better known, much to Vesta's disappointment! While working with the group **Clique** she met producer David Crawford who took her demo tapes to A&M Records. They signed her as a solo artist in 1986, for *Vesta* (1987), including 'Once Bitten, Twice Shy' (UK Top 20), 'Don't Blow A Good Thing', 'You Make Me Want To (Love Again)' and the **Gary Taylor**-penned/produced 'I'm Coming Back' (on CD only), and *Vesta 4 U* (1989), including 'Sweet Sweet Love'.

WILLS, VIOLA
(Singer)

Born in Los Angeles, Viola grew up in a gospel environment before turning to the local club scene. She initially recorded for the Bronco label, where **Barry White** produced her early singles, before joining The Sanctified Sisters in 1972. This vocal group were instigated by Joe Cocker who hired them as his backing singers.

She moved to London where she recorded as a solo artist briefly for the Goodyear label (including 'Without You', later issued by Charly). Her major success came in 1979 when she recorded the 1957 Patience & Prudence hit 'Gonna Get Along Without You Now' (UK Top 10) on the Ariola/Hansa label. The B-side of a follow-up was 'Somebody's Eyes' (1980), much sought after by UK soul fans in later years.

In 1985 she scored UK success again with 'Dare To Dream' (Top 40) for Streetwave Records.

WILSON, BOBBY
(Singer)

Bobby recorded one album, *I'll Be Your Rainbow*, released by Buddah Records in 1975. It was recorded in Detroit, Philadelphia and Miami, produced by **Vernon Bullock**, orchestrated by **Paul Riser**, with backing vocals by **The Jones Girls**. From the album, 'Deeper And Deeper' was popular on the UK soul scene.

WILSON, FRANK
(Songwriter/Producer)

Born in Los Angeles, Frank was involved in the running of Motown in Los Angeles during the '60s while the label was still officially based in Detroit. As a solo artist he recorded 'Do I Love You (Indeed I Do)' on the Soul label subsidiary (1965), but scored greater success with his songs and/or productions for artists including **Eddie Kendricks** ('Keep On Truckin''), **Jimmy Ruffin/David Ruffin** (duet 'Stand By Me'), **The Four Tops**, **New Birth** (*Behold The Mighty Army*), **Smokey Robinson** ('Still Water') and **The Supremes** ('Up The Ladder To The Roof' and 'Stoned Love').

Aside from his work at Motown he wrote and/or produced for artists including **Lenny Williams** ('Shoo Doo Fu Fu Ooh') and **Marilyn McCoo & Billy Davis Jr**. Returning to his solo career, he recorded 'Promises To Keep' for the UK Motorcity label in 1990.

WILSON, JACKIE
(Singer)
Born in Detroit in 1934, Jackie grew up listening to blues and originally began a career as a boxer. He later worked on the assembly-line at a car factory before replacing **Clyde McPhatter** as lead singer of The Dominoes in 1953 (the group's Billy Ward becoming his vocal tutor). Here he stayed for three years and made a chart debut with 'St Therese Of The Roses'.

In 1956 he met **Berry Gordy**, at the time an unknown songwriter, who offered Jackie some songs, the first of which, 'Reet Petite' (UK Top 10, 1957), secured Jackie a deal with the Brunswick label (Coral in the UK). Follow-ups were 'To Be Loved' (UK Top 25, 1958), 'Lonely Teardrops' (1958), 'That's Why I Love You So' (1959), 'I'll Be Satisfied' (1959), 'You Better Know It' (1959) and 'Talk That Talk' (1959). When Berry formed Motown Records, he and Jackie parted company, Jackie's later hits being 'All My Love' (UK Top 40, 1960) and 'Alone At Last' (UK Top 50, 1960) before he was shot by a female fan in 1961. It took him two years to recover, following which he scored American success with 'Baby Workout' and 'Shake! Shake! Shake!'. He later switched to MCA for 'Higher And Higher' (Top 20, 1969) and 'I Get The Sweetest Feeling' (UK Top 10, 1972).

During a live show at the Latin Casino in New Jersey in 1975 he suffered a heart attack and lay in a coma for eight years before his eventual death in 1984. 'Reet Petite' gave him a UK Christmas No. 1 in 1986, followed by reissues of 'I Get The Sweetest Feeling' (Top 5, 1987) and 'Higher And Higher' (Top 20, 1987).

Jackie was also godfather to **Jody Watley** through being close with her evangelist father, and invited her on stage when she was eight years old.

WILSON, LESETTE
(Pianist/Songwriter/Producer)
Born in New York, Lesette established herself on the jazz fusion circuit in the early '80s. She played keyboards with **Tom Browne** on his *Love Approach* (1980), including 'Funkin' For Jamaica', prior to signing with Headfirst Records for a solo album *Now That I've Got Your Attention* (1981), including 'Caveman Boogie'.

In 1986 she joined forces with **Meli'sa Morgan** and in the capacity of co-writer/producer worked on Meli'sa's albums *Do Me Baby*, including 'Fool's Paradise' and 'Do You Still Love Me', and *Good Love* (1987). Also with Meli'sa, Lesette co-wrote and produced 'All Of My Love' for **Genobia Jeter**, before returning as a solo artist on the Some-1 label with a single 'Look Into Tomorrow'. She has also recorded with **Roy Ayers** (*Africa Center Of The World*, 1981), **Najee** and **Steven Dante**.

WILSON, MARY
(Singer)
Born in Mississippi in 1944, Mary and her family moved to Detroit where she grew up. Aged 14, her friend Florence Ballard invited her to sing with a new group, The Primettes. Another founder member of the group was **Diana Ross**. They sang in local halls and at factory dances in Detroit before becoming **The Supremes**. Mary remained a member of The Supremes from their formation in 1960 until 1976.

From here Mary pursued a solo career, touring the world and working only occasionally in the United States. In 1979 she recorded a debut solo album *Mary Wilson*, including 'Red Hot' (Motown), before leaving Motown to write her memoirs. Her book *Dreamgirl, My Life As A Supreme* tells the story of The Supremes' rapid rise to stardom, how she believes Motown treated its artists – for better or worse, and battles between the groups at the label and among The Supremes themselves. In 1987, Mary took on an extensive promotional tour for the book, taking in numerous radio and TV appearances around the world. The same year, she joined the UK Nightmare/Motorcity label and worked with writer/producer **Ian Levine** on a single 'Don't Get Mad, Get Even'. Her follow-up was 'Oooh Child' (1989).

WILSON, NANCY
(Singer)
Born in Chillicothe, Ohio, in 1940, Nancy was only 15 when she hosted her own TV show, *Skyline Melody*, in Columbus, Ohio. In 1959 she signed to Capitol as a singer, and moved to New York in 1960.

Recognised as a pioneer of adult sophisticated soul, broadening r&b to white audiences (prior to **Dionne Warwick**, although Dionne had more commercial success in the UK), Nancy's highlights over the years include 'Tell Me The Truth' with Cannonball Adderley (1963), 'Face It Girl It's Over' (1968), *I Know I Love Him* (1973), 'All In Love Is Fair' (1974), written by **Stevie Wonder** and produced by **Gene Page**, and 'You're Right As Rain' (1974). In 1982 she signed with CBS, her albums here including *The Two Of Us* (1984), duets with **Ramsey Lewis** produced by **Stanley Clarke**; *Forbidden Lover* (1987), including the title track duet with **Carl Anderson**; and *A Lady With A Song*, which became her fifty-second album release in 1989.

In 1986 she sang 'The Way It Goes' with **The Crusaders**, while over the last thirty years she has been an inspiration to numerous r&b singers.

WILSON, PRECIOUS
(Singer)
Born in Spanish Town, Jamaica, in 1957, Precious spent her childhood in the UK before moving to Connecticut in 1972. Here she developed her vocal skills in a gospel environment before returning to England, where she joined a group The Silent Eruption, later to become **Eruption**, and recorded with producer **Frank Farian**.

Frank later produced her debut solo album for Epic *On The Race Track* (1981), featuring the singles 'If I Loved You Less' and 'I Need You'. In 1985 Precious made her strongest impact on the UK soul scene with 'I'll Be Your Friend', released by Jive Records.

WILSON, REUBEN

(Keyboards/Singer/Songwriter)

During the mid-'70s Reuben Wilson recorded for the Chess label, his albums including *A Groovy Situation*, *The Cisco Kid* and *Reuben Wilson And The Cost Of Living*. The latter, recorded in 1975, included 'Got To Get Your Own', which became a cult track on the UK jazz funk scene of the early '80s. Although he sang backing vocals himself, he hired lead vocalists including Sammy Turner on songs such as 'In The Booth, In The Back, In The Corner, In The Dark'.

WINANS

(Vocal Group)

From Detroit, The Winans are brothers Marvin (chief songwriter), Carvin, Michael and Ronald. Growing up on gospel music, they originally performed as The Testimonial Singers before turning professional as The Winans in 1981. Their recording debut was courtesy of California-based gospel label Light Records for which they recorded three albums, *Introducing The Winans* (1981), *Long Time Comin'* (1983), including 'Don't Be Deceived', and *Tomorrow* (1985).

While in Los Angeles they invited **Quincy Jones** to their concert at The Beverly Theatre. They were signed to Quincy's Qwest label the same year and *The Winans*, including 'Let My People Go', was released in 1985. Further Qwest albums have been *Decisions* (1987), including 'Ain't No Need To Worry' (featuring **Anita Baker**), and *Return* (1990), including producers **Teddy Riley** (on 'It's Time') and **Michael Powell** and also featuring **Stevie Wonder**.

They recorded backgrounds with **Quincy Jones** on **Michael Jackson**'s 'Man In The Mirror', and a duet with **Thelma Houston** on a version of 'Lean On Me' from the soundtrack album of the same name (1989). They are America's most successful gospel family and also have a younger brother and sister who record together as **Be Be & Ce Ce Winans**. Marvin's wife is gospel singer **Vicky Winans**, and Be Be's wife is another gospel singer Debra Winans.

WINBUSH, ANGELA

(Singer/Songwriter/Producer)

From St Louis, Angela began her musical career in local bands, progressing to playing in concert with **Stevie Wonder** and Wonderlove. Moving to Los Angeles she met **Rene Moore**, with whom she began writing and producing from 1977. In 1980 this association led to a recording deal with Capitol, **Rene & Angela** working together until 1986. After a publicized bust-up she signed to the Mercury label as a solo artist and established a relationship with Ronald Isley of **The Isley Brothers**. Her debut album *Sharp* was released in 1987 and featured 'Angel', 'C'est Toi' and a duet with Ronald Isley 'Hello Beloved'. It was followed by *The Real Thing*, including 'It's The Real Thing' and 'Menage A Trois', in 1989.

As writer and/or producer Angela has worked with **Lalah Hathaway** ('Baby Don't Cry' and 'I Gotta Move On'), **Body** ('Body'), **Stephanie Mills** ('I Have Learned To Respect The Power Of Love' and 'Something In The Way You Make Me Feel') and Sheena Easton ('Without You' and 'Fire And Rain'). She has also sung backgrounds with **Ramsey Lewis** (*Ramsey*), **Uncle Louie**, **David Oliver**, **Bobby Lyle**, **Donald Byrd** and **Lenny Williams**, among many others.

WINDJAMMER

(Group)

From New Orleans, Windjammer are Kevin McLin (guitar/producer), Roy Paul Joseph (guitar), Chris Severin (bass), Darrell Winchester (drums), Carl Dennis (lead vocals) and Fred McCray (keyboards). In 1977 Kevin McLin broke into a hotel and gave Tito Jackson of **The Jacksons** a Windjammer demo while riding an escalator. Two years later Jacksons' father/manager Joe Jackson signed them to his management company.

A debut single 'Stay' sold well around New Orleans before the group were signed by MCA in 1982, the year *Windjammer* was released. In 1984 *Windjammer II* featured 'Tossing And Turning', a UK Top 20 hit. The song was remixed and re-released by Debut Records in 1989.

WINGATE, ED

(Songwriter/Producer/Label Boss)

Born in Detroit in 1925, Ed established himself as an astute businessman before venturing into the music business in the '60s. By this time he owned property around the city including Twenty Grand, a nightclub and recording venue for The Detroit Symphony Orchestra.

His love for black music led to his purchase of Golden World Records, a small label which released productions by fellow Detroiter Leonard Reed between 1962 and 1963. Ed Wingate's success with the company led to five spinoff labels including J&W, Wingate and the highly acclaimed Ric Tic. His artist roster included **Edwin Starr** and **J.J. Barnes**, while Motown viewed the company as competition!

Berry Gordy, not wishing to have his supremacy at Motown threatened in any way, bought out all the Golden World contracts in 1966, although Ed maintained his studio and Ric Tic label for another two years, continuing to do well with artists including **Fantastic Four**. In 1968 Berry stepped in again to purchase Ric Tic and Ed's studio for around $1 million, although Ed maintained the names Ric Tic and Golden World. The Golden World studio became Motown's 'Studio B'.

Ed Wingate now owns racehorses, property and department stores around Detroit and is a multi-millionaire.

WINTERS, ROBERT
(Singer)
Based in Los Angeles, handicapped singer Robert Winters initially recorded as Robert Winters And Fall. In 1981 he made an impression on the soul scene with *Magic Man* for Buddah Records. He later switched to Casablanca for *L.O.V.E.* (1982).

WISH
(Studio Group)
At the end of the disco era, **Greg Carmichael** produced 'Nice & Soft' (1981) for Wish, a UK floor-filler in the early '80s. The group featured the lead vocals of **La-Rita Gaskin** on the song and album *Wish* for the Perspective label.

WITHERS, BILL
(Singer/Songwriter)
Born in 1938, Bill signed to the Sussex label in 1971, but still maintained a day job fitting toilets into airplanes! During time off he recorded his debut album *Just As I Am*, produced by **Booker T. Jones**. It featured the hit 'Ain't No Sunshine' (later recorded by **Michael Jackson** and others), which alongside 'Grandma's Hands' and 'Use Me' established Bill in the early '70s. From his second album *Still Bill* (1972), 'Lean On Me' reached the Top 20 in the UK where it was released by A&M. In 1974 his song 'Let Me In Your Life' became the title track of an album for **Aretha Franklin**, then in 1975 he signed to CBS.

In 1977 his song 'The Same Love That Made Me Laugh' was recorded by **Diana Ross** on *Baby It's Me*. A year later Bill was in the UK Top 10 with 'Lovely Day', a song which was remixed in 1988 to reach the UK Top 5 that year. The record went gold on both occasions. In 1981 Bill was the voice on the Grammy-winning **Grover Washington** release 'Just The Two Of Us', and later guested with **The Crusaders** on 'Soul Shadows', and with **Ralph MacDonald** on 'In The Name Of Love'.

In 1985 he released *Watching You, Watching Me* for CBS which featured the popular 'Oh Yeah'. The same year he toured with backing vocalists James Varner and Lynn Roderick. At one show producer Stan Sheppard was in the audience, and he persuaded them to form the group **By All Means**.

His songs have also been recorded by **Creative Source** ('Who Is He And What Is He To You'), **Margie Joseph** ('The Same Love That Made Me Laugh'), **Thelma Houston/The Winans** ('Lean On Me'), Blossoms ('Grandma's Hands') and others.

WOLINSKI, DAVID 'HAWK'
(Songwriter/Producer/Keyboards)
David was the original keyboard player with the Chicago-based group **Rufus** for whom he also wrote songs including 'Do You Love What You Feel' and 'Ain't Nobody'. Upon his departure from the group he wrote and/or produced songs through the '70s and '80s including 'I Really Don't Need No Light' and 'Plane Love' (**Jeffrey Osborne**), 'Betcha Say That To All The Girls' (**Sister Sledge**), 'The Medicine Song' (**Stephanie Mills**), 'Razzle Dazzle' (**Michael Jeffries**), 'Giving Myself To You' (**Glenn Jones**), 'Don't Wanna Be Normal' (**Randy Crawford**), and songs for **Shalamar** and **Easy Pieces**.

He also runs a group called World Citizens and played keyboards with **Michael Jackson** on 'Rock With You'.

WOMACK & WOMACK
(Duo/Songwriters/Producers)
Based in Los Angeles, Womack & Womack are husband and wife **Cecil** (pronounced See-Sil) **Womack** and Linda Womack. Linda is the daughter of **Sam Cooke**, and Cecil first met her when she was eight years old!

When Linda was 14 she wrote 'I'm In Love' for **Wilson Pickett**, following which she wrote the duet 'A Woman's Gotta Have It' for **James Taylor** and **Bobby Womack**. Cecil and Linda first began writing songs together in the mid-'60s, and prior to becoming recording artists Womack & Womack worked for Philadelphia International Records, co-writing and producing for **The O'Jays** ('I Just Want To Satisfy You'), **Teddy Pendergrass** ('Love T.K.O.') and **Patti Labelle** ('Love Symphony' and 'Love Bankrupt').

In 1983 they signed with Elektra Records and released *Love Wars* produced by **Stewart Levine**. The title track made the UK Top 20 in 1984 while 'Baby I'm Scared Of You' reached the UK Top 75 the same year. The album also included their own version of 'Love T.K.O.' (later recorded by Blondie). In 1985 the self-produced *Radio M.U.S.C. Man* was released by Elektra before they left the label to sign with Manhattan (via EMI). Here *Starbright* (1986) included a UK Top 60 single 'Soul Love/Soul Man'. The same year they wrote and produced 'Hurting Inside' for **Ruby Turner** (later writing 'Sexy' for her).

In the UK, their greatest commercial success came in 1988 after signing to Island Records. *Conscience* included 'Teardrops' (Top 5), 'Life Is Just A Ballgame' (Top 40) and 'MPB (Missing Persons Bureau)'.

WOMACK, BOBBY
(Singer/Songwriter/Guitar)
Born in Cleveland, Ohio, in 1944, Bobby began his musical career with his family group **The Valentinos**, writing many of their songs and becoming the group's lead vocalist from the late '50s through to the late '60s. While on tour The Valentinos met **Sam Cooke** who later signed the group to his Sar label. Outside of the group Bobby broadened his experience by involving himself in numerous sessions as a freelance guitarist with **Sam Cooke**, **Aretha Franklin**, **Ray Charles** and many others.

The Valentinos split up following the death of Sam Cooke, at which point Bobby pursued a solo career full-time. His early recordings were for Him, Checker, Atlantic ('How Does It Feel' and 'Find Me Somebody'), Keymen and Minit (two 1967 albums including the songs 'Fly Me

To The Moon' and 'Take Me'), before he eventually settled at United Artists. Here he recorded numerous albums from 1971 to 1975, but while building a following among UK soul fans never achieved any chart hits. His memorable albums include *Communication* (1971); *Understanding* (1972), including 'Harry Hippie'; *I Can't Understand It* (1972); *Facts Of Life* (1973); *Lookin' For Love Again* (1974), including 'You're Welcome, Stop On By' and 'I Don't Wanna Be Hurt By Ya Love Again'; *Check It Out* (1975); *Across 110th Street* (1975), movie soundtrack; *BW Goes C&W*; and *I Don't Know What The World Is Coming To*.

From here he switched to CBS for *Home Is Where The Heart Is* (1976) and *Pieces* (1978), including 'Trust Your Heart' and 'Caught Up In The Middle'. In 1979 Bobby began a recording affiliation with **Patrick Moten**, and upon signing to Arista delivered *Roads Of Life*. Featuring 'How Could You Break My Heart', 'Give It Up' and 'The Roots In Me' (later released in the UK as a 12" EP in 1987), the album established a formula that was soon to bring him his greatest commercial success in the UK. In 1981 Bobby signed with the Los Angeles-based Beverly Glen label and worked with Patrick again on *The Poet*, generally regarded as his best album (released in the UK by Motown).

The formula was repeated again for *The Poet II* (1984) which included Bobby's only solo UK Top 60 single hit to date, 'Tell Me Why'. The album also featured **Patti Labelle** on three duets (including 'Love Has Finally Come At Last'), but when Bobby toured in support of the album it was **Alltrinna Grayson**, not Patti, who shared the stage with him. Bobby recorded with Alltrinna that year, although the song 'No Matter How High I Get' came from a **Wilton Felder** album *Secrets*. (Bobby had earlier guested with Wilton on the UK Top 40 hit 'Inherit The Wind' in 1980.)

In 1985 Beverly Glen issued *Someday We'll All Be Free*, allegedly a selection of outtakes from the *Poet* sessions. The same year Bobby signed with MCA for *So Many Rivers*, which included 'I Wish He Didn't Trust Me So Much' (UK Top 75). *The Last Soul Man* followed in 1987, from which 'Living In A Box' has been his last UK Top 75 entry to date.

In the meantime Bobby produced **Regina Belle**'s first recording, 'Where Did We Go Wrong' (1986), as a co-lead vocal with **The Manhattans** on the group's *Back To Basics* (on which he also played and contributed songs 'I'm Through Trying To Prove My Love To You' and 'Mr DJ').

Bobby's next recording contract was with Solar Records (via CBS) where to date he has released one album, *Save The Children* (1989). Also in 1989 he teamed up with **Shirley Brown** for a duet 'Ain't Nothin' Like The Lovin' We Got' (released in the UK by Cooltempo), and re-recorded 'Trust Your Heart' (calling it 'Give This Love A Try') for a Japanese album *My Pleasure* by June Yamagishi.

As a songwriter his credits include 'Midnight Mover' (**Wilson Pickett**) and 'Breezin'' (**George Benson**). He has also maintained a relationship with the Rolling Stones since the '60s.

WOMACK, CECIL

(Singer/Songwriter/Producer)
Brother of **Bobby Womack**, Cecil began his professional career in the 1950s as a member of his Philadelphia-based family group **The Valentinos**. He was briefly married to **Mary Wells**, following which they separated and Cecil married Linda Cooke, daughter of **Sam Cooke**. Together they became **Womack & Womack**, while independently Cecil wrote for artists including **Bobby Womack**, **Teddy Pendergrass** and **The Dells**.

WONDER, STEVIE

(Singer/Songwriter/Producer/Harmonica/Drums/Keyboards)
Although born Steveland Morris, blind, in Saginaw, Michigan, in 1950, Stevie and his family had moved to Detroit by the time he was three. Before the age of ten he had mastered keyboards, harmonica and drums while getting to know neighbourhood friend John Glover. John's cousin was Ronnie White, a member of **The Miracles**, and via Ronnie came an audition with **Berry Gordy** who signed Stevie to Motown.

In 1962 he made his recording debut as Little Stevie Wonder. The song was 'I Call It Pretty Music (But The Old People Call It The Blues)' which featured **Marvin Gaye** on drums. His next singles for the Tamla subsidiary of Motown were 'Little Water Boy' and 'Contract On Love', although none were released in the UK at this time. His fourth single, 'Fingertips' (1963), established Stevie across America and reached No. 1 on the American pop charts. Simultaneously, his debut album *The Twelve Year Old Genius* reached No. 1 in the American album charts, while in the UK 'Fingertips' was released on the Oriole label, following which Stevie came to the UK to appear on TV shows *Ready Steady Go* and *Thank Your Lucky Stars*. In 1965 he returned again, this time with the legendary Motortown Revue.

When Stevie's voice broke in 1966, Motown were concerned that he might lose his appeal, but his career was dramatically saved when songwriter **Sylvia Moy** collaborated with him on some new songs. One of these was 'Uptight', which not only put an end to Motown's concern but became Stevie's UK chart debut later in the year when it reached the Top 20. His other 60s UK hit singles were 'Blowin' In The Wind' (Top 40, 1966), 'A Place In The Sun' (Top 20, 1967), 'I Was Made To Love Her' (Top 5, 1967), 'I'm Wondering' (Top 30, 1967), 'Shoo Be Doo Be Doo Da Day' (Top 50, 1968), 'For Once In My Life' (Top 5, 1968), 'I Don't Know Why' (Top 20, 1969), 'My Cherie Amour' (Top 5, 1969) and 'Yester-Me, Yester-You, Yesterday' (Top 5, 1969). His albums were *The Jazz Soul Of Little Stevie* (1962), *Tribute To Uncle Ray* (1962),

Twelve Year Old Genius (1963), *With A Song In My Heart* (1963), *Stevie At The Beach* (1964, renamed *Hey Harmonica Man* in the UK), *Uptight* (1966), *Down To Earth* (1966), *I Was Made To Love Her* (1967), *Someday At Christmas* (1967), *For Once In My Life* (1968), *Eivets Rednow* – 'Stevie Wonder' backwards! (1968), and *My Cherie Amour* (1969). By this time he had also established his commitment to social harmony. He expressed his feelings in the media and through his music which in 1966 included a version of Bob Dylan's 'Blowing In The Wind'.

In 1970 he married **Syreeta** Wright, released the album *Signed Sealed Delivered*, and scored further UK hits through the year with 'Never Had A Dream Come True' (Top 10), the title song of his new album (Top 20) and 'Heaven Help Us All' (Top 30). In 1971 he signed a new agreement with Motown allowing him more creative freedom over his recordings. The first of these was *Where I'm Coming From*, which not only established him on the rock scene (with singles including his cover of The Beatles' 'We Can Work It Out', UK Top 30, 1971), but led to a tour with The Rolling Stones and sessions with Jeff Beck, Eric Clapton and Steven Stills. Stevie became fascinated by the Moog synthesizer, a new keyboard invention which led to what became a unique Stevie Wonder style. Part soul, part rock, he first put it to the test on *Music Of My Mind* (1972), a critically acclaimed album on which he played virtually every instrument himself.

In 1973 he took this formula further and scored UK hit singles with 'Superstition' (Top 20), 'You Are The Sunshine Of My Life' (Top 10) and 'Higher Ground' (Top 30), while releasing *Talking Book* and *Innervisions*. Three days after the release of the latter album, Stevie was involved in a bad car accident which left him in a coma for four days, and a semi-coma for a further week. Remarkably, two months later he was jamming on stage with Elton John at a concert at New York's Madison Square Garden.

'Living For The City' (Top 20) and 'He's Misstra Know It All' (Top 10) got 1974 off to a good start in the UK in advance of a new album, *Fulfillingness First Finale*, including 'Creepin'' and 'Boogie On Reggae Woman' (UK Top 20), which entered the American album charts at No. 1. The album featured **The Jackson 5**, **Minnie Riperton** and **Deniece Williams**, the latter two singers being part of what had become Wonderlove, Stevie's backing group, and an institution for star talent. *Songs In The Key Of Life* (1976) became his most successful album, winning a number of Grammys and including 'Isn't She Lovely' and the UK hits 'I Wish' (Top 5), 'Sir Duke' (Top 5, 1977) and 'Another Star' (Top 30, 1977). His next album was *Journey Through The Secret Life Of Plants* (1979), a soundtrack for a documentary of the same name which featured the UK Top 75 songs 'Send One Your Love', 'Black Orchid' and 'Outside My Window'.

In 1980 he returned to the UK for the first time in six years and played the Wembley Arena where on the last night he was joined on stage by **Marvin Gaye** and **Diana Ross**. The same year he delivered the album *Hotter Than July* and scored further UK chart success with 'Masterblaster' (Top 5), 'I Ain't Gonna Stand For It' (Top 10) and 'Lately' (Top 5), followed by 'Happy Birthday' (Top 5, 1981), a campaign song to turn Dr Martin Luther King's birthday (15 January) into an American national holiday. In 1981 and 1982 he sponsored two marches in Washington to demand this holiday be granted (later to return in 1984 to celebrate the passing of the bill).

His greatest hits to this point were released on a double album *Original Musiquarium* (1982), each side containing one new song. From these he scored UK chart success with 'That Girl' (Top 40) and 'Do I Do' (Top 10). Also in 1982 he went to No. 1 in the UK charts with 'Ebony And Ivory', a duet with Paul McCartney, before a two-year break. In 1984 Stevie returned with a soundtrack album to the movie *The Woman In Red*, scoring his first solo UK No. 1 hit with 'I Just Called To Say I Love You'. Also from the album, 'Love Light In Flight' reached the UK Top 50, 'Don't Drive Drunk' the UK Top 75. His next albums were *In Square Circle* (1985), including 'Part Time Lover' (UK Top 5) and 'Go Home' (UK Top 75); *Characters* (1987), including 'Skeletons' (UK Top 60), 'You Will Know' and 'Get It', a duet with **Michael Jackson** (UK Top 40); *Jungle Fever* (1991), including 'Gotta Have You' and 'If She Breaks Your Heart'; and *Conversation Pieces* (1991), including 'Keep Our Love Alive'.

More recently he sang/produced the duets 'It's You' and 'Weakness' with **Dionne Warwick** on her *Without Your Love* (1985), and sang 'We Didn't Know' with **Whitney Houston** on her *I'm Your Baby Tonight* (1990).

As a writer and/or co-writer over the years, his songs recorded by other artists include 'It's A Shame' (**The Detroit Spinners**), 'Tell Me Something Good' (**Rufus**), 'Loving You Is Sweeter Than Ever' (**The Four Tops**), 'I Can See The Sun In Late December' and 'Don't Make Me Wait Too Long' (**Roberta Flack**), 'Perfect Angel' and 'Take A Little Trip' (**Minnie Riperton**), 'Betcha Wouldn't Hurt Me' (**Quincy Jones**) and 'Buttercup' (**Carl Anderson**).

As a producer he has worked with **Jermaine Jackson** ('Let's Get Serious'), **Syreeta** ('Your Kiss Is Sweet'), **Third World** ('Try Jah Love') and **Minnie Riperton** ('Loving You'), among many others, while in 1983 he attempted to start his own label Wondirection with 'The Crown' by **Gary Byrd**. To date it remains the label's only release.

WOO, GERRY

(Singer)

Gerry's family are from the Philippines, but he grew up in Detroit prior to signing to Polydor in 1988. Here he delivered *Listen To My Heart Beat*.

WOO, PHILIP
(Keyboards)
Growing up in Seattle, Washington, Philip attended the same high school as **Kenny G**, with whom he formed several bands. He was given his first professional break by **Roy Ayers** who hired him to play keyboards in his group Ubiquity from 1975 to 1979. His song 'Simple And Sweet' was recorded by Roy on *Fever*.

Philip played keyboards with **Ashford & Simpson** before becoming a member of **Maze** in the mid-'80s. He has also recorded with **George Howard** and **Jeffrey Osborne**.

WOOD BRASS & STEEL
(Group)
Wood Brass & Steel were a West Coast mid-'70s funk band comprising Douglas Winbush (bass), Otha Stokes (sax/vocal), Randy Bost (trumpet/flugelhorn), Craig Derry (congas/vocals), Bernard 'Skip' McDonald (lead vocals), Barton Campbell (guitar), Harold Sargent (drums/percussion/vocals) and Hubert Powell (keyboards/vocals). In 1976 their *Wood Brass & Steel* on Turbo Records stirred interest on the UK jazz funk scene with their version of the **Ronnie Laws** classic 'Always There'.

The following year they made an appearance on an album by 'Sylvia' playing horns on 'The Lollipop Man', a rendition of the theme to the TV series *Kojak*.

WOOD, BRENTON
(Singer)
Brenton released one album *Come Softly* for the Los Angeles-based Cream label in 1977. It featured songs by **Frederick Knight** with **Wilton Felder** among the guest musicians.

WOOTENS
(Group)
From Dallas, Texas, The Wootens are brothers Gary Wooten (keyboards), George Wooten (lead vocals) and Louis Wooten (lead vocals). After building up a local following during the mid-'80s and releasing a debut single on their own D-Town label, they moved to Los Angeles where they signed to A&M Records in 1990. Here they released *Try My Love* (1990), including 'We Could Be Together' and 'Tell Me'.

WORKING WEEK
(Group)
From London, Working Week were instigated by Simon Booth (lead guitar) and Larry Stabbins (sax) in the early '80s. Playing jazz, they signed to the Paladin label (via Virgin) and soon acquired the services of singer **Juliet Roberts** (vocals). Introducing r&b elements into their music, the group established themselves on the UK jazz/soul scenes with 'Venceremos – We Will Win' (UK Top 75, 1984). Juliet later became a host on UK TV's *Soul Train* and recorded as a solo artist. Meanwhile Simon and Larry continue the group, 'Positive' being a single release in 1991.

WORLD PREMIERE
(Group)
From Brooklyn, New York, World Premiere were Douglas Pittman (drums), Bernard Bullock (guitar/vocals), and brothers Norman 'Skip' Wright (lead singer/guitar) and Anthony Lamar Wright (bass/guitar). In their early days they played cover versions of **Kool & The Gang**, **Earth Wind & Fire** and **Brothers Johnson** hits in local clubs prior to writing their own material and finding a record deal with the Easy Street label. Here they delivered one single 'Share The Night', released in the UK by Epic where it became a Top 50 hit in 1984. It was a very popular dance record that year in New York and the UK.

Individually the group have also been session musicians, their clients over the years including **Luther Vandross**, David Bowie, The Del Vikings and The Shirelles.

WRIGHT, BERNARD
(Keyboards/Songwriter/Producer)
From Queens, New York, Bernard took to playing keyboards at a very young age. At eight he joined a local jazz ensemble The Junior Firebolts as their youngest member (the eldest was 12!), and by the age of 13 he was touring with **Lenny White**. By now he had also made his recording debut as keyboard player on 'The Vampire And The Dentist' by **Weldon Irvine**. Soon afterwards, neighbourhood friend trumpeter **Tom Browne** signed to GRP (via Arista), and Bernard was invited to play keyboards on his debut album. Impressed, the label's owners/producers **Dave Grusin** and Larry Rosen signed Bernard as a solo artist too.

Combining funk, jazz and vocals, Bernard made his debut in 1981 with an album *Nard* which created an immediate impression on the UK jazz funk scene with tracks 'Haboglabotribin'' and 'Firebolt Hustle'. The album was produced by **Grusin/Rosen**, but as with his other albums to date, it was not released in the UK. His other American albums were *Funky Beat* (Arista, 1983) and *Mr Wright* (Manhattan/EMI, 1985). On the former, Bernard collaborated again with **Lenny White** (with whom Bernard wrote 'Blow' for **Bobby M** in 1982). On the latter he collaborated with **Marcus Miller**.

He also co-wrote and sang the duet 'We'll Keep Striving' with **La La** (1987) and has recorded with **Cameo**, **Bobby Brown**, **Pieces Of A Dream** and **Charles Earland** among others.

WRIGHT, BETTY
(Singer)
Born in Miami, Florida, in 1953, Betty joined her sister's gospel group The Echoes of Joy by the age of three! The group also featured her four brothers. At the age of

eleven she was entering talent shows and was brought to the attention of producers Willie Clarke and **Clarence Reid**.

With the permission of her mother, Betty started off by singing backing vocals for the producer's Deep City label, recording her first single success 'Paralyzed' in 1967.

In 1968 'Girls Can't Do What The Guys Do' was an American r&b hit, and in 1971 she scored her first American gold record with 'Clean Up Woman' (from the Atlantic album *I Love The Way You Love*). Also in 1971 she was signed to co-host a talk and music show on Miami's ABC-TV.

Still with producers Clarke and Reid, her music began to take on a more powerful, assertive vocal approach. This direction continued with 'Babysitter' and 'Secretary'. In 1975 she visited the UK with her band, The Clean Up Men, and received a Grammy the same year for co-writing 'Where Is The Love' with Clarke and Reid. The song was a Top 25 follow-up to her UK chart debut that year 'Shoorah Shoorah' (Top 30), both singles released by RCA.

She now entered a quiet period of her career, taking time to get married and have children. In 1978 she returned to recording for her first of two albums for TK Records, *Betty Wright* (1978) and *Travellin' In The Wright Circle* (1979) before she signed to Epic. Here she released a second album called *Betty Wright* (1981), including 'Make Me Love The Rain', before another break from recording.

She guested with **Percy Larkins** (*Music Of Passion*), and appeared with **Richard 'Dimples' Fields** on 'She's Got Papers On Me' before her 1986 album for First String Records, *Sevens*. The album included 'Pain' (released in the UK by Cooltempo, Top 50), 'Share My Love', 'Are You Gonna Stand By Me' and 'The Sun Don't Shine'.

Having established herself in the industry as an astute businesswoman, it came as little surprise when Betty launched her own label, Ms B Records, in 1987. Now in full control of her own recordings she has to date released three albums on the label, *Mother Wit* (1987), including 'No Pain, No Gain'; *4U2NJoy* (1989); and *Passion And Compassion* (1990), including 'I Miss Ya' and 'No Good But So Good'.

WRIGHT, CHARLES

(Singer/Songwriter/Keyboards/Guitar/Producer)

From Los Angeles, Charles Wright formed Charles Wright & The Watts 103rd Street Rhythm Band in the late '60s. Featuring **James Gadson** (drums) and **Al McKay** (guitar), the group signed to Warner Brothers in 1969 for *Express Yourself*. The title track song was an American Top 20 hit (1970), while in the UK it became an in-demand 'rare groove' in the mid-'80s. More recently it was sampled by rap troupe N.W.A. on their own version of the song.

WRIGHT, O.V.

(Singer)

Born Overton Vertis Wright in Memphis, Tennessee, in 1939, O.V. began his singing career with various gospel groups. These included The Sunset Travellers (with whom he recorded), The Spirit of Memphis Quartet and The Highway QCs. As a solo artist his recording career began in the early 1960s, an early release being 'That's How Strong My Love Is'. The song was later an American hit for **Otis Redding**, but O.V. recorded the original in 1964 for the American Goldwax label (which also released his single 'There Goes My Used To Be').

In 1965 he signed with the Backbeat label, for whom he had American r&b hits with 'You're Gonna Make Me Cry' and '8 Men 4 Women'. He also released *Nucleus Of Soul* before switching to the Hi label.

Working with writer/producer **Willie Mitchell** (responsible for numerous hits with **Al Green**), O.V. recorded with Hi through to 1978, his albums including *A Nickel, A Nail And The Ace Of Spades* (1972), *Into Something* and *The Bottom Line*. He died in 1980.

WRIGHT, ROBERT

(Songwriter/Producer)

During the '70s Robert Byron Wright was employed as an independent writer and producer by **Maurice White** and his Kalimba Productions. At this time he co-wrote 'Baby Baby My Love's All For You' for **Deniece Williams** (1977) and 'Take It On Up' for **The Pockets** (1978), also co-writing and producing The Pockets' album *So Delicious* (1979) with Verdine White of **Earth Wind & Fire**.

In 1980 he joined RCA as an in-house r&b producer, becoming vice-president of A&R in 1983. Here he wrote and/or produced for **Glenn Jones** ('I Am Somebody'), **The Jones Girls** (*On Target*), **Fonzi Thornton**, **Evelyn 'Champagne' King**, **Pleasure** and **Genobia Jeter** ('Together'), among many others. In 1985 he wrote and produced 'Fall Down' and 'In The Morning Time' for **Tramaine**, after which he developed cancer and died in 1987.

WRIGHT, SANDRA

(Singer)

From Nashville, Sandra sang on the local club scene prior to a deal with Stax's Truth subsidiary in 1974. The following year a single 'Wounded Woman' was issued, shortly followed by 'Lovin' You, Lovin' Me'. Unfortunately Sandra's timing at Stax was bad as the label shortly went out of business. This left her disillusioned, and it was only in 1989 that a selection of her early recordings was issued as *Wounded Woman* by Demon Records in the UK.

WYCOFF, MICHAEL

(Singer/Guitar/Keyboards/Producer)

Based in Los Angeles, Michael Wycoff first made an impression as a solo artist on the soul scene in 1980 after signing to RCA. His albums were *Come To My World* (1980), featuring **Merry Clayton**; *Love Conquers All* (1982), produced by **Webster Lewis**, including 'Looking Up To You'; and *On The Line* (1983), including 'Tell Me Love'. In 1984 he switched to the independent Valley Vue label where he released 'I Wanna Be Loved By You'.

As a writer and/or producer he has worked with artists including **Jerry Bell** (*Winter Love Affair*, including 'Tell Me You'll Stay'), **The Manhattans** and **Bobby McClure** ('It Feels So Good To Be Back Home'). He has also worked as a session musician with artists including **Yarbrough & Peoples** ('Don't Stop The Music') and **Bobby Womack** (*The Poet II*).

WYLIE, RICHARD 'POPCORN'
(Singer/Songwriter/Producer)
Born in Detroit, Richard was one of the early signings to the Motown label where his singles included 'Custer's Last Stand', 'Money, That's What I Want' and 'Real Good Lovin'' during the early '60s. He also became an A&R man at the label before forming his own label Soul Hawk where artists included **The Holidays**. Resuming his solo career, 'Rosemary What Happened' and 'Lost Time' became popular on the UK 'Northern soul' scene before he rejoined Motown in 1971 for American success with 'Funky Rubber Band'.

As a producer his work includes 'With This Ring' (The Platters), 'School's All Over' (Adorables), 'Like Columbus Did' (The Reflections) and 'Just A Little Loving' (The Manhattans, not to be confused with **The Manhattans**), and various projects for the Ric Tic and Golden World labels during the mid-'60s. More recently he has signed to the UK Motorcity label and worked with writer/producer **Ian Levine** on singles including 'See This Man In Love'.

WYNNE, PHILIPPE
(Singer)
Born in Detroit in 1941, Philippe Wynne grew up in a gospel environment, later becoming a member of the **Bootsy Collins** group The Pacesetters in 1968. The following year he became a member of **James Brown**'s group The JBs where he stayed for two years. In 1971 he became the lead singer of **The Detroit Spinners**, taking the group on to a string of hits including 'I'll Be Around' and 'Could It Be I'm Falling In Love'. He remained with them until 1977 when he signed to the Cotillion label as a solo artist.

Here he recorded *Starting All Over* (1977) before teaming up with **George Clinton** to tour and record with **Funkadelic** on '(Not Just) Knee Deep'. In 1983 he recorded 'You Ain't Going Anywhere But Gone', written and produced by **Bunny Sigler** and released by Sugarhill Records. In 1984 he collapsed while on stage in Oakland, California, and was pronounced dead on arrival at hospital.

XYZ

YARBROUGH AND PEOPLES
(Duo)

From Dallas, Texas, Cavin Yarbrough and Alisa Peoples met in early childhood through their mutual piano teacher. They later sang in the same church choir, following which Cavin joined a local group The Lost Band. Through meeting members of **The Gap Band**, The Lost Band worked with Leon Russell and Mary McCrary before Cavin left to work with Alisa as Yarbrough & Peoples.

The group crossed paths with **The Gap Band** again in 1979, resulting in a trip to Los Angeles where they met **Lonnie Simmons**. Through Lonnie's production company they signed to Mercury Records, and their debut release was a gold album *The Two Of Us* (1980), including 'Don't Stop The Music' (UK Top 10) and 'You're My Song'. Recording directly for the Total Experience label (via Phonogram), their next albums were *Heartbeats* (1982), *Be A Winner* (1984), including 'Don't Waste Your Time' (UK Top 75), and *Guilty* (1986), including 'I Wouldn't Lie' (UK Top 75) and the title track single (UK Top 75).

Also at Total Experience they wrote 'Ready Or Not' for **Robert 'Goodie' Whitfield**.

YELLOW JACKETS
(Group)

West Coast fusion jazz trio Yellow Jackets were originally top session musicians **Ricky Lawson** (drums), Jimmy Haslip (bass) and Russell Ferrante (keyboards). Signing to Warner Brothers in the early '80s they made an impact on the UK jazz funk scene with two **Tommy LiPuma**-produced albums, *Yellow Jackets* (1981) and *Mirage A Trois* (1983). More recently William Kennedy became the trio's drummer for *Greenhouse*, released by GRP Records in 1991.

YELLOW SUNSHINE
(Group)

From Philadelphia, Yellow Sunshine were formed by brothers Karl and Roland Chambers, both top session musicians (drums and guitar respectively) who played at times with **M.F.S.B.** Roland had also played with **Kenny Gamble** in **The Romeos** and worked as the musical director on tour with **Marvin Gaye** and **Tammi Terrell**. Yellow Sunshine was formed in 1973 and featured the brothers alongside **Dexter Wansel** (keyboards), Idrees Young (bass), Lester Young (percussion) and Ron Harding (sax). They recorded one album *Yellow Sunshine* (1973) on the Philadelphia International label.

YEOW
(Group)

The Yeow band were Dennis Andrews (vocals), Curtis Lugay (guitar), Mike Timothy (keyboards), Jumbo Barker (bass) and Leroy Dublin (drums). Although Dennis was from Chicago, the group were essentially a British funk band and were called Inch By Inch before becoming Yeow in 1981. Their debut single 'Prepare Yourself' was released on their own Yeow label in 1982, followed by 'Has Anyone Seen Dennis' (1982), before 'Give My Heart Away' was released on the Rumble label in 1983.

YOUNG & CO
(Group)

From New Jersey, brothers Kenny, Mike and Billy Young originally worked together locally as Young Movement. In 1980 they became Young & Co for the popular disco release 'I Like What You're Doing To Me' (UK Top 20) on the Excalibur label.

YOUNG SIRS
(Vocal Group)

This late '60s Detroit vocal group recorded one single 'There's Something The Matter With Your Heart' for the local Magic City label and featured lead vocals by **Oliver Cheatham**. The group then changed their name to **Butch And The New Ports**.

YOUNG, EARL
(Drums/Singer/Songwriter/Producer)

Born in Philadelphia, Earl joined **Norman Harris** as part of **Baker/Harris/Young** (BHY), three musicians, songwriters and producers who played an integral part on the Philly soul scene from the mid-'60s to the late '70s. One of the early Philly groups BHY worked with was The Volcanos, whom Earl groomed into **The Trammps** after the departure of their original lead singer. Earl became drummer with The Trammps in addition to his other session duties with **First Choice** and in particular **M.F.S.B.**

YOUNG, KAREN

(Singer)

Based in New York, Karen recorded for the West End label during the late '70s where she made an impression on the disco scene with her single 'Hot Shot' (UK Top 40, 1978, via Atlantic) from her album of the same name. In 1981 she returned with 'Dynamite' for the Sunshine label.

YOUNG, LARRY

(Keyboards)

Born in New Jersey, Larry first studied classical music before broadening into jazz, inspired by such organists as **Jimmy Smith** (whose repertoire he included at early club gigs). While working with UK guitarist John McLaughlin in 1969, he met Jimi Hendrix with whom he played organ on a few sessions. He also played with John Coltrane (though this was never recorded). During the early days of jazz fusion in the early '70s he played with **Tony Williams** in a group Lifetime, and later recorded with **Miles Davis** on his *Bitches Brew*.

From here he recorded two solo albums for Arista, *Larry Young's Fuel* (1975), including 'Turn Off The Lights', and *Spaceball* (1976), both highly collectable 'rare grooves' among UK funk, soul and jazz fans.

YOUNG, VAL

(Singer/Songwriter)

Formerly a Bride Of Funkenstein, and backing singer with **The Gap Band** and **Roy Ayers**, Val became a solo artist after meeting writer/producer **Rick James**. Signing her to Motown, Rick worked with her on a debut album *Seduction* (1985) which included 'If You Should Ever Be Lonely'.

YOUNGHEARTS

(Vocal Group)

Formed in Los Angeles, The Younghearts were a vocal group who recorded for the 20th Century label in the early '70s. Their albums include *Do You Have The Time* (1973), with songs arranged, produced and co-written by Vernon Bullock.

YOUNG–HOLT UNLIMITED

(Duo)

From Chicago, Young–Holt Unlimited were Eldee Young (bass) and Red Holt (drums), who initially played together with **Ramsey Lewis** as two-thirds of the Ramsey Lewis Trio. In 1969 they signed with Brunswick (via MCA) and worked with **Barbara Acklin** on a track 'Soulful Strut'. However, upon release Barbara's vocal was removed and the instrumental side to Barbara's record (credited as Young–Holt Unlimited) proved more popular than 'Am I The Same Girl' on the top side; indeed it charted in the USA. It was produced by **Carl Davis** and **Eugene Record**.

ZAGER, MICHAEL

(Producer/Arranger/Singer/Songwriter)

From the mid-'70s through to the early '80s Michael Zager was prolific on the r&b and disco scene, primarily as a producer. During this period he worked with artists including **Peabo Bryson** (debut album in 1975), **Johnny 'Guitar' Watson** (*That's What Time It Is*), **Patti Day**, **Ronnie Dyson**, **Saint & Stephanie** (1979), **Cissy Houston** (1979), **The Detroit Spinners** ('Cupid – I've Loved You For A Long Time', 1980) and **Alvin Fields** (*Special Delivery*, 1981).

As an artist he formed The Michael Zager Band and scored a disco hit with 'Let's All Chant' (UK Top 10) on the Private Stock label in 1978. In 1980 his album *Zager* included the single 'Time Heals Every Wound' featuring the lead vocals of **Deniece Williams**. The album also featured two co-lead vocal performances by **Luther Vandross**.

ZAPP

(Group)

From Ohio, Zapp were formed by **Roger Troutman** in 1981 and consisted of Roger Troutman (vocals/talk box/guitar), Larry Troutman (congas/percussion), Zapp Troutman (bass/keyboards), Lester Troutman (drums), **Bobby Glover** (vocals), Gregory Jackson (vocals), and the horn section of Jerome Derrickson, Eddie Barber, Sherman Fleetwood, Jannetta Boyce and Michael Warren. With their unusual blend of funk (Roger singing his vocals through a vocoder-style talk box), the group signed to Warner Brothers and released a series of albums, *Zapp* (1981), *Zapp II* (1982) and *Zapp III* (1983), before Bobby took on a solo career and the line-up was amended to Damien Black (drums), Aaron Blackmon (guitar), Robert 'Kumba' Jones (percussion) and **Shirley Murdoch** (vocals) for *The New Zapp IV U*, including 'It Really Doesn't Matter' and 'Computer Love', both UK Top 75 hits in 1986.

ZINGARA

(Group)

Zingara were Wali Ali (vocals/guitar), Karen Coleman (violin/percussion/vocals), Rick Jones (bass/vocals) and Minor Williams (drums/vocals). In 1981 they recorded *Zingara* for the American Wheel label. It featured 'I Surrender' and 'Love's Calling', written and produced by **Lamont Dozier**.

ZUICE

(Group)

From North London, Zuice were Michael St Luce (bass), Tony James Black (keyboards), Steve Corsial (lead guitar), Hazel Fernandez (vocals) and Steve Carmichael (keyboards/vocals). Michael and the two Steves met at school where they put a band together called Deja Vous. After leaving school they toured with the group Clint Eastwood & General Saint. Tony joined the group after a stint with **Juliet Roberts**, and later Hazel was added to the team. They signed to Phonogram in 1985, their debut single release being 'Everyone A Winner', produced by Nathan Watts (a bass player with **Stevie Wonder**) and Bobby Brooks. Follow-up singles were 'I'm Burning' (1976) and the **Lenny White**-produced 'I'm A Survivor' (1987).

Steve Carmichael and Hazel Fernandez later formed a group **The Affair**.

ZUSHII

(Duo)

Formerly the nucleus of the group Cue, London-based soul duo Jason Halliday and Carol McLeod formed the partnership in 1986. Their Debut Records single 'Surprise Surprise' was released later that year, and scored dancefloor success in the UK a year or so later. Follow-ups were 'Say Goodnight' (1987), also on Debut, then 'There Ain't Enough Love' on First Base Records in 1989.